Brazil's Revolution in Commerce

Brazil's Revolution in Commerce

*Creating Consumer Capitalism
in the American Century*

JAMES P. WOODARD

The University of North Carolina Press
Chapel Hill

© 2020 The University of North Carolina Press
All rights reserved

Set in Adobe Text Pro by Westchester Publishing Services
Manufactured in the United States of America

The University of North Carolina Press has been a member of the
Green Press Initiative since 2003.

Library of Congress Cataloging-in-Publication Data
Names: Woodard, James P., 1975– author.
Title: Brazil's revolution in commerce : creating consumer capitalism in
    the American century / James P. Woodard.
Description: Chapel Hill : The University of North Carolina Press, 2020. |
    Includes bibliographical references and index.
Identifiers: LCCN 2019035097 | ISBN 9781469656366 (cloth) |
    ISBN 9781469656434 (paperback) | ISBN 9781469656373 (ebook)
Subjects: LCSH: Capitalism—Brazil. | Consumption (Economics)—Brazil. |
    Brazil—Economic conditions—20th century. | Brazil—Commerce—United
    States. | United States—Commerce—Brazil. |
    Brazil—Civilization—American influences. | Brazil—Relations—United
    States. | Brazil—Social life and customs—20th century. | United
    States—Relations—Brazil.
Classification: LCC HC187 .W636 2020 | DDC 381.0981—dc23
LC record available at https://lccn.loc.gov/2019035097

Cover illustration: Chico Albuquerque, *Campanha para automóvel
Willys-Overland* (1962). Chico Albuquerque / Convênio Museu da Imagem e do
Som–SP / Instituto Moreira Salles Collection.

For Louis A. Pérez Jr.
Scholar, Mentor, and Friend

They like almost all our products, from hot dogs to automobiles, from chain stores to trailer camps. They want to make Brazil another United States of America: with more motion picture shows, radio and television, modern plumbing, electric refrigerators and everything else we have.
—*Nation's Business*, January 1945

They only know American methods and know nothing of Brazilian peculiarities. . . . We know Brazilian peculiarities and also American methods, which are not an obscure subject matter and which are at our disposal in libraries and bookstores.
—Auricélio Penteado (1951)

We accept the business philosophy that has communication with the masses as its greatest premise. We repeat for the hundredth time: we are an advertising-minded people.
—Manoel de Vasconcellos (1956)

They are agents of the economic development of the Country, for it is well known that advertising is one of the most useful instruments in the expansion of productive activities today. They learned that difficult art with the Americans and transmitted their experience to other Brazilians.
—*Boletim Cambial*, August 1959

We are beginning to be a people of consumers. The workers are beginning to have a, shall we say, middle-class consciousness. They are beginning to become consumers and the "class struggle" is nothing more than an outdated *slogan*.
—Carlos Lacerda (1964)

If we continue on the same path, if we are able to transmit to the Brazilians an ever-greater repertoire of needs; if we are able to mobilize our own energies to attend to these needs, then we will create an internal market that will sustain the Brazilian economy.
—Antonio Delfim Netto (1971)

"It is they."
"They who?"
"The white enemies."
"I don't understand."
"Wait."
—José de Alencar, *O Guarani* (1857), pt. 2, chap. 12

Who is this "we," Kemosabe?
—Americanism, n.d.

Contents

Tables

Abbreviations in Text

ABA	Brazilian Association of Advertisers
ABAP	Brazilian Association of Advertising Agencies
ABI	Brazilian Press Association
ABP	Brazilian Advertising Association
ACADE	Association of Merchants of Household Electrical Appliances
ADVB	Association of Sales Directors of Brazil
AMCE	Alcântara Machado Comércio e Empreendimentos
ANL	National Liberating Alliance
APP	Paulista Advertising Association
CEIMA	Automotive Materials Industry Executive Commission
CIN	Companhia de Incremento dos Negócios
CNP	National Advertising Council
DDB	Doyle, Dane & Bernbach
EAESP	São Paulo School of Business Administration
EEB	Emprezas Electricas Brasileiras
ESPM	Higher Advertising and Marketing School
FENIT	National Textile Industry Fair
FIESP	São Paulo State Federation of Industries
GEIA	Automobile Industry Executive Group
HBS	Harvard Business School
IBOPE	Instituto Brasileiro de Opinião Pública e Estatística (Brazilian Institute of Public Opinion and Statistics)
INESE	Instituto de Estudos Sociais e Econômicos
IPOM	Instituto de Pesquisas de Opinião e Mercado
ISEB	Higher Institute of Brazilian Studies
JWT	J. Walter Thompson Company
MASP	São Paulo Museum of Art
NCB	National City Bank

NCR	National Cash Register
OCIAA	Office of the Coordinator of Inter-American Affairs
RBP	Royal Baking Powder
SAPS	Serviço de Abastecimento da Previdência Social
SCPC	Central Credit Protection Service
SENAC	National Commercial Apprenticeship Service
UD	National Domestic Utility Fair
UEB	União de Empresas Brasileiras
URAPEL	Union of Electrical Appliance Retailers
USP	University of São Paulo

Preface

A classe C vai ao paraíso!
("Class C goes to paradise!")

The words were everywhere in Brazil as the first decade of the twenty-first century ended. Few literate Brazilians could have escaped seeing them or hearing them, and everyone apparently knew what they meant. Indeed, even Brazilians who contested the statement's basis in fact knew exactly what it was supposed to signify.

That meaning, of course, was not immediately apparent to visitors from abroad or most observers from afar. Who made up "class C"? What sort of paradise—terrestrial or other—had they encountered? The answers to these two questions, in plain English, would be that class C was the working poor, a majority of Brazil's population, in cities and towns from the Amazon to the pampas of the south, for whom paradise consisted in having, for the first time in their country's history, sufficient means to become full-fledged participants in the world of consumer goods and services epitomized by an abundance of home appliances and access to household credit, culminating, for the truly fortunate, in a late-model family car. That was what the statement meant to Brazilians, who used the term "class C" as social shorthand and took it for granted that heaven on earth resided in the products and promotions of consumer capitalism.

By why "class C"? Where does the term come from? How did it attain such ubiquity? How, indeed, did practices and patterns of thought associated with what was once called "the consumer society" come to predominate—or at least come to be seen as predominating—among Brazilians of radically unequal means, strikingly different backgrounds, and structurally divergent life chances?

Answers to these questions lie in Brazil's twentieth-century encounter with the United States and its ramifications down through the decades. Though its origins are forgotten, the idea of dividing society into letter-denominated strata A, B, C, and D had been introduced in the interwar years by the local office of a Madison Avenue advertising agency, to be taken up by commercial and cultural impresarios of all types over the years to come, years that witnessed the creation of a Brazilian consumer capitalism modeled on the United States that was, in national-cultural terms, at least as dominant as its North American analogue. The creation of this commercial and cultural edifice, which by the mid-1970s featured one of the world's largest cohorts of advertising, sales, and marketing specialists, working for and in cooperation with the most powerful media conglomerate to be found anywhere outside of the United States, is the great untold story of Brazil's twentieth century, and one key to its twenty-first.

———

Any telling of that story would be incomprehensible without further explication, and so chapter 1 of this book provides a more developed introduction, including an overview of Brazil's twentieth century—one of dramatic changes in society and politics, culture and the economy, accompanying the development of the country's consumer capitalism—to which are added description of Brazilian commercial cultures of the early twentieth century and explanation of U.S. interest in Brazil at the same point in time. The four chapters immediately following trace the development of Brazilian consumer capitalism from the U.S. eclipse of European influence in the interwar years through the Brazilianization of much that was once exotic over the following decades, chapter 2 looking at the period between the 1910s and 1930s; chapter 3, the 1930s and 1940s; chapter 4, the 1940s and 1950s; and chapter 5 bridging the 1950s and 1970s. Chapter 6 arrests some of the movement through time of the preceding chapters to look more closely at the major agents of Brazil's consumer capitalism, at intellectual criticism of what their commercial and cultural work produced, and at creative portrayals of the same. A postscript extends the story into our time while gesturing toward summary.

Brazil's Revolution in Commerce

Chapter 1

Of the Other America

Over a four-year period spanning 1918–1922, Brazil's oldest continuously published newspaper ran a series of reports from the United States. In doing so, the *Diario de Pernambuco* provided a forum for a young man named Gilberto Freyre, a native son—born in the Pernambucan state capital of Recife in 1900—who opted to pursue an undergraduate education in Texas, followed by a master's degree at Columbia University, at a time when his peers' academic ambitions typically ended at the local law school, a musty temple to tradition founded in 1827. Under the title "Da outra America"—of and from the other America—Freyre gave readers his impressions of campus life and times, of differing religious traditions and their implications, and of North American urbanism and intellectual life, to name only a few things that caught his attention. Sometimes sober and buttoned up, playful when it came to such subjects as snowfall, skyscrapers, and the opposite sex, Freyre's missives were reprinted in other newspapers throughout Brazil. As such, "Da outra America" is one piece of evidence of increased interest in the United States in an era in which the European lodestar to Brazilian high culture went dark, Freyre endorsing U.S. intervention in the war to end all wars along the way. Here and there, the series is also suggestive of the appeal of that other America's emerging commercial civilization, for amid portraits of Princeton and the New York Public Library, Amy Lowell and H. L. Mencken, Freyre's epistles recorded the flash, comfort, and abundance of the North American culture of consumer capitalism, its getting and spending, together with traces of its essential promotionalism, so foreign to readers in Recife as to require explanation.[1]

An early outline of a day's flânerie in Manhattan began at Wall Street, went north to Times Square, and ended in Midtown, "to stop before Fifth Avenue's luxurious shopwindows," among the "examples of varied sensations of color and of scenery that one receives in New York." At nighttime, there was "New York in its dress clothes—which are its illuminated advertisements." In July, there were summer clothes and soda-fountain drinks. "Folks here dress according to the weather," Freyre remarked of the former, inviting readers to make envious comparisons with the heavy northern European apparel that they wore year-round, while "delicious soft drinks" were a sensation without Pernambucan parallel: "Americans are crazy about them." Further on, as his first springtime brought fresh fashions, Freyre was less taken with

North American styles, even as he exulted in the change of seasons and acknowledged Yankee retail acumen: "Each season arrives with its color, its tone, its fruit, its flavors. And it makes a revolution in the 'shopwindows' of the shrewd American storekeepers. It seems that one of this spring's novelties is the loud color of silk shirts, of neckties, of hatbands, of collars."[2]

More than once, Freyre turned his readers' attentions to Christmas as commemorated in the United States, with gift-giving and festooned fir trees, greeting cards and candies, the bustle of spending and the spectacle of shopwindows. "All of this is Christmas in the United States," he explained, though more than anything else he seems to have been carried away by the commercial magic enveloping Manhattan:

> For two weeks it has been impossible to enter a store on Fifth Avenue without being thronged with people. And how pretty were the New York shopwindows for Christmas! They dazzled. They enchanted the eyes. They lent the person who stopped to look at them the stupid desire to have more money, to be filthy rich. They say that Americans don't know how to do anything beyond the purely mechanical. And these Fifth Avenue shopwindows? Fifth Avenue is a museum of art. Here is Avendon's shopwindow that enchants us: ladies' dresses that look as if they were made by fairies. Then the shopwindow of Page & Shaw, full of beautiful boxes of bon-bons and cans of "glacé" sweets. In the shopwindow of the Holden's store one sees, in fine cages, birds with multicolor plumage and fluffy little dogs; the Persian rugs in the Harris shopwindow seduce us; the boxes of cigars in the window of the tobacconist on the ground floor of the Flat Iron seduce us; silverware shines amid wine-colored velvet in the window of the Gatcham jewelers; and what elegant, fragile, artistic things—watches, laceworks, furniture, flowers— our eyes take in greedily as we walk Fifth Avenue! For Christmas, these shopwindows were tempting, diabolically tempting. And, of what was there, folks acquired many things, at great expense.[3]

Amid explanations of Christmas spending and other exotic aspects of his host country, Freyre also noted North American professional-associational life and informed his readers of ways of making a living scarcely known in Brazil. Even in Texas, there was an Ad Club, "made of folks who write or draw commercial advertisements for the press or for posters." It was, he noted, "work for which good money is paid in the United States," adding, "It is also a pleasure to read certain advertisements, written with true knowledge of the psychology of the public and in strong, incisive language." And then there was the commercial press in which these advertisements were published, its daily broadsheets of upward of fifty pages each, chock-a-block with scandal, sports, and comic strips—all of "What the Public Wants"—epitomized by the Hearst newspapers.[4]

Beyond their glimpses of a commercial civilization unknown to most Brazilians and serving as evidence of increased interest in matters North American, installments of "Da outra America" have additional significance. Timidly, even hesitantly at first, they were experiments in writing by a young man attempting to find his voice, trying on different poses and personas, essaying varied styles and subject matters. As such, they proved fundamental to Brazilian culture and intellectual life in the broadest sense, as Freyre went on to become a, and perhaps the, leading figure in twentieth-century Brazilian letters, best known for a trio of works first published in 1933, 1936, and 1959. These three books offered eclectically documented, exuberant, sentimental, often-striking reflections—at once literary, ethnographic, and mythopoeic—on Brazil's history as a Portuguese colony, as a singular South American kingdom in the nineteenth century, and in the turn from that century to the twentieth, from monarchy to republic, from African slavery to diverse systems of labor supply and social organization. Through this trilogy and in countless other fora, Freyre came to argue that the Portuguese possessed a special genius for interethnic mixture and tropical colonization that had been bequeathed to Brazil, making for a unique civilization—a New World in the Tropics, in his terms—characterized by a relative absence of racial prejudice and thus the peaceful intermingling of peoples of every hue, but especially Portuguese and Africans, masters and slaves, denizens of the "Big House" and the slave quarters, in the terms that provided the title for his first book.[5]

Freyre had anticipated making his trilogy a tetralogy, and so it was somewhat in the spirit of his unfinished work that the coauthors of an English-language biography drew up a list of "topics to be considered in a possible Freyrean history of contemporary Brazil." But the listing they assembled, though it began with housing patterns and the continued coexistence of descendants of Europeans and Africans—thus echoing Freyre's work—owed little to Portuguese legacies, Luso-African encounters, or tropical idyllism. Instead, its most important items—"the shopping mall," "the supermarket," "the rise of North American fast food," "new forms of dress," "transport [of the automotive variety]," "modern advertising," "and of course new media of communication and new genres of communication such as the Brazilian soap opera (*telenovela*)"—pointed to other sources of inspiration. Indeed, the listing may be read as a topical arc running from the U.S.-style shopping center to the *telenovela*, an entertainment born of the expansion of Brazilian television modeled on that of the United States. Small wonder, then, that Freyre, whom a doting mentor had called an "American product" in 1921 but over time an increasingly vocal defender of Luso-Brazilian tradition, had planned to complete his tetralogy with a study of burial practices and attitudes toward death over the centuries already covered in the earlier volumes, rather than extend his work any further past the 1910s.[6]

For in looking at Brazil between the 1910s and the 1970s—from Freyre's adolescence to his senescence—it is the implantation and adaptation of institutions, practices, products, and modes of thought originally associated with the consumer capitalism of the United States, some of which he observed firsthand in 1918–1922, that stand out among the most salient developments in that country's history. Beginning in the interwar years, the United States replaced Britain and France as the country's most important trading partner and the tastemaker of its better-heeled citizens. Luxurious carriages and cabriolets in Old World styles were replaced by Chevrolets and Fords, cartmen became truckers, and the building and maintenance of railways were put aside in a mania for cheap automobile roads. Even as U.S. advertising agencies introduced the methods and metaphors of Madison Avenue during these years, they helped lay the bases for a national communications network of commercial radio, publicity-driven magazines, and commercial television programming. The first Brazilian five-and-dime opened its doors in 1930, the first Sears, Roebuck store in 1949, the first supermarket in 1953, and the first shopping mall in 1965. Within Brazilian homes, the very fabric of existence—including foodways, furnishings, domestic leisure, and household labor—was rewoven, with commerce reaching into the deepest spheres of family life, touching conditions as intimate as maternity and as innocent as childhood. Along the way, new professions were summoned out of little more than thin air, and with them ever-more elaborate techniques for the monitoring of consumer behavior and the encouragement of additional consumption. Some Brazilians delighted in these changes, others rued them, but into the postwar era, few could fail to notice them or regard them with indifference. Soon enough, however, the results of the changes thus wrought would be seen as ordinary, and even Brazilian, as the development of the country's consumer capitalism came to intertwine with processes of state-making, industrialization, interregional migration, class formation, and the elaboration of a national cultural repertoire.

Arguably most affected by and certainly most attentive to the changes involved in the creation of a Brazilian consumer capitalism in the image of the United States were the practitioners of the new professions brought into being along the way: commercial advertising, retail sales, market research; later, public relations, media management, and the omnibus of marketing; but especially advertising. Between the 1920s and the 1970s, this group grew from its origins in a small circle of advertising men (and they were all men) to become an outsized professional cohort that included women as well as men across these fields, its leaders lavishly paid and patronized by Brazil's greatest holders of economic and political power, bearers of the latter increasingly engaged in state projects running parallel to and drawing upon the cultural work of the new professionals. Americanization, many called it, but it was the work of Brazilians more than of anyone else.

That is not to say that it was unimportant to the United States or to U.S. actors, or that the development in Brazil of a consumer culture fashioned after that of the United States is without interest to historians of the latter country, or even its elusive educated public. U.S. officialdom, through its promotion of Washington's economic and geopolitical interests, assisted in the efforts of North American firms to build their businesses in Brazil, from Detroit's "Big Three" automakers to the major U.S. advertising agencies, the Hollywood studios to the publishers of *Reader's Digest*. These firms, along with U.S.-based manufacturers of desktop lamps, disposable razors, radio sets, canned foods, cosmetics, automobile tires, toothpaste, condensed milk, bar soap, shaving cream, chocolate flavoring, chewing gum, and carbonated soft drinks pursued a commercial El Dorado in Brazil with varying levels of zeal, in the process helping to create markets for all these goods, and much else besides. The advance of U.S. business into Brazil was exemplary of a larger pattern of U.S. economic expansion in Latin America, but it was also exceptional, as it occurred more quickly, less problematically, and with more thoroughgoing effects than in any other country in the region. Its rapidity was such that by the late 1950s, Brazil—a laggard at the turn of the twentieth century—ranked second only to the Venezuelan petrostate in the amount of U.S. foreign direct investment it had absorbed. By that point, only the Cubans had embraced the culture of U.S. consumer capitalism more completely than Brazilians, but a majority of Cuba's people would soon reject capitalism itself when faced with the choice between the prospect of national redemption and such neocolonial comforts as they had been able to afford. In the interwar years, from the perspective of the General Motors Corporation and the J. Walter Thompson Company advertising agency—the worldwide leaders in their respective fields—the Argentine market had been a much greater prize than the Brazilian one, but neither firm made anything like the impact in Argentina that they would make on society and culture in Brazil.

In some ways, Brazil's experience looms larger than Latin America, and not only because the origins of the *telenovelas* seen in more than a hundred countries worldwide may be found in the efforts of North American promotional experts to reach Brazilian consumers and the exertions of Brazilian businessmen bent on creating a U.S.-style commercial television network. Even most specialists in the history of the United States in the world—as the field of U.S. foreign relations is now often referred to—are unaware that in 1914 Rio de Janeiro was selected alongside London, Paris, and Berlin to host one of the United States' first seven commercial attachés amid a larger push to support U.S. business abroad. But so it was that Rio was chosen alongside the great European capitals as a strategically important point in the development of a worldwide commercial imperium. Thereafter, the growth of U.S.-style consumerism in Brazil—and Cuba, and even Argentina—occurred concurrently with or even ahead of similar developments in Western Europe, contrary to the established wisdom.[7]

That growth, and the efforts of varied interests that helped bring it about, may not have always stood out as the most salient aspect of U.S. engagement with the world beyond its borders. Liberalism and conservatism, imperialism and militarism, nationalism and racism all loomed at least as large as consumerism at particular moments in the making of the global power and presence of the United States across the twentieth century. However, if one considers all these isms alongside one another—none of them yet "wasms"—of only consumerism can it credibly be claimed that it was conceived in the United States, that it was a U.S. invention. Looking at the United States from within, it is the one that has been most thoroughly applied domestically and most widely embraced by its peoples in their own lives. It is the country's creed, more so even than its foundational and abiding racism. Examining its application and growth in another of the world's most significant countries might speak to the development of the United States, and to the limits and liabilities of its most characteristic contribution to the modern world.

Turning back to Brazil, although the country's consumerism was often attributed to the United States and referred to as "Americanization," the actual transfers of institutions, cultural practices, and even personnel occurred transnationally—that is, through rather than between territorially bounded nation-states and fixed national citizenships. To be sure, U.S. corporations operating in Brazil retained "American" identities through these years and, when pressed, as in World War II and at points in the Cold War, their managers acted in what they were told was their parent companies' national interest. But their "know-how," to use a locution very much of the era, was easily—and eagerly—taken up by European and Brazilian interests, first- and second-hand. Well-traveled Brazilian entrepreneurs borrowed from the United States directly, but also from the shifting commercial cultures of Buenos Aires and Paris, and from these cities acquired indirect influence of North American ways that those Spanish American and European cultures had already endured. What mattered in the early overseas expansion of twentieth-century consumer capitalism—and this was true not only of Brazil but of the world at large—was that its actualities appeared American. As one authority explained in 1931, having made specific reference to installment selling and chain stores: "All these marketing devices are not particularly recent inventions, nor are they especially of American origin. Yet here again, the pace set by the United States has been the determining factor in their wide and rapid acceptance and adoption." This authority was an immigrant to the United States from the Russian Empire with no specific interest in Brazil, but he would have recognized similar experiences in the emigres and expatriates—other men and women of shifting or uncertain nationality—who played key roles in the development of a Brazilian culture of consumer capitalism modeled on the United States but arising at the intersections of transnational circuits of knowledge, experience, and capital. In other words, a good deal of the cultural work that went into re-creating U.S.-style consumerism in Brazil was carried out by men and women who were becoming Brazilian. And their work was becoming Brazilian also.[8]

How these processes unfolded, identifying and understanding their principal agents, tracing the growth of Brazilian consumer capitalism and the processes by which it became national and contributed to the making of modern Brazil is the major thrust of the chapters that follow. The subjects of the making of consumerism in Rio de Janeiro, São Paulo, and elsewhere were men and women, most of them Brazilian, who believed that their cultural work in the service of an emergent consumer capitalism was making way for modernity. Tracking their triumphs and realizations nevertheless bears upon a problem that should be of vital interest to all historians. That problem, of course, is power, to be approached through the tracing of connections between different spheres of power, namely the economic, political, and cultural; examining how power is compacted among or, more rarely, contested between different elite groups; charting how certain kinds of cultural power—authority and expertise, identity and esprit de corps—are established and maintained; through what infrastructures these kinds of power operate, to what ends, and with what effects.[9]

Brazil in the Twentieth Century

Brazil, as the last century began to unfold, was the second-most populous country in the Americas, its seventeen million people spread over a territory larger than the continental United States, but with their greatest concentrations in the coastal northeast, which had been the old colonial pole of sugarcane plantations and Portuguese administration, and the southeast, where coffee displaced cane and to which the country's center of gravity had swung beginning in the eighteenth century. In both these regions, as in the Amazonian north, in northeastern backlands inhabited by more cattle than people, and in the variegated territories of the far south, the overwhelming majority of the population was made up of rural folks, as befit the "essentially agricultural country" identified by spokesmen for landed interests. That the country's people were largely rural, however, obscured a multiplicity of experiences and lifeways, from former slaves and their descendants working in the cane fields of the northeast to mostly immigrant small farmers in parts of the south, as well as rubber-tappers in the Amazon, herdsmen and sharecroppers of the northeastern backcountry (the *sertão*), and the tenants of southeastern plantations—called *colonos*—whose routines were split between tending coffee bushes and raising staple crops. Hired hands, squatters, vagrants, piece-workers, stockmen, muleteers, carters, maritime and riverine fishing folk, and subsistence farmers of all kinds rounded out the human geography of Brazil's rural expanses. In the coffee-growing southeast, highly mobile *colono* families shuttled about by rail, through towns and cities, including the port of Santos, at which most of them first arrived in Brazil from Italy, Spain, and farther afield; mobility and ease of communication were considerably lower elsewhere, and transport between the country's regions precarious at best, limited to coastwise shipping, the cities of the Amazon nearer to the North Atlantic than to the national capital of Rio de Janeiro, the extreme south in closer contact with Uruguay and Argentina than much of Brazil.[10]

Despite the essential agrarianism that characterized Brazil's past and constituted its present, which many assumed would abide indefinitely into the future, industry had grown up at certain interstices of Brazil's agrarian capitalism and its networks of cities, towns, and rail links, producing voluminous amounts of textiles and processed foods. In São Paulo, mostly immigrant middlemen branched out into manufacturing, their sweated labor force building what boosters called "the largest industrial center in South America." Along the way, São Paulo, with its hinterland of moderately prosperous coffee towns, overtook Rio as the leading site of Brazilian industry, but even in the national capital fortunes were to be had apart from public administration, the import-export trade, finance, and the conjoined businesses of real estate and construction, which received an early twentieth-century boost through Parisian-inspired urban reform, as "Rio civilized itself," in the bon mot of the era. Indeed, even in the northeast and the far south some captains of industry could be found. Throughout the Brazilian subcontinent, these new men and their families converged with the country's old regime of landlords and state administrators, as had earlier parvenus.

By the 1930s, this old regime—preternaturally unified in the face of challenges from below but segmented regionally and divided in other ways as well—found itself facing its second systemic crisis. The first, which had stretched across the last two decades of the nineteenth century, involved the ending of slavery and the establishment of a republic on the ruins of the Rio-based monarchy founded in 1822. The second, which unfolded from the 1910s, had at its center the shortcomings of the republican order instituted in the 1890s, but it intersected with labor unrest and generational self-assertion, and involved the bursting forth of tremendous intellectual and social energies, in literary modernism and new modalities of public engagement, all of these molded and mediated by the country's characteristically uneven development and its varied regional loyalties, to which was added, in 1929–1930, the impact of the Great Depression. Amid these overlapping crises, the third of Brazil's nineteenth-century institutions—its military, the only national institution left standing after the abolition of slavery and the elimination of monarchy in 1888–1889—asserted an autonomy it had never before enjoyed, as elements among the army officer corps aimed to unify the country and make of it a nation of sorts. For a time, they had as their partner the civilian politician Getúlio Vargas, a stumpy product of the old regime from Brazil's southernmost state, who found himself provisional president in November 1930 and who came to share the centralizing, modernizing aims of his uniformed counterparts. In late 1937, in advance of elections that would have produced Vargas's successor, the military intervened, canceling the elections and banning all political parties while maintaining Vargas in office, with considerable authority in nonmilitary matters, including foreign affairs. That the military plotters' pre-coup artifices had included an anti-Semitic forgery, and that the most powerful among them were open admirers of the worst of the European regimes of the interwar years, was indicative of what kind of nation they wanted to build. The imprint provided by Vargas's civilian entourage—labor legislation borrowed from Mussolini's Italy, the cult of personality built around their own unlikely *Duce*—suggests that they agreed.

Nonetheless, as continental Europe fell to fascism's advance, Vargas did not enact the pro-Axis foreign policy favored by many around him. Instead, he led Brazil into an alliance with the United States, eventually sending twenty-five thousand men to fight under U.S. command in the Italian campaign. Geopolitical considerations factored in Vargas's decision, but so did economic diplomacy. The United States desperately needed access to territory in the Brazilian northeast for naval and air bases crucial to transatlantic communication and transport; it also needed Brazilian raw materials for the war effort and wanted a united, anti-Axis hemisphere. And so Vargas's government found itself in a relatively favorable position as far as bargaining with Washington was concerned, thereby obtaining military and economic assistance of unprecedented scale and scope, most notably financial aid and technical expertise for the building of a modern steel-producing complex, to stand at the center of a state-capitalist sector that would drive domestic manufacturing from light industry into capital-goods production.

Meanwhile, the war years were a boom time for private industry, which built on the advances of the 1930s, when it benefited from the inadvertent protection provided by the Great Depression in combination with national policy initiatives, pushing along what would come to be called import-substituting industrialization. As industry's share of production grew, surpassing 50 percent for the first time, so too did the industrial working class, though it would peak at around 15 percent of the labor force, and then only in the mid-1970s. State-building, economic diversification, and increasing urbanization were also conducive to the expansion of other strata, composed of professional, managerial, and administrative personnel, as well as their clerical subordinates, concentrated in the urban southeast but present in cities throughout what was already being called the Brazilian archipelago, the chain of island-like provinces and provincial centers connected by coastwise shipping, telegraphy, and not much else.

Despite the growth of an urban working class and of nonmanual intermediate strata, Brazilian languages of class and class structure did not match the North Atlantic model of a tripartite division of society between upper, middle, and working classes, even in the major southeastern cities of Rio and São Paulo. Instead, urbanites were divided into "upper classes"—plural—of varied origins and overlapping portfolios (agriculture, ranching, and absentee landholding; commerce, finance, industry, and urban real estate; high-status liberal professionalism, the patrimony of state administration), a "middle class" that stood as the mean between members of the former group and "the worker" formally employed in manufacturing, transportation, or construction, and finally, the group from which household servants were drawn, to serve members of the first two groups in particular, hence, from their point of view, "the *criadagem.*"[11] Ex-slaves and the children and grandchildren of freedmen and freedwomen in the late nineteenth century, often in service to the very families to which slavery and its legacies linked them, this class was swollen by rural to urban migration, exceeding the organizing capacity of established patron-client ties, even as changing circumstances summoned forth new patterns of deference, exploitation, and unequal but mutual dependence reminiscent of the forms inherited from plantation households. Beyond quarters in the homes of the servant-employing classes—an essential part of the floorplan of any apartment house well into the turn to high-rise living—the *criadagem* and migrants to the cities more generally turned to housing they built themselves, the iconic shacks, shanties, and eventually brick-and-mortar homes of the hillsides of Rio known as *favelas*, which would spread to every Brazilian city of any size over the second half of the twentieth century.

That spread would occur under an array of political leaders and regime types. The fascist-inspired but eventually anti-Axis government headed by Vargas did not long survive the end of World War II, falling in late 1945 with the withdrawal of military support. Vargas's first elected successor was one of the most pro-Axis conspirators of 1937, a career army officer named Eurico Gaspar Dutra who soon outpaced even the North Americans in his rush into the Cold War while presiding over a government that maintained, then built on, the repressive capacity of the preceding regime. Dutra's successor—the first to be elected under the Constitution of 1946—was none other than Vargas, following a campaign that played on labor-friendly aspects of the later years of his previous turn in office. Old, increasingly out of touch, and facing a less favorable geopolitical scene than he had previously—as well as an un-muzzled, often-manic domestic opposition—Vargas did not serve out his term, choosing an exemplary suicide over a second ouster from office after his government was caught up in a series of scandals culminating in a political murder traced back to a member of his palace guard. Of Vargas's successors under the Constitution of 1946, only two are worth mentioning. The first, Juscelino Kubitschek, was elected to the presidency in 1955 on the promise of fifty years' worth of progress in a single five-year term. The second, João Goulart, was raised from the vice presidency to the presidency in 1961 when Kubitschek's successor resigned. A protégé of Vargas, Goulart had served as minister of labor under the old man and was identified with a union move-ment seeking to build on earlier advances. He took office in even more try-ing national and international circumstances than his mentor had faced, the Cuban Revolution having had an unhinging effect in each arena. Stymied by Washington and his domestic opponents in his attempts to govern from the center left, Goulart was overthrown in early 1964 following a half-hearted radical parry, to be followed by a series of presidents drawn from the upper reaches of the army officer corps. Brazil thus succumbed to two decades of military dictatorship, leading the South American turn to the continent's characteristic political form of the 1970s and 1980s. At its most repressive between the late 1960s and the early 1970s, when it faced only the token opposition of small groups of armed radicals, Brazil's military regime began to let up around its decennial anniversary, having "won" its dirty war against those would-be revolutionaries, eventually leading a glacially paced opening, or *abertura*, to culminate in a return to civilian, constitutional rule in the 1980s.

If anything, the economic record of these years is even more dramatic than the political one. The postwar did not bring the economic assistance from the United States that Brazilians had been led to believe was their due for their contributions to the war effort. Instead, U.S. officials preached "self-help" and openness to foreign direct investment by what were coming to be called multinational corporations. Dutra came around to both (secondhand military equipment, it would seem, excited him more than economic matters), but Vargas was diffident. He was not an opponent of foreign investment—he welcomed it in various sectors—but he was not going to abandon Brazilian state capitalism either. Indeed, on his watch, if not entirely on his initiative, a petrochemical company was added to the government's portfolio. Vargas also sought to ensure a place at the table for Brazilian private capital, which would be faced by increasingly unfair competition under Kubitschek, as the floodgates were opened to direct investment by global corporations, swamping native capital's family-based economic groups. This volume of investment, however, could not offset the sums flowing out of the country, and so the economic boom times of the Kubitschek presidency were accompanied by ballooning inflation. Goulart would inherit the latter, but not much of the former, as political uncertainty made for jittery markets. Full-on recession came in 1964, as the first military government attempted to end inflation through rigid austerity measures. Subsequent administrations were less dogmatic, tolerating a measure of inflation in exchange for economic growth, bought at the expense of working families as employers' wage bills were held down as a matter of policy. Thus came the economic miracle, the period beginning in 1968—overlapping nearly exactly with the years of greatest political repression under the generals—in which annual growth rates exceeded 10 percent, even as critics coined the expression "savage capitalism" to describe conditions on the ground. The miracle would come to its unavoidable end in 1973 with the first oil shock. Rather than a soft landing, however, the country's military rulers and the civilian economists who served them opted to push for continued high rates of growth at the price of mounting indebtedness. With the second oil shock and higher interest rates in 1979–1981, the bill came due, but by then the generals had one boot out the door, and it would be the Brazilian people who would pay, and pay dearly, as the long-term economic growth that had characterized the twentieth century to that point came to an end, while inflation surged upward through the 1980s.

The hundred years of growth that began in the late nineteenth century and now skidded to a halt had witnessed massive demographic growth alongside epochal changes in social life, infrastructure, and culture. Brazil's population of under twenty million in 1900 grew to more than thirty million in 1920, more than forty million in 1940, and more than seventy million in 1960, crossing the one hundred million mark in the early 1970s. Transitions that took centuries in other national histories occurred nearly overnight. Mass migration out of the countryside led to the population of cities and towns outstripping rural areas at some point between 1960 and 1970, a process that within a few decades would make Brazil more urban than the United States. The decade of the 1960s was likewise the first one in which a bare majority of Brazilian adults were classed as literate, whereas a half-century earlier only a small minority could read; this educational milestone crossed, Brazil would soon be a country, like the United States, in which most citizens possess at least some literacy but prefer not to read. Brazil's demographic transition—from high to low mortality and natality rates—occurred nearly overnight, racing ahead of its struggle for women's equality, unfinished there, as elsewhere. These changes operated through new infrastructures of national scope: radio broadcasting by the 1940s, automobile roads from the 1950s, and satellite television in the 1970s, the last and most crucial of these a technology undreamed of by the centralizers of the earlier twentieth century. In the resultant movement of ideas, people, and images trafficked the elusive encodings of national belonging and the mass metonymy of nationhood. Some of these have become so universally recognized as to be nearly banal: the music, social dance, and pre-Lenten festivity of Rio summoned up by the words *Carnaval* and *samba* standing in for Brazil, for example. Others are so intangible as to defy documentation: conviviality and melancholy, dissemblance and creativity, sensualism and a capacity for cultural assimilation so great as to be characterized as cannibalistic. At the midrange between these two registers are the regionalisms of a continental-sized country as building blocks of nationality, the fashioning of a mythical common history, and British association football becoming national, alongside American dreams that infiltrated the imaginations of millions of Brazilians and acted to make Brazil what it became, marking modern Brazil, making Brazilian modernity.

Commercial Cultures of the Brazilian Archipelago

Dreams extruding from or inspired by U.S. consumer capitalism did not operate on a blank slate. Rather, the re-creation of institutions, practices, and patterns of thought related to the interlocking worlds of commerce, material life, and leisure occurred in, around, and atop commercial cultures that had been fashioned amid the Atlantic exchanges fundamental to colonial and nineteenth-century Brazil. From the tellingly titled Belle Époque of the turn of the twentieth century onward, these cultures would exert their influence, even as they were reshaped.

For many, probably most of Brazil's literate, comfortable minority, a single Rio street represented the national center of commercial splendor and leisure as the twentieth century began, a position it had held for decades. In the words of a nineteenth-century diarist, "Rio de Janeiro is Brazil, and the

Rua do Ouvidor is Rio de Janeiro,—that is a sentence full of truth." He continued,

> On the narrow and almost always shaded street, one finds the best part of Rio's retail trade; brilliant shopwindows show off the products of European industry and innumerous luxury articles are displayed in them. The great shops for fashions, such as the "Notre Dame de Paris" or the "Grande Mágico," may compare with the best of Paris and Berlin; the jewelry stores overflow with gold, silver, and precious stones. Fruit shops exhibit fruits from all climes, pineapples and mangos alongside grapes from Portugal and pears from Montevideo. Bookstores and shops of objets d'art call one's attention with their luxury editions, their copper and steel tables, etc.; ultimately, as narrow and dark as the old street may be, the stores are brilliant for their content and presentation.

As the store name "Notre Dame de Paris" suggests, the reigning influence was French, a legacy of émigré stylists, seamstresses, tailors, and "shopkeepers of various specialties" who began to arrive in Rio in the early 1800s, then set about remaking Rua do Ouvidor and the tastes of the richest of the city's residents—known as *Cariocas* regardless of their means—at a time when the national capital set the fashion for the rest of the country. But although French models predominated, they did not exclude other influences, not even on the Rua do Ouvidor, where the memoirist Luiz Edmundo recalled a Café Londres, an early cinema belonging to the Italian immigrant Paschoal Segreto, and the Casa Edison, a store specializing in phonographs and other gadgets founded by a Bohemian-born businessman who came to Brazil via the United States.[12]

The urban reforms of the early twentieth century, and with them the building of a broad Avenida Central—soon renamed the Avenida Rio Branco—bisecting the Rua do Ouvidor, hardly dented the commercial and cultural centrality of the narrow, shaded walking street, even as commerce spread laterally onto Uruguaiana and Gonçalves Dias Streets, and eventually Rio Branco as well. As a visitor from Ohio wrote in 1910, "The famous Ouvidor still remains, and during all the business hours of the day is filled with a throng of shoppers, business men and the idle who spend their waking hours in the cafés or other resorts. It is still the great shopping as well as gossiping street. . . . It still possesses some of the best stores and the best of everything that pleases the Brazilians." It was, a countryman wrote, sui generis, "a delightful combination of shopping district and an open air club," and perhaps even a key to Brazil: "If one can read national character through the kind of shops the people frequent, the historic Street of the Auditor is an unveiling; with its windows filled with flashing gems, diamonds home-grown, tourmalines and the like; with its rich silks and satins from the finest looms of France and Italy; with its book-shops where the tables groan with their weight of literary lore in classic Portuguese, and the latest French romances as well; and we can never forget the flower stores."[13]

In São Paulo, well established as Brazil's second city by that point, *le coeur de la ville est la rue 15 de Novembro, cette rue de Ouvidor de São Paulo*. "It is the city's principal street, the one with the most commerce and animation," wrote a Brazilian visitor, who made the same comparison to Rua do Ouvidor, of which it was "at least the equal," for its "more sumptuous buildings, magnificent cafés, shops for fashions and jewelry stores; and at night it offers, along with brilliant and lively lighting, more animation than the Federal Capital's principal street, that at that hour is a dead street." With São Bento and Direita Streets, 15 de Novembro formed the Triângulo, or "Triangle," that marked off the commercial and cultural center of São Paulo in the early twentieth century. On these streets were São Paulo's own Notre Dame de Paris and Au Palais Royal, as well as its Casa Alemã (literally, "German Shop"), founded by an immigrant from the Reich in 1883 as a hardware dealership but which became a department store of sorts. In 1913, Rua 15 de Novembro would be the site chosen for the opening of Mappin, a British-owned department store that promised "to supply Brazil with everything having to do with items for the use of ladies and children, in the latest styles from London and Paris." Even before the latter addition to the city's commercial scene, its cosmopolitan vibrancy was stressed by visitors: "At once, I come across a *Rôtisserie Sportsman*, national restaurants, and a beer hall that answers to the quick cognomen of *O Chopp*. It is a consortium of languages, a small Babel, with redundant names and monstrous commercial hyperboles." British-owned Mappin would itself become a Babel of sorts, its floorings department headed by an Italian who had previously worked in an Argentine department store, its seamstresses led by *"une dame français avant beaucoup d'experience,"* and its beauty shop referred to as the "Salon de Beauté 'Mappin.'" By that point, proud São Paulo residents—to be called *Paulistanos*, or *Paulistas*, as residents of the state, though outsiders often overlooked the distinction—bragged, "Look, until a little while ago, all fashionable people dressed themselves in Rio, or in Europe. Now we have good seamstresses and tailors, and very well stocked stores: Casa Alemã, Casa Paiva, Dona Juanita, the Favorita, Casa Lemke, Mundo Elegante, Casa Bonilha, Pigmalio, Casa Genin."[14]

Commercial centers and residential areas catering to smart-set Paulistanos and Cariocas were the sites of annual pre-Lenten Carnaval festivities and the daily strolls referred to by the English word "footing." "On the Avenida Rio Branco (on the shaded side) one did the 'footing,' 'like in London' (there were ladies who would say in French, 'faire le trottoir'). On Botafogo beach, 'like in Nice,' battles of flowers were joined. On the beaches of Lapa, Flamengo, and Botafogo, one did the 'Corso,' 'like on the Riviera.' São Paulo did the 'footing' on Avenida Higienópolis, the battles of flowers and the Corso on Avenida Paulista."[15]

Year-round, from early morning to fall of night, residential streets would be traversed by a profusion of ambulatory vendors, each with their distinctive call, or *pregão*: newspaperboys, knife-sharpeners, milkmen leading their cows or goats, greengrocers, sweetsellers, tinkers, basket-weavers, broom-makers, haberdashers; dealers in fish, fowl, fruit, meat, and fresh-baked bread, a day's worth of ice, a week's worth of firewood; buyers of empty bottles and used clothes, the clerks of neighborhood corner stores, and other middlemen of every possible description. "And there was the Italian who carried a chest over his shoulder, lined with a very white piece of cloth full of potatoes: *Batata assata al forno!*" remembered one Paulistana of her childhood, along with the Portuguese seller of brooms "singing like a bass: *Vassouras, espanadores!*" and the Italian truck farmer "*Ma que bela tomata da chacra mia!*" The Rio counterparts of these men were less fondly remembered by José Maria Bello, who identified the city's scenic beauty and the better shops of the Rua do Ouvidor as its only worthwhile sights when he arrived from Pernambuco in 1905: "Despite the affectations of its new 'civilization,' the city had not yet freed itself from many of its colonial aspects: sordid kiosks, resisting the opposition of municipal authorities, the melopoeia of ambulant sellers of all possible kinds of things, from live turkeys to *fós . . . fósfos . . . baratos . . .* ['cheap matches'] and candies and caramels." Eight years later, a new city ordinance identified eighty-six goods and services together with the licensing fees that their mostly immigrant and Afro-Brazilian providers were to pay, the goods ranging from "confetti and other seasonal carnival goods" to artificial flowers, but also including most of life's necessities. Regulation represented official acknowledgment of the fact that brick-and-mortar municipal markets and the neighborhood stores called *armazens* or *mercearias* were incapable of provisioning Brazil's largest cities on their own, an acknowledgment that was seconded by the formalization of open-air markets called *feiras-livres* that were hastily assembled every morning to serve a different neighborhood each day of the week.[16] But even after the coming of the feiras-livres, the *pregões* rang on:

> The cry *verdureiro!* means that the vegetable man is coming, his back loaded down with fresh vegetables. *Galinha gorda!* means fat chicken and we see a barefooted man coming along with two large baskets of them hanging from the ends of the pole resting on his shoulders. The

whistle of the sweetmeats man brings all the youngsters of the neighbor-hood to his heels. The scissors grinder touches a piece of metal to his emery wheel every little while to attract attention. The ice merchant strikes a steel triangle. The tinman shakes a sort of frying pan with a clapper inside. The seller of dry goods and clothing slaps two sticks together.[17]

Beyond Rio and São Paulo were regional variations on the commercial cul-tures of the two great cities. In Paraná's capital of Curitiba, a local Rua 15 de Novembro featured shops named Au Petit Bazar, A La Ville de Paris, and O Louvre, owned by Syrian-Lebanese-, Spanish-, and German-surnamed men, respectively. Several hundred miles north, in Belo Horizonte, the newly founded model capital of the state of Minas Gerais, the approximation of Rio's high-end commerce found a broad Rua da Bahia standing in for narrow Ou-vidor, with such shops as Salão Parisiense, Notre-Dame de Belo Horizonte, and Parc Royal, the last an affiliate of an identically named Rio store. From the beginning, however, Belo Horizonte's streetselling was distinct from Rio and São Paulo's in that nearly all its practitioners were native-born Brazilians, which would have been true of any city to its north, and was increasingly the case in the two southeastern capitals as well.[18]

Elsewhere, even high commerce retained a familiar air. The memoirist Cyro dos Anjos, for one, remembered the shops of his native Montes Claros as having "a patriarchal air of half-business, half-family: boys played behind the counter, servant girls came and went with messages from their mistress to her husband, toddlers with pacifiers in their mouths disarranged the contents of the lowest shelves, adult sons served the clientele." The stock of such stores, found in cities and towns throughout Brazil, would have been almost en-tirely imported. As a merchant's son recalled of his father's stock, in a rail-way town in the northeastern interior: "At that time almost everything came from outside of the country, including foodstuffs and beverages. There was French butter of the 'Le Pelletier' and 'Brétel' brands, Carolina rice from It-aly, Dutch cheese, Felippe Canaud petit-pois, imported potatoes, Brandão Gomes preserves and sardines from Portugal, Portuguese onions and garlic, Veuve Clicquot and Pommery champagne, Guinness and Hamburg beer, Fo-ckink gin, Apolinaris mineral water."[19]

In small towns, rural hamlets, and crossroads, a narrower selection of some of the same goods would appear in rustic general stores, or *vendas*, that served as social centers as much as sites of commerce. The "venda at the crossroads," recalled Nelson Palma Travassos of the interior of São Paulo state in the 1910s, "was the 'club' of the caboclo"—the backwoods rustic—and "one of the most typical institutions," just as the vendas of the "colonial" zones of the far south were spaces of male sociability for German, Italian, and Eastern European immigrants. In one or the other, and in vendas serving the backlanders of the northeastern interior, the most crucial item on sale was sugarcane liquor served in short glasses or fired-clay cups. The vendas' less-essential merchandise varied considerably by region. In the colonial zones, according to the historian João Carlos Tedesco, it ran from clogs to cured sausages, tobacco to tinned sardines. The one Travassos remembered, belonging to a stereotypical *turco*, as Syrian-Lebanese immigrants and their children were referred to indiscriminately, sold "wet and dry goods, with a haberdashery section, shelves with hardware and kitchen items, and with the ceiling covered in hooks where there hung wooden water-barrels, zinc buckets, and enameled chamber pots." In the cattle lands of the northeast and the extreme south, the offerings of an early twentieth-century venda would have been considerably poorer, as befit a material culture not far removed from the nineteenth-century "leather age" described by Limeira Tejo: "In certain zones, domestic utensils were made of fired clay: pans, bowls, jugs, plates, cups, chamber pots. In others—where indigenous artistry had not been passed on—such gear was even more rudimentary, made of wood, or using gourds. In cold regions, wool—spun and sewn at home—was the dominant item in the confection of clothes, ponchos, shirts, and even camisoles and drawers. In the tropics, clothes were made with fiber sacks, or the ones wheat flour was sold in, and with a bit of cheap cotton cloth that came from England, passing through the hands of the Portuguese wholesaler, the shopkeeper of the interior, and the peddler."[20]

Vendas owned by native Brazilians, new immigrants from Europe, and Syrian-Lebanese peddlers who made good on the road and were able to settle down; the establishments of local shopkeepers of major cities and of the towns of the country's seemingly endless interior; streetselling lines with trades and techniques owing much to Africa, to southern Europe, and to Luso-indigenous caboclo or *caipira* tradition, but which were opened to newer arrivals, including from east Asia, in the new century; *mercearias* and *armazens* run especially by recent Portuguese immigrants and their Brazilian-born kin; luxurious emporia owned by French, British, German, Portuguese, Italian, and other, the proportions of particular nationalities varying by city— all these constituted the local and regional commercial cultures of the Brazilian subcontinent in the early twentieth century. Their variety defies all but the broadest of generalizations. One would be the European, especially French, orientation of its high commerce, which radiated outward from the Rua do Ouvidor. It was in referring to this lasting influence that a midcentury anthropologist, writing from Rio, declared, "The European concept of 'civilization' was bequeathed to us by France," such that "fashion, especially women's fashion, reflects decisive French influences. Same for the market in certain commercial goods, identified in Brazilian capitals, in the so-called 'shops for fashions,' such as dresses, hats, *lingerie*, perfumes, and other articles for *toilette*. French expressions are common in this kind of trade." Indeed, one such expression had become so common that its French origins were overlooked by this authority: the term *magasin*, used in Brazil for stores catering to upper- and upper-middle-class customers, especially if those stores specialized in apparel and one or more other lines of goods. Such was the influence of France over Rio and, initially at least, of Rio over the rest of the country, that the term came to be used even in cities where the commercial landscape had been less dominated by the French, including São Paulo, where Mappin's British managers used the term to refer to their store.[21]

Significantly, streetsellers of nonessential goods also were rechristened using a French word, as the seller of cheap, shoddy goods (*camelote*) was generally referred to as a *camelot*. The French term would never have been used for the seller of life's essentials, whether ambulatory or in an open-air market, but—just as significantly—Portuguese words of African origin could and often would be used for such sellers, their place of business, and their goods: *quitandeiras*, for the (female) persons, and *quitanda*, for the place or products. Neither these Kimbundu-derived terms nor *camelot* would disappear from Brazil's regional vernaculars, though the Gallicism would eventually be Brazilianized to *camelô*. Along with the enduring Francophilia of high commerce, then, the deep influence of African custom on provisioning is a second potential generalization to be made about Brazil's regionalized commercial cultures. A third may be made regarding Brazilian commerce generally. It was profoundly cosmopolitan, though with recognizably regional patterns (for example, German influence increased the farther south one went). Its cosmopolitanism was such that Brazilian merchants were easy to overlook. As a critic complained of the nineteenth century, "Business establishments multiplied: English ones, Italian ones, French ones, German ones, with their respective specialties in hardware, haberdashery, dishware, textiles, not to mention the peddling Turk, with a beat-up chest on his back or astride a half-skinned mare." This "invasion carried out by the locusts of commercialism," our critic now exaggerated, had eliminated Brazilians from their own country's commerce: "There's the characteristic English commerce; there's the French, the Italian, the Japanese, the North American; but not the Brazilian." From there, he charged, it extended to the streets: "Even the cries of the ambulant sellers are characteristic of each country. Some are sharp and without rhythm, others are melancholy, soft, steeped in suggestive sadnesses that recall native breezes, distant landscapes fading in the final blaze of twilight, extreme nostalgias, sobs of farewells for evermore . . ."[22]

Brazil's American Century

These were the commercial and cultural conditions existing as the interwar upsurge of U.S. interest in Brazil and of Brazilian interest in the United States began. Geopolitics mattered a great deal in these mutual interests: Europe's self-destruction presented tremendous opportunities to North American business worldwide, even as it spurred Brazilians to reconsider their long-established Europhilia. But there were other prompts to U.S. interest in Brazil. To start with, the North American coffee habit made for an unfavorable balance of trade that worried Washington policymakers and their allies in finance. Brazil, though overwhelmingly poor in per capita terms, had a relatively large population of wealthy and near-wealthy families concentrated in the urban southeast, in Rio, São Paulo, and the latter city's satellites. That this market, attractive as an aggregate, was served by shipping lines that had Buenos Aires as their terminus at a time when the massive wealth of the Argentine upper class made it one of the richest cities in the world was an additional lure. Finally, as U.S. stakes in Brazil were established, even hard-hearted businessmen proved susceptible to national fantasies of dormant gigantism. "Brazil is the great and powerful country of South America—a great sleeping giant," were the words of one such observer. "Vast in area," noted a trade-press writer, "Brazil is no less so in the possibilities for commercial development in many directions." In statements like these was faith beyond evidence akin to that which had gripped nineteenth-century believers in the China market: surely a country occupying such a sizable portion of the globe must be home to customers by the teeming millions, if not in the present, then certainly in the not-too-distant future.[23]

The interwar era was marked by encounters between Brazilian conditions and U.S. consumer capitalism resulting from these interests and illusions. Between the 1910s and the 1930s, the major U.S. automakers expanded into Brazil, bringing with them the promotional and organizational apparatus of Madison Avenue, at the encouragement of U.S. officialdom and other adjutants to big business. Dramatic changes in the Brazilian press unfolded, together with the development of commercial radio broadcasting, while Hollywood solidified its place as leisure-time draw and source of daydreams for city-dwellers, all three commercial media enjoying the indulgence of Brazilian governments. At this early stage, the history of Brazilian consumer capitalism was already a transnational tale, one that involved Dutch and Canadian concerns, as well as a Spanish-born entrepreneur who sponsored the remaking of a section of Rio in the image of Broadway, just as the urban reformers of the dawn of the century had evoked the avenues of Haussmann's Paris.

By the mid-1930s, American influence borne by Brazilian merchants was recasting the same city's commercial thoroughfares, even the Rua do Ouvidor, amid a larger emulation of North American retailing in Rio, São Paulo, and other Brazilian cities. These developments were part of a larger Brazilian romance with the United States between the 1930s and 1940s, a spell that would be broken, and then only in part, when the war-era alliance failed to yield even a measure of postwar prosperity or abundance as recompense for wartime shortages and the surrender of sovereignty over strategically crucial northeastern bases. Against this backdrop occurred many developments of lasting impact and importance, among them the growth and early professionalization of advertising and sales promotion, as well as the continued commercialization of the press and the rise of commercial radio to the status of national institution, buoyed by radio soap operas inspired by Cuban and Argentine examples and broadcast on behalf of Brazilian and North American manufacturers of branded goods, their audiences measured by the country's premiere market-research firm.

In the aftermath of World War II, U.S. models of retail shopping and its promotion were demonstrably ascendant as the North American department store was re-created in São Paulo, Rio, and other urban centers by U.S., Brazilian, and mixed-capital Euro-Brazilian interests. Having already colonized Carnaval, commercialism now advanced upon Brazil's end-of-year festivities and created new commemorations, reaching deep into the intimacies of family life along the way, aided by media old and new, and bearing products that would reshape domestic space and color relations between the servant-employing classes and the people they called *criadas*. Beginning in the 1950s, the supermarket's introduction made way for changes in food shopping and nonfood retailing. Throughout were the activities of the new professionals in advertising, sales promotion, media, and market research, as protagonists and self-promotors claiming for themselves the roles of experts in and of prosperity, as their North American exemplars had done before them.

Between the 1950s and the 1970s, Brazil experienced some of the most wrenching changes in its twentieth-century history. Although these bookended decades are usually considered separately from one another, there were marked cultural and economic correspondences between the Kubitschek presidency, the fifty years of progress in five that delivered on the dream of domestic passenger-car production, and the economic miracle of the late 1960s and early 1970s, which was the object of further fantasies of imminent ascension to the First World. Television's expansion and its consolidation as a national medium, the wholesale adoption of "marketing" as business practice and modernizing worldview, the arrival of the new professionals to the position of influence, affluence, and prestige they had long sought, in part as reward for their role in the creation of the over-the-top economic patriotism identified with the military regime at its peak—these were some of the most salient developments of this era, along with the early malling of Brazilian cities, as shopping centers inspired by the United States, Western Europe, and Japan were assembled in Rio and São Paulo beginning in the mid-1960s. The essential features of contemporary Brazil's culture of consumption would be in place within ten years of the opening of the first *shopping*, as the new cathedrals of consumption were soon called, but something of the hollowness of that culture was already apparent. It would only become more so over time and, indeed, by the late 1970s, this hollowness was apparent even to some among the new professionals, themselves products and promotors of Brazilian consumer capitalism.

———

In the 1910s and 1920s, such disenchantment was unimaginable. Even as Gilberto Freyre explained the other America, exotic elements were being eagerly absorbed into Brazilian culture and commerce, especially in the urban southeast, in ways that anticipated developments to come. In a figurative sense, Brazil's American Century was beginning and—indeed—the term itself was coined in a literal sense in Rio simultaneously with Freyre's stateside reporting, two decades before Henry Luce's boastful prospectus of 1941. Its author was not North American, nor was he a native Brazilian, but rather a French émigré named Alberto Rosenvald, who started out in life managing his mother's luxurious flower shop, which catered to the self-styled aristocrats of Rio's Francophile upper class. Some ten years after overseeing the move of Mme. Rosenvald's famed shop from the Rua do Ouvidor to the future Avenida Rio Branco in 1905, Alberto was hired to represent Fox Films, becoming the head of its Rio office in 1916 and continuing to lead its operations in Brazil through the following decade and into the 1930s, a time in which the Brazilian market was second only to the U.S. one as far as Hollywood was concerned. Along the way, he developed what a reporter called a "very American 'shake-hands.'" Eventually, this Frenchman-turned-Brazilian would become a director of the Commercial Association of Rio de Janeiro—Brazil's most venerable associational body—and an officer of the local Rotary Club, as well as acquire an interest in the automotive trade. But it was much earlier than that, in June 1922, that he applied the idea of an "American Century" to the "North American infiltration which is being observed in all parts of the world" as "men of other countries, the sons of other races are adopting

American habits and ways." Turning to Brazil specifically, and to potential knock-on effects of the silent films he promoted as a matter of professional course, Rosenvald continued: "There is, in our country and principally in Rio—the magnificent heart of this gigantic body—progress and thirst for progress, for rapid progress, for the prodigious progress of the Americans. This is, possibly, one of the results of the suggestion of the films. If such is the case, it is a blessed influence." And so it was that Brazil's American century began.[24]

Chapter 2

One of the Great Automobile Countries in the World

In 1922 and 1927, James Mooney traveled to Brazil for the General Motors Corporation. His first trip left him impressed. "I am amazed at the wonderful possibilities of the motor car industry in this country," he declared. "I am positive, once the people as a whole realize the true value of the automobile, Brazil will become one of the great automobile countries of the world." Mooney's second trip provided something as important as impressions and the beginnings of business plans: it gave him a story, one he told more than once, the particulars shifting, but the outline and implications remaining the same. The story began with a trip from Rio "through the vast state of Minas Gerais," where, amid the wild vastness of the interior, Mooney happened upon a hamlet featuring two reminders of home. The first was "what we would know here as the 'general store.'" The owner of this rustic store—a *venda*, in Brazilian terms—"had prospered, in his way," and acquired another sight for Mooney's sore eyes, "an American touring car." The automobile—purchased a year before Mooney's visit—had brought further change. Where before it had taken the store owner nearly a week to reach the nearest railway depot, a journey that his wife and daughter had made twice, he now "motors to the railroad town at least once a week and he takes his family with him." The "little village of 200 souls" was now home to nine other automobiles, which took produce to market and introduced additional innovations, including three radio sets. The storekeeper's wife and daughter, who had gone "barefoot, dressed in the simplest calico," now "wear silk stockings and emulate the latest Paris fashions." More than mere traveler's tale, the story represented, for Mooney, "one illustration . . . of what the American automobile is doing to change the lives and increase the happiness and prosperity of foreign peoples."[1]

Mooney's satisfaction leaps off the page, but assumedly at least some among his stateside audiences were as pleased by his story. For in its implications, it offered corporate executives, their institutional boosters in chambers of commerce and the halls of government, and other Americans sharing in the business ethos an appealing narrative about their country's overseas economic expansion. U.S. businessmen were no Babbitts; they were "restless pioneers," in Mooney's patriotic idiom, for whom "business in foreign lands became the great adventure." Theirs was a romance twinned with patriotic satisfactions, for they were "building a great American commercial empire."

Romance and patriotism, to say nothing of profits, were untinged by guilt, for "the American business man in export trade" worked "without a thought of the appropriation of territory," and his work was "a great constructive force for the world at large—bringing about economic development with unprecedented rapidity and certainty." In Brazil, as in Asia, Africa, and benighted corners of Europe, "backward peoples" received more than motorcars. "Prosperity"—a category encompassing automobiles, economic development, and the consumer goods that both brought with them—carried with it "certainly a higher degree of happiness," an assertion that served as balm for unmentionable anxieties (for if prosperity produces a higher degree of happiness, then certainly North Americans in the 1920s were happier than ever?) and assurance "that human nature is pretty much the same the world over."

Some of Mooney's satisfaction sprang from personal circumstance, for over the previous decade he had made a swift climb to the summit of business success. Within three years at General Motors, he was president of the General Motors Export Company and a vice president in the parent corporation, soon joining what a journalist called "the General Motors group of millionaires." Mooney accomplished all this before reaching the age of forty, his success sweetened by comparison with earlier struggles as a mining engineer in California and Mexico.[2]

Beyond Mooney's personal success, which was in full bloom by the time of his second Brazil trip, there was General Motors' place in the automotive industry and the U.S. economy. In 1925, GM's Chevrolet outsold the Ford Model T for the first time, making General Motors the world's leading automobile manufacturer. The following year, its profits more than doubled Ford's. By 1927, GM was producing around one-third of the automobiles rolling off U.S. assembly lines; in 1928, its stockholders reportedly received the largest dividends ever distributed.[3]

News of GM's growth at Ford's expense was bigger than the business pages, for it reflected changes in the structure of the U.S. economy and the texture of North American culture. The family-owned and owner-operated Ford Motor Company, directed idiosyncratically by Henry Ford since its founding in 1903, had been bested by a new, decentralized conglomerate run by salaried managers working on their own behalf and for other holders of publicly traded stock. The cultural contrast was equally stark. Ford had famously remarked that customers could have a Model T in any color they wanted, provided it was black. He held to a rustic distrust of artifice and aspired to simplicity in his person and his product. In contrast, GM offered Chevrolets in myriad colors, outfitted with an increasing number of gadgets and gewgaws while holding out the promise of a "car for every purse and purpose" in ascending orders of luxury culminating in the Cadillac.

Beyond its besting of Ford's workmanlike dependability, GM's price-tiered flash matched the United States in the 1920s, awash in money and all too aware of its preeminence. For the United States had emerged from its participation in World War I, which Ford had opposed in increasingly lonely fashion, as the world's most powerful nation, while the European belligerents had been bled white. Europe's economies would struggle, and for the most part fail, to approximate their pre-1914 levels through the 1920s, while the U.S. economy bounded on to ever-dizzying heights. Affluence might generate anxieties, but it also summoned the bravado evident in Mooney's account of Minas.

And what of Brazil? Culturally and socially it remained the archipelago it had long been, its island-like regional centers separated save for shipping and telegraphy. Economically, too, it presented a set of separate, insular vistas. Some regions—the coffee-exporting atolls of the southeast, for example— seemed to recover satisfactorily from the war's external shock and the downturn of the early postwar. Other regions languished. National statistics showed a favorable trade balance; export-import merchants noted built-up demand in export-producing regions for goods, including automobiles and automobile parts, that had become scarce since the United States entered the war. Among Brazilian statesmen, enthusiasm for automobilism ran high.

This, then, was the scene against which Mooney took his Brazilian trips and spun his traveler's tale. And while his self-serving story was hardly representative of conditions across Brazil—indeed, it was not even representative of conditions across Minas Gerais—these were crucial years in the development of something approximating Mooney's "great American commercial empire" in parts of Brazil, and with it the transfer of products, practices, and patterns of thought associated with the emergent consumer capitalism of the interwar United States. The representatives of U.S. automakers and the would-be opinion leaders of the Brazilian press were key actors in this process, followed by agents of the United States' largest, most important advertising firms. All three groups were abetted by U.S. government agencies, quasi-official business-interest groups, and New York banking interests newly freed to operate abroad, as well as by the private utility companies that provided Brazilian cities and towns with electricity. The radio, as a product, was probably second only to the automobile as a marker of modern consumption in interwar Brazil, and while the car could broadcast certain figurative messages about the good life, commercial radio—born in Brazil between the 1920s and 1930s—could do so aurally. As for projecting images of that world of goods, there was Hollywood cinema.

Detroit Dreams

Mooney's 1922 visit made Brazil the first foreign country ever visited by a General Motors executive. GM, however, was not the first U.S. automaker to establish itself in Brazil. Ford had arrived earlier and remained a leader in the distribution and sale of automobiles, while now-forgotten makes and models—Studebaker, Packard, Nash—also found their way south. GM, however, despite its late start, would play a larger, more impressive role through its pairing of the American automobile and a promotional apparatus unseen in Brazil to that point.[4]

Until the mid-1910s, Brazil's automobile market was tiny, dominated on the supply side by European automakers, on the demand side by car-for-hire services, and centered on Rio. In 1907, a mere 366 cars were reportedly imported into the country, most of them from France. The import statistics of five years later reveal that French automakers had been narrowly overtaken by German ones, which supplied 1,060 to France's 1,011, while the United States lagged in a distant third place, with 783 cars. Only the outbreak of World War I allowed U.S. automakers to slip into first place.[5]

In 1915, one year into the war and the U.S. dominance of the automobile market that went with it, a Rio newspaper reported that there were 2,274 registered automobiles in the city, excluding official vehicles. Of this total, 1,336 were cars for hire, 245 were cargo vehicles, 10 were listed as being "for demonstration purposes," and the balance of 683 were held privately for personal use.[6] Between 1916 and 1920, Brazil imported an annual average of 3,614 automobiles valued at $1,890,000. Over the next five-year period, from 1921 through 1925, the respective figures were 16,925 and $8,220,000. From 1926 through 1929, an annual average of 39,963 automobiles were imported at an annual average value of $21,280,000.[7] In the record year of 1929 alone, by which point European competition was deemed "scarcely worthy of consideration" and U.S.-style service stations were lending Rio "quite an American air," Brazil imported a total of 53,928 automobiles.[8]

The rapid increase in automotive imports thus brought further changes. In 1923, insiders estimated that Brazil had the world's fifteenth-largest automobile fleet (sixteenth, including the United States); in late 1928, it was tied for ninth, the size of its active fleet having increased five and one-half times over the same number of years. The 1920s also saw São Paulo, with its larger and more prosperous hinterland, overtake Rio as an automobile market. Over the same years, the proportion of automobiles used as cars for hire declined relative to privately owned passenger cars, even as greater numbers of trucks and buses were imported.[9]

Increasingly, such vehicles were shipped to Brazil "knocked down" (industry jargon for partially assembled), with final assembly taking place in local workshops and factories. The savings to be had by more efficient use of shipping space meant larger profits for companies that set up assembly operations, and so Ford installed a makeshift plant in a converted skating rink near São Paulo's city center in 1920, less than a year after employees of the automaker's Argentine subsidiary had founded an office there. The construction of a three-story assembly plant, "modern in every detail," followed. Founded with $25,000 in capital, by 1923 Ford's Brazilian branch held $1.4 million in assets and, in its manager's words, "had the country covered with a good dealer organization." In 1924, 16,828 Fords were sold in the country, a figure that jumped to 23,499 the following year.[10]

Henry Ford may have professed a disdain for show, but his agents in Brazil demonstrated a promotional eagerness that appeared to pay off. In 1925, when Rio's Automobile Club hosted a "Grand Exposition of Automobiles," the local Ford organization contributed the largest exhibit, which offered visitors the opportunity to see Ford trucks, tractors, and the Model T up close, and had as its centerpiece a working assembly line, at which "the awed Brazilian public watched the cars come into being," a gratifying response that "showed the value of propaganda work."[11] In 1926, the automobile company took a similar show on the road, a sixteen-vehicle caravan that traveled 1,400 kilometers through the interior of São Paulo state, reaching a total audience of some one hundred thousand at twenty-five stops, "demonstrating the vehicles' capabilities by day while entertaining evening audiences with films depicting the Ford factories and the building of good roads."[12]

Ford's producerist promotionalism would be increasingly outdazzled by the work of representatives of General Motors. GM executives may have arrived in Brazil at a lag but lost no time in introducing their company's price-ordered "aura of affluence" to local audiences through displays that emphasized entertainment over education and leisure over labor. More fully in tune with the business and culture of the North American 1920s, GM was also better positioned to appeal to Brazilian urbanites who were modern minded but not necessarily industrially inclined.[13]

In 1925, General Motors opened its first assembly plant, in an outlying São Paulo district, and sold 5,597 vehicles. Chevrolet cars and trucks were the plant's mainstay, but soon other makes and models were coming off the line as well. In 1928, 25,162 vehicles were sold, and it became clear that a larger plant was needed. Construction of a "model plant for [GM's] world wide organization" began in nearby São Caetano soon thereafter. By late 1929, it was already in operation. Described as "one of the finest erected by the automobile industry anywhere," it could turn out fifty thousand vehicles a day and was a source of wonder for visitors, who "carry back with them to every part of the country glowing accounts of American manufacturing and producing methods."[14]

Alongside its assembly operations, GM built a sales organization to rival Ford's. By 1929, it included a network of dealers throughout the country, divided into four districts overseen by regional managers. The latter headed the company's "large and prosperous branches" in São Paulo, Porto Alegre, Recife, and Salvador and met quarterly to "exchange . . . ideas for the expansion of General Motors in Brazil."[15]

Assembly operations and distribution networks were joined by a department specializing in advertising, promotion, and publicity, which grew from five employees in 1926 to thirty-four in 1928. While the department started out as a clearinghouse that published monthly bulletins and provided dealers with pamphlets, translations of imported catalogues, and plates for the publication of advertisements in local newspapers, it came to provide all the services of a New York advertising agency: preparing original artwork and text ("copy") for publication in major newspapers; offering regular supplies of advertisements to dealers in smaller cities and towns; creating and maintaining billboards, car cards, and neon signage (which together were referred to as "outdoor" advertising); placing publicity pieces in news outlets large and small; and publishing a magazine for GM dealers, employees, owners, and enthusiasts.

Over these years, journalists and would-be journalists, caricaturists and other starving artists, along with more than a few young men hired for their command of English alone, became what former employees would identify as Brazil's first real cohort of advertising professionals. Their most formative experience, another ex-employee claimed, was provided by its first North American manager, who made the department "a true practical school of advertising." Beginning at around the same time, GM's International Department regularly sent the Brazilian office "manuals, books and magazines" on advertising, while the enthusiasm of the new Brazilian devotees was such that by 1928, "it was the young men themselves who ordered technical books from New York." The new knowledge and systemic practices—"all of the experience of the competitive American advertising market"—that GM brought to São Paulo was summed up by a specialist as "a new school of advertising thought, using odd expressions like *layout, copywriter, slogan, market-research, headline, caption* and so many others. Commercial advertising technique, already richly developed by 'Uncle Sam,' finally reached Brazil."[16]

While advertising was the department's main order of business, promotional activities ranked a close second. These activities included a showy debut of new automobile lines timed for the close of GM's first full year of business in Brazil. It was followed by further spectacles that brought entertainment and the glamour of the cars for every purse and purpose to audiences throughout southeastern Brazil.

The grand debut of 1926 began quietly. Through early December, advertisements in São Paulo newspapers promised "the greatest event of its kind, which no other private firm has ever attempted," but provided few clues as to what awaited. On December 10, a Friday, a convoy of dozens of new GM automobiles, their chassis shrouded in white fabric, weaved through the city streets, while a biplane crossed the skies, scattering invitations to "The Greatest Exposition of New Automobile Models Ever Realized in Brazil." That evening, special guests and the holders of the air-borne invitations were welcomed to the exposition's inaugural, where sixty makes and models of automobiles—"of every type and price," but each "of impeccable elegance"—were on display in a refitted warehouse, at the center of which stood a Cadillac, the "most beautiful General Motors car." According to one account, many of the now-unshrouded cars were not yet available to the U.S. public and would only be launched in 1927, "simultaneously, in S. Paulo and the United States," in recognition of Brazil's reception of GM products, "providing purchasers of its cars the opportunity to acquire the most modern models, which feature all the latest improvements." On December 11, the exposition was opened to the public, and over the course of the following days, more than forty thousand visitors lined up to see the latest in automobile style and participate in the raffle of an Oldsmobile convertible. Newspaper reports mentioned the "practical demonstrations" of automobiles at work (engineering displays that would not have been out of place at earlier Ford-sponsored shows) while also noting the exposition's emphasis on "the beauty of the automobile, as well as the advantages that come from the improvements now introduced in the latest models." The exposition thus constituted "a veritable showroom of the choicest cars, of elegant lines. . . . There is the superb Cadillac, the elegant Oakland, the popular Buick, the speedy Chevrolet, the graceful Oldsmobile and the new Pontiac, a modern make of automobile that has just been launched in Brazil." For display alone, it was "worth seeing," a reporter counseled. "The new car models, the modern color-finishing of the chassis, their impeccable upholstery in leather and velour, the elegant structural lines, be they of the high-end cars, or of the common kinds, all this was cause for the public's admiration."[17]

Where Ford had sent a caravan of cars, trucks, and tractors into the interior of São Paulo to carry out practical demonstrations followed by films promoting good roads and assembly-line production, GM's publicity men had their caravan accompanied by the "Grand Chevrolet Circus." This caravan toured the state of São Paulo, as well as portions of Minas Gerais and Rio de

Janeiro, and at each stop provided an automobile exhibition for prospective buyers and the invited guests of the local GM dealer, followed by circus acts, musical numbers, and dramatic and comedic performances, all put on for free, with scarcely a mention of the virtues of good roads or the efficiency of U.S. assembly lines. The spectacle itself was the point.[18]

Ford's management in Brazil, like Henry Ford back in Dearborn, was slow to recognize the competition's advance. In December 1926, for example, as GM set São Paulo abuzz, Ford advertisements, unaccompanied by product illustrations or other adornments, provided the sober promise of "New Improvements in Ford Cars and Trucks without Any Increase in Their Prices." Before too long, however, both the parent company and its Brazilian subsidiary faced up to GM's challenge. The first step, taken in the United States, was the introduction of the Model A, to provide car enthusiasts worldwide with the same features as a Chevrolet; it soon drew attention even in some of Brazil's deepest reaches for its "new *design*, with a variety of colors." A second step was the improvement of the Brazilian affiliate's promotional apparatus, which was accomplished in part by the hiring away of an employee of the GM advertising department to assist in Ford's advertising and sales promotion.[19]

By that point—mid-1928—the slide toward depression that began in Brazil with a softening of coffee prices was little more than a year away. When the crash of October 1929 followed, it brought an immediate drop-off in automobile imports and sales, but the Great Depression did not prompt Ford or GM to abandon Brazil. Rather, Detroit's big two were joined in the automobile-assembly business by Chrysler in 1935–1936. Manufacturers of key components—tires, for example—were similarly bullish about prospects.[20]

Depression did not destroy the automobile dream, though the desires of many car buyers were downsized. By the early 1930s, even for some among the idly affluent, "the day of the Packard sports car came and went. Now it's the Chevrolet." To the extent that basic U.S. makes faced any competition in the decade following 1929, it came from downscale European models, but even here the U.S. connection was key: the most popular of these European cars was the Opel, manufactured in Germany by a GM-owned company, but "advertised locally as 'a product of General Motors,'" such was the perceived appeal of its U.S. connection. At mid-decade, the strength of automotive product sales relative to other imported goods was taken to be "encouraging proof of Brazil's increasing dependence on the motor vehicle as being no longer a luxury but a decided necessity" and that "there is no question of the future importance of this market."[21]

The road to automobile ownership was shortened by credit. In the mid-1920s, interested parties lamented the lack of financing facilities in Brazil, a situation that was little changed when the economy fell into depression. By 1936, however, the U.S. automakers had expanded their local credit organizations, each offering "substantially the same facilities" (for financing retail sales for periods of up to eighteen months), and GM's representatives claimed "that they are now financing more passenger cars and trucks than has ever been the case."[22]

To the convenience of credit were added accessories and new finishes. For buyers of low-priced cars, in particular, add-ons like radios and clocks constituted "a badge of affluence," while as the Brazilian economy rebounded, matching its performance of 1928–1929, observers noted an increased preference for "more vivid colors," a "trend in finishes [that] continued toward bright colors in all price fields." Here, in a Brazilian journalist's words, were "the demands for progress of these faster-paced days," the "unusual interest, for it reaches all classes, awakened by the appearance of a new model of car" featuring a "technical or aesthetic detail that renders a year-old model obsolete."[23]

Meet the Press

In 1929, on the eve of the crash, GM was publishing advertisements in 350 newspapers, some of which had at most a couple of hundred readers, others reaching as many as two hundred thousand people on peak days.[24] That was not the extent of the unevenness of the Brazilian press. Few newspapers sold enough copies to cover their expenses, and while additional income—from political subventions, movie listings, blackmail, classifieds, and reclames (the French term for advertisements, in telling use into the 1920s)—kept some out of the red, at least for a time, many newspapers lived on the edge of insolvency. The situation for journalists was similar. Few newspapermen could survive by their writing alone, no matter how much hackwork they churned out; among the more popular sidelines, ranked from most to least desirable, were absentee jobs in public administration, lawyering, actual jobs in public administration, shystering, brokering space for reclames, and teaching. Successful journalists occupied one of two poles: they were political-literary true believers or absolutely amoral in their approach to the craft. Notwithstanding, journalism remained a dream for many, if not most, among the relatively slight percentage of young men in Brazil who were fortunate enough to learn to read and write; proof may be found in the sheer number of new titles published every year, from school newspapers to the one-off annuals of clubs, teams, and other associations. The press, in Brazil as elsewhere, continued to exert a romantic attraction, even if as an aggregate it delivered little romance and still less in the way of a decent livelihood.

This somewhat grim portrait should not be taken as the last word, accurate as it may be in its outlines. To start with, early twentieth-century Brazil was home to some very fine newspapers. Indeed, when one keeps in mind the limits imposed by the country's poverty and the illiteracy of most of its inhabitants, the scene appears more impressive than abject. Moving on, and more to the point, the early decades of the twentieth century, especially the period beginning in the 1910s, were a period of great quantitative growth and tremendous qualitative change in Brazilian journalism.

The growth of the press may be illustrated by figures compiled by the Ministry of Labor's Department of Statistics. In 1912 there were 1,377 periodical titles published in Brazil, 882 of which were newspapers, the remainder made up of almanacs, house organs, and reviews of various sorts. In 1930, the respective figures were 2,959 and 1,519. The circulations of individual titles also grew, the estimated circulation of São Paulo's leading title jumping from twenty thousand copies per day in 1910 to upward of ninety thousand in 1931. It was, however, a geographically uneven growth, as the circulation of even the weakest São Paulo and Rio dailies approached or even left behind the circulations of extraregional newspapers: in 1931–1932, the leading newspapers in Minas Gerais and Bahia, then the most-populous and third-most-populous states, respectively, had an estimated daily circulation of around ten thousand.[25]

As far as the character of journalism goes, it too changed dramatically and unevenly. Indeed, qualitative change was probably even more uneven than quantitative change, so much so that any overview risks caricature, however necessary a big picture might be. At the turn of the twentieth century, to refer to the Brazilian press meant to refer, in the main, to morning newspapers, published in Rio and the larger state capitals for local or, at most, regional distribution. Many of the more important of these newspapers had been founded decades earlier (the *Diario de Pernambuco* in 1825, Rio's *Jornal do Commercio* in 1827, the *Correio Paulistano* in 1854). Even more recently founded outlets of Brazil's grand press gave the appearance of belonging to an earlier era. Such was the case of *O Estado de S. Paulo* (1875), with its narrow columns, quiet headlines, diminutive type, and sober masthead. It may have been liberal in politics, but it was conservative in style and everyday content, emphasizing those portions of the news (the international wires, the coffee trade, high culture) least likely to be of interest to ordinary city-dwellers. Rio's *Jornal do Brasil*, founded in 1891, presented a similar profile. By the 1910s, however, changes were afoot. New newspapers, many of them published in the afternoon or evening rather than the morning, offered urban everymen more varied fare presented in reader-friendly fashion, with cover-page photographs and nonstandard typefaces. That was the case of

A Noite (1911) and *A Epoca* (1912), both published in Rio, as well as of several São Paulo titles. For-the-people reporting, a censorious attitude toward the authorities, and a brisk trade in scandal led critics to bandy about the term "yellow press," an epithet embraced by some ink-stained, would-be tribunes. Over time, however, such "popular" outlets either toned down their muckraking and rabble-rousing or were overtaken by newspapers that adopted some of their scandal mongering and populist appeal, while shedding the exclusivity and edge of the earlier muckrakers: women and children readers were now addressed directly, through columns dedicated to their perceived interests, and editors were more attentive to advertiser concerns regarding news coverage and printing quality. Wrested from the hands of its founder, the veteran journalist Irineu Marinho, *A Noite* became a very big business in the 1920s, while *A Época* and its São Paulo counterparts disappeared, the latter overtaken by the *Folha da Noite* (1921) and *Folha da Manhã* (1925), known as the *Folhas*. Even older newspaper interests took notice, *O Estado de S. Paulo* launching a livelier evening edition and shifting its morning edition's coverage to appeal to a broader public, including through enhanced sports coverage.

This incipient massification was sometimes accompanied by a depersonalization of newspapers' editorial lines. Where before a given newspaper had been identified with a single figure or family (whether or not he or they were sole proprietors), it became more common to find locutions the likes of "Sociedade Anonima" on newspaper mastheads. At its 1912 founding, Rio's lavishly illustrated *O Imparcial* was identified as belonging to a "Companhia Brasileira de Publicidade." In 1925, when *O Globo*, also of Rio de Janeiro, was launched, it was thoroughly identified with Irineu Marinho—the name of the "editor-proprietor" featuring prominently on the masthead—but after the unlucky journalist died suddenly only weeks later, it was run by committee and its masthead fell silent regarding ownership. Through 1930, the *Folhas* were the property of an eponymous limited-liability firm, but they were identified in the popular mind with their cartoon mascot, Juca Pato, a harried Paulistano taken to be typical of his fellows.

Arguably more important than depersonalization and massification were the twin forces of concentration and professionalization. Though these developments came relatively late to Brazilian journalism, they nevertheless came to exert a significant influence in the 1920s and 1930s. These beginnings set the stage for the greater concentration and professionalization of the postwar era.

The early concentration of Brazilian journalism is synonymous with the career of one magnate, Assis Chateaubriand, a diminutive publisher from northeastern Brazil known to intimates, acquaintances, and some readers as

Chatô (he thus stands as a noteworthy exception to the general trend of de-personalization). Beginning in 1924, when he took over Rio's *O Jornal*, Chatô laid the basis for Brazil's first media empire, the Diários Associados, or "Associated Dailies," until its expansion into radio, when it became the Diários e Emissoras Associados (Associated dailies and broadcasting stations). By late 1929, the empire-to-be included six newspapers, published in Rio, São Paulo, Porto Alegre, and Belo Horizonte, each of which ran four-color supplements on a regular basis, as well as *O Cruzeiro*, a magazine with pretensions of "national" status founded the year before as simply *Cruzeiro*. As an aspiring press baron, Chatô made his way by a combination of wit, charm, ruthlessness, and connections to the powerful (leading politicians, captains of industry and corporate executives, newspaper-proprietors of the "grand" press), but he was also an eager student of things North American. Soon after acquiring *O Jornal* he hired Dermot Fitzgibbon, the advertising head of Hearst's *New York American*, to organize an advertising department for the Rio newspaper and, in Chatô's words, "help me put an end to doctrinaire journalism, belonging to the last century." Addressing Fitzgibbon directly, he said, "With your help, I want to establish North American methods of selling merchandise through the daily press. We are going to impose new ways of doing their advertisements on high-end shops [*magasins*]. Whoever doesn't follow us is going to starve." Fitzgibbon's efforts soon payed off, as *O Jornal*'s advertising revenues doubled within the year, its pages filled with commercial appeals on behalf of cars and trucks, patent medicines, and *magasins*. In 1927, a special issue commemorating what boosters called Brazil's Bi-Centennial of Coffee ran to 192 pages, more than half of them taken up by advertisements. With *Cruzeiro*'s debut in 1928, advertising, promotion, and publicity were joined: late afternoon on December 5, as Rio's downtown filled with home-bound commuters, four million pamphlets were dropped from the roofs of the city's high-rises, promising a weekly magazine "belonging to [the age of] the skyscrapers," one that "knows all, sees all," and would deliver it in color. The pamphlets themselves carried advertisements, as would the magazine, everything done, in Fitzgibbon's words, according to "the most modern American process for the infiltration of the consciousness of consumers." Perhaps the most impressive publicity feat of all came five days later, when a distribution network featuring a rented bi-motor plane made it possible to put the magazine on sale in state capitals from Belém to Porto Alegre simultaneously. Little wonder that insiders point to *O Cruzeiro* as having played a singular role in the making of Brazil's commercial, advertising-driven media.[26]

As the example of *O Cruzeiro* suggests, Brazilian magazines began to come into their own in the 1920s and 1930s, not in competition with newspapers, but as complementary means of advertising, often published by newspaper interests. While Chateaubriand had *O Cruzeiro* (to be joined, in coming years, by other weekly and monthly magazines), *A Noite* began publishing a weekly rotogravure supplement in 1930, an experiment that soon led to the publication of two magazines, *Carioca* and *Vamos Ler*.

The new magazines and broader expansion of the press translated into greater professionalization, or at least professionalization of a sort. The proliferation of press outlets meant more opportunities for aspiring journalists, and while the latter's numbers always exceeded the number of paying jobs, the situation of the lucky few improved over time. While few journalists could live from their craft, the expansion of government employment through the 1930s helped the cause, as did the establishment of government-mandated minimum salaries for different classes of journalists.[27]

Tenuous professionalization, increasing centralization, and other forces at work in Brazilian journalism in the 1920s and 1930s combined to make for a press that was more favorable to business. Not that a friendliness toward or spokesmanship for leading economic interests was novel (recall that Brazil's second-oldest continually published newspaper was titled *Jornal do Commercio*); what was new was a friendliness toward consumer-oriented businesses, affiliated with U.S. corporations or otherwise inspired by North American models, and an increasing emphasis on promotion over production, spectacle over substance. Even the most staid newspapers would eventually promote consumption in the present more prominently than they reported on coffee futures. Along the way, advertising began to shed some of its less savory associations and, by the mid-1930s, upstanding members of the grand, nineteenth-century press were announcing their services to advertisers. By then, an older equation of newspaper-reading with gentility and civilization had been joined by a more meretricious calculus of the money to be made off the comparatively comfortable classes from which the newspaper-reading public sprung. Here, as predicted by a Minas-based businessman, was the "stimulation of the present media, helped by good advertising, into wider and more general circulation," showing "the wide-awake business man . . . that the printed word is to be his best sales help."[28]

In 1925, on the occasion of Brazil's first automotive exposition, the Rio press had joined Ford, GM, and local dealers of cars, trucks, tires, lubricants, and related goods in the promotion of automobilism. Chateaubriand's *O Jornal* had sponsored the exposition's two professional auto races, while amateur races were sponsored by sportsmen's magazines, the *Gazeta de Noticias*, and—in the case of the "Ladies' Automobile race" consisting of "tests of skill, with obstacles"—the homemaker's monthly *Vida Doméstica*.[29]

The event's motorcycle race was sponsored by the late Irineu Marinho's *O Globo*. An evening newspaper with roots in the popular, crusading journalism of the 1910s—at its debut it forswore any links "to capitalist groups or individual plutocrats"—*O Globo* nevertheless emerged as a vocal advocate of automobile imports from the United States and of Ford's Brazilian interests in particular. Among *O Globo*'s principal figures was Herbert Moses, himself of North American ancestry and a self-described "Attorney at Law representing American interests in Brazil," though Roberto Marinho, son and heir to Irineu, would emerge as the newspaper's unquestioned leader.[30]

Connections like those existing between *O Globo*'s Herbert Moses—soon to be the head of the Brazilian Press Association—and the local representatives of U.S. business were hardly unique to the new afternoon newspaper. At the time, *O Globo* was outdone by the Diários Associados, the local representatives of General Electric, Metro-Goldwyn-Mayer, and Standard Oil numbering among Chateaubriand's deep-pocketed backers. In turn, these interests' behind-the-scenes contributions and ready resort to advertising expenditures were rewarded with friendly editorial matter. But that was not the extent of the connections. It was the president of GE's Brazilian subsidiary who introduced Chateaubriand to Dermot Fitzgibbon, the New York advertising veteran hired to "to establish North American methods of selling merchandise through the daily press." Thereafter, success came readily to Chateaubriand as he sold the press to merchandisers at every step in the building of his empire. As a foreign observer remarked, his "sense of the value of advertising [was] impeccable. Newspapers had regarded business as being vaguely vulgar until Chateaubriand came along. He was quick to see that business was here to stay and would pay off in advertising. He has been friendly to big business and with big businessmen, and it has paid off."[31]

By the mid-1930s, it was a commonplace among interested observers that the press, despite continued technical difficulties and other limitations, was the best way to reach the relatively deep-pocketed public that had drawn companies like GM and Ford to Brazil, even if the size and composition of that public were ill-defined. Back in 1921, a representative of a New York–based advertisers' association had reported that the 20 percent of the Brazilian population that was literate "represent a strong buying power." It was a wildly optimistic estimate, but in its miscalculation and its conclusion it highlighted the scarcity of reliable market-related information in Brazil and anticipated the belief that among those Brazilians privileged enough to attain literacy were to be found the smaller proportion of the population from which consumers could be recruited. As another North American observer remarked of Recife, newspaper advertising "does not reach more than a small part of the population owing to the high rate of illiteracy, but the fact remains that purchasers for automobiles are to be found almost exclusively among the upper, educated classes." By 1937, another automobile-related inquiry estimated that newspaper and magazine advertising reached "approximately 1,462,000 readers . . . which comprise probably the most select buying group in the country."[32]

Madison Avenue Arrives

Hedging aside ("approximately," "probably"), the estimate for 1937 was a significant advance on the hopeful guess of 1921. The U.S. automobile manufacturers' activities in Brazil, especially in advertising, sales, and distribution, were one impetus to that advance. Another, initially sponsored by those automakers, was the opening of São Paulo and Rio offices by some of the United States' leading advertising agencies. The J. Walter Thompson Company, from 1929, N. W. Ayer & Son, from 1931, and McCann-Erickson, from 1935, built on the work carried out by GM's advertising department, introducing new professional standards and making the first sustained efforts to map local markets and media. Along the way, the U.S. agencies trained a generation of Brazilian advertising men, who would be increasingly influential in years to come.

The installation of the J. Walter Thompson Company (most often called JWT in the United States and "Thompson" in Brazil) resulted from a pact committing the agency to open an office in every city outside of the United States where General Motors built or assembled cars, but that agreement had sprung from an existing interest in foreign markets on JWT's part. Its New York executives had long held forth on the necessity or even inevitability of overseas economic expansion by the United States, as well as the gains to be made by awakening the "same desires and passions [that] rule one and all alike," using "intensive selling coupled with intensive advertising" to unloose "the latent demands . . . which [will] build our markets abroad."[33] For Stanley Resor, the agency's president, advertising was "an essential component of American culture" that would be exported abroad as "more and more American technicians in advertising, selling, transportation, and manufacturing were to live and work throughout the world, helping local people develop their skills in various fields." This faith in advertising and Americanism—an admirer described it as "persistent and devout"—tied in with enthusiasm for what some critics dared call monopoly capitalism, in which "America would take over the financial leadership of the world . . . financed by Wall St., and there would be world-wide super-giants in the economic sense. There would be General Motors, for example, which would supply the major portion of automobiles throughout the world; an international General Foods or Standard Brands would dominate the specialty food market throughout the world; a couple of American tire companies would supply the world with tires, and so on. And along with these worldwide American industrial octopuses would, naturally, be JWT—ready to serve them in any place they needed to be."[34]

To serve General Motors in South America, Resor sent an executive named Henry Flower to Argentina, then Brazil. At São Paulo's port city of Santos, Flower was met by J. Maxwell Kennard, the son of a U.S. diplomat chosen for his command of Portuguese. Flower was to supervise the outfitting and staffing of the new office, while Kennard was to take over once it was up and running, though he probably did not foresee that he would soon be replaced by older advertising hands sent down from New York, the most noteworthy of whom was Harry Gordon. Gordon, Kennard, and Flower, like their colleagues in New York, shared the upbringing and educational experiences of "sons . . . of the late-nineteenth-century liberal Protestant elite," which bequeathed them "a faith in inevitable progress unfolding as if in accordance with some divine plan," some of which would be adopted by their Brazilian understudies.[35]

JWT's first São Paulo office was in a newly built high-rise facing the city's Parisian-styled Municipal Theater, its interior decked out "in the very latest style, with the very best that America can produce in the furnishings and fittings." For staffing, the office drew on GM's advertising department, an obvious recruiting pool, as its newspaper-advertising operations would be shut down under the terms of the agreement with JWT, the remaining employees reorganized into a sales-promotion department.[36]

Over time, however, this pool of recruits proved insufficient, for reasons including JWT's growth, other opportunities open to the GM veterans, and the need for employees based in Rio beginning in 1931, when the agency opened a suboffice serving the national capital. As a solution, JWT turned to what Brazilian professionals would refer to for decades as the *trainee* system, in which new hires worked their way through each of the office's departments— media, traffic, copy, art, research, accounts, and more as the number of departments grew over the years—learning on the job in each one. In the words of one ex-trainee, hired in 1933 at age seventeen, "JWT was my school of advertising. Thompson people were my teachers, Thompson literature and informational material were my school books."[37]

Over the agency's first fifteen years in Brazil, the São Paulo office grew from eight employees in 1929 to twenty-eight in 1935 and thirty-three in 1944. In Rio, the suboffice founded with a handful of employees in 1931 came to have a twenty-two-person staff of its own by 1944. These tallies leave uncounted considerable numbers of employees who took their training with them when richer prospects emerged.[38] In that training, two sets of ideas were important at the time and lastingly influential. One was called the "T-Square"; the other was a schema for classifying potential consumers.

Invented by Stanley Resor, the T-Square was defined as "five questions that must be answered before any plan for an advertising campaign can be made": "1. What Are We Selling?"; "2. How Are We Selling?"; "3. To Whom Are We Selling?"; "4. When Are We Selling?"; and "5. Where Are We Selling?" Here, as simple as any catechism and blessed with the imprimatur of an organization that prided itself on operating "from the center of every large population area in every land," was a set of questions that could be asked by any aspiring professional with the promise that, if answered thoroughly, success awaited.[39]

Even more lastingly influential was the classification schema used in the answering of the T-Square's most crucial question, "To Whom Are We Selling?" As described by a New York executive, this schema was based on "apparent income and standard of living," dividing families into four groups: "Class A is the very wealthy, clearly able to afford expensive luxuries. The other extreme is class D, the poorer families represented by day laborers and foreigners. This leaves the intermediate B and C classes, with the B class sitting just above the level of the skilled workmen." Initially in Brazil, the groups were defined by income: class A families had incomes above twenty-four thousand milreis per year; class B, between twelve thousand and twenty-four thousand; class C, between five thousand and twelve thousand; and class D, under five thousand.[40]

Of the men who imparted the general training based around the T-Square and the class A–D categorization scheme, Harry Gordon was remembered as a "living school of experience" and "one of the great boosters of modern advertising in Brazil." When additional technical specialization was required, his in-office training was complemented by the efforts of new emissaries from North America, who provided short, intensive workshops to impart specific skills. In 1930, one emissary's efforts were credited with providing the São Paulo office with "an experienced layout man in charge of the studio, a draftsman and a new figure man who gives promise of great usefulness."[41]

Training was only a small part of JWT's work. While new hires were drilled in draftsmanship, the rest of the office would have been busy with the search for clients, with attempts to map Brazil's uncharted markets, and with the production and placement of advertising. These activities were more immediately impactful in spreading Thompson's influence beyond its São Paulo office.

JWT's first non-GM client was the local branch of National City Bank, for which turning away the automaker's new agency would have been difficult. It was thus an easy prize, but not a particularly fat purse, as the bank was not a heavy advertiser. Over the next few years, however, and despite the economic collapse that began shortly after the opening of the São Paulo office and continued through the Rio opening, new clients were sought out and signed up. In 1935, by which time Brazil, if not the United States, had emerged from the Depression, the agency's client roster listed the local offices of U.S. corporations with profiles complementing General Motors'—Atlantic Refining Company, Firestone Tire & Rubber—together with other North American companies, including Kodak, Johnson & Johnson, Pond's, and Northam Warren. Consumer-oriented European firms, such as Coty and Lever, had also been signed, as had the British transatlantic carrier Blue Star Line. As a rule, foreign clients were favored for their deeper pockets, but Brazilian interests were courted to the degree that they were tied to U.S. corporations and, more importantly, that they allowed the U.S.-owned company to "begin to say . . . we're a Brazilian agency." Assumpção & Cia., a São Paulo dealer in electrical goods, fit both descriptions, while Brahma and Fontoura, manufacturers of beer and patent medicine, respectively, missed on the first but more than made up for it on the second. Each Brazilian client, of course, also meant an increase in billings. Indeed, print-advertising space suggests that Brahma contributed more to JWT's success in Brazil than did many of the more favored foreign interests.[42]

As far as situating the agency in its new setting was concerned, the first order of business was establishing contacts with newspapermen and printers, to be followed by the surveying of local markets. Indeed, the former occurred alongside the pursuit of clients, and by August, a staffer claimed, "We have established ourselves with about 80 of the most important newspapers in the country." Sizing up markets began with firsthand observation of São Paulo and Rio, consulting with GM veterans and other old hands, and gathering such statistical material as could be found; it continued with reconnaissance further afield. To the media chief of the São Paulo office fell the thankless task of a late-winter trip to Brazil's southernmost states, "to collect facts and figures that will enrich our store of information," while his assistant toured the country's north. Who was sent where is revealing of the perceived importance of the two regions relative to one another—the underling relegated to the country's poorer northern reaches—but in both cases the "investigators secured population statistics and fairly accurate estimates of the possible purchasing power of each state and municipality. They counted the number of retail stores and classified them by the kind of product that is sold. They visited banks and secured figures which show fairly well the movement of money from season to season and from year to year. They observed the types of people who read each paper." And, finally, "They went to the people themselves to secure firsthand answers to their questions."[43]

Investigations carried out for clients offered the prospect of greater detail. It has become a truism that such investigative work does not deal in pure facts but rather represents the creation of knowledge, but it is nevertheless one worth keeping in mind, especially as JWT's São Paulo office was almost certainly the first institution to formally investigate and thereby create knowledge about aspects of Brazilian life that would be continually remapped and remade in the years that followed.

Of surviving investigations, the most interesting in these respects was carried out in 1931 for Lehn and Fink, the North American manufacturer of cosmetics, toilet preparations, and Lysol-brand disinfectant. The resulting report brought together statistical material from the files of JWT's local Research Department and the results of "approximately 25 consumer interviews with young women." These sources were complemented by interviews with nineteen doctors, eight wholesale druggists, two midwives, and one veterinarian, as well as at seven beauty parlors, six perfumeries, and ten retail pharmacies and in-store beauty counters.[44]

The report aspired to science, noting with clinical aloofness such facts as the prevalence of birth control, with "ergot products used extensively," and that in Brazil—as in the United States—there was a gulf between legality and customary practice when it came to abortion and contraception. More often, however, North American prejudices announced themselves, as in passing mention of the "Brazilian theory . . . that the best way to surmount the color line is literally to wash it out by encouraging inter-marriage between the races" and in the assertion that "all types" of skin are to be found in Brazil, "with the majority dark-skinned and inclined to be oily, as might be expected from a people largely of southern European origin." In other cases, it would be difficult to distinguish between newly imported prejudices and those long characteristic of the southeastern Brazilian upper crust among whom the U.S. advertising men lived and worked; climatic determinism, for example, had great purchase among both groups, and was apparent in the assertion that "the southern states" demonstrated "greater activity and general health, while in the north the people are comparatively indolent and more subject to disease."

In this assertion, the report relied upon the geographic division of Brazil into two halves, "North" and "South," though at other points it used a scheme discerning "three general trading areas: north, center, and south," with the middle category embracing the Federal District centered on Rio and the states of Rio de Janeiro, São Paulo, Minas Gerais, and Espírito Santo. Population estimates for 1929, income tax returns for 1928, and automobile registrations for 1930 were cross-listed to rank the territorial jurisdictions within these areas and identify the most desirable ones. Ranked by population size, they were Minas Gerais, São Paulo, Bahia, Rio Grande do Sul, Pernambuco, Rio de Janeiro, the Federal District, Santa Catarina, Paraná, and Espírito Santo, which represented "75.9% of the total population, 87.5% of income tax returns and 95.3% of the automobile registrations." Within these nine states and the Federal District were "approximately 193,244 families with an annual income of 12:000$000 or more—one fifth of the total number of literate families"; this "buying power" was concentrated in the cities of Rio and São Paulo, "with Porto Alegre rapidly increasing in importance" and "the northern cities apparently slightly decreasing." As far as sales went, a manufacturing concern based in São Paulo or Rio with representatives in Porto Alegre and Recife would "do approximately 70% of his business in the central market, 20% in the south and 10% in the north." North, south, and central, "it is probable that a more satisfactory net profit can be secured by concentrating on the small, wealthy section of the population."

To approach this population, the report offered information on newspapers in Rio, São Paulo, Santos, Belo Horizonte, Salvador, Recife, Fortaleza, Belém, and Porto Alegre, including circulation, geographic distribution, advertising rates, general appearance, and whether their readers fell into class A, B, or C. Rio and São Paulo's magazines received the same treatment, with special mention made of those read primarily by women. Total numbers of perfumeries, beauty shops, and pharmacies were listed for Rio and São Paulo, and the names and addresses of leading cosmetics distributors in the two cities were provided, as was information on expected margins for wholesalers and retailers, their merchandising efforts, and their nationality. Since Lysol would be used in hospitals, and physicians and other caregivers might use their practices for product promotion, the report also included statistics on hospitals and offered lists of Brazil's eight thousand physicians and the two major cities' 132 registered midwives.

The bulk of the report, however, was concerned with what women did and what products they might be persuaded to buy. Class A women drove their own cars and received periodic facial treatments. They used two or three brands of facial creams regularly, as well as hand lotion, had their nails painted, and practiced "feminine hygiene." They did not work inside or outside the home. Class B women did not drive or receive beauty-parlor facials. They used "one and sometimes two" facial creams, painted their nails, and practiced feminine hygiene; were likely to work outside the home as well as perform some household work; and used much the same kinds of cosmetics as class A women. Class C women were considered only inasmuch as they consumed some of the same goods as their social betters: national-brand facial creams; bar soap; lipstick, rouge, and powder (but not the compacts used by classes A and B); household disinfectants. While most women of classes A and B gave "special care to their skin" before leaving the house and "before retiring," only "some" class C women did; the same was reported of the practice of feminine hygiene. As class D was excluded altogether, the report could assert that makeup was used "extensively" by women of "all classes" and that all women "shopped."

While JWT's investigations aimed at mapping actual and potential consuming publics, its advertising sought to make potential consumers into paying customers and to shape public choices and tastes in more general ways. The increase in JWT's advertising was reflected in the growth of its client list and increases in its billings, which more than tripled over the 1930s. Qualitative changes can also be observed. The effectiveness of testimonial advertising was noted early on by JWT's staff. At first, such advertising—"so unusual in the Brazilian press that [it] attract[ed] a great deal of attention"—was limited to society and specialist appeals: men of standing endorsing the Chevrolet's "comfortable ride," men of science hailing its fuel efficiency, the head barman of Munich's Regina-Palast Hotel testifying to the excellence of Brahma beer, "A triumph of Brazilian industry!" These testimonials were soon joined by the cinematic glamour of appeals featuring Hollywood celebrities. "Reason-why" advertising was deployed on behalf of GM's entire line of automobiles, as well as for Atlantic motor oil and Goodrich Silvertown tires. Photography increasingly vied with line drawing in advertisements, despite its comparative expense, the difficulty of achieving good-quality photographic reproduction on newsprint, and a lack of professional models. "Class A" audiences were offered the comforts of the Blue Star Line; striving members of "class B," more time at home and an end to the inconvenience of public transport through the "fully attainable pleasure" of owning a GM Opel.[45]

N. W. Ayer followed JWT to Brazil, opening an office in São Paulo in 1931 and one in Rio soon thereafter. Ayer's arrival was, in part, a function of Ford playing catch-up and acquiring overseas representation by a single U.S. agency, as GM had with JWT. In another parallel, the Ayer executive sent to head the São Paulo office, a Canadian-born veteran named Ingriff Diez "I. D." Carson, found the ex-employees of the GM advertising department an indispensable staffing source. "The best advertising school yet in Brazil," Carson supposedly remarked more than once, "was that early General Motors section." In turn, Carson, like JWT's Gordon, was recalled as a "living school of experience," a "teacher of many good folks," the "legendary Major Carson."[46]

In São Paulo, Ayer was installed in the Martinelli building, the city's first true skyscraper and "the most glamorous building of the time," where Carson and his staff gave "finishing courses" to holders of "'diplomas' from GM's Advertising Department." In Rio, Ayer's office was housed in the *A Noite* building, another of South America's earliest skyscrapers. By 1935, the two offices had around twenty employees, "gripped . . . by fascination with American technique. It represented then the greatest *know-how* in the world. It laid down the rules. It pontificated. And all of us came to work according to its guidebook."[47]

While the bulk of the agency's work was for Ford, Ayer also created and placed advertisements for firms ranging from Gessy (a Brazilian soap manufacturer) to U.S. Steel.[48] Over a four-month period in 1934, Ayer also undertook what for years would be called "the largest investigation ever taken of the Brazilian market," carried out for the government's National Department of Coffee "with the aim of verifying . . . the habits of the Brazilian people in relation to coffee consumption and . . . the possibility of promoting, within Brazil itself, the consumption of its principal product." Through it, the advertising men "sounded out public opinion to find out what were the most efficient means of advertising for the timely divulging of advice and instructions that could make the Brazilian a bigger consumer of coffee." Working under the direction of five chief investigators, 228 questionnaire-carrying "local investigators" in cities and towns from the banks of the Amazon to the Uruguayan border reached 10,743 families (of classes A, B, and C, Ayer having adopted JWT's schema), representing 71,733 actual or potential consumers, as well as 376 roasters and 152 wholesalers. Back at Ayer's offices, twelve staff members compiled, catalogued, and analyzed 566,750 responses to questions ranging from methods of coffee preparation to newspaper readership. Here, again, was the creation of knowledge about subjects scarcely pondered by earlier business interests or the administrative elite of Brazil's old regime.[49]

Nor did Ayer's staff in Brazil neglect the work of establishing and maintaining cordial relations with the press. As a Ford executive wrote, "N. W. Ayer & Son we feel stands out in front of all of the advertising agencies in Brazil, and no matter which part of the country is visited by the writer we always find that the local newspapers are willing and ready to cooperate with this agency by publishing all articles and news stories submitted by them free of charge and without hesitation." Through its press contacts, copywriting, and other activities, the agency was "giving outstanding service in their field at the present time so much so that they have been able to obtain some of the best local accounts" and had come to be "considered an independent Brazilian corporation established to serve local firms."[50]

The third of the three U.S. advertising agencies to enter the Brazilian market during these years was McCann-Erickson, brought to Brazil to serve the Standard Oil Company. Unlike JWT and Ayer, it was based in Rio, in an office in Standard Oil's newly built Art Deco skyscraper, and initially maintained only a small subsidiary office in São Paulo. More noteworthy still was McCann's break with the "colonial empire" model insisted upon by Resor for JWT and followed by Ayer in São Paulo, in which offices were opened and managed by North American executives overseeing a staff made up mostly of "natives." Instead, the head of McCann's Buenos Aires office hired Armando de Moraes Sarmento, a former Ayer staffer, to head the agency's Brazilian operations beginning in 1935.[51]

At that point, the specialist common sense was that "the gradual transition from casual and poorly organized advertising to the present-day improved standard of sales promotion was due to a large extent to the influence of American agencies and their methods." As one authority described it: "Although relatively recent, this development has had a far-reaching influence. Not only have newspapers, magazines, and other published media found it necessary to improve their physical make-up and general appearance in order to meet the more exacting requirements of advertisers, but the consumer has been educated to expect attractive and original advertising, and his buying habits are influenced accordingly." A small cohort of Brazilian advertising men had been trained and were held to be "as able as one could hope to find in any country": "As they augment their numbers through training and experience, modern advertising, as we understand it in the United States, will become a widely employed and profitable aid to Brazilian commercial and industrial endeavor." Amid these developments, "American products sold in Brazil have benefited to the greatest extent from this almost indispensable aid to merchandising."[52]

Helping Hands

The overseas expansion of U.S. business that began in the 1910s and continued, in Brazil, through the 1930s was abetted by a host of institutions. The Commerce Department, which grew to mammoth size after Herbert Hoover was made secretary of commerce in 1921, was one. The State Department also pitched in, principally through its consular representatives. Although ostensibly private, American Chambers of Commerce in Brazil worked in close cooperation with U.S. officials for the benefit of business. The first U.S. banks authorized to function abroad performed valuable services in the overseas expansion of U.S. corporations. Each of these three types of institutions—banks, businessmen's associations, and branches of government—assisted in the re-creation of elements of U.S. consumer culture abroad, including in Brazil, where they were joined in their mission by utility companies owned by corporations based in the United States and Canada.

Hoover, like GM's James Mooney, had been a globetrotting mining engineer early in his professional life, though a much more successful one. Before heading the Commerce Department, his most significant experience in Washington had been as chief of the Food Administration during World War I, when he brought the full force of the nascent profession of public relations "to educate and direct public opinion," including through cooperation with JWT and the Hollywood studios. As secretary of commerce, Hoover matched this war-born love of publicity with an unabashed enthusiasm for mass-produced consumer durables and time-saving efficiency, declaring that a "man who has a standard automobile, a standard telephone, a standard bathtub, a standard electric light, a standard radio, and one and one-half hours less average daily labor is more of a man and has a fuller life and more individuality than he has without them." While unmentionable anxieties regarding manliness, fulfillment, and individualism were implicit in this claim, they scarcely stayed Hoover's massificationist zeal.[53]

A key part of Hoover's remaking of the Commerce Department was his overhaul of its Bureau of Foreign and Domestic Commerce. In 1921, in his words, it was "a feeble agency . . . presided over by an ineffective appointee." Over the next eight years its staff grew from 100 to 2,500, while its congressional budgeting rose from $100,000 to over $8,000,000.[54]

For the bureau's directorship, Hoover chose Julius Klein, by his lights "not only a most able economist but a great administrator—a perfect public servant." Klein was also that oddest of birds, an Ivy League–trained historian who was perfectly attuned to his age's passions, interests, and illusions. He could thus, without a twinge of shame or regret, single out national advertisers as "spokesmen of our whole scheme of civilization," and serenely intone as 1929 staggered to an end, "I think we are moving forward, as individuals, as business men and as a nation. I believe in no time in history has man had as much consideration for his fellow-man, as much genuine generosity, as much idealism or frankness, as he has today."[55]

Klein also brought an existing interest in Latin America to the bureau's directorship. In 1915, he topped off his graduate studies at Harvard with a tour that took him across the Spanish- and Portuguese-speaking Americas, following which he returned to Harvard, but not for very long. In 1917, he was recruited by the bureau to serve as its Washington-based expert on Latin America; in 1919–1920, he served the bureau in the field at Buenos Aires. As the bureau's director, and later as assistant secretary of commerce, he used every available medium—newspapers, magazines, academic journals, motion pictures, even a weekly radio show—to steer his countrymen's attention to the "harmonious, mutually beneficial exchange of commodities" between the United States and Latin America, a "New Pan-Americanism" that was "operating fully as much to the advantage of the Latin American countries as to our own," while telling the kinds of stories of "America Motorizing Mankind" of which James Mooney was so fond.[56]

The bureau's interest in Brazil predated Klein's directorship and, indeed, the Hoover-led expansion of which it was a part. After 1914, when the bureau convinced Congress to fund diplomatically accredited commercial attachés who would serve "at posts especially important to our export trade," Rio was among their "ten pioneer posts." Under Hoover and Klein, a subsidiary office was opened in São Paulo, headed by a trade commissioner. The two offices were staffed by assistant trade commissioners and Brazilian and Anglo-American clerks. Elsewhere, from Manaus to Porto Alegre, the State Department's consular officers played similar roles.[57]

This cohort, numbering some two to three dozen officials and employees at any one time, was responsible for regular reports on specific subjects, as well as answering inquiries from U.S. firms interested in Brazil, providing direct assistance to U.S. business interests, and occasional reporting on local businesses and any developments that might be of interest to the bureau, to which were added, a former trade commissioner remembered, "creating 'good will for American goods'" and serving as an "Ambassador of Trade" more generally.[58]

A listing of the topics on which the commercial attaché in Rio was required to submit periodic reports included "radio development," "American representation in Brazil," "power developments and prospects," and "department store organization and methods." Automobiles were, of course, the subject of detailed reporting, as were tires, fuel, and road conditions.[59]

In 1921–1922, the Rio office submitted 199 formal reports to the bureau, in addition to 357 letters, 103 telegrams, and thirty-eight "trade lists" of Brazilian mercantile houses and manufacturing firms. During the same fiscal year, the office provided 275 direct responses to firms in the United States. In 1922–1923, it submitted 354 reports, over four hundred letters, and fifty telegrams to the bureau, as well as around four hundred letters sent to U.S. firms in response to direct inquiries. Beginning in late 1922, reports from Rio incorporated reporting from the newly opened São Paulo office, which increasingly submitted correspondence directly to the bureau as well as to interested parties in the United States.[60]

As U.S. business expanded in Brazil, the bureau's officers, their local staff, and allied consular officials provided direct, on-the-ground contact and counsel for every kind of interest and agency. In 1923, Julius Klein himself commended the attaché in Rio for the "more militant sort of assistance . . . given the Gillette Safety Razor Company, the Singer Sewing Machine Company, and the Davis Baking Powder Company" (in the latter case, the attaché's efforts were key in circumventing a government ban on imports). Two years later, the trade commissioner at São Paulo assisted GM's representatives as they prepared to establish assembly operations.[61]

Despite belt-tightening at the Commerce Department after 1929, these kinds of services continued to be offered. In 1930–1931, the São Paulo office hosted 182 businessmen visiting from the United States. During the second half of the 1931 calendar year, it answered queries from U.S. interests ranging from the American Association of Advertising Agencies to the Player-Tone Talking Machine Company, while also providing assistance to a new Ford dealership and to I. D. Carson as he set up Ayer's local office. Through the 1930s, such "Outstanding Examples of Service to American Business" were repeated.[62]

Creating goodwill for the products and practices of U.S. consumer capitalism entailed more work for bureau, consular, and diplomatic officials. In 1921–1922, it meant drumming up support among businessmen for contributions to the U.S. pavilions at Brazil's Centennial Exposition. Opened in December 1922, the pavilions included a cinema auditorium and displays by 182 U.S.-based firms, including "manufacturers of steel products, locomotives, railway cars and accessories, automobiles, trucks, tractors and accessories, machinery, tools, explosives, rubber products, paint, floor coverings, typewriters and office equipment, sewing machines, phonographs, school supplies, yarns, pharmaceutical products, safety razors, flour, baking powder, beverages, and toilet articles."[63] Two years later in São Paulo, similar if less strenuous work was required by the coordination of local dealers of U.S.-made automobiles as the trade commissioner and his staff helped organize one of the city's first automotive shows.[64] On a day-to-day basis, the bureau's staff maintained relationships with specialty-interest journalists such as the editors of *Automobilismo*, with whom the São Paulo office maintained "close contact" by "constantly feeding them material from the United States" that might tend "towards bringing out the qualities of the American product." The result was that the monthly magazine was "strongly pro-American and . . . a good share of the articles smack of American origin." With the broader press, the favored approach was indirect: "working through such individuals as the manager for J. Walter Thompson, and the public relations officers of the local General Motors and Ford assembly plants. These people bat 100% with local newspapers, owing to their extensive advertising," as the trade commissioner found when he "made the rounds one night" with one of GM's public-relations men. Returning the favor, the trade commissioner "worked up an article to appear in the General Motors house organ."[65]

The task of maintaining cordial relations with government fell to staffers in Rio, who "found it necessary to frequently call on Brazilian Government officials and officials of the Federal District for information and help in the preparation of reports and occasionally interceded with some of these officials on behalf of American business concerns." These favors were returned as well, as the office of the commercial attaché "was frequently called on by Brazilian Government officials for information or assistance in their work."[66]

Along with currying favor with officials, journalists, and the broader public, representatives of the U.S. government acted in and alongside the local
affiliates of the American Chamber of Commerce. Indeed, these ostensibly
unofficial groups were conceived, midwifed, and nurtured by U.S. officials
with an eye toward establishing "that co-operation and community of interest which American business men are realizing to be as essential in foreign
trade, if not more so, as it is in domestic trade."[67] Here was another set of helping hands.

The founding and early organization of the Rio chamber was mostly the
work of the U.S. consul general, to whom fell the task of obtaining a model
constitution in May 1915. Affiliation with the U.S. chamber at Washington was
achieved in November and was followed by recognition by the Brazilian government in 1916. At its founding, the Rio chamber was described as having
"as its nucleus the local representatives of such concerns as the Standard Oil
Company, United States Steel Products Company, United States and Brazil
Steamship Line, Singer Sewing Machine Company, General Electric Company, the American Consulate-General, the National City Bank (Rio de Janeiro Branch), the United States Banknote Company, Otis Elevator Company,
Caloric Oil Company, New York Life Insurance Company, and others—in
short, the representative American establishments working on Brazilian soil."
By 1922, the chamber's membership had climbed to around 250, "steadily
increasing" and including "43 alien members who are representatives of
American interests"; two of these "aliens" also served as directors. From
its downtown offices, the chamber provided "considerable service to American trade interests," including through "trade-mark protection work," "the
furtherance of American shipping interests," and "the conclusion of a commercial arbitration agreement" between the U.S. chamber and Rio's Commercial Association, which had among its legal counselors Herbert Moses, of
O Globo, who was also a member of the chamber and counsel to several of its
corporate sponsors.[68]

The founding of a São Paulo chamber was encouraged by the local commercial attaché in early 1919 as part of larger efforts "in trade reconstruction
work and the maintenance of American influence and prestige" and to provide "the Embassy and the Commercial Attaché another valuable aid." By
December, the São Paulo chamber employed a full-time managing secretary, who worked out of a downtown office that included meeting space and a
reading room for the use of the chamber's two hundred members. Like the
Rio chamber, the São Paulo office was active in the brokering of information
and more general assistance to U.S. business: "It is active in matters of trade
inquiries, securing agents for American firms, compiling commercial information, [and] adjustment of commercial disputes."[69]

From the beginning, the São Paulo chamber was led by automobile executives and distributors. At the end of its first decade of activities, the chamber's corporate and institutional membership was a who's who of consumer-oriented U.S. firms and their local agents. Among the former were not only Ford and General Motors but also Goodyear, Firestone, B. F. Goodrich, Columbia Phonograph, Victor Talking Machine, General Electric, Standard Oil, Atlantic Refining, the Texas Company, and the Hollywood studios. Among the latter were Brazilian and expatriate commercial interests (Assumpção & Cia., Byington & Co., Paul J. Christoph & Co.), the executives of U.S. firms, and corporate lawyers the likes of Herbert Moses, who corresponded from Rio. As Moses's presence suggests, the members and officers of the Rio chamber were no less convinced that "the Brazilian importer, merchant and consumer are coming to realize and appreciate the distinctively American style, finish and quality of many articles peculiar to the United States, which were [virtually] unknown here before the war," including automobile accessories, household appliances, motion pictures, toilet preparations, and canned goods, demand for which "will continue to increase with the increasing number of potential consumers who are enabled to become actual purchasers through better wages and more equitable distribution of the profits of industry and agricultural development in Brazil."[70]

The Chambermen, in other words, were of the same mind as Herbert Hoover and Julius Klein, whose writings and speeches they eagerly quoted and reprinted in publications distributed in business circles. The first issue of the Rio chamber's magazine noted, correctly, that "one of the greatest publicity agents developed during the war was Herbert Hoover," adding, equally correctly, "Commercial and industrial interests have good reason to expect some highly beneficial and interesting developments during Hoover's tenure of office as Secretary of Commerce." In 1925, *Brazilian Business* summarized Hoover's remarks on the elimination of "wastes which . . . are responsible for huge annual losses in both the productive and distributive phases of business" in the United States, remarks that were held to be equally applicable to foreign trade "in these days when the margin of success . . . depends increasingly more on efficient industrial and sales technique." An expatriate spin on an old homily drove the point home: "We are all headed for the City of the Ideal. Many of us will never reach it. But the suburbs—they are very beautiful." Klein's words received equally reverent treatment, his homilies including the appeal to service rather than speculation and the identification of "reciprocal advantages, that with every upward lift of American sales or investment there must be commensurate improvement in the economic well-being of the peoples" of Latin America. In merchandising and sales, in particular, Klein argued, the key was to apply "engineering precision to distribution" through "painstaking industrial and marketing research."[71]

The appreciation was mutual, Klein ranking the work of the Chambers of Commerce just behind the overseas activities of U.S. banks as "contributions to American commercial advancement." The opening of branch banks abroad was only possible beginning in 1914, following the passage of the Federal Reserve Act of 1913. National City Bank (NCB) was the first to enter the Brazilian credit market and, by late 1916, operated branches in Rio, São Paulo, Santos, and Bahia. By mid-1920, these had been joined by other NCB branches in Porto Alegre and Recife. The branch banks not only provided the credit facilities that made expanded trade possible; they also—like the advertising agencies, Chambers of Commerce, and State and Commerce Departments— served as brokers of information and promoters of the further expansion of U.S. business, not only in the export-import trade but also in local manufacturing, assembly, and merchandising. This extrafinancial brokering and promotion continued into the 1930s, despite straitened economic circumstances and the closing of some NCB branches.[72]

During these same years, there was increasing concentration in Brazil's utility sector, as local power, transport, gas, and telephone companies were absorbed by two conglomerates, the Emprezas Electricas Brasileiras (EEB, wholly owned by the Electric Bond and Share Company of New York) and the Brazilian Traction, Light and Power Company (a holding company chartered in Toronto, "nourished on a mixture of North American promotion and technical expertise combined with large injections of capital from both sides of the Atlantic," and referred to universally in Brazil as "the Light"). This concentration resulted in "better and more economic utilization of natural resources" and more "uniform conditions of production," as a Chamber of Commerce organ pointed out, while affording economies of scale that allowed the two conglomerates to invest in the promotion of consumption.[73]

The utility companies' need to attend to such promotion was recognized in 1926 by a São Paulo–based engineer: "Our problem is no longer one of producing ample power but of *selling* it. . . . It is impossible to apply too much attention and effort to this commercial end of the business." In the case of the EEB, this situation meant the eclipse of "engineers primarily interested in the mechanics of current production and distribution" and so "a new experienced manager has been placed in charge in São Paulo with instructions to push sales, the old manager being left as superintendent in charge of construction and production." As far north as Pernambuco, an EEB employee recalled, "The Americans readied themselves to put their commercial methods into effect." Their efforts paid off, electricity consumption in Rio and São

Paulo growing by 28 and 78 percent, respectively, between 1928 and 1935, despite the catastrophic economic conditions of the early 1930s.[74]

In order to stimulate greater household use of electricity, the Brazilian Traction, Light and Power Company and EEB sought to popularize the use of electric light and especially of home appliances, "acquainting the consumer with modern electric labor-saving devices, and to inform the people in the communities served concerning the many ways that electricity can be used to relieve the housewife of drudgery." In 1930, EEB "maintain[ed] in about 100 cities and towns, showrooms where all kinds of electrical appliances for industries and for the home are demonstrated and offered for sale"—"stores, even those in the smaller towns, [that] are modern in every respect, and compare very favorably with stores of a similar nature in the United States." Over the next two years, EEB continued "aggressively developing its appliance sales," more than doubling the number of its nationwide showrooms.[75] Meanwhile, Paulistanos could visit "an extensive display," featuring "lamps, irons, toasters, wiring devices, etc.," on the ground floor of the São Paulo Tramway, Light & Power's headquarters, "the most modern and perhaps the best situated building in the city," kitty-corner from JWT's office.[76]

Each utility company worked in cooperation with the Brazilian subsidiary of the General Electric Company, which had its headquarters in Rio and offices in Belo Horizonte, Porto Alegre, Salvador, and São Paulo. Along with employing "a number of sales and engineering specialists who work very closely with the utility companies wherever possible, with a view toward increasing sales, through the most modern and effective sales methods," GE created its own advertising department—founded in 1926, and thus second only to GM's—which placed advertisements for goods ranging from refrigerators to radios in newspapers throughout the country. *O Cruzeiro* and the Chateaubriand newspapers were particularly favored, as one might expect given the friendly relationship between Chatô and GE. In the 1930s, GE and EEB would employ N. W. Ayer's services in promoting appliance sales and "creating demand for the increase in consumption of electrical energy," work that a Brazilian employee of the utility company would recall as a revelation, "as they put me in contact with an organized standard of service and with a system of planning at that point nonexistent in our midst."[77]

To these efforts were added "modern efficiency sales methods, including house to house canvassing" and other "direct sales methods," plus "five or six sales campaigns" per year, "each one specializing on [*sic*] some article of domestic application, such as refrigerators, irons, etc." By the early 1930s, installment buying (previously unknown for household durables, with the partial exception of sewing machines) had "obtained considerable volume with regard to commodities used in homes," including through the "collecting of monthly payments by adding them to the lighting bills of consumers." Indeed, one observer claimed, "Due to sales methods employed by utility companies to increase their outputs, homes are being gradually equipped, through the operation of these methods, with radios, refrigerators and other appliances." In a sense, these developments dwarfed electricity usage and appliance sales: "In fact, the development of the Brazilian market from a sales point of view at the present time is proceeding as rapidly as possible, and in a number of centers the same type of effort, with corresponding results, is being employed as is currently practiced in the United States."[78]

Radio, Radio

Among the devices that the utility companies and General Electric were able to promote and sell in increasing volume were radio sets. This process began, for GE, with "carrying on a campaign of education at Rio." For Brazil, radio broadcasting began in Rio as well, with a demonstration put on by the Westinghouse Corporation for the Centennial Exposition of 1922. Thereafter, radio ownership, audience size, broadcasting facilities, and programming grew at a nearly geometric rate. Rio would remain the national center of Brazil's advertising-supported broadcasting stations, though São Paulo developed its own commercial networks serving its hinterland, while cities to the north and south came to have commercial stations of their own.[79]

In 1924, one of the Bureau of Foreign and Domestic Commerce's assistant trade commissioners estimated that there were slightly more than three thousand radio sets in Brazil, around two thousand of them in Rio, most of them made by hobbyists. He nevertheless noted a "great deal of interest" in radio, not only in Rio but also in Bahia, Pernambuco, and Rio Grande do Sul, in the last of which he saw "unrealized opportunities" for potential radio sales, "although not exactly a virgin field" because of the state's proximity to the commercial poles of Buenos Aires and Montevideo. In São Paulo, which had more radios than any other city but Rio, he reported that "enthusiasm is running high," adding that "one American salesman who recently returned from a trip to that market described it as radio mad."[80]

From these beginnings emerged an explosion in radio ownership and listening. Factory-made sets—imported, locally assembled, and Brazilian made—replaced amateur kits, with the path to ownership shortened by installment sales. In 1930 the U.S. trade commissioner at São Paulo reported that the value of radio-set imports through Santos in 1928 reached $137,500, the U.S. portion of which was over $113,000, while "dealers estimate[d] that imports in 1929 exceeded in value those of the previous year by at least 30%."

São Paulo had outpaced Rio in radio sales, and "numerous trade estimates would place the total sets in use in the State of São Paulo at about 40,000."[81]

The increase in radio sales was undeterred by the collapse of 1929 and the poor economic conditions that followed, a U.S. official reporting in 1932 that "the growth of radio sales during the past two years" was an "outstanding phenomenon": "Distributors and retailers have perfected a sales method based upon long term installment buying and the success which has been made by the better known American makes has stimulated importers to bring in a wide variety." By the mid-1930s, there were an estimated three hundred thousand sets in use in Brazil (45 percent of them in São Paulo, 40 percent in the city and state of Rio de Janeiro, and the remainder split among Brazil's other eighteen states), an increase attributed in large part to credit sales. The result was that "Brazil is today one of the world's best markets for radio receivers," accounting for more than 20 percent of U.S. radio exports in 1935, as well as increasing numbers of sets manufactured in the Netherlands by the Philips company. Meanwhile, Brazilian factories turned out domestically branded Cacique, Imperator, and Metrotone sets.[82]

Expanding demand over the first half of the 1930s was credited to "the ability of the Brazilians, despite the low exchange value of their currency, to purchase luxury items," as well as the importance of "more intensive merchandising methods." To the extent that Philips made itself competitive with U.S. manufacturers, it was "not only by offering a wide range of excellent sets at prices lower than some of the well known American makes," it was "also by attracting dealers by more liberal credit terms and an aggressive propaganda campaign" (that is, by adopting the competition's methods).[83]

By 1937, there were an estimated 420,000 sets in use, reaching between 1.8 and 2.5 million people, "a majority of which fall into the higher income groups" previously pursued through the press, and demand for new sets showed no sign of slackening, with imports running at between 6,500 and 7,000 sets per month. At that point, between 90 and 95 percent of new receivers were purchased on installments. Over the next two years, "notable upswings in sales" of electric devices, including "an almost spectacular increase" in radio sales, led to a doubling of the number of sets in use, to an estimated 850,000 in 1939.[84]

Accompanying the growth of radio ownership expanded between the 1920s and the 1930s was a tremendous expansion of broadcasting facilities. In 1924, there had been only two stations in Rio, one the property of the national government, the other privately owned, and a single station in São Paulo. By the mid-1930s, there were fifty-seven, from Pará to Rio Grande do Sul. Six more joined the scene in 1936, and in early 1937 the first successful experiment in chain broadcasting resulted in simultaneous broadcasting by fourteen stations belonging to a network owned by São Paulo's Byington group, distributor for such U.S. firms as Westinghouse and Columbia Records, headed by a Harvard alumnus of North American ancestry. The network's broadcasts covered an area ranging from Curitiba to Campos.[85]

Along the way, stations' broadcasting strength and programming quality improved considerably. Second only to credit as an explanation for the ability of Brazilians to continue buying radio sets through the darkest days of the depression was the fact that increasingly inexpensive "midget" sets could pick up local stations in Rio and São Paulo. These stations, rather than the European, North American, and Argentine shortwave broadcasts that had been sought after by Brazil's amateur pioneers, drew most of the growing radio-listening public. Building on amateur origins characterized by improvised shows and heavy dependence on prerecorded music, Brazil's better stations came to offer an array of entertainment programming, including live performances of popular and orchestral music, as well as dramatic and comedic sketches. Sports coverage increased and improved in quality, and in 1938 the Byington group's Rádio Clube do Brasil brought play-by-play coverage of the World Cup to Brazilian audiences. Ever obliging, *O Globo* provided the front-page headline, "Todos a postos nos radios!"[86]

Thus Brazilian radio became a fully commercial medium, modeled expressly on that of the United States, the source of most of Brazil's broadcasting equipment and many of its early experts in radio technology and programming. As Bryan McCann has argued, it could not have been otherwise: given the government's lack of resources, and despite the statist inclination of its leaders during much of the 1930s and 1940s, the country's radio would be either commercial or entirely amateur, and, if the latter, its broadcasts would be drowned out by stations broadcasting out of Buenos Aires. That overdetermination, however, should not obscure that while commercialization encouraged vibrant cultural production, it also exerted lasting effects on other media and the country's larger cultural life.[87]

There is a tradition in Brazilian media studies that dates the commercialization of radio to a 1932 decree that legalized broadcast advertising, while seeking to regulate it, limiting commercial appeals to 10 percent of a station's on-air time, but adherence to the letter of the law was lacking on either side of the decree's issuance. In 1924, Rio's government-owned station was itself broadcasting advertising material alongside martial music performed by bands on loan from the armed services. São Paulo's first station, Rádio Educadora Paulista, was promoting the sale of branded patent medicine as early as September 1927; not long thereafter, it offered musical programming sponsored by one of the city's leading radio dealers. Rádio Sociedade Record, a relative newcomer to the São Paulo market whose technical director was the

U.S.-born brother-in-law of the manager of the local NCB, broadcast material sponsored by such firms as Firestone and Lever, including, for the latter, a "program on hygiene, aimed at housewives."[88] By that point, mid-1931, several U.S. companies, including General Motors, had begun to include radio in their advertising appropriations, and dealers of U.S.- and European-made goods were using radio intensively to promote sales of automobiles, toilet preparations, patent medicines, record players, and records, as well as the latest radio-set models. Brazilian-made products, including branded toilet preparations, patent medicines, and cigarettes, were advertised in the same fashion. Indeed, radio had joined the press as a means to reach "better-class" consumers with appeals to buy "luxury items and other goods falling into a price class beyond the reach of mass buying power."[89] Given the sums of money involved, it is little wonder that the 10 percent limit on advertising time specified in the 1932 decree was ignored. Nor should anyone be shocked that the national government doubled the legal limit to 20 percent in 1934 and that officials were "inclined to be liberal" as far as enforcement was concerned.[90]

From the early 1930s onward, there was a consistent increase in the use of radio advertising to reach potential consumers. In 1936, it was estimated that "approximately 1,000,000 prospective buyers falling into the medium and high spending brackets can currently be reached through this medium." At that point, radio advertising revenues were estimated at 1,500 contos per month (approximately $85,000 in 1936 dollars), 70 percent of which was absorbed by Rio and São Paulo stations.[91]

By then, Ayer staffers had quizzed thousands of Brazilians on radio ownership and their favorite stations. The firm had also established regular simultaneous broadcasts on Rio's Radio Mayrink Veiga and São Paulo's Radio Record. Among the artists featured in these broadcasts were Carmen Miranda and Mário Reis, national singing sensations whose performances were sponsored by Ford and General Electric.[92]

Where GE was to be found, the Chateaubriand group would not be far behind, inaugurating Rádio Tupi in Rio in 1935, expanding into the São Paulo market two years later, and hiring Carmen Miranda away from Mayrink Veiga for good measure. By decade's end, the Emissoras and Diários Associados had become the country's first true media empire, including a national wire service and dozens of newspapers and magazines published in cities from Fortaleza to Porto Alegre, as well as the stations broadcasting from Rio and São Paulo. The advertising revenue that fueled this burst of expansion not only came from GE's generous patronage; it also issued forth in increasing amounts from businesses belonging to Chateaubriand: patent-medicine and perfume laboratories, a soft-drink bottler, a chocolate factory.[93]

Other Brazilian industrial and commercial interests took part in the expansion of radio advertising. The Gessy soap-manufacturing concern, for example, sponsored Ayer's simultaneous Rio–São Paulo broadcasts along with Ford and GE. European firms, including Philips, Lever, and Nestlé, were just as active, if not more so. But the guiding (not to say gadarene) spirit came from the United States. As one radioman-turned-advertising-agent remembered, "Back then it was proper to use some terms from American radio jargon: *broadcasting, speaker, spot, jingle, background.*" "How much of the United States' progress does it owe to radio!" a booster asked, adding that through "commercial advertising in *our* Country new horizons were opened, while innumerable opportunities emerged for merchants and manufacturers, who witnessed the rapid and efficient diffusion of their products, becoming known throughout the country over the radio," but emphasizing more than anything else "the importance that this invention had *there*," in the United States.[94]

Radio's power had not been lost *there*, particularly not as far as the information-brokering boosters of U.S. business were concerned. As secretary of commerce, Hoover had been a key player in making U.S. radio, nascent when he took office in 1921, a commercial, advertising-driven medium dominated by large broadcasting companies, while his overseas understudy, Julius Klein, had made much of "The Romance of World Radio": "The development of radio throughout the world will, I am sure, afford further opportunities for triumphs of American merchandising. And, like every other aspect of swift and easy communication, it will be of incalculable benefit to the expansion of general commercial operations."[95]

Movies and Mores

Klein was nearly as sanguine regarding the cinema, writing, "Motion pictures are the latest form of silent salesman, not so much perhaps for the goods of some individual firm as for classes and kinds of goods as a whole." "In spite of the fact that there is no conscious trade propaganda in the entertainment picture," he added, "it is proving a considerable force in helping to arouse on the part of the buying public a desire for the many types of products most commonly shown on the screen." An admirer chimed in, drawing a parallel between the leading U.S. export and the movies: "Like the automobile . . . the motion picture is more than a mere export product. It is a real trade envoy—an active salesman for other lines of goods." A contributor to the American Chamber of Commerce's monthly magazine made the same point more circumspectly: "The scenes which these films present to foreign eyes do not, to be sure, always give a correct impression of life in America. They do, however, arouse curiosity which translates itself into wants." All were outdone by the *Saturday Evening Post*: "The pictures have become a factor in international trade. They are making the United States the best-known and most widely advertised country to the very remotest habitations of man on the globe." "Trade," the *Post* trumpeted, with specific reference to Brazil, "follows the film."[96]

That film would drive commerce and that U.S. film would dominate Brazilian markets and entertain ever-growing audiences for decades to come were not foregone conclusions when cinema was introduced to the country, at the dawn of the twentieth century. Then, the most widely viewed productions were European, as films by Nordisk (Copenhagen), Pathé Frères (Paris), Gaumont (Paris), Cines (Rome), and Pasquali (Turin) dominated theaters in Brazil's major cities, as well as improvised showing-rooms elsewhere. By one estimate, 90 percent of the films imported into the country in 1913 were French or Italian.[97]

World War I, however, destroyed the European producers' pride of place and catapulted U.S. films into a position of dominance they would not soon lose. First Fox Films and later Paramount, Universal, and other U.S. studios entered the market and "unloosed the craze for American stars and consequently for the films from the United States." The result, according to the commercial attaché at Rio, was that "American [films] dominate this field." "American productions are more popular than European [ones]" in every genre, reported the U.S. consul at São Paulo in 1923, and there "is hardly a steamer coming from the United States which does not bring a good sized shipment." In statistical terms, Hollywood provided 67 percent of the motion-picture film sent to Brazil in 1920, 65 percent in 1924, and 80 percent in 1925, figures based on film tonnage, which thus fail to account for the much higher value (and cost) of the U.S. films. In 1925, when the United States provided 80 percent of the motion-picture film imported into Brazil by weight, it provided more than 88 percent of the total by dollar value. For 1926, the figures were 87 percent and 94 percent; for 1927, they were 88 percent and 91 percent.[98]

By that point, the pattern had been set and U.S.-made cinema had bested all competitors. Even the crash of 1929 failed to slow the U.S. advance, as film exports to Brazil continued to increase through the 1930s. Indeed, at mid-decade, insiders could afford to be magnanimous regarding local competition (much of it involving U.S. expatriate technicians and capital), noting that 1934 may have been the "best year in the history of this national industry," but the "progress made in local productions . . . in no way affected the position of American films. Developments in distribution and exhibition followed their normal course, with an increase notable in receipts of both branches of the business."[99]

Hollywood's ascendance was abetted by government and by local allies who lobbied Brazilian officialdom. As early as 1931, representatives of the Hollywood studios received a sympathetic hearing from President Getúlio Vargas. In 1938, the U.S. embassy and especially the U.S. commercial attaché cooperated with the Associação Brasileira Cinematographica in lobbying the national government to exclude motion pictures from new taxes. As a result of this activity and much more like it, executives of RKO Pictures, Twentieth Century Fox, and Warner Brothers were able to take time out of a 1939 junket to inform a U.S. embassy staffer "that the treatment of American motion picture films in Brazil is better than in any other important country in Latin America," noting the lack of import restrictions, the government's light hand as far as censorship was concerned, and the companies' easy access to dollar exchange for profit remittances.[100]

By then, movies had become a kind of "popular necessity" that a Rio-based writer described, before an audience of his peers, as thoroughly "incorporated among our needs," something that those younger than twenty imagined as having always existed. In the first of his assertions, this Rio film aficionado was beaten to the punch by at least a part of the "working-class population" of São Paulo, who two decades earlier identified the cinema as something necessary "to pass in diversion the leisure hours that it has."[101]

The vast social distance between working-class São Paulo and the intellectual circles of the nation's capital was spanned by cinema spectatorship, which reached further multitudes outside of the Rio–São Paulo axis. The two cities were home to the largest, most luxurious Brazilian movie palaces, along with smaller neighborhood theaters, but by 1935 multiple large-scale, sound-wired theaters existed in the country's next three-largest cities as well, while 1,155 additional movie houses were spread throughout the rest of the country, for a national total of 1,351. Eight U.S. film companies operated distribution centers in Rio, with branches in São Paulo, Salvador, Recife, Porto Alegre, and Ribeirão Preto.[102]

From Parnaíba to the north to São Pedro do Rio Grande in the far south—two very different urban spaces—Brazilian children grew up watching Tom Mix westerns and playing Cowboys and Indians. After their generation moved on to more grown-up pursuits, other boys and girls, in provincial towns like theirs and in very different cities elsewhere in Brazil, spent their weekend afternoons cheering "for Flash Gordon against Ming and we stomped our feet frantically on the floor when good guys like Buck Jones, Ken Maynard, Charles Starrett, William Boyd (Hopalong Cassidy), Gene Autry and Bob Steele chased the bad guys."[103]

The rise of cinema-going as leisure-time pursuit for Brazilians of all ages was accompanied by a remaking of Rio led by the Spanish-born entrepreneur

Francisco Serrador, who initiated a spree of cinema-house openings beginning in the mid-1920s, in the process changing nearly beyond recognition a part of the city that would be known as "Cinelândia." Here, steps from Rio's Municipal Theater, designed and built in the image of the Paris Opera, were new motion-picture theaters, housed in the ground floors of skyscrapers constructed expressly for the purpose, in an attempt "to recreate the atmosphere of Broadway and the magical world of Hollywood," which Serrador had experienced firsthand earlier in the decade. While in the United States, Serrador had "investigated construction, styles, etc., and decided to use the Capitol Theater in New York City as a model." Now, on Brazilian shores, he aimed to provide "cinema theaters of the most modern kind, reproducing the best of what I saw abroad." Thus were born the Capitólio, the Alhambra, the Broadway, the Império, the Odeon, the Rex, and others, in the image of Broadway and Times Square.[104] The results convinced at least one North American visitor, who found that Cinelândia "looks like a moving-picture district in New York or Hollywood. The tall new buildings house a number of fine picture theatres and at night great electric signs wink and blaze." To this reordering of space and re-creation of foreign spectacle was added the remaking of urban tastes, as the Serrador group was credited with introducing the hot dog to local palates, a culinary development noted in Lamartine Babo and Ari Barroso's Carnaval march, "Cachorro quente" (1929).[105]

As powerful and influential as Serrador was (and he owned theaters not only in Rio but throughout southeastern Brazil, including Alhambras and Odeons in São Paulo), the concrete and culinary changes that his group effected were a small part of larger social and cultural developments. The films from the United States that dominated Brazilian screens were, in one writer's words, "the best and most beautiful advertising that has yet been done of its industries, of its practices and customs, of every aspect of its spiritual and material, moral, social and economic life."[106] Cinema as a business and as a setter of fashions led to new developments in the press and helped shape radio programming, while movie-going encouraged new deportments and kindled new desires.

The creation of novel press outlets was among the more immediately striking results of cinema's rise. The publication of short-lived fanzines and distributor-published compilations of advertisements testify to enthusiasm on the part of amateurs and the perception of interested parties that such enthusiasm could be profitably exploited. But the long runs of other magazines dedicated to matters filmic demonstrates sustained interest on the part of advertisers and readers. Two such magazines were published in Rio. The first, *A Scena Muda*, was founded in 1920 and, its title notwithstanding, continued to be published by the Companhia Editora America well into the sound-cinema era. By 1932, its weekly, forty-eight-page issues were published in runs of sixty thousand copies, according to the interested estimate of the J. Walter Thompson Company and the U.S. trade commissioner at São Paulo, an estimate that put it ahead of most of the country's newspapers. The second such magazine, *Cinearte*, was founded in 1926. Dedicated "primarily to American cinema," *Cinearte*'s aspirations were summed up in its motto, "A country's progress is measured by the number of cinema halls it has."[107]

Just as the cinema summoned new publications into existence, so too did it influence the existing press. Motion pictures were promoted by international and national distributors, as well as by local exhibitors, which meant that Hollywood releases were "generously advertised in the newspapers in São Paulo and Rio." In return, nearly all the country's big-city newspapers carried movie reviews in motion-picture sections in which studio press releases ran alongside "any item of news interest emanating from Hollywood."[108]

From the point of view of Hollywood's local representatives and their helping hands in the State and Commerce Departments, the results of these arrangements were more than satisfactory. As a U.S. consul wrote of First National Pictures, "The success which their pictures have obtained in Brazil is due not only to the popularity of such actors as Norma Talmadge, Jackie Coogan, Katherine MacDonald and others, but also to the activity of the company's representatives in São Paulo in making the films known through extensive advertisements in the *O Estado de São Paulo* and other daily papers." More broadly, the "general attitude of the Brazilian press," oiled by advertising revenue, was "sympathetic and cooperative." "This was amply demonstrated," according to a Bureau of Foreign and Domestic Commerce officer, "by the support given to the industry during its recent campaign to secure a reduction of customs duties on prints."[109]

Even radio, a newer medium than cinema, was influenced by Hollywood. The introduction of sound cinema increased the popularity of imported records, thereby increasing sales and, one guesses, airplay, in what was further attested to have been a "valuable instance of the way in which American films help to sell other lines of goods." Meanwhile, radio producers adopted the U.S. practice of "presenting episodes from outstanding movies, giving still greater impetus to the Hollywood exports."[110]

Brazilians and North Americans alike remarked on the influence of Hollywood motion pictures, as did some moviegoers whose lives bridged the two countries. Among the latter was the Brazilian-born daughter of Baptist missionaries, who years later remembered the impact that "the important attraction for the masses" had on her in the 1910s in Rio: "What the films did for me was to prove graphically everything that mother had tried to teach me about America. All the people in the films were Americans, and they certainly were beautiful and good and very rich. They dressed with so much style, had such lovely homes, and the men were demigods." "Why, the United States was a paradise," she wrote, "the land flowing with milk and honey . . . where there was no poverty or injustice, where all the men and women were healthy and beautiful."[111]

For the psychologist, educator, and historian Manoel Bomfim, it was apparent in 1922 that "American films, by their inherent qualities, have impressed upon the attention of the entire world the life and customs of the American, providing the basis for new opinions and tastes," with the result that in Rio, "and in the other large cities of Brazil as well, the influence of the ideals and things American is manifest," in men's apparel and in young women assuming new public roles. "Nor could it be otherwise," he wrote. "There are millions and millions of Brazilians who have, hundreds of times, throbbed to the emotional appeal of episodes in American life."[112]

These episodes, according to the writer and publisher Monteiro Lobato, soon to declare that he felt at home for the first time upon visiting the United States, contained the very making of modern Brazil: "The Brazil of tomorrow is thus not made here. It comes from Los Angeles, on filmstrips, packed in cans like guava paste. And 'yankee' domination goes on working in an agreeable way, without the assimilated noticing." Within a dozen years, this domination would work in such a way that even a critic might be found "in a bar delightedly sipping an *ice cream soda*, very well put together in his *Palm Beach* suit. . . . After the *ice* he'll go to the Capitólio to see Gloria Swanson in *Folia*," as the Brazilian release of *The Coast of Folly* was titled. Along the way, a Buick "allowed him to fly pleasantly to Leblon in minutes."[113]

Even before the introduction of sound, the cinema constituted a compulsory, if elementary, form of English lesson, through movie posters and theatergoers' desires to accurately pronounce their idols' names. Thus was imposed an "apprenticeship in a new language and an unknown type of life was divulged—English and the United States. European influence began to die." As European cinema artists were eclipsed by Hollywood stars, the "French elegance of the 'smarts,' completely made of a starched conventionalism," was replaced by the "sporty inelegance" characteristic of the North Americans, with their Neolin-soled shoes and convertible coupes. Along the way, the automobile "came to be indispensable" even in coffee towns in the interior of the state of São Paulo.[114]

In the city of São Paulo, the opening of new cinema houses defined neighborhood sociability and generational styles, "in the coming together of traditional French influences and the North American ones divulged by the cinema." According to a Piauí-born migrant, who arrived in São Paulo in the 1930s, "Young people attended the cinema houses—the Alhambra, the Odeon, the Paramount, the Rosário, all upholstered in red with gilt fleur-de-lis, and began to dream the dreams of Hollywood. French culture gave way to the American invasion." By that point, in the words of another adoptive Paulistano, the "general tendency" was to believe that "that which was good came from Hollywood or from Detroit."[115]

Back in Rio, World War I had brought the "rapid publicizing of North American life, through the cinema." Thus, the U.S. example "facilitated a new style, which is reflected in outward habits and in one's dress. Women see themselves as freer from old prejudices, beginning to compete with men in various professions, principally in public employment. . . . Yesterday's *smarts* trade in their solemn overcoats and tails for lightweight, light-colored cashmeres and linen cloth. *Foot-ball* clubs proliferate."[116]

That Hollywood cinema was directed "above all at the masses" was its great strength, in the words of Anibal Machado, a professor at Rio's premiere normal school. "Thus its influence upon human behaviour, in how life is conceived, in the way one feels and loves, in customs and practices and dress. The *gaúchos* change their characteristic clothing, trading the *bombacha* for the cowboy's chaps. Our city Negroes dance like their brothers in America. Even girls in the most remote provinces keep up with the latest hairstyles in Hollywood." In this context, the cinema was taken to be "one of the greatest vehicles of civilization. If the girl from the outskirts of town, the scullery maid back at home . . . begin to dress better, it is because they saw the styles and the elegance of the actors in the movies." While girls from the purlieus were dressing better, their social superiors from the city proper were putting themselves together more modernly: "The pretty *Carioca* is learning to wear slacks and shorts; she buys her dresses modeled in North American style as a direct consequence of Hollywood's taking over Paris' leadership in fashion; she combs her hair according to Lana Turner's, Hedy Lamar's, Jean Arthur's, or Joan Fontaine's hair-do in the latest screen appearance."[117]

It seemed to be proceeding as predicted by Fox Films's Alberto Rosenvald in his descrying the dawn of an "American Century" twenty years earlier. In Rio in 1922, Rosenvald saw "that American predominance is fed by public preference. The force of suggestion . . . is producing its first fruit in our country. One film shows us how an automobile is made in the United States, thus exercising direct propaganda; others, of a purely entertaining nature, show us types of vehicles of this species in use by rich people and in streets and squares which are crowded with American cars." In hairstyles and home furnishings too, North American influence was apparent. Across the country, the influence of film was such "that a great part of Brazil would remain unaffected by modern progress were it not for the motion pictures, which for this reason enjoy an enormous field for development." Brazil offered Rosenvald evidence for his prediction that "within a few years, but with an effect which will endure for many decades, the Americanization of the world will be accomplished."[118]

––––––––

Rosenvald's observations from Rio recall James Mooney's storytelling for stateside audiences. The year 1939 offers an apt moment for assessing how well the two executives' claims held up. On the one hand, the "great commercial empire" Mooney had foreseen was a work in progress; a typical week of that work, as reflected in the schedule of the Commerce Department's Rio-based personnel, included meetings with and on behalf of representatives of Chrysler, Ford, Studebaker, Firestone, Standard Oil, and seven Hollywood studios. On the other hand, many of the developments Mooney and Rosenvald had observed in the 1920s had become the stuff of history, with the rise of the automobile in Rio considered alongside the urban reforms that preceded it and the "North American–style skyscrapers" of Cinelândia having become as characteristic of the city as earlier architectural forms: "Here, an old colonial section, recalling the era of the vice-roys; there, a certain corner of the imperial city of Pedro II; further on, the likeness of a Levantine port, and, here, a vision evoking New York." "The number of automotive vehicles increased by the thousands" and "men and women began to abandon the solemn and tormenting clothes of the last century." These changes led an editorialist to argue that the old turn of phrase, "Rio civilized itself," no longer fit: "It would be more exact today to say that Rio Americanized itself, seeking to reproduce the models that the United States imposed nearly everywhere." In this context, the growing appeal of the North American cocktail, the declining popularity of traditional refreshments, the opening of hotel bars, and the closing of the sugar-cane-juice stand in the Avenida Hotel and its replacement with "a pop-corn establishment, equipped with pop-corn machines made in the U.S.A.," was identified as "a turning point in the social history of the city."[119]

In 1922, Rosenvald had noted the beginning of the influence of Hollywood film on home-building: "Bungalow houses, hitherto unknown in this country, are now appearing here and there." He was seconded in 1924 and in 1926 by the local mouthpiece of the American Chamber of Commerce and by Julius Klein. That the bungalow represented "the last word in modern comfort" was such a commonplace by 1929 that the words appeared in a leftist journalist's semiautobiographical novel. Eight years on, however, the bungalow belonged to a seemingly remote past, an advertising man remembering, "There was a time in which, due to American influence, one didn't speak of residential houses anymore. One spoke of *bungalows*." Now, however, the bungalow itself was "anachronistic, almost incomprehensible."[120]

This sense of changes in everyday life as belonging to history, in one or the other of the word's two senses, and of new practices and patterns of thought passing from the exotic to the everyday, from "North American" to normal, was ubiquitous during these years. At Brazil's Centennial Exposition of 1922, Fox and Universal films shown out of doors and in an improvised auditorium had been by far the most popular attraction, drawing huge crowds day after day. Nearly ten years later, a film executive noted that, far from being satisfied with its "very fine modern [cinema] houses in the downtown section of the city," the "São Paulo theatre-going public is very rapidly Americanising its tastes [further], and will soon be demanding more comfortable and more luxurious theatres." As the finishing touches were put on a new Rio theater in 1932, a press release promised, "The Rex will follow in the least details the most artistic and comfortable lines. We wish to distinguish the capital of this Republic with a theater which will rival the most luxurious and comfortable theaters of the large North American and European cities." Over the next decade, residents of Rio and São Paulo alike would witness the inauguration of ever-larger and better-equipped theaters, with air conditioning, wall-to-wall carpeting, concessions, and other improvements unknown to their spellbound compatriots of 1922. Cinema's progress in Brazil might not match that in North America, but it "already represents something considerable."[121]

The first automobiles imported into the country, nearly all of them European makes, had occasioned wonderment and terror. Within two decades, young women in Mato Grosso could be heard humming a ditty beseeching Saint Anthony—the matchmaker saint—to send them Chevrolet-driving husbands and, by the 1930s, from Cuiabá to Cachoeiro de Itapemirim, the automobile had incorporated itself into the celebration of Brazil's pre-Lenten Carnaval, the run-up to the national fete becoming a peak time for car purchases, as well as for sales of radio-phonograph sets, records, and cosmetics, and for the tailoring of costumes modeled on promotional stills from Hollywood.[122]

As a Rio resident remarked, "the number of things American in constant use steadily grows. A well-known American sewing machine and phonographs from the United States are daily necessities, the electrical refrigerator, toaster, iron and other articles are widely used as a result of clever advertising." GE was manufacturing "millions of electric lamps annually in its plant near Rio" and the Kodak-brand camera "is as popular here as in the United States," with the word "Kodak" becoming a metaphorical referent for any modern or modernistic slice of life. "American drugs and toilet articles are widely used," while "Brazilian youths affect American styles."[123] Despite the chastened economic circumstances of the early 1930s, interested observers could claim that "the desire of ownership of those articles which go to make life easier, more comfortable and agreeable, is just as pronounced as ever," citing "the ever increasing sale of radios, electric refrigerators, electric sewing machines and modern household equipment generally in Brazil," to say nothing of "the increasing number of very late model automobiles already running in the streets of Rio and S. Paulo," even as dealers were "protesting against a lack of stock of the new models."[124] Visiting São Paulo at decade's end, a traveler "checked every car parked along several blocks and every one was an American model"; along the same streets, she found "palatial moving picture houses" displaying Hollywood films and soda fountains serving American-style confections. Moving on to Rio, there too she noted the influence of Hollywood movies, changing modes of dress and models of deportment, and the increasing popularity of U.S. goods. What lay behind these developments? "We like American things," a Carioca told her.[125]

But Rio and São Paulo were the country's two largest urban centers. Cachoeiro de Itapemirim was a regional pole linked to Rio by rail, and even Cuiabá was a state capital. What of the country's farther reaches, far from the Serrador and Chateaubriand skyscrapers of Cinelândia? In 1937, Hermes Lima had the chance to find out for himself, when, for the first time in eleven years, he returned to the interior of Bahia, where he was born and his parents still lived, traveling by train north from Rio to Montes Claros and from there "cutting through about a half-dozen counties of Minas and Bahia in the cab of a truck." Much that he found was new. In terms of "commodity," he wrote, "the greatest backland development is the presence of the refrigerator. Since the discovery of the kerosene-burning refrigerator, the backlands received an important element in its social life. The refrigerator is too expensive for private use. The fridge ended up, in this way, creating the bar, an improvement upon the old, picturesque 'venda.'" Here, the most basic commercial institution of the Brazilian interior was remade and, in Lima's eyes at least, improved.[126]

For all that, however, the kerosene-burning refrigerator was outdone by the radio. By law, municipal governments in Minas and Bahia had to have a radio receiving set, and while this regulation had not met with universal compliance, Lima predicted that soon every town and village would have at least one, fitted with loudspeakers for public use. Already, "in the backlands one dances to music from Rio. Sometimes . . . one dances to music from Berlin or the United States. One has to be there to appreciate how radio gave the backlander a feeling of approximation, of finding himself in the world, which is certainly the most pleasing of his contemporary sensations." "The radio is, for the backlands," Lima observed, "what the cinema is for us here in Rio. Just as here we talk of Greta Garbo, of Loretta Young, of Clark Gable, of [Robert] Montgomery, there one talks of Carmen Miranda, of Chico Alves. The backland listeners are 'fans' of all these radio personalities."

Hermes Lima's observations speak to the condition of that part of the interior that he traveled through and especially the gap between conditions in the counties he saw and the country's great urban centers. His point of view dovetails with Mooney's in that both men projected onto the interior a sense of pastness, of existing at an earlier stage of history than the United States (for Mooney) and the urban Brazil represented by Rio (for Lima), of the backlander as having just "found himself" in but not of the contemporary world. The temporal fancifulness of this framing, however, is not what is most interesting or relevant. What is most interesting and relevant is what Lima's account reveals about urban Brazil, the world of the writer and the audience he was writing for. There is the easy resort to English, unlikely twenty years earlier, unthinkable forty years earlier: "fan," still enclosed in quotation marks; *bar*, so naturalized as to obviate the need for italics or inverted commas. There is radio as something "ours," as part of everyday life. Then there are the performers, Carmen Miranda and Greta Garbo, Francisco "Chico" Alves and Clark Gable, to whom no national labels are assigned, who are understood as belonging to their listeners and viewers, the actors figuring in the everyday dialogues and dreams of urbanites, the singers playing similar roles for their country cousins but implicitly belonging to both publics. Commerce is attached to the venda-turned-*bar*, but not to the performers; that Carmen Miranda was an Odeon recording artist who performed exclusively on Chateaubriand's radio stations, between spots hawking the products of General Electric and General Motors, went unmentioned; the same is true of Greta Garbo's connection to Metro-Goldwyn-Mayer, then engaged in a monumental expansion of its Brazilian cinema facilities. Connections and commercial infrastructures like these enabled the changes observed by Hermes Lima, initiating Brazil's American century and fulfilling fables of the kind told by James Mooney ten years earlier.[127]

Chapter 3

Between the Two Great American Countries

In mid-1938, a businessman named Lauro de Souza Carvalho sat down with a reporter for Rio's *Diario de Noticias*. The subject of their interview was the United States, a country Lauro had visited twice over the last half-decade. Both times he had traveled in search of merchandise and ideas for his *magasin*, A Exposição, but each time he brought back a good deal more. To start with, there was his first impression: "New York was a 'punch in the stomach.' A shock, an impression of greatness and, despite this, of humanity, never before felt with such intensity." Then there was the rest of the country, from the rush of Chicago to a roadside retail outlet in upstate New York. Most inspiringly, there was the "gigantic North American commercial apparatus": "The great retail-trade organizations, the so-called 'Department Stores,' like Macy's, of New York, and Marshall Field, of Chicago, to cite only two examples, are gigantic bee-hives, in which thousands of bees work." Despite the latter characterization, department-store employees were no drones. Rather, they were "experienced men, who had attended professional schools where they learned every detail of the art of serving the public." Of these stores, Macy's, in particular, was a revelation: "Fifty years ago, Macy's was a small establishment. Due to good management, with 'to sell at low prices to sell more' as its guiding idea . . . Macy's didn't stop growing. A gigantic establishment today, it continues to grow." That example led Lauro to declare, "A great establishment cannot stop. It must always progress," while his overall impression was, "North America is a great school for those who want to learn."

The comparison with Brazil rankled. Lauro did not expect Rio to rival Manhattan, at least not yet, but he saw no reason for it to lag behind third-order towns in upstate New York: "When you see cities like Troy, with 50,000 inhabitants and 6 large department stores, and then arrive in Rio, with 2 million inhabitants and no establishment that one could call a Department Store, comparison is inevitable. . . . Here, the retail trade is tiny. . . . The very expression 'retail' has here a sense of commercial mediocrity." Part of the explanation for this situation, Lauro acknowledged, lay in Brazil's relative poverty, as he estimated that among Rio's inhabitants were only two hundred thousand potential department-store customers. Even so, he pointed out, U.S. cities with smaller populations than that had department stores of their own.

These comparisons and his North American experience kindled a consuming desire to create a store worthy of comparison with Macy's: "My desire to organize a Department Store in Rio is no longer a personal ambition, as I am satisfied with what I have. It is the drive to leave something behind." His experience also led him to urge Brazilians to "buy more from those who buy the most from us": "We should buy more and more from America. I buy more and more from the United States. Not only to find better values, but also as my duty as a Brazilian. They are our biggest and best customers."[1]

As his willingness to dispense advice and announce his ambitions suggests, Lauro was riding high. Born in the northeastern interior, he had been brought to Rio two decades earlier by his brother Milton, a retail merchant whom the writer Humberto de Campos had called "that American from Ceará" for his business acumen. In Rio, Lauro had started out as a junior partner to Milton, establishing increasingly profitable menswear stores, first on the Rua do Ouvidor, then on neighboring streets, including a shop called "Casa Yankee." In 1931, Lauro set off on his own, taking with him a single store, which he promptly renamed "A Exposição," the São Paulo rights to which he extended to another brother, Nilo, who had been in business in that city since 1921 under the name "A Capital," an appeal to civic pride that had the unfortunate whiff of Marxism to it amid the deliria of the early 1930s. At the time of Lauro's interview, all three brothers were prospering, and in the years that followed Lauro and Nilo did particularly well. By the mid-1940s, Lauro's operation included two successful Rio stores under the A Exposição name (one for men, the other for women), while Nilo owned two thriving São Paulo stores, A Exposição (for men) and Clipper (for women and children).[2]

Taking a broad view of the 1930s and 1940s, Lauro's interview for the *Diario de Noticias* was more than a chapter in one businessman's biography or twist in the tale of his family's role in the remaking of Brazilian retailing. Rather, it captures a particular moment in Brazil's mid-twentieth-century history. While U.S. business interests turned to Brazil in greater numbers through the 1910s and 1920s, Brazilian businessmen increasingly directed their attention away from Europe and toward the United States during the years that followed. Retailing in Rio and São Paulo reflected this shift, an influence registered not only in nationally owned businesses but in European-owned outlets and a chain of five-and-dime stores founded by a North American expatriate as well. Similar developments were afoot in advertising, in which Brazilian and European agencies applied lessons garnered from Lauro's "great school" to the north, while Brazilian advertising men employed by interests of every nationality bid for professional standing and public recognition. The press felt the influence of these developments, even as particular media outlets sought to encourage them. Indeed, it is to this period that we may date the Luso-Brazilian neologism that would eventually be spelled *mídia*, its monitoring by a nationally owned Gallup-style organization, and the accession of radio to the importance of cinema as a commercialized mode of leisure and entertainment, the latter epitomized by the re-creation of the soap opera on behalf of manufacturers and distributors of branded goods, North American and Brazilian, amid a larger profusion of trademarks, slogans, and advertising fora.

In all, the years between the mid-1930s and the mid-1940s may have been the high-water mark of Brazilian "Americanism." Geostrategic logics were at work, on the part of each country's governments, but consumer-oriented business—Brazilian and North American, expatriate and European—was enmeshed in the making of Brazil's plural inter-Americanisms as well. At an early point in the country's midcentury romance with the United States, Lauro de Carvalho's *Diario de Noticias* interview figured in a monthlong series explicating the "Factors of Friendship"—as described by businessmen and other notables—"Between the Two Great American Countries." Further on, Brazilians were given the promise of "A Ford in Your Future." The latter promise went unfulfilled, and the expectation of friendly assistance in the postwar died hard, but the moment of which both dreams were part was lastingly important.

A monographic account of any one of these developments—changes in retail business culture, the founding of trade associations and the fabrication of professional identities, the profusion of branded goods, commercial appeals to Americanisms of varying types—might satisfy a scholarly curiosity or suffice for an academic thesis, but it would come up short as far as tracing the ties among them, which created a commercial and cultural edifice more impressive than the sum of its parts would suggest. The turn by Rio retail merchants to the United States led them to a new emphasis on advertising and increased patronage of Brazilian specialists, who in bidding for professional standing sought strength in numbers, adding "sales" to their specialist purview. Brazilian market and media research was born as an adjunct to advertising; the country's premiere research firm subsequently served holders of the trademarks of branded goods (on whose behalf Brazil's first national media outlet broadcast entertainment programming), together with Lauro de Carvalho's A Exposição and other retail concerns. These developments intersected with and built upon other initiatives: the Brazilian-owned advertising agencies were founded by veterans of General Electric, General Motors, and the U.S. agencies established beginning in 1929; as a professional cohort, in their associations and the pages of their trade publications, Brazilian advertising men made no distinction between employees of the nationally and U.S.-owned agencies, and they welcomed to their ranks the executives of other commercial, industrial, and media concerns. Consumer-oriented businessmen of all types took on something of the missionary outlook absorbed by the first generation of Brazilian advertising men during their training at the U.S. agencies, while copywriters, commercial artists, soap-opera script-writers, and reporters sought to refract for their own purposes something of the glamorous glimmer pouring from the projection booths of Hollywood-happy movie houses.

The accumulation of these connections was one factor in the strength of an increasingly imposing market culture. Another was that so many of the new developments of the 1930s and 1940s were the work of Brazilians. Even in the age of the wartime alliance and its capitalized Inter-Americanism, Brazilian actions tended to speak louder than the sweet-sounding words of U.S. propaganda. In the postwar, Brazilian desires kindled during hostilities would burst forth, to be dampened, but not extinguished, and not before illuminating much that had changed and even more that had not.

Travelers, Traders, and Thieves

North American commercial travelers of the 1910s and 1920s were unanimous in taking a dim view of Brazilian retail. Store design and decor, shop-window dressing, sales techniques and training, the use of advertising and sales promotion—all were seen as falling short of U.S. standards. At worst, local practices were simply deplorable. At best, they were "European" and would have to yield to U.S. influence as was occurring or would occur in cities and towns across the Old World. "The arrangement of stores and store windows does not provide for the modern American type of window displays," sniffed one such traveler, apparently unimpressed by the nineteenth-century luxuries piled atop one another in the shopwindows of the Rua do Ouvidor, beckoning to a fortunate few in their signaling of quasi-aristocratic exclusiveness. "The idea of a store as a permanent exposition of merchandise—beautiful things to be looked at even by those who cannot afford to buy—is still novel," noted another, who added, "it shows in antiquated window dressing and the scarcity of counter and interior displays." In store signage, there was little use of electric light. Instead, one found lettering reminiscent of Italy and Portugal, "but no American styles." "Fascination of merchandise never gets a chance to work through the printed word," as even stores that invested in newspaper advertising "seldom select attractive offerings for individual description, much less build themselves up institutionally, like our great stores."[3]

The country's "staid British department stores"—there was, in fact, only one such outlet, São Paulo's Mappin—"remind[ed] one of London before Mr. Selfridge invaded it from Chicago." "Energetic retail is needed . . . to cut profit margins, increase turnover, and give the public service." In other words, there was a need for the "extension of American retail methods" and the founding, under U.S. auspices, of "department stores, five-and-ten-cent stores, chain stores, and the like, managed in our characteristic way."[4]

As it happened, much of the extension of such retail methods fell to Brazilian and European interests, who drew on U.S. models of store design, décor and display, product styles and services provided, sales promotion and employee training, and advertising and publicity. In developing the Brazilian five-and-dime, a former Woolworth's manager from Pennsylvania played a key role, but he soon encountered native-born competitors equally eager to steal a page from his former employer's business plan.

Innovations in store design, décor, and display were noted in Rio soon after Lauro de Carvalho first returned from the United States. Early 1934 saw what was described as "an unusual amount of activity . . . in the remodeling of store fronts." On the Avenida Rio Branco alone, "no less than ten shops have constructed modern store fronts during the past few months, and numerous additional projects are in process of construction throughout the business center of the city." Work in marble, copper, bronze, chrome-plated steel, wrought iron, and glass made these store fronts "conform closely to the modern American type." Over the next few years, parallel developments in "the modernization of store fronts . . . on a large scale" were seen in "many of the more exclusive shops" in São Paulo and other cities, resulting in "more ample window space."[5]

As far as the displays featured in these windows were concerned, Lauro de Carvalho and his cohort were even more zealous, Lauro having returned from the United States convinced that "shopwindows should become salesmen" rather than "static showcases of merchandise." It was at this point, remembered a former employee of the Carvalho brothers, that "more life, more light, more beauty, [and] more functionality came to be seen in the shopwindows of Avenida Rio Branco and Ouvidor, Uruguaiana, and Gonçalves Dias streets, with A Exposição in the lead." This was far from an individual or even a family affair, as retailers generally were "manifesting an increasing appreciation of the value of attractive window displays as an aid to merchandising," resulting in "a tendency on the part of local merchants to prepare attractive displays."[6] As a spur to employee creativity in shopwindow design, storeowners held U.S.-style window-dressing contests, while surviving photographic evidence reveals the adoption of U.S. accents and even the use of North American themes and English-language signage in displays.[7] One type of signage, however, was always in Portuguese: that indicating prices, a borrowing of the "American practice of conspicuous signs to show the prices of the various items of merchandise on sale" that, by 1936, helped make São Paulo's Mappin the country's "only large American type department store." In Rio, such signage answered Lauro de Carvalho's U.S.-born belief that "the people want to know the price of what's in the store windows, check their wallets to count the money they have on them at the time and stride confidently into the store to request the displayed merchandise."[8]

The influence of the United States was also seen in the goods and services on offer. U.S. catalogs were pored over by retailers, among whom it was a given that "America, assisted by the moving fashion plate that is the cinema, spread through the world the style of sportswear, of light and comfortable cuts of clothing, of a less elaborate style of dress."[9] With the wartime cutoff of trade with Europe, lines of goods once shipped from France, Britain, and Germany were imported from the United States: "North American novelties," proclaimed Mappin, in introducing Peter Pan and Kaycraft cloth. There were Arrow shirts for men and short-sleeved "Springtime Blouses" for women, also from the United States; and, for children, at the outlets of the once-French, now-Brazilian Mesbla S.A., a "rich and varied collection of beautiful American toys."[10] In 1939, a traveler observed, "In the feminine world the products of the United States vie with those of Paris. . . . The few ready-made dresses, aside from expensive French models, come from New York." In 1941–1942, the owner of São Paulo's Casa Vogue made several trips to the United States, returning as enthused as Lauro de Carvalho with the "fashion market of the United States" and his ability to obtain "the most enchanting novelties for S. Paulo, visiting not only the formidable New York market but also Los Angeles's great fashion centers." Soon enough, "North American Fashion" was "At Full Zenith," with patterns from Hollywood and New York predominating.[11]

New services included female attendants for female shoppers (an innovation that owed much to U.S. influence), in-store beauty shops featuring U.S.-brand cosmetics, and live fashion shows featuring the latest from Marjorie Montgomery and Bergdorf Goodman. Here were new spaces for female employment, sociability, and entertainment, all at the service of consumption. With the opening of Mappin's Elizabeth Arden Beauty Salon, women of means could avail themselves of "the scientific methods employed by this North American organization for skin treatments and the products especially created for these treatments," a service that placed São Paulo "on the same level as the great North American and European centers." Clipper's fashion shows were "a model of the best that can be done in advertising, 'public relations,' sales promotion, and entertainment, all at the same time," offering the store's "famed national products" alongside imports from the United States and Argentina.[12]

Beginning in 1939, men could take cocktails at Mappin's "American Bar" while their wives and daughters patronized its *salão de chá*, as generations of Paulistanos did from the 1914 opening of the store's "English Tea Room" until well into the postwar era. Men and women were encouraged to frequent Clipper's in-store, after-hours nightclub, where they could thrill to local "crooners." Attempting to address its heretofore Europhile customers' geographic shift in interests, Mappin sponsored a 1939 trip to the United States.[13]

New sales-promotion techniques reflected additional inspiration from the north. Lauro de Carvalho's A Exposição came to be synonymous with the "Big Liquidação," timed for Rio's changes of season and aimed at selling off existing stocks of seasonal goods, exposing bargain shoppers to other, non-sale products, and attracting publicity generally, thereby impressing the store's "personality" upon the public.[14] The Big Liquidação was complemented by the "Item of the Day" sale. Modeled on Macy's "Dollar Days," this promotion involved a single item sold at a price only slightly above its cost "with the principal objective of promoting traffic in its various departments, based on that elementary principle that someone who enters a store to buy one thing, could perfectly well end up buying something else also . . . everything depending upon what the Americans call 'sales by suggestion.'"[15]

As suggested in Lauro de Carvalho's testimony of 1938, employee training remained an intramural, somewhat informal affair. Implementing sales promotions the likes of the "Item of the Day" and such services as Mappin's Elizabeth Arden salon had owners and managers instructing employees in elements of what they had seen in the United States or read about from afar. Trade journals were avidly consumed by employees and managers (Cincinnati's *Display World* was a favorite), while business manuals were required reading for ambitious executives. As a nephew of Lauro de Carvalho remembered, "I discovered North America at the Civilização Brasileira bookstore, buying American books on retail." Employees who did not read English consulted Portuguese-language texts on "scientific administration" and "the art of selling" compiled by a Boston University graduate and American Management Association member named Louis James.[16]

At Lauro de Carvalho's invitation, James provided A Exposição employees with what one trainee would call "theoretical, almost scientific lessons" in "the art of retail selling and in executive management." Years later, the same ex-trainee would remember James's A Exposição–sponsored course as the point in his life at which "were revealed the mysteries that perchance existed surrounding that which is so familiar to him today and which he emphatically refers to in English as 'marketing,' 'merchandising,' etc."[17] As the war wound down and restrictions on airline travel were loosened, executives and employees would be sent to the United States to intern at Macy's, to take classes in retailing at New York University, and to visit the offices of the National Retail Dry Goods Association. Upon returning to Brazil, these travelers would further disseminate the lessons of "the great school."

Other changes were afoot in retail advertising and publicity. Here, perhaps more than in other fields, São Paulo and Rio presented distinct starting points. Beginning with Mappin's founding in 1913, if not earlier, high-end retail advertising had been carried out regularly by São Paulo's leading outlets. The situation in Rio, however, was different. As Milton de Carvalho remembered of the 1910s and 1920s, "merchants almost never advertised and when they did it was with the greatest parsimony." Hence the impression that U.S. retail advertising had on Lauro de Carvalho. Thereafter, the two cities' retail trades converged as each sought to apply the lessons of the "great school" in advertising and store publicity, and the directors of Rio's A Exposição were remembered as having "achieved their objectives assisted by advertising inspired by the most modern North American patterns," while Modas A Exposição Clipper, its advertising department headed by a former Ayer staffer, outpaced Mappin to become São Paulo's largest retail advertiser, "applying sales-promotion methods inspired by the North American system."[18]

In both cities, retailers showed as great an enthusiasm for radio advertising as they did for print. Milton de Carvalho, for one, prided himself on having been an early radio advertiser. In the early 1930s, his firm sponsored shows broadcast biweekly from an in-store studio. Thereafter, retail-interest radio advertising increased in volume and sophistication, in Rio and São Paulo. When Nilo de Carvalho introduced his brother's "Item of the Day" sale to São Paulo in 1946, Modas Clipper advertised over the airwaves, while in Rio Lauro was described as having "went the Americans one better" in radio advertising, including regular "Big Broadcasts" and "Big Broadcastings."[19]

As these titles suggest, advertising often aimed at establishing links between retail establishments and the United States. Even British-owned Mappin took this tack, noting in Portuguese-language advertising of 1933 that it was "modeled on the same principles as the great 'magasins'" of London, Paris, and New York. Similar appeals were made in other kinds of publicity, as in 1931, when Rio's traditional Casa York closed its doors, only to reopen as "A Nova York."[20]

Installment selling and retail-credit systems introduced in the 1920s were of European and Argentine inspiration but also bore North American imprimaturs. Milton de Carvalho encountered installment selling in 1927 in Paris, where he learned all he could about it, then returned to Brazil via the United States, where he admired similar credit-sales systems. The "new way of carrying on retail business appeared excellent to me," he recalled, and so he introduced it in Rio "with intelligent advertising in newspapers and magazines, handsome signage in the shopwindows, [and] well-instructed employees," to gratifying results: "in no time installment sales under the new process were voluminous, confirming a total acceptance on the part of the public." Nilo de Carvalho, who introduced the same system in São Paulo eight months later, found his inspiration in Buenos Aires, having traveled south to study installment selling. Like Milton, Nilo found credit sales to be "one of the most modern and practical systems for commercial transactions," noting that it "was already adopted and is very common in the United States." It fell to Lauro, however, sensitive to shady, down-market connotations of the word "credit," to provide a pleasant-sounding name for the operation, the contraction *crediário*, from "crédito diário" (daily credit). In São Paulo and Rio, the brothers introduced the same system, in which the listed price of goods was divided into ten payments, the first two due at point of sale and the remaining eight due monthly beginning two months later, such that customers would pay off the balance over ten months. Its success led Lauro de Carvalho to confide that installment sales were the only retail-related matter of which he learned nothing in the United States.[21]

The Carvalhos' stores, Mappin, and shops like Casa Vogue had been founded to serve well-off clienteles. Some gestured toward lower-income groups through the practice of signaling prices, as did A Exposição's slogan for store credit, "It's Enough to Be an Upstanding Young Man," but these overtures came after the stores' foundings and contrasted with institutional tradition and exclusive in-store services (salons, for example). The first retail outlets created to serve middling Brazilian urbanites, however, belong to this same historical moment and influenced the operations of the tonier stores. They were, in U.S. terms, five-and-dimes, the first of which was called Lojas Americanas ("American Stores").

Lojas Americanas was founded by James Marshall, an ex-Woolworth's manager from Pennsylvania, who landed in Rio in 1929 with the aim of serving the "thousands of government clerks, army officers and employees of big companies who did not earn very much money but earned it steadily," people who could not afford to shop in the city's magasins. He was especially keen on reaching "the housewife with a dozen items on her list [who] might have to go to half a dozen untidy little stores and often take what was offered rather than what she wanted." Along the way, this archetypal Brazilian housewife, as Marshall described her, would be forced to haggle with a male shopkeeper whose attitude was condescending at best. Here was an opportunity for selling a feminine public inexpensive, fixed-priced goods in neat, well-maintained stores located in less exclusive areas, staffed by young unmarried women, who would make female customers feel at ease while earning bargain-basement wages.[22]

The first store was opened in 1929, far from the Rua do Ouvidor, in the city of Niterói, facing Rio across Guanabara Bay. The store's name, Lojas Americanas, not only evoked Marshall's distant home; it was also distinctive in that most lower-end retail outlets, and many higher-end ones, identified as "Casas" (Casa Vogue, for example). The difference is as slight as that between "store" and "shop," but it set the new establishment apart initially. To the distinctive name was added a copyrighted store slogan, "Nada Além de 2$000," indicating that everything in the store could be had for two milreis or less (about US$0.25 in 1929 terms), and the spectacle of open counters, "laden with cheap trinkets, household goods, gewgaws." The store was an immediate success, prompting the opening of four more stores in the city of Rio de Janeiro in short succession. The first São Paulo store opened a year after the Niterói store, the second two months later, in a smokestack-studded district east of downtown. Despite the economic gloom of the early 1930s, sales grew year after year, even as the sum indicated in its slogan inched upward with the weakening of Brazil's currency. By 1944, the chain had grown to twenty-six stores, some featuring the novelty of in-store lunch counters selling "Brazil's biggest ice cream volume" and a gut-busting quantity of hot dogs.[23]

Lojas Americanas's success spawned imitators. In 1931, a Rio businessman bankrolled an eponymously named "Lojas Victor," to "handle exclusively merchandise of the 5 and 10 cent class as implied by their sales slogan 'tudo até 2$000'" ("Everything up to 2$000"), a riff on Lojas Americanas's slogan. Its owner left the running of the store to a U.S. expatriate with a resume similar to James Marshall's. For a time, Lojas Victor competed with Lojas Americanas, but it eventually was absorbed by the larger chain.[24]

With Lojas Americanas as a model, it took no leap of imagination for would-be entrepreneurs to dream up "Lojas Brasileiras" as a name for similar stores specializing in "articles of popular consumption." Some attempts failed, but one, begun in Recife, showed remarkable staying power, expanding into Lojas Americanas's southeastern markets, as well as attracting imitators of its own. This Lojas Brasileiras was the brainchild of a former teller who had read of the five-and-dime store as it existed in the United States and elsewhere, learned of the early successes of the Lojas Americanas, and opened his own store in 1930, with the slogan "Tudo Até 4$400" (Everything up to 4 milreis and 4 tostões, 100 reis—or a *tostão*—being the half-nickel decimal part of the milreis). The success of his first store led him to open a second Recife outlet in 1931, together with three stores in Bahia and one in Ceará. The following year, two more stores were added to the chain, in Belém and Macéio, and in 1933 the company entered the Rio market, while also moving its headquarters from Recife to the national capital. In 1934, the first Lojas Brasileiras was opened in São Paulo, its "55 salesgirls chosen among the most able of those who have already worked in shops of this type," staffing eighteen departments. Over the next ten years, the chain opened an average of two stores a year, for a total of twenty-eight stores spread throughout Brazil.

Imitators ranged from an unaffiliated "Lojas Brasileiras" founded in an outlying São Paulo neighborhood in 1938 to the Lojas de Variedades chain organized in Fortaleza by a former Lojas Brasileiras manager beginning in 1944. Unlike its counterparts farther south, the Fortaleza-based chain invested heavily in radio advertising, a break with the five-and-dime practice of limiting promotional expenditures and an early example of how retail models aimed at North Atlantic everymen and, initially, the middling sort of southeastern Brazil became more expensive, and thus exclusive, over time, particularly as they were assembled elsewhere in the country.[25]

At the time, a comment on such incongruities would have sounded the wrong note. Back then, the stores seemed an unmitigated triumph. As a long-time resident of São Paulo chirped, "We even have five-and-ten-cent stores," adding, "the five-and-ten-cent stores are exact reproductions of the American edition in variety of goods, arrangement on the counters, and even to the distinctive 'five-and-ten smell.'"[26]

The "Lojas" appellation was so successful that it was adopted in lines well beyond "Tudo Até 4$400." In order to promote household-appliance sales, General Electric opened its own "Lojas G.E." in 1931 and operated the chain through much of the decade. Here was a case of the local promotional arm of a mighty U.S. corporation, including GE's sales department and the Ayer advertising agency, availing itself of the merchandising experience of a relatively puny expatriate-headed firm and its Brazilian imitators.[27]

The same groups influenced the operations of other Brazilian retail outlets. More traditional merchants in Belo Horizonte, for example, established "everything up to 2$000" sections on their shopfloors in the 1930s.[28] When Lauro de Carvalho branched out from menswear into women's fashion, the precedent set by the *lojas* in hiring young women to serve as salesgirls no doubt made staffing easier. The chains' mounting sales of large amounts of merchandise at low markups may also have prompted Lauro's interest in selling to social strata that he and his brothers had underserved, to say nothing of potential customers beyond the Rio–São Paulo axis. In such changes were premonitions of retail revolutions to come.

Friendly Competition

Lauro de Carvalho was not the only Rio-based businessman asked to speak of his U.S. experiences for the *Diario de Noticias*' readership. Cícero Leuenroth was another. Like Lauro, Leuenroth spoke glowingly of the United States, smitten with its roadways and railroads, service and skyscrapers, optimism and automobiles. He too noted the "principal lessons" he had learned there. Like Milton de Carvalho (another interviewee), he mentioned the demonstration effect of U.S. film on Brazilian wardrobes, pleased by cinema's influence on his country's "mentality." However, Leuenroth's business was not the Carvalhos', or, rather, it was not the whole of their business. Leuenroth's business was advertising, and he reserved his greatest enthusiasm for advertising's standards and standing in the United States. Like countless JWT, Ayer, and McCann executives, he held that "advertising, with its rules, its definitions, its precepts, is the work of the Americans."[29]

Perhaps surprisingly, Leuenroth was not an executive of any of those agencies. Nor was he an ex-employee, out to profit on his experience. Rather, Leuenroth was the head of a substantial agency of his own. Years earlier, he had started out working for his father, Eugênio, a partner in a firm that acted as a broker between publishers and advertisers, taking commissions from the former on the newspaper space sold to businessmen for the publication of *réclames*. Over time, the firm became an advertising agency of sorts, with the French-inspired name A Ecléctica, while Cícero had ideas of his own and ambition to match. He traveled to the United States, studied advertising and business administration at Columbia University, and worked on Madison Avenue and Wall Street. At some point, he also worked for National City Bank in Brazil. These were the experiences he drew on in founding his agency in 1933.[30]

The experiences of the two Leuenroths, father and son, add a further layer of complexity to the early history of the profusion and professionalization of advertising in Brazil. Alongside and inspired by the U.S. advertising agencies onward were nationally owned agencies. Some, like A Ecléctica, bore the influence of European commercial cultures. Others, like Cícero Leuenroth's, were all but all-American. One was wholly owned by a European corporation. Each contributed to the adoption of U.S. standards and to the cultural moment epitomized by Lauro de Carvalho's American epiphanies.

A Ecléctica emerged in the 1910s out of the São Paulo firm Castaldi & Bennaton. The firm's namesakes, João Castaldi and Jocelyn Bennaton (the publisher of a yellow-press newspaper and a local jack-of-all-trades, respectively), were soon joined by Eugênio Leuenroth, a journalist, advertising-space broker, and former printer. First Bennaton, then Castaldi, left A Ecléctica, which received a new managing partner in Júlio Cosi, a former art student. For years thereafter, A Ecléctica represented publishers as well as advertisers, a divergence from the U.S. model that led some observers not to consider it a true advertising agency. That divergence notwithstanding, the firm increasingly drew from the United States. For Cosi, this process began with "studying and examining the foreign magazines that gave us some idea of advertising's progress." Later, taking advantage of a 1926 junket to the First Pan-American Conference of Journalists, in Washington, he traveled throughout the United States, "visiting the principal newspapers and the great advertising agencies, with the aim of perfecting his knowledge of the line of business and in search of suggestions and ideas to be adapted to our milieu." Ten years later, such ideas could be found closer to home, and so Leuenroth and Cosi hired Orígenes Lessa away from J. Walter Thompson, availing themselves of his experience with JWT, Ayer, and GM. Somewhat earlier, they had hired a North American "expert" of their own, Victor Hawkins, who carried out "surveys" of the country's markets. By that point, A Ecléctica was second only to JWT and Ayer in São Paulo billings, boasting a roster of Brazilian and North American clients. Of the latter, a staffer wrote, "We should feel satisfied to work with capable and progressive businessmen like the Americans, for all of us come out ahead with this cooperation." In the same spirit, another employee noted his pride in working in advertising, "one of the true foundations of a modern economic system," an activity "responsible, as one of the presidents of the United States of America pointed out, for the industrial restructuring of that great country."[31]

Another leading Brazilian-owned agency, A. D'Almeida, was founded in Rio by Armando d'Almeida. An aspiring engineer, d'Almeida began working for General Electric in 1924, aiming to enter polytechnic school later. His English led to a transfer from GE's technical section to its advertising department, as well as encouragement from the longtime head of its Brazilian operations, Ralph Harrison Greenwood. When d'Almeida insisted that he wanted to become an engineer, Greenwood replied, "Advertising is an advanced kind of engineering. It builds more quickly and for larger numbers of people." Thereafter, d'Almeida was "educated in the North American school" of advertising "through the reading of American books." His successes led him to receive the highest of compliments from the newspaper magnate Assis Chateaubriand, who called him "a Brazilian who knows his trade and who has the fertile spirit of invention of an American." Leaving GE in 1929 to found his own agency, Armando d'Almeida secured the Brazilian representation for New York's Foreign Advertising and Service Bureau and won several North American clients, including the Gillette Safety Razor Company. Thereafter, the D'Almeida agency "felt the influence of the American agencies, that is of American technique in advertising matters," but d'Almeida continued to insist on the primacy of industrial concerns such as GE and Gillette in providing the initial impulse behind advertising's professionalization in Brazil. Despite this distinction, the resulting patterns of thought were much the same. In 1940, when d'Almeida opened a campaign to double his firm's capital, renovate its physical plant, and hire new personnel, he quoted Calvin Coolidge while pointing to the need to "create demand" through advertising and sales promotion, adding, "It is on this foundation of the increase of production as a result of demand generated by advertising, that rests, in large part, the success of North America's industrial system."[32]

Then there was Cícero Leuenroth's agency, founded four years after d'Almeida's. While d'Almeida had given his name to his agency, Cícero and his partners resisted that immortalizing urge. Instead, Cícero chose the name Empreza de Propaganda Standard (later Standard Propaganda S.A.). He explained, "If I [called it] Leuenroth, Souza Ramos & Campos, or anything like that, [people] would associate the firm with something else, with an automobile dealership, perhaps. But Standard seemed to me to indicate an advertising agency at once. And a little bit of Standard Oil's fame rubbed off." Unlike A Ecléctica, which started out with a São Paulo office and later opened a branch in Rio, and A. D'Almeida, founded in Rio, only to expand into São Paulo subsequently, Standard counted on offices in each city at its founding. By 1937, Standard also had a long list of clients, including U.S. and Brazilian firms. Among the clients obtained over the following decade was Modas A Exposição Clipper. Along the way, Standard's staff came to include former employees of Ayer and JWT, "disciples," in Cícero's words, of the U.S. advertising agencies that "introduced modern methods."[33]

Here, then, in friendly competition with JWT, Ayer, and McCann, were Standard, A. D'Almeida, and A Ecléctica. In 1937, when a Rio monthly noted, "There are already at work a half-dozen firms specializing in the theoretical and practical knowledge of advertising, whose work of improvement and technique are contributing decisively to a transformation of commercial advertising," it was referring to these three Brazilian-owned agencies and the three U.S. ones.[34] Beyond this half-dozen were many more. There was the Empresa Nacional de Propaganda, founded by former employees of the GM advertising department who claimed to head the "first Brazilian agency to set out to work according to American methods" but who gave up the ghost to join Ayer. There was Pan América, its name soon shortened to Panam, founded in 1938 by João Alfredo de Souza Ramos, a former partner in Standard. By 1939, there were reportedly fifty-six agencies operating in Rio and São Paulo, including all the above-mentioned (save the short-lived Empresa Nacional de Propaganda), plus "A Americana," "Moderna," and "Printer." The degree to which these agencies' names represented their founders' dreams or the perceived interests of potential advertisers is unclear and, indeed, immaterial, in both senses of the word, and in the case of a contemporary agency of fleeting existence, one gets a sense of this tandem immateriality. São Paulo's Propaganda Eficiente was the brainchild of Paulo Siqueira, who took as his agency's name an adjective that had become a watchword so quickly that many took it for a neologism. The agency's name, like the services it provided, stemmed from a U.S. sojourn. As a colleague recalled, "Paulo had spent some time in the United States and from there he brought back all the "know-how" of modern American communication. He had an acute merchandising sense and he gave his clients complete assistance, from the design of trademarks and packaging to point-of-sales promotion."[35]

That colleague of Siqueira's was a young man from Rio Grande do Sul named Rodolfo Lima Martensen, who in 1937 accepted an invitation to join the advertising department of Irmãos Lever, the Brazilian subsidiary of the Anglo-Dutch behemoth Unilever. Despite its European origins and ownership, Lever was committed to the American "know-how" espoused by Paulo Siqueira, evidenced in its founding an in-house advertising agency in 1931. Like similar outfits affiliated with other Unilever subsidiaries, it was called Lintas (*Lever International Advertising Service*), but unlike most, it failed, so Lever retained JWT beginning in 1933. Thompson went on to conduct several grand campaigns for Lever, notably one featuring testimonials from a bevy of Hollywood starlets: Barbara Stanwyk and Irene Dunne, Ginger Rogers and Kay Francis, Lupe Velez and Carole Lombard. Martensen's 1937 hiring represented a first step toward creating a new in-house advertising agency, another Lintas that would provide Lever all JWT did and more. To that end, Lever's president deluged Martensen with English-language advertising handbooks and "all of the . . . magazines subscribed to by Lever." Decades later, Martensen would remember taking these magazines home and reading late into the night, dictionary in hand: *Advertising Age*, *Advertising Agency*, *Advertising and Selling*, *Art & Industry*, *Graphis*, *Printers Ink*, and *Tide*, together with the Art Directors Club of New York's *Annual of Advertising Art*, the *Modern Packaging Encyclopedia*, and *Art & Industry*'s annual *Modern Publicity* survey.[36]

For Martensen, "It was these sources of information and the intense day-to-day work of advertising that acted as my school of advertising. . . . I had to pursue the theoretical grounding that I lacked in books published in the United States and England." By 1945, he was the head of Brazil's leading in-house agency, which combined sophisticated research with "a bit of Hollywood." As an admiring journalist remarked, "Lintas looks like it's O.K."[37]

Mission, Institutionalization, and Esprit de Corps

As should be clear, there was an emerging cohort of Brazilian professionals who had been profoundly shaped by the extrusion of some of the key institutions of U.S. consumer capitalism and the global demonstration effects of the United States as exemplar of modern consumerism. It was, in Jackson Lears's terms, a professional-managerial elite in its incipience. Like their U.S. forebears, its members faced the problems of mission and esprit de corps, if in very different settings. Their new professions—advertising, sales promotion, and others to come—still had more than a whiff about them of the shady, the underhanded, the déclassé. Advertising men had nowhere near the standing of established members of the liberal professions, while Brazil's disparate publics had yet to be convinced of the utility of their services. One response, on the part of the new professionals, was to adopt the missionary zeal that their U.S. counterparts had expressed as they set out abroad. Where James Mooney's international automobile dealers and Stanley Resor's Madison Avenue men were going to carry less progressive peoples into modern civilization, Brazilian professionals were going to do the same for their countrymen.[38] Thus, the problem of mission was addressed, in a seemingly unproblematic fashion, together with part of the problem of esprit de corps. Another solution to the two problems was institutionalization, the creation of associations and specialist publications to respond to and reflect the needs, wants, and anxieties of the new professionals. Still another was the search for allies in other fields.

Advertising men (there were no female advertising executives in Brazil until the 1950s) faced the problems of mission and corporate identity earlier than other members of their incipient elite, though they would soon receive collaboration from specialists in other fields. That so many copywriters and layoutmen had aspired to be authors and artists meant that their profession faced these problems precociously. Orígenes Lessa, a would-be writer when he joined GM's advertising department, eventually an author of national renown, remembered colleagues seeking to hide the fact that they worked in advertising. Renato Castelo Branco, who joined Ayer in 1935 after answering a classified advertisement for a *redator* (staff writer), recalled his disappointment upon learning that the position involved writing advertisements: "Instead of debating political theses, or literary theories, I would be writing to sell soap, shaving cream, or sausage." He needed the work, yet still he felt "prostituted."[39]

Then there was the comparison with the United States, where, as Lessa recalled, "advertising was already a profession, a *most advanced technique*— and big business." On the one hand, the contrast could be galling; on the other, it could be inspiring. Modern advertising, after all, had been a North American creation, and a recent one at that: "It is the Americans who, with their civilization of specialization, systematized sparse knowledge, developing and rationalizing their methods of work and action. The pioneering Agencies emerged. Economists, psychologists, mathematicians, artists, men of letters . . . an entire army of efficient collaborators was called to contribute to the new art." By "bolstering their production with such intense advertising . . . the Yankees have been able to maintain their indus-trial superiority in the world."[40]

One lesson was that professional standing could be claimed, even con-quered, as the new professionals set about re-creating the perceived suc-cesses of the United States on native ground. As Armando d'Almeida explained, in terms that could have been broadcast from Madison Avenue, "advertising has a well-defined social function: through psychological influ-ence and through the force of its contribution to commercial technique, it cre-ates needs, awakens desires, identifies, deepens, explores, and consolidates markets." D'Almeida's twinning of "advertising and national development," however, would have echoed oddly in New York; here was a Brazilian twist to the problem of mission, to make an underdeveloped country a "developed" one. The same problem had emerged for at least one employee of GM's ad-vertising department: "I imagined myself joining, in my advertising work, the noble civilizing work of automobiles and roads with our people's aspirations for progress."[41]

Emulation of the U.S. example was also at work in the advertising men's founding institutional groupings and professional publications. These asso-ciations and trade magazines were to bring together true believers and po-tential converts. In so doing, they aided in the accrual of professional standing and spread the word.

The Brazilian Advertising Association (ABP) and the Paulista Advertis-ing Association (APP) were founded within two months of one another, in Rio and São Paulo, respectively. Their founding groups were of similar profile: employees of McCann, Ayer, and JWT, the founders of D'Almeida, Ecléctica, and Standard. "We struggled, at that point, for the very recogni-tion of the Agency and of Advertising as a line of business," remembered a founding member of both groups. But there was more to it: "We needed to create an image of our profession, to have a professional appearance, and we needed to have a 'status' as good as that of the physician, the engineer, and the lawyer." They needed, in other words, "an entity that would bring the adver-tising man certain advantages, that would situate him at a decent profes-sional level, that would place what he deserved within his reach, that would give him the 'status' of any other profession." The goal was "the valorization of the advertising man," demonstrating his role as an agent of economic well-being, "as opposed to the idea then in vogue that the advertising pro-fessional exercised an activity that was merely, shall we say, *parasitic*."[42]

While society-wide recognition and respect were long-term goals, valori-zation of the profession was envisioned as beginning among its practitioners. As Orígenes Lessa put it, as the APP's first president: "One of the great aims of the Paulista Advertising Association is to dignify the profession of the advertising specialist [*propagandista*] among us. The situation of our specialists is so false in appearance, or has been so prejudiced by arrivistes, that they are terrified of the word *propagandista* for fear of being ill perceived. They introduce themselves, in English, as 'advertising men.'" This rare disavowal of an Americanism aside, it was clear that the ultimate frame of reference was North American and that only by appealing to that example might Lessa's audience be as convinced as he appeared to be of their mission and worth: "It is for this reason that advertising in the United States brings together a true elite of worthies. It is carried out by technicians, draftsmen, painters, writers, experts in graphic arts, experts in market research, specialists in analyzing advertising vehicles, men distinguished for the acuity of their vision and their power to see ahead." Advertising was, in other words, an "eminently modern line of work" that called for keen-eyed, far-sighted men possessed of special skills: "It is these men who come together now to found the Paulista Advertising Association." Not for nothing did an early member describe it as "an emotional treasure." "It was," he said, "an institution where we, professionals in advertising, accepted advertising as a profession, with standards and as a career, and not a marginal activity that one passes through."[43]

The associations provided services as well as emotional rewards. English lessons were an early offering of the APP, as were lectures and luncheons. Formal courses followed, including, by the 1940s, coursework in "Media" and "Market Research" taught by a JWT staffer.[44] In 1946, the inaugural lecture in the APP's course on advertising—by then a yearlong curriculum based on U.S. and Argentine models—was titled "Advertising at the Service of the Consumer," the keynote explaining his profession's role in drawing public attention to "all that can improve its living conditions," namely, "articles for nutrition, for comfort, for commodity, for the preservation of health and for man's joy, that facilitate life, making it less arduous, more efficient, and more pleasant." That such "means of realizing sales" were educational was driven home by the presence of the federal minister of education at the inauguration of an ABP course in 1946.[45]

Ten years earlier, just a few months after its founding, the ABP sponsored an advertising campaign aimed at educating newspaper-reading Brazilians. In 1937, the words "public relations" did not yet flow from the lips of the new professionals, and so the campaign was described as "advertising for advertising." It began with an advertisement likely cribbed from the U.S. trade magazines and in-house primers in circulation in São Paulo and Rio since the 1920s: "Mass production, and the resulting need for consumer markets, created a new profession on the world stage—advertising. In all the civilized countries, the professionals of this new art work, study, and perfect their knowledge, seeking to serve the always increasing demands of Commerce and Industry." In their work, these professionals drew on carefully compiled statistics, rational administration, graphic artistry, and "the science of Psychology," making their craft "a respectable profession, for the abundance of knowledge it requires, for the activity it demands, and for the results it provides." Old prejudices aside, advertising "is not the streetseller's shout [*pregão*], is not scandal, is not a gilded lie." Rather, it was a service to business and to Brazil: "a capital investment that provides results to the advertiser and to the public, fomenting the progress and wealth of the country."[46]

In 1938, the ABP unveiled its "First Brazilian Advertising Salon." Held at the hall of the Brazilian Press Association—the model associational body as far as Brazil's advertising men were concerned—the display of "all of the best of what we have in advertising material" reportedly "succeeded in attracting the attention of a large audience." While the attendance of potential advertisers was welcomed, the goal was to reach "the greater public" so that it might assign to advertising "the just value that it deserves and possesses—in all the cultured and advanced nations—not only as a powerful weapon in the competitions of Commerce, but also a true factor of Education and Progress."[47]

The same aims informed the two groups' annual commemoration of "Advertising Day" on December 4. So too did placing advertising-related publicity in the press and on the radio. In 1938, readers of São Paulo's largest-circulation daily stood to learn that there were in Brazil "hundreds, perhaps thousands, of families" headed by advertising men, who lent an "inestimable service to the press, to radio, and principally to commerce and the consuming public." Beginning not long thereafter, readers of Brazil's leading businessmen's magazine—founded by the head of IBM's subsidiary and modeled after Henry Luce's *Fortune*—were treated to a regular column by the ABP founder Walter Ramos Poyares. In 1944, the same magazine's lead editorial would note advertising's universal role "stimulating the consumption necessary for the development of production" and the presence of "modern advertising markets" in Brazil, "where until a few years ago we had almost nothing solid."[48]

The founding of specialist publications, at first oriented to advertising alone, later addressing other lines of business, was another aspect of institutionalization. The new periodicals also aimed to enhance professional standing and morale. Initiated by the same men who had founded the ABP and APP, trade publishing was an extension of that project, one that became steadily more ambitious over time.

Published by the same group that had founded the APP, the magazine *Propaganda* aimed "to place in relief what has already been done among us in the field of advertising and what could be done in order to raise the standard of this branch of activity, so complex and so necessary to the development of industry and commerce." *Publicidade*, founded in Rio, included among its collaborators some of the ABP and the APP's founders; its editors sought "an organ in which all those who dedicate themselves to this specialization may debate their points of view, mutually stimulating one another and showing commerce and industry that without advertising there is no progress, there is no prosperity." Looking back, an early staffer, later one of *Publicidade*'s publishers, wrote, "The basic objective of the magazine from its founding in 1940 until 1947 was precisely to build up [advertising], to begin by defining it and, at the same time, to make advertising men aware of the importance of their activity's social role."[49]

As these lines suggest, the magazines' features complemented the services and psychic benefits offered by the two associations. Agency employees were told that their profession made them part businessman, part artist; that they were working "toward the education of the masses" and "the improvement of economic conditions"; and that advertising was "one of the conquests of modern commercial technique, given that it is essentially, *the art of creating buyers* . . . and, from a purely philosophical point of view, it is psychology expressed as a practical corollary." Readers who found the idea of "creating buyers" too mechanistic might warm to other framings: "It is . . . a great *creator* of desire, which is to say, creator of new needs and new habits." Advertising was thus part of a larger civilizing mission: "*Comfort and ease of communication* are considered by many to be the two great *tendencies of Western civilization*, above all in America. In this sector, advertising plays a role. Raising the standard of living, it *civilizes*."[50]

Whether advertising was depicted as civilizing mission or science, art or technique, the United States was paradigmatic, and not only when it came to that "modern creation of the American people." As Salvador Pintaudi, a contributor to both magazines, declared, "These days we cannot express ourselves regarding any problem of the economic order, of the capitalist economy, without having the United States of North America in mind. . . . In any study undertaken having to do with the production, circulation, and consumption of useful goods, we must have this marvelous social grouping in mind." Consciously or not, Pintaudi was describing himself and many of his fellows when he claimed that "observance in theory and practice of the methods of the North Americans" was an effect of the "natural influence of the spirit of this highly evolved social group over other groupings, though, oftentimes, independently of the latter's will, who receive that influence as if by enchantment." The allure of the U.S. example was such that even a call to use commercial advertising "to liberate national production from its position of inferiority" by appealing to consumers' patriotism took a Standard Oil campaign as its main point of reference. A more striking, perhaps even comic, example of the same came in *Publicidade*'s debut issue, in which a guest contribution by an Argentine specialist was offset by a photograph of the Manhattan skyline and the caption "New York—the capital of advertising."[51]

It was not a joke, however. Nor were readers who received the magazine as members of one of the two advertising associations likely to laugh. Not knowing what was to come, they likewise could read the optimistic pronouncements of the mid-1940s without feeling pity, embarrassment, or regret: "Advertising is a force used for the well-being of the greatest number, and the age of the common man, of the average citizen, is coming into being across the entire world." In 1944, in *Publicidade*, such pronouncements might serve as further appeal to advertisers' budgets and advertising men's amour propre.[52]

Like the professional associations, the trade publications needed to offer benefits beyond "emotional treasure" and talking points on advertising's supposed social importance. Translations of English-language material, from "The Ten Commandments of the Copywriter" to articles from New York's trade press, put precious knowledge in the hands of novices and non-English speakers. Features on advertising jargon, from "copy theme" to "novelty advertising," "O.K." to "reset," performed the same function. Statistical surveys of advertising and listings of media outlets put useful data in reach. By 1946, with the eased communications and transport of the postwar, faithful readers could expect an ever-more-rapid initiation in the latest "science" as it applied to their work, such as the peacetime application of the new "science of colors," which a columnist dubbed *cromotécnica*.[53]

The technical application of color to commerce, of course, went beyond advertising. It would be as useful, if not more so, in retail settings, to be manipulated by managers and employees in order to draw customers into stores. Closely allied to the advertising men, these sales professionals were also pursued by the new trade press. In 1938, *Propaganda* reprinted portions of Orígenes Lessa's handbook *O livro do vendedor* (The salesperson's handbook), first published in 1931 and based on the author's work with the GM advertising department. The following year, the magazine helped bring out a third edition, with its instructions—not yet, in Brazil, reminders—that the salesman himself was "an item on sale" and the "satisfied customer" was "the best and most effective of advertisements." By 1939, the word *vendas* (sales) had been added to the magazine's masthead; the serialized dictionary of Americanisms published that year included such retail terms as "outlet" and "merchandising." In Rio, the editors of *Publicidade* identified their magazine as covering "advertising and sales" from the beginning, and while months passed in the early 1940s without retail-related material appearing in its pages, in 1944 it launched a monthly column on shopwindow dressing, featuring lavish photography. Thereafter, excerpts and adaptations from *Display World* were a familiar presence in the magazine's pages, just as translations and other borrowings from *Printer's Ink* had been from the beginning.[54]

If the advertising professionals' attitude toward retail staffers was at once imperial and solicitous, their relations with retail merchants were entirely accommodating. The Carvalhos and men like them were sought out as patrons and held up as paragons, "men of the new mentality, perfectly integrated into their profession," who "have shown themselves to be good judges of the real value of advertising." The same was true of advertising-minded industrialists. Beyond advertising budgets and employment opportunities, connections with captains of industry and commerce offered the new professionals more powerful allies as they bid for status and standing, for themselves and their profession.[55]

Through 1945, the APP and ABP also ran interference with federal- and state-level propaganda and censorship machines established under the corporatist order implanted in Brazil in the 1930s. Smoothing out potential problems for advertisers was another of their services. Nor were these the extent of the benefits of ties to state functionaries. If, in an earlier period, "investigating the market, surveys, departments of economic investigations seemed to be luxuries to us Brazilians"—"to our eyes an ostentation of North American organization"—by the 1940s, a somewhat more imposing state had stores of information on hand that might prove useful to the new professionals.[56] In a statist system, a public relationship with government conferred prestige, hence the advertising associations' cultivating relations with key officials. In any political order, identification with a seemingly popular leader or policy promised similar benefits: "President Getúlio Vargas and Advertising"; the state-led expansion into the backlands called the "March to the West" and the "renovating cultural mission" of print advertising; state-sponsored industrialization and the profession's capacity "to provoke large-scale consumption, raising the standard of living, and lowering the cost of production."[57]

There was not yet any apparent contradiction between national-patriotic appeals like these and the new professionals' identification with and emulation of the United States. Young patriots could note the "lucid 'advertising spirit' of our neighbors from North America" while calling for "reproducing in Brazil the case of the United States." Those were the thoughts of an ABP president-to-be and *Publicidade* contributor, a self-described "passionate Americanophile, at least as much as my father was Francophile": "What an enthusiast I was of the generous people of the North! What admiration I nourished for the things that I read about the life, customs, history, everything that had to do with the United States! I learned, between the ages of 20 and

22, notions of economy and of advertising technique from American compendia." Abroad, even as World War II imposed strict limits on travel, ABP officers sought to strengthen connections with their U.S. counterparts.[58]

At home, establishing links with practitioners of other professions was another strategy aimed at fulfilling the aspirations behind the founding of the advertising associations and trade publications. Among the founders of *Propaganda* was the editor-in-chief of the *Revista Paulista de Contabilidade*, published by the São Paulo Accountancy Institute since 1922; some years later, in a *Publicidade* article titled "Estudos de mercados (Market Analysis)," he called for cooperation between "those most interested in the preparation of such studies and the technique of bringing them to a good conclusion—economists, accountants, and advertising professionals." There were, however, serious obstacles to such cooperation, the most important of which was that economics as a profession scarcely existed in Brazil in the 1940s.[59] Likewise, Brazilian advertising men were fond of referring to the "science of psychology," but that field was similarly underdeveloped, thinly peopled by pedagogists and physicians who dabbled in psychiatry. Some members of these groups could be convinced to cooperate with the ABP's efforts, but most physicians had their eyes set on attaining the prestige enjoyed by jurists trained at the country's two traditional law schools, an aspiration to augustness that could well be undermined by association with market-minded new professionals, many of them without academic degrees of any kind.[60]

Media Matters

There was, however, one established professional grouping the new professionals could rely upon in their bid for public esteem and power. By the 1940s, even the most quixotic of Brazilian journalists recognized that the outlets that carried their work depended on advertising revenue, just one of several factors linking the two professions. That newspapers and magazines would be mentioned in the same breath as radio, however, accompanied by the neologism soon spelled *mídia*, was something new, as was the stunning expansion of commercial radio.

At the ABP's 1937 founding, it took the Brazilian Press Association (ABI) as its model. Founded some thirty years earlier, the ABI was led from 1931 on by the businessmen's lawyer, American Chamber of Commerce member, and *O Globo* cofounder Herbert Moses, who drew on his connections in business and government to make the ABI the country's best-known and most generously funded private association, based in a daringly modernistic skyscraper steps from Cinelândia. Under Moses's long tenure as president, the ABI hosted the ABP's "First Brazilian Advertising Salon" and its technical courses, while Moses was a reliable source for speeches lauding the new profession.[61]

By that point, *O Globo* and Rio's other grand daily newspapers—*A Noite*, the *Correio da Manhã*, the *Diario de Noticias*—were thoroughly dependent on advertising revenue, as were their São Paulo counterparts. As a longtime resident of São Paulo told a New York audience, "The Sunday newspaper in my town . . . has thirty-six to forty pages. I can see there is a lot of advertising in those forty pages. I can see month by month and year by year a tremendous improvement coming about in advertising, through the ideas and techniques that American advertising agencies have brought to Brazil." These changes inhered in the "transformation of the press in the industrial age," in which the "installation of machines, the acquisition of paper that is more expensive every day, the maintenance of a large number of journalists, functionaries and workers, the organization of distribution, the struggle for advertising, are factors that demand the employ of large capital." The press, in other words, had become a big business, as in the United States— the "Fatherland of the great modern newspaper"—and its "services do not differ in their origin from those provided by the railroads or by industry." In the process, advertising became a "decisive factor" in the "life of the modern newspaper."[62]

Among the greatest beneficiaries were Assis Chateaubriand and his Diários Associados. By the mid-1940s, it was a commonplace that "Dr. Chateaubriand was an enthusiastic pioneer" of U.S.-style advertising and that his chain, in Armando d'Almeida's words, was "the organization that instilled confidence in the advertising business among us." By that point, Chatô's *O Cruzeiro* was considered "obligatory for national [advertising] coverage," the magazine's back cover especially sought after by advertisers, the "great disputed space" often reserved a year in advance.[63]

To the extent that *O Cruzeiro* had any competition among Brazilian magazines during these years, it was *Diretrizes*, founded in 1938 with an under-the-table subvention from "the Light" and described as Brazil's "first magazine of national political prominence." But while *O Cruzeiro* was known "for being lively, focusing on current subjects, concerned with women and the home, having good illustrators, good colors, well-laid-out pages," *Diretrizes* was "well written, full of interest, varied, of an informative and instructional character, cheap." It requires little imagination to guess which magazine reached more readers and received a larger share of advertising, though *Diretrizes* made valiant efforts to attract agency and advertiser interest, including through a series of interviews with leading advertising men.[64]

Magazines and newspapers were increasingly grouped together in the new portmanteau term "media," which would eclipse "the press" over time. In

1939, the word was featured in *Propaganda*'s running glossary of specialized terms, with the translation "specific advertising vehicles." It was soon assimilated, and while it took time for "media" to be nationalized as *mídia*, currency had already been achieved by the North American sense of the word, bringing together press outlets and radio stations as channels through which commercial appeals could reach consumers.[65]

The 1940s were years of growing importance for radio. Radio ownership, the number of stations, and the range of programming all increased. Even more so than for the press, the United States was radio's frame of reference, though the medium was also described as especially suited to national needs, an opinion shared by government officials, who availed themselves of U.S.-style commercial radio as a means to tie the country together, fostering the growth of a station that was "national" in name and nearly in fact, which in turn set the standard for the field.

Estimates of radio ownership in the 1940s vary considerably, but they all indicate growth, the number of receivers climbing above one million despite wartime shortages of components. Beginning in the late-war years and continuing thereafter, the country's stock of radio sets grew, reaching some 1.5 million in 1947. By 1941, for "the suburban home" seen as typical of Rio, "the radio represents something serious, something tremendous and irreplaceable. The domestic world can no longer do without the songs, the plays, the voices, and even the advertisements that circulate implacably through the ether"—at least according to the aspiring playwright Nelson Rodrigues. Meanwhile, according to a São Paulo journalist, local radio "possessed a wide experience, it already divulged popular idols, it already constituted a relevant factor, it played an indispensable role in the life of the common citizen, beginning to penetrate the rural sphere." Looking back from the late twentieth century, "it was as important as television today, the radio set in the living room or the kitchen was part of the furniture."[66]

The radio's rise to such status, at once iconic and everyday, was accompanied by the proliferation of stations, with new ones founded every year. A tally based on official data records an average of 7.5 new stations founded annually between 1940 and 1945. In 1946, an unprecedented 26 stations were founded, to be outdone by 42 in 1947 and 49 in 1948, while the total number of active stations climbed from 106 in 1944 to 300 in 1950.[67]

The United States remained the model. A 1935 primer informed readers that "in the United States fabulous quantities are spent on radio advertisements, there being, indeed, large firms that affiliate and set up radio stations for the advertisement of their products," whereas "we are still far from reaching the perfection of the American radio stations." "We should look, therefore, to American radio in search of the great lesson," wrote a contributor to

Publicidade, the lesson being ever-greater cooperation between stations and advertising agencies. A lesson learned, it would seem, by 1948, when a government expert who had witnessed U.S. broadcasting firsthand informed the *Revista do Rádio* that "Brazil has one of the most improved, if not the most complete radio-broadcasting service in the world," based, an amanuensis added, on "the support of commercial advertising." It was "commercial radio, financed by advertisements, that has best satisfied the interests and desires of national listeners."[68]

Even as insiders took the measure of their radio against the U.S. model, they argued that the medium was particularly suited to Brazil's needs. Surveying "various advertising vehicles," a business columnist wrote, "Radio is especially worthy of mention. Adapting itself marvelously to our environment, due to the lack of entertainments, due to the weak habit of reading, radio invaded the homes, the places of business, the public squares. Radio did not have to face the problem of transport over great distances that so hampered the expansion of the press down to today. It splits the ether." A director of São Paulo's Rádio América—a telling choice of name—agreed: "In a country like Brazil, of vast territorial extension, of rudimentary means of communication, where the rate of education is still very precarious, there falls to radio a relevant role and, more than that, a decisive role as the vehicle of culture, of progress . . . and of commercial advertising!"[69]

Government officials were of similar opinion. In 1940, the nationalization of an indebted railroad conglomerate established state control over properties that the mostly foreign-owned concern had acquired from its debtors, including *A Noite* and a radio station called Rádio Nacional. Thereafter, assets of the presciently named station remained on the government's books, but it was run with a minimum of interference, a regime that had aspired to totalitarianism settling for the connaturalizing influence of commercial radio, and so the station's format remained advertiser-supported entertainment. Freed from the need to turn a profit, the station's managers were able to direct its ample advertising revenues toward investments in technology and talent.

From its first broadcast, which featured a guest appearance by the ABI's Herbert Moses, Rádio Nacional boasted one of Brazil's most powerful transmitters, mounted atop Rio's tallest skyscraper. Even before that debut, print advertising promised "the most complete and improved technical equipment" and "the most powerful and complete 'broadcasting' organization." Upgrades following the station's change in ownership left no doubt that Rádio Nacional had Brazil's most powerful broadcasting setup, including short-wave transmitters that beamed the programming heard in Rio throughout the country. Likewise, at its founding the station was billed as having "the largest and most select 'cast' of exclusive artists." After 1940, its deep pockets made it nearly impossible for owners of rival stations to lure away on- and off-air talent, though some tried, including Assis Chateaubriand.[70]

In the 1940s, Rádio Nacional's producers strove to re-create the successes of U.S. broadcasting and the United States' cultural industries more generally. As the producer Haroldo Barbosa recalled, "Rádio Nacional's great programs were based more or less on the great American broadcasts. I had a very good radio, I tuned it to the short waves, and listened to the *hit parade*. . . . Programs that I heard, adapted, and made in my own way." Radamés Gnattali's band was renamed the Orquestra Brasileira de Radamés Gnattali, "to personalize the program, give it an American style, like Benny Goodman and his Orchestra." Each day after work, Barbosa and a coproducer would head to Cinelândia for song-and-dance movies from Hollywood: "Every day a movie house. We listened to everything, discussed it, then picked up the acoustic guitar, [and] reproduced what we had heard." The results lasted past their on-air performances, as Rádio Nacional's reach meant that recordings of the songs it broadcast live sold well. According to the radioman-turned-historian Luiz Carlos Saroldi, advertisers lined up to sponsor programming for the first time in Brazil. Powerful U.S. interests sponsored long-running programs on Rádio Nacional, as did some key Brazilian firms, while smaller concerns scrambled to place "spots" hawking patent medicines and shirt-collars, candies, and colognes.[71]

Amid these spots and sponsored shows, the state-owned station delivered what a trade writer, fresh from a visit to the United States, described as "our good-quality radio," nearly the equivalent of that country's NBC. For listeners, among them thousands of Brazilians who addressed letters to Rádio Nacional and its performers each year, it appears to have meant much, one memoirist evoking "the station that at that time condensed practically all Brazilian dreams," and another remembering his neighborhood's pride in being the site of factories belonging to two Rádio Nacional advertisers. For their part, advertisers used its shortwave broadcasts to reach beyond the hardscrabble districts of Rio's northern suburbs: "it was the immense Brazilian interior, great font of listeners and future customers for the sponsors of the broadcast schedule, that was taken into account." According to *A Noite*'s weekly magazine, that was the intended reach of Rádio Nacional's services.[72]

Private media groups could not match Rádio Nacional's resources, but the station nevertheless stood as a benchmark. It was with Rádio Nacional in mind that *O Globo*'s directors founded a station in 1944. São Paulo stations attempted to reproduce the leading Rio station's sound, even while playing on state pride to stake a near-exclusive claim to regional listeners. Chatô not only sought to bolster his standing with advertisers by poaching talent from Rádio Nacional; he also attempted to end-run the station's provincial predominance by establishing Emissoras Associadas stations farther and farther from Rio, in Belo Horizonte, Porto Alegre, Salvador, and beyond.[73]

The standard for these stations had been set, according to an executive, by "American technicians," especially in advertising, who beginning in the 1930s "came to Brazil and who did much for our modern radio," the latter, though he would have been loath to admit it, exemplified by Rádio Nacional. While stations showed "great interest for this aspect of radio, selecting and contracting specialized writers for their commercial-scripts service," advertising agencies were as enthusiastic, Ayer having taken an early lead (hence the "American technicians"), to be followed, then overtaken, by Lintas and Standard.[74]

At one point in the mid-1940s, Standard did 65 percent of its business in radio. While this percentage soon fell, the specter of advertisers opting for one medium or the other rather than backing both did inspire an overheated denunciation of comparisons between "different advertising vehicles." Such comparisons were "impossible, and thus false." They were, paraphrasing a North American authority, a "disservice to advertising" that might divide publishers, broadcasters, agencies, and advertisers. Indeed, it was "senseless to compare the direct or isolated effects of different advertising vehicles, like radio, the press, signage, and direct advertising." The media, after all, were one.[75]

Counting Heads

Increasing numbers of vehicles, growing budgets, and the pressures of professionalization combined to convince Brazilian specialists that existing market and media investigations were insufficient. Certain agencies had carried out landmark studies—JWT beginning in 1929, Ayer for the National Department of Coffee a few years later—and the information-gathering powers of the state had been enhanced, but if the new professionals were to master Brazil's disparate markets, they would require greater stores of objective, verifiable data. Faced with wary publics and dissembling private interests, the solution was increased application of research methods developed abroad, particularly in the United States.

In his 1938 interview with the *Diario de Noticias*, Standard Propaganda's Cícero Leuenroth provided a comparative perspective on Brazilian market research:

> Let us imagine, for example, a market investigation that advertising
> agencies require in order to study the circumstances for a large-scale
> advertising campaign. In the United States, the agent knocks on the
> door of a woman's house. She answers. The agent asks what kind of

cooking oil she uses.—"This one," she replies.—"Are you satisfied with the product?"—She replies yes or no.—"How much do you pay for the product?" he asks.—"This much," she replies. In such a way, filling out one checklist after another, an advertising agency can carry out a real market investigation. And so on.

In Brazil, with some exceptions—fortunately, every day more numerous—picture an agent seeking basic information as part of a market investigation. He knocks on the door of a house. The maid answers, the housewife remaining in the background, spying, untrusting. . . . The maid passes on the message:—"I don't know who he is, ma'am; no, he's not panhandling, no ma'am. No, he's not trying to sell anything, no ma'am. I don't know what he's after. . . ."

"Well you tell him that my husband isn't home. And he'd better not insist."

So the agent leaves, frustrated with the results of his investigation.[76]

Two years later, *O Observador Econômico e Financeiro* noted Brazil's lack of "'market researchers,' as the North Americans call them." The solution, according to a contributor to *Publicidade*, was "to seek out ideas of our own on *market studies* precisely in the country where such studies are carried out with the greatest reach and depth and see for ourselves the feasibility of adapting them to Brazil." One such seeker, recently returned from working for the New York office of the Brazilian government's trade-promotion bureau, emphasized the importance of "well-organized statistics . . . to the efficiency of advertising campaigns." As he put it, "advertising, the twin sister of commercial enterprise, cannot do without statistics."[77]

By that point, market research and media research were so intertwined in the minds of interested parties as to be nearly inseparable. Just as *O Observador* lamented that Brazil had no "market researchers," so too it noted the country's lack of "a 'bureau' of circulation" that could provide reliable information on newspapers' print runs. If basic circulation statistics were tough to obtain, reliable information on "the publicizing capacity of press organs" was almost impossible to come by, while measuring radio stations' effectiveness was even more of a conundrum. As Júlio Cosi would recall, "during the period 1939–1940, advertising was already done in Brazil, but there were symptomatic differences between Brazil and the United States principally having to do with the wealth of figures and Media information, in contraposition to the almost total absence of numbers on national vehicles." "Despite this," Cosi added, "A Ecléctica did its own *Ibope*."[78]

The term *Ibope* (pronounced something like "ee-BOP"), which rolled off Cosi's tongue in the early 1970s, did not yet exist in 1939–1940. As an acronym for Instituto Brasileiro de Opinião Pública e Estatística (Brazilian Institute of Public Opinion and Statistics, or IBOPE), a polling organization founded in São Paulo in 1942, it was a linguistic artifact of the 1940s and 1950s, when IBOPE established itself as the country's premiere media- and market-research firm.

IBOPE was founded by Auricélio Penteado, a judge's son who followed in his father's footsteps just far enough to obtain a lifelong sinecure lawyering for the federal government. Along the way, Penteado tried his hand as a radio announcer, an advertising copywriter, and an automobile-racing promoter. In the 1930s, he co-founded São Paulo's Rádio Kosmos. The station's lack of success introduced Penteado to the problem of measuring the reach of media outlets and their influence on audiences, which led him to methods developed by George Gallup in the United States. Penteado was an enthusiastic convert, reading everything he could on public-opinion polling and consumer research, and eventually traveling to the United States to top off his distance education.[79]

Soon after its founding, Penteado's IBOPE absorbed an earlier experiment in media research, Empresa CIPEX. Founded by a successful radio scriptwriter, CIPEX offered subscribers a monthly survey of print advertising for the cities of São Paulo, Santos, and Campinas, listing the top advertisers by volume and according to product line, as well as ranking the three cities' newspapers according to the volume of advertisements they published. In so doing, and through its editorial statements, CIPEX styled itself as working toward "the evolution and progress of Advertising in Brazil" alongside the APP and the ABP.[80]

CIPEX may not have delivered on this pledge—it left few traces in its time and has since been forgotten—but IBOPE contributed mightily to the efforts of advertisers, advertising agencies, media outlets, and captains of industry to create the kind of practical data called for by Cícero Leuenroth and *O Observador Econômico e Financeiro*. From the beginning, IBOPE did so on a larger scale: whereas CIPEX had limited its focus to the daily press of the three largest cities in the state of São Paulo, IBOPE investigated radio as well as the press, offered consumer investigations independent of its media studies, and extended its operations to Rio, to which its headquarters were transferred.

Given that the fortunes of Rádio Kosmos were what led Penteado to investigate "the public's habits, tastes, and preferences," it should come as no surprise that establishing the size and composition of São Paulo radio audiences was IBOPE's earliest concern. Patterned directly on Gallup's techniques, this work was described by IBOPE's directors as a "permanent research service on the habits and preferences of radio listeners," based on "what the Americans call 'coincidental radio checking,'" carried out through door-to-door visits. Door-to-door visits and "coincidental" checking were deemed most appropriate for Brazil because of low rates of telephone ownership and because the method offered "on-the-spot control of the truth of the information given." As Penteado explained, "the public's behavior is not always in accord with its opinion." Put more plainly: if quizzed on preference, in a neutral setting, an interviewee would likely claim that he or she preferred broadcasts of classical music; if asked on the spot what the radio was tuned to at that moment, the set perhaps within earshot of the doorstep, the interviewee would be likelier to come clean.[81]

The next question was how many other people were listening to the broadcast and whether they were men, women, or children. As described by Penteado, a successful interview took one minute, so an IBOPE investigator would be able to make forty-eight household visits in an hour (including visits to households at which no one was at home, the radio was not turned on, or—rare in the two southeastern capitals by the 1940s—there was no radio set). By 1949, IBOPE had a staff of ten radio investigators working in Rio and seven in São Paulo, covering all airplay from 9 A.M. to 10:30 P.M. through fifty thousand household interviews each month.[82]

Another advantage of the door-to-door method was described as the "perfect coverage of all social and economic and geographic areas" that its investigators provided as they "roam[ed] from wealthy homes where there are as many as seven radios, to shacks in the *morro* [hillside] where almost the only piece of furniture is the table on which the radio sits." Over the course of a day, investigators were instructed to make a certain number of visits to households belonging to specific socioeconomic groups, aided by IBOPE's citywide classification of neighborhoods according to the "class" of its residents. Under this schema, Rio was divided into forty-nine neighborhoods, "including the working-class districts": seven "Class A," six "Class AB," four "Class B," and thirty-two belonging to "Class BC" or "Class C." Homes in designated "Class A" neighborhoods were assumed to be occupied by "Class A" families, whereas in "Class AB" neighborhoods it would be up to the investigator to provide "direct evaluation . . . of the social-economic pattern of each house visited," the same rules applying to B, BC, and C neighborhoods.[83]

The A, B, C classification system was a clear case of IBOPE borrowing from JWT, which had developed the scheme in the United States and extended it to Brazil in 1929. By the mid-1940s, it was in much wider use in Brazil than it ever had been in the United States, appearing in studies with no apparent connection to IBOPE or JWT, or to any advertising agency, for that matter. And alongside the Brazilian media- and market-research firm's contributions to the diffusion of the A, B, C schema, its founder provided a more explicit rationale for the view of society underlying it: "Research by the sample system is based on two known laws: (1) individuals of the same class show visibly similar reactions; and (2) to analyze a total it is sufficient to analyze a representative part."[84]

As Penteado's explanation suggests, the data collected by investigators was tabulated, processed, and analyzed at IBOPE's offices. Through the 1940s, monthly reports distributed to clients listed the leading programs, the best times for reaching the greatest number of listeners, and, crucially, "the purchasing power of the average listener [of] a given program." Whereas IBOPE had initially confronted the hostility of station directors, resentful of a firm selling information that might deflate claims made about their broadcasts, and perhaps leery of Penteado's identification with a rival station, by 1945 every station in São Paulo was an IBOPE subscriber, as were all the major Rio stations.[85]

Alongside its monthly investigations of Rio and São Paulo radio-listening, IBOPE produced quarterly studies of consumer preferences in the two cities and semestral surveys of the same in Santos, Belo Horizonte, Porto Alegre, Recife, and Salvador, also based on door-to-door investigations. For its quarterly studies, IBOPE's investigators reached six hundred housewives in Rio and São Paulo, of classes A, B, and C in proportion to their supposed weight among the consuming public, asking them their preferred brands of perfume, toothpaste, lipstick, face cream, nail polish, rouge, aspirin, cough syrup, tomato extract, cooking oil, floor wax, dish soap, and radio set. In 1948, the semestral investigations included information on these products and additional ones—baking powder, condensed and powdered milk, magazines, morning and evening newspapers, refrigerators, even automobiles— gathered through 2,286 interviews, 16 percent of them in class A, 37 percent in class B, and 47 percent in class C.[86]

While IBOPE's semestral, quarterly, and monthly reports were available for purchase by anyone, the firm also conducted investigations on a contract basis. By its own count, IBOPE undertook "almost a hundred market studies and public-opinion polls, in Rio de Janeiro, in São Paulo, and in the interior" between 1942 and 1944. These investigations were carried out in strict confidentiality on IBOPE's part, but the results could be divulged at the contracting firm's discretion, and results cherry-picked from studies showing the popularity of a given product or service were soon trumpeted in advertisements.[87]

Thus, from relatively humble beginnings, IBOPE claimed quick successes, as investigations produced an ever-growing mass of statistical information that its directors and paid subscribers could use to study, sway, or otherwise influence city-dwelling Brazilians. Amid the political opening and relative retreat of statism that characterized the immediate postwar years, a member of IBOPE's São Paulo advisory board—founder of the Panam agency and an early investor in the market-research firm—took the luxury of decrying the usefulness of the government's statistical services, the fruits of which had been sought after not long before.[88]

Along the way, IBOPE enjoyed honors from abroad. In 1946, an invitation to affiliate with Gallup's American Institute of Public Opinion was a coup for Penteado and a point of pride for Brazilian professionals generally, as was an IBOPE profile in the New York advertising magazine *Tide*. By 1948, IBOPE had also established cooperative relationships with Gallup Institutes in Canada, Australia, and Europe, where it was also affiliated with non-Gallup firms.[89]

Back in Brazil, the advertising agencies of Rio and São Paulo had supported IBOPE, some from the start. Given his call for door-to-door research, it should be little surprise that Cícero Leuenroth backed the new firm. While his Standard Propaganda was the first advertising agency to do business with IBOPE, Leuenroth himself provided the firm with direct financial support, his name appearing on an early list of minority shareholders. The trail to IBOPE's door blazed by Standard was traveled by a long list of agencies, including Lintas (the first foreign concern to contract with the market-research firm), JWT (the first North American one), and A Ecléctica, while Armando d'Almeida and the head of McCann-Erickson's Rio office were also IBOPE shareholders.[90]

Manufacturing firms also retained IBOPE's services. Among U.S. companies, the most important was Colgate-Palmolive-Peet; the most important Brazilian concern was probably Gessy, a soap and cosmetics firm whose owners prided themselves on their "modern, scientific, organized advertising," including in cooperation with Ayer and A Ecléctica. Colgate, Gessy, and other consumer-goods manufacturers were joined by retailers, including Lauro de Carvalho's A Exposição, whose directors studied IBOPE's radio surveys and consumer-preference reports.[91]

That was not the extent of Brazilian business's patronage. In a 1948 interview, Penteado made special mention of the "moral and material support" provided by four benefactors. Three were advertising men, but the fourth did not represent the world of promotion, publicity, and media, at least not directly. Indeed, advertising and related activities probably seemed to many to be beneath Brasílio Machado Neto, president of the São Paulo Commercial Association and the São Paulo State Federation of Commerce, founding officer of the National Confederation of Commerce, and scion to a proud São Paulo clan. Machado Neto nevertheless "lent steady, precious assistance to IBOPE," on his own and as an officer of three leading trade organizations.

Machado Neto's presence on IBOPE's board likely served as a stimulus for representatives of many of the country's other family-based economic groups to support the market- and media-research firm.[92]

IBOPE's directors could thus speak directly to captains of industry and commerce, as well as address themselves to kindred professionals in advertising, media, and related fields. That was not the extent of their reach, however. The resumption of electoral politics in 1945 meant that the firm's services were sought after by politicians. Thus, when IBOPE launched a weekly digest "of everything one can find out through public-opinion research," the decision to title it the *Boletim das Classes Dirigentes* (Bulletin of the ruling classes) was not the empty boast it might otherwise have seemed.[93]

Radio Romance

An early issue of the *Boletim* informed readers that Brazil's radio audience was "predominantly feminine." Ten years earlier that fact might have been received by members of the country's "ruling classes" as trivia, perhaps definitive proof that radio was an unserious business, hardly the idea that IBOPE wanted to convey. There were, however, good reasons why men of affairs were now interested. A month earlier, Brazil's second direct presidential election in which women were able to vote had taken place. More importantly, over the preceding decade radio programming oriented to women, as listeners and consumers, had become a lucrative business, for stations, advertisers, writers, actors, musicians, and other professionals. The key development here was the creation of the Brazilian *radionovela*, or radio soap opera, which borrowed from foreign and domestic forerunners and with which Standard Propaganda, Rádio Nacional, and Colgate-Palmolive-Peet were closely identified.[94]

Before the radionovela came *radioteatro* or *teatro em casa*, short, one-off dramatic performances, some original, others adaptations of novels, plays, and Hollywood films. Sponsors were to be had—*radioteatro* would not have been broadcast otherwise—and some of these advertisers no doubt profited handsomely, among them, Perfumaria Myrta, manufacturer of Eucalol, Brazil's leading bath soap. But nonserial shows were hit or miss, and most advertisers held that the evening, when entire families could be reached, was preferred over daytime for advertising. Teatro Eucalol, to take only one example, aired in the evenings.[95]

The reversal of this situation was due in part to a North American executive named Richard Penn, who came to Brazil from Cuba for Colgate-Palmolive-Peet in 1940. In Cuba, where he also worked for the soap and toothpaste conglomerate, Penn helped popularize U.S.-style dramatic serials, performed over the radio on behalf of his employer (hence the term "soap opera"). In Cuba and the United States, the soap opera had been designed specifically to appeal to female listeners, particularly housewives, the domestic decision-makers when it came to Colgate-Palmolive-Peet's products. Penn was determined to repeat their success in Brazil, bringing with him a Cuban script, *En busca de la felicidad*, by the Spanish exile writer Leandro Blanco. Years later, a Brazilian collaborator would remember him insisting, soon after his arrival, "We are going to reach women one way or another."[96]

Colgate's advertising agency was Standard Propaganda, with its in-house studio and seasoned radio staffers. Standard's writer-producers were charged with translating Blanco's script and adapting it to local tastes, while talent was lined up and midmorning airtime was booked, of which a Colgate executive would recall: "Rádio Nacional had given it to us almost for free, as the audience [at that hour] was tiny."[97] That would soon change.

Each Monday, Wednesday, and Friday at 10:30 A.M., for a two-year period beginning in 1941, an episode of *Em busca da felicidade* was broadcast from Standard's Rio studio over Rádio Nacional's airwaves. From the first episode on, female listeners were addressed on behalf of the show's sponsor: "Madams and misses, Rádio Nacional of Rio de Janeiro presents 'Em busca da felicidade,'" sponsored by Colgate toothpaste, "the maker of the most beautiful smiles." The show's success was attested to by the press, which noted that "three times a week . . . in the great majority of homes the same scene repeated itself," as housewives, their daughters, and women in general tuned in. No one was more pleased than Richard Penn, who boasted that it was "the most listened-to program on Brazilian Radio." The volume of fan mail it provoked was unprecedented, sometimes more than one thousand letters per day in a majority-illiterate country in which the postal service had long been an object of derision. Over the show's run, Rádio Nacional received more than half a million letters from every corner of the country reached by its multiple broadcasts.[98]

The success of *Em busca da felicidade* prompted Rádio Nacional to launch an evening *novela* close on its heels. In 1942, the station premiered six more (including another Leandro Blanco adaptation, this one at 10:30 A.M. on Tuesdays, Thursdays, and Saturdays), a number that jumped to twenty-two in 1943, thirty-five in 1944, and fifty-two in 1945. All told, Rádio Nacional broadcast 2,985 novela episodes between 1943 and 1945, while the station's advertising revenues more than doubled. As the writer Mario Lago recalled, "the novelas were already a nearly religious fanaticism from one end of the country to the other and Nacional became the headquarters of the serials, the advertising agencies disputing their sponsorship and the commercial management allowing itself the luxury, at certain moments, of announcing to the four winds that no airtime was available for commercials." Popular acclamation was such that Standard-distributed recordings were rebroadcast free of charge, complete with the promotional appeals made for commercial sponsors. According to a Colgate executive, "many stations from the Interior and from other state Capitals asked to broadcast them without us having to pay anything."[99]

São Paulo, of course, was not among those "other state Capitals." It remained, in radio terms, a special case, even in the age of the novela. Nevertheless, the same forces were at work, and many of the same patterns emerged. As in Rio, adaptation from Spanish America occurred, but it came via the River Plate rather than the Caribbean, and its agent was a Brazilian writer rather than a U.S. executive. In Argentina in the 1930s, the São Paulo–born playwright Oduvaldo Vianna had acquired direct experience of a more sophisticated media market. Returning to Brazil in 1940, he parlayed that experience into a directorship at Rádio São Paulo, promising its listeners programming novelties. Among the new programs was the "radial novela," a term he borrowed from Argentine Spanish. Its Portuguese cognate did not take, but the programming did. Sponsored by Carlos de Britto & Cia., a manufacturer of processed foods under the brand name Peixe and a Standard Propaganda client since the 1930s, Rádio São Paulo's *Teatro de Romance Peixe* was so successful that it was moved from its original 11:00 A.M. slot to what its creator would call the "so-called primetime" of 9:00 P.M. as the station spun off similar daytime programming.[100]

While Brazil's two major radio markets were distinct, São Paulo and Rio were hardly isolated from one other in programming terms. Six months after Rádio Nacional's initial broadcast of *Em busca da felicidade*, it began its first run in São Paulo, acted out before the microphones of Assis Chateaubriand's Rádio Difusora for Colgate toothpaste; thereafter, Richard Penn took a personal role in São Paulo's radio scene, holding forth with Standard's staff in-studio and at Mappin's tea room. Another six months on, Standard brought Oduvaldo Vianna's work to audiences in Rio and beyond when Rádio Nacional began producing its own *Teatro de Romance Peixe* as the men behind Peixe products—"Brazilians who see Brazil's radiophony ranking among the best of the world . . . great industrialists who see in radio a great advertising vehicle"—prepared to introduce branded "Pickles" and "Ketchup."[101]

That the shows promoting these delicacies came to occupy an important place in the lives of Brazil's disparate publics is attested to by memoirists and actors, foreign visitors and writers for the domestic press. Decades later, Paulo Francis (b. Franz Paulo Trannin Heilborn, 1930, Rio) would recall listening to six Rádio Nacional novelas with his mother, memories retouched with regret at her unhappiness and early, preventable death and hints of his own sexual awakening, just as Mario Lago (b. 1911, Rio) evoked the serials' importance to his own mother. The actor Saint-Clair Lopes, interviewed in 1978, emphasized the success of *Em busca da felicidade*—"a gripping novela . . . for two years a 'big hit' in this country"—then turned to the genre's broader implications: "The novela was something uncommon, no one had seen or heard of it before. All of a sudden, one came to listen to the play in their own homes. You can imagine what radio broadcasting did out there, throughout this entire country. A country, for example, divided into tremendously differentiated economic strata. For example: terrible misery alongside shocking wealth in São Paulo and Rio de Janeiro. Those people in misery . . . all of a sudden came to listen to the theater in their very own home, hearing that message as if it was a message for them."[102]

That these "tremendously differentiated economic strata" were found within the same households was indicated by a North American writer, who set the pattern for his compatriots for years to come in portraying his domestic servant as representative of Brazilians numbering in the millions: "Soap operas flourish too. . . . Housework stops while the maids weep, sigh and exult into their mops, listening to their 'romawnces.' Our maid regarded the radio as the most precious object in the house. She polished it daily and kept us informed of the best programs. During the evening, the kitchen door was always slightly ajar, while she sat sewing or shining the silverware with one ear cocked to the radio."[103]

While the reach that commercial radio programming achieved through the soap opera was celebrated by insiders, the new professionals felt some embarrassment at what they had wrought. Radio, an ABP founder wrote, "goes everywhere, to the house of the rich, to the house of the poor. If we wanted to highlight a typical fact, it would be enough to recall what has happened with the radio novelas—a true fever, not only of sentimental young girls, but of many responsible folks." Eliding the role of advertising men in creating the form, he continued, "The stations burst out shouting the most sensational, fabulous, and romanesque novelas of all times. Because there are advertisers willing to sponsor these novelas. And, unfortunately, in general at least there is a public for them." Radio melodrama might be embarrassing, even regrettable, but it was to have been expected. After all, "the press also had its era of 'vaudevillism.'" More important than the foreseeable poor taste of a new medium was the pattern revealed by its growth: "this means that businessmen are opening their eyes and beginning to consider, for their output, great masses of consumers, with whom they communicate through advertising."[104]

Standard Brands

The advertising that this writer had in mind—radio commercials and print advertisements—was not the only means through which business interests communicated with consumers. The branding and packaging of trademarked goods were complementary channels. Endorsements by radio and cinema stars reached the public through the same means as other promotional material, but were designed to foster the illusion of unmediated communication between "celebrity" and consumer, thereby affording the fantasy of the latter approaching the former. The "slogan" echoed from radios and, set to a tune, became a "jingle," another neologism of the era. In locales without radio stations of their own, jingles reached listeners publicly through a medium unknown to North Americans, while in Rio, larger state capitals, and their environs, familiar forms of "outdoor advertising" established branding's ubiquity.

Trademarks were not new to Brazil. For respectable townsfolk of the early twentieth century, even in the northeastern interior, "butter was French," as was toothpaste, branded Bretel Frères and Lubin, respectively. Readers of São Paulo's irreverent press of the 1910s associated lighthearted caricatures of their rulers with the fizz of Guaraná Espumante soft drink. The following decade, when Limeira Tejo moved to Rio to enroll in engineering school, social entrée was eased by certain fluencies: "It also wasn't difficult for me to become an expert in brands of French perfume and of automobiles, or to discuss movie artists and films using their titles in their original English."[105]

By the 1930s, many consumer goods, nearly all of them manufactured in Brazil, were packaged to appeal to larger publics. As the Commerce Department reported, "manufacturers of many products have found it advantageous to stress the visual presentation of their trademarks or identify their products by trade names which can easily be remembered." Their gambit succeeded: "many trade names have become synonymous with a particular product and a large proportion of the illiterate element of the population will order goods by mentioning a trade-mark, such as 'Peixe' (fish), 'Indio' (Indian), 'Gato' (cat)."[106]

If the presence of branded goods on Brazilian shores, and even in remote parts of the interior, was no novelty, there were new developments afoot. The sheer number of trademarks, the attention paid to branding, and the meanings attached to goods generally, as well as to particular brands, all set the 1930s and 1940s off from preceding years. The branding of Brazil now began in earnest.

In 1927, some two thousand trademark applications were approved by the Brazilian government. Ten years later, more than five thousand met with official approval. In the first half of 1938 alone, nearly 2,300 were granted, despite Carnaval and the other distractions keeping functionaries from their desks early in the year. Thousands of other applications were rejected, while the government pocketed the equivalent of hundreds of thousands of dollars in fees. Little wonder, then, that branding was a matter of heightened interest.[107]

The year 1938 was also noteworthy for publication of an article by Hermano Durval, a lawyer who focused on commercial rather than juridical aspects of trademarking. His premises were twofold. First: "The increasing rationalization of modes of production, the modern resources of grand advertising, and the accentuated trend toward assembly-line production, which, creating a new mentality, came to imprint upon the trademark a function surpassing that which was reserved for it until then." Second: "Even in Brazil— 'an essentially agricultural country . . .'—one notes this trend toward trademarked products," and it behooved Brazilian businessmen to pay attention to branding.[108]

The trademark, as Durval described it, worked on two levels. Objectively, it served to distinguish one product from another in markets in which similar goods circulated. Subjectively, matters were more complex: "It allows the consumer to identify the product by its intrinsic qualities, qualities that become factors that they may not have been at the time of fabrication. . . . There is an American phrase that ably summarizes this subjective side of the factory trademark:—'good will.'" Drawing on *The Theory of Business Enterprise* (1904), perhaps directly and indirectly, perhaps through a French primer alone, Durval identified the trademark as enabling Thorstein Veblen's "class of monopolies . . . not usually classed as such," those "of a less definite character resting on custom and prestige (good-will)."[109]

A brand's prestige and goodwill were fostered, most importantly, through advertising. Here, Durval again echoed Veblen, though without the slightest hint of his contempt for "the growth of the industrially parasitic lines of business just spoken of." For Durval, it was the way of the modern-day business world: "Advertising becomes the instrument of diffusion and notoriety of the trademark, valorizing it. . . . Hence the need for the trademark to be suited to advertising." The valorization of the trademark, in turn, transcended sales promotion; it increased a firm's value and might become a tradable asset.[110]

In passing, Durval also noted the multiplication of brands as "the intensity of modern life in the great urban centers and the increasing emancipation of women in contemporary society made possible a greater expansion of internal consuming markets, lessening certain kinds of domestic activities to the advantage of rationalized industry." He also distinguished between product-specific trademarks and ones "applied to an entire series of different products, but of a single producer," which "help advertising . . . and even transmit to less important articles a part of the prestige involving the more important ones, thereby inspiring greater confidence in the consumer." GE was his examplar of this kind of trademark.[111]

Durval closed by considering Brazilian brands comparatively. French trademarks were artful, German ones impressive, while "American trademarks seek to produce the most advertising projection." Brazilian trademarks, on the other hand, "have that provincial 'air' that characterizes the Dutch trademark." Germany and the United States were therefore held up for emulation in Brazil: "In order to create and maintain a sales monopoly, the brand must be *modern*, that is it must endow itself with a strongly impressive advertising character." Only then could the trademark carry out "its mission in consonance with the progress of the industrial and commercial environment."[112]

Durval's brief for the brand was just that, a lawyer's case for his client, replete with learned references to precedent and other forms of authority. Inconvenient evidence was ignored, as it would have been unhelpful to acknowledge the success of Carlos de Britto and Perfumaria Myrta in making Peixe and Eucalol household names and their products (guava paste and tomato extract, toilet soap and toothpaste, respectively) indispensable items of consumption in many homes. For the historian, Durval's brief is most useful as evidence of growing interest in the trademark and a window onto the making of the meanings of goods—branded in Brazil and abroad—that had been ongoing for over a decade.

R. M. Ferreira, writing in *Propaganda*, pointed out that in the United States even the most basic foodstuffs were packaged and sold under brand names, merchandising that created "large fortunes . . . for a large number of industrialists." Turning to Brazil, Ferreira could only cite one comparable case, that of Assucar Perola, which by 1919 was billed as "Refined granulated— American type." Still, he was convinced that "thousands and thousands of housewives would be inclined to spend a little more to buy rice, potatoes, etc., that were advertised as pure, because they passed through certain processes of refining and are sold in packages, free of contact with cockroaches, or flies," to the profit of Brazilian businessmen. But that was not all. Writing for fellow advertising managers, Ferreira took the U.S. model as proof that their role was to "get in touch with the consuming public, the public that buys the article and comments, says if they are satisfied or unhappy, if they prefer a packet or a box, a bottle or a can," while making a special case for one kind of packaging: "boxes, bottles, etc., with dual uses. Boxes that once acquired can be used for other ends." "In the land of Uncle Sam," he pointed out, "many manufacturers made fortunes selling their products in little boxes, cans, etc., with dual uses."[113]

For Mario Angelini, writing in *Publicidade*, packaging was a second-order concern. The trademark had developed, as he saw it, to protect industrialists' investments, including in sales promotion. Brands resulted, in his words, from manufacturers' need to curtail "illicit or parasitic competition." "And in turn," he argued, "brands made the work of advertising even more necessary." On this basis, Angelini simplified his argument, applying it globally: "The appearance of advertising thus made the trademarked product inevitable. The trademarked product appears, affirms itself, expands, becomes popular, first in the United States and then in Germany, in England, in France. If the trademark owes its affirmation to advertising, the latter provided it enormous benefits in exchange."[114]

The identificative elements of the brand were present in Brazil from the late nineteenth century onward. "Peixe" stood for Carlos de Britto's guava paste going back to 1897, a tribute to the company's base in the town of Pesqueira, subsequently trademarked and extended to additional products, most notably tomato extract, years before *Publicidade* was launched. Likewise, the Brazilian trademark for Nestlé's signature product was coined by customers long before the firm turned its fuller attentions to the country and began producing condensed milk in the interior of São Paulo: as the foreign script on the imported cans' labels was indecipherable to many, including most tradesmen, the milkmaid featured on them stood in and the product came to be called "Moça" (Miss), long before it became a formal trademark. In 1948, IBOPE judged the once-improvised brand to be "better known than the manufacturer's name."[115]

Distinctive packaging of branded goods in order to prevent the "illicit or parasitic competition" identified by Angelini was also well established. Bars of Eucalol soap came sealed, stamped, and labeled, with a strip of red ribbon as additional proof of authenticity. Advertisements warned consumers of imitations and instructed them to "demand the red-ribbon guarantee." In 1933, some of the first Eucalol advertisements produced by Standard Propaganda reminded readers of the "red-ribbon guarantee," adding, "Refuse imitations and remember that only good things are imitated."[116]

JWT took a similar approach with Royal Baking Powder (RBP) after taking over advertising for Standard Brands. RBP's major competitor was a German product that had been introduced as "Backpulver," with its own distinctive packaging, but, due to RBP's popularity, "Backpulver" was dropped from advertising and packaging, the former now featuring the term "Baking-Powder" while the latter was altered to look like "Royal packing containers." JWT's first advertisements for Standard Brands informed readers, "It is not legitimate Royal, if it does not have the name 'Royal' on the label."[117]

Contracting an advertising agency was not the end of the matter for manufacturers of branded goods. As they sought to protect their trademarks and expand their brands' reach, manufacturing firms were increasingly involved in sales and distribution, including such basic matters as pricing. These firms displayed an increasing in-house concern with advertising, despite contracting with independent agencies. Retailers and middlemen, as much as rival firms, were viewed with distrust, and where possible, local merchants were monitored by sales agents and independent distributors replaced by direct distribution networks. Thus Nestlé, its initial manufacturing operations based in the state of São Paulo, founded offices in Recife, Porto Alegre, Belém, Fortaleza, Salvador, Curitiba, and Belo Horizonte between 1927 and 1938. By 1939, Standard Brands had grown to have "seventeen branches and 79 agencies, installed in the country's principal cities." These networks allowed the monitoring of sales and service nationally, such that in 1940 Nestlé could carry out a country-wide investigation that uncovered the sale, "on the part of some businessmen in the bar and café line," of ersatz chocolate-flavored drinks under the proprietary name Nescau: "That being the case, in defense of the product and, consequently, of the very consumer, the Branches came to take measures. These measures may be summarized as a quick fiscalization, by surprise, preferably done by the Branch's Manager, these measures offering excellent results." Even new companies with relatively puny sales organizations could monitor pricing in their immediate bailiwick: for one, the Santiago Development Corporation, manufacturer of a Nescau-like product called Toddy.[118]

Any size company could use advertising to enlist consumers in efforts to eliminate middlemen from decision-making on pricing by publishing prices in their advertisements. Standard's first advertisements for Eucalol-brand bath soap and toothpaste thus indicated the prices that consumers should expect to pay in the city of Rio de Janeiro. Toddy was launched amid what its competition would call "the largest Advertising Campaign yet seen in the Country, carried out through all possible media"; prices figured prominently in these advertisements as well. In 1937, when Palmolive "came to Brazil to stay," the price of the soap recommended by "20,723 beauty specialists" figured prominently in advertising, as did the price for tubes of Colgate in advertisements for the conglomerate's other major product. On Richard Penn's watch, advertisements for the two lines of Colgate-Palmolive-Peet products carried pricing for the cities of Rio and São Paulo. Coty S.A.B., subsidiary of the French cosmetics and fragrances firm of the same name, went further and imposed a nationwide price chart on retailers, enforced through its agents and through pricing in its advertisements, while taking some of the sting out of the imposition with turnover-based givebacks and the sales assistance provided by advertising campaigns handled by JWT beginning in 1934.[119]

Advertising offered manufacturers of branded goods the opportunity to instruct consumers on product usage. From its first sales campaigns, RBP incorporated recipes into its advertisements; in the 1930s, its advertising also included suggestions that best results would be achieved by using "wheat flour in little sacks, sold in all grocery stores," with its baking powder. Toddy was to be taken hot first thing in the morning and cold after every meal. Palmolive's "rich and smooth suds" were to be massaged into the skin, which then, thoroughly rinsed and lightly dried, would "acquire more beauty, exuberance, and youthfulness." That was not all: Palmolive soap could also be used as a shampoo. By suggesting alternate uses for products already in consumers' homes, advertisers would increase turnover and sales, and so, years before the pressure cooker became a fixture in Brazilian kitchens, a teaspoon of RBP added to the household's pot of beans was advertised as ensuring that the staple "would cook more quickly and turn out tenderer."[120]

The consumption of branded goods thus promised to save time and provide superior results. Cleanliness may have been next to godliness, but youthfulness was closer still to the divine: "Everything about her breathes youth," or so claimed Standard Propaganda for Palmolive. More than a soap, Eucalol was a "beauty product." Gessy-brand toothpaste—made with Milk of Magnesia—promised total asepsis of the mouth, in addition to a "fascinating smile," while Colgate's foam contained a "*new ingredient* that penetrates into the hidden gaps between the teeth." In addition to "the unmistakable taste of ripe tomato," Peixe tomato extract offered health, "through the precious vitamins A, B, C, and G . . . entirely conserved, due to the exclusive modern processes of its fabrication." "No other food is as beneficial, practical and nutritious as Moça condensed milk," or so JWT claimed on Nestlé's behalf, while Toddy was "an ideal food all year round," promising increased vitality, firm muscles, and a higher red blood cell count, while "strengthen[ing] the cerebrum and invigorat[ing] the nerves."[121]

Star-powered testimonials were another approach. Carmen Miranda endorsed Eucalol's entire line, while Madeleine Carroll favored Lever soap— "Its perfume is simply adorable!"—alongside "9 out of 10 movie stars." "There are few products of everyday use which are not advertised as being favored by one star or the other," was a foreign correspondent's hyperbole, but he was not entirely mistaken: "If a new toothpaste is brought on the market, it may be touted as helpful in developing a 'Tyrone Power' smile; or if new cosmetics are sold, they may be publicized as Alice Faye's favorite. And it is a serious mistake to think that this technique does not influence sales."[122]

If celebrity endorsements and the promise of everything from vigorous nerves to tender beans were not enough, consumers of branded goods were offered giveaways. By 1939, a kitchen's worth of cookbooks had been offered Brazil's "good housewives" on behalf of a laundry list of brand name products: Royal Baking Powder, Backpulver, Maizena Duryea, Leite Moça, Gordura de Coco Carioca. Alongside these volumes might be found Johnson & Johnson's *Primeiro Livro do Bebê* (First baby book) and a home-economics sequel to RBP's recipe compendia. In 1939, Colgate-Palmolive-Peet offered free bars of Palmolive soap with purchase of Colgate toothpaste for the debut of an unnamed "new ingredient," while purchasers of Palmolive were given a "precious calendar for 1940" along with the product's "gift of beauty." By that point, the nationally owned competition had incorporated collectible cards into the already-busy packaging of Eucalol products, a giveaway that some believe was more fundamental to Perfumaria Myrta's success than any other promotion. At one remove from these premiums were contests sponsored by Toddy and Peixe that awarded valuable prizes—porcelain sets, radios, even cash—to collectors of proofs of purchase and other bits of branded packaging.[123]

"Peixe in your mouth is money in your pocket," went one contest *slogan*, a word only then entering the Brazilian vernacular and to which increased consideration was being given. A contributor to *Publicidade* explained its importance through analogy: "If advertising as a technique . . . is a modern creation of the American people, the 'slogan' that is its most persuasive and most superior form is, legitimately, a creation of American advertising." But what was the slogan? It was "the most perfect synthesis that exists": "because it synthesizes on both sides, on the side of the one who buys and on the side of the one who sells." Indeed, it was "concentrated truth, proven truth, truthful truth." The journalist Ary Kerner was less prolix. In his view, the "slogan" (he too maintained the quotation marks) was a "convincing affirmation" communicated through "an interesting and harmonious phrase." According to the São Paulo Commercial Association's *Digesto Econômico*, it was the key element in advertising aimed at "a less cultured class"; "seeking the vulgarization of the item's name," such advertising worked "through a 'slogan' repeated infinitely until it becomes a psychological tic."[124]

Manic or epiphanic, brand name slogans became ubiquitous during these years. Standard Propaganda was especially active in their spread, dubbing the signature scent of Royal Briar products "a perfume that leaves behind *saudades*" (a not-quite-translatable Portuguese word indicating a keen feeling of longing), and translating Palmolive's "head to toe" promise as "embeleza dos pés à cabeça!" (literally, "beautifies from feet to head"). Early Eucalol advertisements employed an ingredient-explaining slogan ("Made with Eucalyptus"), which Standard would replace with the claim-staking "The Best-Selling Soap in All of Brazil" (shortened to "The Soap of Brazil" at around the time the two companies parted ways).[125]

The Omega-Tissot (JWT) was "the antimagnetic watch," while the Mido Multifort (Standard) "is a Swiss watch." Peixe tomato extract (Standard) had "a fount of vitamins in every can," Toddy was "light and easy to digest," and Brahma's Malzbier "complements any meal." In the case of the ice cream and frozen novelties introduced in the 1940s by the U.S. Harkson Company, the trademark itself was the simplest of slogans: Kibon ("How Good!"). And, as listeners of *Em busca da felicidade* remembered, Colgate toothpaste was the "maker of the most beautiful smiles"[126]

As the latter suggests, the slogan lent itself to broadcast as well as print advertising. For the radio, there was also the "jingle," yet another neologism. Like the radionovela, there were Brazilian precedents for the jingle (the streetseller's *pregão*, to start with), but the consensus among insiders was "that the jingle was imported from the United States," as the slogan had been. It was not the U.S. agencies, however, that were most responsible for its early spread. Rather it was Brazilian radio directors, composers, and musicians, soon joined by Lintas and Standard, as they turned out ditties on behalf of the Brahma and Antarctica breweries and the makers of Gessy, Carnaval, Lifebuoy, and Palmolive soaps. If anything, the results exceeded those seen in the United States, "radio singing commercials" administering an "exhilarating shock" or a special torment to listeners every fifteen minutes. That these jingles soon transcended the airwaves was indicated by a North American correspondent: "As comical as the Brazilians think these little songs are, they are still happily and swiftly spreading," hummed by streetcar passengers in Rio and São Paulo.[127]

Beyond the two southeastern centers, recordings of these jingles and of radio programming generally were disseminated by an alternate route: loudspeakers mounted in busy parts of town to provide a kind of improvised local radio service. By the 1940s, such *serviços de alto-falantes* had been largely banished from Rio and São Paulo, but they were important in cities and towns with no local or regional broadcasting facilities of their own and for brand name advertisers attempting to reach such places, which included state capitals in the north and northeast, as well as most municipalities in populous Minas Gerais. Indeed, the loudspeaker services remained important in some towns even after the success of local radio stations.[128]

By that point, in Rio, São Paulo, and their environs, and in other locales as well, visual out-of-doors advertising was similarly inescapable. Streetcar advertising, billboards, and neon signage were the most widely used of an array of forms designed to establish the brand's ubiquity.

In 1931, two decades after a former engineer for Light introduced streetcar advertising to Brazil, JWT reported: "Car cards are now used to a great extent by toilet and cosmetic manufacturers. It is possible to get a very complete coverage in Rio and São Paulo." Backed by an exclusive concession, by 1937 a specialist firm offered "the facilities of a well-equipped art department" and the attention of nearly two million daily fares, "for the 'reminder' advertising of a number of imported products, among which automobiles, foodstuffs, radios, automobile tires, petroleum products, and household insecticides are the most prominent." Five years on, wartime fuel shortages and restrictions on automobile traffic made streetcar advertising more attractive still: "The war, which brought so many difficulties to other advertising vehicles, indirectly benefits this one, increasing the already enormous public of streetcar advertisements."[129]

Cornering roadside billboard advertising in the southeast fell to a native son, Antônio Augusto de Macedo, who would recall being struck by "one of these classic 'million dollar ideas'" driving from Santos to São Paulo in 1926: "Why not sow the road with happy, well-made signs for advertising, as was already done throughout the world, principally in the United States?" With the support of GM and Ford, Macedo extracted an exclusive concession from the state of São Paulo, which he later extended to cover the roads linking São Paulo with Rio and Rio and Juiz de Fora. "Today advertising on highway roads is absolutely victorious," he declared in 1939, by which time billboards by the hundreds dotted these roadways, "lending interest and color to long voyages on our interminable roads. Our signs shout the virtues of an infinity of products. Not only automobiles, tires, the brands of gasoline and oil interest the drivers who pass, often with four or five passengers in the car, four or five attention spans, four or five potential buyers." Meanwhile, a sideline in urban "outdoor advertising" became so successful that Macedo spun it off into a separate business handling the billboarding of Rio, São Paulo, and Belo Horizonte.[130]

In Rio and São Paulo especially, billboards jostled for space with the electric signage that commercial travelers had once seen as lacking. "Rio by day needs no dressing up," wrote a visitor in 1929, "but at night the large number of brilliant electric signs, backed by the myriads of lights bedecking the fantastically-shaped hills in festive array, make a night view of the harbor a never-to-be-forgotten sight, a veritable glimpse of fairyland." No one, then or since, mistook São Paulo for anything out of a fairy tale, but a proud local nevertheless boasted of his hometown's branded electric signage: "As far as illuminated advertisements, we have notable examples in our beautiful

Capital. There is seen in Anhangabaú the large and beautiful one of 'Chevrolet' automobiles; on the Martinelli building, the *neon gas* ones of 'Goodyear' tires and of 'Gessy' toothpaste and soap." Between Rio and São Paulo, the business of building and raising neon signs occupied "two sizeable firms," and soon "all of the desirable space" on the cities' major buildings was fitted with electric signage. While there were no exclusive concessions to be had, interested parties—advertisers, agencies, and agents of the Bureau of Foreign and Domestic Commerce—could point to favors from municipal powers-that-be: a tax holiday on illuminated advertising during Rio's Carnaval festivities (official recognition of the importance of commercial signage for the city's image) and a loosening of the fiscal burden on electric-light advertising in São Paulo.[131]

The proliferation of these forms of what advertising insiders called "outdoor" would have been overwhelming to earlier generations. At the turn of the twentieth century, billboards and electric-light signage were unknown in São Paulo. Three decades later, a municipal inspector revealed that there were nearly 1,800 electric signs at work in the city, most of them neon, blazing over surfaces that totaled more than four thousand square meters in area, while billboards covered another eight thousand square meters of the city's sightlines.[132]

At the same time, the profusion of "outdoor" made the unfamiliar familiar to outsiders. In 1941, a U.S. correspondent wrote of his arrival in Rio, "As an old advertising man, I habitually look at signs. Before we reached the hotel we had passed dozens that look just like the ones on Main Street—Goodyear, Kodak, Palmolive, to name three at random."[133]

Had he arrived two years later, it is likely that our correspondent would have added a fourth brand name to his list, as Brazilian professionals would marvel for decades to come at the imposition of Coca-Cola's brand on their country. Billboards, posters, neon signs, and newspaper and magazine advertisements impressed themselves upon the eyes of city dwellers, first in Rio, then São Paulo, then throughout the country, while jingles, spots, and a Coca-Cola-sponsored show on Rádio Nacional echoed in listeners' ears wherever radio sets were found. This promotional torrent might have given the impression that there was hardly a plan in place or method at work, but it resulted from careful coordination between the Coca-Cola Export Sales Company, McCann-Erickson, the Macedo outdoor-advertising interests, radio stations, and, by 1948, local bottlers in fourteen Brazilian cities, from Porto Alegre to Fortaleza. Coca-Cola's show on Rádio Nacional was particularly important, as *Um milhão de melodias* (A million melodies) acted as the firm's "spearhead," its performances of contemporary Brazilian and North American music presented so as to emphasize the quality of the show and the "personality" of the product. *Um milhão de melodias*, according to one of Rádio Nacional's producers, "avoided the star, the big name, to valorize the product. Music, and Coca-Cola." The parent company's deep pockets meant that these campaigns did not have to turn a profit. Indeed, according to a McCann staffer, "Coca-Cola was launched in Brazil, investing practically 100% of their anticipated sales volume in advertising." Also noteworthy was that the product was packaged in individual-serving sizes priced well below the larger bottles of soft drinks sold by local breweries as a sideline to their main business; here too the wealth of the parent company was key in establishing an idea of the brand, in this case that it was "essentially popular." It has been suggested that the company may even have lost money in its early years, but in the process it built a sales organization described as "among the best in the world," with red and white salescarts on streetcorners, on beaches, and at recreational and professional sporting events, as well as similarly color-coded bottle dispensers in government offices and other public buildings.[134]

According to a critic, the fashionable beachfront of Rio's south side was first to succumb to Coca-Cola's promotionalism: "Copacabana fell first, like an assaulted bastion: society folks were seen sipping the insupportable drug in bars, with great airs of enjoyment and flickerings of the tongue to hide their grimaces." Then came points north: "The suburban walls and fences turned up one day invaded by signs exhibiting women who were so lifelike they palpitated. They assumed irresistible airs, wearing bathing suits and shouting to those who passed: 'I drink ice-cold Coca-Cola.' How to resist? The suburb fell, the entire city had fallen."[135]

In São Paulo, "'Coca-Cola' was written on everything on which anything could be written. The only way to not read 'Coca-Cola' was to close one's eyes, and even then the brand that the entire world knows paraded through the darkness of our mind, for it had already installed itself there. To free oneself of the obsession, only drinking 'Coca-Cola,' the price of liberation. From then on, one no longer had any awareness, the mechanism had already become unconscious. One had succumbed, consumed." And so was born the "invincible will to drink that modern soft drink, full of 'charm' and involving a slight feeling of daring and eccentricity. All this is what the illuminated advertisements, the billboards, and the healthy young women in the advertisements insinuated."[136]

For insiders, the birth of Coca-Cola's brand was a before-and-after moment. "After Coca-Cola came to Brazil, soft-drinks became something of great importance in advertising circles. While the colored signs of the American drink beautified the places in Rio de Janeiro of greatest visibility, other soft-drink manufacturers emerged, all of them attempting more or less similar methods. . . . There came Guará, Sonny-Boy, Ginja-Cola, Nossa, Crush, Grapette, and so many others." In 1949, the ABP founder Walter Poyares addressed the subject, not for the first time: "One may never fail to recognize that this colossal North American organization 'opened' the market for low-priced soft drinks in this country." Imitators kept coming, as nothing seemed easier than introducing a trademarked soft drink: "Practice, however, revealed the opposite. It is important to impress upon each one of them some characteristics that will constitute its personality in the imagination and will of the consumer. For this, not only do the particular taste, the original bottle, matter, plus the colors frequently used in advertising, the texts, the kind of advertising and other little matters that must be carefully tended to." Of these matters, a soft drink's formula was the slightest: "The secret of each one is its greater fastening on the subconsciousness of the consumer."[137]

Two, Three, Many Inter-Americanisms

In 1928, Julius Klein had taken to the airwaves to tell his compatriots of "the New Pan-Americanism"—"a harmonious, mutually beneficial exchange of commodities, operating fully as much to the advantage of the Latin American countries as to our own."[138] More famously, over a four-year period beginning in 1940, Nelson Rockefeller was entrusted with the coordination of "Inter-American Affairs" out of the Commerce Department building, Klein's old base in Washington. In both cases, the Americanism in question was to be encouraged at home, as well as abroad. But Americanism—"Pan-," "Inter-," or other—is an idea at once shifting and slippery, and Brazilians were never passive recipients of Washington propaganda. Americanism, in the sense of contradistinction from Europe, had emerged periodically in Brazilian political discourse from the nineteenth century onward; between the 1930s and the 1940s, variations on the theme emerged in the writings of some of the country's most revered intellectuals.[139] Political and intellectual Americanisms, however, were only tangentially related to the making and remaking of Brazilian media and markets in the years between Klein's Pan-American promotionalism and Rockefeller's coordination of Inter-American affairs, the latter of which was ostensibly a matter of war-era geopolitics rather than commerce. The vernacular Americanism effected by Hollywood talkies was more closely related to these changes, but it was also influenced by North American print culture and music, and these changes intersected with commercial and cultural appeals to Americanism that had been "made in Brazil."

Visitors were quick to note the influence of U.S. sound cinema on Brazilian Portuguese. "It is difficult to find a youngster in Rio de Janeiro who has not added at least a few Americanisms to his speech. Such slang as 'O.K. baby,' 'kid,' 'yeah man,' is not missing from his vocabulary, even if he knows no other English." Expressions such as "'okay' have become Portuguese words." To critics who might complain of the corruption of the national language, Hollywood's boosters in the press responded, "The talking pictures in English . . . gave the Brazilian public an opportunity to get convenient lessons in the most important commercial language in the world."[140]

"American movies have made Brazilians feel that they know the U.S.," proclaimed *Fortune* magazine, while they also provoked curiosity about other carriers of North American culture: "American books and magazines have followed in the wake of the interest thus created." Thus was fostered "a vast and increasing enthusiasm for the U.S. Because he reads American magazines and books and sees American movies, every literate Brazilian feels that he knows Americans—how they live, what they wear, what the country looks like." Brazilian authorities and expatriate journalists agreed, while U.S. visitors thrilled to the idea that such familiarity might yield contentment. In Rio in 1939, Anne Peck encountered a "like refrain" from Cariocas: "You Americans are so efficient—you have such a high standard of living." Returning to the United States, she informed her compatriots that Brazilians "believe that 'the United States is Brazil's best customer and best friend,'" leading one to wonder if Lauro de Carvalho was one of her contacts. Decades later, the Communist ex-military man Nelson Werneck Sodré recalled Brazilians' "warm sympathy" for the United States during these years: "It was the great moment of this ample, generalized, spontaneous, popular sympathy." To sympathy was added curiosity, "an ever-increasing interest on the part of Brazilians who are eager to see anything bearing a United States trademark or dealing with the American way of life."[141]

The Americanism of U.S. trademarks, magazines, books, and movies was hardly a bolt from the blue, as made-in-Brazil commercial Americanism went back decades. Cinelândia's Americana ice-cream shop predated the introduction of sound cinema, as did the Orquestra Pan-Americana, Odeon's session band on several classic samba recordings. In Rio's retail world, there was the precedent of the Carvalho family's Casa Yankee (1917), while Salvador's largest magasin was called Duas Américas ("Two Americas"), founded in the same year, not coincidentally one in which the United States and Brazil had also found themselves at war with Germany. The 1930s and 1940s do, however, appear to have seen an upsurge in Brazilian-made commercial Americanism.[142]

Nilo de Carvalho's flagship store for women was one example. He wanted a glamorous, modern, cosmopolitan name for his seven-story emporium, which "Clipper" appeared to deliver through its evocation of Pan American Airways' U.S.-to-Brazil service, one of many borrowings of Pan Am's signature route by Brazilian branders. Clipper-brand cigarettes and mattresses made their debuts during these years, as did Hollywood-trademarked lines of both products; in the days of the postcoital cancer stick, the juxtaposition was perhaps not as strange as it seems today. Among the other Americanist cigarette brands to hit the market during these years were Continental ("a national preference" was soon its slogan) and Lincoln ("a good cigarette"—whether it was named in tribute to the gigantic automobile or the Great Emancipator is unclear), together with an updated take on the Liberty cigarette, which had been around for years. According to a Brazilian official, these brands benefited from "more aggressive advertising campaigns undertaken by the manufacturers," including "the giving of premiums . . . in order to attract buyers" and "the mention of certain characteristics such as *tipo americano* (American type)." More Brazilians, especially women, were taking up the habit, prompted by Hollywood but also by "the increased interest manifested in 'things non-French.' Formerly the center of interest in matters foreign was France: today other centers have greater appeal to the Brazilian. This may be said to be particularly true of 'things American.'"[143]

Such things needed not actually be from the United States. Indeed, the impression one gets from the reports produced by the U.S. embassy clerk charged with scouring the Brazilian government's daily gazette for potential trademark infringements is that any English-language or seemingly English-language term seemed a decent bet. Among the English-language trademark registrations flagged in February 1942 were "Bambi" (candies), "Universal" (chalk), "Scarlett" (cosmetics), and "Airline" (shoes), while the Portuguese-language trademarks "Americano" (shoes) and "Laranjada Americana" (orangeade) also made the cut. Applicants only became more inventive, or unhinged, as time went on, evidenced by a three-month stretch that yielded Kiddy, Golden Malt, Marshmallow Gardenia, Extramint, Cream Cracker, Tropical Biscuit, and King, among food trademarks; Show, Charme, Crack, Duplex, Sunset, Tank, Waldorf, and Lady, among clothing trademarks, the first of them for Lauro de Carvalho's A Exposição; Jane, Hollywood, and Made, among furniture trademarks; Botany, Officer, and King in the cotton-piece goods category; Clipper and Clip Cola in the soft-drink category; and Tractor, Rapid, and Big, in the capacious category defined by U.S. trademark authorities as "Matches. Candles, common and detergent soap. Starch, blueing and other preparations for washing." "Clock" was a sane enough name for a pressure-cooker (which may explain why the trademark has never lapsed), but the same cannot be said of "Sex-Appeal" for "Instruments, apparatus and appliances, medicinal, surgical, veterinary for curative purposes or in relation to the health of man or animals."[144]

European-branded products might also wrap themselves in the stars and stripes, Leite Moça being one example. That Nestlé transferred operations from Switzerland to the United States during the European war was good business; that the words "Registered Trademark Belonging to Nestlé's Milk Products, Inc., New York," figured prominently on the Brazilian labels of its most important product was apparently good business also. Better still would have been a label with the magic words "Made in U.S.A.," for as a *Publicidade* staffer remarked, "We have a true inclination for everything that comes to us with the 'made in . . .'"[145]

Newspapermen abetted this fascination in their pursuit of reader interest and advertising revenue, as in the *Diario de Noticias* interviews explicating "Factors of Friendship between the Two Great American Countries," an embassy official remarking privately of the newspaper's publisher, "Of course he had in mind the possibility of advertising support from American companies." Much the same could have been said of *Diretrizes*'s sponsorship of a Pan-American Cultural Competition, which awarded a trip to New York for the best essay on "the development of economic and cultural relations between Brazil and the United States," as judged by a panel featuring Herbert Moses.[146]

Diretrizes's liaison in the United States was Armando d'Almeida, who had renamed his agency Inter-Americana shortly before representing the *Diario de Noticias* on an earlier U.S. trip. He was hardly alone among his colleagues in his Americanist enthusiasms, Cícero Leuenroth having issued an early call for Brazilians to join the Americas ("We have to live the life of the Americas, so that we may create and develop a great civilization here"); two years later, when Standard opened a U.S. office, *Publicidade* greeted "one more concrete work in the strengthening of inter-American relations." As for Pan-Americanism, it was evident in the founding of Pan América by the former head of Standard's São Paulo office, who soon shortened his agency's name to Panam, as well as in the rechristening of the trade's "Advertising Day" as "Pan American Advertising Day."[147]

A most candid take on this Pan-Americanist profusion came from an A Ecléctica executive. "Let us lay aside old and spent Europe and dedicate ourselves, confidently and insistently, to the great approximation between Brazil and North America, because the results of this approximation can only be favorable and beneficial to us," wrote Ottilo Polato. "We, advertising men, should become 'propagandists' of American-Brazilian sympathies, and we will have carried out, with this, a labor to our own benefit and in favor of our profession."[148]

Five years later, Polato's boss at A Ecléctica helped found São Paulo's Rádio Pan-Americana. The idea seems to have belonged to the radionovela writer Oduvaldo Vianna, who received a government license for a station with that name in 1942, winning the congratulations of Herbert Moses along the way. Despite this endorsement, it took time to get the project off the ground, and so early 1943 found Vianna stringing together work, translating Shirley Temple movies for radio reenactments sponsored by Nilo de Carvalho's A Exposição, an experience that built upon his having studied film production in the United States. Finally, in 1944, the station went on the air, to be joined by Rádio América (also in São Paulo) and Rádio Continental (in Rio).[149]

For all their enthusiastic Americanism, the three newer stations could not match the reach of Rádio Nacional. In addition to deeper pockets and more powerful equipment, Nacional counted on a lasting draw in the show Repórter Esso, created by McCann-Erickson for Standard Oil in order to keep its brand in the public eye despite war-induced shortages. Benefiting from avid wartime interest in international news, the show with the slogan "The first to provide the latest" soon became as essential to everyday life as the radionovela.[150]

Joining Repórter Esso as product and pastime in 1942 was *Seleções de Reader's Digest*, a monthly printed in the United States for export to Brazil. Served by JWT from the first, *Seleções* offered Brazilians of classes A and B similar fare to that found in the parent magazine. By all accounts, it was an immediate success, "beating all sales *records*": "Having greater resources, with advertising billed according to foreign rates, made overseas with better paper and graphic material, and giving advertising its due worth, this publication beat all national magazines." Or, as Armando d'Almeida put it: "What happened, in the case of *Seleções*, was the application of rational advertising to the selling of a magazine. Offering good merchandise, intense advertising was used to convince the Brazilian reader to buy it." Like Liberty, Hollywood, and Pan Am's Clipper, *Seleções* even inspired a brand of cigarette.[151]

Nelson Werneck Sodré was then a young officer serving in Bahia. Years later, in his first foray into memoir, he would recall, "Over the radio and through the newspapers, we kept up with news from the war, on all fronts: the *American way of life* presented us with two new and characteristic sources: the *Repórter Esso*, on the radio, and *Seleções*, in the press,—the propaganda they developed was efficacious."[152]

Additional propaganda poured forth from Hollywood, the Chambers of Commerce, private foundations, wire services, and U.S. government agencies, all of it coordinated, at least in theory, by Nelson Rockefeller's Office of the Coordinator of Inter-American Affairs (OCIAA). Advised and officered by U.S. expatriates, including representatives of GE, the Light, Gillette, GM, Standard Brands, and the Hollywood studios, the Brazilian branch of the OCIAA also contracted with JWT's local offices, which saw billings double between 1941 and 1943. Brazilian advertising professionals offered their services independently of JWT, as did their counterparts in journalism and broadcasting. Much of the OCIAA's work in Brazil, however, was only indirectly related to media interests or mercantile concerns. Even its propaganda had more to do with the war effort than "the *American way of life*" from 1942 through Allied victory in North Africa in 1943. Rockefeller and the OCIAA nevertheless played an important role in the remaking of Brazilian media and markets in the 1940s. In the first place, it is unlikely that Repórter Esso would have been broadcast or that *Reader's Digest* would have launched a Portuguese-language edition had it not been for Rockefeller. Second, the OCIAA secured a Treasury Department ruling that made North American companies' Latin American advertising tax-deductible in the United States, encouraging corporations "to maintain abroad their trademarks and the knowledge of the qualities and virtues of their products," as well as "to maintain the good will that has been built up." Some U.S. firms cut their advertising anyway, citing straightened circumstances and an inability to ship goods; others, such as the Hollywood studios, only mildly affected by shipping-space limitations and wartime factory refitting, immediately increased their Latin American advertising. In Brazil specifically, where Ford responded with nationwide newspaper advertising, it is difficult to imagine that Coca-Cola's promotional bonanza was uninfluenced by the Treasury Department's giveaway, or that the OCIAA's efforts to enlist local business interests were fruitless.[153]

A Ford in Your Future

Just as 1943 marked a turn in the war, with German forces turned back at Stalingrad and driven from North Africa, so too it marked a shift in war-themed advertising in Brazil. The first fruits of what insiders called "the Rockefeller Advertising Plan" were that "a much wider spirit oriented advertising into the war's orbit . . . contributing to the psychological formation of the spirit required for man's resistance to the difficulties and contingencies occasioned by the conflict that envelops the world." This "advertising of ideas, of principles," did not disappear from the pages of Brazilian periodicals in mid-1943, nor did local advertisers ranging from shoe stores to cooking-oil concerns give up on identifying themselves with the alliance with the United States or the war effort generally. But a new theme did emerge in advertisements published in Brazil by U.S. concerns, and at least one nationally owned firm, as the end of the war came into view.[154]

"Electricity," declared a GE advertisement of August 1943, "key to progress . . ." There was nothing novel about this appeal. What was new was in the small print, which noted the war-effort work underway in GE labs and factories, yielding "discoveries and improvements" that "will contribute even more so that the postwar world, through new electric devices, enjoys comfort unknown until now." The wartime balance of forces furnished the subject for a sequel, an advertisement featuring two sets of illustrations. The primary set consisted of pictures of a well-dressed urbanite, whom the reader was invited to identify with as he read of victories over the Axis from the Sahara to Ukraine. The secondary set pictured a full line of GE products, including an electric iron, toaster, washing machine, vacuum cleaner, stove, dishwasher, and refrigerator. "What was your part in these victories?" the caption asked. The answer? No more than understanding "that General Electric had a more important objective than making domestic appliances." But with the war's coming conclusion: "GE's friends will be rewarded. Entirely at the service of Peace, using new conquests and discoveries . . . G.E. will be able to offer articles of greater utility, efficiency, and value in every sector of electricity"—that is, all the products pictured in the secondary set of illustrations. "In every sense Victory is worth waiting for!"[155]

The editors of *Publicidade* exulted, calling the campaign "an inestimable contribution of its advertising to the comprehension of the war effort on the part of their clients, now prevented from acquiring the articles that have become more necessary on the combat fronts." They too looked forward to the postwar, when "we will once again possess the devices that contribute so much to all of our well-being," anticipation heightened in 1944 by a new GE radio show, *O mundo de amanhã* (The world of tomorrow). Philco answered with similar advertisements published in *Seleções*: "Today—Philco dedicates all of its vast research and manufacturing facilities to produce the most essential articles for the war, in the field of electronics and its derivatives." As for tomorrow, "Tomorrow—the improvements arising from Philco's war research will be introduced in new and sensational enterprises in television, radio, refrigeration, and air conditioning." Other advertisements guaranteed the "many friends and admirers" of Zenith-brand radios "that the many improvements made by Zenith engineers during this time of war will be incorporated in the sets that will be manufactured after the war." With the end of the war in Europe, Zenith's São Paulo distributor announced that a "new and sensational" line of sets was "On the Way!" Days before Japan's surrender, GM announced, "The World of Tomorrow—Begins Today!": "the day is coming on which we will once again be able to enjoy the benefits of peace—the peace that will place within your reach products that will contribute to a more ample, more comfortable, and more abundant life." A listing of product lines, from Chevrolets to domestic appliances followed: "General Motors presents here a list of the products that it will distribute in the future and congratulates itself with Brazil's millions of consumers on the coming appearance of the useful things created *today* for the world of *tomorrow*."[156]

U.S. public relations—official and extraofficial—encouraged the belief that the products of the future were on the way. Writing before V-J Day, Fred Gardner of the Office of Inter-American Affairs (as the OCIAA was renamed earlier in 1945) assured Brazilian readers that wartime shortages would soon be resolved. Press coverage of the movements and utterances of visiting businessmen fostered similar expectations of comforts to come. "When the promises of the postwar are fulfilled, advertising will continue to lend its assistance," declared one such visitor, who added that in Brazil "a real spirit of advertising predominates" and that Brazilians and North Americans would soon be cooperating "for the well-being of the greatest number."[157]

Brazilian advertising men agreed. "The world will once again do business in peace," wrote Walter Poyares, his words printed opposite a GE advertisement promising power, production, light, leisure, transportation, and comfort to postwar consumers. "In Brazil, the ever more extensive diffusion of the commercial advertisement will raise the general standard of living in all of the country, will make possible the existence of strong commercial and industrial organizations, lowering the cost of manufacture and distribution." Celso Kelly, formerly of Rádio Nacional, more recently the founder of the Continental agency, took a similar view: "This notion of comfort is one of the characteristics of American civilization, which already exerts such a great influence among us, an influence that will make itself felt even more in the near future." Addressing readers on behalf of Carlos de Britto and Peixebrand products, Standard's copywriters expressed their faith that the coming year would see "a better tomorrow and the full satisfaction of all of humanity's yearnings, for which the United Nations are fighting," and that Christmas heralded "a new era of PROSPERITY for Brazil."[158]

Readers might struggle to distinguish between copywriters' appeals and editorial matter. "It is foreseen that with the end of the war, and given the economic development of Brazil, a higher standard of living will be possible for the various social classes, which will permit, naturally, greater individual spending," declared a business journalist. "Such spending, as is logical, will be directed toward human comfort itself." At first seemingly less assured, *Diretrizes* noted, "The 'slogan' of a 'Better World' exerts a profound influence over the popular imagination" and asked, "Will a Better Brazil Be a Part of a Better World"? Yet a reply in the negative was obviously unimaginable. Rather, it was a question of what such a world would look like and how— rather than if—Brazil would share in the "higher standard of living" needed for anyone's "share of happiness."[159]

With Japan's surrender, the expectation seemed to be that good times were around the corner. "IMPORTATION," screamed a full-page GM advertisement: "Brazil's ports are now open ports!" "The good days of gasoline are back!" proclaimed the Brazilian subsidiary of the Atlantic Refining Company: "Brazilian motorists may once more freely obtain Atlantic products." Most famously of all, Brazilians were promised, "There's a Ford in Your Future!"[160]

This campaign was the work of J. Walter Thompson, which had taken over worldwide advertising for the Ford Motor Company in 1943. In São Paulo and Rio, the campaign was translated by JWT's Brazilian staff, who would recall their work fondly for years. As of December 1945, the postwar Ford was to be "Soon on Display," with "notable improvements": different grillwork, two-tone upholstery, and new shocks and brakes. Careful-reading car enthusiasts might thereby discern that the "new and magnificent Ford" was a prewar chassis upon which an "ample and comfortable interior, richly finished with new fabrics and plastic materials," had been mounted. That fact, however, likely escaped most readers, who were offered "*more* in every sense" to be "put on sale very soon." In early 1946, the first display models arrived: "Come get to know, now, Ford's 1946 models, and . . . don't alter your plans—don't be satisfied with less . . . for *there is a Ford in your future*." By April, however, advertisements were kindling desire and counseling patience in equal measure: "If you desire beautiful lines . . . a comfortable ride . . . security . . . power . . . savings . . . don't alter your plans—wait for your Ford!" The "Ford in your future" was not yet available to buyers, though potential buyers were encouraged to "visit your Ford Dealer and get to know the Ford of your future!" Here too, advertisements promising mechanized beauty and comfort were reinforced by the public-relations work of U.S. advertising men, who assured their Brazilian counterparts that better days were ahead.[161]

"After the war . . ." ran the caption in a 1946 issue of *O Observador*, alongside photographs of the latest U.S. appliances: "In recent years, whenever we wanted to acquire one of these modern machines, which contribute to the comfort of the home and are an effective need in the life of modern man, we were most of the time forced to desist: small stocks, high prices, old models. So the hope was 'after the war.' . . . The war ended and with it our hopes are reborn. When will the first machines for domestic use arrive?" Seven months later, the same journal mentioned the lack of automobile imports, noting that wartime shortages had led to "the absolute wearing out of existing ones, in such a way that the entire country calls for motor vehicles for various collective and private activities."[162]

According to the private correspondence of a U.S. advertising man, dealers continued to converge on Ford's São Paulo offices in early 1947, "waiting to see . . . about getting some cars," having been "duly prepared for post-war business" by the automaker's representatives. That patience had its limits was suggested by Arnold Tschudy, a GM executive who had headed the OCIAA in São Paulo. Referring to "the situation in Brazil . . . now that that victory has dimmed the spirit of brotherhood with the United States which prevailed during the war," he noted that Brazilians "resent continued shortages in goods which they had expected the United States to supply." Fearing the undoing of "Brazilian-American friendship," Tschudy singled out his counterparts in U.S. business: "It is necessary, therefore, for North American commerce and industry to measure up to the present expectations of Brazilians and allocate a reasonable share of its production for current export to the country."[163]

Still, the cars did not come. "The importance of the American automobile in the life of Brazil, both socially and industrially, is emphasized in the present acute shortage of these exports to Brazil," a New York journal indicated in mid-1948. "Review of the outlook for the balance of 1948 with respect to American passenger car export[s] to Brazil offers little relief. It is unlikely that more than a few of the people in Brazil who are hoping for new cars this year will be able to gratify that wish." The magazine of the U.S. Chambers of Commerce in Brazil advised, "If you have a car take good care of it, because chances are that you will not get the shiny new one you have been dreaming about for some time to come." Notwithstanding, the "hope of new cars aplenty" died hard, while the black market in such automobiles as were available flourished: "This has greatly disappointed Brazilians who expected American automobiles to enter this country in large quantities at low prices as soon as the war was over."[164]

No Brazilians were more anguished by the lack of automobile imports and the prosperity for which they had stood than the advertising men. In 1947, Manoel de Vasconcellos wrote that the preceding year "may now be defined as having been the year of expectations." With the end of the war, "a great time for business was expected. The new materials developed during the conflict, new experiments in industry that would now be put to everyday use, hundreds of new products that would eventually be launched on the market, all this put the business world in a state of suspense and made one suppose that 1946 would mark the beginning of a new era of prosperity for the entire world. However, things did not happen so idyllically."[165]

As a co-editor of *Publicidade*, which had so encouraged the idyllic view, Vasconcellos may have felt a twinge of guilt. He might have been disappointed at not having a new car of his own. But weightier matters nagged at him also: the fate of business generally and of advertising specifically, agency revenues looking to appear as scarce as prosperity itself. Vasconcellos nevertheless allowed himself a measure of that greatest stock in trade, hope: "It is very possible that many plans that have been awaited up to now enter into development during the present year, many new products be launched in the Brazilian market, the automotive industry may supply us with vehicles for the transport of our riches, and commercial competition be reestablished, greatly increasing the volume of advertising in Brazil."[166]

A year and a half later, such hopes endured, as in an interview with the advertising manager of Rio's *Correio da Manhã*. Looking back over a thirty-year career, Georgino Sandes Pérez touched on early cinema advertising, the U.S. agencies, their Brazilian counterparts, and advertisers of various kinds. He recalled, fondly, a time when U.S. automobile manufacturers introduced new models, "before the war," adding, in a turn from memory to prophecy—perhaps attributed to him in the editorial process—"as they certainly will do again."[167]

By decade's end, the subject had become something of a joke, if not a laughing matter. "There's a Ford in Your Future! But . . . when?" asked the publishers of *Publicidade & Negócios*—as *Publicidade* was retitled in 1947—before rehearsing the campaign for their readers: "One of the 'slogans' that became most popular in these postwar years was that happy discovery of those responsible for Ford's advertising—'There's a Ford in your future.' Even before the war ended, the grand manufacturer began promising us a beautiful automobile, with all the improvements that industry could introduce once its efforts on behalf of military production ended. . . . And all of us were taken in by the beautiful promise contained in that phrase."[168]

———

The Fords did not come, at least not in the anticipated volume and at the anticipated prices. Nor did Chevrolets or other of the North American makes that had come to symbolize peacetime prosperity and comfort. They did not come in 1945–1947 because of delays in the return to civilian production, industrial conflict in the United States, and Detroit's prioritizing of its domestic market once assembly lines were running. Beginning in mid-1947, the cars did not come due to exchange controls imposed by the Brazilian government in a tardy attempt to induce some rationality in the country's import trade. Through the postwar quinquennium, on either side of the imposition of exchange controls, the prosperity symbolized by the "Ford in Your Future," the "World of Tomorrow," the "Better World" failed to materialize for all but a few Brazilians. Many others, not without reason, felt they had been duped. Having given of their resources and sovereignty, endured wartime shortages and privation, and thrilled to their own army's participation in the wartime struggle against a gray autarky and for Freedom from Want, they now expected some measure of the advancing civilization and well-being that had been promised. Hundreds of millions of dollars in foreign exchange, accumulated over the course of the war, and Washington's earlier pledges of postwar assistance seemed sound bases upon which to begin to build the "Better Brazil" of propaganda and press commentary.

The U.S. government's commitment to Brazilian development vanished almost overnight, while Brazil's foreign reserves disappeared nearly as quickly, in an episode that one writer called the "cycle of the superfluous" and another, the "Flight of the Dollar": "this due to the purchases of products of no benefit to the national economy, luxury products, trinkets, which they threw at us right after the war due to the unpardonable neglect of those responsible for the subject." "Made in U.S.A. in the *feiras livres*"—the open-air markets of cities and towns—and "The price of fashion" were the captions added by the editors of *O Observador Econômico e Financeiro*, who went on to explain, in the first case, "The sidewalks of Rio, the *feiras* of the suburbs, the shelves of stores throughout the country, came to be populated by all sorts of objects, even those for domestic use, made of plastic material, in the United States"; in the second, "Female elegance turned to American patterns, and this cost us the sacrifice of precious exchange." According to *Publicidade*'s 1947 annual: "We invested much of our good foreign exchange, accumulated at great cost during the war years, in useless gewgaws of every kind of shiny metal and plastic material."[169]

The moment would not soon be forgotten. For years thereafter, the "flight of the dollars" was evoked, rued, and regretted. Writing in 1949, the critic Limeira Tejo recalled, "Aspirin and harmonicas—a veritable torrent of trinkets, so tumultuous that just one year after the war ended, hundreds of millions of dollars' worth of our commercial credits had been liquidated." "We ended the Second World War with a 650 million dollar credit in our commercial balance and the prospect of increasing it," wrote a Rio businessman ten years later, describing the blowing of that balance as an accumulation of "follies and imprudences" epitomized in imports of plastic yo-yos. A similar description figures in a memoir published decades later: "They were the years in which Brazil wasted the dollar reserves that it had in the United States— 600 million—importing consumer articles, most of them luxury goods, and even raisins and yo-yo's that were sold on the streets of São Paulo." Gerson Moura was only six years old when the war ended, and so it was as a historian that he wrote, "Between 1946 and 1947 Brazil was inundated with *made in USA* products and their advertisements, from luxury cars to bars of soap, cereal, gelatin, lenses, brushes, pomades, beauty products, insecticides, medicines, paints, cloth, office materials, electric appliances, and even the famous plastic gewgaws—the most modern American creation—in the end, all the paraphernalia of American consumerism. The foreign reserves accumulated during the war were in good measure flushed away in this furious importation."[170]

That the disappearance of Brazil's overseas balances came to be universally decried does not mean that contemporaries were of one mind regarding what spending was wasteful and what was worthwhile. Indeed, there seems to have been some bad faith on the part of the *O Observador* editor who projected waste upon the feminine worlds of fashion, housewares, and shopping for the home rather than the importers who had ordered products consumed by their countrymen and countrywomen alike. For B. de Aragão, there were additional distinctions to be made: "We have already shown that the purchases of machines, tools, railway cars and passenger vehicles were smaller than those of automobiles for individual use and goods related to them, pyrex, objects made of plastic materials, so-called European fruits, beverages, perfumes, silks, radios, electric appliances for domestic use, etc." Similarly, if more angrily, Limeira Tejo wrote, "Having at our disposal resources overseas with which to acquire material for transportation, agricultural machines, electric equipment, we used them for the acquisition of radios, soap dishes, suspenders, tooth brushes. We permitted the free importation of canned foods when, at much lower cost, we could have refitted and increased domestic production." Brazilian officialdom adopted a more clinical tone: "Many superfluous products, of which the country had been deprived during many years, have entered lately on a relatively excessive scale." Apparently uninfluenced by the "Ford in Your Future" campaign, the Federal Council of Foreign Trade's *Brazil Trade Journal* identified automobiles as the principal example of the "present confusion," citing the fact that they made up nearly 10 percent of imports in 1947 as opposed to less than 3 percent in 1938, while adding that radio- and phonograph-set imports had also risen disproportionately. For the publishers of *Publicidade*, however, passenger cars, radio sets, and refrigerators were "useful things," and the insufficient supply of them that had arrived in 1946–1947 was to be distinguished from imports of canned foods and plastics. The latter, but not the former, were an unproductive drain on foreign exchange.[171]

To disagreement was added recrimination, the search for causes and assignment of blame, with all their radical potential. In 1947, *O Observador Econômico e Financeiro* sought to head off radical inquiry, while providing an answer of sorts to the question of who bore responsibility:

We had some millions of dollars that we accumulated during the war because we could not purchase what we needed. The war ended and we, armed with those millions, sought a market where we could acquire things. We left home shielded by the excuse that we were well-mannered young men and we were going to spend our money well. As it happens, however, we arrived there and, before we spotted what we most needed we saw new things made of plastic material, the latest novelty; we saw preserves in pretty cans; we saw dog biscuits; and we saw this and that other thing. The truth is that we were neither cured of curiosity nor immune to the temptation of all that. And as there was no restriction on the way in which we should spend our money, we started buying. Until one day we woke up to the news that the available balances had come to an end. And then it was cried out in protest that we had been victims of economic imperialism. Imperialism had sold us gewgaws, fragrances, instead of machines, vehicles, and other things of this kind.[172]

That was not *O Observador*'s position. Rather than blame imperialism, Brazilians should blame themselves: "No one forced us to buy those things, or would only sell us a machine if at the same time we bought so many thousand combs, so many thousand bracelets, so many thousand necklaces, and so many thousand pendants made of Lucite or some other similar material. And even if someone had made such an imposition upon us, it was up to us to repel it, to resist." At fault was "our own imperialism": "Imperialism, according to this line of reasoning, is not a thing or a word that is imposed upon us, but something that we subject ourselves to or that we lend consistency." Collective spendthriftness was attributed to cultural values: "We were raised on the theory that what we make is worthless, is more expensive; any product carrying the label 'made in Brazil' is a definitively inferior product, which we consume compulsorily due to tariff barriers. Who created this theory?"

By 1947, the premises framing this question were no longer correct (there were domestically manufactured goods considered as good as or better than their foreign equivalents), but the question imposes itself regardless. No definitive answer may be had, given that the valuing of foreign-made over Brazilian-made goods goes back centuries, and it was not only for that reason that *O Observador*'s writer sidestepped it ("No one knows" was his reply). But if one leaves aside worrying after origins and probes the issue of inculcation, it becomes clear that its obverse—the valuing of "Made in U.S.A."—received powerful reinforcement over the preceding decade.

From wartime Inter-Americanism to prewar Pan-Americanism, and ranging through commercial and vernacular Americanisms, such reinforcement may be found. It was also at hand in the profusion of branded goods and in the making and monitoring of Brazilian media. Retail merchants, radio personalities, advertising professionals, publishers, and associational spokesmen all contributed.

The contrasts and contradictions of the war era likewise bear reemphasis. These were years in which Brazilian cities experienced shortages of sugar, even as U.S.-style ice cream novelties made their debut. For many urbanites, the taste of white bread and butter became a matter of memory, but "North American shirts and English cashmeres never ceased to be on display." Rationing and other restrictions meant that Rio's 1944 Carnaval was celebrated without the gasoline-powered automobiles that had become such a central part of festivities, but there were plenty of hot dogs and Coca-Cola to be had. Forty years later, childhood memories of wartime Copacabana twinned fears fanned by blackouts and the gaiety of the first Kibon and Coca-Cola-brand carts, selling Eskimo Pies and the pause that refreshes, respectively. Culturally, Brazil's Americanist moment made it possible to contrast the eclipse of European influence with the adoption of U.S. ways, the former representing the country's "progressive liberation from various foreign influences" and the latter the sharing of "habits and customs and tastes among peoples" of supposedly similar outlook, experience, and affect. Even as consumer-goods shortages were felt, consumerism gave further impetus to an incipient cultural industry. In 1941, Nelson Rodrigues was the aspiring playwright for whom "even . . . the advertisements that circulate implacably through the ether" contributed to "something tremendous and irreplaceable" in Rio's northern suburbs; by 1945, his work was being adapted to the radionovela format by Standard for Rádio Tamoio's *Teatro-Romance dos Produtos Marca Peixe*.[173]

Also by 1945, despite the wartime shrinking of Brazil's automobile fleet, the car was "considered an article of indispensable use—that is, definitively incorporated into life's average necessities." No longer a luxury item, it was part of Brazilians' "sense of comfort," and so it was that "the public is getting more and more interested on [*sic*] news from the States about new car production," even as business conditions remained, in the words of a Ford executive, "unchanged."[174]

Even as the promise of postwar automobiles evaporated, Brazil remained "very definitely an automobile-conscious nation." "The automobile is the aspiration of every individual of our time," a journalist opined in 1949. "Or at least of most of them." This desire was further excited by the manufacturers of trademarked goods—Lever, U.S. Harkson, and Brazilian bottling interests—on behalf of Lifebuoy soap, Kibon ice cream, and the Guará soft drink, offering consumers the chance to win a new Chevrolet, Dodge, or other make and model.[175]

Meanwhile, retail consumers were pursued using all manner of advertising, through signage, in the press, and over the airwaves. In 1947, during the Rio conference, delegates from the twenty-one "American republics" who wandered into the city's downtown were greeted by a profusion of A Exposição signs, "all bearing the announcement BIG LIQUIDAÇÃO." By this point, it appears that Lauro de Carvalho had delivered on his Macy's-inspired ambition: while in 1938 he had despaired that there was not a single shop in Rio worthy of the name "department store," advertisements for his A Exposição locations now referred to them explicitly as such. In the 1930s, Lauro had been shocked by an "almost-Communist campaign" that he saw put on by picketers in Manhattan. A decade on, the Communist Party's *Tribuna Popular* figured in his stores' advertising plan, alongside mainstream newspapers and several radio stations. Between 1945 and 1947, A Exposição advertising offered such men's items as Gillette-brand razor blades, Williams shaving cream, and Aqua Velva aftershave; plastic watchbands and Parker pens; suits made with "Legitimate, American," Palm Beach cloth; "Short-Life" brand shorts and Jantzen bathing suits, "American style" slacks and "American cut" sport coats, as well as sport shirts bearing the brand names "Camping" and "Miami." Female shoppers were offered "Items of the Day" that included Johnson & Johnson talcum powder ("100% pure"—"the best for you and your baby"), two-in-one nail clippers and files ("the latest American novelty"), "American side combs, in turtle-shell plastic," and imported elastic girdles in English-language sizes "small, medium and large." On Christmas Eve 1946, women and men may have thrilled together to the "Sensational Item of the Day" available at both A Exposição stores: Air King radio sets, "imported directly from the U.S. to satisfy 100% of your demands."[176]

Thus did commerce and culture intertwine in Brazil's postwar, in what would be seen as the making of a new Brazil, if not the "Better Brazil" dreamed of in wartime. "Right after the Second World War," remembered Walter Clark Bueno, "there began to emerge in Brazil the fantastic American novelties that we only knew from magazines: the fishtail Cadillac, the blender, the yo-yo." It was in an "atmosphere of fascination" that Brazilians "revealed themselves to be curious about technological advances and had an immediate interest in everything that appeared, even if they were trinkets like the yo-yo." Cecílio Elias Netto, born in 1940 in a moderately prosperous town in the interior of the state of São Paulo, presented his memories of the era in the third person: "So then, the boy saw the new Brazil, of the postwar. There was a new beverage . . . Coca-Cola." Traditional, locally made soft drinks scarcely stood a chance, and with Coca-Cola came "'nylon' stockings [and] Cadillacs. . . . It was as if, in Brazilian culture, there had been a sudden reversal: France left, in came the United States. And they came with the fantasies of Hollywood, consumer products, with technological novelties and an infinity of superfluous things."[177]

Writing amid these developments, the anthropologist Arthur Ramos provided a quick evaluation of their impact. "Since the first world war, and especially since the second," he wrote, "French influence has been increasingly counterbalanced by North American influence, which today imbues the preferences of the middle classes of the entire world." U.S. influence—"in food-ways, in men's fashion"—likewise eclipsed the earlier influence of the English, "today . . . barely distinguished from the other, more recent one, brought by the cultural invasion of the North Americans." This "new wave of cultural Americanization" was borne primarily by Hollywood movies and commerce and was clear in various cultural forms: "in the notion of 'comfort' in modern life (new styles of home, bathroom and kitchen, skyscrapers, electric appliances, telephones, refrigerators, automobiles, the multiple 'gadgets' . . .)"; in "foods and drinks (*ice creams, coca-cola, chewing-gum,* the *whisky-and-soda,* the *cocktails* . . .)"; and in "men's and women's fashion." Cinema was a means of cultural transmission and a cultural outcome, as were "the new style of *parties,*" "the multiple linguistic North-Americanisms," and "the loosening of customs, relative sexual freedom, a philosophy of life sometimes in conflict with certain traditional standards of Brazilian life"[178]

Ramos made these comments in passing, as asides in a massive survey of Brazilian anthropology. He recognized that in its novelty and scope, "Americanization" exceeded the attention he could give it. Readers may also sense some discomfort in his writing, stemming from a larger discomfort with the subject. These limits and tensions may explain apparent logical failings. On the one hand, Americanization represented the eclipse of French and English influence; on the other, it was the "latest tendency in the process of Europeanization." It was a matter for the middle class at one point, for entire populations at another, and it was process, work-in-progress, and fait accompli all at once. It was an "invasion" and, by analogy, "from an anthropological point of view . . . less of a true 'cultural' influence with the spontaneous exchange of experiences, than of the type of a 'civilization' imposed, from above," yet Ramos persisted in using term "influence" while dropping his scare quotes from the word "cultural."[179]

It seems that memories of actual war were too recent and the developments Ramos described too near at hand for the martial metaphor of "invasion" to be a comfortable fit. Any reasoned attempt to make it work would bring one face-to-face with a fifth column outnumbering anything identifiable as a foreign expeditionary force and no capital-"R" Resistance to speak of, nor even the ruins of overrun fortifications, only Maginot lines that on closer inspection revealed themselves to have been erected by local partisans of once-imposing commercial cultures. Perhaps revolution would be a better metaphor.

Chapter 4

A True Revolution in Consumption and Commerce

"Rarely has the Paulista Capital seen an event of such great proportions." The verdict of São Paulo's largest-circulation newspaper was an exaggeration, but not that great of one, for it was undoubtedly the most impressive store opening in the city's history. On the morning of March 15, 1949, awaiting an eleven o'clock ribbon-cutting, thousands of people—men, women, and children—crowded outside a massive new structure looming over what until recently had been a quiet intersection in an entirely residential part of the city. Some members of the crowd had strolled there, the site having been picked because it stood at the hinge of neighborhoods where large numbers of wealthy and near-wealthy families lived. More had driven, the location offering plenty of free parking. Most, however, had taken public transport, the new store's managers having convinced city hall to reroute streetcar and bus lines for the occasion. While the crowds waited, many of the women among them bearing parasols against the bright, late-summer sun, a police band played to the captive audience. Among the onlookers, a well-positioned few could eye enormous display windows, each displaying a specific kind of merchandise and the slogan *De tudo para todos*, suggesting something for everyone in every imaginable line of goods. No one, not latecomers, nor passersby, nor drivers caught in snarled traffic, could have missed the streamers, banners, and bunting, or the bold lettering on the towering façade: S-E-A-R-S R-O-E-B-U-C-K.[1]

Representing the parent company was its chairman, Robert Wood, in the late stages of a career that saw Sears's greatest expansion, from a mostly mail-order business to the world's second-largest retail concern. Also in attendance, on government loan to Sears to serve as a living symbol of U.S.-Brazilian collaboration, was General Mark Clark, under whom Brazilian troops had fought in the Italian campaign. Flying the flag for the U.S. diplomatic corps was the consul-general for São Paulo, while higher authority still was represented by São Paulo's archbishop, on hand to bless the new store. Perhaps toughest to miss would have been São Paulo governor Adhemar de Barros, to whom Sears's chairman took an instant liking, eased by the politico's fluent English, professed anticommunism, and backslapping venality, the latter no doubt a reminder of Chicago, where Sears was based. As Wood later remarked, "He is a politician pure and simple."[2]

At the appointed hour, Barros performed the ribbon cutting and shoppers streamed into the store's thirty-odd departments. More than eighty thousand people passed through Sears's doors that day, with thousands left waiting outside when the store closed at five, its staff exhausted, shelves and shop-counters nearly bare. Almost sixty thousand more "Paulistas in Wonderland" visited the store the following day, "to shop and look, and to become indoctrinated in Sears['s] unique methods of merchandising." Thereafter, Sears continued to draw crowds of a thousand or more awaiting each 9:00 A.M. opening.[3]

All the while, cash registers jangled and clanged, and "any doubt that the São Paulo store would be a success vanished." The stock of refrigerators sold out almost immediately, set upon by "hundreds of women . . . screaming and waving money," but even before the bulky white appliances could be delivered to customers' homes, other goods flew from the racks—dresses and nylons, baby clothes, men's suits, linens for bed and bath, every kind of kitchenware. Meanwhile, additional deliverables, from carpets to card tables, bureaus to box springs, awaited their turn at the store's warehouse.[4]

Three months later, the scene repeated itself in Rio, where an even more imposing structure had been built overlooking Botafogo Beach, a strategically chosen point halfway between Rio's downtown and the toniest neighborhoods of its southern reaches. Once again, spiritual and secular authorities turned out, the ranking politician, General Antonio Mendes de Morais, calling the store "one of the greatest public services" the city had ever known, oblivious as to what that might say about his performance as mayor. To Morais's good fortune, the massive crowds that had gathered beginning at dawn showed little interest in parsing his words. Rather, they were intent upon the moment when the doors would swing open, allowing them to rush in. Over the course of the day, more than 120,000 people followed, more shoppers than at any of Sears's previous 637 retail openings. It was an event as manic as it was massive, with crowds erupting into tumult—"near riots in the model kitchen"—and the store's escalators astounding shoppers. As in São Paulo, refrigerators were the hottest item, but impulsive shoppers reportedly "marched home with everything from absorbent cotton to zinnia seeds," rung up on National Cash Register machines to the tune of $550,000.00, for opening-day sales exceeding 10 percent of Sears's initial investment.[5]

As the dust settled, and some of the novelty wore off, interested parties began to consider Sears's impact. The company's view, expressed to stockholders, was that "the stores are operating profitably and the need for them has been demonstrated." A Brazilian journalist was more expressive. Sears, in his words, had provoked "a true revolution in consumption and commerce."[6]

Revolutionary or not, the two openings were no bolt from the blue. Beginning years earlier, during Sears's earliest exploration of Brazil, people took notice. Within months of the purchase of the site in Botafogo, local retailers were "studying counter-measures to meet this serious threat." Advertising men were intrigued. By 1947, when Sears's chairman visited for the first time, the firm's plans were an open secret. Industrialists, in particular, had been forewarned by Wood's handpicked representative, who had "already made the rounds of Brazilian factories," and so Wood was feted in São Paulo by a group that included the industrial engineer Armando de Arruda Pereira and the advertising man João Alfredo de Souza Ramos. Even Ford executives, not usually given to retail-watching, kept an eye on the construction of Sears's stores.[7]

In 1948, following more than a year's anticipation, Sears began to establish formal contacts with the press. Its instrument was Ruy de Barros Chalmers, a Brazilian of English ancestry recently returned from sales-promotion training in the United States. In December, Chalmers met with representatives of the advertising departments of São Paulo's leading newspapers to begin planning for the campaign that would herald Sears's opening. By February, insiders were nearly giddy at the prospect of a major new advertiser.[8]

In each city, full-page newspaper advertisements introduced Sears to readers a month in advance of the opening of the local store. Once a date for the event had been picked, smaller advertisements, reprinted constantly, served as reminders, while dozens of radio spots produced the same effect over the airwaves. For the final push, the cities' most important newspapers were picked for catalog-like advertisements running over multiple pages highlighting the range of merchandise to be sold, the features of unknown or less-well-known goods, the prices of everything on offer, and the slogan *De tudo para todos*.[9]

This advertising onslaught was unprecedented in scale. The bargains that Sears's deep pockets allowed the two stores to offer, including refrigerators at prices 35 percent below the going rate, nylons at 40 percent, and men's shirts at nearly half price, were unheard of. In both areas—advertising and pricing—the aim was a public stir rather than immediate profits.[10]

It was therefore to be expected that *O Observador Econômico e Financeiro*'s staff writer, having coined the pretty hyperbole "a true revolution in consumption and commerce," would draw down some claims regarding Sears's impact: "We must reexamine that which we called a revolution in commerce." Such a revolution, he continued, could be dated back to the founding of the Woolworth's-style *lojas*. More recently, he argued, Rio's "great stores, even before Sears," had introduced sales-promotion techniques as effective as any deployed by the U.S. firm. As one example, he cited Lauro de Carvalho's A Exposição and its introduction of the "Item of the Day"; as another, he mentioned large-scale installment selling, so ubiquitous that he was apparently unaware of its origins.[11]

Taking a longer view, Sears's São Paulo and Rio debuts are best understood as episodes in a series of changes affecting not only commerce and consumption but the society and culture of the urban southeast generally. The 1940s and 1950s were characterized by innovations in store location, services, design, and technology. Sales promotions old and new were employed to draw consumers into stores and the world of goods more broadly. Goods never before manufactured in Brazil came to appear on counters and in shopwindows. Employee training became more sophisticated, as did techniques for monitoring customers, stocks, the competition, and especially consumer credit, the use of which grew exponentially amid rising inflation. Throughout, the United States—Lauro de Carvalho's "great school" of 1938—remained the central point of reference and regard for retail merchants and their salaried managers, but other influences surfaced too. Europhilia, never erased even at the high point of Brazil's midcentury romance with the United States, appeared anew in matters commercial, even as the country's most important European-owned commercial concerns became Brazilian. Conditions peculiar to Brazil likewise influenced the retail revolutions of the country's postwar, and even the most obstinate foreign interests—Sears, for one—remade their plans accordingly.

The retail trade was one sponsor of commerce's reaching out of the sphere of publicity and into private life, a process most apparent in the colonization of traditional holidays and the creation of new commemorative dates. The advertising profession was an eager cosponsor, backed by newspapers and radio stations. Local government also assisted in the promotion of commercial commemorations.

The sales promotionalism and retail revolutions of these years arose alongside changes in media. General-interest newspapers strove ever-harder to appeal to readers as consumers, even as new broadsheets and tabloids sought to corner specific markets. Old magazines and new ones kept after the holy grail of national coverage and the advertising revenue that would accompany it, even as particular publishers were increasingly aware of the profits to be had by reaching niche audiences. In radio, the 1940s saw the peak popularity of the commercial jingle, while the 1950s witnessed the last, bright blaze of the medium's "golden age." Television, introduced in 1950, did not replace radio all at once, either as advertising medium or mode of mass entertainment, but it did establish a foothold in the southeast.

Together with the electric refrigerator, the television set was the biggest of so-called big tickets—large, bulky, and especially expensive household goods. In 1949–1950, these consumer durables were luxuries only available on an import basis, thus the excitement caused by the below-market prices available at the two Sears stores. Within ten years, electric appliances large and small, as well as all kinds of nonelectric durable household goods, would be turned out by Brazilian factories producing nearly exclusively for the domestic market. Existing retail outlets demonstrated increased attention to such goods, even as new commercial concerns entered the growing field. Expanded consumer credit enlarged markets, while advertising and sales-promotion techniques sought to create consumers. Here, perhaps more than in any other area, the new professionals' self-appointed role as educators of a buying public came to dominate publicity work.

Pedagogic promotionalism was similarly important in the last of the major developments in retailing between the 1940s and 1950s. Beginning in 1953, U.S.-style supermarket shopping was brought to Brazilian consumers. By decade's end, supermarkets owned and managed by native-born Brazilians, immigrants, and expatriates played prominent roles in the provisioning of parts of São Paulo and Rio. In a less tangible sense, they had also become part of everyday life for many urbanites. The model presented by these metropolitan markets, in turn, had been taken up elsewhere in the country, including locales passed over in earlier retail revolutions.

These developments, ranging from the opening of Sears stores to the spread of supermarketing, were inseparable from broader spatial and social shifts. The cityscapes of São Paulo and Rio experienced changes more radical than they had seen in a generation. Smaller southeastern cities—satellites of the megacities-to-be, as well as Belo Horizonte, the capital of Minas Gerais—were contemplated by some of the captains of Brazil's new commercial culture. Further expansion of the characteristic institutions of that culture, to cities north and south, occurred as well, often at the initiative of locals rather than southeastern emissaries.

Amid these changes, at once its creature and its creator, was the growing cohort of new professionals. Market researchers, sales-promotion specialists, and advertising men and women thrilled to changes in the structure and culture of business, markets, media, and everyday life. Further reaching for allies and esteem, advertising executives in particular—*profissionais da prosperidade*, professionals in and of prosperity, in a cute alliteration that nearly caught fire during these years—seemed on the cusp of achieving all that they had aspired to in the 1930s and 1940s, for themselves and their country. If only it could last.

Retail Revolutions

Sears's openings in São Paulo and Rio were star turns before a backdrop of general retail-sector euphoria, fueled by the innovations of preceding years, the delayed gratification of wartime, the postwar influx of imported merchandise, and the novelty of wage-earners' ability to push for long-delayed pay increases in a relatively open political environment. "Retail trade is booming," a local source reported in 1948, "with department store sales setting a new record." While accurate statistical series isolating retail from wholesale sales were impossible to establish, an early study of the field—"the least-investigated sector of commercial activity"—concluded that Rio retail sales in 1948 were about four times greater than in 1940.[12] They would increase even more dramatically over the next decade, encouraged by changes in retail staging and structure.

Perhaps the most oft-noted of Sears's innovations, at least by retail-watchers in Rio, was its Botafogo location, far from the traditional shopping district centered on Rua do Ouvidor. But had such observers a better grasp on recent changes in the commercial geography of São Paulo, they might have been less likely to attribute innovation to the U.S. firm. Ten years earlier, São Paulo's Mappin—the great British-owned department store—had transferred the site of its flagship from the "old" city center to a new location a few hundred yards to the west in what was considered a "new" downtown. Four years later, when Nilo de Carvalho's Clipper opened its doors, it was in Santa Cecília, more than a mile from the traditional shopping district.[13]

Following Sears's opening at a location two miles south of that established shopping district, retail expansion into the city's residential districts continued apace. By 1951, Nilo de Carvalho operated A Exposição stores in Brás and Belém. In Brás, Nilo's store competed directly with a magasin belonging to the Casa José Silva group, as well as an outlet of his brother Lauro's A Sensação, a store designed "to serve the populous borough of Brás with the same articles for women and the home that are found in the grand stores of the city center." The three stores would not encounter competition from Sears for another five years, the U.S. company only opening a local branch in 1956. By that point, Sears was also operating a large store in the Agua Branca neighborhood, while A Sensação had opened a Vila Mariana outlet. In the meantime, Mappin—nationally owned beginning in 1950, its British investors having sold out to a Brazilian group—opened a second São Paulo location in a retooled movie palace on a busy thoroughfare west of downtown, dubbed Mappin-Odeon in homage to the building's earlier function. It was Nilo de Carvalho's Modas A Exposição Clipper, however, that was the pacesetter, opening stores in the outermost neighborhoods in which middle-class consumers could be found and laying the groundwork for a chain of stores encompassing the state's most important interior cities.[14]

In Rio, even before "the appearance of Sears with its store 'of all for all,' situated in Botafogo, a residential neighborhood, that no one believed in, as merchants, customers, and even the indifferent thought that the *ponto*, in the heart [of the city], was what made things sell," retail groups had begun establishing stores outside of downtown. These stores—typically located in upper-middle-class Méier, northwest of downtown, and Copacabana, on the city's southern beachfront—operated initially as adjuncts to the downtown stores, but by the mid-1950s, some were self-supporting. Indeed, the Copacabana outlets became luxurious destinations in their own right, the Casa Barbosa Freitas's location dwarfing its downtown stores and Casa José Silva's hailed as "fitting tribute to Copacabana's progress, to its growth as a veritable city within the city itself."[15]

Of all the commercial interests active in Rio, however, Mesbla established itself most boldly beyond the confines of the old downtown shopping district. The giant mercantile company had once been the Brazilian affiliate of the French firm Mestre et Blatgé, though by the postwar most of its shares were held by Brazilians. For decades, Mesbla had dealt in almost every line of imported goods, including automobiles, which is why GM's James Mooney had paid a visit in 1922 and why Mesbla's management maintained close relations with U.S. consular representatives. Wholesale trading and the distribution of heavy durable products—machinery, passenger cars, even airplanes—were Mesbla's focus, and thus the portion of its Rio headquarters that was open to the public was more of a showroom than a shop. This situation changed notably, however, in 1952, with the opening of Magazine Mesbla, the English-language spelling of *magasin* chosen to suggest a synthesis of European style and North American service. The store occupied a site south of Rio's shopping district where its 120 meters of display windows would be seen from the major north-south routes linking downtown and the fashionable neighborhoods of the Atlantic beachfront. The store continued to grow after opening its doors, as new floors were finished and opened to the public, in the process creating what a European-born executive boasted was Rio's first "complete 'department store'"—using the English-language term in Portuguese conversation—because of its many departments and policy of possessing "complete stocks in its departments, including articles that are sold less often, but that by their existence in a department of Mesbla, give the customer the widest possible choice." While Magazine Mesbla was designed to draw customers from throughout Rio, with a focus on the comfortable classes of its southern reaches, a smaller store in upper-middle-class Tijuca, dubbed Mesblinha ("Little Mesbla"), was to serve as a beacon to consumption in points west from its 1958 opening onward. Here was a parallel with Sears, which had opened a midsized department store in Méier a year earlier for similar reasons.[16]

The problem of keeping these increasingly large department-store operations stocked with goods led administrators in different directions. At one point, supply had presented no problem at all. As a boastful scion of the Carvalho clan recalled, "I went to the USA and brought back nylon stockings, Cannon towels, women's dresses. The dollar was a trifle, so cheap that a pair of nylon stockings came out for us with customs and everything 5$000 and we sold them for 12$000. . . . And so I came to have a marvelous life. I went to the USA two times a year." After the postwar import binge and the disappearance of Brazil's dollar reserves, it was clear that imports on such a scale would be impossible, at least for the foreseeable future, and the local manufacture of ready-to-wear clothing would be necessary. Sears took a minority stake in a local firm, Indústria de Roupas Regência, and provided it and other suppliers with technical assistance, as well as, in Regência's case, "approximately $100,000 worth of the latest most-up-to-the-minute machinery." Casa José Silva, which had been the exclusive Rio dealer for clothes manufactured by the A. J. Renner group since the 1930s, created its own workshop for the making of Epsom-brand shirts during the war; in 1948, the firm sent technical staff to the United States for training, purchased new machinery, and contracted a North American industrial-engineering firm. In the same year, a factory owned by Rio's Casa Tavares began turning out ready-to-wear suits. Of the Carvalhos, Nilo was the first to branch out into manufacturing, but Lauro soon followed, returning from the United States in 1949 having bought machinery for what was billed as a "most modern factory . . . the largest in South America," with "one of the greatest U.S. technicians" contracted to oversee production. Experts in design followed, increasingly from Europe as England and France came to provide Brazilian fashion plates.[17]

That these plants could produce more clothing than the department stores could sell led to the creation of new sales organizations, including chains of menswear stores featuring some elements of department-store shopping alongside a more limited line of products. The Renner group created a nearly nationwide network of agents alongside its regional arrangement with Casa José Silva; it also established an eponymous chain of stores in Rio Grande do Sul. By 1958, Casa José Silva had a network of eight hundred dealers and agents for its Epsom-brand shirts. Alongside Regência's dealings with Sears, and in the run-up to a Sears-brokered deal in which it would receive investment funding from Nelson Rockefeller's International Basic Economy Corporation, the clothing manufacturer founded a retail arm called Lojas Garbo. Even before Regência's deal with Sears was formalized, Lojas Garbo had created a promotional apparatus aimed at convincing customers of the quality of its Brazilian-made ready-to-wear suits, including a dry-cleaning business and "advertising programs . . . in order to draw people into the shop and to provide an opportunity to show the merchandise." While Lojas Garbo grew in and around São Paulo, Rio's A Exposição Modas was spurred by its manufacturing operation to create its own chain of menswear stores, Lojas Ducal. Like so much else about the group's operations, the chain's name was inspired by a U.S. company, in this case Bond Stores' offer of a second pair of pants free with a purchase of a suit, thus *du*as *cal*ças (two pairs of pants), or *ducal*, the contraction forming a word with the same meaning as its English cognate, and thus the implication of near-regal style. But there was more in the way of U.S. influence than a clever store name inspired by a bygone promotion. The chain's executives also applied what they learned studying retailing at New York University, among them Ducal's president, José de Carvalho. As early as 1947, members of the A Exposição group also traveled to New York to study department chain-store organization in situ. Follow-up trips provided additional pointers for a growing organization active in manufacturing, retailing, and wholesale distribution, as did José de Carvalho's membership in the National Retail Dry Goods Association. In his words, "I had the satisfaction of being . . . the 1st South American member of this association that affords excellent services to its members, keeping them informed through publications and periodic pamphlets of all that is new in retail." Within ten years of the opening of the first Ducal store, José de Carvalho had appropriated his father's Good Neighbor–era turn of phrase: "I recommend to my retail colleagues, to all businessmen involved in distribution, to advertising men, periodic immersion lessons in the great school that is the United States."[18]

By that point, such advice was hardly needed. The owners and managers of stores large and small, foreign-owned and nationally owned, were intent upon the U.S. example, not only in store location and product design but especially in sales promotion. Retail advertising became more aggressively promotional from the late 1940s onward, aiming to attract potential customers' attention to specific sales and sale items, rather than impress a particular store's presence and "personality" upon the public. According to one estimate, the portion of large-scale retail advertising in São Paulo newspapers that was promotional doubled between 1948 and 1957, by the latter year "accounting for over seventy per cent of the retail advertisements."[19] Institutional advertising remained important in radio, but in print for a its principal motifs—store slogans, images of store's exteriors—came to figure alongside or below sales-promoting appeals.

As far as specific sales promotions were concerned, the sheer number of them daunts the researcher, just as the promotions themselves were meant to dazzle consumers. New and old schemes to get customers into stores, sell particular goods, and move additional wares filled newspapers and the radio waves, even as other appeals—in-store, ephemeral, and word-of-mouth—went unrecorded and have thus been lost. When Sears set up shop in Brazil, its executives tut-tutted at their competition's reliance on liquidation sales, no doubt thinking of A Exposição's Big Liquidação, but the U.S. company soon came to employ the same promotional device, even as Nilo de Carvalho's A Exposição Clipper sent an executive to the United States to examine liquidation sales, where his study yielded nothing new in that well-explored field.[20]

Another nearly shopworn promotion was even more widely diffused, as the "Item of the Day" sale became a national institution. Competing with A Exposição's Item of the Day were the "Temptation of the Day," the "Advantage of the Day," and the "Purchase of the Day," each offered by a different São Paulo retailer, while A Sensação made an alliterative change of timescale to offer the "Sensação da Semana" (Sensation of the Week). Thus, in one retail-watcher's words, did these stores address "the no. 1 problem of the retail trade . . . which the Americans call 'store traffic' or 'customer traffic.'" The item in question was secondary: "above all they seek to maintain (and increase) the daily flow of customers in the respective stores, because the presence of the customer in the store *leads to the purchase of many other products*, and it is the sale of the latter that makes the *business profitable and compensates for the expenses made on Advertising.*" Sears's management in Rio adopted the same promotion, using the name "Bota-Fogo Sears," in a play on the name of the store's neighborhood and the "red-hot" price of the item on sale. Ten years later, a trade magazine identified more than forty retail outlets offering variations on the Item of the Day, including stores in Belo Horizonte, Recife, Campinas, Niterói, and Curitiba. It was by then a given that such sales were "excellent means to create *movement* in stores or, as one now says, American-style, to create *traffic.*"[21]

By that point, dozens of other gimmicks, giveaways, and discounts featured in Brazilian retailing. Something for nothing, something nearly for nothing, or—more often than not—the illusion of one or the other aimed to increase "traffic" and foster "impulse" buying. In 1955, when Rio's Casa Tavares opened a third store, its McCann-Erickson-designed advertisements featured "an original promotion: clients who shopped during the 'Inauguration Month' received a Founding Client certificate and came to enjoy, from then on, a discount on the purchases they make." Sears's São Paulo store offered a more frugal path to discounts, offering housewives credits toward new cookware in exchange for old pots and pans. In 1956, Modas A Exposição Clipper and Lojas Garbo promoted head-to-head giveaways aimed at boys, young men, and their parents' pocketbooks, giving away an association football and their favorite team's jersey, respectively, with each purchase of a jacket, shirt, and pants. São Paulo's Loja Isnard offered a promotion in cooperation with Probel, a manufacturer of innerspring mattresses and furniture: the purchase of a Probel mattress, sofa, or divan gave customers the chance to win a thirty-day trip to the United States. By Isnard's estimate, the results were "very satisfactory."[22]

In-store events, tie-ins with out-of-store occasions, and spectacles bridging in-store and out-of-store spaces served as progressively less direct means to impel sales. By the 1950s, in-store fashion shows were such well-established features of Rio and São Paulo's retail world as to seem ordinary to urban sophisticates. That fact was not necessarily a drawback in sales-promotion terms as shoppers accustomed to the showier side of such events might have their attention focused more intently upon the fashions for sale while new customers—generational turnover alone would account for thousands more every year—gave themselves over to wonder. That customers could be made to find the familiar format thrilling was shown by a 1956 event cosponsored by Mappin, Metro-Goldwyn-Mayer, and Max Factor of Hollywood. This show, held at Mappin's Odeon store, featured its new ready-to-wear line, modeled by the Goldwyn Girls, on tour to promote *Guys and Dolls*. An audience of eight thousand attended, an unspecified number having been turned away, in what was an unqualified success for all three firms.[23]

Events with no inherently commercial content were also turned to sales-promoting ends. In 1955, for example, when Rio hosted the Thirty-Sixth International Eucharist Congress, a world gathering of the Catholic faithful, the city's merchants "felt enthused by the great promotional happening . . . producing some advertisements that will certainly be multiplied in the future." Five years earlier, Rio had hosted an even holier event, its retailers reaping greater commercial rewards. The 1950 World Cup, played at Maracanã Stadium, provided irresistible fodder for tie-ins, with A Exposição the pacesetter, creating Brasil-brand suits, hosting a Championship of Prices, and buying the right to display the Jules Rimet Cup in its shopwindows.[24]

The display of the Rimet Cup built on a tradition of A Exposição trading on Carioca sporting fanaticism, but it was more impressive than earlier efforts. Indeed, an insider described it as a "scoop," in which the store's owners and managers had created an attention-grabbing, sales-promoting event out of circumstances no one had yet thought to exploit. That the Rimet Cup would have to be in Rio for the tournament would have been obvious to any sports fan, but that it could and should be put on display alongside merchandise as an incitement to retail sales did not seem so obvious. By the very nature of the shopwindow, the Rimet display was also a spectacle that transcended the store's commercial space, bringing passersby and one of the public's greatest enthusiasms into its orbit. Both gambits—the "scoop" and the bridging of shopfloor and public square—were also exploited in novel ways in São Paulo, notably at Mappin in 1955–1959, when the store's advertising department was headed by Alex Periscinoto, formerly of Standard Propaganda, and before that, of Sears. One of Periscinoto's "scoops," likely lifted from the U.S. department-store advertisements he pored over in his off hours, was to make a commercial event out of Mappin's anniversary, using the slogan "'It's our birthday, but you are the one who receives gifts' and . . . spectacular offers of merchandise and prices. It was an *estouro*" (literally, an explosion). Making it an even bigger *estouro* was making the store's façade into a gigantic mock-birthday cake. For Mappin's "Fortnight of Carpets," an adjoining square at the meeting point of the city's old center and its newer one was covered in gigantic, multihued, mock rugs. Most provocatively, given the cultural conservatism of the era, Periscinoto placed live models in Mappin's shopwindows to publicize no-run nylon stockings.[25]

Mappin and A Exposição's ability to create popular furor through their shopwindow displays depended upon their stores' locations. For large stores outside city centers, there was a need for attractions that would make them destinations. For Mesbla's general manager, a Dutchman who had worked in retail in Zurich, London, and New York before settling in Rio, the point was "to make the store a complete unit in itself," such that "a lady will not only be able to do all her shopping there, but will also be able to have lunch and tea, go to the beauty parlor, and take in a fashion show or a movie in the auditorium." Even more than that, he wanted to make Mesbla "a kind of civic center," with expositions ranging from rare orchids to sacred art, the latter coinciding with the Eucharist Congress. By that point, Mesbla's panoramic rooftop restaurant vied with Sears's "Sky Terrace" for the title of Rio's most scenic eatery, and while São Paulo had nothing comparable in the way of vistas, Sears's flagship offered dining and entertainment in its "Blue Room." Upscale restaurants had not been part of Sears's plans for Brazil; indeed, one reporter came away from the first store's opening surprised by how spare its company-standard features were. Rather, the Sky Terrace and the Blue Room were something Sears's tonier Brazilian clientele demanded of retail outlets situated at a distance from such amenities, as were the bars installed in the two stores, the first ever featured in any Sears. Tearooms and in-store eateries more generally, at stores from Clipper to the Woolworth's-styled lojas, were not merely services, as their locations could make them inducements to traffic: "a tearoom, in the innermost part of the store, is another means of attraction, because it will make the customers pass through the entire establishment and see the displays, with open possibilities for purchases."[26]

As with its tearoom, so with child-friendly features: Clipper's management never let up on making its store more accommodating to children. Child-friendly services and entertainments brought mothers into the store with their children, at which point they might purchase goods from any of its departments. Thus, from the 1940s onward, Clipper's kids-only hair-cuttery was a São Paulo institution. Beginning the following decade, Clipper sponsored a "Children's Festival" during the otherwise slow month of June, with performances by circus clowns, free balloons, and Duchen-brand cookies. Tying it all together was the slogan "Bring Your Children to Enjoy Themselves for Real!" By the 1960s, the Clipper Children's Festival had become an institution as well, celebrated "with daily shows and free gifts . . . a cooperative promotion with Arco Flex (shoes), Seven Up (soft drink), Estrela (toys), and Semp (electronic appliances for the home)." In the meantime, Magazine Mesbla adopted some of the same facilities and hosted similar spectacles, so that mothers could "park Junior in the barber shop" or at a "Children's Cinema" while they shopped. Mesbla's Tijuca location also featured in-store movies, as well as a weekly "Mesblinha 'Show'" put on by a famous clown.[27]

At Sears, according to Luiz Fernando Furquim (b. 1940), the goods themselves were the main attraction: "Children, who hated going shopping with their mothers, found themselves eager to accompany them, for this could represent a few more marbles . . . or mean a cat's eye reflector, as was only manufactured in the United States, to equip their Philips, Triumph, or Bianchi bicycle." As those children grew, Sears became a site for the "footing" that had once taken adolescents downtown, a place "of leisure for young people," where they gathered to see and be seen by members of the opposite sex.[28]

That Sears and other department stores lent themselves to "footing" and to the spotting of such novelties as Furquim's made-in-the-USA reflectors was a function of store-design and shop-display techniques, many of them adopted under the inspiration of U.S. models or the instruction of U.S. experts. The point, often aided by imported technology, was the offer of ostentatious comfort and convenience, combined with the subtle steering of consumers' movements and attentions.

From the beginning, Magazine Mesbla—"frankly designed to appeal to upper and upper middle class customers"—was "modeled on the finest European and American stores." That these customers would be women led one journalist to wax rhapsodic: "A great store should always, above all, attract ladies. Fashion, the goddess around whom the devotion of all women revolves, always tends to be the dominant attraction of the great 'department stores.'" From Mesbla executives' point of view, the firm's identification with the masculine world of wholesaling made it imperative "to feminize the new store and distinguish it as far as was advisable from the traditional Mesbla." Their success was attested to by the Chamber of Commerce's monthly magazine: "The aisles are wide and spacious, goods are prominently displayed so that customers can play the old game of 'just looking,' and all the clever and eye-catching tricks of modern display and merchandising are used to make the store attractive and the merchandise appealing." Indeed, "Mesbla's main floor, with its wide spacious aisles, gleaming show cases, tasteful display of merchandise, and courteous sales girls, makes Americans think of Saks, Bonwits, or their favorite hometown department store." That was the point, according to Mesbla George Wahl, who compared the store "to B. Altman, of New York, or Marshall Field, to cite two great American stores." "In Europe," he added, "I would compare it to 'Trois Quartier,' of Paris, or with 'La Rinascente,' of Milan, or even with Harrods, of London."[29]

Such commercial cosmopolitanism was the aim of the investors and managers who opened the Galeria Carioca de Modas on the corner of Ouvidor and Gonçalves Dias in 1949. At the heart of Rio's traditional shopping district, "folks who understand commerce and who are linked to various stores famous the world over, like 'Galeries Lafayette,' in Paris, 'Bon Genie' and 'Innovation,' in Switzerland, and grand department stores in England, in the United States, and in other parts," sought—an executive claimed—to make the new store part of Rio's "living patrimony." "The spirit of the establishment," an admiring journalist declared, "is European. If you enter the store, however, you note that the physical plant is entirely American. The 'display' follows the style of the great stores of the United States, in its form, layout, shopcounters, in the presentation of its merchandise." The result was "one of the best-outfitted department stores in Brazil. Ample use was made of the modern decorating trend of bringing together different colors and styles in a single setting. . . . Florescent lighting and the brightness of the furnishings . . . giv[e] a pleasant impression. . . . The establishment's entire surface is carpeted. One moves easily through its interior."[30]

The feeling of movement was particularly important at Sears, as its adoption as a site for *footing* suggests. While the décor of the São Paulo store had disappointed a Rio-based journalist who wrote that it reminded him of "a great big 'five and ten cent' store," he had to recognize that it worked: "We appreciated one thing about the American store: its 'lay-out.' The shopcounters are laid out within the store in such a way as to permit the transit of thousands of people without great confusion." Initially, that was the most crucial point. Thereafter, displays and other fixtures could be upgraded, and so the store was remembered as "a great big amusement park, happy and carefree, that contrasted with the boringness of the antiquated stores of the time."[31]

In Rio and São Paulo, the managers of Lauro de Carvalho's A Exposição and its offshoots—the Ducal chain, A Sensação—drew on their knowledge of the "great school" of the United States and "profound study of the new American commercial techniques" for the remodeling of their stores and the design of new ones. "The client needs to see, to examine the merchandise," José Luiz Moreira de Souza declared in 1954. "Their desire to buy is stimulated by the presence of the merchandise." If this was commonsensical, it had not always been, nor were its implications always apparent: "It is not so simple for us to *really* convince ourselves of the importance of principles and to carry out everything within their limits. Every time we return from the United States, for example, we bring ideas like this one, but they are forgotten in a few months. You cannot imagine how different a store can be, if one remembers the principle of displaying merchandise in keeping with the study of each property and each lighting point." These principles were reflected in the layout of the Ducal store on Praça Tiradentes, billed as Rio's "largest store for articles for men" and described as a "a luxurious establishment, laid out in accord with modern North American display technique," a store "with ample open spaces for the traffic of clients and employees," in which "one feels at ease, as merchandise is displayed in such a way that clearly indicates that it can be touched." Even as that store was readied for opening, the expansion of the group's flagship department store for women was underway. Amid that expansion, A Exposição Modas contracted the services of a New York architectural firm that had served Macy's, among other department stores, "to be able to offer greater comfort to its clients, through better presentation of its goods and easier traffic on its eleven floors." Arriving in Rio, the firm's Columbia-trained engineer told reporters, "My principal work will be precisely that of planning the internal organization of the various departments with special attention to illumination." Ahead of opening São Paulo's first Ducal store, the group sent its architect to the United States to study retail-store design and imported a "great authority in the facilities of modern stores in the United States" to oversee the outlet's decoration. The results were hailed in the press: "The commercial facilities of the recently inaugurated magasin, which occupy five floors, were planned and built according to the modern technique for stores of this kind, in which mirrors predominate, with merchandise laid out openly, functional furnishings, wall-to-wall carpeting in lively colors, direct and indirect lighting, florescent and by incandescent bulbs, in addition to other modern decorative and architectural characteristics."[32]

Technology was thereby employed to move customers through stores and their gazes over goods on offer. Another technology—air conditioning—was used to enhance customers' comfort. Air conditioning had been installed in local movie palaces for years but was only extended to retailing in 1949, by Galeria Carioca de Modas, then Sears's Rio store, an occasion for remonstrance by one retail-watcher: "In the Federal District there are about 100 office buildings with air conditioning for the comfort of those who work in them. First-class cinemas also offer this comfort to moviegoers. But stores, until now, have not even thought of this, in a city in which it is 90 or 100 degrees in the shade on hot days! Galeria Carioca, followed by Sears, is the first to do this thing that should be compulsory. All the stores of any importance that we have just visited in the United States offer the comfort of air conditioning to their customers."[33]

By the mid-1950s, air conditioning had been installed in several retail outlets, including Sears's original São Paulo location and its Agua Branca store, A Exposição's downtown menswear store, Casa Barbosa Freitas's Copacabana location, and two of the Lojas Brasileiras chain stores, one in Copacabana, the other, more surprisingly, in north-zone Bonsucesso, prompting the chain's founder to explain: "Everyone told us that the public from the suburb wouldn't look kindly upon a store with such a luxury. But it is not a luxury. We only want to give the housewife of that suburb a place where she can do her shopping in comfort, and we are certain that this will open up a new field in suburban commerce." For the actress Tônia Carrero, speaking on behalf of the "feminine consuming public," air conditioning was a necessity. "In a climate like ours," she declared, "one cannot shop in a place where one is dying of heat. Air conditioning is not a luxury. It is indispensable."[34]

To the comfort of cooled air was added the dulcet tones of piped music. By 1958, dozens of São Paulo establishments were subscribers to the Promúsica service, including Mappin, both Sears locations, and all six A Sensação stores. In Rio, Mesbla was among the first retailers to retain the services of a similar company "organized in Rio on the bases of North American firms of the same type." By 1959, the use of ambient music was Ducal policy, its stores reporting increased sales with the introduction of "programs of functional music as a 'back-ground' . . . providing an agreeable atmosphere for their clients."[35]

Shopping bags came into use at virtually the same moment as elevator music, and for some of the same reasons. As a U.S. Embassy staffer reported, "Their use (an innovation for department stores in Brazil) has become particularly widespread since the opening of American department stores at Rio de Janeiro and São Paulo. The latter consume about 140,000 paper bags and about 2,000 kilograms of kraft wrapping paper per month." To such basic technology was attributed tremendous import and influence on sales: "The use of bags for purchases ('shopping-bag') began in the United States, less than twenty years ago and is today so widespread that it is part of the everyday scenes of American life. Even so, American stores and magasins seek to increase, more and more, the number of clients who carry their purchases away with them. The advantages to the stores are enormous: not only are operational costs lowered, alleviating the home-delivery service and the inevitable annoyances on both parts (client and store), while also provoking a greater buying atmosphere within the establishment due to the fact that the customers take the merchandise that they have bought with them. Sales technicians sensed that the 'shopping-bag' stimulates and increases the number of these customers." According to a Brazilian specialist, "Sales promotion is not just advertising and bringing the public to the store. One must provide comfort and elegance in the transport of the merchandise." Shopping bags with plastic handles met those standards while serving as a means for retailers—Mappin was one—to advertise, their customers making their way home bearing ornamented kraft-paper bags.[36]

Once again, the emphasis was on movement, in this case a simple technology enhancing the movement of people and goods, to which were added customer comfort, payroll savings, and sales promotion. The cash register was a more advanced technology applied to the cause of efficient accounting and limiting employee fraud, but it too was employed as a means of moving people, products, and money. Placing at least one cash register in each department was a novelty when Sears opened its doors. "No one was used to that system of picking up the merchandise, putting it under one's arm, and paying at the cash register," recalled one of the technicians who installed the machines. "You could pick it up and then you went to pay at the cash register."[37]

The escalators that made such an impression when Sears opened in Rio were another application of technology to the movement of people and goods, each capable of moving six thousand persons hourly, though statistics were irrelevant to the teenagers for whom "everything came to be cool." "It was cool," remembered one, "to ride on the pioneering escalator." In São Paulo, Clipper was the pioneer, its status highlighted in a "Great Escalator Inaugural Sale." Doubling down on the fascination the escalator exerted on children, the toy department was situated at its summit. The escalator was soon seen as "indispensable, today, in a department store," and installed in five-and-dime stores as well. As Lojas Brasileiras's founder explained, "The escalator is, then, a way of attracting customers' attention to certain parts of the establishment."[38]

Other stores adapted simpler technology to the same ends. For Casa José Silva's Méier location, it was an elevator, introduced with a ribbon-cutting performed by "two genteel female clients." São Paulo's Eletro-Radiobraz department store—"a new and sumptuous Department store, which presents really revolutionary and never-before-seen architectural and functional features"—used ramps rather than escalators to move shoppers through its nine stories of air-conditioned shopfloor. Combined with the store's lighting and its open layout, the effect was to "allow a complete view of the entire store, from whatever point within it an observer places himself." Its encasement in an entirely glass façade had the added effect of providing customers the feeling of being "within the very display window of the store."[39]

For the man or woman in the street, the customers were within the display window, and in this respect Eletro-Radiobraz's ultramodern design was only the latest shopwindow bid for attracting attention and inducing movement from street to store. Mesbla's façade, for example, was described as "a veritable gallery of shopwindows." Tended by an autonomous department that received 20 percent of the store's promotional budget, its 120 linear meters of show windows were reportedly "such a strong sales element that they force passersby, firmly persuaded, to head for the entrance." By the 1950s, window-dressing was becoming a profession, practiced by Brazilian artists and European-expatriate specialists, taught in government-sponsored institutes, the subject of specialized publications. "Rio de Janeiro is, without a doubt, one of the cities of the world that has made the most progress in the art of the shopwindow," wrote a women's-interest columnist. "How long ago were those times in which everything that was sold in a store was laid out, lined up, hung up, piled up! Just a few years ago, nothing was known about the art of window-decorating among us." Since then, the situation had been reversed, "and today we stroll on rua Gonçalves Dias, on avenida Copacabana or on rua Visconde de Pirajá, stopping to admire the internal architecture of the stores, the originality of the constantly changing presentations, and shopwindows that, without a doubt, lead many people to buy objects that they did not intend to acquire." A writer for *Propaganda* provided a view from the other side of the glass: "Today, it is fair to suppose that there is not a single retailer, advertising man, or any citizen involved in commerce, who has not gauged exactly the importance that the shopwindow exercises in sales."[40]

Comparing European and Brazilian window-dressing styles, an Italian-born decorator employed by Casa Barbosa Freitas pointed to the greater "American influence" in his new homeland. That influence, combined with "the Brazilian people's own mentality," made for the most striking difference between European and Brazilian approaches: "In European shopwindows, the conception is more closely linked to art than to commerce. In ours, the commercial interest is more alive and the conception has a more commercial feeling." "The shopwindow is the mirror of the store," he added. "The shopwindow has a life of its own and it would be an error to think that it does not leave in the mind and heart of the passerby a memory, a remembrance that, expressed, means the desire to purchase." He might have been echoing Lauro de Carvalho, whose U.S. experience had convinced him of the importance of shopwindow-dressing, a lesson extended to the Ducal chain: "The passerby is attracted to the store from the street, as his natural desire to buy is stimulated to the maximum." By that point, the professionally decorated shopwindow—in Rio's city center and outlying neighborhoods, in São Paulo and points south—was seen as "a great natural salesperson," exercising "its powerful influence on passersby."[41]

In increasingly decentered, motorized cities, passersby were no longer necessarily, or even primarily, on foot. To take only one example, the greatest part of Mesbla's 120 meters of display-windows faced a busy thoroughfare, trafficked by buses and cars. The need to accommodate customers as users of public transport and automobile owners was clear in 1949 in Sears's petitioning for the rerouting of public transportation and on its storefront, the lettering "Estacionamento Grátis" (free parking) appearing over the entrance to its private garage. By that point, Modas A Exposição Clipper operated shuttles that whisked customers from the Praça Ramos de Azevedo—literally in front of Mappin—to Clipper. With the opening of Mappin-Odeon in 1955, the once-British, now-Brazilian department store offered ample parking, "a very modern innovation and a useful one for car-owning customers." Such customers could leave their cars parked while they examined Mappin-Odeon's stock of appliances and furniture, then take a shuttle to the flagship store, leading a trade columnist to remark, "Thus the esteemed Paulista establishment follows the trend of the great North American 'magasins' and fulfills a capital precept of Sales Promotion: to facilitate access to the store." Or, as a local newspaper put it, the solution to "the automobile parking problem" was part of Mappin's mission as "A Democratic Empire."[42]

Retail commerce not only expanded into previously unexploited spaces, department stores also offered extended shopping hours. Beginning in 1947, Rio's A Exposição followed up on the success of its "Big Liquidação" with the "Big Night," a sales-promotion event that took place once per week, on Wednesdays, when the group's stores stayed open late into the evening. A Exposição was not Rio's first retail outlet to offer nighttime shopping, but it was "the first to advertise especially to attract customers between 7 and 10 at night," with advertisements offering shoppers "more time to buy," topped off by free movie passes. One observer reported, in language that no doubt gladdened A Exposição's sales-promotion staff: "Remaining open until 10 o'clock on Wednesdays is *a service* that *A Exposição* is providing its clientele. All advertising that offers a service to the customer is destined to succeed." This success was doubly assured as "the prizes ... are an object of powerful attraction, really capable of causing women to come downtown with two purposes: to go shopping and to go to the movies."[43]

In 1949, Sears successfully lobbied São Paulo's city government for permission to offer nighttime shopping. Thereafter, competing stores extended their hours past the traditional 6:30 P.M. closing time, with mixed results: "The volume of night business for Sears has been constantly growing because Sears is located outside of the downtown shopping area, with adequate parking space for cars in its own parking lot and on surrounding streets. . . . The downtown stores, on the other hand, have not secured any very great increase in business as a result of the night openings. Even at night parking is very congested and it is usually necessary to walk seven or eight blocks after parking your car in order to reach a downtown store."[44]

In Rio, where Sears also offered free parking, nighttime shopping was a huge success, an executive exaggerating only slightly in referring to nights "when it is almost impossible to walk through the aisles." There was, however, a key difference between Rio and São Paulo as far as nighttime shopping was concerned. As of the early 1950s, nearly all Rio retailers benefited from nighttime shopping. In São Paulo, where downtown stores lost money trying to vye with Sears for evening shoppers, an ungainly coalition of retail interests, ambitious politicians, and labor leaders put an end to nighttime shopping in 1952. For nearly two decades thereafter—increasingly to the chagrin of all retailers—São Paulo stores closed at 6:30 except for a four-week period around the end-of-year holidays, when they stayed open until 10, while Rio retailing was ever less bound by legal or customary restraints.[45]

Novelties from nighttime shopping to crosstown shuttles and comforts and conveniences the likes of air-conditioning and escalators—these were features of Brazil's postwar retail revolutions that were apparent to all concerned. Other innovations took place outside of the public's attention. Methods and systems of monitoring merchandise, customers, and the competition were purposefully hidden from view. The behind-the-scenes training of managers and employees was increasingly systematized, though demand for skilled personnel remained sufficiently high for predatory hiring to be standard practice. In retail credit, meanwhile, open competition yielded to cooperation in the monitoring of would-be consumers.

The monitoring of merchandise involved U.S.-inspired systems of accounting, purchasing, and stock control that took turnover rather than markup as the measure of a firm's well-being. In 1949, José de Carvalho bragged of A Exposição's "analytical accounting" and especially its "stock control under the American system, which provides the situation of the merchandise at any given moment, doing so with scientific rigor." Professional buyers used this information to time purchasing so as to minimize stocks and the time goods spent on store shelves, A Exposição drawing on the services of a Brazilian graduate of Macy's executive training course, though it would soon lose him to Mesbla, where he would supervise a group of fourteen buyers charged with purchasing for its thirty-seven departments. In the meantime, as the Ducal chain branched off from A Exposição, it renewed the parent firm's emphasis on stock control, an executive explaining, "The Ducal stores, like the modern North American retail organizations, pay special attention to planned purchasing and to stock control." Turnover was coordinated with advertising, on which Ducal spent 5 percent of its gross sales, again in emulation of U.S. methods: "The American already has a precise awareness that advertising, by accelerating the pace of stock turnover, makes prices go down." As in sales promotion, so in stock control, the aim was to keep up with the latest from the United States, and so in 1956 the Lauro de Carvalho group sent A Exposição's commercial director and the head of its merchandise division to the "fabulous world of New York's retail trade" to observe "the latest programs of American retail, principally those having to do with methods and systems." Macy's was on their itinerary, of course, but their most important stop was at the headquarters of the National Retail Dry Goods Association, where the two executives met with in-house experts, most importantly the ones responsible for stock control and accounting, "to obtain broader knowledge about how to establish a 'Lifo Index,'" a "Last in, first out" method of calculating costs and a "most modern system of 'stock' control" especially suited to the inflationary cycle predominating in Brazil. Other Rio-based merchants adopted "The Retail Inventory Method," also of North American provenance. These systems provided managers with information that would allow the coordination of increasingly rapid movements of goods.[46]

"In summary," explained Ducal's commercial director, "accelerating 'turnover,' which is almost synonymous with increasing profits, is to buy the *right* merchandise, in the *right* quantities, at the *right* times, and to sell them as quickly as possible. To schematize and coordinate the means necessary to reach these objectives constitutes the basic task of the modern merchant." Inflation encouraged the spread of this approach: "There emerged, at that point, brought from the United States . . . a magic word—'turnover'—that little by little was crystalized in the Brazilian expression—*rotação de estoque*. In synthesis, this ideally means sales so rapid that they allow the retailer to pay the supplier with the consumer's money." This arrangement was dressed up in the language of "service": "Once he understood this, the retailer ceased to be an agent of the supplier, ceased to make voluminous purchases, with voluminous investments of capital, to become an agent of the consumer, from whom, truly, he receives a commission for the work of selecting the merchandise that he offers." Indeed, a retailer who could turn over his stock four times a year "is not interested in increasing the price of merchandise; to the contrary. He wants to speed up sales and low prices will always mean larger swathes of the market to serve." The latter assertion was debatable, but there was no doubt that turnover was increasingly central to retail strategy. If, in 1959, a Ducal executive described turnover as nearly synonymous with profits, by 1961, Casa Barbosa Freitas's director claimed, "the retailer's profits come exclusively from stock rotation."[47]

Monitoring potential consumers, actual customers, and in-store crowds was simpler. Unlike stock control and accounting, it could be accomplished without resort to systems or formulas, at least on the part of retailers. Executives availed themselves of IBOPE's services, as they had going back to the 1940s, allowing the research firm to do the math for them. For example, six months after Ducal's mid-1956 debut of a new line, its advertising director pointed to an IBOPE study indicating "87.2% of the Carioca population are already aware of the 'New Suit.'" By that point, IBOPE was not alone in offering retail-oriented consumer research. Advertising agencies had increased their profile in the field, the larger ones creating research departments. Some of these departments grew into independent or quasi-independent organizations, while other freestanding research institutes emerged through other means. One result was that IBOPE faced half an alphabet's worth of competition, including Empresa Nacional de Organização e Pesquisa (ENOP), Instituto de Estudos Sociais e Econômicos (INESE), Instituto de Pesquisas de Opinião e Mercado (IPOM), and Marplan–Pesquisas e Estudos de Mercado.[48] To reach actual customers, retail stores carried out in-store research. One such investigation, conducted alongside "an external study, among the grand public, by a specialized institute," took place in four stores belonging to an unnamed São Paulo firm. It was directed by a Brazilian public-relations consultant and executed by store employees, who obtained 1,300 responses to a questionnaire adapted from Verne Burnett's public-relations primer, *You and Your Public*, which were "most useful" to store executives.[49]

Research methods like these also yielded information on competing firms. A more direct approach involved sending employees into rival stores disguised as customers. Professional "shoppers," as they were called, in English, provided pricing information that allowed their employers to ensure that stocks were optimally priced. If statements of store policy were to be believed, such reconnaissance should have been used only to underbid the competition, but the opposite was sometimes the case, a Sears executive explaining: "We have two shoppers who shop our competition daily. I have found them to be very beneficial in keeping us competitive and also occasionally find opportunity of taking additional mark up." By 1954, a "'shopping' group" was on Magazine Mesbla's payroll as well: "They are ladies and some gentlemen who investigate the trade daily, observing the articles sold at the other stores and the prices that are being charged. Every day they write up a report that is given to management."[50]

At Mesbla and Sears, the training of "shoppers" and in-store functionaries, from department heads to floor personnel, was carried out by managers who passed on what they had learned working in the United States and the major western European capitals. Members of Mesbla's mostly female workforce were subjected to a test "to reveal their level of sociability, inclination to deal with the public, and other requisites of education and good appearance" (the latter a Brazilian euphemism for whiteness), in some cases complemented by psychotechnical exams. Thereafter, store employees attended "special courses on 'merchandising' and sales in all sectors." In 1948–1949, as Sears prepared to open its doors, its customer-service staff underwent an eight-month program of daily instruction in salesmanship: "a marvel," said the friend of one company employee, a "great school." Sears's in-store employee training paralleled the technical assistance it provided manufacturers and the pedagogic promotionalism directed at potential consumers. "Sears' problem is definitely one of education," a company executive explained. "Teaching people to make goods is manufacturing; teaching people to want goods is selling; teaching people to work together is organization; and let me add a fourth—teaching employees to understand Sears and its policy is selling Sears." As Sears's operations expanded, its in-store training was complemented by sending employees north: "some to attend courses of instruction along with people from stores in U.S. cities; others to Sears stores in the U.S.A. for specific job experience; and still others to the Sears headquarters for 'graduate courses' in buying, sales promotion, and personnel management."[51]

At Rio's A Exposição and its offshoots, employee training had been more improvisational. Through the mid-1940s, attempts to indoctrinate employees in aspects of what Lauro de Carvalho and his junior partners had observed abroad were complemented by occasional resort to foreign experts. This situation changed in 1948, when the group hired an ex-JWT copywriter with substantial sales experience to create a training department "to administer to sales personnel and supervisors the practical knowledge essential to their profession." Two years later, the training department was transformed into a formal school, accredited by the quasi-official National Commercial Apprenticeship Service, or SENAC, and run by an A Exposição employee who had recently completed a business degree at New York University. Admission required same kind of psychotechnical testing applied at Mesbla, following which sales personnel took a "finishing course" covering everything from merchandise presentation to the correct way to address customers, while department heads confronted curricula in executive management, sales promotion, purchasing, and advertising. Both courses were taught by A Exposição executives, who drew on such texts as Charles Edwards and William Howard's *Retail Advertising and Sales Promotion.*[52]

The proliferation of these courses (which by the 1960s almost invariably began with psychotechnical testing), the adoption of streamlined instructional methods (Mesbla adopted the Training within Industry system in 1958), and the use of company organs and conventions to keep employees and executives up to date proved to be insufficient, particularly when it came to retaining skilled personnel. Competition between firms continued to lead to the poaching of employees, a boon to the new professionals. When Alex Periscinoto left Sears to work on the Modas A Exposição Clipper account at Standard in 1951, his salary increased tenfold; when he moved on to Mappin a few years later, his salary bumped upward again. Pedro Nunes had a similar experience as he moved from A Exposição to McCann and on to Galeria Carioca.[53]

As critical as executive staffing and personnel training were to the operations of increasingly complex retail firms, consumer credit was more important. Ultimately, installment selling was what fueled retail growth. At Lauro de Carvalho's A Exposição, credit sales as a proportion of total sales doubled between 1949 and 1952, to more than two-thirds of the total. Between 1954 and 1958, Ducal credit sales increased from 60 to 75 percent of total sales. By 1958, 65 percent of sales at Modas A Exposição Clipper's stores were made on credit. At Mappin, credit sales increased from 22 to 43 percent between 1952–1953 and 1955, while the figures for Sears for 1952 and 1958 were 31.3 and 57 percent.[54] By 1949, A Exposição claimed to be the largest personal credit organization in South America, its files containing information on a half-million registered users. By 1957, the Lauro de Carvalho group claimed more than three million "crediaristas." Managing the mountains of data that lay behind this figure was eased by Hollerith tabulating machines, a U.S. technology brought to bear on an Argentine- and European-inspired system introduced by a network of Brazilian firms, then adopted universally.[55]

In Milton de Carvalho's words, "This system, which I had the pleasure of introducing at A Capital . . . is diffused in such a way, not only in Rio but in all of Brazil, that retailers that haven't adopted it are very rare." "The Carioca retail trade is currently going through a period that one could call the era of individual credit," another Rio-based retailer claimed, "and the merchant has seen appear, as if through a trick of sleight of hand, the acquisitive capacity of his market, suddenly increased." "The Crediário took over

Rio," crowed a proud Carioca. "It is so generalized that there is no one who doesn't know of it and, save for few exceptions, who hasn't already used it." Meanwhile, a São Paulo executive noted, "The business policy of the great majority of São Paulo and Rio de Janeiro stores is based principally upon their installment-sales plans."[56]

Initially, installment sales were an area of intense competition. Firms jealously guarded the information they had on customers' credit-worthiness. Through the 1950s, advertisers' emphasis on the special advantages of their credit facilities only increased. Sears executives complained privately that they were at a disadvantage when it came to obtaining financing because of the personalistic nature of the Brazilian banking system, but this was no barrier to the Carvalho clan or to Mesbla, nor was it a problem for the deep-pocketed Brazilian group that purchased Mappin in 1950.[57]

Competition, however, yielded to cooperation in one area. In 1955, representatives of São Paulo's leading retail firms founded the Central Credit Protection Service (SCPC). Housed by the São Paulo Commercial Association and funded largely by subscriptions, the SCPC was a clearinghouse for records on delinquent account-holders. Rather than relying on their own investigations of potential customers' credit-worthiness, participating firms would now inquire, by messenger or telephone, whether someone's name figured in the SCPC's files as either "negative" (more than three months in arrears) or "rehabilitated" (currently paid up, but with a recent record of having been "negative"). Under the agreement entered into by all of São Paulo's major retailers, a response of "negative" would lead to the denial of credit until the existing debt was paid. In the service's first full year of operations, it received 285,773 inquiries from 175 stores, figures that climbed to 828,404 inquiries and 315 stores by 1959. From the point of view of São Paulo retailers, it was a tremendous success: losses declined, in-house credit departments cut investigative staff, and customer credit was extended more quickly. Attuned to this success, Rio's thirty largest firms founded their own Credit Protection Service (SPC) in 1957, in cooperation with the Brazilian Advertising Association. In the early 1960s, there were twenty-one SPCs in Brazil; by 1965, there were sixty.[58]

Happy Days

By that point, the SCPC's services were so sought after that its income from subscriptions and other user fees exceeded its operating expenses, including the salaries of its fifty-person staff. The surplus was deposited into a promotional-date fund, another cooperative venture involving retailers and advertising professionals, this one aimed at lending a more commercial air to existing holidays and creating new occasions for the exchange of store-bought gifts.[59]

Going back to the 1920s, the run-up to Carnaval had been a peak time for car sales, "due to the part the automobile has come to play in the greatest of all Brazilian 'festas.'" By the 1930s, radio sales were as important, the sets "charged with general synchronization," in the writer Alvaro Moreyra's words. "It is the radios, from morning calisthenics to bedtime, that sear into the memory of the Carioca land its true national anthems." Brightly colored fabrics and branded cosmetics were in even higher demand. In 1933, São Paulo's A Exposição advertised the "triumphant crediário system" for the purchase of Carnaval clothing, while leading up to the following year's festivities *O Paiz* ran a "Carnaval Guide" listing merchandise for sale at dozens of Rio retailers. By mid-decade, it was clear: "Carnaval is for Rio de Janeiro's commerce what Christmas is for the great North American and European capitals, an optimal occasion for exceptional business."[60]

In the postwar, several firms sought to make it an even bigger commercial event, Rio's A Exposição leading the way with a "*Big* Carnaval Sale," hawking factory-made costumes and sportswear for women, men, and children. In 1950, the firm introduced Samba-brand dresses for women and Superman costumes for boys, the latter available as an Item of the Day. Shopwindows featured these Carnaval promotions and more, while saleswomen worked in costume ahead of the festivities. Meanwhile, Galeria Carioca was involved in some of that year's most notable, not to say notorious, Carnaval developments, publicizing the "Nêga Maluca" (Crazy Negress) costume in cooperation with the radio artist Linda Batista, singer of the samba of the same title: "To *Galeria Carioca*'s good fortune, 'Nêga Maluca' was the samba that won first prize in this year's Carnaval music contest. *Galeria Carioca* also managed to be the store that was chosen to display the prizes for the most beautiful costumes of the Municipal Theater's Ball in its shopwindows. In a well-done window, it placed some splendid costumes alongside the luxurious presents. And this made it such that traffic sometimes became difficult on the stretch of Ouvidor at Gonçalves Dias. Still not satisfied, it placed a Samba School under its central awning, with which it succeeding in attracting the attention of all who passed."[61]

These campaigns, relatively buoyant economic times, and the financial support of city government made for extravagant celebrations. "There's never been a Carnaval like this one!—we heard from many people. And the monthly balance of some great Rio stores must have indicated the same thing," a trade columnist wrote, highlighting the role of the public purse: "Every large Carnaval club or small group of dancers subsidized by the mayor's office had to buy costumes, a thousand adornments, traditional musical instruments, materials for decorations, in a word: an infinity of things, leading to lots of business for the trade. The prospect of a great Carnaval stimulated everyone. And, in Rio de Janeiro, the public took to the streets to buy. Carnaval is, incontestably, a great occasion for sales promotion for the retail trade."[62]

In 1951, A Exposição and Galeria Carioca were joined by stores in Brazil's "principal urban centers," including Mappin, Sears, and Clipper. Soon enough, even insiders felt that Carnaval's commercialization had gone too far. As Standard Propaganda's Sangirardi Jr. half-joked, "Carnaval, these days, is not something spontaneous: it's only the product of advertising. If it wasn't for this well-planned advertising, of records played over the radio, of carnavalesque columns in the newspapers, of shopwindows and banners in the stores, the people wouldn't come out into the streets."[63]

The mid-1950s saw a scaling back of Carnaval promotions, accompanying changes in how Brazilians commemorated the holiday, particularly the relative decline of Rio's downtown festivities and the drawing power of other attractions as more Cariocas of coveted classes A and B opted to spend the long weekend on the beach or in the mountains, while poorer city residents could resort to Rádio Nacional's novelas, which ran uninterruptedly through the traditional three days of revelry. While stores in Rio's northern suburbs still found it worthwhile to deck out their shopwindows and façades, downtown retailers seem to have reasoned that the city government's decorations would serve as reminder enough for sales of mostly low-end goods: cheap cloth, clothing, and costumes that would bear the brunt of the festivities. Carnaval was not dead, nor was it dying, but it was changing. It was no longer Brazil's commercial equivalent of Christmas. Christmas now occupied that role.[64]

Christmas had thus come to Brazil, but not from out of the blue. Brazil's pre-1930s yuletide traditions were many and varied. The most widepread Luso-Brazilian traditions were the crèche, homemade sweets, and midnight mass, to which Brazilians of more recent immigrant stock, in some regions and among some families, had added Christmas trees and tales of a kindly old man, most often called St. Nicholas (São Nicolau) rather than Santa Claus (Papai Noel). Gifts, when they were given, were modest, often homemade, and only destined for children. By the later 1930s, however, Lauro de Carvalho, having been impressed by Christmastime sales in the United States, began to promote generalized gift-giving in advertisements featuring Papai Noel, as did other retailers, and in the process Santa became an increasingly ubiquitous figure in urban culture. Thus was unleashed "the greatest promotional idea of all times," the editors of *Publicidade & Negócios* explained, one with "all the right qualities for a special sale."[65]

Rio's municipal government—its mayor named by the national president—contributed to promoting Christmas festivities, as did the press. Beginning in the 1950s, the Rio government put up Christmas-themed decorations from downtown to Copacabana, while cooperating with *O Globo* and the ABP in an annual competition awarding prizes to the best-decorated shopwindows and storefronts. According to the longtime head of *O Globo*'s advertising department, the campaign was an instant success: "We achieved our objective entirely. . . . We enlivened commerce, we stimulated the civic feelings of our businessmen, who attended to our appeal warmly, well beyond our expectations. Practically all Rio's shops displayed Christmas decorations, whether in their shopwindows or on their façades." A Exposição carried the honors in 1952, while the following year—in which Herbert Moses served as a judge alongside representatives of the ABP, the municipal tourism department, and the retail-merchant's syndicate—Mesbla won for best shopwindows and Sears for best storefront. All the while, according to a semiofficial institute, Christmas sales continued to increase, reflecting a "growing interest in the habit of giving gifts for Christmas" that researchers attributed primarily to advertising. Installment sales led the way, credit having become a more important consideration than end-of-year bonuses when it came to holiday sales, while publicity sought to convince customers to start their holiday shopping earlier and earlier.[66]

As the years passed, Christmastime was marked by in-store events and public spectacles. In 1954, Magazine Mesbla was described as having "gone all out on Christmas." Along with "delightful decorations" that lent "a real Stateside Christmas look," its toy department featured "a real live Santa Claus." Not to be outdone, Mesbla's São Paulo outlet launched "Santa Claus in a [Hot-Air] Balloon" in 1955: "The balloon and the cabin were set up inside the store so that in order to speak with the kindly old man it was necessary to enter the 'magasin,' where [one's] eyes were soon focused on the varied assortment of toys." In Rio, a forty-meter-tall electric-lighted billboard of Santa Claus—the "biggest Santa Claus yet seen in this country"—was inaugurated by Santa himself, who was also to visit all the city's neighborhoods, starting with Copacabana, while the *Correio da Manhã* sponsored a live nativity scene featuring three hundred figures and a parade of the Magi on each of the four Saturdays preceding Christmas, "a spectacular living demonstration of its modern promotional mentality and its desire to contribute so that the Christmastime festivities have greater salience, [as] sources of joy for the collectivity and catalysts of sales in the retail trade."[67]

In 1958, arriving in Rio by Brazilian Air Force helicopter, Santa was met by a crowd of fifty thousand, including the mayor, who presented the kindly figure with a key to the city. The following year, half a million Cariocas were on hand when Santa Claus touched down. In receipt, once more, of the key to the city, Santa "got on a magnificent float" created by a famed set designer, then led a parade that included two hundred troops of Brazil's most storied army battalion, its marine band, and hundreds of clowns. Thereafter, children bused in from throughout the city attended a "gigantic 'show'" featuring acrobats, contortionists, and jugglers on stages decorated by the filmmaker Chianca de Garcia. These spectacles were put on by the city's retailers and its tourism bureau, in cooperation with the mayor's office.[68]

By then, it was clear that Brazilian Christmas commemorations had changed significantly, at least in the cities of the southeast and south. "Christmas celebrations," as an insider wrote in 1956, "revived and created new enthusiasm in the last 10 or 15 years, thanks in large part to the efforts of commerce itself in promoting the sales of toys and items for gifts, efforts supported by the Press and Radio." "A list of local advertisers that are using Christmas as the theme of their end-of-year advertising would be excessively long and, even so, incomplete," noted a copywriter. "Practically everyone who has something on their shelves and something between their ears as well, since Christmas is the great sales-promotion occasion." But it was not just retailers: "What leaps out at you most if you flip through a December issue of *O Cruzeiro* . . . is the application of the Christmas theme to an ever-greater number of items." Once toys and other likely gift ideas were the only products featured in yuletide advertisements: "These days, tires and pans, meat grinders and plastic dishware, mesh shirts and perfumes, are all advertised as suggestions for presents." That was the "promotional magic of Christmas," the poet Décio Pignatari argued: "Advertising did nothing more or less than organize it rationally, replacing surprise with the correct choice and steering this formidable collective will . . . toward buying [gifts] that created a historic, automatic, even compulsive habit." "Commerce and advertising brought into being a Christmas and New Year spirit that the sweet Christian legends, the Midnight Mass, the Crèche, and the tree were not able to create on their own," was how the writer Elsie Lessa described the process, even as she lamented of Rio's favelas, "Santa Claus doesn't always climb the hillside and continues to overlook the way to its huts and hovels." Such locales remained off Santa Claus's well-beaten path, though it would not be long before his annual helicopter ride would end at Maracanã Stadium, with its two-hundred-thousand-spectator capacity, and specialists would claim, "In Brazil Christmas is celebrated with a greater furor than in any other South American nation."[69]

By then, Brazil was also distinguished by its dedication to Mother's Day. The idea of dedicating the second Sunday in May to commemorating motherhood had been imported from the United States early in the twentieth century by the Brazilian branch of the Young Men's Christian Association. Thereafter, it was observed by the tiny membership of Brazil's mainline Protestant churches, but it was unknown to the vast majority of Brazilians, despite a 1932 edict that announced its recognition by the national government and sporadic efforts by educational and commercial institutions to make more of the date. This situation changed in the late 1940s following a trip to the United States by Modas A Exposição Clipper's commercial director, for whom "creating something new was required." Among the novelties he brought back was Mother's Day as commercial event, introduced by a Standard-designed advertising campaign, ostensibly put on by a lay Catholic organization, but funded by Clipper, other retailers, the city's retail-merchant syndicate, and the São Paulo Commercial Association. By 1951, the campaign was so successful and the retail sales accompanying it so great that Standard's president bragged to colleagues of his agency's role while highlighting the commemoration's larger meaning: "The function of selling is a social function. It creates new habits."[70]

In Rio, *O Globo* adopted the idea of popularizing Mother's Day. Along with direct appeals, the newspaper sponsored awards for Mother's Day–themed posters, the best window-displays, and the Mother of the Year. In their efforts, *O Globo*'s staff, including a brand-new Department of Promotions and Public Relations created by the ABP founder Walter Poyares, counted on the support of downtown and Copacabana retailers, Brazilian and North American advertising agencies, the municipal tourism commission, and city hall. As *O Globo*'s advertising revenues swelled, so did agency billings, retail sales volume, and the interest of other media outlets. At mid-decade, a columnist claimed, "Year after year, Mother's Day becomes more a part of the customs of our people." A year later, the same writer judged it a "promotional and sentimental event, which one may already consider to be a respected and established tradition."[71]

Although receiving less respect in Brazil, as elsewhere, Father's Day was imported by some of the same agents and implanted by many of the same means. The major difference was that while Mother's Day was celebrated on the same date as in the United States, Father's Day was scheduled for August rather than June because the former was a slow month for sales and the latter already had a commercial commemoration of its own. This commemoration was another Clipper-created borrowing from the United States, a Sweethearts' Day modeled on Valentine's Day but scheduled for June 12 rather than February 14 so as not to conflict with Carnaval, with boosters offering the additional excuse that it was the eve of Saint Anthony's Day and therefore hallowed by the matchmaker saint. At its introduction, a trade columnist lamented the lack of sales-generating seasonal changes and commemorations in Brazil:

> Our commerce is poor in sales prompts. To start with, we don't have well-defined seasons. At most a hot season and a cold season in which stores launch the designs for Summer and the designs for Winter. But where is Spring, with well-defined characteristics to the point that it may serve as a theme for advertising? Where are we going to find sufficient differentiation between Summer and Fall, so that we may launch articles suited to the latter season?
>
> We also lack an "Independence Day," like there is in the United States. And we also lacked a "Valentine's Day," as there exists in the country of Uncle Sam. Yes, we lacked. Because now we have it, at least in São Paulo, and with repercussion in Rio de Janeiro. "Valentine's Day" was translated as Sweethearts' Day.

The first campaign for the newly invented commemoration was designed by Standard for Modas A Exposição Clipper, with the São Paulo Commercial Association contributing as well. Paulistano newspapers provided free inserts and ample coverage, while radio broadcasts made repeated mention of the occasion in the days leading up to June 12. "It is not only with kisses with which one proves their love," cooed Cupid-adorned advertisements. "Give 'him' or 'her' a memento . . . so that, in both your hearts, the happy memory of the times when you were sweethearts lives on forever!" A success in São Paulo from the beginning, it was implanted in Rio by A Exposição, Galeria Carioca, Magazine Mesbla, Rádio Nacional, and *O Globo*, among other institutions.[72]

The same interests—advertising, entertainment, media, and retail—did not need to invent Easter, though they did have a harder time attaching a sales-promotional message to painful death and resurrection than to the other Christian holiday's miraculous birth and celebration. The creepy eugenicist associations of the Day of the Race (October 12) and the Week of the Child in which it fell were easier to shake, beginning with their 1956 consolidation into a Day of the Child commemorated by JWT for Kibon and Johnson & Johnson, as well as by other concerns. Thereafter, the holiday was increasingly associated with gift giving due to promotions begun by the Estrela toy-manufacturing concern in 1958. The following year, as newspapers throughout the country contributed free publicity, an admirer wrote, "Behind this support is not only commercial interest in the creation of one more prompt for advertising promotion, but, above all, the desire that one have, in Brazil, a deeper consciousness of our responsibilities to children. The gesture of giving them a toy as a gift certainly has much greater significance than it may seem at first glance. It is a contribution to their psychic adjustment and to their belief in human solidarity."[73] He was not kidding.

Civic holidays—the anniversaries of Rio's founding, of Independence, and of the Republic, even Brazil's observation of the international day of labor on May 1—were pressed into the service of sales, along with dates recognizing teachers, public functionaries, and commercial employees, as retail merchants and the new professionals hammered away at the possibilities. Occasions from the beginning of the school year to the cluster of saints' days celebrated in June were monetized alongside seasonal changes that scarcely existed in large parts of the country. "Because the truth is that, in addition to its normal and peculiar qualities, each product has many other occasions in which its sales may expand," a sales-promotion specialist argued. "On the promotional calendar there are . . . innumerable dates that are favorable to all kinds of articles, that is, innumerable opportunities for the businessman to capitalize on the interest, the enthusiasm of the public around a commemoration."[74] Lojas Brasileiras's founder singled out window-dressing specialists:

> A good window-dresser should ally his store, whatever its line may be, with all the special times of the year and all local festivities, as well as the different seasons. During the school year, one should take advantage of everything students use, from a handkerchief, a shoe, a shirt, to typical items such as pencils, erasers, and notebooks. At Carnaval, one not only sells costumes and [other] timely items, but also automobile parts and medicines for "after the carousal." At Eastertime, presents and decorative objects, as well as chocolate eggs. At the time of the saints' days in June, not only miniature hot-air balloons and various fireworks, but also perfumes, shoes, cloth, and dresses for dances. Other festive dates, such as the Week of the Child, of Aviation, of the Fatherland, Mother's Day, Sweethearts' Day, national festivities, Christmas, New Year's, the Olympics, university games, a conference, a famous singer who receives a contract from a broadcasting station, a philanthropic festival, everything should serve to present opportunities for the realization of new sales, taking advantage of the "opportune moment." Every retailer, whatever his line may be, always has an item that may be adapted to any of these occasions. The shopwindow reminds the customer and keeps the store in touch with the season.[75]

A São Paulo–based specialist made a more general case: "Concentrate all our 'batteries' on promotion. Advertising, shopwindow decoration, and the internal decoration of the shop should be in absolute harmony." Prices needed to be set below the competition's, and sales personnel needed to be informed "of everything that the store will do during the promotion," which might involve a religious holiday or another occasion, "it being enough that the promotion is of a kind to interest the local population." The dates mattered little, a colleague argued: "What is important is to know how to take advantage of them, linking them with the products for sale and giving them the indispensable publicity. On this particular, it is not a bad idea for us to be inspired by the example of the United States, where the days, weeks, and months of this and that are copious and most varied."[76]

More and more merchants were so inspired. In 1949, asked about his firm's promotional schedule, an executive responded, "A Exposição does sales promotion from the 1st of January to the 31st of December of each year," from Carnaval to Christmas, from "Back to School" to the *avante-premiêre* of women's fashion." Mesbla made a killing at Christmas, while also commemorating all the more recently invented dates and redubbing the sales doldrums of July a "Marvelous Month" that led into August's "Great Home Sale." These promotions not only concerned large retail interests, as an "annual calendar of promotions" featuring "'natural' sale opportunities" like Christmas and "especially created dates, like Mother's Day, Sweethearts' Day and Father's Day" increasingly engaged all retail outlets of substance and many small ones, in Porto Alegre and Belo Horizonte, as well as Rio, São Paulo, and their satellites, while the Lojas Brasileiras organization extended the influence of these traditions to northern and northeastern cities as well. Although the processes by which these promotions were replicated involved imitation and improvisation, store owners and employees also received instruction on an increasingly uniform promotional calendar from magazines, newsletters, and books.[77]

Retailers measured the success of this promotional calendar in traffic, turnover, and receipts, notwithstanding bromides of its working "to strengthen family sentiments, the cornerstone of human society."[78] Its broader impact is more difficult to gauge. Contemporary fiction may or may not offer a window onto the society for which it was written, but it does indicate that authors believed that Santa Claus had worked his way into the imagination of Brazilian boys and girls, that Brazilian parents dedicated themselves wholeheartedly to the commercial commemoration of Christmas, and that Brazilian children were moved by merchandisers' appeals to Mother's Day. Evidence suggests that not only the idea of Mother's Day but that of Father's Day found its way into the mental calendar of some of the poorest Paulistanos—members of merchandisers' class D—within ten years of their introduction. Memorial and testimonial literature offer examples of women whose political formation might have steeled them against consumer-capitalist appeals feeling Mother's Day to be an intimate part of their lives and dressing up as Santa Claus for nieces and nephews, grandnieces and grandnephews. By the 1960s and 1970s, middle-aged and elderly interviewees felt it important to inform their interlocutors that much of what passed for Christmas tradition was once new to them, as well as from where it all came. "Santa Claus and tinseled tree[s] were not a part of my Christmas," stated Raimundo Araujo (b. 1928). "When I was a child we had the crèche." "Santa Claus, Christmas trees are something recent," declared D. Risolea (b. 1900). Christmas was a holiday spent with family, secluded from the outside world, remembered D. Brites (b. 1903): "Later, with commercial advertising, there began to be this Christmas and this Easter." Recalling her early twentieth-century childhood, D. Alice took care to point out, "Santa Claus came much later, it's an American thing."[79]

Media Old and New

D. Brites also remembered the press. By the 1950s, it had changed irrevocably, with many "American things" figuring in these changes. Brazilian newspapers, remembered Cláudio Abramo, were "much influenced by American newspapers." North American influence was one reason that 1951's *Anuário Brasileiro de Imprensa* examined the U.S. press, "which exerts the greatest influence over Brazil's newspapers and magazines." This influence was felt most acutely in advertising and attempts on the part of editors, publishers, and staffers to attract greater advertising revenue, where the parallels with radio and the emergent medium of television were apparent by mid-decade. As a Brazilian-born, Columbia-trained historian wrote in 1956, "Radio and T.V., and, especially, North American–type advertising have been domesticated in Brazil and today have left some of the models behind."[80]

Much has been written about the renovation of the Brazilian press in the 1950s, as some of the country's most venerable newspapers imported new machinery and methods, upgrading their appearance and offerings to appeal to greater numbers of readers, to stake claims to burgeoning advertising revenue. The same newspapers' promotionalism has been less noted, perhaps even undersold, by historians of Brazilian journalism, but technical improvements and promotional bonanzas complemented one another. Of the great morning newspapers, *O Estado de S. Paulo* led the way in upgrading its physical plant, though the *Jornal do Brasil*'s renovation is better remembered, because it occurred in the nation's capital and featured the celebrity touch of a countess-owner at the helm. The *Correio da Manhã* also imported new machinery from the United States during these years. All three newspapers modified their editorial standards to match U.S. standards, as did the *Diario de Noticias*, the *Folha da Manhã*, and the *Diario Carioca*, which introduced the "lede." Alongside these qualitative changes, newspapers ballooned in size, providing what an old hand called the "impression that we had a press comparable to that of the United States, with newspapers of up to 120 or more pages per issue." Newsstand prices went up, which led to lower sales, but income from sales was beside the point: more pages meant more room for advertising—"an orgy of space," the same critic called it—which meant more revenue. In this category, *O Estado de S. Paulo* came out well ahead, by mid-decade winning a greater volume of advertising than any of the country's other newspapers, its care entrusted to a ten-person Advertising Department.[81]

Of Brazil's established press outlets, however, *O Globo* remained the "Promotion Champion." With little in the way of tradition holding them back, *O Globo*'s executives missed few opportunities to pander to the fancies of the new professionals and the businesses they served. It is difficult to imagine *O Estado de S. Paulo* or the *Correio da Manhã* devoting a cover story to Mother's Day, much less Father's Day, to which *O Globo* dedicated two front-page items in a single day.[82]

New afternoon newspapers attempted to replicate *O Globo*'s success, including the *Tribuna da Imprensa*, brainchild of the unbalanced Communist-turned-conservative Carlos Lacerda, who had dabbled in advertising earlier in life. At his newspaper's December 1949 founding, as visions of advertising revenue danced in his head, Lacerda declared: "Having as a pioneer A Exposição, now spectacularly followed by Sears, Roebuck, press advertising is evolving in the direction of the predominance of retail stores. This is the country's progress as much as the press's—as it is true that the two are forever linked. It is the phase in which the advertisement rises from the level of the favor to that of the verification of the number of copies printed per issue combined with the examination of the newspaper's authority. It is the phase of the agencies. Of the newspaper-as-industry." The *Tribuna da Imprensa*, however, never became much of a business, in part because it failed to attract readers beyond a narrow cohort devoted to Lacerda's politics, less manic versions of which were on offer in most Rio newspapers.[83]

Ultima Hora was more successful, to Lacerda's exasperation. At its founding by Samuel Wainer—formerly of *Diretrizes*, more recently of the Diários Associados—*Ultima Hora*'s raison d'etre was to support the government of Getúlio Vargas, elected in 1950 on a for-the-people program despite the opposition of Brazil's major press outlets, as well the *Tribuna da Imprensa*. Politics aside, *Ultima Hora* in many ways recalled the populist style of *O Globo*'s yellow-press origins, with its scandal-mongering, reader-friendly features, and claims to speak for "the people," who were offered comics, sports coverage, Hollywood gossip, and drawings in which readers could win prizes "for the whole family." The newspaper was a success, quickly becoming Rio's second-largest circulating afternoon newspaper and leading to expansion into other markets, with increasing numbers of regional editions and a Rio radio station run by Júlio Cosi, of the A Ecléctica advertising agency. Meanwhile, the Rio edition's vice president, Armando Daudt d'Oliveira (son of a leading figure in the National Confederation of Commerce), oversaw a six-man advertising department that promised advertisers that "35% of the newspaper is reserved for advertising, so that advertisements come out well-placed" and that the newspaper constituted a "'round-table' of all the social classes." For his part, Wainer indicated, "*Ultima Hora* is a vehicle for advertising banks and international travel (the class 'A' public) as well to sell ready-to-wear clothes (the class 'B' and 'C' public)." *Ultima Hora* followed *O Globo* in promoting Mother's Day, adding a labor-friendly spin in 1954 by noting that it was the day's coincidence with a minimum-wage hike that "change[d] the face of [Rio's] commerce."[84]

The greatest newspaper sensation of the 1950s was not an afternoon or a morning daily, but a weekly. Titled *Shopping News*, it was inspired by a San Francisco newspaper of the same name, and like its U.S. exemplar was entirely funded by advertising and distributed free of charge. Launched in 1952 in São Paulo, it was warmly welcomed by retailers—including Clipper, Mappin, and Sears—and by advertisers generally. As a JWT executive explained, "Thompson received *Shopping News* with much sympathy, as its high circulation offers good coverage of the public, especially the feminine public. We have newspapers with large circulations, but not with these accentuatedly feminine characteristics." Once each week, in a matter of hours, the São Paulo edition's early runs of one hundred thousand were delivered to preidentified high-income homes throughout the city by a team of 150 men on forty-five trucks working routes designed in consultation with an engineer. Alongside its many advertisements (which per editorial policy had to feature the prices of goods so that readers could comparison shop from home), each issue of *Shopping News* featured celebrity news, the week's radio and television listings, and retail-friendly fashion reporting, as well somewhat more sophisticated cultural features than could be found in similar U.S. periodicals. By mid-decade, the São Paulo edition had been joined by one in Rio, each distributed in runs of 120,000. These circulations allowed the publisher to boast that it was "the first newspaper in Brazil to regularly reach a million and a half readers," with issues featuring a "great mass of information on Fashion, Cooking, Sewing, Decor, Pediatrics, Child Psychology, Cinema, Theater, Travel, Arts, Letters." By late 1957, the two editions were published in runs of 130,000 and the São Paulo edition featured three thousand to four thousand advertisements per week, ranging from multipage spreads for Sears and Eletro-Radiobraz to hundreds of classifieds. By that point, *Shopping News* had become one of Brazil's most profitable publishing ventures and—for its campaigns on behalf of lower-priced foodstuffs and cheaper gas for home cooking—"made itself, in the opinion of almost all the leaders of women's associations in the State, the most legitimate mouthpiece of housewives." Crowning those successes, according to a study carried out in cooperation with São Paulo's most prominent academic statistician, was *Shopping News* achieving a "higher rate of readership among women of a certain social level than any of the state capital's other dailies."[85]

Shopping News's successes led established press outlets to expand their coverage of matters deemed "feminine." Beginning in 1953, *O Estado de S. Paulo*'s sixteen-page "Feminine Supplement" reached newsstands and subscribers' homes each Friday morning, a day ahead of *Shopping News*. Readers received fashion news from New York and Paris, menu ideas, guidance on child-rearing, and tips on home care and decor, as well as incitements to spend by "Mary" in a column named "Compare e . . . compre" (Compare and . . . purchase), a title coined by the winner of a reader contest. São Paulo's largest-circulation newspaper was not alone in offering a *Shopping News*–like supplement aimed at women as consumers. The same ideas lay behind the creation of the *Jornal do Brasil*'s Sunday supplement in 1956, as well as the coverage in *Ultima Hora*'s tabloid supplement.[86]

All the while, newspaper advertising grew rapidly. Between 1953 and 1957, according to one study, retail advertising in São Paulo's Diários Associados newspapers, *Folhas*, and *Shopping News* more than doubled in volume. Non-retail advertising seems to have grown just as quickly, perhaps more quickly. For some time, newspapers retained the largest proportion of advertising revenues, and even when magazines, radio, and television increased their shares of the total, newspaper billings continued to rise in absolute terms. Little wonder, then, that publishers and their agents reacted swiftly to any proposed changes to the existing order. In 1955, for example, when a congressman proposed that foreign-owned advertising agencies be nationalized, *Ultima Hora*'s Samuel Wainer decried the effort as a "political" one that showed a lack of awareness of the "progressive, renovating role played by foreign advertising agencies in our country." On this issue, *O Globo* found common ground with its antagonist, one of its executives arguing: "The proposal reflects a total lack of knowledge of the subject on the part of its author and aims at the elimination of a class—that of advertising men, a hard-working class that is the master spring of our economic development." For his part, *Shopping News*'s advertising head remarked, "The foreign agencies are an ideal school for us advertising professionals." Two years later, Herbert Moses reported, on behalf of the press as a whole, that educational progress was being made: "We are taking long strides toward achieving in newspapers and magazines that which is constant in the United States: 2/3 of advertising in each vehicle for 1/3 of editorial text. That is to say that the press, like radio and television, has sought in advertising true freedom of action, which begins with economic freedom."[87]

That Moses, an old newspaperman, would mention magazines alongside newspapers was more than fulfillment of his duties as ABI president. It was also an indication of the importance of a wider range of magazines among the press's "advertising vehicles." As a behind-the-scenes article explained: "Products, whether for men, whether for women, as long as they have national distribution, find their cheapest, most efficient vehicle in magazines. That occurs in the United States. It will occur in Brazil, which learns from the North American primer."[88]

O Cruzeiro continued to be a successful application of those lessons, the circulation of the Diários Associados weekly doubling between 1948 and 1958, when it was printed in runs of over a half a million and was the country's most widely distributed commercial publication of any kind. Through the mid-1950s, its attractiveness to advertisers only grew. Asked in 1951 about changes in Brazil over the three years he had lived there, a U.S.-born JWT executive mentioned the weekly: "A single issue of the magazine *O Cruzeiro* . . . displays five or six competing brands, and each brand has its own agency." Indeed, the magazine had its own agency, McCann-Erickson. At mid-decade, the advertisements published in *O Cruzeiro* were taken as the country's standard, in manufacturing and merchandising, cosmetics and kitchen appliances. While those advertisements promoted goods, the magazine's columns promoted advertising: "Advertising Firms have a commitment to the public and know how to respect it: they only advertise products, articles, or services of proven quality." Such complementarity of editorial content and advertising copy was a part of what a thirtieth-anniversary retrospective called "a revolution in the spirit and technique of journalism" that introduced "a new style that would come to free the domestic press from a rigid obedience to the tradition of the European schools."[89]

O Cruzeiro's allusive Americanism of 1958 may be counterposed to the Brazilianization of its main rival over the preceding decade, *Seleções de Reader's Digest*, printed in Brazil from 1950, represented by JWT, and increasingly tailored to national tastes. "The printing of the magazine in Brazil," an executive explained, "allowed us to provide much better service to local advertisers. As a result, advertising increased greatly." The magazine's Brazilian circulation surpassed three hundred thousand in 1951, while it continued to follow "the old and wise North American commercial process of making everything easy for the consumer and of surrounding him with all the conveniences for him to obtain what he desires." At that point, the editorial responsibilities of the magazine's Brazil-based staff was limited to choosing among articles from the U.S. edition, which were translated by an executive who had spent years in the United States working for NBC. By 1953, however, editorial policy had changed, with issues carrying Brazil-themed cover stories and other nationally specific features. Another innovation was *Seleções*'s "'Merchandising' Plan"—in the advertising director's words: "This plan consists in establishing a link between the advertising published in *Seleções*, its dealers, and its product at the point of sale. The plan provides more prestige to the advertised product and promotes greater sales and even for this the advertiser does not pay anything [additional]. He has a credit in proportion to the number of pages [of advertising] that are published and which give him the right to a certain quantity of sales-promotion material, such as 'displays,' 'reprints,' 'cover-folders,' 'dealer-letters,' small posters etc." Meanwhile, the magazine's circulation and readership continued to climb, to the delight of the executive charged with monitoring both, a former assistant to *O Globo*'s advertising manager who had also worked at McCann and Sears. In 1953, *Seleções*'s print runs reached 410,000, with executives guaranteeing advertisers that each run would sell at least 340,000 copies and estimating, based on the results of reader questionnaires, that each of these copies would reach an average of six people, divided equally between men and women, four of them belonging to the same household, two visitors or neighbors. By 1957, the magazine's monthly circulation was 455,000 issues, distributed to mostly comfortable households, almost 80 percent of which owned refrigerators, a firm indicator of urban middle-class arrival.[90]

By that point, *Seleções* and *O Cruzeiro* had been joined at the peak of general-interest magazine success by *Manchete*, which had made its debut five years earlier, heralded by a campaign designed by the Inter-Americana agency. Whereas *O Cruzeiro* had long been unabashedly influenced by the North American press and *Seleções* was a U.S. implant, *Manchete* took its cues secondhand, from *Paris-Match*, the French knockoff of *Life* magazine. Like *Paris-Match* and *Life*, *Manchete* emphasized imagery over textual content, offering an unprecedented amount of lavish, full-color photography designed, in the first instance, to appeal to the eye rather than complement editorial copy. The magazine's publisher, a Ukrainian immigrant named Adolpho Bloch, was the owner of a major printing concern that churned out everything from Communist Party propaganda to Esso's in-house newsletter. He also craved the power and social prominence of the Diários Associados's Assis Chateaubriand. This combination of resources and ambition meant that no expense was spared in making *Manchete* Brazil's most visually impressive periodical, at precisely the moment in which its photography-first approach would complement new styles of image-driven advertising that overtook the text-based "reason-why" formula that JWT and other U.S. agencies had done so much to diffuse. It was therefore *Manchete*, more than any other periodical, that led an insider to pronounce: "Some time ago, commercial advertising took the lead on the Brazilian press. These days, the press is responding, in grand style." If the magazine did not immediately fulfill all Bloch's ambitions, it soon became one of the country's most sought-after advertising vehicles.[91]

Beginning the year before *Manchete*'s founding, in 1951, the Rio women's magazine *Grande Hotel* made a big splash with imported "fotonovelas," comic-like photographic narratives, complete with speech balloons translated into Portuguese but typically featuring romantic stories rather than humorous material or adventure tales. The "Magical Magazine of Love" prospered, reaching a circulation of one hundred thousand by 1953 and finding a place in the programming of the country's most important advertisers. In the words of its advertising manager, who had previously worked for a U.S. film company and JWT: "I would say that it is a magazine that plays the same role that the soap opera plays on the radio." And so it was, *Grande Hotel*'s fotonovelas offering readers similarly plotted melodramas and advertisers access to its audience. Making it still more attractive to advertisers was its provision of merchandising-friendly materials like those found in *Shopping News*.[92]

Capricho—the greatest publishing sensation of the period—adopted that strategy beginning in 1952, when it was launched by Victor Civita's Abril publishing group. Civita, a dual U.S.-Italian national, had arrived in Brazil two years earlier with the rights to publish Walt Disney comics in Portuguese, a runaway success that led him to declare to all who would listen that children were "the best customers in the world." *Capricho* was Abril's first venture in publishing expressly for women, its every issue featuring "a complete fotonovela, varieties, fashion, cinema, beauty, and other interesting subjects." As was the case for *Grande Hotel*, most of *Capricho*'s fotonovelas came from Italy, while its writers on fashion looked to France and the United States as well. While sales of its earliest issues lagged behind initial runs of 90,000, they rose rapidly thereafter, reaching 240,000 in 1956. By 1958, the circulation of the "Monthly Magazine of the Modern Woman" had risen to 506,000, an unprecedented figure. Civita attributed much of this success to research and advertising (the latter handled by JWT from the beginning). "Advertising," he explained, "has been very effective, because it follows a different program for *each region* of Brazil." In some cities and towns, Abril advertised the magazine on the radio or over loudspeaker services; in others, newspapers, signage, and other ephemera were used, depending upon data gathered by circulation personnel and the magazine's distributor. Readers were the object of further research: "We did statistical studies, analyses of the magazine's penetration throughout Brazil, research on the taste and mentality of the Brazilian woman and we maintained and continue to maintain innumerable direct and indirect contacts with the public, through contests, correspondence with hundreds of readers, etc." This "ascendant trajectory," the aim "to always give the women of Brazil a healthy and entertaining read," and the revenue figures that Civita shared publicly, proud "to belong to the American school, in which there are no secrets," prompted expansion, Abril adding *Você, Ilusão*, and *Manequim* to its list of women's titles between 1956 and 1959.[93]

These titles were part of a surge of periodicals aimed at women of differing interests and ages, and from somewhat-varied economic positions, from *Casa e Jardim* (1953) to a long list of fashion-and-fotonovela magazines that included *O Globo*'s *Querida* (1954) and *Garôtas* (1959), as well as two titles launched by *Manchete* in 1958, *Jóia* and *Sétimo Céu*, the latter the first magazine to publish Brazilian-made fotonovelas rather than Italian or Spanish-American ones. While women's periodicals were hardly new, there had never been so many, nor had earlier experiments—even the most successful ones—been so commercially savvy or sought after by readers. *O Globo*'s titles played on the experience and resources of the parent company, including its promotional departments, contacts with advertisers, and free or at-cost advertising, with *Querida* coordinating a "Festival of Fashions" at Magazine Mesbla and contributing to each year's Mother's Day commemoration alongside *Shopping News* and *Manchete*. At *Querida*'s sixth anniversary, its advertising department cited an IPOM study indicating that 80 percent of its readership belonged to classes A and B as proof that it was "Brazil's best feminine magazine." Meanwhile, Abril's magazines for women were touted as integral to the movement of all variety of goods, for "directly or indirectly, women are the masters of the market."[94]

In late 1959, the Christmas edition of *Casa e Jardim* was touted as "a veritable holiday for Media [executives]," one of many appeals playing on magazines' reach among female consumers. The word "media," in turn, summons a system of which magazines were becoming a part. Alongside newspapers and magazines as bearers of modern tidings and invitations to consume were increasing numbers of radio stations and the country's first experiments in television.[95]

In 1950, IBOPE reported to readers of the *Boletim das Classes Dirigentes* that in Rio and São Paulo 95 percent of families—"poor or rich"—owned radio sets, a figure that was certainly inflated, but closer to the truth than many estimates of radio ownership for Brazil as a whole, which present discrepancies of a million or more sets. Where these estimates converge, however, is in demonstrating increasing ownership, which accompanied the turn from imports to local assembly and eventually production. In 1948, the year immediately preceding a surge in domestic output, no more than one-third of families owned radio sets; by the late 1950s, following a ten-year period in which the output of Brazilian factories was measured in the hundreds of thousands of sets per year, somewhat more than half of the country's families owned a radio, a larger proportion than in many Latin American countries with higher per capita incomes. Credit sales were an integral part of expanding ownership, enabling the household set—manufactured in European-, U.S.-, and Brazilian-owned factories—to become "a must in Brazil," with "almost every family in civilized areas . . . ha[ving] access to a radio."[96]

Establishing the number of stations available to radio listeners is an easier task than estimating the number of sets in use. The 300 stations in operation in 1950 grew to 524 by 1960, with a further 126 awaiting licensing or otherwise preparing to go on the air. Most of these stations reached only local audiences, but some broadcast across the country's vastness. Rádio Nacional remained the most important, as its golden age of the 1940s stretched into the following decade, but by the late 1950s its command of national airwaves was no longer what it had been, nor could it count on local dominance in Rio.[97]

In the first half of the decade, however, the "Station of the Multitudes" was as popular as ever: "Rádio Nacional set the tone, imposed fashions, massproduced idols. From 1951 to 1954, under the command of Victor Costa, the so-called PRE-8 reached its peak: its average audience in 1952, in Rio, reached the mark of 50.2% of all sets." It was, recalled Walter Clark Bueno, "Brazil's best broadcasting station—glorious, complete, with attractions for all segments of the public." Between 1945 and 1955, the station received nearly eight million letters from listeners, which a specialized "correspondence section" replied to for the station's hundreds of bandleaders, announcers, musicians, actors, actresses, producers, and singers. All the while, Rádio Nacional's writers worked away, their labors portrayed in a station-produced report: "The idea is our raw material. This is our factory, where eighteen privileged artists work. . . . They mount their production, develop it, and the merchandise, which is the program, is ready for sale. . . . This . . . is placed at the service of the weekly consumption of a spectacle." Interweaving ideas and industry, production and consumption—here was a vision of the writer's craft consonant with the self-image of the copyeditors and advertising-agency contacts whom Rádio Nacional's employees worked alongside. That the station was such a commercial success, bringing in more than twice the advertising revenue of its nearest rival, meant that its influence would be decisive. For two generations of professionals—in advertising, radio, and eventually television—"Rádio Nacional was the great school," in the words of Gualter

Leão, whose career began at Rádio Nacional before taking off at JWT's Radio Department.[98]

The radio that resulted was profoundly commercial. As a semiofficial gazette explained, "radio broadcasting keeps the public in immediate contact with competitions, happenings, and spectacles, making it interested all the time, which makes it a magnificent means of advertising." Such was progress: "Every day, radio achieves new technical victories that permit it to improve and amplify radio broadcasting, receivers are improved and become cheaper; the economic base of radio broadcasting becomes stronger at each turn, with increasing numbers of listeners and consequent rise in advertising." The latter was also an important source of programming, with one-fifth of the country's broadcast time taken up by advertising, more than any other category of programming except music.[99]

The remainder mixed new and old. On Rádio Nacional, Paulo Roberto "was the symbol of the modern producer, who brought novelties from the United States and made genial programs," including an adaptation of "This Is Your Life." While the inspiration for such programming was unmistakable, audience shows and related happenings assumed a greater importance in Rio than they did in the United States, becoming, in the musicologist José Ramos Tinhorão's words, "a type of spectacle of absolutely Brazilian characteristics." A thriving black market emerged for tickets to live radio performances held at station-owned auditoriums, where listeners, organized in fan clubs, could see their idols up close and participate in radio production—singing along, cheering, and dancing in the aisles—as well as win prizes and receive free samples of sponsors' products. With *A felicidade bate à sua porta*, Rádio Nacional offered a spectacle that bridged its 634-seat auditorium, listeners' living rooms, and the down-market neighborhoods in which most of its audience lived. Raffles provided fans the opportunity to be visited at home by the show's producer, "and if the raffle winner had all of the sponsor's products he received cash and a number of prizes." While the lucky fan gathered those prizes, a Rádio Nacional singer would perform for passersby, the performance broadcast nationwide. The show's success inspired another, titled *Ronda dos bairros*, in which the station broadcast a live show from a different Rio neighborhood each Sunday: "From ten to noon, Paulo Gracindo and Carlos Pallut transmitted, always live, direct from one of the city's cinemas, an electrifying auditorium program. The itinerant spectacle drew multitudes with prizes, crooners, female singers, and actors from the *cast* of the station's radionovelas." Attendees wearing Alpargatas-brand shoes (the country's cheapest variety of factory-made footwear) were eligible "to participate in the drawing for four-liter pressure cookers, lengths of printed nylon organza, and Superball-brand balls for association football."[100]

For a brief period in the early to mid-1950s, then, an "increasing approximation of radio with the humbler public of Carioca neighborhoods" had created shows that resembled nothing so much as "a veritable popular fair." In the process, much had changed in radio broadcasting, but not all. The radionovela continued to enjoy its weekday pride of place. On Rádio Nacional, *O direito de nascer* continued in the tradition established by *Em busca da felicidade*: a melodrama was imported from Cuba on behalf of Colgate-Palmolive, translated into Portuguese, and acted out over the air, becoming a national sensation. Like *Em busca da felicidade*, *O direito de nascer* was broadcast three times a week and aimed expressly at a female audience. Unlike *Em busca da felicidade*, it aired at nighttime and so reached an even larger audience—"Businessmen, ladies who are not very accustomed to the common vice of listening to radio systematically, marriage-minded misses, young men who have other things to think of, grandparents and old maids, all cling to the receiver." In retrospect, it was the peak of the radionovela's success, though the genre remained profitable after the show's 314-episode run. Indeed, the genre's importance to Rádio Nacional appears to have increased in the later 1950s, a 1958 feature story indicating that it broadcast a daily average of fourteen radionovela episodes, which filled more than half of the station's airtime and provided two-thirds of its revenue. This increased importance probably responded to a well-documented backlash against the auditorium shows' participatory aspects and plebeian fan base on the part of advertisers, critics, and some radio professionals.[101]

By the time of the audience show's eclipse, another craze of the 1940s and early 1950s had passed its peak, that of the commercial jingle imported from the United States. "These days the most efficient and most modern kind of advertising is without a doubt the 'jingle,' or better put, advertising set to music, and we have outstanding successes in this veritable avalanche of little marching songs," reported *A Noite Ilustrada* in 1948. The editors of *Publicidade & Negócios* agreed: "The 'jingles' or advertisements set to music and with the use of mnemonic effects are being used by practically all the great radio advertisers." Along with the insecticide Detefon and the analgesic Melhoral, there were Coca-Cola and its competitors, Gessy soap and shaving cream, and Chiclets-brand chewing gum. Jingles inspired and were inspired by popular song, including Carnaval marches and sambas, and their perceived efficacy led to an explosion in their use in local, state, and national electoral campaigns. By the mid-1950s, "jingles were produced for everything and everyone," according to José Scatena, the principal owner of the country's first studio to specialize in recording commercial shorts, who lamented that the form's profusion had led to a decline in quality. This decline notwithstanding, Scatena argued, it remained an invaluable resource. "The message is standardized for all of Brazil, from North to South," he pointed out, something that could not be said of "spot" advertising. Once broadcast, "the melody burrows into the subconscious and with the power of repetition it ends up overcoming the listener's resistance." For all these reasons, and for its "awakening new desires and keeping these desires burning, the jingle . . . has been the modality of advertising that produces the best and most rapid results." Scatena was hardly a disinterested observer, but one may also quote the testimony of a North American observer who first visited Brazil in the early 1950s. Not given to comparisons that would favor his hosts, he nevertheless wrote, "The advertising jingle is perhaps better utilized in Brazil than in the United States.[102]

The list of products advertised by jingle and the continued importance of the soap opera identify key interests that used radio to promote their goods. "Radio was colonized by the big firms of the area of toothpaste and bar soap," a fan recalled. As far as radio stations in the second- and third-tier cities and towns of Rio de Janeiro and São Paulo were concerned, a 1951 poll of the country's largest brokers in local commercial airtime produced a list that included many of the country's leading branded goods—its beers and cigarettes, floor waxes and patent medicines, as well as the soap and toothpaste manufacturers Lever, Gessy, and Colgate-Palmolive. The picture that remains, however, is incomplete, for it omits the firms that were remaking the retail trades and cityscapes of Rio and São Paulo, which were also major advertisers. In a 1954 promotional push, for example, Mesbla reached radio listeners through thirty-five jingles a day on Rádio Jornal do Brasil, together with spots and jingles on four other stations. After Lauro de Carvalho's group spun off its Ducal stores, the chain sponsored a Rádio Nacional program, then contracted McCann to create its "Divertimento Ducal" (Ducal Entertainment), broadcast on five stations. In São Paulo, "fans of North American music" tuned into nightly broadcasts of the *Midnight Mappin* show.[103]

By the time of *Midnight Mappin*'s 1953 debut, radio faced fresh competition in its pursuit of advertising billings. Television had arrived in Brazil three years earlier, directly from the United States, and while it would take two decades to achieve national coverage, it soon became a fixture in the lives of many southeastern urbanites and a promotional vehicle of increasing importance. A dozen years on, it would be indispensable.

Brazilian television broadcasting dates from 1950, when TV-Tupi of São Paulo debuted, to be followed by an identically named Rio station in 1951. Both grew out of Assis Chateaubriand's Emissoras and Diários Associados, whose founder had taken a personal interest in bringing television to Brazil while other bigwigs took a wait-and-see approach. The two stations were created in characteristic manner, Chateaubriand shaking down business interests and calling in favors from government, using official credit to import equipment and technicians from the United States, and manipulating his newspapers, magazines, and radio stations—"51 advertising vehicles," in the words of the group's highest-ranking executive—to maximum promotional effect. "Only Chateaubriand had the courage to take on TV," was how an admirer put it. The same observer expressed his satisfaction that Brazilian television, like U.S. television but unlike European television, had been born commercial, a source of lasting pride: "In Brazil, television was born as a business, as a commercial television that has to sell its product and survives on the sale of this product. And it has to be good, otherwise it doesn't sell." Such was "The Power of Advertising" that this model was followed by Chateaubriand's early competition, TV-Paulista and TV-Record, which began broadcasting from São Paulo in 1952–1953, and TV-Rio, which began broadcasting in 1955, to coincide with the Eucharist Congress. Also in 1955, Chateaubriand took the template to Minas Gerais, declaring ahead of the first transmission by Belo Horizonte's TV-Itacolomi—named for a landmark rock formation—"It is with advertising, made and sold, that we raised massive monuments of the solidity of this Itacolomi."[104]

The television sets that would allow Brazilians to view TV-Tupi's programming were an afterthought as preparations were made for the station's inaugural broadcast. Reminded of their importance, Chateaubriand hurriedly arranged for two hundred sets to be flown in from the United States in circumvention of import-licensing restrictions. Just under half the sets were presented to Brazilian grandees, including President Eurico Gaspar Dutra; half were distributed among São Paulo retailers; of the remaining sets, four were installed in local bars and one was placed in the lobby of the Associados building. The number of sets in operation grew thereafter, though a considerable volume of illicit imports made establishing the total a difficult task. Advertising-agency sources estimated that there were 5,000 apiece in São Paulo and Rio in late 1951, figures that grew to 25,000 to 30,000 and 20,000, respectively, in just over a year. By 1954, a "conservative guess" placed the number in each city at 40,000, for a national total of upward of 80,000 (São Paulo broadcasts, in particular, reached viewers well beyond municipal limits). In 1955, according to an advertising-agency handbook, there were 130,000 in Brazil. In 1956, the United States Information Agency estimated that there were 405,000. A year later, estimates ran as high as half a million, with McCann providing the conservative estimate that there were somewhat fewer, with 180,000 in São Paulo and 150,000 in Rio. In 1958, the *New York Times*'s Tad Szulc (almost certainly relying on advertising-agency sources) reported that estimates had risen to 550,000 total sets: 250,000 in São Paulo,

150,000 in Rio, 50,000 in Belo Horizonte, and the remaining 100,000 "in localities around the three cities."[105]

As far as the number of viewers was concerned, JWT estimated seven viewers per set in private homes and twenty per set in public facilities in 1951. The estimated proportion of viewers per set fell over the course of the 1950s (in 1957, McCann estimated 3.5 per set), but the dramatic increase in the total number of sets meant that overall viewership rose dramatically, in absolute and proportional terms. In 1954, with an estimated five viewers per set in Rio and São Paulo, television reached less than 10 percent of the two cities' populations, whereas in 1957, McCann's estimated 3.5 viewers per set covered a third of each city's population. In 1950–1951 in São Paulo, the actress Lélia Abramo remembered, "The number of people who owned TVs was very small, but success was measured by the gathering in front of the shopwindows of stores in which the sets were turned on during the novela's slot." Far more importantly, from the point of view of advertisers, was the number of people watching in private homes, who were assumed to belong to classes A and B, and who included the "televisitor," the neighbor, friend, or relative who did not own a television but who was an integral part of an audience "rated economically as having greater purchasing power than the public known for radio-listening."[106]

The programming that this audience viewed was a dog's breakfast of shows, spectacles, and promotional fare, nearly all of it performed live, save for imported feature films, a few made-in-Brazil commercial shorts, and some animated material. The first stations recruited most of their personnel from radio, but attempts to translate radio's successes to the new medium came up short, with the exception of news programming, as Repórter Esso quickly established itself on television. The first telenovela aired in 1951, but it would be a dozen years before the genre approached the success of its radio counterpart. Until then, the dominant dramatic programming was live theater, initially performed by some of the troupes bidding to raise the Brazilian stage to the standards of Europe and the United States. Game shows, often patterned after U.S. programs, were early popular successes, including *O ceu é o limite* and *Um milhão Probel* (based on *The $64,000 Question* and *The Big Surprise*, respectively), as was *Boliche Royal*, a bowling program that was a proven success in Cuba. Musical shows were easier to produce than game shows, but offered little beyond existing radio offerings. Live-broadcasting association football matches, by contrast, was trying, but every step of the process of trial and error proved to be enormously popular, as well as lucrative for stations: sponsors were eager to be associated with the national pastime and at first neither teams nor leagues nor stadiums collected broadcast rights. Another area in which television quickly outdid radio was in children's programming. One early success was *Circo Bombril*, a circus-themed show sponsored by a company already synonymous with steel wool, featuring some of the same clowns featured at Clipper's Children's Festival. Another was *O Sítio do Picapau Amarelo*, an adaptation of a beloved children's book series, whose author had predicted that "the Brazil of tomorrow" would be made by the U.S. film industry. Hollywood's direct influence on Brazilian television was felt through the airing of old films, while one show in particular made elements of Rio's posh nightlife visible to less exclusive audiences, the long-running *Noite de gala*.[107]

Advertisers not only were important for sponsorship; they also played key roles in programming and production. Indeed, following an early improvisational period, it was customary for advertisers and advertising agencies to create and produce shows rather than simply sponsor them. To that end, the U.S. agencies borrowed specialists from their parent firms and sent Brazilian executives to the United States. According to one account, within a half-dozen years of Tupi-Rio's first broadcast, "all the biggest advertising agencies" had "television departments staffed with U.S.-trained specialists" acting as "talent scouts, script writers, drama directors, and even on occasion as announcers." A group of these specialists at JWT's São Paulo office developed *O Sítio do Picapau Amarelo* for the ice-cream manufacturer Kibon, an attempt "to win over directly the children's market most receptive to its products," directed by a physician who specialized in child psychology, "who makes of children's theater a field of study and education for the children." JWT-Rio took on translating Standard Brand's *Boliche Royal* from Cuban Spanish to Brazilian Portuguese, while McCann's staff transposed Repórter Esso from radio to the new medium and scripted Coca-Cola's Brazilian television debut.[108]

Then there were the commercials. Few advertisers were free-spending enough to invest in production of filmed commercial shorts in the early years of Brazilian television. Ford, however, was, Thompson producing its first filmed commercials for the automaker in 1952, a collaboration between a New York–based executive, JWT's Brazilian staff, and the Vera Cruz motion-picture studio. Most commercials, like most entertainment programming and all news, were broadcast live, with two varieties predominating. The first was the "slide," featuring a still image of a given product's brand name, with or without a voice-over: Nestlé, Peixe, Firestone, Gessy. The second was a live commercial in which an attractive young woman would model, demonstrate, or otherwise extol the virtues of a dress, sofa, or soap. Commercial television thus "created the new profession of *garota propaganda*" (advertising girl). Whether hired by the station, the advertiser, or an advertising agency—or in rare cases working on a freelance basis—for more than a dozen years these women were as integral to the functioning of the new medium as cameramen or scriptwriters and as widely recognized as quiz-show announcers and teletheater actors.[109]

The celebrity of *garotas-propaganda* was interpreted to mean, in the words of a U.S. correspondent, that "Brazilian television finds itself firmly entrenched as a profitable industry and an important medium for mass communications and entertainment." Another telling development, perhaps a turning point, came in 1956, when the longtime voice of Rádio Nacional's Repórter Esso announced his leaving radio "for the superior stage of TV, which is without a doubt the greatest force of the century": "Today, in São Paulo, in Rio and in Belo Horizonte, the impact of television is so serious that one may see with the naked eye the transformations in the life of the collectivity provided by this marvelous invention." Then, he turned to comparison and prognostication: "In the United States, in which popular education is several points higher than ours, TV is the most constant fact in the life of each family, at every hour of the day. The very Brazilian tendency to exaggerate things will create a state of spirit that will become dazed unto fanaticism when television can reach the cities of the interior and its programs are presented with greater perfection and objectivity. At that point, nothing will be done in this country without television poking its nose in."[110]

By then, the Tupi stations were turning a handsome profit. São Paulo's TV-Record was already making its founders money. Each issue of Thompson's confidential internal-distribution bulletin announced another advertiser's commitment to the new medium. In a 1956 visit to the company's New York offices, a Brazilian executive identified television's growth as the major recent development in his country, noting that the Rio and São Paulo stations were "firmly established." São Paulo—larger and wealthier than Rio—was a particularly attractive field for advertisers. "No other vehicle has the power of TV, in São Paulo's particular conditions," another advertising executive asserted, remarking on Ducal's use of television to publicize the opening of its first São Paulo store. "It's a moving shopwindow in the home. Beyond this, television in São Paulo has great coverage, the buying power of Paulista television-viewers being very high."[111]

The year 1957 saw no letup, agency sources indicating that the Tupi stations—which broadcast twelve hours daily, longer than any stations in the world outside of the United States—had become "one of the three biggest advertising media" in the country, alongside Rádio Nacional and *O Cruzeiro*. Advertisers and advertising professionals were convinced "that there is nothing like TV to sell one's wares." Asked about recent developments in advertising, Cícero Leuenroth remarked, "The most important media development in 1957 was the expansion of television." Nor did any letup follow, TV-Rio's revenues increasing 400 percent between 1955 and 1959.[112]

At around the time of Leuenroth's remark, the television producer Abelardo Figueira returned from a month in the United States. Back in Brazil, Figueira held forth on all he had seen, but announced he would chart his own path: "I am radically opposed to this copy mentality, this mania of copying what is done by others, principally the North Americans. I never did that and I will not under any circumstances." Why, then, had he gone to the United States? Why not Europe? "Here the TVs depend upon the advertiser. . . . For this reason, perhaps, European TV could not serve as a model for us. Our TV is commercialized, just like the North American one."[113]

Big Tickets and Creature Comforts

The television set was itself a product, one of the biggest of "big tickets"— North American slang for expensive consumer durables, a category that also included the refrigerators that had been the greatest draw at Sears's Brazilian openings, as well as washing machines and high-fidelity sets. These goods were only available as imports in the 1940s, but were manufactured domestically thereafter. Gas ovens and ranges—Brazilian-made for years—were produced in increasing numbers and styles during the postwar, replacing wood-burning stoves in hundreds of thousands of homes amid what a highbrow journal called "the true domestic revolution occurring among us." Small electrical appliances—blenders, floor-polishers, vacuum cleaners, cake mixers, electric irons, freestanding and table-top fans, shower-head hot-water heaters—were turned out by the millions. Brazilian-made pressure-cookers and Pyrex dishware also contributed to the refashioning of kitchens and foodways. Mass-produced detergents replaced unbranded bar soap in many homes. By the late 1950s, the innerspring mattress had come to be seen as "indispensable" even among the "population with lower purchasing power (class C)," while the better off lounged on domestically produced living-room sets.[114]

The popularization of these goods was no more spontaneous than their manufacture. A case for "modern comfort" had to be made before appliances, furnishings, and detergents could "symbolize the civilization of modern times, constituting a victory of commodity and of comfort."[115] Manufacturing interests had an obvious stake in making that case, alongside department stores and specialty shops. These businesses, assisted by advertising and media executives, adopted a pedagogic approach to creating wants, transforming wants into needs, and making these needs felt more deeply. That nearly all these devices were invented elsewhere—that they were artifacts of a different culture, though one long-familiar to movie fans—meant that the new professionals had to present them in different ways than in the United States. That Brazilians, even middle-class Brazilians, enjoyed less disposable income than their North American counterparts meant that consumer credit would be more important, used even for items as inexpensive as pressure cookers. The inflationary conditions peculiar to Brazil would likewise play a key role in these revolutions in the country's material culture, enhancing the attractiveness of installment-purchasing. Credit, in turn, became a cause around which appliance-retailing interests and their allies united, to defend its use and monitor consumer behavior.

The history of the manufacture of durable consumer goods in Brazil remains to be written, though press accounts may be assembled into an outline that includes some disposable novelties toward its end. Of the big-ticket items, the first to be built in Brazil was the refrigerator, followed by the television, the washing machine, and the hi-fi set. Foreign corporations predominated, though there was room for national manufacturing, aided by the fact that the U.S. home-appliance industry was not as oligopolistic as it would become, making licenses and patents more affordable than they would otherwise be. When it came to smaller electrical appliances, with the partial exception of the radio, Brazilian firms predominated. The Walita company, which turned out a few dozen blenders in 1944, would produce a million over the next fifteen years, most of them after ramping up production in 1952–1953. Other Walita-brand devices—floor polishers, cake mixers, fans, irons, vacuums—composed not Brazil's, but "America's largest line of home-electrical appliances." The success of the "Walita Family" prompted imitators, the most important of which was Arno, which received technical assistance from Sears. The bulk of stoves and innerspring mattresses meant that their manufacture was initially the business of small, localized firms. Indeed, it was only in 1957 that Probel, São Paulo's leading mattress producer, began to sell its products in Rio, by which time its full line of goods included "North American style" sofa beds and armchairs. Pressure cookers were first mass-produced in Brazil in 1949 by a single company at Sears's behest but were soon manufactured by several firms. Bombril, synonymous with steel wool, was churned out by a Brazilian concern beginning in the 1940s. Pyrex dishware was manufactured in São Paulo from 1953 through a joint venture between Corning Glassworks and the Companhia Vidraria Santa Marina, the premiere industrial holding of the proud but declining Silva Prado group. At around the same time, Lever introduced Rinso powdered soap, followed by OMO-brand synthetic detergent.[116]

With some exceptions (most importantly, the refrigerator) these goods were all but unknown in Brazil before their domestic production. Their utility needed to be defined and explained, their modes of use taught. In some cases, the product name needed to be invented. The Portuguese word for "blender" (*liquidificador*) was probably invented by Walita. Early advertisements highlighting the nutritional benefits to be had as "Fruits + vegetables = VITAMINS," in a "delicious 'cocktail,'" led to the coining of *vitamina* decades before American English's "smoothie." Arno emphasized the same themes in McCann-produced campaigns, as did Mesbla's 1951 Christmas catalog, touting the blender's utility "for the quick preparation of vitamin juice, from vegetables and from fruits, so essential in the nourishment of children." Within fifteen years of the device's domestic manufacture, an admiring journalist explained: "This universalized the use of the blender and created the habit of drinking *vitaminas de frutas*, the famous juices, today as well received as the traditional *cafèzinho*." Not all business interests benefited. In 1957, faced with declining sales of its chocolate-flavored powdered milk, Nestlé launched an investigation that found "'Vitaminas' grew vertiginously in popular consumption and were above all promoted by blender manufacturers. . . . The public's eating habits were thus changing, the former coming to ingest more cereals and/or fruits with milk."[117]

Whereas blender advertisements emphasized nutrition, especially children's nutrition, advertising for other goods entangled pleasure, practicality, modernity, comfort, efficiency, preservation of health and beauty, and pride in the appearance of home and family. An A Exposição advertisement for Walita's floor polisher called on women to "Make 'House Waxing Day' . . . a day of pleasure . . . with the best floor-polisher": "Modern comfort demands that you make housework easier and less tiring! And the work of waxing the house, with the heavy brush—harmful to your health and to the beauty of your hands—becomes an agreeable task taking only a few minutes—with a WALITA FLOOR POLISHER!" Drawings representing "Yesterday . . ." (a woman doubled over, wielding a long-handled brush) and "Today . . ." (a smiling woman, standing upright, managing an electric floor-polisher with one hand) contrasted "the old system, slow and harmful to your health," with the new, which would make the floor "a mirror at your feet!" An early advertisement for Bombril steel wool—"the magic sponge"—promised that it would make "all difficult cleaning easy" and pots and pans "a daily surprise for all— complete cleanliness and the nice shine of new things," while freeing housewives "from acidic ingredients, so harmful to your pretty hands!" Much-admired advertisements created by the Norton agency for Bendix-brand washing machines minimized their expense: "To squander your health is to pay the highest price for the washing of clothes." The accompanying text promised the machine would "preserve your womanly charms," while addressing the fact that any household that could afford to buy one could also afford hired help: "Perhaps you are a determined housewife who, in order not to rely on anyone, flings herself at the harsh task of the laundry tub. Have you thought, however, how much it costs you? The mark of fatigue remains on your face. On your nails and hands, the devastation caused by the alkaline from the soap. On your body, the consequences of hours of exertions in anti-hygienic conditions."[118]

A short film that Norton produced as part of the same campaign played on old fears of contamination among the servant-employing classes. Titled *The Invisible Enemy*, the film "showed the washerwoman from the favela mixing bed linens from a sophisticated neighborhood with the clothes of sick people, which could provoke contamination." The winner of international prizes, this commercial short and the "educational" campaign of which it was a part were successful in other ways. In addition to drawing attention to Bendix and promoting washing-machine sales, the campaign appears to have led GE to retain Norton, a major coup for a small, Brazilian-owned agency. It also prompted other firms to take up similar themes, leading an advertising executive to declare, "We educated housewives about the human side of the machine"—while dehumanizing their African-descended servants—"and about how undesirable it is to wash all your clothes together in a tub."[119]

Thus, as described by another advertising man, did advertising contribute "to the creation of new riches, to the implantation and growth of new habits." It was a process epitomized by the popularization of the blender, "a classic example . . . which emphatically illustrates this indisputable reality." With "assembly-line production, advertising undertook to sell blenders on a large scale, in the short term, creating, solidly, the habit of 'liquidification.' New industries emerged and in Brazilian homes today the blender has the same importance of more common items. Thus occurred with the refrigerator, with radio sets, with the television and with detergents." It was nothing less than a "true pedagogical crusade of well-being."[120]

There was more than metaphor at work in references to "educating" housewives and to advertising-as-pedagogy. Considerable instruction occurred, not only through print advertising and in ephemera aimed at retail personnel but inside stores, in other settings, and over the airwaves as well. Some in-store demonstrations were simple affairs, in which employees walked customers through the functioning of washing machines. Others were spectacles. Among the latter was the Panex Dinner, held at A Exposição's Rua do Ouvidor location in 1953 to promote the Panex-brand pressure cooker. Helena Sangirardi, a celebrity chef avant la lettre for her column in *O Cruzeiro*, and the wife of a longtime Standard executive, hosted the dinner. The event's "hook" was that Sangirardi would not start cooking until all her guests—celebrities, journalists, and businessmen—had arrived, then prepare a full meal in thirty minutes, while her efforts and her guests' commentary were broadcast over Rádio Jornal do Brasil. Beginning the same year, Walita sponsored a "little school" (Escolinha Walita) in São Paulo and Rio in which women learned "to make greater use of the advantages offered by Blenders and will get to know the new appliances." By 1959, the promotion was said to have "crowned with success a permanent effort to educate consumers, more than 150,000 housewives" having enrolled. This total included women from cities and towns throughout Brazil, as the "little school" and its nutritionist-instructors administered courses on the road, in coordination with sales-promotion specialists and Walita-sponsored musical acts, as well as the "Walita Shopwindow" broadcast on Rádio Nacional and commercials in which *garotas-propaganda* showed off appliances amid programming produced by JWT.[121]

That the Escolinha Walita was directed at women who would have overseen one or more household servants is plain. Indeed, a Walita advertisement published in Rio's *Ultima Hora* made much of the blender's utility "when the maid is off . . ." and claimed that "1 Walita Blender Is Worth 2 Maids," while inviting homemakers to attend the Walita Escolinha. The understanding appears to have been, as in Brazilian cookbooks and home-economics texts, that the housewife-graduate of the "little school" would be prepared to direct servants in the proper execution of recipes and use of household appliances, as well as use the devices on their own, for pleasure or on the maid's day off, with their labor-saving features perhaps allowing for a smaller household staff, freeing up that portion of the family's budget for spending on other goods. These issues surfaced in a 1957 campaign led by São Paulo's A Sensação do Lar, a home appliances and furnishings spin-off of the women's-wear chain. This "Grand Sale of Electric Appliances" included an invitation "to get to know the practical-lesson salon of Sensação do Lar, where Marialice Prestes, São Paulo's greatest authority in the culinary arts, and her team of specialist instructors will teach you and your domestic helpers how to get the most out of the work of your electric servants, on a daily basis, for free." This appeal was issued at an odd moment in the social history of twentieth-century Brazil, a brief period in which domestic service in São Paulo, and to a lesser extent in Rio, was relatively scarce and dear, encouraging some families to improve the conditions of their household staff, who were—as A Sensação described them—"domestic helpers" rather than "servants," a term reserved for the machines that would now ease their labors: "Teach your domestic helpers to use 'Electric Servants.' You will live more happily, because everything in your house will be always in order, come out better, in much less time. Working with less exertion, your domestic helpers will achieve the indispensable 'joy of living,' and will remain in your household forever." Among these "Electric Servants" were the Walita blender "that will prepare your children's foods, preserving all the vitamins," the Prima washing machine "which will wash all your laundry within the home, avoiding contagions that are highly dangerous to the health of your family," and the Brastemp refrigerator "that preserves foods and provides more health and well-being to your entire family." "'Philips' electric servant"—a television set—would entertain the entire family, while "avoiding the expenses and inconveniences of going out"; before long, another trademarked set was touted as "The Best Nanny in the World."[122]

A Sensação do Lar was one of an increasing number of stores focused on appliances. The growth of Eletro-Radiobraz, of the all-glass façade, was in some ways a mirror image of A Sensação's: as its name suggests, Eletro-Radiobraz started out in outlying Brás and with a focus on radio sets, but over the course of the 1950s expanded into every department-store line and opened a "modern outlet" in downtown São Paulo. The two firms' shops represented a small proportion of the growing number of retailers dedicated to household-appliance sales. In the run-up to TV-Tupi's first broadcast, there had been a mere seventeen stores selling televisions in São Paulo. Within ten years, there were at least seventy-five major firms engaged in the retail sale of washing machines (the newest of the major appliances, seen as much more of a luxury than the television or the refrigerator), many of them operating multiple stores in locations throughout the city. By then, Rio's Association of Merchants of Household Electrical Appliances (ACADE) counted ninety member firms, exclusive of wholesalers and manufacturers. Among the most important were Ponto Frio and O Rei da Voz (named for Sears's Coldspot refrigerator and the Brazilian crooner Francisco Alves, respectively, aptly illustrating the origins and orientations of Brazil's new commercial civilization). Ponto Frio was noteworthy for its growth (from a single store in 1949 to more than a dozen by the mid-1950s), O Rei da Voz for its owner, ACADE president Abraão Medina, who provided Rio's Christmas parade with the slogan "With 'Them' Life Is Better": "suggesting to the people how to live better through the most modern forms of comfort, hygiene, and entertainment provided by Electric Home Appliances."[123]

Medina also led the way in improving the quality of Rio's television programming, reasoning that it would lead more Cariocas to buy televisions. Best of all, he was able to do so without spending his own money, approaching the subsidiaries of Philips and Philco with a proposal: rather than him taking the customary 5 percent discount that manufacturers offered retailers, they would give him 10 percent of the value of his order in cash and he would spend it on "advertising"—that is, on producing the high-end variety show *Noite de gala*. The sums involved meant that Medina's production team could have their pick of local talent while also importing costly equipment and contracting foreign performers without agonizing over their expense. Memoirists count among the results "amazed television-viewers," a higher profile for TV-Rio, and increased television sales.[124]

By any other name, this was "cooperative advertising," insider's jargon for collaboration between industrial and commercial interests, most often advised by advertising agencies, in the placement of local appeals. The term also applies to Walita's in-store demonstrations, advertised by Mappin and Mesbla, their managers prizing the "traffic" these events created, as well as advertisements for Brastemp refrigerators and Gasbras stoves featuring the names and addresses of local retailers. According to McCann's Armando de Moraes Sarmento, the "heavy growth" of such advertising outside of Rio and São Paulo was an outstanding recent development as of 1958.[125]

In industry argot, "cooperative advertising" refers to promotions involving local retailers and national- or regional-level manufacturers. To laymen, however, other promotions appear every bit as "cooperative," even when they involved no retailers at all or the commercial interests had a larger profile than the industrial ones. Most notable among the former were Lintas-produced advertisements for Rinso powdered soap featuring endorsements from washing-machine manufacturers. Among the latter were giveaways: Mesbla of São Paulo giving away six months' worth of Antarctica-brand soft drinks and beer with the purchase of a Brastemp refrigerator; Sears-Rio promising the weekly delivery of a case of Coca-Cola with purchase of an increasingly rare imported Coldspot; and, less practically, Sears–São Paulo offering "6 pairs of the finest nylon stockings" with a Gasbras-made Kenmore-brand stove.[126]

More important than all these giveaways, however, more important even than delivery, installation, and service, was credit. Manufacturers, merchants, and their allies agreed that installment purchasing was fundamental to sales of household goods, while critics of the crediário decried its influence on "the people" and unnecessary spending on superfluous appliances. Alfredo Monteverde of Ponto Frio claimed that his firm had been the first to sell refrigerators on long installment terms, to which he attributed much of his success: "My merit was believing that the poor also like comfort, or in other words, would also like to own refrigerators." Although his early refrigerator customers were scarcely "poor" in any meaningful sense—they would have been classed as "B" by IBOPE—he later began selling gas stoves by crediário to poorer families and found that "class 'C' repaid our trust one hundred percent." Looking back from 1961, the director of a São Paulo furniture-manufacturing concern declared: "About ten years ago, approximately, the appearance of credit transactions on a large scale, directly with the consumer, brought a great stimulus to the furniture trade throughout the country. Business growth, in some years, was 100%." The co-owner of the Rio store A Televisão, which sold kitchen appliances alongside its namesake good, was happy to be called "an apologist for commerce by credit" in the countdown to Christmas 1952. "Modern civilization," he explained, "created innumerous necessities, entirely unknown to our grandparents." Credit had become a defining characteristic and a necessity of its own when it came to big-ticket items. "Today, credit is an established institution," explained a Mesbla executive. "There are sections in a department store where it is imperative, as in the case of furniture, refrigerators, television and the like." A São Paulo advertising man agreed: "This practice has been stimulating considerably the sale of certain products, the sale of which for cash in hand would be simply prohibitive . . . the case, for example, of refrigerators, televisions, etc." Indeed, wrote the journalist Fernando Cerqueira Lemos, the idea that Brazilian retailers "could sell radios, televisions, refrigerators" on a cash-and-carry basis was "pure demagogy." Francisco Garcia de Garcia, who got his start selling Fords and Goodyear tires before founding Casa Victor, a Porto Alegre institution in the radio and refrigerator trade, spoke from decades of experience when he claimed that the crediário had become "a powerful sales factor. . . . It produces greater diffusion of appliances and contributes, in this way, to the raising of the standard of living." Senator Auro Moura Andrade, a fortunate son of the hard-driving bourgeoisie of northern São Paulo state, probably saw eye to eye with Garcia on many subjects, but not this one. "Present-day crediários exist [only] for the superfluous," he argued, adding, in a sop to nationalism flecked with paternalism: "For Brazil, a 'Sears' store isn't even worth the taxes that it pays. In 80% it is a crediário for futile things; it is 100% an extremely poor school of savings for our people." Even critics attested to the importance of credit in the diffusion of consumer durables, while recognizing the pedagogic side of the new commercial culture.[127]

All the while, dealers in home appliances and furnishings vied to offer consumers what appeared to be the most favorable deals (the lowest down payments and longest terms, though the fine print often hid additional charges), and the number of installments stretched on. In 1952, A Televisão did most of its credit sales in ten or twelve installments, while A Exposição advertised floor-polishers in ten monthly installments with no initial payment (the claim "no money down" could not be made because of associated fees). By mid-decade, this standard had shifted, A Exposição offering household goods on fifteen payments, and up to eighteen for gas stoves, washing machines, and refrigerators, with the usual charges and a payment equaling 10 to 20 percent due immediately. Much of this detail would have been lost on consumers until they were far along in the purchasing process, while many members of Rio's newspaper-reading, radio-listening, and television-viewing publics remained blissfully unaware, due to advertisements that led even a supportive trade columnist to complain: "There are advertisements—like one recently done by one of our large stores, to sell refrigerators—that don't so much as inform the total price of the merchandise; they only say the value of the monthly payments, without saying at least how many there will have to be." The columnist came to his senses (given Brazilian inflation, he wrote, "credit is a way of making up for the loss of value, allowing the maintenance and even the raising of the population's standard of living"), but as he made up his mind, the length of installment plans grew: from twenty-three months for televisions at Casa Barbosa Freitas in 1956 to thirty months at Ponto Frio in 1957, increasing thereafter.[128]

The importance of longer-term credit sales of "big tickets" was part of what drove São Paulo retailers to form the SCPC and made the specialty firms eager participants in its growth. In Rio, the appliance-dealers' association (ACADE) was an early advocate of the creation of a similar organization. After the local SPC's founding, owners and managers of specialty stores were overrepresented on its board.[129]

The importance of credit sales also made these business interests and their allies zealous defenders of consumer credit when it appeared that the government might seek to slow inflation by restricting the commercial banking loans from which much retail credit derived. Ponto Frio's Alfredo Monteverde defended consumer credit vehemently, telling an interviewer, "Look . . . how national [i.e., Brazilian] factories of sewing machines, refrigerators, floor waxers, and pressure cookers have developed. Today, these industries are mass-producing and can, therefore, offer their products at lower prices because mass consumption also exists. And who makes this mass consumption possible? Who places this merchandise in reach of a larger number of people? It is the stores that sell through the 'crediário'!" The thirty-six member firms of Belo Horizonte's Union of Electrical Appliance Retailers (URAPEL) agreed, protesting plans "to restrict the activities of those who offer consumer credit," as "given Brazilians' low purchasing power, only installment selling makes buying possible for the greatest number." As recounted for a third party, URAPEL's appeal combined old tropes on the special utility of wireless communication in Brazil with newer, more universal ones: "The inestimable services that radio lent and television is now already lending to this Nation of such vast territory and difficult communication are evident. On the other hand, one cannot help but recognize that Brazilians' 'standard' of living must be improved and that not only a minority, an insignificant and ridiculously small minority, should enjoy the benefits provided by modern electric implements for domestic use." Arguments by and for advertising professionals paralleled those of retail interests. "Industry would come to a standstill without installment sales," was the view of the Brazilian Advertising Association's president, while the country's longest-running trade magazine asked, "What will become of the poor and those of modest means if they cannot buy clothes, furniture, radios, stoves, and refrigerators by installment anymore?" It was a question that hardly warranted a direct response, only an affirmation of the place of credit in national life: "'Buy now, pay later' is one of the most useful and consequential 'slogans' created by Advertising. It works to benefit millions of people in this country of sub-consumers. It has contributed to introducing greater comfort, health, and well-being into thousands of Brazilian homes. We should develop the 'crediário' and not shrink it."[130]

If, on the one hand, Brazilian deprivation was cited as justification for extending consumer credit, on the other, as inspiration and example, there was the United States, where credit was "a *philosophy for life*." As described by an admirer, "This philosophy—which we may call that of 'material well-being'—establishes that *people should enjoy the most comfort as soon as possible*. If you—the North Americans think—could have your own house, automobile, refrigerator, washing machine, television, etc., *today*, buying on installments, why wait months or years until you can acquire all these things paying in cash? Life is short and you only live once. Therefore, take care to enjoy your material well-being this very day . . . buying on credit." Rio newspapers—*O Globo* was one—eagerly ran reporting from the United States to this effect amid challenges to the crediário, suggesting that the U.S. example settled any controversy. The correspondent Wilson Velloso, based in Washington, implied as much in his reporting: "A fair share of American prosperity can be attributed to consumer credit. Without it, there wouldn't be the fabulous quantity of automobiles, television sets, washing machines, refrigerators, boats, outboard motors, etc., that there are in the country." At a gathering of Brazilian retail managers and owners, the former head of Sears's radio and television department made the case for credit by quoting from a New York State Commerce Department tract: "Credit is thus an important part of the consumer's purchasing power." That was enough for him as far as the importance of installment buying was concerned: "No one can question, therefore, the indispensability of credit." As far as credit spurring inflation, he quoted an article that Eugênio Gudin, Brazil's most prominent monetarist, had recently published in *O Globo*. "Without the creation of large-scale consumer credit," Gudin wrote, "industry would have to reduce its production considerably, as is threatening to occur at this moment."[131]

Many specialists were aware that installment terms were much shorter in the United States than in Brazil, but they scarcely advertised the fact. Had a critic made the point, however, he would have been met with a familiar argument, that credit, the flywheel of U.S. consumerism, was even more important in Brazil than in the United States. In the words of URAPEL's president: "We may cite the fact that in the United States a television receiver costs less than 200 dollars and the earnings of a middle-class citizen are more than 400, but even so such devices are sold on installments when this citizen could buy TWO receivers with ONE month's earnings. In our Country, the average price of a receiver is 50,000 cruzeiros and middle-class earnings are lower than 10,000 cruzeiros and there you have the evidence of a contrast so clamorous that it is inconceivable that the Government should resolve to interfere in the subject to make it more difficult instead of making it easier."[132]

Supermarketing

Another area in which the United States served as exemplar was food selling. The supermarket—created in the United States in the 1930s, conjured up elsewhere in the early postwar—began to be assembled in Brazil in the mid-1950s. Its introduction meant fundamental changes in sales techniques hinging on the introduction of new technology and ways of structuring space, as well as the imposition of new meanings on the trade in foodstuffs and other items. At the technical level, supermarketing depended upon three new ideas—"self-service," "one-stop shopping," and "cash and carry"—that defined a series of interlinked practices: unattended customers choosing items from a large stock of prepackaged, fixed-price products, including but not limited to goods customarily acquired from butchers, fishmongers, poulterers, greengrocers, fruitsellers, bakers, milkmen, and confectioners, or from open-air markets and neighborhood stores dealing in more than one of these lines; then taking them to a cashier who would calculate the total due, which would be paid without recourse to credit, whereupon the goods would be the customer's property and responsibility. The supermarket's capacity for bulk purchasing and skimping on labor costs meant that it could sell its goods at a lower markup while profiting on the stock rotation effected by the attractiveness of its prices. These techniques, in turn, required or came to require new technologies: the cash register, for tallying customers' totals and minimizing cashier theft; stores designed to accommodate a variety of departments and ease movement through them; baskets and carts for customers to carry larger amounts of goods; refrigerated displays and cellophane wrapping to protect perishable foods while maximizing customer access to them. In most U.S. contexts, but not necessarily elsewhere, parking for passenger automobiles was another exigency. To the resulting assemblage of new technologies, techniques, and practices were attributed superior values, as supermarketing was presented as a better way of procuring foodstuffs—more hygienic, convenient, comfortable, and efficient. More "modern," in every imaginable way, the supermarket was also portrayed as the site of pleasant, even pleasurable experiences, in contrast to traditional neighborhood stores.

That supermarket shopping would be a pleasure was, however, a third-order consideration for the parties interested in its Brazilianization. Manufacturers of technological inputs were interested in selling more of their wares, thus the National Cash Register company, which had operated a Brazilian subsidiary since 1936 and done well with the expansion of department-store operations, encouraged commercial concerns and would-be entrepreneurs to experiment with "self-service" in general and supermarketing in particular, offering promotional literature and training. Suppliers of marketable goods had a similar stake, the key example being the country's mostly foreign-owned meatpacking plants, which sought to streamline their distribution of chilled and frozen beef while growing the market for canned foods rendered from unmentionable by-products. Local, regional, and national governments were interested in arresting runaway price increases and making scarce goods available to consumers: a key step was the federal government's Industrial Development Commission contracting a team of U.S. experts to study Brazilian food-supply and distribution systems; the report of the so-called Klein & Saks mission, among other things, called for reorganizing the retail trade in foodstuffs, including creating regional chain-stores as a preliminary to a nationwide transition to supermarketing. Where there was government, there were politicians—actual and aspiring—keen to gain popularity by "solving" the problem of retail food distribution. Finally, as in other fields, there were men and women on the make, Brazilians, North Americans, and Europeans who saw the promise of wealth in supermarketing. Out of the conjugation of these interests emerged Brazil's earliest experiments with the form, which came to attract the interest of other parties as the first successes emerged: Sirva-se and Peg-Pag in São Paulo in 1953–1954; the supermarket of the Serviço de Abastecimento da Previdência Social (SAPS), a semipublic model assembled in Rio in 1954 and elsewhere in Brazil thereafter; Supermercado Copacabana and the Disco chain in Rio from 1955–1956, the latter founded by Augusto Frederico Schmidt, a well-connected businessman who had led the government board to which the Klein & Saks mission reported.[133]

In retrospect, the supermarket's success seemed foreordained: "As could not be otherwise, Brazilian commerce was inevitably drawn to the American novelty." Amid the introduction of the "revolutionary method" of "Self-Service" in Rio, the *Correio da Manhã* made the same case: "As could not but have happened, Brazil imported the new method, through sensible merchants of progressive spirit." Two years later, the same newspaper made a booster-ish case for the North American model's acceptance in the fastest-growing neighborhood of the city's fashionable south side: "An institution renowned around the world, the supermarket could not fail to appear in Brazil, and, principally, it could not fail to appear in Copacabana. A modern neighborhood, up to date with progress, Copacabana had to receive the supermarket with open arms."[134]

In these accounts and others like them, much was made of the influence of Hollywood films and North American periodicals: "The knowledge we had of supermarkets was not more than a few years old, from newspaper stories, and specialist magazines and in the curiosity sections of popular magazines. Thereafter, cinema reinforced the interest that existed in the subject, presenting to Brazil the fabulous American 'self-service' establishments, through various films, some of them in color. Thus occurred the definitive lodging of the supermarket in the curiosity of the people, who saw starlet 'x' and star 'y' making their purchases there and enjoying the benefits of the novelty." "There is not a vehicle that has provided the Brazilian housewife with a better idea of the facilities and comfort that the American woman has at her disposal than the cinema, with its portrait of modern kitchens, its vision of the practical and economic system of purchasing," according to the *Correio da Manhã*. "This awareness of a solution suited to the demands and rhythm of life in the age of aerodynamism and atomic power . . . has been a constant dream, the example cited by all women at all hours." There seemed no other way to describe "Copacabana's fabulous Super-Market": "It looks like something from the movies. The produce counter reminds one of American magazines."[135]

However spontaneous or overdetermined it might appear, there was a good deal of work involved in assembling the supermarket. In-store tableaux might resemble Hollywood stills or photographs from *Life* magazine, but their makers required greater experience of the United States than could be had at the movies or a newsstand. As Raul Borges, who planned Sirva-se and Peg-Pag, explained, it involved direct study of "turnover" and supermarket organization in the United States. In the run-up to Sirva-se's opening, Borges's partner, Fernando Pacheco de Castro, spent three months in the United States: "He visited innumerable supermarkets and got in contact with factories making refrigerating equipment, as well as producers of shopping carts, machinery, stock-control systems, etc. The smallest details were studied, since we did not want to have to improvise." A Nestlé executive remembered, "Raul Borges, the man who managed part of this Sirva-se group, trained in the United States, to bring back *know-how*, like Fernando Pacheco." The head of the group's meat department spent time in the United States as well, learning about U.S.-style cuts and the packaging of ready-to-cook meat in cellophane.[136] In Rio, the official responsible for the SAPS supermarket—"the Federal District's first supermarket"—built on an earlier experiment in self-service foodselling carried out for the state government of Rio Grande do Sul and observation of "similar organizations in Canada and the United States." The Disco chain was similarly modeled. "The Disco Supermarkets represent five years of study and observation," the group's advertising director declared: "Our directors traveled to the United States several times so as to be informed of all the new things relative to supermarkets."[137]

The results did not disappoint. The first São Paulo supermarkets were hailed as "absolutely authentic copies" of U.S. supermarkets. An academic authority agreed, noting, "The Paulista supermarkets, at their origins, were a faithful copy of the North American supermarkets." As Fernando Pacheco's widow, who had accompanied him to the United States, remembered, "Everything was done exactly within the standards of American supermarkets," despite the rush to open the store "at the best time of year" (just before Christmas). And so "the lay-out, the self-service, the products laid out for sale and many other typical characteristics of the North American supermarket were transplanted to the São Paulo supermarket in its initial period of operations, the latest innovations being adopted, within the limits of the possible, through information from specialist magazines or through knowledge acquired 'in loco' by the most dynamic businessmen." In Rio, SAPS's director proclaimed that his state-owned store was "a patrimony of the people" and "a Model Super-Market and that a similar one could only be found in the United States." That the SAPS supermarket could sell workers "essential items and merchandise of all kinds, including metal goods, toys, and others," through the "system adopted at the grand American grocery stores" led the aldermen of Santos to propose that the system be assembled in their city. The inauguration of Disco's second location had *Ultima Hora* predicting that the firm's growth would produce a citywide chain that "would not owe anything to the Supermarkets of the great American centers," but in the meantime the organization "followed American technique closely." "One observes in them the preoccupation with respecting all the rules laid down by the years of experience of US technicians," wrote a trade journalist, noting the "buildings especially built for that end, with functional architecture, with good lighting, comfort, and space for the consumer's circulation."[138]

It was not enough, however, to create stores in the likeness of U.S. super-markets. Brazilians had to be enticed to enter them. Once inside, they had to be made to adapt themselves to self-service shopping, the names of the leading São Paulo firms offering the briefest of suggestions: "Help yourself" (*Sirva-se*), "Pick and pay" (*Peg-Pag*). Hollywood films might have given fans attractive images of U.S. supermarkets, but they did not explain why movie-goers should patronize Brazilian supermarkets or how they should behave within them. That all the early supermarkets but SAPS's were located in wealthy or near-wealthy neighborhoods helped, as "a large part of those who had already traveled [to the United States] thought that was great, 'what was lacking in Brazil, finally!,'" but the firsthand experience of a handful of hemispheric travelers only went so far. As the manager of the first Sirva-se store recalled, many Paulistanos "did not know what it was." A turnstile at the entrance left the impression that admission would be charged, while men "felt as if they were feminized if they had to push a cart." And so for the first six months of the store's operations, he stationed himself, "for a good part of business hours at the entrance, to talk with the people who arrived, approached, were in doubt, to get the shopping cart, to get going together." Thereafter, the store provided "a kind of in-store assistant, to show off the store; she helped push the cart, went along showing the sections, talking about what a supermarket was."[139]

Eager to serve, the press featured stories describing how supermarketing worked, while the major privately owned supermarkets worked closely with advertising agencies: Sirva-se with Grant and Companhia de Incremento dos Negócios (CIN), Peg-Pag with Alcântara Machado, and Disco with Grant. Advertisements comparing supermarket prices and the going rates for particular goods aimed to convince readers to try the new system; although the privately owned supermarkets could not compete with corner stores or open-air markets when it came to the pricing of unbranded staples, they could offer cut-rate trademarked goods: Bombril steel wool, Swift canned peas, Royal gelatin. Rio's SAPS supermarket, though it had an edge on privately owned stores when it came to unbranded goods, offered similar comparative advertising for Quaker oats, Peixe canned pears, and Nestlé powdered milk. From comparative advertising, it was a short step to cooperative advertising and trademarked celebrations of store openings: Kolynos toothpaste, União sugar, and Lincoln cigarettes for Sirva-se, "a model 'supermarket,' installed with all modern resources to offer the maximum cleanliness, quality, and comfort"; Kibon, Armour, and Johnson & Johnson for Peg-Pag, "providing modern comfort, more quality and savings for the home." Similarly, the first anniversary of the opening of Disco's flagship was celebrated by Nestlé, Gillette, and Alpargatas, among other firms. When Brejeiro-brand rice was introduced to

Rio, cooperative advertising announced its availability, "in hermetically sealed packages," at Disco supermarkets. Television advertising, cooperative or independent, aimed to maintain a connection with the public while offering instruction on the preparation of canned, bagged, and cellophane-wrapped novelties: TV-Tupi's daily *Sessão das Cinco*, "Brazil's greatest and most complete feminine Television program," produced by Grant for Disco; TV-Paulista's cooking show featuring Helena Sangirardi, produced by CIN for Sirva-se. In-store promotions, giveaways, and services sought the same results as print and television advertising, while also seeking to create "traffic." At Peg-Pag's opening, "in addition to vast advertising in the Press and on the Radio," there was a drawing sponsored by a home-appliance dealer, offering customers the chance to win coveted "big tickets" and smaller electric devices: a Frigidaire refrigerator, an RCA-Victor radio-phonograph set, vacuum cleaners, floor waxers, radio sets, blenders. Variations on the time-honored Item of the Day included Peg-Pag's Deal of the Month. At Disco, homemakers learned to make Kibon sundaes and a "revolutionary dressmaking method," while "Mary" of the "Compare e . . . compre" column endorsed in-store tastings of Armour's canned concoction of *feijoada*, Brazil's national dish, hosted by Sirva-se. Customers could take home recipe cards and booklets from Peg-Pag and Sirva-Se, where they would hear the same piped music as at Sears and A Sensação, while at Christmastime at Peg-Pag children could meet Santa Claus and see a performance by the clown Arrelia, a star on TV-Record.[140]

Amid these promotions, shoppers streamed into the stores. Sirva-se's prize drawing, according to a trade columnist, produced "a large number of female customers." At Rio's SAPS, where the only giveaways were booklets listing prices and dispensing nutritional advice, twenty-five thousand customers were served in the store's first four days in operation, a headcount that soon jumped to ten thousand per day, despite long lines, the store having been engineered to handle half as many people. The first Disco supermarket claimed 121,675 paying customers in its first month, a figure that became the standard by which Rio's south-zone supermarkets were measured. By mid-1957, all the major privately owned firms—Sirva-Se, Peg-Pag, Disco, Supermercados Copacabana—operated multiple stores. Imitators emerged, in Rio, São Paulo, and elsewhere, the supermarket becoming an "index of progress"; in an illustration of its allure and perhaps of misplaced priorities, pressure from the servant-employing class led to the creation of a city-run store in one of Salvador's wealthiest neighborhoods. Many upstart firms failed; some succeeded; all emulated their predecessors' promotionalism, through radio spots and store names like "Pague Pouco," which combined a riff on Peg-Pag and the promise of low prices.[141]

By 1958, there were more than a dozen supermarkets in Rio and at least as many in São Paulo. Nationwide, according to a National Cash Register executive, there were one hundred self-service foodstores. If, on the one hand, relatively few of these would have been large enough or offered a wide enough variety of goods to meet a strict definition of the term "supermarket," others no doubt escaped the NCR's attention, given how many small retailers adopted self-service. Of the multidepartment, self-service food stores, most catered to upper- and middle-class customers. Indeed, even the government-run stores aimed at workers served the least poor among them. Very few families obtained all or even most of their food from supermarkets. Despite claims that the new institution was "revolutionizing retail food marketing in Brazil's big cities," supermarketing was only a measured success.[142]

It had, however, already proven to be culturally important, most obviously in language, where the store names Peg-Pag and Disco became shorthand for self-service food shopping. Other clues to the supermarket's cultural import come in how language was used, as in advertising's shift from gender-neutral forms of address to specific appeals to women as housewives, a shift reflected in how journalists referred to supermarket customers.[143] The supermarket came to be thought of as a place that was not only sanitary but sociable, from which the demotic aspects of the open-air market and the sharp dealing of dank neighborhood stores had been expunged. While the U.S. supermarket was founded in the depths of the Great Depression, self-service and cash-and-carry offering middle- and working-class families savings on their grocery bills only to take on an aura of prosperity and comfort later, in Brazil the entire package of the postwar U.S. supermarket arrived at once. Its exotic origins meant that women who never stooped to visit the butcher or greengrocer (tasks left to retinues of servants) would at least experiment with supermarketing, a maid in tow to push the shopping cart. Sirva-se's manager observed "that his customers seem to find it fun to buy in a supermarket" and "they admit they buy more than they had planned." After his first visit to a supermarket, the writer Rubem Braga explained, "The attraction that the super-market exerts is simple: in a clean and agreeable atmosphere, a person can buy almost everything they need." A journalist charged with explaining Disco's success went further: "Glamour, as a contributing factor in sales, is present in the supermarkets." In the chain's "luxurious" supermarkets, "within North American standards of functionality, we see an environment that oozes comfort, cleanliness, of relative silence, in which shopping is done in a calm absorption, which provokes—in women, especially—that state of 'acquisitive delirium' responsible for extra sales." Delirium-inducing or not, supermarkets—unlike old-fashioned grocery stores, but like open-air markets—became spaces that married commerce and female sociability, "since the atmosphere is pleasant and a chat is part of the new experience."[144]

Elements of supermarketing were re-created in other retail stores. In 1956, Magazine Mesbla created a self-service record department, one of that year's "two revolutions in the record market" (the other was the domestically produced 45 rpm single); it also introduced self-service in more traditional lines, with open carts serving as "display counters, from which customers serve themselves." At around the same time, O Camizeiro began transitioning to self-service, creating a "Super-Market of Shirts" in its ancient flagship store. As one of the firm's principals explained, "I was in the United States, studying the American market, and I reached the conclusion that 'self-service' is the best solution for a retail store's problems." The first Lojas Helal outlet opened in 1957, selling domestic appliances, toys, and, in its founder's words, "what the Americans call *general merchandising*"; it operated on a self-service basis from the start, a fact advertised in the pages of *Ultima Hora*, *O Globo*, and *Shopping News*, as well as on TV-Tupi. Thus did "the pick-and-pay system leave the relatively restricted fields of selling items for the pantry and kitchen, and begin to be adopted in other lines of business."[145]

National Cash Register (NCR) was more closely identified with this expansion than any other firm, its executives, salesmen, and staff offering assistance in "Modern Merchandising Methods." Growing sales helped prompt NCR's transition from the assembly of imported machines to their manufacture in a new plant near downtown São Paulo. Flush times also attracted competition from European manufacturers and their agents.[146]

Real estate interests were only tangentially involved in early supermarket operations, through the Simonsen economic group, which put up some of the initial capital for Sirva-se, then took over the firm once it proved profitable. Property owners, brokers, and builders were quick to see advantages in the location and construction of supermarkets, thereby providing advocates for the system of self-service, cash-and-carry, one-stop shopping who were infinitely more powerful than the early supermarket entrepreneurs.[147]

Among the earliest enthusiasts for the assembly of supermarketing had been Brazil's advertising professionals. In 1953, their leading trading magazine published one of the first pieces of Portuguese-language reporting on the U.S. supermarket, which made much of the round-the-clock convenience of California stores. Sequels introduced Rio readers to the São Paulo supermarket and complained that Carioca housewives were deprived of the modern facilities available to their Paulistana counterparts. Reporting called on consumers to be more discriminating—by demanding the facilities available in São Paulo and the United States—and asked why the government did not use its regulating commission to create supermarkets, thus "accompanying the modern sales processes." When supermarketing reached Rio, the response was ecstatic: "The truth is that the ample installations, the cleanliness, the freedom of choice that is provided the buyer, in sum the entirety of large and small things that make the supermarket different, all this operates, provoking a 'flight' from the old business methods." For advertising men and professionals in adjacent fields, the supermarket's success in Brazil was proof of the superiority of the North American system, but it was also comforting evidence of the universalism they had made their own: "The North American mean is not far from the Brazilian one, because as we have already had the opportunity to mention in earlier articles, the population is just one, in Rio as in New York, in Paris as in London, and even in Japan. Cinema and rapid means of communication have contributed to unifying the habits of the peoples. Progress, today, is not limited to one city, to one country, or to one continent. What is good for an American female customer is good for any other female customer in any part of the world."[148]

Prosperity Professionals

Between swooning over supermarkets, endorsing installment sales, producing television programming, and inventing commercial commemorations, Brazil's advertising professionals watched their trade grow. Having reported "boom conditions" in 1951, they were "unanimous in their feeling that the business is still in its infancy, a very healthy infancy, with every prospect of continuing and increasing growth," in 1952. Between 1947 and 1953, advertising expenditures increased four and one half times over, while McCann's billings doubled between 1950 and 1952. In the early 1950s, JWT's billings increased at an average of 15 to 20 percent per year; by 1955, budgets were increasing "at the rate of almost a third annually," according to Caio de Alcântara Machado of the Almap agency. Part of this growth was fictitious, reflecting the diminishing value of Brazil's currency, but part was real, increases in advertising budgets remaining ahead of the rate of inflation, and the total output of advertising increasing as well. Indeed, the volume of advertising was increasing so quickly that U.S.- and Brazilian-owned agencies, including JWT and Almap, were forced to turn away business.[149]

The number of agencies and the size of the professional cohort increased in these boom times, as did salaries. The cohort's composition changed too, in response to the latter incentive and in connection with broader social changes. Meanwhile, the profession extended its ken into adjacent fields of endeavor and underexploited regions of the country. Alongside these changes was the continued work of bidding for standing and status, and for the fuller professionalization of the field and its recognition by Brazilian publics and powerholders.

In 1950, there were an estimated 101 advertising agencies in Rio and São Paulo, a number that grew to 120 in 1952, 130 in 1954, and 188 in 1960. By the latter point, estimates of the total number of persons employed in Brazilian advertising ran as high as five thousand.[150] Burgeoning salaries meant that agency work attracted candidates who would otherwise have looked down their noses at the once-grubby business, a "considerable number of old journalists, writers and even poets," who remained respected figures in their fields even as they took to copywriting. As elsewhere, women's salaries lagged behind men's, but the female presence in advertising nevertheless increased over Brazil's long postwar, matching the increased presence of women in white-collar work generally and reflecting advertisers' increased interest in reaching women. Hilda Ulbrich Schützer (hired by Grant as a secretary in 1947, at JWT from 1952, including a three-month traineeship in New York) may have been underpaid and often underestimated, but she attributed part of her cohort of women executives' success to "some things that only their sensibilities, their condition's natural intuition can provide." And so, "woman broadens her field of labor, adding to her purely technical collaboration her practical knowledge, her domestic existence, of great worth in studies of the advertising strategies to be adopted." Such practical knowledge was also applied at Standard, where Haydée Guersoni found work on her return from eighteen months in the United States, where she studied advertising and public relations at Wayne State University and worked in automotive advertising. Her presence was one basis for Standard's claim to be "always informed of [women's] tastes and their daily needs as housewives."[151]

The same Standard advertisement noted the agency's activity in other fields (market research, public relations, economic analysis, and sales promotion) and its offices outside the Rio–São Paulo axis, in Belo Horizonte and Porto Alegre, varieties of expansion that were generalized. Grant beat Standard to Porto Alegre, and while McCann was slower in its transition from relying on local representatives to opening full-scale offices outside of Rio and São Paulo, by 1958 it had offices in Belo Horizonte, Porto Alegre, and Curitiba, to which were added Recife and Salvador by 1960. At that point, Norton was also operating a Porto Alegre office, while CIN had offices in Belo Horizonte and Salvador, as well as Porto Alegre.[152] JWT was a laggard in geographic terms, but a pioneer in offering new services, identifying itself "as a merchandising organization as well as an advertising agency" in 1951: "In a country where advertising and sales organizations are generally unsophisticated it is necessary that advertising service go far beyond normal agency functions. This extends to product and distribution studies, packaging, sales meetings, salesmen's portfolios and government contracts." Inter-Americana offered similar services: "What is your problem? Advertising? Distribution? Branch manufacturing? Our office is well equipped and staffed to take care of your needs—from initial market research, to determine the chances of your product down here, to creation, production and final placing of advertising." By 1959, the range of facilities and services offered by advertising agencies had expanded further, not, as JWT's assessment indicated, because of a lack of sophistication, but because of the very dynamism of the field. CIN, for example, boasted an autonomous department specializing in the planning and design of packaging, while Publitec, another rapidly growing Brazilian agency, offered market analysis, public-opinion research, and industrial rationalization, as well as public relations and sales promotion.[153]

At the same time, countervailing trends were in evidence, as the sales-promotion field, born as an adjunct to advertising, bid for a sort of independence with the founding of the Association of Sales Directors of Brazil (ADVB) in 1956. Modeled on the New York–based National Sales Executives, Inc., and affiliated with its international arm, the ADVB brought together representatives of U.S.-, European-, and Brazilian-owned concerns, including Colgate-Palmolive, Arno, Walita, Lever, Probel, Sears, and Peg-Pag, "in the sense of improving their methods." If the ADVB represented a dilution of the advertising associations' claims to speak for sales professionals, it was nevertheless committed to the same consumerist values and the mission of "better advertising, better sales, more affordable products." By 1957, JWT, McCann, and the Almap agency were paid-up member firms, as were the advertising-dependent *Seleções* organization and the Abril group.[154]

Just as the ADVB's founding represented a countertrend to agencies offering services in other fields, the trajectory of the MPM agency was a counterpoint to the expansion of São Paulo—and Rio-based advertising firms beyond the country's southeast. At its 1957 founding by two ex-employees of Grant's Porto Alegre office, MPM was backed by the Renner textile concern and the Ipiranga petroleum company, making it a major presence in Brazil's far south. Its founders' aim, to create the first Rio Grande do Sul agency of national scope, was realized more quickly than anticipated when Ipiranga acquired Gulf Oil's distribution network in 1959; with filling stations throughout the southeast to promote, MPM opened a Rio office almost immediately.[155]

As these developments unfolded, the new professionals kept up the push for allies and esteem, chalking up some victories early in the postwar: in 1946, when the founder of the Panam agency was elected to the São Paulo Commercial Association's board of directors; in 1949, when the Standard executive João Doria represented the São Paulo State Federation of Industries at the National Conference of the Productive Classes. Official recognition

ensued: in 1953, when the APP was recognized by São Paulo's state government; in 1957, when the ABP received the same honor from Rio's mayor. Ballooning salaries also inflated the advertising professionals' amour propre, as
did acknowledgment of their kind "in the country of the masters of advertising": a Brazilian serving as art director in JWT's Miami office, the election
of McCann's local head to a vice presidency of the parent company.[156]

The advertising professionals lost few opportunities to proselytize, assid-
uously contributing to the general-interest press, even as their own magazines continued to be their major forum, its purview and reach expanding
with time. The monthly *Publicidade* became *Publicidade & Negócios* (Advertising & business) in 1947; in 1950, it began to be published on a fortnightly
basis, its publishers calling it "Brazil's Only *Business* Magazine" (their emphasis distinguishing *Publicidade & Negócios* from magazines concerned with
"economics," in allusion to *Digesto Econômico* and *O Observador Econômico
e Financeiro*). In the same year, the magazine was printed in runs of ten thousand issues, over half of which were sent to paid subscribers: those figures
and the first half of its title made it the largest-circulating advertising magazine published outside the United States. By 1955, when the print run of each
issue was increased to fifteen thousand, its title had been shortened to *PN*. In
1957, print runs reached twenty-five thousand and the magazine began to be
published as a weekly. The following year, printings increased again, to forty
thousand, more than half of which were distributed to subscribers, with
nearly all the rest sold at newsstands. By then, *PN* faced new competition,
the São Paulo monthly *Propaganda* having been revived in 1956. Whereas an
earlier generation only had resort to U.S. and European publications, and
many professionals continued to subscribe to them, "most of them pursue
their theoretical knowledge . . . in the two national magazines": *PN*, "a veritable school of advertising men"; *Propaganda*, "an excellent vehicle that, like
PN, has carried out a great training effort."[157]

The two magazines reported dutifully on the activities of the major trade
associations, the ABP and the APP, as well as the Brazilian Association of Advertising Agencies (ABAP), founded in 1949 in the face of a proposed tax on
agencies by Rio's city government. The latter threat was beaten back in cooperation with JWT; thereafter, the three associations continued the work
of bolstering the profession's image and boosting the morale of its practitioners through time-tested means, as well as in new fora. Larger memberships—
including representatives of publishing and broadcasting interests—were
offered seminars and formal coursework, access to specialist libraries, and
attendance at increasingly high-profile social events, the most important of
which remained the annual commemoration of Pan-American Advertising
Day. At the ABP's 1951 commemoration, Lauro de Carvalho gave the keynote,

the self-described "merchant and industrialist who in time discovered the power of advertising, and used it to grow his businesses" declaring: "The interests of those who manufacture, those who sell, and those who establish the connection between the seller and the consumer—the advertising professionals—are the same. Advertising men all seek the same objective: the quicker and cheaper flow of consumer goods or, in other words, the increase of well-being to the greatest number." At the São Paulo fete, the APP's president made a similar case: "In the economic field, especially, advertising is the basic factor that counterbalances wealth, equating the fundamental elements of material progress in an almost mathematical formula, that may expressed in these terms: Production—Advertising—Consumption." That "production depends upon advertising" was "the great secret and the great technique of rational economic organization, that has produced the extraordinary advance of certain countries, from the point of view of material wealth, among which I would like to cite the United States of North America, whose economic rise has marked the history of Humanity as the greatest and most marvelous boom of progress, impressive in the breadth of its proportions."[158]

The associations' officers were increasingly successful in expanding the audience for such pronouncements. At the ABP's 1954 banquet, for example, the group's president could thank the federal minister of labor, industry, and commerce for attending, before crowning *O Globo*'s advertising director the "Advertising Man of the Year." Meanwhile, in São Paulo, the ABP and APP collaborated on a "round-table on advertising" broadcast on TV-Record in which the president of the São Paulo Commercial Association made the same case for advertising that Lauro de Carvalho and the APP's president had made two years earlier, praising the "technicians, whose knowledge, experience, vision, judgment, discernment, power of imagination—which are all essential requirements for the advertising men—has raised them in Brazil to a level that today is on par with that of the most advanced countries in the world."[159]

The press amplified these pronouncements through coverage of associational activities. In 1956, newspaper readers encountered a McCann-designed advertising campaign sponsored by the ABAP and ABP. "Which one of these don't you need?" was the caption of an advertisement illustrated with mass-produced goods (including a toothbrush, lipstick, and a bottle with Coca-Cola's familiar curves). "In your conception of comfort, which of these is unnecessary to modern life?" The answer was plain: "In truth, you already can't go without them, because they are among the things that simply became a part of your habits and your higher standard of living. In order for this standard of comfort to constantly rise, and for you to be always up to date and minutely informed of all the good things that Commerce and Industry place within your reach, a class of men works in one of the most intense modern professions—Advertising." Another advertisement in the series made the case that "what was a luxury for Cleopatra" (a perfumed bath) was ordinary for readers, thanks to advertising-driven competition between manufacturers of mass-produced soap. Perhaps the most lastingly influential of the campaign's advertisements was one illustrated with a park bench in the cold light of a streetlamp. "You'll never sleep on this bench . . ." it informed the reader, "but have you ever thought that, aside from your personal value, fully recognized by your bosses, there exists another, very important motive that guarantees the stability of your employment?" That motive was "the prosperity that allows there to be more and more jobs, and that derives from the fact that Commerce and Industry can sell more and more, more quickly!" "Our function—that of Advertising men—is exactly that of continually and incessantly enlarging the conditions for this prosperity; discovering markets, enlarging markets, bringing forth more consumers." The cadres represented by ABP and ABAP were thus *profissionais da prosperidade*—professionals in and of prosperity, "prosperity's professionals" or simply "prosperity professionals"—and they saluted "all of the other citizens who contribute, with their creative capacity, to Brazil's progress."[160]

Alongside this campaign, the ABP and *Ultima Hora* cosponsored the First National Salon of Advertising Artists. Held on the first floor of the Ministry of Education building, a landmark of Rio's modernist architecture, the exhibition of posters, sketches, and other visual materials was supported by the Inter-Americana agency, the Época print works, *PN*, and *Propaganda*, as well as *Shopping News*, the *Correio da Manhã*, and TV-Rio. In Samuel Wainer's words, "*Ultima Hora* is honored to pay homage to the artists who make art a factor in commercial development." According to a McCann layoutman, it was "a decisive step toward the very advertising of national advertising." The head of Inter-Americana's art department agreed, adding that it showed "the team spirit that predominates in Advertising." "Formidable," exclaimed Lintas's Rodolfo Lima Martensen, "it is a great initiative!"[161]

Martensen knew better than most, for he had been closely involved with an earlier advertising-related exposition, the National Salon of Advertising held in São Paulo in 1950. Carried out independently of the ABP and with minimal input from the APP, it nevertheless made more of an impact than the Rio exhibition. It emerged out of an interest in commercial art and design on the part of Pietro Bardi, an Italian art dealer of shady origins whom Assis Chateaubriand invited to be the founding director of the São Paulo Museum of Art (MASP) in 1947. Chateaubriand's gift for shaking down the deep-pocketed meant that Bardi and his wife, the architect Lina Bo, had spared no expense in creating one of the world's great museums, while Chateaubriand's stake in the Diários Associados meant that the Bardis were free to lead MASP into commercial territory untouched by traditional galleries: fashion shows, clothing design, courses on window-dressing. In 1950, amid such slumming, MASP hosted the National Salon, composed of three parts: an exhibition on the history of commercial art, a display of contemporary advertising artwork, and lectures by advertising men, including Martensen. If the published version of Martensen's speech is any guide, an off-putting case for the trade was on display alongside lithographs and sketch boards, in which he emphasized advertising's manufacture of dissatisfaction as a means of creating wants: "To those who pay rent, advertising beckons with a house of their own. To those who have straight hair, it seeks to sell the Toni-brand permanent treatment. To the pedestrian, it suggests a bicycle. For the cyclist, an automobile and for the automobile owner, a new model every year."[162]

Turning to the consequences of this beckoning, Martensen asked his listeners to imagine a working-class couple who had achieved their dream of replacing their icebox with a refrigerator after years of longing. Their idyll was short-lived, for scarcely was the new refrigerator plugged in when a radio spot announced "new, revolutionary refrigerators" that kept food fresh using shortwave valves instead of cooling components, "which inevitably destroy flavor and vitamins." The couple is now dissatisfied with what they had striven for, leading Martensen to head off a criticism: "This creation of new needs and of new demands at the price of insatisfaction oftentimes has been singled out as a downside of advertising. Analyzed properly, however, we shall see that human dissatisfaction created by advertising is exactly its greatest virtue." It was this "basic sentiment that drove human evolution," through which "advertising places itself definitively alongside evolution for the good of humanity itself."[163]

The salon was a success. Thousands visited the exhibitions, and while it is unclear if any visitors swallowed Martensen's view of human progress, their presence made a deep impression on Bardi. "While my Rembrandt, Velasquez, Goya, Picasso, Renoir, are drawing flies, awaiting the few visitors to the Museum, you people from advertising fill up the eyes of the people with all sorts of garbage," was his retort, to which he added an invitation: "Rodolfo, wouldn't you like to organize a course in advertising art to help the Museum to improve the artistic level of this country's advertising?"[164]

While thinking it over, Martensen decided that "a little course on advertising art" would be insufficient and that "the poor taste of advertisements and billboards, which so shocked Prof. Bardi, was only a consequence—and perhaps the least harmful one—of a much broader problem, with serious socio-economic implications." What Brazil needed was "an efficient advertising structure, capable of promoting the products and services that are now being produced here." While the raising of this structure would take time, a sound basis could be laid with the founding of a school of advertising, a professional aspiration of long standing. Given the opportunity to make it a reality, Martensen went to work. He interviewed advertisers, suppliers, and the representatives of publishing and broadcasting interests, as well as his fellow advertising men. The Brazil–United States Cultural Institute provided Martensen with introductions to U.S. experts, who offered advice on how to organize a professional course of study. After almost a year of off-hours work, Martensen presented Bardi with his proposal.[165]

The ten-page document outlined Martensen's design for the school's administration, curriculum, teaching regimen, and faculty, as well as for a publicity department. Between periodicals and books, its bibliography ran to thirty-three items, from *Advertising Agency* to Eugene Seehafer and Jack Laemmar's *Successful Radio and Television Advertising*; three of these titles were published in London, one apiece in Zurich and Rio; of the remaining twenty-eight, two were published in Chicago and the rest in New York. The briefest of budgets indicated that the school could be self-supporting, beyond MASP's provision of rent-free space, based on nominal student fees. The most important sections of the proposal dealt with the curriculum and teaching regimen: ten subjects (Elements of Advertising, Layout, Art Direction, Graphic Arts and Production, Copywriting, Media, Statistics, Sales Promotion, Psychology, and Radio, Cinema and Television) to be taught through faculty lectures, seminars led by outside speakers, hands-on training at local agencies, and guided visits to businesses (from pulp plants and print shops to radio and television studios). All courses would be taught by working professionals, with the exception of psychology, for which Martensen enlisted a professor from the University of São Paulo (USP).[166]

Bardi was impressed, passing the proposal on to the Diários Associados's local advertising manager (a founding contributor to the original *Propaganda* in 1937), who placed it in Assis Chateaubriand's hands. The diminutive tycoon accepted the proposal, provided Martensen commit to leading the school for five years, and so the plan was put into effect much as it had been outlined, leavened by additional consultation with USP experts in pedagogy. The first sixty-student cohort matriculated in 1952. Thereafter, not everything went according to plan (to start with, the school soon outgrew MASP, becoming the autonomous São Paulo School of Advertising in 1955), but newly minted professionals emerged from the course each year, alongside agency staffers who enrolled to get ahead. Guest lectures reaffirmed old alliances and cemented new ones: among the outside speakers during the school's inaugural year were IBOPE's Auricélio Penteado and the banker and real-estate magnate Orozimbo Loureiro. That these seminars were open to the public made them all the more worthwhile from a promotional point of view; the relationships with USP were a similar source of prestige, augmented in 1959 when its

Faculty of Economics and Administration invited Martensen's unaccredited instructional staff to offer a course on advertising. In the same year, four hundred candidates competed for seventy-five spots in the Advertising School's entering class.[167]

If, on the one hand, annual enrollments fell short of student demand; then on the other, the Advertising School's alumni did not come close to fulfilling the need for trained professionals. Particularly in Rio, the trainee system remained the major source for entry-level employees, while bidding wars over top executives were the rule everywhere. The problem that had so exercised Bardi in 1951—the quality of advertising artwork—found a piecemeal solution beyond his imagination, as foreign agencies imported gifted artists from Spanish-speaking countries with offices of lesser importance.[168] Despite these qualifications, the founding of the MASP Advertising School and its growth into the São Paulo Advertising School were not only the fulfillment of an old professional aspiration; they were also the most important institutional outgrowth of the pursuit of allies and esteem dating to the 1930s.

Another old aspiration was the holding of a national convention of advertising professionals, an aim fulfilled in 1957, when the First Brazilian Advertising Congress met in Rio. Organized by the three major trade associations and held at the great hall of the Brazilian Press Association, it was funded, in approximately equal measure, by registration fees and donations from interested firms (as an aggregate, Chateaubriand's empire was the largest donor, followed by Rádio Nacional, *O Globo*, and the Inter-Americana agency in a three-way tie for second). The 427 registrants represented all Brazil's largest advertising agencies and many smaller ones, as well as advertisers from Bombril to Toddy and media interests from Abril to *Ultima Hora*. A half-dozen women's names appear on the list of registrants, representing agencies (including A Ecléctica) and newspapers (*Shopping News, O Globo*), a numerically insignificant yet telling presence, for had the congress been held ten years earlier it would almost certainly have been a male-only event. Relative to their tiny number among registrants, women were overrepresented among presenters, with the representatives of the two newspapers submitting presentations on advertising education and the ex-suffragette jane-of-all-trades Miêtta Santiago addressing the question of an "Advertising Code of Ethics." Geographically, most attendees hailed from Rio and São Paulo, but registrants also represented every state of the seaboard from Rio Grande do Sul to Bahia, as well as Pernambuco, Ceará, Pará, Goiás, and Minas Gerais. Through three days of plenaries and presentations, attendees were saluted by the president of Rio's Commercial Association and officeholders representing each of the country's three major political parties. At intermissions, "stands" offered soft drinks, instant coffee, and analgesics courtesy of

Coca-Cola, Nestlé, and Sydney Ross; the Antarctica bottling interest also offered six months' worth of its trademark guaraná-derived soft drink to attendees' families, "an Antarctica toast to the prosperity professionals." This publicity and the promise of more to come, as in a missive from *O Estado de S. Paulo* indicating that the newspaper would create a section dedicated to advertising, ultimately mattered more than any discussion of ethics, education, or best practices. Indeed, even the most enthusiastic attendees would one day agree that the conference was, in practical terms, "not very productive." More than anything else, the congress was the opportunity for the performance of professionalism, the public marshaling of honors, and the bidding for recognition of advertising's importance and its practitioners' position as Brazil's prosperity professionals.[169]

———

From Sears, Roebuck to the prosperity professionals—here were signs of the consolidation of aspects of a Brazilian culture of consumption. At the opening of Sears's second outlet, a Rio housewife, invited to give her impressions of the store over a radio microphone, had answered, "Eu gosto de você" (I like you). One need not take her at her word—this was, after all, part of a publicity event—or that she was representative of a larger group, but it is noteworthy that she addressed the store directly, as a person, as it had addressed her through its advertising. A few weeks later, a Sears executive wrote, "Unquestionably we have captured the Brazilians' fancy." In a 1950 diary entry, a U.S. consular official's wife recorded her impressions of the Rio store and Sears's broader impact. "After entering the building, I felt as if I were back home. Everything was presented for sale in the manner to which I was accustomed," she wrote. "Sears of Rio, as well as their store in São Paulo, is very popular now among all classes." At mid-decade, a journalist observed: "Younger people show a more visible attachment to things American. . . . They regard Cadillacs and Coke, blue jeans, be-bop and even Sears, Roebuck as belonging to them naturally." By the late 1950s, even an otherwise unremitting critique of the "packaged civilization" of the United States would make an exception for "our well-known Sears Roebuck."[170]

In addressing Sears as a person, the housewife of 1949 may have been helped along by years of A Exposição's attempts to create a personality for "the magasin in the heart of the city," like the stores Lauro de Carvalho had admired in the great school to the north. That said, the retail revolutions of the postwar involved more than simple north-south, U.S.-Brazilian transmission of methods and models, as witnessed by the admixtures of European and North American commercial cultures at work in the flagship department store of once-French Mesbla, or at European- and Brazilian-capital Galeria

Carioca. In the case of São Paulo's once-British Mappin, becoming Brazilian—after the original owners sold off their shares—meant hiring a North American agency (JWT) to establish a new, national identity for the store. It was amid these changes that a former commercial attaché observed, "The mechanics of retail trade are improving steadily, and merchandizing outlets everywhere are modernizing their appearance and methods." The spread of such methods may be charted by the diffusion of promotions based on the "Item of the Day" promotion that Lauro de Carvalho adapted from Macy's, from beyond Rio and São Paulo to Belo Horizonte, Recife, Curitiba, Niterói, Campinas, and Salvador.[171]

In São Paulo and Rio, "modernizing" retail structure and service contributed to deep changes in the two cityscapes. By 1950, the "new" downtown west of São Paulo's old center was the "heart of the city," and so the slogan A Sensação borrowed from A Exposição could be used there. In a limited sense, the stores that had spearheaded the move out of the old downtown—Mappin, Clipper, and later Sears—were more "democratic" than their predecessors and previous incarnations, and so distinction migrated elsewhere, to boutiques on Rua Augusta, distant from the new downtown and not yet problematic as far as "parqueamento" (parking) was concerned. Parallel developments were underway in Rio, to be celebrated by a Copacabana-based journalist: "Women no longer need to take the tunnel to go shopping. The great shops that were once sought after on Rua do Ouvidor . . . today have their outlets in Copacabana. Copacabana's elegant ladies and lasses can stay on this side of the Tunnel." "In Rio de Janeiro," wrote a longtime retail-watcher long after the fact, "those who did not keep up with urban development and insisted upon maintaining their store in the old commercial center, found themselves compelled, in most cases, to close their doors." However, he continued, "those who moved to Copacabana, Ipanema, Leblon, in the south zone, or Méier and Madureira, in the north zone, did well." When Sears opened its first Brazilian store, *Publicidade & Negócios* had predicted that shoppers would forever fill the streets of São Paulo's old city center; thirteen years later, insiders bemoaned "the emptying out of the downtown."[172]

The shift out of the two cities' older, mostly nonresidential downtowns and into residential neighborhoods brought commerce closer to more people's homes, part of a larger thrust into everyday, familiar, and even intimate aspects of their lives. That was the ideal, at least from the perspective of an A Exposição executive, who pointed to the ties between his business and the public, "so linked through activities that sometimes exceeded commercial limits, to penetrate the intimacy of the great Brazilian family, sharing its aspirations and helping it to realize them," through commercial credit, a mission blessed by the local diocese. This thrust into family life was most apparent in commercial commemorations of Christmas and motherhood, but it may also be seen in apparently spontaneous responses to the milestones of marriage and childbirth: a stocked, new-model refrigerator as an especially generous, but not unheard-of, wedding gift among Copacabana's upper-middle class, to be restocked at the local Disco supermarket; the Walita or Arno blender, as a present upon the birth of a child. Within such homes, another big-ticket item would bring moving images into the domestic realm, accompanied by other influences, with a more pronounced impact than the radio sets of an earlier era. "The diffusion of domestic habits," the psychologist Anna Veronica Mautner remembered of her São Paulo girlhood, "occurred then, in the early 1950s, through television, technicolor cinema, and the four-color magazines, ever-better distributed through the four corners of the country. Thus was created an intimacy with what happened within the four walls of other people's homes. It was in this era that mimetism, once an object of shame, became the rule. One observed and imitated."[173]

Intimate, seemingly spontaneous, apparently the product of transnational diffusion, many of these changes depended upon the hidden hand of the Brazilian state. The national government's subsidizing newsprint imports enabled the ballooning size of advertising-happy dailies and weeklies, from the *Jornal do Brasil* to *Shopping News*, making journalism a license to print money. The quasi-official SENAC collaborated in the training of retail personnel. Rio's municipal government, under an ostensibly nationalist mayor appointed by the president, was key to the popularization of Santa Claus's Christmas, while São Paulo's rerouted bus and streetcar lines to accommodate Sears stores distant from the city center. Supermarketing in Rio began as a state project; later, when Augusto Frederico Schmidt made it his business, he relied on the experience of the federally funded Klein & Saks mission. The latter, but not the former, presaged further changes, as did the homage paid by politicos at the First Brazilian Advertising Congress.

The conference's greatest coup came a few days after its close, with the winning of an audience with President Juscelino Kubitschek for a commission headed by Genival Rabelo, the ABP president and *PN* copublisher, who brought "the salutations of the advertising class" to a popular leader beginning to deliver on his promise of fifty years of progress in a five-year presidential term. "Your Excellency knows that advertising, in its primordial function of promoting sales and stimulating new consumption habits, has been contributing in a decisive way to the acceleration of our economic progress, it perhaps not being an exaggeration to affirm that, thanks to it, Brazil will have its name stricken from the unflattering list of underdeveloped countries." In the letter they presented Kubitschek, Rabelo and his peers thereby married their work to the president's developmentalist project, then went on to review their field's progress as measured in advertising expenditures, periodical circulation, and the "advertising mentality" of Brazilian businessmen ("as evolved as that of the heralds of advertising: the United States"). A brief history of Brazilian advertising, a case for its cultural and economic importance, and an overview of the congress's aims gave way to the latest catechism: "We carry on the faith to such an extent that when it happens that we must define the advertising man we are not reluctant to call him the Prosperity Professional."[174]

Chapter 5

An Economy of Abundance

On January 31, 1961, Juscelino Kubitschek handed over power to his democratically elected successor. The changing of the guard inspired myriad retrospectives on his presidency, unique in having begun and ended more or less as prescribed by the Constitution of 1946, ambitious in its promise of a half-century's worth of progress in a single term. Among the contributors was Genival Rabelo, who had led the advertising-congress delegation that met with Kubitschek three years earlier. In June, Rabelo weighed in with an overview that glossed the most salient aspects of Kubitschek's presidency while addressing his cohort's particular concerns. Rabelo's treatment of the government's inflationary monetary policy and his claim that Kubitschek created "a climate of optimism" could have been written by any defender of the ex-president's achievements. Likewise Rabelo's mention of road construction, investment in energy production, and capital-goods industrialization, but to these accomplishments was added an achievement omitted by Brazilian political economists of the postwar era: "What stands out most about the operating philosophy of the previous government was its influence stimulating consumption." This turn led Rabelo to the prosperity professionals' favorite comparison and to appeals to advertising, retail credit, and consumerist values: "Wasn't that the 'recipe' of the exceptional economic development of the United States? Why is the technique of advertising so developed in that country? Why are all marketing processes studied so seriously there and so much importance attributed to them? Why did the system of credit sales reach such elasticity and such popular acceptance? The importance of consumption cannot go unnoticed to those who study the phenomenon of the economy of abundance. 'Nothing happens'—prescribe the North American economic primers—'until the product reaches the consumer's hands.' Thus, what is important is not production, but consumption."[1]

Many of the same touches featured in a column by Rabelo's copublisher, Manoel de Vasconcellos, who took their venture as his subject in late 1960. The occasion was doubly significant: first, the twentieth anniversary of their flagship magazine; second, the coming launch of a new title, *Indústria & Mercados*, to complete a transition begun in 1959 with the release of *Vendas e Varejo*, following which the flagship would deliver weekly news to the business world while the two monthlies focused on specialist concerns. And so, Vasconcellos looked back: "20 years also allowed us to form a philosophy. And we discovered in advertising the most efficient means of promoting an economy of abundance." Advertising was the instrument for distributing mass-produced goods, making them available to more people, such that "the producer himself has an interest in the raising of the standard of living of the population, through better remuneration to labor," a scenario that would have seemed bizarre to many Brazilian industrialists. Looking forward, Vasconcellos proclaimed that Empresa Journalística *PN* would hew to the philosophy forged over the previous decades: "This way of viewing national progress will be a constant."[2]

In the two retrospectives, one finds Vasconcellos's and Rabelo's matching, almost-incantatory resort to the "economy of abundance," an expression employed by Rabelo in other contexts in ways that make clear that it had been unmoored from its origins in Veblenian economics and kindred technocratic radicalism, in which business had been a problem rather than the solution. Instead, Rabelo used "economy of abundance" synonymously with "the mass-consumption revolution," "the American way of life," and "this age of consumerism in which we live."[3] The pairing of professional mission and the achievements of the Kubitschek presidency was also more than mere promotional bid, for there was a deep affinity between the Kubitschek moment and the dreams, desires, and ambitions of the cohort to which *PN*'s publishers belonged. While nearly all of Kubitschek's "Targets Plan" for time-bending progress dealt with infrastructure, agriculture, and capital goods, the subsequently developed mechanisms for the automotive industry's transition from assembly of imported vehicles to full-scale manufacturing came to involve passenger cars as well as trucks, buses, and other utility vehicles, which many felt to be fulfillment of Brazil becoming "one of the great automobile countries of the world," the vision announced by GM's James Mooney in 1922 and internalized by three generations of Brazilian advertising men, together with hundreds of thousands of their compatriots who had no professional stake in the matter. Automobilism was also inseparable from the fabrication of Brasília, the unsidewalked, ultramodern forward capital designed by Oscar Niemeyer and Lúcio Costa and sold as the "synthesis" of the Targets Plan. That Kubitschek was the first Brazilian president to make effective use of television only heightened his appeal among the new professionals, eager to believe that their country was on the cusp of civilizational arrival and keen to spread such ideas. As Vasconcellos wrote in 1958, "Living in today's Brazil is a fascinating experience. We feel like a giant breaking through the last obstacles to civilization, modernizing itself, placing itself on par with other peoples' technical and scientific progress, deepening its voice and beginning to speak like an adult. And President Juscelino Kubitschek is present for all of it. Not only in Rio de Janeiro, but in the most distant parts of the country."

In São Paulo in 1960, Kubitschek presented his own overview, which a *PN* reporter referred to as "the accounting of a philosophy": "We witnessed, at last, an entire transformation, glorious and mortifying at the same time, of a country that grows, that multiplies its people, that enriches itself in the constant increase of the number of consumers." A month later, Kubitschek invited Rabelo and Vasconcellos to meet with him. "*PN*," he said, in advance of a carefully staged photo opportunity, "is the press organ that best understood the meaning of developmentalism. I know that it will always be battling so that Brazil does not interrupt the pace of its growth and progress." In 1962, as a senator and an aspirant to return to the presidency, Kubitschek took part in a capital campaign aimed at sustaining the growth of *PN*'s parent firm amid rising inflation and increased competition. "It was a pleasure to acquire shares in the Empresa Jornalística *PN* S/A because it has been in the vanguard in the defense of the ideas most applicable to Brazil," he explained. "While Brazilian economists, still submerged in the shadows of the Middle Ages, want to force us into models that would keep us as slaves of foreign powers, the magazine *PN* fought for the new philosophy of Development, which steered my government and thanks to which we broke the chains of misery and began a new march to redemption."[4]

More was at work than collaboration between a born politician and *PN*'s publishers, as suggested by Kubitschek's concern, expressed the same year in conversation with a longtime collaborator, that International Monetary Fund orthodoxy stood in the way of Brazil developing "an internal market of consumers" like that of the United States.[5] Advertising executives unconnected to *PN* thrilled to Kubitschek-era accomplishments. Media elites, especially in television and magazine publishing, collaborated eagerly in the making of the president's image. The turn from automotive assembly to manufacture involved nearly a dozen foreign companies and many more nationally owned firms engaged in parts production. Relatively few Brazilians obtained passenger cars under Kubitschek, but for hundreds of thousands, the domestically produced family car became somewhat less imaginary than the "Ford in Your Future" of unhappy memory through industrial fairs that were a leisure-time site for aspirational consumption.

These fairs' alluring presentations of goods and implicit promise of their future delivery matched well with the cultivated optimism of the Kubitschek quinquennium, as did media developments. That the president was able to "appear everywhere" in his last years in office was due to a massive expansion of television-broadcasting facilities. A few years on—having overthrown the postwar constitutional order—Brazil's military rulers eagerly adopted the project of increasing television's reach, making it a national medium in the early 1970s. Along the way, contemporary broadcast programming took shape, not only in television but in radio as well, while the second half of the Kubitschek presidency witnessed shifts in publishing that were cemented between the late 1960s and early 1970s.

Another way in which Rabelo and Vasconcellos's retrospectives of 1960–1961 proved to be bigger than their moment and of a piece with developments spanning the 1950s and 1970s concerns the magazine on their drawing boards. *Indústria & Mercados* would be Brazil's first magazine dedicated to "marketing," a term introduced to Portuguese from North American English and subjected to countless attempts at translation before its verbatim adoption. Marketing soon became a framework for business and, indeed, for society. That marketing qua marketing was global in the sense of encompassing nearly every aspect of business, on either side of the production-consumption trajectory, made it enormously appealing to the new professionals; that it was also global in the universalizing sense heightened this appeal and matched it to multinationalizing trends in political economy.

Marketing's rise to globalism, in both senses of the word, occurred alongside what can only be described as the arrival of the cohort of experts in advertising and adjacent fields. Well-paid and professionalized, sought after by industry, recognized by government, and identified with marketing's allure, advertising executives and their peers in sales promotion, market research, and public relations now enjoyed the standing they had long sought, while their allies and employers among the owner-administrators of retail and media concerns did even better.

Media owners and managers were keen partners with military-led governments in the formulation of what has been called the ideology of *Brasil Grande* ("Great Brazil," "Greater Brazil," or simply "Big Brazil"). Indeed, they were even more enthused by the economistic über-patriotism of the miracle years than they had been by Kubitschek's developmentalist optimism, which shared some of the same tropes. Although the boosterism of the miracle years focused on memorable metrics of grandiosity and pharaonic construction projects, consumer-oriented business was present in the planning for greatness that represented the policy implementation of Brasil Grande ideas, as in the credit-driven expansion of passenger-car production that began in 1967, the signal achievement of Kubitschek's government becoming a point of pride and legitimacy for the regime that had stripped him of his political rights and blocked his return to the presidency. But there were other consumer-oriented aspects of military-government policy, including the engineering of the supermarket's triumph and the export of the Brazilian "hypermarket." In non-food retail, the regime aimed to create *zaibatsu* (Japanese-style conglomerated firms) with the economic group founded by Lauro de Carvalho as their principal agent.

The most lastingly influential retail development of the period was the creation of the Brazilian shopping center. Commerce and leisure were remade as a result, the former ratifying its hold over the latter and the shopping mall remaking urban space generally. Geographic unevenness and inequality embedded in new forms of shopping were among the most salient changes in Brazilian commercial culture bridging the 1950s and 1970s.

Geographic inequality, in turn, raises the question of social inequities, which also deepened during these years. Their deepening summoned apologetics, excuses, and some long nights of the soul for participant-observers of the development of Brazilian consumer capitalism. It also led to experimentation with the A, B, C, D system introduced by JWT in the interwar years, diffused by IBOPE beginning in the 1940s, and employed thereafter by virtually every inhabitant of the interlinked worlds of advertising, retailing, marketing, and media.

Until the aftereffects of the first oil shock were plain, no amount of evidence of inequity—not to say iniquity—in Brazilian consumer capitalism could deter enthusiasts from the belief that their country was on the cusp of an arrival of its own. As surely as D followed C, they maintained that an economy of abundance was imminent, that consumerism was incipient, and that a Brazilian consumer society was at hand. Such a belief may be the most telling aspect of the phenomenon of the economy of abundance identified by Genival Rabelo two decades earlier.

Modernity Shows

Affinities between Kubitschek and the new professionals would have been apparent to followers of the business press generally. In 1959, writing in *O Observador Econômico e Financeiro*, a Standard Propaganda executive declared, "The best public-relations man that Brazil has right now is named Juscelino Kubitschek," beating *PN* to the punch, for it would be nearly a year before the latter's in-house expert identified the president as one of Brazil's "authentic public-relations men." Readers of *Propaganda*'s poll of São Paulo executives regarding the "greatest advertising events" of 1960 would have spied João Doria's vote for Kubitschek's state-of-the-nation-style summary of his government's achievements, delivered "through a chain of radio and television broadcasting stations, which, at a certain moment, raised the President to the position of the country's most popular politician." For Doria, that achievement earned Kubitschek "the title of 'advertising professional of the year.'" Similarly, Rodolfo Lima Martensen called Kubitschek's inauguration of Brasília "the most splendorous product-launch advertising ever carried out in our land."[6]

Hardly a passing fancy, the Kubitschek administration's media savvy and its televised unveiling of the new capital left a lasting impression among advertising professionals and their allies. Walter Clark Bueno, a young Inter-Americana staffer when Kubitschek took office, recalled his performances decades later: "I remember having watched him on TV, using posters, maps, panels and everything else that the embryonic technology allowed, to show the roads and hydroelectric plants that he planned to build. Despite precarious resources, ridiculous if compared with those of today's TV, that was a show of modernity." "The golden age of advertising in Brazil is owed to the fact of having a president like Juça," was the case a television producer made in conversation with the advertising man Renato Ignácio da Silva, using a diminutive nickname for the ex-president. Silva agreed, adding, "The inauguration of Brasília, as I see it, was Brazilian advertising's prettiest day."[7]

That these impressions were so lasting was no accident. Their impact resulted from advertising-agency work and the support of producers and writers. As *Manchete* reported in 1958, "An advertising firm (J.W.T.) is organizing an enormous plan for programs on the achievements of his government that the president of the Republic will personally present on television." In 1960, one of the same magazine's writers made apt comparisons: "On television, for two and a half hours, he speaks as if he was a perfect 'show-man,' or an excellent advertising-boy [*garoto-propaganda*], used to the cameras, the 'booms,' the angles, the 'closes,' the 'slides,' and the cuts." As deficit spending on Brasília fueled inflation, it was argued that the new capital—"audacious, intelligent, star-like in its advance through time"—was perfectly suited to the country's people, credit happy and undaunted by overspending: "Brasília is in perfect agreement with Brazilian psychology. It is our poor man's luxury, at a time in which to owe more or owe less doesn't matter in the final accounting. It is our magnanimous ostentation to amaze the rest of the world." For the sales-promotion expert A. P. Carvalho, "Brasília was born under the sign of Advertising. Its daring urban layout, the modernity of its great architectural works . . . were from the beginning, and continue to be, excellent subjects for publicity." "Brasília is our new packaging," declared Martensen, fusing promotional metaphor and patriotism. "It is a demonstration of our vigor as a people, of our irrepressible creative capacity, capable of building a city of tomorrow today."[8]

Even as Brasília was being built, a visitor wrote, "the only thing one sees upon leaving the small airport . . . is a long row of billboards, where the bright colors and gigantic letters of 'Cinzano' stand out, while farther on at the beginning of the road that leads to the city there stands out, isolated, one for Firestone." Along the roads leading to the new capital, billboards proliferated, on new byways and old ones undergoing their first paving, as Kubitschek, according to the director of the Ecal billboarding works, was doing outdoor advertising a great service: "We, as advertising men, those who are called 'prosperity professionals,' can only applaud the government's achievements." In the makeshift settlement housing Brasília's builders "once more emerge, on the wooden walls of improvised stores and kiosks planted in the middle of the streets, posters for innumerable products. . . . The stores' walls . . . are, for their part, enormous billboards advertising the items on sale." This merchandise included "life's essential goods, as well as many of the items that one may live without, but which modern habits have made indispensable, or at least very desirable: electrical appliances for the home, accordions, inner-spring mattresses. . . . And many of these things are already offered for sale on installments, including through advertisements on Rádio Nacional, which has a broadcasting station there." Thus did "Radio's voice . . . make itself heard and with it commercial texts, hammering away with a product's trademark or issuing invitations to a 'special sale.'"[9]

Brasília's inauguration was not just a media event; it was an occasion for celebrating the world of goods. As a foreign correspondent remarked of the crowds, "The teen-aged girls, as everywhere, were blue-jeaned. . . . Hokeypokey men peddled Eskimo pies, trade-named Kibon and Antarctica." Trucks passed with banners, "This FORD helped build Brasília," a utility-vehicle appeal that soon figured in print advertising alongside tie-ins with the characteristic consumer products of the Brazilian postwar: Amaral-brand Christmas baskets, Philco television sets, and furniture made to match these latter-day household gods. McCann placed Brasília-themed advertisements for Bombril and Nestlé, Doria for Clark shoes, and Norton for Cosmopolita stoves, a "modern comfort" for the "capital of the modern world."[10]

Advertisements for Wolff silverware announced the Alvorada line of utensils, designed in homage to the new presidential palace. This link between Brasília and product design was not unique, visual cues from the city's architecture also appearing in Widevision television sets and Walita appliances. In the latter case, advertisements for the signature blender promised "absolute perfection . . . a perfect helper for your home" featuring "the modern lines of the future." They did not reveal that the blender's design was the work of a commercial artist rather than industrial engineers, information reserved for insiders, to whom a JWT executive confided, "I am pleased to inform you that the new 'Walita' blender, which displays the influence of Alvorada Palace, was designed by Thompson's art director." Kubitschek probably appreciated the indirect tribute, having boasted: "Never before have Brazilians had so many televisions, so many refrigerators, so many radios, so many automobiles."[11]

There was good reason for the president's consumer-product crescendo to peak with the passenger car, for while the home-appliance industry stirred fantasies of modern comfort, the automotive industry had a stronger hold on Brazilian imaginations, with its matching of national greatness and personal success embodied in vehicles representing a triumph of domestic industry and the acme of upper-middle-class arrival. The automobile thus was, in the apt expression of the cultural historian Sérgio Augusto, "the principal totem of Kubitschek-era prosperity." He remembered these years fondly, while a somewhat older eyewitness provided a jaded perspective: "Brazil busied itself with the idea that it was becoming 'American,' buying cars, televisions, and other trappings of newfound wealth." At the time, however, even well-traveled men of affairs waxed enthusiastic over the automobile and its meanings. For the director of the national steel company, his countrymen's acceptance of automobilism was proof of their progressiveness: "The Brazilian is open to progress. As soon as his pocketbook permitted, he . . . motorized himself." For Lúcio Meira, a powerful executive-branch official, the automobile was the "most characteristic creation of our way of life," a first-person-plural phrasing that set Brazil in the western world's "civilization of the automobile."[12]

While the automobile was emblematic of civilizational belonging and totemic in the hold it exerted, the implantation of the automotive industry beginning in 1956–1957 lent itself to additional metaphors and conceits. Automobile production, as one retrospective described its meaning in the 1950s, was "a kind of passport to modernity." For Meira, it brought "a social and economic revolution." Indeed, as he described it on another occasion, the creation of the automobile industry was one of those rare, transformative, before-and-after moments: "the Brazil of after the creation of the automotive industry . . . is not the same sleepy and settled Brazil of yesteryear. It awoke, became aware of its strength, and transformed itself." This sense of transformation was shared by a foreign-born observer: "All this is going on too quickly. Brazil is changing a lot with the emergence of the automotive industry. It is bringing an entirely new social structure, a new way of life." For *Manchete*, it was the "most sensational" item in the Kubitschek government's five-year plan. For Manoel de Vasconcellos, it marked the country's coming of age: "No other industry indicates more properly the economic maturation of a country than the automotive industry." Subsequently, others among the new professionals made similar cases for the epochal importance of automobile manufacturing, while Ernani Silva Bruno's multivolume history of Portuguese-speaking America across the ages ranked it among the most important developments in the country's recent past.[13]

At publication of Silva Bruno's history, Brazil's automotive industry was exactly ten years old, having been conceived early in the Kubitschek presidency. In 1958, the first full year of production, 60,983 motor vehicles were produced, a figure that included only a few thousand passenger cars; in 1960, Kubitschek's last full year in office, motor-vehicle production rose to 133,041, nearly a third of which were classed as passenger cars.[14] Automobile manufacturing was thus, in a very real way, an accomplishment of the Kubitschek government. That signal accomplishment, however, built on preexisting dreams and arose amid the initiatives and impediments of earlier governments.

In 1950, amid a burst of interest on the part of Brazilian industrialists, *O Observador Econômico e Financeiro* referred to automobile manufacturing as "one of the oldest national aspirations." Over the following months, the magazine highlighted the contributions of domestic industry to the assembly of imported vehicles, even as rumors whirred that one or more manufacturing plants would soon be installed, which *Publicidade & Negócios* took to mean "that the public is anxiously awaiting one of the large industrial groups to install itself in the country." Like yesteryear's "Ford in Your Future," continued publicity only heightened enthusiasm, with news of interest on the part of foreign firms failing to conjure up even the slightest nationalist reaction through early 1951, when Getúlio Vargas's popularly elected government took office. Vargas had an interest in automobile manufacture going back decades, to when he had put a GM staffer on the spot by asking what the automobile company produced in Brazil: "Practically nothing," was the flustered response. Vargas's follow-up question had been when automobiles would be manufactured domestically, the reply to which was "Within twenty years."[15]

It was not the latter deadline that heightened Vargas's interest in the question on his return to the presidency. Rather, it was the country's dependence on automotive transport and the pressure that motor vehicle imports placed on foreign reserves that made domestic manufacturing a pressing concern. Popular enthusiasm, the lobbying of parts-manufacturing interests, and the embarrassing fact that the state seemed powerless to stop illegal imports made it more pressing still. In 1952, the government's Industrial Development Commission (the same group that contracted the Klein & Saks study of food production and distribution) nominated a subcommission to look at the issue. With Lúcio Meira at its head, the subcommission concluded that the domestic market could absorb one hundred thousand vehicles per year and, not for that reason alone, Brazil needed its own automotive industry.[16] Acting on the subcommission's recommendations, Vargas's government further restricted imports of parts that could be manufactured nationally, offered incentives to companies that invested in domestic production, and prevented firms from importing assembled or semiassembled vehicles. In 1954, the government gave the go-ahead for the creation of the Automotive Materials Industry Executive Commission (CEIMA), headed by Meira and given advisory and decision-making authority over motor-vehicle manufacturing and the automotive-parts industry.

The closest Brazil came to a deal for domestic production under CEIMA came later that year, when the industrialist Henry Kaiser flew down to Rio as part of a scheme to unload his increasingly uncompetitive automotive-manufacturing plants. Kaiser was received cordially by Vargas, in a meeting attended by the omnipresent Herbert Moses and by Oswaldo Aranha, an old Vargas ally whose family had a stake in the Willys Overland do Brasil assembly plant, which imported Jeep kits purchased from a Kaiser-owned plant in Ohio. It seems likely that Kaiser would have received every executive-branch assurance and consideration had unrelated political scandal not led the president to commit suicide a few days later. Undeterred, Kaiser, the Aranha family, and a Brazilian investment interest with close ties to Rockefeller's International Basic Economy Corporation worked out a deal that would have provided the two Brazilian groups with 55 percent of a reorganized Willys Overland do Brasil outfitted with U.S. machinery for the manufacture of Jeeps and passenger cars. This plan, however, was undone even before it was finalized by a dollar-saving giveaway to foreign investors that prevented the Brazilians from buying Kaiser's Jeep-manufacturing equipment.[17] And so the midwifing of domestic automobile manufacture fell to the Kubitschek government, no less pinched by dollar shortages and prodded by parts manufacturers, and even more intent upon the political gains to be had from popular enthusiasm for the idea.

Still, there was significant continuity between the efforts of the Vargas government and the automobile-manufacturing achievements of 1956–1961. To start with there was Lúcio Meira, who advised Kubitschek during his presidential campaign, urging that motor-vehicle manufacturing figure in his five-year plan. Once in office, Kubitschek made Meira his minister of transportation and head of a successor group to CEIMA, the Automobile Industry Executive Group (GEIA). GEIA was responsible for devising guidelines for the turn to manufacturing and reviewing proposals by firms interested in establishing Brazilian plants. In July 1956, the interdepartmental group issued guidelines for trucks, jeeps, and utility vehicles; it was not until February 1957 that guidelines for passenger-car production were released, though the distinction between the latter two categories obscures the fact that many of the vehicles in the "utility" category—station wagons and ultralight trucks with closed cabins rather than pickup beds—would be used as family cars. The four sets of guidelines called for firms to increase the proportion of their vehicles' total weight that was made up of Brazilian-made components, proportions that would be ratcheted up over time, from 35 to 90 percent between 1956 and 1960 for heavy trucks, the essential category as far as developmental priorities were concerned, and from 50 to 95 percent between 1957 and 1960 for cars, the most symbolically important kind of vehicle. All the firms active in domestic assembly submitted proposals to meet these requirements, as did others with little stake in the country. In the passenger-car category, the only U.S. proposal was a joint Chrysler-Willys partnership; the remainder came from European firms and mixed-capital Euro-Brazilian groups. Ford and GM's reluctance to build Brazilian cars (by Detroit's lights, the market was too small and existing arrangements too profitable) meant that the door was left open to Willys, which remained committed to car manufacture after Chrysler opted out, and to transatlantic competitors.[18]

Cars and car-like utility vehicles were soon coming off production lines. There were DKW-Vemag station wagons and passenger cars, "as much ours" as Carnaval or coffee, and thus "authentic Brazilian citizens." Classed as a utility vehicle, the Rural Willys was sold as the "ideal vehicle for the Brazilian family" and evidence "that the national automotive industry advances . . . toward total emancipation." Willys's plant, inaugurated by Kubitschek "in a ceremony that had the character of a national holiday," also manufactured Dauphines—"with quite a continental look"—under license from Renault. The tiny, Italian-designed Isetta was built in the interior of São Paulo by the Romi group, "the first passenger car manufactured in Brazil" more than meeting guidelines for nationally made components without submitting to GEIA authority. In 1959, Brazilians had their first look at the nationally made Simca Chambord, outdone the following year by the Simca Présidence, a Gaullist land-yacht available by special order. Brazil's president received his own luxury car tribute in the JK-2000, built by the undercapitalized National Motors Factory under license from Alfa Romeo, which would absorb the once-successful state-capitalist concern some years later. Meanwhile, as a point of pride for his government, Kubitschek kept trying to convince Ford to build an American-model sedan in Brazil. He failed, but he had the consolation of Willys's release of the Aero, a U.S. car no longer produced in the United States, which likely figured in his decision to award the company's director with the Order of the Southern Cross—the highest honor the Brazilian government can grant a noncitizen—"affirming . . . that Willys is one of his government's lasting glories." It was the Aero Willys and the Volkswagen "Beetle," which went into production in 1959, that would be the most coveted of the first generation of nationally made cars.[19]

Willys relied on the Brazilian advertising agency P. A. Nascimento–Acar through the Aero's launch and Multi, a thinly disguised McCann spinoff, thereafter. Introducing the Aero, P. A. Nascimento–Acar lauded the appearance of "the big Brazilian car," the country's first, "inspired by the modern conquests of space and comfort" and "one more affirmation of the extraordinary development of the Brazilian automobile industry." Multi's campaigns for the Aero-Willys offered streamlined advertising, from which developmental-industrial appeals and, indeed, any mention of mechanics had been jettisoned. As a Multi executive explained, "We sought to present the automobile in the greatest simplicity, which was achieved by its placement in certain angles . . . seeking to identify it with the type of buyer from classes A and B." Spare copy complemented this approach, while background illustrations—the entryway to a stately home, the suggestion of a tennis court, "symbols of a public of a little higher 'status'"—played on desires for social ascent and the stability available to the most fortunate of all.[20]

Early campaigns for the Volkswagen Beetle, produced by Almap, contrasted with Aero-Willys advertising. They also broke with tradition: while earlier advertising for European makes—Opels, Peugeots—had suggested near-American technology and style, advertisements for the tiny sedan, soon to be called a *fusca*, emphasized its practical features, often with a humorous touch, nearly always in black and white, a presentation suited to the practicality of its subject. The approach might seem un-American, but it belonged to the New York agency Doyle, Dane & Bernbach, where Almap's creative director, Alex Periscinoto, had interned in 1958 on paid leave from Mappin. Some professionals grumbled. Others defended the campaign, including McCann's Júlio Cosi Júnior: "The great responsibility is to the national agency's credit, that of facing up to a campaign by Doyle, Dane, as well as the production in Brazil of an excellent campaign that is the equal, in its advertisements, to those that were totally produced in the United States."[21]

Something like Cosi's sense of automobile advertisements illustrating Brazilian greatness by approaching international standards was on display at a pair of events held in 1960–1961. The First Automobile Salon, held in 1960, brought a half-million visitors to a 20,000 m² hall in São Paulo's Ibirapuera Park. All the country's vehicle-manufacturing interests and many of its parts-producing firms contributed "stands" feting the achievements of the preceding four years alongside such novelties as the Willys "Saci" convertible and a Kombi van-turned-bar-car, while extramural entertainments included a classic-car rally and Volkswagen's demonstration of an amphibious *fusca* in one of the park's decorative ponds. Early the following year, in Rio, Kubitschek inaugurated the Museum of Modern Art's Automotive Exposition. Sponsored by GEIA and the manufacturing interests that had made the São Paulo salon such a success, the Rio event was smaller and more didactic, its layout emphasizing national achievement over popular entertainment. It was nevertheless hailed by Lúcio Meira and the Museum of Modern Art's president as having exceeded expectations, the curator asserting that it was fulfillment of the alliance of "ART and INDUSTRY in a work of interpenetration, in which both forms of human activity benefit." Taken together, the two events represented another kind of modernity show, commercial expositions that became leisure-time occupations and incitements to consumption.[22]

Events like these, of course, had been put on before the Kubitschek years. The Centennial Exposition of 1922, at which radio made its domestic debut, was an early example. More recently, in 1954, commemorations of the four hundredth anniversary of the founding of São Paulo had included an exposition held in the pavilion that would host the First Automobile Salon, a structure designed, as Brasília would be, by Oscar Niemeyer, on his way to becoming Brazil's most famous architect. Nor were Cariocas immune to such blandishments, though the more successful expositions took place before or after peak beach-going season and at a distance from the attractions of Rio's southern shores. Thus the U.S. Exposition of 1963, with its fashion shows, kitchen of the future, and depictions of "Mr. John Worker, USA," and his "purchasing power for consumer items" took place from July to October on a site west of downtown, its success hailed by *Ultima Hora*'s Samuel Wainer as evidence in an argument with a young Trotskyist in his employ. The throngs lined up for the "exposition of products from the USA" were Wainer's proof that revolution—permanent or other—was not in the cards. "In one week, around a half a million people, out of a total of three million inhabitants, went to see it," remembered a chastened Paulo Francis. "Samuel brandished these figures in my face."[23]

But it was in São Paulo beginning in 1958 that commercial fairs became happenings, leisure-time draws in which entertainment took on civic airs and offered actual and virtual consumption to Brazilian families, who came to be dazzled as domestically produced goods took star turns surrounded by human celebrities—beauty-pageant winners, singer-songwriters, famous musicians—directed by advertising, public-relations, and media executives. These events were the work of the former advertising man Caio de Alcântara Machado, who sold his eponymously named agency in 1956 and founded a new business with an interest in international-trade promotion called Alcântara Machado Comércio e Empreendimentos (AMCE). Alcântara Machado's connections led the Kubitschek government to have AMCE represent Brazil at the 1957 World Trade Fair in New York, but he failed utterly at obtaining the support of Brazilian industry, and so the resulting display was bare boned. As Alcântara Machado recalled, "There were used shoes, used clothes, used machinery, everything improvised, no industry, but there was Brasília and it worked." Beyond the latter consolation was a prompt to new business, for while in New York Alcântara Machado became convinced that Brazil was ready for commercial fairs of its own. In 1958, AMCE put on its first, the National Textile Industry Fair, or FENIT, at the Ibirapuera Park pavilion. According to Alcântara Machado, FENIT turned a profit in 1963; by then, AMCE had launched the Automobile Salon, a National Domestic Utility Fair, and a Children's Salon, each an instant success, gate receipts alone providing guaranteed profits, enhanced by the fees paid by participating firms.[24]

These were major events, "great promotional novelt[ies]" in one staffer's words. FENIT was conceived as a forum for the country's oldest, most traditional industry, a meeting-place for suppliers, manufacturers, and wholesale customers, but it became the site where each year's fashions were set, in carefully produced shows featuring beauty-pageant contestants, popular musicians, and the country's first professional models. Attendance climbed from 177,000 in 1959 to 600,000 in 1964, reaching 1,000,000 in 1968. By then, despite the sponsorship of the textile-manufacturers' association and the support of all the major firms in the field, FENIT was synonymous with a single company, the subsidiary of the French firm Rhône-Poulenc, known in Brazil as Rhodia. Rhodia executives, drawing on the experience and expertise of Standard Propaganda, had made the fair their own in bidding to convince Brazilian women to wear synthetic fabrics, launching a new line at FENIT every year beginning in 1962, each bearing an English-language title: Brazilian Nature, Brazilian Look, Brazilian Style, Brazilian Primitive, Brazilian Fashion Team, Brazilian Fashion Follies. In 1968, Rhodia's Momento 68—cosponsored by Shell, Ford, and Willys—was introduced with performances by the most important of the musicians who had invented Brazilian Tropicalism, while 1969 belonged to the Stravaganza Fashion Circus. As the leading women's magazine described it, "To show off the 'Stravaganza fashion' nothing was spared, an entire circus was assembled, circus rings, trapeze artists, jugglers, lions, tigers, beasts from all over. Sensational clowns. And more. The text by Carlos Drummond de Andrade, the Tropicalist joy of the great artist Gal Costa. The artful narration by the actor Raul Cortez, and much, much more."[25]

Rhodia was so identified with AMCE that it contributed fashion shows to the other fairs as well, including the domestic utilities fair (UD). The UD, sponsored by the São Paulo industrialists' federation (FIESP), was billed as an "exposition of everything that makes a modern home—from the indispensable to the superfluous," displayed in stands installed for the country's leading retail and manufacturing concerns. Posters promised that UD would be "a never-before-seen display of everything practical and good that Brazil produces for the comfort of the home," while newspaper advertisements called on housewives to attend the on-site cooking lessons ministered by Helena

Sangirardi and *Casa e Jardim* provided a tour: "General Electric showed off its entire line, from refrigerators, televisions, large radios and portable ones, to fans. Another great factory is Ibesa, showing off its Gelomatic refrigerators. . . . Isnard & Cia. Ltda., representing Climax—Brazil's most accessibly priced refrigerator, with its perfect, efficient working. General Motors with the famous Frigidaire. . . . Right thereafter, Brastemp's large stand displaying the 'bossa nova' line."[26]

At the first UD, 114 manufacturing firms contributed some 200 stands; the following year 240 firms were represented at 383 stands, visited by 350,000 people. Advertising agencies competed to design the most creative stands, vying for public attention with displays of larger-than-life Pyrex plates, mock television sets, and, in 1963, a Brastemp washing machine made of translucent acrylic material that allowed attendees to see its inner workings. Live-action re-creations of commercial films gave visitors the feeling of being in the world of what had become the most important home appliance, as did the use of closed-circuit television, while musical spectacles allowed fans to see their idols live.[27]

From the first, the Automobile Salon was credited with making Brazilians believe in their country's arrival in the industrial age. For contemporaries, this achievement, more than the wonder and thirst inspired by such four-wheeled oddities as the amphibious *fusca* and the bar-car Kombi, mattered most. The inaugural fair, according to *PN*, "completely met its principal objective, which was to show visitors that Brazilian industry is an incontestable reality. Visiting the Salon's numerous *stands* . . . folks from all social classes could observe the 26 vehicles produced by the twelve firms currently operating in Brazil, plus the new vehicles about to be launched, as well as the colors that will be used in the 1961 models." The salon was also noteworthy for its inspiration, for while FENIT had been prompted by Alcântara Machado's experience in New York, the main referent for the automotive fair was Europe: "it followed, in its organization, the style of the great European automobile fairs, from the distribution of the vehicles and components on display, to the decoration of their surroundings." Brightly colored curtains and carpets enhanced the pavilion's modernist lines, offset by illumination described as fairylike, marvelous, and magical (*feérica*), while "photographic panels and mock-ups provide an exact idea of São Paulo's grand industrial park." Attendance jumped from 500,000 in 1960 to 1.2 million in 1968, when São Paulo's population was five million, the fair drawing thousands of people who did not belong to car-owning families.[28]

At the First Automobile Salon, children drove Brazilian-made go-carts. At FENIT and UD, distractions borrowed from retailing and the mass media beckoned. Beginning in 1961, AMCE went one better, offering an exposition especially for boys and girls, held for two weeks in October around the Day of the Child. Co-sponsored by FIESP and the state and municipal governments, the Children's Salon was a showcase for manufacturing and publishing interests. Like UD and the automotive salon, it was an instant success, the *Correio da Manhã* reporting, "Toys, clothes, shoes, treats, magazines, books and other products for the young public are attracting a considerable multitude to Ibirapuera." In addition to stands dispensing Coca-Cola, Kibon ice cream, and Nestlé and Toddy chocolate-milk drinks, there were playgrounds, pony rides, bicycle races, and roller-skating contests. Magic shows, circus performances, and exhibitions of cartoons and short films were other attractions, as were opportunities to meet beloved clowns and the stars of popular television series. Children could "play, see clowns, watch skating 'shows,' eat sweets," their joy leading São Paulo's middlebrow poet laureate to remark, "Caio gave the children of São Paulo an extra Christmas." The 1962 sequel was even more elaborate, "undeniably the greatest advertising event of October." The salon retained that status for years, "for the advertisements published in newspapers and magazines, 'jingles' on the radio and television broadcasting stations, and posters placed on the streets," and the diversions that made it "different from the other expositions—a mixture of fair and amusement park." For Alex Periscinoto, that distinction was its great strength: "Everyone receives the messages without noticing, and that is advertising's principal end."[29]

By the late 1960s, a common feature of the Children's Salon and the other consumer-friendly expositions loomed larger than distinctions between them. With attendances running upward of a million, AMCE's fairs had outgrown the infrastructure built for São Paulo's quadricentennial, despite extensions and add-ons. The solution was the building of a new complex on the north bank of the Tietê River, the Tupi name for which it claimed as its own. At its 1970 inauguration, timed for the opening of the Automobile Salon, Anhembi's promoters boasted that its 67,000 m² hall was sheltered by the "largest metal structure in the world" and could accommodate crowds of two million people. It was, according to an advertisement produced by Almap, "the largest exposition palace in the Americas."[30]

Ten years earlier, the cars on display at the first salon constituted proof of Brazil's arrival in the world of modern industry. Now, a structure built for the fairs and Fords of the future was emblematic of national greatness. The emphasis on structure, and in the advertisement's illustrations of the squat, smooth-lined exposition center, the world of architectural design, was noteworthy, as the fairs had increasingly emphasized design, especially visual design, industrial design, and fashion design, three other areas in which Brazil was believed to be coming into its own, with the founding of the country's first design firm in 1958, the creation of Rio's Higher Industrial Design School in 1963, and the *avants-premières* of experiments in export-quality fashion. Art and industry—or, better put, commercial artistry and manufacturing—were thereby joined much as the Museum of Modern Art's curator had envisioned in 1961.[31]

Over the same years, the presence of leaders of national standing had lent the expositions airs of civic communion: Kubitschek inaugurating FENIT and receiving a hero's welcome at the second Automobile Salon; his former vice president, João Goulart, attending the Children's Salon and Automobile Salon as president in his own right; a series of hard-faced presidents and ministers on hand for automotive fairs thereafter.[32] In this respect, a journalist's pairing of Kubitschek and the creator of the São Paulo expositions was not entirely fanciful: "It is difficult to say if Caio de Alcântara was the Juscelino of the business world or if Juscelino was the Caio of politics. Not by chance, the two were involved with the automobile industry, then the most expressive symbol of the advance of Brazilian industrialization. The Automobile Salons, among other fairs, made São Paulo the most important exposition center in Latin America." The expositions also, in a man-in-the-street view from the third UD, "make any Brazilian proud."[33]

As important as such patriotic effects were, they were only part of what made the fairs so successful. In a beachless Brazilian city underserved by public recreational facilities, the fairs offered relatively accessible, seemingly wholesome entertainment to middle-class families, attendance costing the equivalent of a movie ticket. Even Paulistanos of considerable means might attend an event, like FENIT, that featured live music by national attractions. At the UD, families not only could shop (some stands sold as well as displayed goods); they could comparison shop with an ease unknown since the days when São Paulo's retail trade was concentrated in a few downtown blocks. Free samples, something-for-nothing souvenirs, and other promotional giveaways made consumers even of attendees tapped out by the entrance fee. Prize drawings—five cars at the 1960 automotive fair, fourteen the following year—offered the chance to claim grander goods. To actual consumption were added virtual variants as attendees were encouraged to dream of being "future buyers" of new-model cars and futuristic kitchen sets. Beyond consuming dreams were entirely abstract responses to "a marvelous world of colors, lights, shapes, and movement." "The Fair," in an observer's words, "is a festival, the Fair is color, the Fair is people, the Fair is free gifts. It doesn't matter what gifts. At the Fair we get things. It doesn't matter what things. The Fair is fascinating."[34]

Media Mastery

While the AMCE fairs exerted their fascination over a single metropolitan area, increasing numbers of regional audiences came to be absorbed by television. Beginning in 1959, broadcasting expanded out of the southeast. Through the 1960s, Brazilian programming took shape, overseen by advertising and sales professionals. In the 1970s, the television business assumed its definitive structure with the consolidation of Rede Globo as the country's premiere national network. Over the same decades, developments in radio and publishing were conditioned by television's rise. Radio reached greater numbers than ever before, but as a poor adjunct to an ascendant medium. Magazine publishers split their efforts between addressing a shrinking general readership and serving segmented audiences. Despite a long-term contraction in the reach of general-interest magazines, publishers and their new-professional employees did well for themselves, as did the money men and managers of the newspaper trade, where a mass extinction of titles made way for near-monopoly.

After the inauguration of TV-Rio and TV-Itacolomi in 1955, there was a lull in the expansion of broadcasting facilities that lasted until 1959, when three new stations debuted, including the first two in Brazil's far south, in Porto Alegre and Curitiba. More than a dozen stations began broadcasting the following year, from Fortaleza to Londrina, including three Brasília stations. Amid this growth, São Paulo's fifth station, TV-Excelsior, debuted with a show-business premiere called Bossa Nove, in a play on the station's channel number (*nove*/nine) and the made-in-Brazil musical genre; among the show's attractions was a filmed short in which Kubitschek offered his best wishes. As *Propaganda* magazine had predicted, 1960 was "an authentic 'golden year'" for television, insiders ranking the expansion of broadcasting facilities as the year's most important development.[35]

Television's expansion continued thereafter, the number of broadcasting stations climbing from twenty-five in 1961 to thirty-eight in 1967, then reaching forty in 1968, fifty-three in 1970, and seventy-five in 1974. By the latter year, according to official sources, there was a station in every state except Alagoas.[36] The largest number of these stations belonged to the Associados group founded by Assis Chateaubriand, but ownership within that group had become less centralized than in 1955, when Chatô had exercised direct control over stations in São Paulo, Rio, and Belo Horizonte. Between 1959 and 1968, the tycoon's sloppy succession, serially debilitating strokes, and tardy demise made the Associados stations the "associates" indicated in the group's name: independently operated, loosely affiliated fiefs that responded to no single direction. The Associados group would thus be overtaken by better-connected, more tightly organized firms. All the major broadcasting groups, however, were akin in operating commercial stations true to their medium's U.S.-inspired origins.

The growth of broadcasting facilities was accompanied by increasing rates of television ownership. From a starting point of somewhere between six hundred thousand and seven hundred thousand sets in 1959, the number of televisions in Brazil reached one million between 1960 and 1961. The two-million mark was passed in the mid-1960s, the four-million mark by 1969–1970, a period in which boosters claimed that Brazil's market for television sets grew more quickly than that of any other country. By 1975, there were no fewer than ten million sets in Brazil, located in every corner of the country but concentrated in the urban southeast.[37] In proportional terms, fewer than one in ten households owned televisions in 1960; by 1970, a quarter did; by 1972, a third.[38] Between 1961 and 1970, São Paulo's household ownership rates increased from 45 to 85 percent, while Rio's increased from 42 to 82 percent.[39] Perhaps more remarkably, household ownership rates for the Rio metropolitan area, which joined grindingly poor suburbs and a few mostly rural counties with the former national capital and its sister city of Niterói, increased from 51.3 percent to 77.8 percent between 1967–1968 and 1974.[40]

Adding the question of viewership to that of ownership, it had been axiomatic that Brazil's television audience of about two million people in 1957–1958 was overwhelmingly upper and middle class. As the advertising executive Marcos Margulies remarked, confident that the expense of household sets would prevent sudden shifts in ownership, "94% of television-watchers belong to classes A and B." He was mistaken, however, as poorer Brazilians in the urban southeast came to buy televisions as soon as credit facilities afforded them the chance, just as had been the case with radios a generation earlier, while public accommodations reached audiences nearly as far afield as Hermes Lima's radio fans of 1938. "Thus, television, which at first was a privilege of class A, then becoming to be common among class B, is now becoming much more apparent in neighborhoods that lean toward C," according to a business journalist. "In São Paulo . . . strictly industrial districts present strong concentrations of antennas." He went on to cite a photograph of a Rio favela, recently the subject of much comment: "There were no cinderblock or brick walls, but the television antennas were innumerable." Called upon to explain the fact that there were more sets in Rio's northern districts than its southern beachfront, an IBOPE executive explained, "The poor watch more television than the rich." By 1961, according to an IBOPE study, 38 percent of Rio's television sets were in the hands of class C and D families, a figure that rose to 43 percent in São Paulo. Many non-television-owners taxed their neighbors' patience as "televisitors," while others watched on public sets, a Minas correspondent of 1960 reporting that in TV-Itacolomi's broadcast area, "every self-respecting bar has its own television set."[41]

All the while, the number of viewers increased, passing the twenty-million mark in the late 1960s and reaching twenty-five million soon thereafter. By the mid-1970s, Brazil's television audience was estimated at forty-five million people, by which point 60 percent of its sets belonged to members of the "lower classes" identified by letters C and D. The democratization of television ownership, however, did not alter the logic behind Margulies's assertion that 94 percent of viewers belonged to classes A and B. By 1963, "about 35 to 40 percent" of Brazilian consumers could be reached by television. Eleven years later, a similar, if more precise, case was made: "TV reaches more than 40% of the Country's population and 64.28% of its active consumer market."[42]

Margulies's logic was that television provided advertisers access to sizable proportions of the country's wealthy and near-wealthy people. In what might seem paradoxical at first, media managers created a more effective commercial vehicle by limiting advertisers' roles to sponsorship and the purchase of airtime for commercials and by establishing ceilings on advertising's airtime. Stations, having asserted control over production and programming, established uniform, audience-friendly schedules. By the early 1970s, viewers could turn on their sets knowing that they would only be subjected to twelve to fifteen minutes' worth of recorded commercial shorts per hour, whereas fifteen years earlier spots, slides, and the sales pitches of *garotas-propaganda* might stretch on for a half hour or more. Many of the executives that effected this transition had worked in advertising; some had direct experience of North American broadcasting. The Brazilian television they created obeyed the same rationalizing, standardizing, professionalizing impulse.[43]

Advertisers responded with increased spending. In 1963, for the first time, more was spent on television advertising than in any other forum, the audiovisual medium establishing a commercial dominance it would not relinquish. In the early 1970s, television absorbed one-half of all billings, eclipsing the total spent on radio, magazines, and newspapers. During this turn from relative dominance to absolute dominion, television became a much more commercially efficient vehicle, the per-household cost of broadcast advertising dropping between 1971 and 1974.[44]

The years bridging the 1960s and 1970s saw the emergence of programming patterns that held for decades. The year 1960, in particular, witnessed two key developments: a deluge of North American programs and the introduction of videotape. The imported shows, called *enlatados* in Portuguese translation of "canned," played an outsized role, as viewers encountered such delights as *Bonanza, Lassie, Father Knows Best, The Untouchables, The Donna Reed Show, The Flintstones, Johnny Quest, Tom & Jerry, Superman, Mr. Ed,* and *Bewitched*. Videotape, meanwhile, was a spur to local production. The most widely viewed moving images of Brasília's inauguration, for example, were captured on videotapes flown to stations throughout the country. Videotape also provided Rio- and São Paulo–produced comedy shows with audiences throughout Brazil.[45]

In 1961, work began on Brazil's first serial, developed by Norton, sponsored by Nestlé, and directed by a young Paulistano who cut his teeth making commercial films featuring Willys cars and Climax washing machines. Titled *O Vigilante Rodoviário*, it followed a law-loving highway patrolman as he pursued evildoers in a Brazilian-made Simca. According to its producer, "We created a Brazilian hero who could compete with the imported ones . . . so as to counterbalance the avalanche of foreign films and demonstrate the potential of Brazilian cinema for TV," with a Lassie-like mascot "who does the same stunts as its counterparts on American TV." Star and sidekick were a success on the Associados stations and in a spin-off comic book, drawing crowds at the AMCE Children's Salon.[46]

Even as experiments in filmed and taped production continued, live programming remained crucial. Live-audience variety shows, despite handwringing over particularly tasteless bits, delivered reliably high IBOPE-verified ratings that executives manipulated to make their stations more attractive to advertisers, and thus the hosts Chacrinha, Hebe Camargo, and Sílvio Santos became fixtures. More elite audiences were reached by Repórter Esso's heirs, news broadcasts produced by stations rather than advertisers but no less amenable to business interests. In the 1960s, musical broadcasting became more prominent, perhaps due in part to the importance of costumed performance to some of the decade's new musical forms, from the *iê-iê-iê* of the mop-topped Jovem Guarda to the theatrics of the counter-cultural Tropicalistas who were such draws at the AMCE fairs; whatever the reason, musical programming was successful on a scale unseen up to that point, delivering young, middle-class audiences to stations and advertisers. Sports broadcasting, on the other hand, was already a proven success. By 1960, audiences of 1.5 million for weekend association-football broadcasts in Rio and São Paulo were common. Early linkups between the two cities created larger audiences for intermunicipal games, but the live broadcast of international matches awaited the creation of a nationwide telecommunications network in 1969–1970.[47]

At that point, international football's only rival in IBOPE-measured audience share was the telenovela. Videotape enabled nightly broadcasts of relatively well-produced novelas of a hundred or more episodes in Brazil's largest cities even before the national telecommunication network went online. The genre's breakthrough hit was a remake of the radionovela *O direito de nascer*, put on in 1964–1965 for Unilever's Brazilian subsidiary. The influence of the Cuban tradition imported for Colgate did not end with script or sponsor type. Through the 1960s, the Cuban exile Gloria Magadan, formerly of Colgate-Palmolive, was Brazil's most prolific scriptwriter, typing up Spanish-language dramas set in faraway lands that were translated into Portuguese by an assistant. Magadan's work, however, increasingly lost ground to scripts by native-born writers, helped by research on audience preference, which permitted the replotting of series as they aired.[48]

Although no one station was responsible for all these developments, they have come to be identified with a single network, Rede Globo, which grew out of the Rio station TV-Globo, founded in 1965. As their names suggest, network and station alike were offshoots of the media group based around *O Globo*, the "champion of promotions" captained by Roberto Marinho. But they were more than that. At the origins of the Globo group's involvement in television was a partnership with Time-Life, part of a broader Latin American push by the media conglomerate, which had gotten a late start in television in the United States and now sought to make up for lost time abroad. The partnership between Globo and Time-Life was illegal under Brazil's postwar constitution (and thus subjected to various artifices), but that proved no impediment. For Marinho and TV-Globo, the deal was more than worthwhile, providing the station with ample funds to import state-of-the-art technology, raid rival stations for talent, and expand beyond Rio. The relationship also eased access to "know-how" and programming (early on, TV-Globo was deeply dependent on *enlatados*). However, it did not produce income for Time-Life, whose U.S.-based executives were increasingly frustrated by the lack of profits, puzzled by Brazilian inflation, and spooked by the fallout from investigations into the illegality of their investment and its potential to tarnish their "brand" back in the United States. And so Time-Life sold out to Marinho at a moment when, unbeknownst to the executives in New York, his incipient network was poised to become Brazil's largest and most profitable. According to Joe Wallach, whom Time-Life sent to Brazil in 1965 but who ended up on the Globo side of the split-up, the U.S. company, having spent about $5 million in Brazil, received $3.85 million under terms worked out in 1969–1970. This sum, however, did not come from a sell-off of joint properties, much less out of Marinho's pockets; it came from Brazilian bankers, at the encouragement of Minister of Finance Antonio Delfim Netto. Even as the relationship between Time-Life and Globo came apart, the first section of the national telecommunications network went online; before the ink on the divorce was dry, TV-Globo was turning a profit; by the time the

1970–1974 payment schedule negotiated by Wallach had run out, Rede Globo was Brazil's most important network, its leading advertising vehicle, and a very big business in its own right.[49]

The question of how much of Globo's success was owed to the Time-Life deal may be unanswerable. Many of the programming changes identified with Globo were pioneered by other stations. Aside from Wallach, all the key personnel in Globo's rise had learned the business working at those stations and for Brazilian-, U.S.-, and European-owned advertising agencies. The weakness of Globo's rivals in the 1960s and 1970s may have been as important as Time-Life's contributions: the Associados were rudderless, while TV-Excelsior suffered from its own succession issues and associations with the political order eliminated between 1964 and 1965, while TV-Globo and its sister stations were amenable to centralized direction and the Globo group was well connected politically, as illustrated by Delfim Netto's loan-procuring assistance.

Whatever the balance between these factors and others (good fortune and insurance fraud seem to have also been important), the outcome was Rede Globo becoming the country's first truly national medium by the mid-1970s, reaching nearly every Brazilian state and an area containing 99 percent of its television sets with eighteen hours of programming per day over the telecommunications system created by the military government. More of this programming was Brazilian-produced than not: *enlatados* and Hollywood movies had been important at first, but in the longer term, novelas and live-audience shows were cheaper and more profitable.[50] National coverage, nationally produced programming, and the fact that a majority of the country's televisions were tuned to Globo at any one time led observers to see the network as delivering on older aspirations for Brazilian mass communications: that radio, and later television, would make the country one. Globo executives, for their part, encouraged the perception of television serving "as the country's integrating force."[51]

Beyond Rio, São Paulo, Belo Horizonte, Brasília, and Recife, where Globo owned stations outright, the São Paulo one reaching deep into the interior through retransmitters, this national—and nationalizing—coverage was achieved through deals with local affiliates, which surrendered 50 percent of their commercial airtime in exchange for national programming and half of the billings for commercials aired during that airtime. That these arrangements mirrored U.S. standards was no accident. As a network director declared, "Globo's model is the model of an American network, even in advertising. Everything, even the mode of speech, is American. . . . All this comes from the United States, studied and timed. This is the great 'enlatado' of TV in Brazil."[52]

Brazilianization was thus an effect of behind-the-scenes emulation of the United States, the undiluted drive for profits creating a network that was "American" in its structure, standardization, and rationalization, everything that made Rede Globo in some ways as "canned" as the *enlatados*. Here was a telling contrast with the grubbing, even gangsterish early days of Brazilian media. Assis Chateaubriand had shaken down captains of industry in person and used his empire to get himself, and his principal adjutant, elected to the Senate ("Senator Corleone, Governor Corleone . . . ," an old man whispered). Roberto Marinho's executives met with other managers armed with briefing memoranda, charts, and the other ephemera of the corporate boardroom, ready to make their case for advertising-schedule "X" or "Y," while their boss avoided the political limelight, instead operating over the telephone and in private meetings with the country's most powerful men.

Marinho's agency-trained staff also saw fortunes where others had scarcely thought to look, as well as where their predecessors had taken backroom pickings or left them to underlings. One result was a lucrative sideline in the recording industry based on the sale of novela soundtracks. Another was the replacement of informal, payola-like practices that produced on-screen product placement with a formal system called "merchandising," in which firms paid a network-established premium to have their products featured on Globo shows. Likewise, early media groups had been content to rely on research produced by IBOPE or Marplan, perhaps complemented by small, in-house test-audience operations or occasional agency services, while Globo hired a former IBOPE director to create a research division that conducted millions of interviews annually. Globo's new division went beyond measuring audience size and composition in seeking to divine the preferences and motivations of sought-after viewers. According to the research division's findings, the leading figure in the "Brazilian television public" was a married woman in her early thirties, with children, better off than most, but not rich: "It is she that buys everything for the man. The husband only really chooses his suit and tie. The rest, down to his briefs, she buys. She reveals herself to be more understanding and more modern than her companion." As Globo's researchers worked to establish what this moderately modern-minded wife, mother, and purchasing agent wanted to watch, the network's producers and writers tailored programming accordingly, another spur to the emphasis on novela production and a key to Globo's media mastery.[53]

As of the 1950s and early 1960s, however, such developments lay in the future. Even as television billings increased at the expense of radio expenditures, more Brazilians listened to broadcasts of Kubitschek's modernity shows than watched them on television. Developments in radio and the press may have occurred in the shadow of television's rise but were lastingly important on their own, commercially, culturally, and socially.

By certain metrics, radio had never had it so good. In 1958 and 1962, Brazil's stations faced no competition in presenting live broadcasts of the national team's rout of the competition in successive World Cups, claiming audiences in the millions and sponsorships from Gillette, Brahma, Ipiranga, and Firestone, lined up by Inter-Americana, MPM, and JWT.[54] The proportion of households that owned radios continued to rise, even through the mid-1960s recession. Meanwhile, new transistor models put radio within reach of the rural poor, ownership of battery-operated sets reaching the unelectrified hamlets that were home to a majority of Brazilians; thereafter, in the words of an eyewitness to radio's arrival in the Bahian fishing village of Arembepe, "everything changed." In 1964, radio-manufacturing interests reported sales exceeding one million units for the first time; sales dipped the following year, in the pit of that decade's recession, but rose again in 1966, then topped two million in 1970 and three million in 1973. In the mid-1960s, at least 60 percent of households owned radios; by the early 1970s, at least 70 percent; by the mid-1970s, 75 percent. By then, metropolitan listeners with up-to-date sets could choose between the AM bandwidth and FM stations.[55]

Over the same period, however, radio's commercial importance and cultural relevance were in retreat. Advertisers in the southeast began to divert billings to television in the late 1950s, initiating a decline against which the quadrennial splurges of the World Cup were epiphenomena. With sponsors fleeing, the lavishly produced live-music spectacles of the 1940s and 1950s were impossible to sustain; with the success of the telenovela, its all-audio forerunner was an anachronism. Specialization—in news, sports, prerecorded music, or some combination thereof, often designed to appeal to a particular demographic group—was the order of the day. There were some success stories, though it was no coincidence that these were linked to television concerns: Rádio Globo in Rio, and, in São Paulo, the station founded as Rádio Pan-Americana, which became Jovem Pan, a reference to the live-music programming of the Jovem Guarda obtained through its association with TV-Record. But the irresistible trend was decline, epitomized by Rádio Nacional, which lost the opportunity to expand into television and failed to recapture audience share as an explicitly women's-interest Rádio Nacional Mulher. By the 1970s, notwithstanding its name, it was just another local station. Nor was this shrinking of Rádio Nacional's reach exceptional: radio had become an overwhelmingly local medium, if one with a far larger aggregate audience than in its golden age. Among the ironies was that at a point in time at which radio reached more people than ever, audience size no longer mattered as it once did. What might have counted as "good *Ibope*" in the 1950s only added to the perception that radio had become a poor people's medium ten to fifteen years later, at a moment when Brazil's political economy was engineered in consummate indifference to the great mass of its population, a perception paralleled by shifts in domestic material culture and household leisure. Even as radio ownership grew, table-top and cathedral-set ownership rates fell below television ownership rates in São Paulo and Rio, with wealthier households leading the way; for such families, two or three transistor sets could provide occasional distraction to individual family members; for others, radio ceased to be part of home life, replaced by televisions and hi-fi sets.[56]

One or more magazines would still feature in most such homes, as magazine publishing weathered television's onslaught better than radio, retaining greater commercial and cultural relevance, even as circulation fell relative to population. Several features of the medium contributed to its staying power. First, magazines offered advertisers and audiences color, which television, as yet, did not. Second, they were better suited to what would be called "audience segmentation" than radio, television, and newspapers. Third, because magazines required some literacy, they signaled distinction; on this basis, a medium with a smaller readership would be preferred to a larger one by advertisers and image-conscious urbanites. One result was the ever-increasing prosperity of the Bloch and Abril publishing groups.

In the late 1950s, *Manchete* overtook *O Cruzeiro* as Brazil's leading weekly, a process within which Adolpho Bloch's magazine made itself part of the monument-making of the Kubitschek presidency. While Assis Chateaubriand had held out for a government subvention in return for reporting on Brasília, Bloch's magazine threw itself into covering Kubitschek's capital as it rose from the dust, confident that repayment in official favor and public enthusiasm would follow. All five hundred thousand copies of *Manchete*'s first special issue on the building of Brasília sold out in two days; in April 1960, more than seven hundred thousand copies of the issue on its inauguration were sold. These efforts, featuring gorgeous, full-color images that remained etched in Brazilian memories long after the accompanying texts had been forgotten, were praised by the president: "*Manchete* and Brasília are two sisters in optimism and cannot be separated."[57]

Brasília was not the extent of the affinities between *Manchete* and Kubitschek's program. As the cultural historian Cláudia Mesquita pointed out, "The Blochs' magazine embraced the national-developmentalist program of Juscelino, whom they supported in an unrestricted way, helping to divulge its trademarks." Like Kubitschek's developmentalism, *Manchete*'s distribution was focused on the southeast; indeed, it was even more tightly concentrated on Rio and São Paulo. It had meant a lot to Chateaubriand to establish *O Cruzeiro* as a nationally distributed periodical, but Bloch and his staff reasoned that advertisers would prefer a slickly produced vehicle read by a smaller, richer, predominantly urban and southeastern audience, no matter how much higher the venerable weekly's readership was. At that point, Bloch's project and the interests of Kubitschek's pet industry coincided: "The fact is that, with a magazine . . . the circulation of which was concentrated at the peak of the capitalist pyramid of Rio and São Paulo, Bloch convinced the nascent automobile industry, among other industries, that it was better business to advertise to its public than to the dispersed public of *O Cruzeiro*." This "market with greater purchasing power" was offered news of the "jet set" and the latest fashions, including cooperation between Standard and *Manchete* on behalf of Rhodia's winter line for 1961, in which celebrity advertising matched reporting that asked, "What will be *IN* in the winter?" As this collaboration suggests, *Manchete* beat *O Cruzeiro* not only, or even primarily, by becoming identified with the civic fervor of Brasília, but rather because it was more attuned to the interests of the country's advertisers: "what happened was that *Manchete* had better 'merchandising.'"[58]

Alongside *Manchete*, the Bloch group continued to publish the women's-interest titles *Jóia* and *Sétimo Céu*, while Abril put out increasing numbers of titles aimed at specific female audiences. *Capricho* remained the most widely distributed, but downmarket and upmarket women's magazines also sold in the hundreds of thousands to audiences identified by letters A through D, each published on the assumption that "women are the masters of the market." The most significant was launched in 1961 with an appeal to advertisers: "The explosive evolution of the middle class requires a magazine to direct, inform, and support the growing number of housewives who want to (and should) adapt themselves to the pace of modern life. *Claudia* will be aimed at these women and dedicated to finding solutions to their new problems. *Claudia* will not forget, however, that women are more interested in polishers than politics, in the kitchen than contraband, in their own world than other planets." In other words, the new magazine would be an ideal vehicle for advertising goods for the home, the natural habitat of the middle-class woman. Industrial and commercial concerns responded enthusiastically, contributing a volume of advertising that equaled the page count of editorial copy, the latter purposefully difficult to distinguish from the former in an editorial-commercial mix representing what the magazine's founding editor called "the Brazilianizing of a monthly women's magazine formula that had already been applied, for several years, in the USA . . . and in Europe." As in other countries, application of the formula was not without its contradictions: beginning in 1963, *Claudia* provided a forum for the writer Carmen da Silva, whose column addressed women who did not fit the mold of 1961, including unmarried women and women who worked outside the home. Monthly responses to reader queries and quandaries updated the genre, with Carmen da Silva providing a therapeutic approach to correspondents' problems, informed by psychology and sociology, that stood in contrast to the sentimental, traditionalistic stance of conventional advice columnists, while advocating extradomestic work as a matter of personal fulfillment, calling for the legalization of divorce, and introducing comparatively frank discussions of sex and sexuality. These topics could not be discussed in a family newspaper, much less on radio or television, another advantage magazines had in reaching segmented audiences. Given the social conservatism of the Brazilian 1960s, it should not surprise that cultural historians, feminist intellectuals, and others describe Carmen da Silva as playing a key part in sociocultural change. Her success in drawing class A and B readers was such that she could even risk an occasional swipe at the inequities and artificially induced desires of Brazilian consumer capitalism.[59]

Magazines aimed at male audiences were fewer and more exclusive. Abril's *Quatro Rodas*, an automotive-interest monthly launched in 1960, was soon printed in runs of one hundred thousand. The Brazilian edition of *Popular Mechanics* (*Mecânica Popular*) was designed for a similar audience and offered much *Quatro Rodas*–like coverage. These two magazines—each covering the annual Automobile Salon enthusiastically—were aimed at classes A and B, like *Claudia*, but unlike *Claudia* they had no downmarket counterparts. Magazine publishers of the 1960s offered nothing specifically for men whose incomes did not place them in at least the middle class, as such men had lower market profiles than their wives and daughters. More exclusive audiences were reached by magazines aimed at upper-class segments: *Visão*, produced for businessmen generally; *O Dirigente Industrial*, for manufacturers; *O Dirigente Rural*, for captains of rural industry. Each of these publications was owned by a U.S.-based firm and initially distributed to a large section of their target audience for free, though some years after its founding *Visão* became a general-interest weekly, featuring such family-friendly fare as *Shopping News*–style guides to Christmas gifts.[60]

Creating a general-interest weekly on the model of *Time* had fired the ambition of Brazilian publishing interests since the 1940s. Several attempts failed before the Abril group finally succeeded. The ambition belonged to the group's heir apparent, Roberto Civita, of the São Paulo School of Advertising's entering class of 1959, who had interned at Time-Life in New York and served as *Quatro Rodas*'s advertising director. In 1968, he convinced his father that the country was ready for a *Time*-style weekly, to be called *Veja*, into which they poured money, including for a Standard-designed national campaign. After an initial, publicity-driven success, however, *Veja*'s newsstand sales tanked. Only after five years in the red did *Veja* find its place as Brazil's

Time, which made it a major outlet for advertising high-end goods. By then, *Veja* reached a far smaller proportion of the population than that reached by *Manchete* fifteen years earlier, never mind *O Cruzeiro* in the 1940s. But that was the point, Abril having fulfilled half its promise of providing advertisers with "intelligent consumers."[61]

In the meantime, the newspaper world experienced the publishing equivalent of a mass extinction. The fallen included the *Correio da Manhã*, *Diario Carioca*, *Diario de Noticias*, and the most important links in the Diários Associados chain. Rio's *Ultima Hora* survived, if only barely, but its regional editions were shut down or sold off, putting an end to Samuel Wainer's dream of a newspaper of national reach. Many factors contributed to the disappearance of so many newspapers so quickly. Mismanagement, particularly in the Associados group, played a part. Some titles suffered for their owners or contributors' politics, *Ultima Hora* most grievously, but also the *Correio da Manhã*. A long-term decline in the proportion of advertising revenues directed toward the press contributed, though under normal conditions, its effects would have been more evenly spread. As it happened, a longtime aspiration of advertising, sales-promotion, and market-research specialists gave a handful of newspapers the opportunity to establish a de facto oligopoly. For years, the new professionals had sought a Brazilian equivalent of the audit bureau, which they would call the Instituto Verificador de Circulação (IVC), to provide independently verifiable production, sales, and circulation data, while newspaper interests had resisted, as a bloc. In the early 1960s, the most widely circulating Rio newspapers, aware of their position of strength, broke ranks and joined the IVC. Their weaker competition, no less aware of their position, faced a choice between two unhappy alternatives: they could refuse to open their books and lose advertising revenue or they could agree, have their lower circulations exposed, and lose that income all the same. The result, combined with crippling political pressures on *Ultima Hora* and *Correio da Manhã*, which had backed the IVC, was that the country's most important, commercially successful newspapers of the late 1960s retained their position for decades, growing in size as they gorged themselves on advertising aimed at their class A and B audiences, leaving scraps to newspapers reliant upon newsstand sales to working-class men otherwise overlooked by publishers and mass-market advertisers, such as *O Dia* and *A Notícia*.[62]

The four dominant newspapers were *O Globo*, the *Jornal do Brasil*, *O Estado de S. Paulo*, and the *Folha de S. Paulo*, the last representing the consolidation of the *Folhas* titles. In 1973, one of the *Folha de S. Paulo*'s leading figures confessed that while his ideal ratio of editorial copy to advertising was 1:1, the balance often tilted in favor of advertising. Issues of one hundred or more pages could still carry a lot of news, as well as the now-customary complement of horoscopes, comic strips, advice columns, Hollywood gossip, society reportage, and fashion features, but the business of journalism was business for the *Folha*'s leading figure, a former radio salesman and faithful reader of Dale Carnegie's *How to Make Friends and Influence People* named Octávio Frias de Oliveira. "Like Roberto Marinho and Victor Civita," Frias's son remembered, "my father helped bring a business mentality to the seigneurial, pre-capitalist environment of the press of that era. Journalistic firms came to be less the instrument of political power or mundane prestige (when not of shady dealings) to effectively become businesses—aimed at meeting the demands of the consuming public so as to widen their markets and profit margins." These "modernizing entrepreneurs" were *"self-made men. . . .* It was the first generation of Brazilian entrepreneurs whose inspiration was the United States, no longer England. It was also the first to employ rational methods of administration, such as planning associated with predefined goals, cost controls, personnel training, the intensive use of advertising etc." Filial piety and other distortions aside, Frias Filho was on to something.[63]

Keh-tching!

As disparate as these developments may appear, they shared one key feature. The factors in the success of the *Folha de S. Paulo*, Victor Civitas's Abril, and Roberto Marinho's Globo identified by Octávio Frias Filho would elsewhere be called "marketing." *Manchete*'s besting of *O Cruzeiro* was described as a case study for a "student of 'marketing.'" AMCE's fairs were "very efficient *marketing* tools," with which the firm "contributed decisively to the revision of national industry's Marketing practices." Kubitschek's media-savvy performances were an early iteration of what would be called "political marketing," put on as Genival Rabelo and Manoel de Vasconcellos planned "the first Brazilian magazine of 'marketing.'" Launched as *Indústria & Mercados*, on the drawing board its working title had been *Marketing*.[64]

By then, the English-language term had circulated among Brazilian advertising men for two decades, though to a very limited extent before the 1950s. Indeed, its circulation was so limited that many practitioners dated its appearance to much later. In the early 1950s, recalled Walter Clark Bueno, "one didn't even speak of marketing." For Roberto Duailibi, "the concept of *marketing* was nonexistent" until later: "With the arrival of the automobiles, in 1958, came the money. And money creates everything." Caio de Alcântara Machado remembered it emerging later still, declaring of the early 1960s, "At that time the word marketing didn't exist." Turning from personal anecdotes to participant histories, Francisco Gracioso described the 1950s as "a phase of primitive *marketing*," followed by consolidation in the 1960s and expansion in the 1970s. More descriptively, Carlos Roberto Chueiri, who joined JWT in 1958, wrote that at that point "the practice of *marketing*" was incipient, incipience yielding to "deep and perceptible growth of the *marketing* mentality" in the 1960s, with "the total integration of *marketing* within firms" occurring thereafter.[65]

But what was "marketing"? How could it be defined? How might it be translated into Portuguese? In what might seem an inversion of the proper sequence, the first question was often that of Portuguese translation rather than definition in any language, which makes more sense when the protean qualities of the English-language term become clearer. Definition, as often as not, yielded to description and elaborate listings of what marketing entailed. A review of these discussions does not yield a unitary definition of marketing, but it does reveal the principal sources of marketing-related ideas in Brazil, as well as the key circuits through which these ideas traveled, together with some suggestion of their appeal.

The question of Portuguese translation goes back to 1952, when Manoel de Vasconcellos confessed he found "marketing" impossible to translate. Armando de Moraes Sarmento replied with McCann's translation, the *atividade de comerciar* ("activity of carrying on commerce"), which Sarmento later amplified to *atividade global de comerciar* ("global activity of carrying on commerce"). The terms *mercadologia* and *mercadização* ("marketology" and "marketization") were coined somewhat later. *Comercialização* ("commercialization") was applied by 1958, enjoying a long run thereafter, alone and as *comercialização global*. *Mercadagem* ("marketage") did not fare as well, nor did imports from Spanish America, which included *mercadotecnia* ("marketechnique"). Perhaps the most precise of proposed translations was *mercancia*, a term most often used to refer to goods that in an older sense means "to market as an activity"; it met the same fate as *mercadagem* and *mercadotecnia*. In some instances, debate and discussion failed to produce any translation. As an executive remarked of a 1967 conference, "We spent a week arguing over gerunds with which to translate the word. . . . But no one knew what it meant."[66]

Confusion encouraged such incomprehension, as Brazilian definitions of marketing piled up over the years, local professionals citing authories from abroad along the way. McCann's early 1950s definition—borrowed from the American Association of Advertising Agencies—was "the execution of all business activities that serve to direct the flow of goods and services from the producer to the consumer," though Sarmento's "activity of carrying on commerce" and "global activity of carrying on commerce" became definitions in their own right, and variations on all three were widely used. A *PN* columnist provided a pithy summation, treating marketing synonymously with the "process of production and distribution." In 1961, Raimar Richers cited an American Marketing Association definition, though his translation was inexact; he also registered his lack of enthusiasm for that definition, preferring an unconventional tag he attributed to a contributor to *Fortune*: "Marketing is the delivery of a standard of living."[67] A more involved definition, from 1969, was "the complex of operations that involve the life of a product or service, from the moment at which its production or implantation is planned, to the moment at which it is accepted or acquired by the consumer or user." By that point, new definitions were emerging at a clip. In José Maria Campos Manzo's booklength introduction, it was the "technique of winning consumers at the lowest cost and with the highest profit margin," thus, "to sell a lot at a profit." As a contributor to FIESP's monthly magazine put it, "Marketing is an incontestable economic phenomenon that is easy to verify: the rapid shift of the core economic problem to the plane of distribution and consumption." For Harry Simonsen Jr., "marketing necessarily includes all of a firm's activities, from production to sale and the providing of post-sale services to the consumer." In 1971, Abril and McGraw-Hill copublished Simonsen and Duailibi's *Criatividade: A formulação de alternativas em marketing*; the most developed of the book's three stabs at defining the term was "the interaction and the integration of all the firm's operational factors and of all its functional activities, oriented to the consumer of its products, ideas, or services, with the objectives of optimizing its long-term profits and promoting conditions for the survival and expansion of the firm." Writing at around the same time, Francisco Gracioso preferred Unilever's in-house definition—"Marketing is the planning and execution of all aspects of a product (or service), in the consumer's interest, seeking to always maximize consumption and minimize prices, all this resulting in continual, long-term profits for the firm"—while Otto Scherb quoted a definition of unidentified origin: "the technique of identification and measurement of existing opportunities in a market and of generating the means to take advantage of these opportunities."[68]

From early on, definitions of marketing by listing its functions or component parts were as common as attempts to establish any essence the idea may have possessed, the question "What is it?" yielding to "What does it do?" or "What does it consist of?" Thus, in a 1959 primer, Caio Domingues provided a definition like the ones his colleagues attributed to the American Association of Advertising Agencies and the American Marketing Association, but followed it with a description (not, strictly speaking, a definition): *"Marketing* 'covers all the commercial activities necessary to effecting the transfer of property over merchandise (or services) and to achieving its distribution.'" Marketing, he went on to write, included merchandising, advertising, and sales promotion; taking his primer as a whole, it apparently included public relations as well. A contemporary paired an updated version of McCann's translation-turned-definition (the "global activity of carrying on business, with an emphasis on consumption") with a narrative description of what was presented as the functioning of the U.S. economy: "to produce in a race against obsolescence, seeking to satisfy an ever-more demanding public, in an extremely dynamic market, in which the watchword is free competition . . . opening the way to the 'American way of life.'" Another description, this one of European inspiration, held that marketing entailed "a modern conceptualization of production, distribution, promotion, commercialization, and consumption." In what may have been the first book written in Portuguese dealing exclusively and explicitly with marketing, one finds an "account of modern Marketing methods," much description of "the functions of marketing," and even a discussion of "its hermeneutics," but little more than a sideways glance at definition. This volume was soon followed by works featuring more straightforward lists of the component parts of what specialists called the *complexo de marketing* ("marketing complex," a riff on "marketing mix"), ranging from product design to distribution.[69]

There were three main circuits in which these ideas circulated and through which they were diffused. First, there were the new professionals and the institutions they created beginning in the 1930s. Second, there was the São Paulo School of Business Administration. Third, there were the branches of what were beginning to be called multinational corporations. While the three circuits are conceptually discrete—the institutions created by the new professionals were separate from the business school, and both were organizationally distinct from the multinationals—there was considerable overlap of personnel between them.

In Brazil, it was advertising executives who first embraced marketing ideas, building on the experience of their North American counterparts, the "first great prosperity professionals, those meritorious creators of mass consumption." As with this cohort's earlier turns to sales promotion and market research, there was a great deal of auto-didacticism involved: after-hours spent poring over imported texts, following debates in local trade publications and studying rare translations, puzzling over what the term meant and how it might be translated. Prominent in this group were JWT, McCann, and Lintas executives. "In Brazil, the advertising man was," in the words of one such veteran, "the pioneer of modern methods of 'marketing.'" When Rodolfo Lima Martensen drew up a blueprint for what became the São Paulo Advertising School, he cited North American literature on marketing. By the 1960s, marketing had been added to its core curriculum, along with market research, media, and planning; beginning in 1973 it was offered as a separate course of study, a change reflected in the institution's rechristening as the Higher Advertising and Marketing School (ESPM).[70]

Sales professionals explored marketing alongside and independently of these efforts. Ruy Chalmers, formerly of Sears and McCann, and a founding member of the São Paulo Advertising School's faculty, instructed Mappin's managers in marketing in 1955–1956, while also publishing on the subject. In Rio, instruction for sales professionals featuring marketing was offered by a Retail Managers' Club and an institute founded by *PN*'s sales-promotion columnist, which trained more than three thousand people by 1960. Formal courses with a marketing focus were offered in the two cities by their respective sales-professionals' associations, the Association of Sales Directors of Rio de Janeiro having created a Center for Marketing and Management Practices and the ADVB operating a Higher Sales School at its São Paulo headquarters. The ADVB also published a monthly magazine, the *Revista Brasileira de Vendas*, a medium for much marketing-related instruction, renamed *Marketing* in 1967, at which point an "ADVB Federation" joined the São Paulo and Rio groups with associations in Minas Gerais, Paraná, Rio Grande do Sul, and Ceará. Alongside these activities, the ADVB sponsored publication of some of the first Brazilian-authored books on marketing, and so the front matter of Chalmers's *Marketing* (1969) and Roberto Simões's *Iniciação ao marketing* (1970) included a stamp of approval bearing the group's slogan, "A Better Standard of Living for All, through Sales."[71]

Another circuit for marketing's spread was the São Paulo School of Business Administration (EAESP), chartered in 1952 under the auspices of the Getúlio Vargas Foundation, a paragovernmental research and training conglomerate. The business school was a binational undertaking, financed by the Brazilian and U.S. governments, the latter paying the salaries of the North Americans who participated in curriculum design, cotaught the first classes, and trained Brazilian faculty who would replace them, training complemented by graduate study in the United States, also funded by the U.S. government under the Point IV technical-assistance program. The North American faculty, from Michigan State University's school of business, taught marketing, production, finance, and general administration, while Brazilian lawyers provided instruction in commercial and labor law. In 1954, forty-one businessmen enrolled in EAESP's first executive-extension course, consisting of twelve weeks' worth of full-time instruction in all five areas, modeled after Harvard Business School's (HBS) Middle Management Program and emphasizing the case method synonymous with HBS. Offered twice yearly, it was completed by more than six hundred executives by 1960. In the interim, EAESP began offering four-year instruction, while the Brazilian junior faculty, who initially served as translators, took on teaching responsibilities. By

1960, twenty-eight of the school's assistant professors, all of them Brazilian, had received master's degrees in business administration from Michigan State and training in case-method teaching at HBS; some also undertook doctoral-level training in the United States. Upon their return, they taught in all three of EAESP's formal programs of study, the school having added a postgraduate course in 1958, while contributing to its professional journal and directing its research institute. All three fora delivered on the school's larger mission as "a service center for business and government." EAESP was a model for university-level business education elsewhere in Brazil, where copycat curricula were administered by professors trained in São Paulo and at Michigan State in cooperation with the federal ministry of education. Back in São Paulo, the EAESP occupied an increasingly conspicuous geographic presence, moving from space borrowed from the federal government to a twelve-story, 13,000 m² structure designed specifically for it. By the time this facility was inaugurated, thousands of EAESP graduates had gone forth, in the words of one of their professors, "as missionaries in our firms by applying and divulging more modern concepts, such as that of Marketing."[72]

Among these firms were the multinational corporations that were the third circuit for the formation of marketing professionals and the extension of their influence. Here, the in loco translation of practices associated with the parent company's "marketing mix" often fell to Brazilian sales executives. As an EAESP professor observed:

> Someday, while preparing the History of Marketing in Brazil, researchers and doctoral and master's students from Schools of Business will come across a universal truth: Marketing began with Sales Administration. It was the Sales Managers and Sales Directors of a small group of consumer-goods and services firms, most of them subsidiaries of North American and European multinationals, that sought to adapt to Brazilian reality: recruitment techniques and concepts; selection and training of the sales force; compensation systems; establishing forecasts, budgets, and sales quotas; determination of itineraries and scheduling of inspection visits; and the evaluation of the potential of clients. And, throughout this process, simultaneously, to carry out the "lion's share" in credit and billing; to identify trends in the market and in the behavior of the final consumer; to take care of promotion at point of sale (*merchandising*); to provide assistance to clients. At night, in the solitude of boarding-house rooms or in the living-rooms of their homes, it was up to them to finish off their work in the field with the preparation of reports on inspection visits, summaries of requests, accounts of billings, and so many other administrative tasks.[73]

In other cases, multinationals imported specialists to structure consumer-product marketing and train staffers. Nestlé led the way, drawing on its war-imposed U.S. experience and re-creating those lessons in Switzerland, including hiring HBS professors to distill their institution's MBA into an eleven-month course. In Brazil, marketing's influence on Nestlé's training was evident by the mid-1950s, an executive declaring of his experience: "I did very well in that course and was invited, not to be the general inspector of Sales any longer, but to assume a function that was going to be created, this one within Marketing, which was Product Specialist, the 'Product Manager.' At that time, one only spoke of this in the United States. But our Company was very much influenced by the United States, because we had an office that directed all of Latin America in Stamford [Connecticut], in the United States. Brazil was directly subordinate [to it]. And of course we had to undergo the influence of the 'popes' of Marketing who, without any doubt, are the North Americans, whether we wanted to or not."[74]

Beginning at around the same time, U.S.- and European-trained Nestlé executives were sent to Brazil to train regional managers and make the case that "integrated marketing is today as important to a modern firm as its equipment, its personnel, and its physical plant." Between 1962 and 1972, more than a thousand employees took marketing coursework in São Paulo; by then, all Nestlé salespersons received a vade mecum providing a short course in marketing, including planning, market research, advertising, and sales promotion. Over the same period, Nestlé was well represented at AMCE's UD and Children's Salon, while operating a Center for Home Economics within its Marketing Division that was part test kitchen, consumer-research group, and public-relations firm. According to a Swiss executive who arrived in 1969, this work meant that "Nestlé already had relatively sophisticated Marketing, not only in terms of Brazil, but also in worldwide terms, because Nestlé had at its disposal sources of Marketing information and technique that came from the United States and from Europe." The only missing element, as he saw it, was comprehensive market-share data, and so in 1969–1970 Nestlé funded the installation of the A. C. Nielsen Company's bimonthly "store audit" service, which provided sales totals at the retail and wholesale levels for entire lines of goods, broken down by brand. Thus, in the name of marketing, did a U.S. firm, acting on behalf of a European multinational, extend the reach of market research beyond the efforts of Marplan, IBOPE, and the advertising agencies that had introduced the practice beginning in 1929.[75]

The circuits formed by the multinational corporations, EAESP, and prosperity professionals intersected at key points, contributing jointly to the diffusion of marketing ideas and practices. For example, the founding director of the São Paulo Advertising School had received his introduction to marketing while working for Lever's house agency; the Anglo-Dutch parent company is also identified as having introduced modern marketing techniques, in the guise of "scientific marketing," through Gessy-Lever, which also recruited executives from EAESP. Among the leading Brazilian ideologues of marketing was Harry Simonsen Jr., a contributor to professional publications and president of the ADVB who worked for several multinational firms; he was not directly connected with the São Paulo School of Business Administration but held an MBA from Michigan State earned independently of its credentialing of EAESP's faculty; his coauthor Roberto Duailibi was the most successful early alumnus of the São Paulo Advertising School and a vice president of the ADVB. Of the seven EAESP marketing professors interviewed by Alyza Munhoz for her thesis on the study of marketing in Brazil, all of them assistant professors in the 1950s, at least two were active in the ADVB and worked in advertising on the side; another two represented the school at the First Brazilian Advertising Congress. One of the Michigan State marketing professors they worked with had been a JWT vice president; during his two years in São Paulo, he was a participant in Thompson's in-house seminars with executives who were "among the first Brazilians to assimilate, practice, and preach the current principles of *marketing*." Finally, there were multinational corporations, and many Brazilian firms, that "carried out mass recruitment at the agencies to compose their *marketing* departments." Needless to say, these agencies had not begun to offer marketing services simply because of their executives' flair for North American novelties; they did so because they thought potential clients would be more likely to retain an agency offering such facilities.[76]

The results of these efforts were difficult to miss. According to a well-regarded insider, "the hegemony of the concept of 'marketing'" was apparent by 1960, with "the advertising man" integrated "into the very structure of business, as the 'marketing' man he is today." A dozen years later, marketing was "a magic word" for a larger host, "a new mentality that is slowly consolidating itself among Brazilian businessmen." The sources of marketing's appeal were as varied as the term was polyvalent, covering, at the very least, a series of functions, a method of organization or organizational strategy, and an academic field of study (indeed, believers went further, claiming for marketing the status of a philosophy, in addition to a strategy, and a social science rather than an area of academic inquiry). Some sources for marketing's appeal were old and established, others particular to that moment; some ideological, others practical.[77]

Among the latter was the fact that the functions identified with marketing already existed in Brazil, even if some were in their incipience (industrial design) and others, though long hallowed, on the cusp of qualitative change (market research). That these functions already existed made their coordination by marketing directors practical in both senses of the word. In this context, demonstration effects mattered also, as pace-setting multinational firms restructured their Brazilian organizations in order to effect such coordination.[78]

There was also the fact of marketing's fit with Brazilian political economy. Official reliance on the manufacture of high-end consumer durables as the economy's motive force helped create conditions propitious for the introduction of marketing thought and the coordination of marketing functions. In this sense, Duailibi was correct to identify marketing with automobile manufacturing. The survival of *Seleções* through *O Cruzeiro*'s displacement and disappearance may be attributed to marketing strategies, carried out in consultation with McCann and in coordination with Johnson & Johnson and Nestlé, that maintained the monthly's following in classes A and B. Such segmentation complemented the politico-economic trends of the Kubitschek years and the period beginning in 1967. In the mid-1970s, Rede Globo's success was attributed to "10 [years] of marketing victories" achieved through "the marketing of our product" (commercial airtime) with the same seriousness and attention to best practices as "Ford or Lever product managers," especially in research; the results of its research, covering "all of the Globo Network's markets and also of sectoral markets and market situations," was shared with "all of the agencies and advertisers' marketing and media professionals" through the group's marketing magazine, *Mercado Global*.[79]

Market segmentation and competition over the fraction of the population that could afford "big tickets" are not, however, an adequate omnibus explanation for marketing's adoption. Such an explanation would have to account for the turn to marketing by the major manufacturer of low-cost footwear, Alpargatas, which had JWT at work "entirely in accord with the global planning of marketing." The campaign "A Child in Shoes Is a Healthy Child," directed especially at state elites and public servants (educational-ministry bureaucrats and schoolteachers, respectively), but aimed at selling more shoes in rural areas, seems to have resulted from saturated markets in the urban southeast amid tough times for all the country's poorest, who on their own were more concerned with obtaining food than footwear.[80]

Taken together, marketing's applications and organizational structure illustrated one of the two senses in which it was global. Marketing as a set of functions included everything involved in moving any imaginable good or service, beginning with its conception and design. Its practitioners—advertising and sales professionals, to start with—were thus positioned to claim authority over all these functions and their coordination. In this context, marketing, which by that name appeared in the late stages of Alfred Chandler's managerial revolution in U.S. business, was grasped onto by elements in Brazil's professional-managerial cohort at a point in time at which similar movements had yet to appear in nationally owned manufacturing concerns. Special claims to marketing expertise by advertising men issued in this context. The ADVB's touting its course in marketing management as contributing to "our objective . . . to form an elite" was a sales professional's equivalent. For the McCann executive and São Paulo Advertising School director Francisco Gracioso, the "professional administrator" typical of marketing-driven foreign firms was "the great secret" of business success, superior to the "hereditary administrator" of family-owned firms and to Brazilian elites generally, to whom were ascribed a "low cultural level [that] was always the root cause of immobilism and backwardness." Even the most academically inclined of the EAESP's assistant professors left scholarly dispassion aside to exult in the "emancipation of the marketing administrator," liberating himself from "ten centuries of administrative subordination [and] social prejudice." Marketing, as theory and practice, was thus a means for managers to claim authority over empirically minded owners.[81]

As nationally owned firms became increasingly scarce, having been driven from the market, bought out by multinational corporations, or forced to accept foreign concerns as partners in order to survive, the other sense of the term "global" had its appeal. Marketing, by its universalism—the assumedly general applicability of its functions, organizing structure, and study—had every appearance of a match with the society its enthusiasts found themselves in, despite differences between that society and the places of its fullest flourishing, which were impossible to ignore but subjected to ruses ranging from understatement to throat-clearing. A contrast with antecedent approaches to sales promotion is fitting: Ruy Chalmers's *Gerência de loja, técnica varejista e promoção de vendas em lojas de varejo: A experiência brasileira* (1966) and the same author's *Marketing: A experiência universal de marketing na conquista sistemática dos mercados* (1969), with the shift in emphasis from national experience to the universal applicability of what Chalmers called "The Doctrine of Marketing." Marketing might have originated outside of Brazil, but it was applicable in all national contexts, if not synchronically than sequentially, thereby establishing an affinity with conceptions of "development." It was hardly coincidental that one of the first Brazilian-authored books on the subject was titled "Marketing: A Tool for Development" or that W. W. Rostow's ideas were adopted by its author, among other marketing enthusiasts.[82]

As its marriage to modernization theory shows, marketing's U.S. pedigree was hardly incidental to its appeal among Brazilian professionals. Indeed, old habits died hard. However, this identification was less important than it had been in the remaking of retailing, and its valence had changed. A telling piece of evidence is the frequency with which Jean-Jacques Servan-Schreiber's *Le défi américain* was cited in arguments on behalf of marketing and managerialism: the extent of U.S. expertise was acknowledged, but a European imprimatur mattered just as much, as did Servan-Schreiber's call for taking up North American tools to counter a preponderance of U.S. economic power.[83]

Marketing's consumer orientation was another source of its appeal. As with its imbrication with modernization theory and the call for its employ against an "American challenge," marketing ideas may have soothed adherents into believing, in the terms of the time-honored Rotary motto, that their mission valued "service over self"; others among the cohort no doubt thought it was good public relations. One or both were at play in Aldo Xavier da Silva's insistence that with the advent of marketing, "the consumer came to be 'king'" and in Manoel de Vasconcellos's assertion that marketing "puts the client's needs in 1st place." But the mask could slip, revealing the "generalized cynicism" Maria Rita Kehl identified in a speech by one of the country's most well-connected specialists. "We, men of the market," declared Mauro Salles in 1975, "apply a different arithmetic to the country's 106 million inhabitants, removing from this population the inactive, minors, the aged and those who are still at the margin of the consumer society, and we arrive at a consuming Brazil that slightly exceeds 36 million inhabitants." Further whittling led to a final calculation: "National consumers, in *marketing* terms, would number only 25 million."[84]

Among advertising professionals, there was another source for marketing's appeal. As claims for the systematic, even scientific status of advertising rang hollow, including because they flew in the face of the global vogue of "creative" advertising, marketing offered the opportunity for the renewal of such claims. And so, in 1958, Manoel de Vasconcellos claimed to see Brazilian advertising agencies "transforming themselves . . . into 'marketing' organizations," while citing an NYU professor's likening of marketing and industrial engineering. For Carlos Chueiri, writing in 1969, to practice marketing was "to eliminate, by definition, the idea of improvisation." Study and planning were what made marketing a *técnica* (a technique, something performed by a technician) and, perhaps, a science. It was to this end that Simonsen and Duailibi presented an adaptation of Stanley Resor's T-Square as the first step in the systematic collection of marketing data and an enhanced T-Square structure (it added "why" to Resor's what, who, where, when, and how) as the starting point for their own four-stage Heuristic Square, which yielded 90,558 possible questions covering every aspect of a twenty-part "marketing mix" and externalities ranging from legislation to customer demand.[85]

By that point, calls for translation were fewer and less urgently felt. As an authority declared in 1970, the term "incorporated . . . into our language was, actually, the English word, perfectly valid and in current use." Ten years later, Raimar Richers rued his earlier searching for a translation, adding: "Today the word 'Marketing' circulates in Brazil with almost the same frequency and intensity as such expressions as democracy and *goiabada*" (guava paste). In an oft-repeated phrase, "marketing lost its accent." To be precise, it gained a Brazilian one, pronounced "mahrr-keh-*tching*," the last two syllables resounding like the click-and-spring chime of an old-time cash register. Such was marketing.[86]

Arrival

The echo, in classrooms and boardrooms, of *marketing*'s percussive ring heralded the arrival of Brazil's new professionals to the standing to which they long aspired. From the 1950s through the 1970s, executive compensation climbed upward, and with it the prestige of its recipients, old prejudices dissipating along the way. Their cohort grew exponentially, their fields of specialization ever-more sought after, their skills increasingly recognized at home and abroad. Beginning under Kubitschek and accelerating under Brazil's military rulers, government was a partner in the work of advertising professionals, promotional specialists, public-relations experts, and media managers. Advertising and sales-promotion executives, reborn as "marketing men," came to lead, rather than merely serve, some of the country's most important businesses. Parallel to this professional ascent, their employers in leading media groups and retail concerns attained ever-greater power and prestige.

Bernardo Ludermir, writing in 1959, acknowledged that he was often asked about the salaries advertising executives received. His reaction was composed, acknowledging that some salaries were indeed astronomical, by Brazilian standards, but that they were limited to the top fifth of executives at large agencies. For the rest, he noted coolly, after citing salaries that would have been the envy of many of his readers, "These salaries are the same as those obtained by university-level professionals in any large firm." They were not, he added, as high as those paid in New York. Writing in *O Estado de S. Paulo*, Marcus Pereira addressed the same issue: "The opportunity of good salaries offered by professional advertising work is the result, pure and simple, of the workings of the law of supply and demand in a specific labor market." Decades later, Carlos Queiroz Telles recalled the boost in his fortunes when he was hired by Almap in the early 1960s: "It was a never-ending amount of money. It was enough to buy a new VW Beetle every two months." In 1973, having mentioned the rate for sought-after copywriters in Brazil, a correspondent for *Ad-*

vertising Age felt compelled to remind her readers that such positions required "total command of Portuguese" to avoid "a stampede of creative people to Brazil." She went on to compare the salaries of Brazilian executives and their university-trained counterparts in production and the service-oriented social sciences: "A marketing director can command $50,000, while a top art director can expect to earn perhaps $33,000, and an account supervisor about $26,000. For the sake of comparison, an industrial engineer draws an average salary of $17,600 and a psychologist under $9,000."[87]

With ballooning salaries came enhanced standing, a fact decried by the arch-reactionary Catholic writer Gustavo Corção, who declared, "100 years ago . . . only classless individuals practiced [advertising]. Then, advertising went from being shameful to tolerable, and from tolerable to glorified." He went on to predict that misgivings would be erased even among high-status liberal professionals: "Soon lawyers and physicians will be proud to practice advertising." Ten years later, Genival Rabelo confirmed Corção's prediction: "The advertising profession has acquired status. It is no longer the resort of the young man who had nothing else. . . . Its technical demands bring together artists, liberal professionals, PhDs, after all. And today there are thousands upon thousands, spread throughout all of Brazil, who are helping industry produce more and commerce to multiply its sales." By 1960, it was no longer merely, or even primarily, publishing figures that rallied around the "big men" of advertising and related fields, as the twentieth anniversary of *PN*'s founding brought congratulations from prominent industrialists and the president of the country's most powerful union, as well as politicians of national standing ranging from the labor-friendly Fernando Ferrari to Carlos Lacerda, Corção's political favorite. Two years later, the anniversary of the Doria agency inspired a tribute that brought together state legislators from São Paulo's largest party and its traditional opposition, representing the kleptocratic center and the liberal-constitutionalist right, respectively; by that point, the agency's founder, João Doria, had joined the country's left-of-center Christian Democratic Party, which would put him in the national legislature in 1963. Back in the world of business, as McCann's Eliezer Burlá put it: "The advertising man long ceased to be a mere maker of advertisements, a merely subaltern recipient of orders from on high, who carried them out without discussion. Today, seated side by side with the advertiser, sharing in his most serious and intimate problems, collaborating intensively in his problems of administration, 'marketing' and sales—agencies attain a new social dimension and are today as sensitive to economic oscillations and variations as the leaders of industry." An understated verdict on the conjugation of enhanced social standing with ever-higher salaries was provided by Leôncio Basbaum, who wrote of a late 1950s dalliance in the field, "At that time—and I believe still today—advertising was a privileged profession, it conferred prestige, it paid well."[88]

Advertising and related fields not only constituted privileged professions; they were growth areas. In 1958, there were an estimated five thousand people working in advertising in Brazil, a figure that rose to ten thousand by late 1962. Ten years later, the going estimate was thirty-five thousand, including employees of "auxiliary firms," rising to between forty thousand and forty-five thousand by 1975–1976. A more conservative estimate of the number of public-relations practitioners (it included only paid-up members of the main professional association) illustrates the disproportionate size of the new-professional cohort vis-à-vis its U.S. exemplar: in 1975, there were 3,500 such professionals in Brazil, compared with 7,000 in the United States, with an economy some fifteen times larger.[89] In 1958, when *Advertising Age* ranked Brazil sixth in advertising billings (behind the United States, Great Britain, West Germany, France, and Japan), Marcus Pereira explained, "We owe the position we reached in the advertising business not only to the extraordinary vitality of the Brazilian industrial park; nor, not only, on the other hand, to the accelerated expansion of a powerful internal market; we owe it also to the work of an immense team of technicians that joins together the famous writer or artist to the young messenger who delivers stereotype plates." The fact that advertising billings exceeded 1 percent of Brazil's domestic product the following year led Manoel de Vasconcellos to crow: "Outdone by the United States, who invest more than 2% of their GDP in advertising, we are, however, at the level of progressive, industrialized countries such as England, France, Germany, Canada. We are on the right path." The political turmoil and austerity-induced recession of the mid-1960s had Brazilian advertising losing ground, but budgets more than recovered, Brazil rejoining the world's top seven advertising markets in the 1970s. No totals exist for spending on much of the rest of the "marketing mix" (design, market and media research, public relations), though by 1970 sales-promotion expenditures were estimated at just under half advertising expenditures. Attempts at gauging the volume of commercial messages were similarly scarce, with but one authority guessing that between television, radio, newspapers, magazines, movies, and outdoor advertising, "Brazilians of the big cities . . . receive, at the conscious or subconscious level, between 1,000 and 1,500 different [commercial] stimuli every day."[90]

Qualitative indications of the enhanced technique and increased authority of the new professionals abounded. A 1958 debate occasioned by a gentle suggestion that national advertising featured "non-Brazilian" types revealed unanimity on the field's progress. To a man—there was not a woman among them—participants in a *Propaganda*-sponsored debate, including journalists, printers, and artists, agreed that Brazilian advertising was improving in artistic, technical, and even psychological terms. The painter Flávio de Carvalho's response was particular in its points of emphasis but typical of the larger comity: "I think that nationally made illustrated advertisements are improving considerably. An important factor in this improvement was the advent and acceptance of the currents of modern art. . . . Modern art issued a grand appeal to the interests of men for things. As far as the psychology of advertisements, I think that it improved a lot."[91]

In their own attestations of the field's advance, advertising men made comparisons old and new. Returning from New York, Renato Castelo Branco declared, "From the strictly advertising point of view, the level of quality here and there is closer than one might suppose," while Norton's Geraldo Alonso employed a less familiar yardstick: "Today Brazil is the most advanced country in advertising technique and formulation, among the Latin American countries." The two kinds of comparison appeared side by side in an appeal to esprit de corps issued as the mid-1960s recession fostered pessimism. "In Brazil, advertising long ago left behind its heroic phase, the phase of speculation and improvisation, the phase of amateurism. It is now an activity that has perfected itself to the point that it is placed in an honorable third place worldwide. First, the United States, and England in second. In third, there is certainly Brazil." National excellence was so obvious that it would be no surprise at all "if sooner or later the 'exportation' of Brazilian advertising professionals begins to take our contribution to the advertising of other countries, principally the Latin American ones."[92]

The situation was held to be the same in allied fields. Retail sales-promotion, an expert observed, "has already reached a considerable degree of efficiency, it being comparable today, in the methods it employs and the results it obtains, to the promotions of the large North American and European stores."[93] Produced by the vanguard of Brazilian media elites, the "Globo Standard of Quality" embodied international norms in programming, promotion, and airtime sales. The importance of Globo's research division in this cultural work was clear; it was also indicative of new directions in market research, in which manufacturing firms such as Nestlé also took part, the television network and the food-products concern complementing the gathering of objective, quantitative data with explorations of the qualitative and subjective. The extent of this shift is clear in the testimony of a Nestlé Home Economics Center staffer:

Our formal education was varied: one majored in Communications, Social Sciences, another in Nutrition and another in Pedagogy. Together we proposed to observe the consumer's behavior, in their world. . . .

Thus it was indispensable that we were also housewives, mothers, and we also experienced the day-to-day problems of a female consumer. We were trained to perceive up-close the meaning of the small habits of a housewife's everyday routine. . . . Perhaps it has been as a function of this sensibility, which training would only sharpen, that we perceived first that something was changing among us: we saw that the woman was "growing," changing, and a new image was beginning to emerge.

The female consumer that in the 1950s did not even bother to read the labels of products, now began to ask questions, to become interested in nutrition and to want to know more. A new image of woman is emerging every day. Participating in economic life, conscious of her responsibilities, she analyzes, she expresses herself, she questions, she needs to be informed and to be listened to.[94]

The introduction of computerized data storage and processing was a contemporaneous advance in the fields of market and media research and consumer-credit monitoring. In 1971, publication of the first Portuguese-language book on sales forecasting was interpreted as "comforting proof of the progress verified in our country in the area of Marketing. . . . It is a sign that the entire field is becoming professionalized."[95]

Another sign of professionalization was the advance into higher education. Even as advertising agencies, market-research groups, marketing departments, public-relations firms, and media concerns hired from a growing pool of sociology and psychology graduates, universities increasingly offered instruction in marketing and allied fields. Perhaps most remarkably, marketing established a lasting foothold in Brazil's oldest university, the University of São Paulo, while the EAESP served as training station and model for business schools throughout the country. In Rio, beginning in 1964, Walter Poyares, the ABP founder and Globo "brain trust" executive, provided instruction in public relations at the Pontifical Catholic University, the first such university-level coursework to be offered in Brazil. Thirteen years later, there were thirty-two college- and university-level courses in public relations offered in the states of Rio de Janeiro, Rio Grande do Sul, and São Paulo, part of a larger surge in the study of "communications," including at public, confessional, and for-profit institutions. Communications, or "social communications," as it was termed by the Federal Education Council, spanned public relations, journalism, cinema, radio, television, theater, semiotics, and advertising, but there was little doubt that advertising drew more than its share of interest. As Rodolfo Lima Martensen wrote, "The advertising that advertising did for itself had created the image of a charming and lucrative profession among the young public."[96]

As a marker of the new professionals' progress, however, the advance into the academy ranked second to the successes of nationally owned agencies. JWT and McCann's international connections made them too big to fail, and so they remained at the top of the heap, but they were joined there by Brazilian agencies that had overtaken smaller U.S. and European outfits with relative ease. A 1968 retrospective identified Standard, Almap, CIN, and Denison as exponents of the general phenomenon of "new techniques, new methods, and new processes reaching the country through national agencies"; while no introduction is necessary for the first two, CIN was founded in São Paulo in 1954 and was one of Brazil's first agencies to emphasize marketing, while Denison had been founded in Rio as Ducal's house agency in 1957 but became a national presence with a full roster of clients. Among the agencies that *Advertising Age*'s correspondent added to the list five years later were DPZ and Mauro Salles. DPZ enjoyed near-instant success from its 1968 founding onward, based in part on a reputation as a "creative" agency, though its lead partner, Roberto Duailibi, evinced considerable skill in marketing. The Mauro Salles agency enjoyed an even more meteoric rise. Its namesake, the son of a powerful northeastern politician who had twice served as minister of agriculture, had started out in journalism, while also dabbling in advertising and side-jobbing as a fixer when reporters for *Time* and *Life* passed through Rio. In 1961, he helped prepare the special issue of *Mecânica Popular* on the Second Automobile Salon. Federal government appointments in 1961–1963, including as acting minister of industry and commerce, allowed him to build on his family's political connections, while work for the Globo group provided introductions to businessmen. In 1965, he founded the agency that became Mauro Salles Publicidade, another near-instant success, based largely on winning the Willys account; the automaker is also rumored to have received shares in the agency in return for underwriting its startup costs, though Salles insisted his firm was always 100 percent Brazilian. Whichever the case, his connections and clever expedience are indisputable. In 1967—Salles assumed the ABP presidency that same year—he arranged a merger that placed him at the head of Mauro Salles/Inter-Americana de Propaganda, the beginning of the end for Brazil's oldest continuously operating agency. That the new agency could compete with JWT was acknowledged even by *Advertising Age*; few, however, knew that the U.S. agency nearly agreed to a merger between its subsidiary and Salles/Inter-Americana, with Mauro Salles in a leading role in the amalgamated firm.[97]

As suggested by JWT's abortive merger, one response to the rise of nationally owned agencies was foreign firms buying in or establishing operating agreements with domestic ones, an approach that offered a shortcut for U.S. agencies new to Brazil. And so Ogilvy & Mather absorbed Cícero

Leuenroth's ownership of Standard between 1969 and 1972, along with the rights to the name nicked from Standard Oil. Leo Burnett bought a stake in CIN, which it later absorbed, while Kenyon & Eckhart and the British agency CPV set up operating agreements with Salles/Inter-Americana. Proeme—another Brazilian agency identified with the creative boom of the 1960s—was taken over by the Interpublic group beginning in 1975. Meanwhile, cost-cutting in the face of competition, combined with the workings of Brazilian political economy, led JWT and McCann to write off their operations beyond the Rio–São Paulo axis, in which they were followed by the competition, U.S.-, Brazilian-, and binationally owned alike, the period between the 1950s and the 1970s witnessing the "life, suffering, and death of the regional offices of the big agencies."[98]

By the 1960s, international recognition mattered more than maintaining a near-national presence. Armando de Moraes Sarmento's success abroad honored "Brazil's Advertising men" with its "reflection of the improvement and advance that his profession has reached in our country." In 1959, when he was made president of McCann-Erickson International, his promotion was commemorated by a banquet attended by a business and publishing who's-who. Four years later, when he became president of the parent company, *Ultima Hora* explained, "Armando de Moraes Sarmento is a 'Prosperity Professional' . . . and has been executing a brilliant trajectory on advertising's international scene." Another sign of Brazilian advertising's international arrival was the reproduction of nationally produced VW and Kolynos advertisements in the United States. Asked to comment, Sarmento's successor at the helm of McCann-Brazil, Emil Farhat, could only say, "Spectacular." In the 1970s, Brazilian successes in international advertising awards at Cannes and Venice were similarly hailed.[99]

Official recognition and collaboration with state- and national-level powerholders was interpreted as further evidence of arrival. In 1960, advertising executives thrilled to the Kubitschek government's awarding of the Order of the Southern Cross to the longtime head of JWT's Brazilian operations, Robert Merrick, "based on his contribution to the development of the advertising business in Brazil, technically and ethically; to the creation of a highly qualified group of Brazilian professionals; and, through this, to the economic development of the country." Beginning in 1964, the new professionals counted on the support of Minister of Planning Roberto Campos as they organized a National Advertising Council (CNP) modeled on the U.S. Advertising Council. Led initially by JWT's Renato Castelo Branco, the CNP was separate from government but campaigned in support of official aims while raising its constituents' profile. Its first campaign proclaimed, "Exporting Is the Solution," a slogan in line with the early military-led government's emphasis on international trade. Another effort aimed at stimulating consumer spending amid the deflationary policies imposed by Campos: "Buy Today—Keep Brazil Progressing." In Castelo Branco's words, "it is an interpretation of a general feeling in the country and of multiple sectors of national life—producers, distributors, and consumers." Anodyne campaigns in support of reforestation and the struggle against cancer culminated in an "advertising campaign for Advertising" designed by Salles/Inter-Americana and supported by the major trade associations (ABAP, ABP, APP, and the Brazilian Association of Advertisers, founded in 1959) together with groups representing broadcasting, publishing, outdoor-advertising, and public-relations interests. Many of the campaign's claims were reminiscent of earlier efforts, but there were some novelties. One advertisement, for example, featured a photograph of supermarket shelves lined with unlabeled, monochrome packages: "Without competition and without advertising, a supermarket would be one of the most boring places in the world." The accompanying "reason-why" text answered the question, "Do you know why every supermarket always has a festive, joyful air?" "Because all the products that are found there are 'fighting' to win you over. It is competition, which insists on advertising, so that you know everything—really everything—about each product on display." The alternative would be "a supermarket without competition. Without advertising. Where no one was concerned with you. Everything would be just the same. Just the same. The same products, the same brand, no advertising, the same monotony. Would you be glad to return to such a place?" The advertisement's layout was old-fashioned, but its animating ideas were new. Twenty years earlier, the idea that food shopping should be pleasurable or that a grocery store could have a festive air would have been so foreign as to be inadaptable. In 1968, its use in the promotion of the advertising profession served as additional confirmation of consumer capitalism's appeal.[100]

By the time of the CNP's pro-advertising campaign, authority over economic policy-making had passed from Campos to Delfim Netto, a University of São Paulo economics professor whose first job had been as an office boy at Gessy. While Campos had been embraced by Renato Castelo Branco and other professionals, his tight-money policies had hurt smaller agencies and many consumer-oriented firms; an observer described them as a reversal of the "euphoric consumerism" of preceding years. Upon taking over in 1967, Delfim eased credit while holding down wages, fueling upper-middle-class spending without unleashing out-of-control inflation. The new professionals identified with him unambiguously, Geraldo Alonso considering him "Brazil's greatest genius," *Manchete* calling him a "wizard of finance." In 1969, he gave the keynote at the Second Brazilian Advertising Congress, a speech that might well have been produced by the CNP: "Advertising enriched the world. It enriched men, increasing the repertoire of their options . . . and created a powerful stimulant to upward mobility." Advertising, he claimed, reciting time-honored claims, "makes possible mass consumption, without which most benefits of progress would never reach ordinary men." Two years later, Delfim gave the keynote for the São Paulo Advertising School's twentieth entering class, a speech on "Advertising and Development" that identified advertising's three major roles: stimulating consumer desire, disseminating technological progress, and mobilizing public consensus.[101]

If Delfim was the new professionals' favorite among Brazil's civil-military elite, the latter showed a soft spot for Mauro Salles. In 1973, Salles was invited to address Brazil's Higher War College, to the delight of his colleagues. Rather than lecture on advertising alone, he gave a talk on the Brazilian economy's tertiary sector, in which he noted the "importance of commerce and the revolution that it is undergoing," with special mention of department-store shopping, supermarketing, and self-service; he also lauded consumer credit, including São Paulo's SCPC and the relatively novel charge card, and gave a brief on banking, insurance, and financial services before moving on to public services, especially in communications. When he reached the subject of advertising, he could find no more apt authority than Delfim Netto, quoting the minister of finance: "Development is a process during which our desire to consume is always greater than our capacity to produce. It is this which produces development." The growth of Brazilian billings and their contribution to national development was noted, but the case was made that expenditures were still insufficient, including through the newly important comparison with Japan, beneficiary of a more sustained economic miracle that made it the world's second-largest market economy: Brazil's advertising billings were 1.3 percent of its GNP, whereas the figure for Japan was over 2 percent. Here and elsewhere, Salles linked his cohort's interests with national policy, as when he credited advertising with beginning to fulfill the government's aim, as described by Minister of Planning João Paulo dos Reis Veloso, "to progressively construct a mass-consumption society, which means having a large middle class and a working class that are capable of consuming." Claims like this one that allowed Salles to gild over the fact that two-thirds of Brazilians did not count as consumers, "using the word in its more restricted sense, that which we adopt in production and marketing firms." Salles's hosts were sufficiently impressed for him to become a regular presence at the Higher War College.[102]

That was not the extent of connections between the new professionals and the post-1964 state. As Carlos Fico and others have documented, between the late 1960s and mid-1970s, the military government counted on an executive-level group that drew on advertising and public-relations techniques to create sophisticated, relatively subtle pro-regime propaganda. The idea belonged to an army colonel, Hernani d'Aguiar, who had "fallen in love" with public relations while taking a course at Rio's Pontifical Catholic University (PUC) in the mid-1960s; among the specialists he recruited was the PUC professor and Globo promotional guru Walter Poyares. D'Aguiar's successor, Octávio Costa, also an army colonel, expanded the group's operations to include coordination of independently produced publicity, especially commercial advertising, which he described as "the most important part [of communications] for the strengthening of national character," an endorsement that professional spokesmen had scarcely dreamt of two decades earlier.[103]

The arrival of the new professionals, some of whom ascended to the pinnacle of business success, becoming leading figures in media and manufacturing firms, was more than matched by the ascent of these firms' owners. The extent of Roberto Marinho's power, influence, and wealth as of the mid-1970s dwarfed anything Assis Chateaubriand had been able to muster and would have been unimaginable in the afternoon-newspaper milieu in which his father had made his name. As far as manufacturing and mercantile groups were concerned, the rise of the interrelated Carvalho firms was only slightly less impressive. Back in 1944, Lauro de Carvalho had been one merchant among many, aspiring to create Rio's first department store and despairing of attempts to get city government to remove trees obstructing views of his shopwindows. Fifteen years later, when Rio hosted the first national retail convention, its federally appointed mayor gave Lauro's junior partners a key to the city. A year and a half after that, Ducal's José Cândido Moreira de Souza was made secretary of agriculture, commerce, and industry for Guanabara, as metropolitan Rio was known when it was counted as one of Brazil's federal states, while another of Lauro's nephews would become secretary of finance for the state of São Paulo. By 1963, a third nephew was treasurer of the São Paulo Commercial Association, while in 1970 yet another nephew became a member of the executive committee of Rio's Commercial Association, a position he used to publicize his satisfaction with Delfim Netto's call "to return to the empire of consumption."[104]

Big Brazil

The cultural counterpart of the GDP growth identified with Delfim Netto's helmsmanship of the national economy has been called the *Brasil Grande* ideology. Thoroughly ideological, it hardly seems developed enough to constitute a full-fledged worldview or structure of belief, though it certainly reinforced its champion's beliefs. Brasil Grande ideas had roots that went back decades, along the way stretching through the cultivated optimism of the Kubitschek years and the metrics of greatness of his Targets Plan. From then on, the development and spread of Brasil Grande ideas owed much to the cultural work of the new professionals, and while those ideas skewed toward producerist views of the conomy, elements of Brazil's consumer capitalism were also present, and consumer-oriented businesses figured in state policy. Over time, other ideas augmented the economistic conceit: pharaonic public works as agents of national integration, the mass nationalism of international sport, and an ugly, exclusionary vision of national belonging.

Statements of Brazilian greatness date back to Portuguese colonial rule, when they included pastoral odes to natural beauty and nativist catalogs of continental bounty. Their most important line of descent runs through what Brazilians call *ufanismo*, a word suggesting boundless national pride derived from Affonso Celso's *Porque me ufano do meu paiz* (Why I am joyfully proud of my country), a turn-of-the-century tract that took as its starting point the country's size ("Brazil is one of the vastest countries of the globe, the vastest of the Latin race, the vastest of the New World, except for the United States"). After 1900, ufanismo surged forth most notably under Kubitschek. "In the 1950s," a contemporary remarked, "with the surge of optimism generated by the developmentalist targets [of Kubitschek's five-year plan], there was a new vitality . . . which was reflected in the sporting victories we achieved abroad . . . especially in football." For specific groups, as the political scientist Maria Victoria Benevides notes, Kubitschekian developmentalism "represented what later would be identified as the ideology of 'Brasil grande potência'" (great-power Brasil), the foreign-affairs analogue of Brasil Grande. "Brasil grande" was a favorite term of Kubitschek's leading speechwriter, the poet and supermarket impresario Augusto Frederico Schmidt, who coined the slogan "Fifty Years in Five." "Schmidt spoke of Brasil grande, one of his constant subjects," remembered another Kubitschek aide. Schmidt would keep at it down to his death in 1965, "speaking with enthusiasm of 'Brasil grande,' the subject of his last articles on politics and his obsession." Among those listening was Ducal's José Luiz Moreira de Souza, who evoked the "task of transforming the country into a Brasil grande" on the first anniversary of the 1964 coup.[105]

Five years earlier, Emil Farhat had presented McCann's vision of what the 1960s held for Brazil. His speech began with a page from *Porque me ufano do meu paiz*: "Brazil already has, at this moment, the second-largest population in the Western World." Other points would have been equally pleasing to Affonso Celso (predictions of growing world coffee consumption, for example). Still others, perhaps unimaginable in 1900, contained the germ of Brasil Grande ideas in the era of the economic miracle. "Governmental authorities may execute plans for even more gigantic public works. . . . The Federal Government will be able to count on tax receipts that in the year 1970 *should be equivalent to 1 trillion and 300 billion cruzeiros today!* By that point the Gross National Product *will already be around a value, also in present-day cruzeiros, of 11 trillion and 580 billion."* In 1965, few were as optimistic (José Luiz Moreira de Souza evoked "Brasil grande" alongside mild criticism of tight money policies). Admissions of that fact were to be found in unlikely places, as in a *Propaganda* editorial: "The fever of why-I-am-joyfully-proud-of-my-Country still affects some Brazilians, though today a certain sense of inferiority seems to dominate a large part of our people." The new professionals and their allies nevertheless threw themselves into recultivating optimism, *Propaganda* offering Brazilian advertising as a source of national pride, the *Visão* group using a "thumbs-up" motif designed by a JWT art director to indicate that the country's course was sound.[106]

Following this pattern, the first of many Brasil Grande slogans of the late 1960s and early 1970s was launched by Salles/Inter-Americana, in an advertisement that announced, in bold letters, "Brazil is at the edge of the abyss." Smaller type clarified, "according to pessimists, nostalgists, egotists and defeatists," while reason-why text explained that "facts and figures," far from indicating dire straits, "speak the simple and objective language of a Brasil Grande." The twenty-four short paragraphs that followed offered over one hundred figures and facts on subjects ranging from GDP growth to housing construction, bank deposits to the shipping industry, all, until the final paragraph, suggesting unprecedented growth. "But not everything in Brazil grew in 1968. The budget deficit, for example, was the same. And inflation was lower." What did it all mean? "Brazil striding ahead. Very quickly. At the pace of Brasil Grande."[107]

It was, in one account, "the first injection of optimism into the great mass of readers," an attempt to "build confidence in a better future for our country" that had a huge impact, prompting comment in advertising, manufacturing, and official circles. Few readers, however, knew that the advertisement was spurred by "an order from the federal government: to prepare a campaign of optimism." That is, it was created in response to a request by the public-relations arm of the national executive to the CNP, though the government may not have had a direct hand in its conception or publication. Whichever the case, the government's public-relations group encouraged the spread of its slogan, "At the Pace of Brasil Grande," which derived its impact from the fact that the Portuguese word for "pace" is the same as for "rhythm," thus playing upon long-standing associations between dance and national character. State-owned, mixed-capital, and privately held firms in every imaginable field took up the call. Embratel, the state-owned firm at that point preparing the way for national television broadcasting, was at work "at the pace of Brasil Grande." The once state-owned shipper Lloyd Brasileiro, its stock trading on Brazilian exchanges, was "the New Lloyd at the pace of Brasil Grande." São Paulo's Sângia department stores were "friendly folks at the pace of Brasil Grande." In 1969, when construction of the Centro da Barra da Tijuca complex began, on dunes and marshland west of Rio's urban footprint, it was dubbed "the new Guanabara at the pace of Brasil Grande"; that plans for the Centro brought together Oscar Niemeyer and Lúcio Costa linked it with Brasília.[108]

The same advertisement indicated that the Centro da Barra was the work of "private enterprise, fully integrated with the Government's effort and in the *spirit* of Brasil Grande." Capital, state, and nation were thereby linked in a phrase exemplifying how Brasil Grande shorthand worked its way into commercial advertising unloosened from the full "At the Pace . . ." slogan. In a similar vein, the Brazilian subsidiary of British-American Tobacco proclaimed: "Souza Cruz's constant refining of its processes and techniques is a standing invitation to the technicians who are being trained in this Brasil Grande." Even the Civilização Brasileira publishing house, identified with the vanquished nationalist left, went along, adding a sporting metaphor: "Brasil grande. . . . We are also in the play of progress." By then, the term had become incantative, resorted to in myriad contexts by magnates the likes of José Luiz Moreira de Souza, Caio de Alcântara Machado, and the banker Walter Moreira Salles, as well as by obscure letter-writers.[109]

The Brasil Grande idea was most often identified with macroeconomic targets and producerist benchmarks. Before the "At the Pace . . ." slogan, it bears repeating, came twenty-four paragraphs, the first on GDP growth and the last on government spending and inflation, the intervening twenty-two covering everything from manganese exports to agro-pastoral industry. But elements of Brazil's consumer capitalism and selected consumer-oriented businesses were present in the economic developments that lay behind this statistical compendium and in the policymaking that represented the implementation of Brasil Grande ideas: automobilism and the automotive industry, of course, but also food retailing and supermarket concerns, as well as nonfood retail interests.

Salles/Inter-Americana's list of accomplishments worthy of Brasil Grande included the production of 290,000 automotive vehicles and tractors in 1968, as well as the launch of three new automobile models, including Ford's Corcel—the only brand name to make the list—which "inaugurated the era of medium-sized cars in the Country," a qualitative, consumerist appeal amid much quantitative, production-oriented data. Quantitative and qualitative change in the automotive industry and its offerings were among the proudest accomplishments of the Brasil Grande era, the industry Brazil's "dream come true," the "number one pride and joy of the land," the passenger car the "most coveted consumer good," like "the gas stove, the refrigerator, the television" before it. Government policy had much to do with these changes and, indeed, Brazilian generals and technocrats did all they could to take credit for them, as the growth of the automotive sector impelled further economic expansion and diversified lines were offered to segmented southeastern consumers. But Brazilians' responses to demands that they consume were as important, their innovations joining their country's marketing mix.[110]

Eased credit was the government's major contribution to automobile production between the late 1960s and 1973–1974, a period in which the economic growth rate of the miracle was more than doubled by increases in the output of automotive plants. Tax breaks, especially on machinery imports, encouraged more diversified production, starting with the introduction of the Ford Galaxie in 1966–1967. Ford's beginning passenger-car production was tardy recognition that it had erred in allowing VW and Willys to corner the Brazilian market, but Ford also received better terms from the government of the mid-1960s than those offered by any preceding administration, including Kubitschek's. GM and Chrysler followed, with Opalas and Dodge Darts, while Volkswagen arranged to produce an upmarket sedan, even as it planned the public-relations-driven commemoration of the millionth Brazilian Volkswagen to come off the line, of which "everyone [in Brazil] became aware." This milestone and the "confident euphoria" that the *Jornal do Brasil* attributed to it were of a piece with the idea of Brazil approaching the output of "the industrially mature countries." Diversified production, meanwhile, was taken to indicate increasing sophistication. For Delfim Netto, it showed that Brazil had achieved the "grown-up market of any civilized nation." FIESP's monthly magazine agreed: "The process of maturation of the market under the customer's control will certainly be consolidated this year. It is what *marketing* strategists call the approximation of the automobile industry to the reality of the market." The contrast was clear: "It was abnormal for a single make, with a single model, to conquer and maintain control of 80% of the market. Normal is that make's competition—a competition made up of Detroit's big three—unleashing a counter-offensive and contemplating the market with models with updated mechanics and style." The starting point, in a sense, had been the 1966 Automobile Salon, as described by *Manchete*: "The beautiful *stands* of the V Salon hold a series of surprises for visitors, as all the nationally made cars of 1967 present larger or smaller new features. The preoccupation of most manufacturers was to highlight the elegance of their models."[111]

Ten years earlier, when the first Brazilian-made automobiles reached dealers, built-up demand made for a sellers' market. Neither automakers nor dealerships saw the need to finance car-buying, as there were more customers willing to pay cash than there were automobiles being produced, which remained the case into the 1960s. Nor did manufacturers or dealers develop such facilities as the cash-and-carry market softened, largely because existing arrangements had worked so well, though political and economic uncertainty probably bolstered this conservative outlook. Car ownership thus excluded potential purchasers who did not have cash in hand or the means for a hefty down payment and access to an independent source of credit. The tight-money policies adopted by the military government in 1964–1965 aggravated this situation. Popular desire for cars, however, remained high, and so an ingenious solution was devised by ordinary Brazilians—tellers, state functionaries, other white-collar workers—known as the *consórcio* ("consortium"). A group of people—fifty was customary—would commit to contributing a given sum on a monthly basis, the total of which would be the price of an automobile (a consórcio of fifty would demand one-fiftieth of the price of an automobile from each of its members every month). Each month the consórcio would buy an automobile, to be given to one of its members through a lottery, until everyone received their own. No one, then or since, seems to have remarked on the irony of popular cooperativism employed in the acquisition of a consumer good synonymous with possessive individualism, but the ingeniousness of the solution, its affinity with cultural tradition (for over a century, a numbers game known as the *jogo do bicho* has vied with association football for the title of national pastime), and the rapidity with which it spread throughout the country reveal the degree to which automobilism incorporated itself into Brazilian visions of the good life. The model was so successful that dealers and manufacturers created their own consórcios, pairing an auction with the monthly drawing to heighten the gamelike aspects of the operation and halve the length of the term over which all the consórcio's members would be satisfied, in a refinement of what Delfim Netto called "the formidable Brazilian invention." Through the 1960s, more than half the cars sold in Brazil went to consórcio members, and while the proportion would fall with sustained GDP growth and the creation of other credit facilities, it continued to represent a significant slice of small-car sales.[112]

While the automobile industry's role in miracle-era political economy is widely recognized, the place of food retailing in policymaking has been overlooked. Fiscal reform engineered the supermarket's triumph. Further on, the rise of the hypermarket matched the gigantism of Brasil Grande and its export delivered on foreign-policy objectives and the dreams of Augusto Schmidt.

In 1967, tax reforms made supermarkets more competitive with smaller food retailers. Thereafter, their number and market share shot up. In 1967, there were 1,052 supermarkets in Brazil; four years later, there were 3,500. By 1972, supermarkets reportedly handled 70 percent of Rio's retail food sales. Government also provided credit for the establishment of supermarkets and technical assistance in transforming traditional shops into self-service grocery stores, including "superettes" and full-scale supermarkets. Many more shops were forced to close their doors: thousands of corner stores and produce stands vanished from São Paulo's retail scene during the "miracle" years. Chains grew in size, including Peg-Pag and Disco, joined by Pão de Açúcar and Eletro-Radiobraz, which branched out from nonfood retail. In March and May 1971, respectively, Peg-Pag and Pão de Açúcar opened the first hypermarkets—"super-supermarkets," some called them, distinguished from supermarkets by their size, range of offerings, number of customers, and area served. A supermarket, according to the Brazilian standard, would have a shopping area of 500–2,500 m^2, featuring six thousand items for sale to up to six thousand families drawn from the store's immediate environs. The Peg-Pag hypermarket, located in São José dos Campos, on land leased from local government on generous terms, had a sales area of 3,000 m^2, featuring twenty-four thousand items for sale to countless families drawn from throughout the eastern corner of the state of São Paulo to "a fusion of the classic American department store with the Brazilian supermarket, in an attempt to reproduce the French hypermarket, bringing together mass self-service sales with credit sales of durable consumer goods." Pão de Açúcar's "Jumbo" store, in Santo André, on the southeastern fringe of metropolitan São Paulo, had a 6,000 m^2 sales floor, visited by an estimated 6,500 people per day, who were offered fifty thousand products ranging from tinned foods to television sets as they strolled its eight kilometers of aisles. It too represented something new in style and offerings: "Inspired by Mexican and French models, the store does not physically separate the great retail lines, as most North American stores do, and offers everything on self-service."[113]

The model soon spread, including to Rio and São Paulo proper, despite commercial real estate's expense in the two cities. Within two years, there were sixteen Brazilian hypermarkets. For a North American observer, they were "a sign of the affluent times . . . colossal stores of near-Nirvana where the shopper can find almost anything his heart desires." If this proverbial shopper wanted, she could even buy a car; if she could not afford a car, she was not the sort of customer sought by hypermarket managers, the assumption being that their stores would serve the automobile-owning classes exclusively. The selling of hypermarketing thus fit the political economy of the period, just as the stores' enormity matched Brasil Grande, hence Delfim Netto's presence as guest of honor at the inauguration of Pão de Açúcar's Jumbo. From the government's point of view, hypermarketing represented retail modernization, while Pão de Açúcar's overseas expansion was consonant with the drive to increase exports and heighten Brazil's international profile, as the group opened thirteen stores in Portugal in 1970–1973, followed by one in Portuguese-ruled Luanda. Augusto Schmidt's Disco had prided itself on exporting supermarketing "know-how" to Uruguay and Argentina, but Pão de Açúcar's transatlantic expansion was far more impressive as far as Brazilian technocrats and geopoliticians were concerned.[114]

Another way in which consumer-oriented business figured in policies worthy of Brasil Grande was in state encouragement of zaibatsu, Japanese-style conglomerates that would provide economies of scale in everything from administration to distribution. The first and largest of the Brazilian zaibatsu was the petrochemical conglomerate Unipar. In retailing and consumer-goods industry, that position was taken by the União de Empresas Brasileiras (UEB), created in 1970 out of the Ducal chain and Sparta menswear-manufacturing concern, which had their origins in the economic group headed by Lauro de Carvalho. Even before UEB, Ducal was a conglomerate with interests beyond retail and apparel manufacturing, including firms specializing in data processing, appliance manufacturing, and the export-import trade. Ducal was also the beneficiary of government largesse before becoming Delfim Netto's favorite consumer-goods group, Roberto Campos providing tax breaks and generous credit, while the president of Brazil's Central Bank sponsored its association with smaller appliance retailers, promising: "The consuming public will necessarily be the final beneficiary of this process. Lower costs will mean more accessible prices when combined with good business practices and above all when these are combined with the support of Government." In the late 1960s, the fact that the interior minister was brother-in-law to two members of Ducal's leadership troika may have encouraged such support; in 1971, when he retired from the army, the minister-general became a UEB vice president. At its founding, UEB's main concerns were Sparta's clothing factory and seventy stores specializing in menswear and electronics. By 1973, through the absorption of competitors and the opening of new outlets, the group owned 102 stores. Changes in retail operations accompanied this growth as existing and newly acquired stores were refashioned, the smaller ones expanded, transformed into small-scale department stores, featuring women's fashions as well as menswear, furniture as well as electronics. Meanwhile, "popular shows"—"spectacles . . . presented in stadiums everywhere we have stores"—were a new promotional turn; some were televised, as a complement to the group's investment in television programming, including product-placement "merchandising," as in the telenovela *Beto Rockefeller*, a sensation widely seen as signaling the Brazilianization of the genre. Over the same years, massive government incentives fueled UEB's creation of an industrial plant in northeastern Brazil, manufacturing growth complemented by expansion in other fields, at least on paper. In the 1960s, finance had become a major concern of José Luiz Moreira de Souza, who emerged as UEB's leading figure. In 1971, José Luiz brought his Independência-Decred financial group into UEB, while adding interests in insurance brokerage, tourism, and real estate, as well as a scheme to double Paraguayan sugar production.[115]

Alongside UEB's expansion, Brasil Grande ideas acquired texture, if not depth. It was not only advertisers, encouraged by the executive branch's public-relations arm, that took up the call. Media interests, too, committed themselves, none more than *Manchete* and TV-Globo, the "most complete translation of 'Brasil Grande.'"[116] Media interests, advertisers, and the new professionals cooperated with regime functionaries in adding to the stock of images and ideas associated with Brasil Grande beyond conglomerated enterprises, cars, and quantitative benchmarks. Gigantic public works, particularly in transport and communications, were extolled, including as means of national integration, which President Emílio Garrastazu Médici (1970–1974) claimed was his greatest concern. Sport, especially association football, was exploited as never before as a means to rally support for government, even as Brasil Grande was interwoven with openly exclusionary rhetorics. Throughout, elaborations upon Brasil Grande ideas were enveloped in the culture of Brazilian consumer capitalism.

The grandest of the era's transportation-infrastructure projects was the Trans-Amazonian Highway, centerpiece of the National Integration Program unveiled by the Médici government in 1970. Though not unprecedented—a highway from Brasília to Belém had been built under Kubitschek—it was unmatched in its scope and ambition, to stretch from the northeastern state of Paraíba, hundreds of miles east of the Amazon, through the northeast and on, traversing the giant Amazonian states of Pará and Amazonia. As a policy response to conditions in the northeast, it was to encourage land-poor farming folk to settle in the Amazon region, envisioned as Brazil's last frontier, where, rendering rainforest into farmland, they would assist in national development. To these social and developmental priorities were added the exigencies of national security: settlement of the Amazon would deter its colonization by outsiders. The Globo network and other broadcasting interests enlisted as cheerleaders. Bloch rushed a special issue of *Manchete* into print, stressing national greatness, unity, and development, while a cover story in Victor Civita's *Veja* pronounced the 1970s to be the "Decade of Amazonia." Almap produced a prizewinning television commercial for Volkswagen that began with footage of the Trans-Amazonian Highway's construction, the voice-over stressing the richness of the region, the difficulty of taming it, and the comfort in which all types of automobiles would one day travel the highway, where now none but heavy construction vehicles dared venture, at which point a brave tune began playing as a *fusca* entered the picture, driving unimpeded through the rutted course of the road-to-be. Thus were bundled the military government's premiere public-works project and the country's most popular automobile.[117]

In some ways the creation of a national telecommunications infrastructure was even more ambitious than the Trans-Amazonian Highway. It was certainly more expensive and, through its effects on television broadcasting and viewership, more significant as far as "national integration" was concerned. And so the beneficiaries of the Embratel system wrapped themselves in the flag and identified with the regime, as in the speech that the media executive Walter Clark Bueno made as ADVB's "Salesman of the Year" for 1973, at a gala attended by the governor of São Paulo, as well as such marketing luminaries as Mauro Salles and Rodolfo Lima Martensen. Bueno credited the prize to his boss, Roberto Marinho, "director of a firm that, through free enterprise, could carry out . . . an important recommendation of the revolutionary government of President Médici: the constitution and consolidation of a network so that television can fulfill its role as the country's integrating force." While Embratel's reach was embraced by Globo, the government's demand for the earliest possible introduction of color television was unwelcome, as it would require overhauling equipment and production, Bueno explaining years later, "The government was interested in introducing color TV quickly, to reinforce the idea of modernity and clarity that it wanted associated with the regime. Brasil Grande had to have a grand TV, beautiful and in color." Ultimately, the network's delaying tactics could last only so long, and so regular color broadcasting was scheduled to begin on March 31, 1972, while Globo executives negotiated a subvention from television manufacturers. The outcome was a happy one: "Color's principal effect was the consolidation of the Globo Standard of Quality. It made beautiful what was already pretty." It did not occur in a vacuum: "All this coincided with the euphoria of the 'Brazilian miracle.' The standard of quality, the strengthening of an image of modernity and technology, ended up coopting, even without wanting to, the image of 'Brasil Grande,' that the governments of the dictatorship were so interested in."[118]

Even as Brasil Grande came to be embodied in investments in transportation infrastructure and communications technology, it also found a place in the twinning of sport and mass nationalism. Indeed, the two projects—of upgrading Brazil's communications infrastructure and identifying the regime with success in international sport—overlapped, the government announcing in 1968 that the 1970 World Cup would be broadcast over live television, a first in Brazil. Globo executives negotiated broadcasting rights with Emilio

Azcárraga's Telesistema Mexicana, while advertisers fell over themselves to sponsor the transmissions. Initially, the government planned to use the World Cup broadcasts to promote a national lottery, but when JWT and McCann executives complained of unfair competition with "the ordinary advertiser," authorities relented. Esso, Souza Cruz, and Gillette thus won sponsorship rights of the transmissions broadcast on all Brazilian television stations, as well as by five pools of radio stations, the two media sharing a theme song composed by the jingle-writer Miguel Gustavo for JWT, a catchy march that provided a widely deployed slogan of the Brasil Grande era and remains the country's unofficial national anthem of association football: "Noventa milhões em ação / Pra frente Brasil / Do meu coração . . ." ("90 million in action, Onward Brazil, Of my heart . . ."). The song, which made Gustavo the ABP's "Advertising Man of the Year," was only part of a "commercial festival behind the scenes," which also included Abril's launching the sporting weekly *Placar* as its first stab at a mass-market magazine aimed at men who were not necessarily of the car-buying classes, replete with giveaway Pelé medals and posters, and advertisements for Ducal clothes, Continental cigarettes, and Monark bicycles.[119]

It was television, however, that made the Cup as important as it was. A year earlier, Brazilians had watched their first international satellite broadcast, a viewing shared with millions worldwide of flickering images of a foreign spaceman making history on some spectral lunarscape. Now millions more Brazilians than had watched any man-made event viewed another simultaneous international broadcast, featuring a group of men representing them, playing the nation's dearest sport in the world's most important competition. "Nothing less than 25 million spectators, distributed among four million households, watched the greatest event of world football. Brazil linked up to History by satellite." That Brazil won it all, decisively, heightened the exaltation of the occasion: "On the 21st of June of 1970, Brazil lived one of the most thrilling moments of its History. History with an H." Manoel Julião Netto (b. 1902), known to posterity only for having left a memoir, made the Cup its culmination. "The repercussion of this conquest," he wrote, "reached the most distant points of the terrestrial globe; it marks a new era in Brazil! We are no longer an underdeveloped nation. . . . At the end of this decade of the 1970s, listen to me Brazilians! . . . Exult! . . . Be happy! . . . The green-gilt flag will be raised among the five greatest countries in the world!"[120]

As millions danced and cheered in the streets, then welcomed home their heroes, some Brazilians, many of them no doubt equally moved, sought to harness the moment to ends associated with Brasil Grande. "No one can hold this country back," was the line attributed to Médici and propagated by the public-relations group headed by Octávio Costa, who later revealed that he thought it unnecessary to exploit the World Cup in official propaganda. Instead, Costa and his lieutenants asked advertisers and advertising executives to mount campaigns hailing the victory as "an indication of Brazilian success," a request that was met by a season's worth of advertisements, at the end of which *Propaganda* saluted Médici for having coined the "Slogan of the Year": "The President of the Republic's phrase translated an entire national motivation and transformed itself into a symbol of the confidence required to build a great Nation." Amid that transformation, advertisers presented each member of the national team with a new Volkswagen sedan and $4,000 worth of appliances: refrigerators and televisions, radios and hi-fi sets, electric stoves and razors, all the comforts that Brasil Grande's consumer capitalism could provide.[121]

As the fanfare began to subside, Costa summoned the head of every advertising agency of note to his São Paulo office. He addressed them in military style: "We have no World Cup this year and we have to keep our people cheerful and satisfied. I know that the best brains in Brazilian advertising are gathered in this room. The government is counting on your talent and imagination to develop a great civic campaign to stimulate popular confidence in the authorities and in the country. The deadline for handing in texts and *layouts* is February 28. Any questions?" Results were not as obnoxious as some earlier cultural work on behalf of the regime, the lowest point of which was the translation of "Love It or Leave It" into Portuguese (which Almap went on to tweak, tastelessly, in advertising for AMCE's tenth Children's Salon, "Love Them and Let Them Go," enlisting parental love in the service of Brasil Grande and Brazilian consumer capitalism). But they were hardly more uplifting. By 1977, even advertising executives were willing to make mild criticisms of the "Brazil Is Made by Us" slogan, in which the naked antagonism of "Love It or Leave It" was toned down into an implicit "them" working against "us." But not Alex Periscinoto, who defended it, "as a kind of shout, saying: 'Hold on there, no one messes with this place.'"[122]

Comfort Zones

By the time of Periscinoto's intervention, many of the most important Brasil Grande slogans had fallen into disuse. As growth rates fell, "At the Pace of Brasil Grande" no longer hit the right notes; indeed, in changed circumstances it had the capacity to embarrass the regime. But stalwarts did not give up on policies supporting the country's consumer capitalism. In 1977 Minister of Planning Reis Veloso addressed the First Brazilian Marketing and Commercialization Congress, emphasizing the importance of strong, well-structured enterprises. "We support the idea that modern [commercial] mechanisms become increasingly developed," he said, adding that such development was already underway, evidenced by the supermarkets long-supported by government and by "shopping-centers." By that point, Brazil's first enclosed shopping malls had been in business for just over a decade, but the words "shopping center" had been applied to other structures beginning in the 1950s. In doing so, stakeholders in commercial arcades and mixed-use complexes sought to portray these structures as embodying modern convenience and comfort, a prelude to the creation of a "shopping-center culture" in the 1960s and after.[123]

Commercial arcades (*galerias comerciais*) were an increasingly important part of southeastern cityscapes in the 1950s. By 1963, the claim that there was "arcade fever in São Paulo" was no exaggeration, and much the same could have been said of Rio. In São Paulo's "new" downtown, in Rio's city center, and in once-outlying neighborhoods of both cities, commercial arcades were laid out in new buildings and in older ones refurbished to create storefronted retail space where none existed. Curved façades and careful lighting seduced pedestrians, while ramps and escalators funneled crowds to spaces below and above. Arcades linking major thoroughfares were designed to erase the distinction between outside and inside, public and private, while drawing foot traffic past artfully designed shopwindows. Some marketing experts sniffed that they were not true shopping centers, but builders and their backers did handsomely, as shopspaces in prime locations sold off quickly, and while the idea of the commercial arcade harked back to European precedent, North American influence upon their design and promotion was plain. According to its developers, São Paulo's Centro Comercial Grandes Galerias was the result of research on "the most modern 'Shopping Centers' built in the entire world"; its four hundred units sold out in eight hours. The most successful arcades featured leisure as well as commercial activities: cinemas, cafés, restaurants. Along with its "most beautiful air-conditioned restaurant," Rio's Galeria Menescal promised "the greatest facilities for shopping, comfortably and without wasting time."[124]

Some of the property owners, real-estate developers, architects, and builders associated with the commercial-arcade craze were also involved in the design, building, and promotion of mixed-use structures, most often called *conjuntos* ("complexes"). These buildings featured combinations of the retailing typical of *galerias* with office space and/or residential condominiums, usually complemented by leisure facilities and parking. São Paulo's Conjunto Nacional, steps from the chic shopping district of Rua Augusta, included stores, eateries, office space, and a cinema, with the added amenity of elevator music. *PN*'s editors dubbed it a "Sales-Promotion Center"; other authorities called it a "shopping center." Inaugurated by Kubitschek, it became a "symbol of the sophistication of the Paulistano upper strata." In Rio, the Centro

Comercial de Copacabana combined retail, residential, and office space in a structure that the magazine of the American Chamber of Commerce called "Rio's first Shopping Center" and *Ultima Hora* predicted would "revolutionize the habits" of the southern beachfront. Its sequel, the Conjunto Cidade de Copacabana, was even larger, joining office space and six residential buildings perched atop "the 1st Super-Shopping Center in the World." This "social-commercial complex" featured an underground garage, more than two hundred shops, a one thousand–seat movie house, a smaller space for theatrical performances, and a nightclub, as well as gardens and playgrounds, topped off by a futuristic Catholic church, linked by escalators and a grand ramp that evoked the Guggenheim Museum. If residents were to want for nothing, retailers were to receive the "commercial benefits of the newest architectural solution": "convergent traffic" created by the "compulsory flow" of residents, visitors, movie fans, theater buffs, nightclubbers, and churchgoers through the complex's commercial heart.[125]

The *conjuntos* and *galerias* became sites for plenty of shopping, but they differed in important respects from shopping malls as North Americans knew them. In the first place they were unenclosed and thus, though sheltered from the elements, not climate controlled. They were also "unanchored"— that is, they did not feature the large retail chains that served as "anchors" in U.S. malls, drawing customers who would also shop at specialty stores. *Galerias* and *conjuntos* were built in the interests of real-estate owners, developers, contractors, and brokers, who vanished from the scene once the last storefront was sold, if not sooner, leaving behind a storeowners' condominium of limited cohesion. Some of the same groups—builders, for example—would have a short-term interest in particular shopping malls, but the latter would be controlled by a management group that answered to the owners of the property, who were not, or not exclusively, the retailers operating its individual stores. Shopping malls of this variety emerged in Brazil in the 1960s, with early, emblematic examples opening their doors in Rio in 1965 and São Paulo in 1966. Shopping Center do Méier and Shopping Center Iguatemi, as the two malls were known, represented different applications of the idea. Each was a success on its own, though the São Paulo one emerged as the national template, erasing Rio's precedence in such commercial memory as can be said to have existed.

The Shopping Center do Méier, as its name indicates, was located in a leading North Zone neighborhood, the site of earlier retail-interest attention. It was the brainchild of Estanislau Zaremba, a former airline executive who had seen the U.S. mall firsthand and whose family owned real estate on one of Méier's thoroughfares. The location was a proven success for existing retailers, including Sears, which operated a store abutting the site, and so seemed a likely location for an enclosed mall. Construction began following studies of Méier and its population and investigations in the United States. The latter, Zaremba indicated, was key to "adapting the 'shopping center' to the conditions of life in Brazil"; only there could the mall's designers "make valid comparisons between what is practiced there and the particular conditions of our country." Even as the center's foundation was laid, it was pegged as Brazil's "first integrated complex of stores to obey rigorous planning in retail technique and promotional architecture." When construction was completed, there stood a glass-and-concrete structure with the lettering "Shopping Center do Brasil S.A. / MEIER / Brazil's first." Inside, fifty thousand people per day could find everything "from a pin to a car" in dozens of stores, including Peg-Pag and Lojas Brasileiras, which served as internal anchors complementing the external anchor of the street's existing commerce, while remaining shops were curated to enhance the range of in-mall options and maximize traffic between them. Following its inauguration, attended by Governor Carlos Lacerda, hungry shoppers could choose between open-air dining on the third floor, a café, and an outlet of the Bob's fast-food chain, which had been serving Cariocas U.S.-style hamburgers since the 1950s. There were also an auditorium, a bank, a post office, and a "play ground" where mothers could leave their children while they shopped. Escalators linked the three floors, including a parking area with spaces for one hundred cars. A "multitude"— even a "great multitude"—was on hand for the opening of this application of "the idea [that] naturally was born in the United States"; by Christmas, sales reportedly exceeded management's expectations.[126]

From early on, the Méier center had attracted the attention of Alfredo Mathias, whose construction company and development group thrived in São Paulo's *galeria* trade and who invited Zaremba to join a São Paulo–based venture modeled on Shopping Center do Brasil. Zaremba agreed, bringing with him the architect João Henrique Rocha, whose Rio-based firm had designed the Méier shopping center but was probably most famous for coming in second in the competition to design Brasília. The terrain Rocha was given to work with was picked following traffic studies and extensive research on market conditions (including thousands of door-to-door interviews carried out by the INESE market-research firm), and was very different than that in Méier: not only was the lot considerably larger; it was located at the pivot of several thoroughfares abutting newer neighborhoods unserviced by major retailers. What resulted was a larger enclosed mall, triply anchored by a Sears, a Lojas Americanas, and a Pão de Açúcar supermarket, linked by wide galleries featuring nearly two miles of interior shopwindows. Its other businesses included dozens of shops of every kind, two full-service restaurants, two cinemas, a snack bar, and a café. Offering many of the services available at the

Méier mall (banking, a post office), Iguatemi also offered a "pick up" parcel service, two filling stations, and the country's first hands-free automatic car wash, adjacent to parking for nearly one thousand cars. Store transactions were monitored by computer to ensure that rents (calculated according to sales) were paid in full. At its 1966 pre-Christmas opening—attended by the governor, and featuring a mass by the archbishop, followed by music from Chico Buarque and a performance by a television comic—Iguatemi was dubbed "the largest commercial complex in Latin America."[127]

These were not the only shopping-mall experiments of the 1960s—there were others, in Rio and São Paulo—but they were the most important. Each was also a model of sorts. The Méier center was erected in an existing shopping district in a neighborhood losing prestige and some of its most comfortable residents to Rio's southern beachfront. Iguatemi, by contrast, was planned and built at a distance from all but the most rudimentary commerce and services at an early stage in the movement of wealthy and near-wealthy Paulistanos from older neighborhoods near the city center to new districts to the south. Thus, in Méier the mall functioned as a mostly pedestrian extension of local retailing, entertainment, and leisure in an established, middle-class neighborhood, while the Iguatemi center represented the first wave of retail development in an emergent, more exclusive area, and catered almost exclusively to shoppers arriving by automobile: according to an early study, 92 percent of shoppers arrived by family car or taxi, and 85 percent belonged to car-owning households. As Jorge Mathias (director of the Iguatemi mall, brother of its developer and builder, and, decades earlier, a McCann staffer and the leading figure behind the founding of the Paulista Advertising Association) explained, "For a 'shopping center' to be an efficient center for purchases, it should form a whole, selling everything, situated in regions of high purchasing power and that allow easy parking." It would be the Iguatemi model, more or less, that would be assembled elsewhere in Brazil: in Brasília in 1971, in Fortaleza in 1974, and in Salvador in 1975, where the mall in question was designed by João Henrique Rocha, built by Alfredo Mathias, and named Shopping Center Iguatemi Bahia. Back in São Paulo, Shopping Center Continental (1975) represented another take on the Iguatemi template, one that drew on the expertise of an EAESP–Michigan State alumnus, Alberto de Oliveira Lima Filho, "who did the *marketing* coordination," while massive Shopping Center Ibirapuera (1976) represented an even more exclusive, luxurious variation. As another mall's marketing director explained of shopping centers generally: "It is necessary to implant them next to the districts inhabited by class A, so that the middle and C classes come to accept them later on." Myopic when it came to the fact that the goods and services on offer in places like Shopping Center Ibirapuera were out of reach of members of class C, such enthusiasts took a long view when it came to construction: "*Shopping centers* are an irresistible phenomenon. Their creation . . . will be inevitable and will respond to consumers' needs over the next 50 years. Therefore, it is fundamental that the shopping centers designed now be planned in such a way that one doesn't run the risk of their deterioration during that fabulous period of five decades." This view was shared in official circles, where as early as 1972 developers enjoyed government support for shopping-mall construction, including financing from the National Housing Bank. By late 1976, these developers were organized in the Brazilian Association of Shopping Centers.[128]

Along the way, the habit of shopping-center shopping was developed, drawing on earlier retail revolutions and the experience of commercial arcades and multiuse complexes, while overlapping with the hypermarket's rise. Readers had the concept explained to them, in articles and advertisements, while television viewers received images elaborating upon it. Onsite entertainments like those featured at the inauguration of the Iguatemi mall would be a recurrent draw for shoppers, along with other leisure-time activities and community events. All were part of shopping's "marketing mix."

Public-relations pieces and other press items sought to explain how the shopping center worked. Interviewed in 1956, the architect Henrique Mindlin explained that the Super Shopping Center de Copacabana would function as "a new commercial square, for which Copacabana feels such a need," different than existing ones in that it would be "separated from the streets and all of traffic's inconveniences" and feature "its own social life." In 1958, *O Estado de S. Paulo*'s urban-design columnist introduced readers to the malls spreading across the suburban United States, "true cultural centers" featuring "commercial establishments [as well as] beauty salons, cinemas, pastry shops, restaurants." Three years later, in anticipation of the opening of the Super Shopping Center de Copacabana, another architect introduced "this organism that, from a commercial point of view, has characterized the modern life of the American nation." "For the people," he wrote, a mall is "a joyful, musical, and lively environment, where one buys everything, a true display fair," while from the point of view of storeowners "a shopping center represents, above all else, a defense against unfair competition, efficient service, and the growth of their businesses, due to the creation of this new and powerful center of attraction, capable of intensely augmenting the flow of the clientele." At the inauguration of the Méier mall, a society columnist wrote, "a fascinating experience, this center of 40 stores, with the most varied kinds of trade," noting the parking, supermarket, supervised playground, "and even a most refined boutique," featuring "dresses made according to patterns from Paris, of naturally impeccable lines and at ultra-accessible prices." In São

Paulo by then, with *conjuntos* open for business and Iguatemi under construction, "the enterprises of intrinsically commercial character, as are the *shopping centers*, advanced considerably in the process of expansion, providing commerce of the contemporary mold, which presumes three guiding purposes: diversification, ease, and comfort of the purchaser. The placement of cinemas, restaurants, or nightclubs within these architectural blocks acts as a factor of public attraction, determining the flow of occasional purchasers, as a function of the shopwindow and of the fasciation that it exercises over those who have purchasing power to dispose of." Months later, when Shopping Center Iguatemi opened, the *Folha de S. Paulo* devoted half of an eight-paragraph feature to demystifying its "grand commercial world," indicating how its features were to be utilized, while *O Estado de S. Paulo* explained, "It will not be simply a center for shopping; it will join the simple commercial sector to public utility, with various services, and entertainment, with cinemas and other activities."[129]

Advertising performed similar functions. Indeed, as had long been the case, it was difficult to distinguish between editorial material and advertising. An advertisement aimed at interesting retailers in the Méier mall proclaimed that "the great commercial novelty of recent times" would feature "all of the necessary requisites so that the public may be better served in a pleasant, comfortable environment." "What is a 'shopping center'?" asked promotors of a shopping mall for Niterói. It was "a grandiose enclosure in which everything was planned, in which every area is destined for a predetermined type of store . . . an ideal center for purchases, of streets and avenues without sun and without rain, without heat or dust, with chilled air, a telephone center, luncheonette and restaurant, supermarket, cinema and other attractions that make it the community's principal gathering place, multiplying sales through the concentration of powerful promotional factors." Shopping Centers Reunidas do Brasil advertisements provided answers to the same question for investors, store owners, and consumers, its idealization of the experience of members of the third group promising "a grandiose, fairy-like, marvelous and magical [*feérico*] enclosure where the consumer finds everything she needs, from food to perfume, in exceptional conditions of comfort and price. Covered streets and avenues. Background music. Dozens of famous stores. Cinemas, a theater, gardens and 'play-grounds.' Enormous parking areas. A fabulous social center of happy conviviality, a marvelous city of shopping and entertainments!" On the eve of Iguatemi's opening, institutional advertisements declared: "Starting tomorrow you will already be able to experience the joy of doing your shopping in Latin America's most fabulous shopping center. There are 70 of São Paulo's most famous stores selling everything—from flowers to refrigerators—in one place and for the lowest prices. At Iguatemi, yes, you may choose and compare as you like—and make the best buy! The maximum of variety, the maximum of economy, the maximum of comfort." These offerings were the stuff of "modernization"; Shopping Center do Méier was proof of that neighborhood's "eminently progressive spirit"; Iguatemi was "an act of progress . . . the pioneering introduction of the 'shopping center' system in São Paulo, bringing our land up to date with this modern marketing process." In advertisements and editorial copy, the key referent was the United States, the "Recipe for a Shopping Center" beginning with "a good serving of American experience," while the Méier mall was said to "look like the *shopping centers* near New York City."[130]

Television also figured in the shopping center's marketing mix. The mall in general and Iguatemi in particular were the subject of a 1965 show designed "to bring the public messages of optimism composed of the story of entrepreneurial undertakings," a goal that anticipated miracle-era Brasil Grande propaganda. In the show—carried by three São Paulo stations—Mathias pointed to his group's success in selling shares in the mall as evidence "of confidence and optimism in this phase of transition that Brazil is going through" and promised viewers "a planned solution for your sales and consumption problems." Nine years later, changing times and the unprecedented luxury of the Ibirapuera mall demanded grander programming. Produced by the Artplan agency and directed by the filmmaker Maurice Capovilla, with ample funding from the Veplan real-estate and development group, it was titled *Revolução do Consumo*. The concept was to "make a program explaining what a shopping [center] is and show it on the Globo network," an idea that received Globo's support, provided that the finished product meet the "Globo standard." Filmed in color over two months on location in São Paulo, New York, Paris, Tokyo, Munich, and Amsterdam, the hour-long program was broadcast nationwide in prime time in mid-1974. Billed as "a documentary that cannot be ignored by consumers and merchants who want to keep up with what is occurring in the world," it was to demonstrate that "factors that influenced the evolution of habits of consumption in the great urban centers" pointed to the "new concept of consumption, leisure, and services" apparent in Ibirapuera's blueprints.[131]

Community events, festivals, and public entertainments were other means to introduce city dwellers to commercial facilities that were purportedly theirs. The Super Shopping Center de Copacabana was the site of two midnight masses before construction of its church was completed, following which it was the site of regular Sunday services. During the same period, the Super Shopping Center hosted televised literary festivals celebrity-studded by Pelé, Kubitschek, and the bossa-nova idol João Gilberto. The group behind the Super Shopping Center da Guanabara hosted a St. John's Day festival in 1965, featuring popular and mock-folkloric music, dancing, and shows for

children and adults, with televisions spread around the grounds for attendees who might otherwise stay at home to watch *O direito de nascer*; a dozen
years later, after the undercapitalized development finally opened its doors,
the promotor Nelson Motta was lent on-site space he transformed into "Fre-
netic Dancin' Days," Rio's first discotheque, its success inspiring a Globo telenovela. From the beginning, children and their parents were drawn to malls
by the familiar figure of Santa Claus, who arrived at Iguatemi for the first time
days after its opening in a spectacle assembled by the JMM agency. Four years
later, decorations designed by Lotus Propaganda assisted in extraordinary
Christmas sales, motivating "a consuming public already accustomed to all
the comforts it offers."[132]

As Iguatemi's Christmas commemorations suggest, shopping-center administrators drew on established retail practice, even as the enclosed mall was
envisioned as a more elaborate, carefully managed version of the *galeria*. The
development of the mall was also of a piece with the creation of Brazilian hypermarketing, the two institutions offering similar comforts to increasing
numbers of people: upward of five hundred thousand per month at Pão de
Açúcar's Jumbo by mid-1973; more than a million each month at Iguatemi by
1974, when shopping-center developers agreed that "the American invention
of bringing together stores and services in one place" had achieved "conse-
cration" in Brazil.[133]

Thus the experience of shopping-center shopping was re-created in
Brazil. "The simple act of buying," according to one account, came to be
enveloped "in a kind of magic and movement mixed with leisure and entertainment." The effect was deliberate, as *Visão* described the "very modern
and sophisticated solution" to the search for sales: "It is very important that
[shopping centers] provide a comfortable shopping environment, seeking to
always transform the necessity of buying something into the pleasure of
buying." It was the fulfillment of Zaremba and Mathias's promise of a "permanent atmosphere of promotions to be provided to consumers and users of
the first Shopping Center of São Paulo through festivals, contests, expositions, and artistic performances, on a scale unknown in Brazil until now, so
that the new commercial center polarizes the buyer's attention." In 1973, the
trade magazine *Supermercado Moderno* predicted, "The 1970s will be the
decade of the hypermarket and the *shopping center*." Four years on, according
to the mouthpiece of Rio's Commercial Association, the changes the new
institutions brought already belonged to the past: "These great shopping
centers completely transformed consumption habits." The time was not far
off when Minister of Finance Mário Henrique Simonsen would refer to shopping "as a leisure moment" and an old retail hand would go further in addressing a seminar titled "Shopping Center and Social Development": "The

moment of purchase is effectively a moment of pleasure. It is a moment in which we realize a desire, a need. It is a moment in which we gratify ourselves with this pleasure and if we do so it is because we feel that we deserve this gratification. . . . It thus seems to me that the moment of purchase is a socially important moment and it needs to be valued."[134]

Such moments occupied increasingly longer stretches of time. As *O Estado de S. Paulo* explained of Iguatemi, "a family, to stroll it in its entirety, would need more than a day." Indeed, "a person who needs to go shopping can spend the entire day in the center, taking his or her meals or snacks there, taking the opportunity to watch a film or to go to the barber or beauty shop, and to send letters or telegrams while their car is getting its oil changed at one of the service stations." Meanwhile, in the hypermarket world, Eletro-Radiobraz managers estimated that shoppers spent an average of four hours on each visit to its superstore. If hypermarket or shopping-mall customers could be made to spend more time shopping, that was all to the good. As a marketing staffer explained of São Paulo's Continental Center: "Continental was planned in such a way that the buyer does not sense the passage of time when they are in the *shopping*. All the stores face the galleries, the windows are not translucent, and the lighting is artificial, preventing the consumer from perceiving if night is falling, if there's sun or rain. Beyond that, there are no clocks in the galleries. The perfect climate control will not permit one to feel cold or heat. Everything is established in such a way as to create conditions such that the buyer remain inside Continental the maximum amount of time." Continental thus matched *Indústria e Desenvolvimento*'s description of an "introvert mall": "In this modern center, consumers remain almost apart from the outside world, being isolated from rain, cold or heat, and from pollution, disposing of a very diverse array of products to buy."[135]

In Rio, year-round nighttime shopping predated malls and hypermarkets. In São Paulo, they emerged at around the same time, authorities lifting restrictions on nighttime shopping outside of the Christmas season in 1969. "Nighttime commerce is the commerce of the future and will certainly be victorious," a shopping-center manager predicted. Promotions and pressures on customers' time soon proved him right, affecting supermarkets and department stores as well as shopping malls and hypermarkets. "Our objective, ahead of anything else, was to give Paulistanos the possibility of doing their shopping at the hour that is most convenient to them," claimed a spokesman for Pão de Açúcar. The director of Eletro-Radiobraz's supermarket sector agreed: "São Paulo, with its nearly six million inhabitants, needs services of this type, matching a practice in vogue in the other capitals of the world." For a Mappin shopper from outlying Tatuapé, it was a welcome change: "Finally, São Paulo's commerce is becoming human."[136]

To the facility of nighttime shopping were added other comforts and conveniences, including the credit card. That shopping centers, "superstores," and "hyperstores" should emphasize the "providing of services," according to one account, "is occurring because of the sophisticated consumer society that is becoming a reality." That the chain of causality just as often ran in the other direction is clear in responses to the emergence of these institutions. In Rio, according to the geographer Charles Albert de Andrade, Shopping Center do Méier became "a *point* for young people" soon after its opening, a function not envisioned by the mall's planners but that benefited retailers catering to the youth market. In a parallel development, record sales in São Paulo's *galerias* were used to gauge public preference in the emergent genre of Brazilian Popular Music, or MPB. Beyond São Paulo, in Sorocaba, Santo André, and São José dos Campos, the services and social spaces offered by hypermarkets drew "the greater public and not only the consumer." As a result, the traditional *footing* shifted from downtown sites in Santo André and Sorocaba to the new suburban complexes and their environs. Having attracted such crowds, the new institutions became sites for market research, Jumbo becoming a "center for *merchandising* research," where consumer-goods manufacturers test-marketed their products.[137]

Market-researcher interest in the new institutions had as much to do with the composition of these crowds as their size, and here the newish practice of shopping dovetailed with Brazilian political economy. Jumbo, with its strip-mall annex forming a "mini–*shopping center*," attracted a clientele that was 41 percent "class A" and 37 percent "class B." It was no coincidence: the "store's advertising and *merchandising* [were] entirely oriented" to these high-end groups. Early studies of Shopping Center Iguatemi revealed a similar consumer profile, while the Ibirapuera mall aimed at an even more rarefied social set. For Luís Carlos Bresser Pereira, an EAESP professor and a Pão de Açúcar executive, this pattern of retail activity represented a paradox, the "use of mass-distribution techniques to serve an elite." But his was a false paradox: first, because other mass-marketing techniques reached well beyond comfortable classes A and B; second, as Bresser Pereira recognized, because "it is more reasonable to expect that the retail system adopt itself to the Country's economic and social conditions than the inverse"; third, because—as such adaptation occurred—economic, social, and cultural conditions shifted in ways unforeseeable in the worldview that informed his analysis.[138]

A, B, C, D[x]

While Bresser Pereira's premises—a dualistic view of society divided between moderns and marginals—were as false as his paradox, he was right about inequality. In Brazil under the generals, even regime economists had to acknowledge quantitative evidence of increasing inequality, while the extent of qualitative differences made conveying inequality's extent to outsiders so daunting that an observer might scarcely try. "There are," a U.S. correspondent wrote from Brasília in 1970, "signs that the good life is spread thin." In conversation, a Brazilian analyst referred to specific products: "It is a challenging market. . . . You can sell frozen TV dinners in São Paulo, but there is no such thing as a freezer in the interior." Attesting to the importance of goods—and visions of the good—while allowing readers to intuit that only figuration could conjure up the depths of Brasil Grande–era inequality, Elizabeth Hardwick juxtaposed the images of a homeless person, automobile traffic, and the hum of São Paulo: "Around the somnolent beggar the cars whir in a thick migrating stream. And there it is, magic visible, vastness palpable, quantity realized, things delivered." Put in marketing terms, matters were simpler: the ways of life of people described as "class A"—serviced by shopping-mall marketers and automobile manufacturers—were ever-more distant from the living conditions of "class D." This burgeoning inequality coincided with attempts to codify the increasingly ubiquitous A, B, C, D system of classification.[139]

By the 1970s, the system had been in use for decades. From its origins as advertising jargon, it had become social shorthand and, along the way, subjected to reinterpretation and revision. Attempts to target particular strata led to refinement, particularly in "middle class" B. IBOPE's surveys of urban-dwelling Brazilians distinguished between B1, B2, and B3, while the Prodimec research group split the category into B1 and B2. In each schema, B1 would be closer to A than to C. The Norton agency divided households into seven salary-distinguished groups (D, lower C, upper C, lower B, middle B, upper B, lower A), plus a tiny "upper A" in which income derived not from salaries but from what was once called unearned income. In the early 1960s, Marplan routinely omitted class D from its analyses, on the assumption that persons or families thus classed would be of no interest to advertisers. It was a safe assumption, but—if for no other reason than the social-scientific authority that presenting a composite social snapshot provided—other firms continued gathering information on the very poor. Indeed, the undeniable presence of misery invisible to the Madison Avenue men who had created the A, B, C, D system led to the identification of a "class E" by Prodimec in 1962.[140]

The system's flexibility would probably have been welcomed were it not accompanied by imprecision. Everyone knew, or thought they knew, what "A" and "D" meant, or at least how to distinguish between them, but where to draw the line between lower A and B1? Exactly how many B3 consumers were there? These problems were compounded by the absence of common criteria and the tendency to treat demographic data proprietarily. The household head's income was one possible metric, but researchers had different ideas of what constituted a class A or B salary. Family income, which acknowledged the increased contributions of wives and children, was subject to the same problem, as was disposable family income, a criterion attractive to advertisers. To these problems was added the instability induced by runaway inflation, which made it difficult to keep income-based criteria up to date. Sociological criteria—educational achievement, employment type, place of residence—were brought to bear, but also in the absence of common standards. The result was that one agency's lower A might be another's B1, while IBOPE's class B might not correspond to the "middle class" families envisioned by a manufacturing firm's marketing department.[141]

In 1969, representatives of seventeen of the largest private companies operating in Brazil addressed the country's research firms, demanding concerted effort aimed at creating a common standard. Executives from specialist firms answered the call, including IBOPE, Gallup, INESE, IPOM, and Marplan, together with representatives from JWT, Nestlé, and USP's School of Economics and Business Administration. Over the course of nine meetings hosted by the Brazilian Association of Advertisers (ABA), the commission they formed reviewed each institution's experience, discussed past criteria, built a model, tested its efficacy, and presented the outline of a refined, standardized system to the ABA and the seventeen member firms that had issued the call for standardization. The new system was approved and in place by mid-1970.[142]

The new model retained the original division of society into four alphabetized groups, class A (upper), class B (middle), class C (poor), and class D (very poor), but was otherwise different from preceding attempts at classification. While the idea of creating common standards for the use of research firms, advertising agencies, social scientists, and consumer-oriented industry was ambitious, the new system stopped short of earlier attempts at classifying Brazil's diversity of social conditions. There would be no national classification under the new model, for its starting premise was that it only applied to cities of fifty thousand or more inhabitants, of which there were 115; therefore, the populations of thousands of cities, towns, and rural hamlets would go uncounted. Income—personal, household, or disposable—would not figure. Instead, families were ranked using a point system based on ownership of household appliances and automobiles, number of domestic servants, and head of household's level of education, the first three categories grouped together as "Items of Personal Comfort" (see tables 1 and 2). Total scores of 21 and higher rated as A, 7 to 20 as B, 2 to 6 as C, and 0 or 1 as D.[143]

Table 1 Brazilian Association of Advertisers–sponsored social classification model (1970): goods and servants

"Items of personal comfort"	*Score*
Television set	1
Two or more television sets	3
Refrigerator	1
Floor waxer	1
Washing machine	3
Electric mixer	3
Vacuum cleaner	3
One maid	4
Two or more maids	6
Each car worth less than a new VW sedan	4
Each car worth more than a new VW sedan	6

Table 2 Brazilian Association of Advertisers–sponsored social classification model (1970): education

Highest educational level	*Score*
Illiterate or some primary school	0
Completed primary school or partial middle school	1
Completed middle school or partial secondary school	2
Completed secondary school or partial postsecondary school	4
University degree	8

The system was in many ways a brilliant match to Brazil's consumer capitalism and its conditions and cultural trends generally. It ignored the countryside and, indeed, millions of townsfolk. It was based entirely on households' consumption of goods and services—their "standard of consumption"—if one excepts the educational criteria, and even education was increasingly viewed as just another service as the "marketing ideology" identified by Carlos Guilherme Mota took hold in schools. Consumption, in other words, defined class, rather than the other way around. Because the new model did not take incomes or net worth into account, it was immune to inflation and deliberately blind to household indebtedness related to *crediários, consórcios*, and other consumer-credit instruments. Alongside the "big ticket" appliances were placed the creature comforts of household servants, cheapened by massive rural-to-urban migration and the lack of protections for domestic workers. Then there was the zero-kilometer Volkswagen sedan as the measure of an automobile, in the same year the millionth *fusca* came off the line. Finally, there were the new schema's results, which might as well have been produced by Brasil Grande ideologues independently of any data, a survey of São Paulo that used the criteria yielding a population that was divided into classes A, B, C, and D in the proportions 10, 40, 32, 18. Brazil's largest city had thus been transformed into a metropolis half rich and middle class, earlier estimates based on family income having depicted one in which C and D outnumbered B and a tiny A group. This transformation was unaccompanied by any outstanding shifts in income structure, except that away from the lowest-paid workers, but it looked great on paper. Subsequent polls purported to show many B households rising into class A, as class D continued to shrink.[144]

Despite these pleasing, if fanciful, results, the model was contested from the start. IBOPE participated in the model's design, but its executives continued to use in-house criteria rather than the points-based system. Emil Farhat, formerly of McCann, now of Globo, persisted in referring to "households classified with the letters C, D, and E," adding that "they mean *almost nothing* in the world of purchases and sales." The need for the "class E" category—to capture additional degrees of want—was seen as so great that it was included in revised criteria established at the ABA's behest nine years later, now in cooperation with an associational body representing research institutes. But the revised criteria produced no lasting agreement and, indeed, the research-institute association eventually split over how classes A through E should be defined. The solution of 1970, in other words, may have matched elements of Brasil Grande–era culture and political economy, but it could not meet the demands of all interested parties any more than it could represent social conditions across the Brazilian subcontinent. It was important, however, inasmuch as it made consumption the central category of a more "Brazilian" schema and, most of all, contributed to the diffusion of the letter-denominated language of class, which became the dominant way in which social difference was treated in the media from which Brazilians of all walks of life increasingly took their cues. So ingrained did it become that historians and other social scientists, including critics of the culture of Brazilian consumer capitalism, use the terms "class A" and "class D" reflexively, unaware that the terminology is an artifact of that culture.[145]

The question remains of why the terminology took hold in Brazil, while in the United States it never caught on beyond Madison Avenue and fell into disuse even there, dropping out of the advertising profession's argot without having made a larger impression. Answers to such questions are speculative by nature, but two seem more than plausible. First, in institutional and structural terms, there is the relative importance of JWT in the two countries and the development of U.S. consumer capitalism in the 1920s compared with the relatively anemic state of consumer-oriented business in Brazil at the same point in time. In the United States, JWT was one advertising agency among many, its executives hardly expecting other advertising men to adopt their in-house schema, much less that it would be taken up by market researchers, public-opinion pollsters, and media elites. JWT's relative position in Brazil was altogether different. In 1929, it became the first major U.S. agency to operate in the country. The cadre trained at JWT went on to work at other foreign firms, as well as found independent agencies; at both they would eagerly apply such Thompson "know-how" as the A through D scheme. Aspiring media managers, working on a quasi-amateur basis, were happy to borrow professional appurtenances and otherwise please advertising agencies and the advertisers they represented. Beginning in the 1940s, the schema was taken up by the country's first major market- and media-research firm at a moment in which many other institutions, products, and practices associated with U.S.-style consumerism scarcely existed. When they did arise, their managers, manufacturers, and promotors had a schema at hand for use in their own work.

Beyond the issues of relative timing, sequencing, and institutional standing lay an even more important factor having to do with language and culture. In the United States, there was an alternative social shorthand manifest in the idea that it was a "middle-class" country, of happy people in an econosocial happy middle. Advertising executives no longer belonged to the "middle class" that was their most important audience, but many would have identified themselves as having middle class backgrounds, and few households they identified as middle class would have objected to the term. The situation in Brazil was different. Even as North American scholars have applied the techniques of ethnography and cultural history to "middle-class" questions in Brazil, something fundamental has gone missing from their analyses. Try as they might to leave behind their cultural blinders, they have not grasped that the modifier "middle" possesses distinct valence in North American English and Brazilian Portuguese. For North Americans, as Barbara Fields has pointed out, it is identified with the notional, if hardly national, virtue of moderation.[146] Its Brazilian equivalent—the *média* in *classe média*—carries connotations of meanness and mediocrity. Despite this baggage, some Brazilian professionals, admiring as they were of the United States and desirous of making Brazil more like their model, attempted to redeem the term "middle class" by employing it in a North American fashion, but it was a tough sell, particularly for men and women who emerged from Brazil's nonmanual, salaried, but unpedigreed strata. "Class B," on the other hand, presented no such impediments. Technical in its origins, ostensibly neutral, it could be appropriated as a term of distinction approaching the excellence of "A," while denoting merit in a manner similar to "middle" in the U.S. context, particularly when quantification made it a B1. Such a palliative, incomplete and arrived at unconsciously as it no doubt was, at least in part, would have been equally pleasing to the consuming public that was the object of professional-managerial attention, class B consumers who wished not to be identified as mean (in the sense of lowly or small) or mediocre (second rate), but who were more than pleased to see that burden shifted onto their supposed inferiors, including a class C encompassing whatever one might identify as the middle point on Brazil's spectrum of socioeconomic conditions.

An Abundance of Fables

In comfortable corners of the southeast, such nettlesome details could be relegated to the shadows, to vanish as stage lights illuminated another modernity show. But just as marketing and make-believe were indistinguishable in such performances, so too were they difficult to discern from one another in the stories scriptwriters and stagehands told each other behind the scenes. Even as the curtain closed on the economic miracle of 1968–1973, the show went on as the new professionals told themselves and all who would listen that Brazil was beginning to measure up, that its course remained sound, and that the country's consumer society was imminent.

Brazilian advertising professionals had long taken the measure of their cause and country against the United States. The attention shown global advertising-expenditure data and Brazil's ranking therein was one example of this stock-taking. Qualitative judgments surfaced even more often, as when the editors of trade publications seized on the statements of visitors from abroad and Brazilians returning from the United States who suggested that national advertising was approaching or even equaling U.S. standards. Something similar was at work when Walita was proclaimed the world's largest manufacturer of electrical blenders, or the director of the Brasil-América comic-book publishing house claimed, "Brazil is in second place in the world in comic-strip stories. We only lose out to the United States of America." Likewise, when an Englishman claimed that Brazil's recording industry was the equal of that of "the most developed countries of Europe and, even, the United States," his words were amplified in the specialist press. Brazilian professionals, long inured to having their U.S. counterparts address them in poor Spanish and identify Brazil with the Spanish-speaking Americas, were eager to point out that their automotive fleet and advertising surpassed any of their neighbors', while the journalist Hernane Tavares de Sá, writing for a similar audience following five years working for the United Nations, claimed that from the state of São Paulo southward, plus the "triangle" of Rio, Belo Horizonte, and São Paulo's state capital, Brazil "has already reached a per capita income equivalent to that of Italy," with "characteristics of a European nation," in "industrial capacity and standard of living." That these comparisons were of broader interest was clear in *Manchete*'s reporting, the weekly lauding the Automobile Salon for its "magnificent *stands*, endowed with authentic international quality," featuring automobiles "among the world's most beautiful cars."[147]

And so was progress measured. As Manoel de Vasconcellos wrote, on the eve of Brasília's inauguration, "In 1959, Brazil invested nothing less than 20 billion, 516 million cruzeiros in advertisements, which is, in relation to the Gross Domestic Product, a percentage of 1.2%," ranking it behind the United States but alongside many European countries. From Kubitschek's roadbuilding and its spur to outdoor advertising to videotaped commercials on television, Brazil "is on the good path." In 1963, as construction proceeded on Shopping Center do Méier, the preconditions for the rise of the North American mall were supposedly apparent, in population growth and increasing numbers of cars: "One shouldn't be surprised, therefore, by the fact that the 'shopping center' has now arrived in Brazil as well." Indeed, it was asserted that "the social and economic phenomena that had justified the North American 'shopping-centers'" had arisen domestically all at once. A decade on, it seemed likely that the Méier and Iguatemi malls "will be little more than a pale showing of the future that appears to await Brazilian shopping centers. Their example will be that of the United States." Speaking for retailers generally, a Brazilian merchant declared, "Our future is that which you see in the United States." Supermarket owners, managers, and promotors acted on the belief in 1972, nearly sixty of them traveling to Houston to attend the U.S. Super Market Institute's convention "to see what problems they will have tomorrow." A year later, a spokesman for sectoral interests took a similar view: "We are experiencing moments similar to those that occurred in the United States . . . at the beginning of the industrial explosion that will raise us to the condition of a developed Country."[148]

To the arc of the story were added other fancies, reminiscent at points of the traveler's tale spun by GM's James Mooney two generations earlier. In 1955, Emil Farhat indicated that a Copacabana service station was Esso's biggest seller in South America, leading a reporter to reflect: "We do not make automobiles"—this was over a year before plans for passenger-car manufacturing were made public—"but, in Rio and in São Paulo, we can already say that we live in the age of civilization on wheels." By the mid-1960s, the idea of the "economy of abundance" had migrated from *PN*'s pages to the talking points of Minister of Industry and Commerce Daniel Faraco, who discerned one amid the austerity-induced recession of 1964–1965. Among public figures, only Carlos Lacerda outdid Kubitschek in his admiration for the United States' "civilization of abundance," while exceeding Faraco in his mid-1960s fantasies: "Brazil is not an underdeveloped country. That is a false and demagogic blah-blah-blah. Brazil is an unequally developed country. A country where the people are beginning to understand that they have a right to the benefits of civilization and of *técnica*. There is a revolution in Brazil that, besides, has already begun and is not the social revolution. It is the revolution of Technology. This is the revolution we are making. We are beginning to be a people of consumers. Workers are beginning to have a, shall we say, middle-class consciousness. They are beginning to become consumers and the 'class struggle' is nothing more than an outdated *slogan*."[149]

Initially embedded in an angry retort to foreign reporters, Lacerda's identification of this peculiar revolution was expressed more calmly in the speech in which he accepted his party's nomination to run in the abortive presidential election of 1965, where he deployed "this revolution of consumers" as an argument against land reform. By 1973, time's effects ceased to operate as they had, an advertising man recalling: "It is curious to ponder certain things that occur with us and with the country. Only some 10 years have passed . . . and for me it seems like it all happened in another century. . . . Brazil changed a lot from 1964 to now—a totally different country, with a new mentality. . . . Everything seems so distant." Walter Clark Bueno, meanwhile, emphasized the work involved in creating that "new mentality": "We are proud to be actively selling to millions of Brazilians, through free enterprise, a new perspective that before television was reserved to elites alone and today is open to practically all Brazilians." Even as the aftermath of the first oil shock made the miracle years seem distant, the new professionals kept at it, Bueno declaring before a legislative committee: "Advertising is one of the indispensable components of the consumer society, the stimulating instrument for the growth of markets, recognizably educational and informative, to the degree that it carries civilized customs and practices to the most recondite interior of the country."[150]

Most notable among the fantasies of the era was what Bueno called the "consumer society." The term was a late addition to the dream language of Brazilian consumer capitalism, appearing with some frequency in the mainstream press in the 1960s in the context of the worldwide student revolt—the same time and context in which it became a referent in middlebrow discourse in the United States, the synchrony illustrating how closely attuned Brazilian commerce, culture, and media had become to their overseas analogues, the lagtimes of earlier eras eliminated. Earlier, with a long lag and considerable refashioning, "economy of abundance" had been adopted, like "consumer society," in simple cognates. Translating "consumerism" seemed more difficult, as illustrated by the early attempt *consumissionismo* and late references to *consumerismo* alongside the now-consecrate *consumismo*.[151] Problems of translation aside, there is little doubt that consumerist institutions and practices existed in Brazil. Fantasy came into the picture, as in Lacerda's deliria, in imagining that the phenomena were generalized, that Brazil as a whole was moved by dreams and desires characteristic of classes A, B, and sometimes C, and especially that Brazilian society was or was poised to become a consumer *society*.

As should be clear, the earliest exponents of this view were the writers grouped around *PN*, *Vendas e Varejo*, and *Indústria & Mercados*. It was Manoel de Vasconcellos who had hazarded the term *consumissionismo*, inspired by an article in the U.S. trade press. At that point, however, his subject was the U.S. idea of "His Majesty the Consumer" and the belief—Vasconcellos called it "revolutionary"—that "nothing happens in the economy except when a product is consumed," in other words, that consumption and its promotion were as important as production. While it might be argued that this was true of the United States, it would have been fanciful to make a similar case for Brazil, but that did not stop the *PN* group from trying, building on a tradition of U.S.-derived universalism, expressed two years earlier: "The difference between our commercial organization and the American one is more a question of degree than of type. Deep down, we are the same thing, as a capitalist society experiencing the same influences of present-day ideologies." By 1961, Vasconcellos's copublisher, Genival Rabelo, was telling all who would listen that Brazilians, too, were living in the "era of consumerism." Brazil's economy had reached "maturity," a *PN* staffer declared: "Thus, the raising of the purchasing power of its populations—and the increase in the very necessities to be satisfied in the country's various markets—all this can be added to the greater transportation facilities, the increase in the means of financing (providing a more perfect circulation of wealth), as well as the growing *desire to buy* that the improvement of social and economic standards itself provides citizens. Without a doubt, Brazil is entering the most promising stage in its history—whatever the aspect (political, economic, or social) to be considered in one's forecast of the future." It therefore hardly made sense to refer to "capitalism" in Brazil or, it would seem, anywhere else. Rather, *consumismo* had carried the day.[152]

Ten years later, Francisco Gracioso and Mauro Salles made similar cases. For Gracioso, Brazil, no less than the United States and Western Europe, had to be understood in the context of the "consumocracy" of "mass-consumption societies." Acknowledging that "Brazil, as a whole, is still very far from the stage of mass consumption," Gracioso argued that this was "a false perspective," produced by "the continental dimensions of the country and the diversity of socio-economic conditions in different areas." In reality: "There already exist in our country several extremely important 'pockets' of development, representing perhaps some 30 million people, with cultural levels and levels of income comparable to Western Europe's mean. These nuclei are moving quickly toward the stage of mass consumption, after having reached and overcome the stage of economic maturity. To judge from the experience of other peoples, the dynamic of this process will be irreversible in Brazil also." For his part, amid the headiest days of the early 1970s, Mauro Salles made a prima facie case for the same: "Everyone talks about the Brazilian miracle and says that we are at the threshold of becoming a developed country: Brazil is entering the era of consumerism."[153]

Lesser lights chimed in. In 1973, *Supermercado Moderno* made the uncontroversial case that Brazilian retail was "passing through a great transformation" but resorted to fabulous explanations for this change, including that an "improved distribution of wealth and increase in personal income are modifying the current structure of spending of the masses, thereby diminishing the relative participation of spending on subsistence items." This rosy scenario, according to the magazine's editors, was the very definition of the consumer society: "Consumer society: folks with money in their pockets to spend." For a Rio Grande do Sul–based billboard entrepreneur, the situation was plain: "It is undeniable that we are advancing from an agricultural society to a consumer society at greater speed than in any other part of the world." By that point, modeling had emerged as an apparently more attractive adjunct to advertising, and among Brazil's earliest "top" models—supposedly its highest-paid model in 1973—was Bruna Lombardi, a São Paulo Advertising School graduate now, alongside the veteran testimonial maker Edson Arantes do Nascimento (of Pelé, Administração e Propaganda Ltda.), on the "consumer-society team."[154]

The idea that Brazil had become or was poised to become a consumer society was not just trotted out for insider audiences. In a 1969 exercise in futurology, staff writers for *O Estado de S. Paulo* argued that the economic policy-making of the previous five years had prepared Brazil to "definitively enter the age of the consumer society" and that five years hence, barring unforeseeable disruptions, the country would be a "consumer society." As usual, advertising precedent to editorial copy may be found; in this case an announcement published ten months earlier, in which *Seleções* heralded the work of the Second Brazilian Advertising Congress: "Throughout the holding of the meeting, thousands of professionals, representing Agencies, Communication Vehicles, and Advertisers, placed all their creativity in the service of the improvement of one of modern Brazil's most dynamic, important, and technically advanced activities. The results of the theses that were approved will make themselves felt, in all their benefits, over the course of the coming years—at exactly the time in which Brazil will once and for all cross the barriers that separate underdevelopment from the Consumer Society."[155]

In 1971, *O Estado de S. Paulo*'s staff writers returned to the subject: "The emphasis on providing services is occurring because of the sophisticated consumer society that is becoming a reality." Meanwhile, in Rio, the *Jornal do Brasil*'s editors had welcomed the production of the millionth Volkswagen as "the point of departure for a country worthy of being treated as a consumer society." Within a year and a half, that point of departure was left far behind: "In truth we are in a full consumer society." By that point, the universalism espoused in *PN* had been adopted by politicians, a São Paulo state legislator affirming, "The United States is like Brazil, a consumer society, on a larger scale."[156]

At the same time, countervailing evidence was impossible to avoid. In 1965, for example, the *Correio da Manhã*'s reporting on a national retail-sales convention at which Carlos Lacerda made his case that "the great revolution that today's Brazil is going through is that of the consumer, through the progressive increase in the needs and demands of the popular masses," and Daniel Faraco issued his evocation of "an economy of abundance," was printed alongside a story indicating that 99 percent of the state of Sergipe's population suffered from schistosomiasis (an acute parasitic disease), along with a "considerable part" of the populations of other states, including Minas Gerais, where Belo Horizonte's Pampulha reservoir, once a symbol of Americanist modernity, had become "one of the major focal points of the disease." Seven years later, readers of the same newspaper's "marketing" section might have also glanced at a column by João Pinheiro Neto published alongside its motif—a horn of plenty—the column demolishing the idea that wealthy Brazilians' increased share of national income was being reinvested. Rather, it was directed toward "the standard of spending that already makes them world famous as friends of abundant superfluousness and unlimited waste," with results that turned the comparisons favored by the new professionals on their head: "The minorities that in countries like ours situate themselves at the peak of the social and economic pyramid leave behind any North American potentate, or Western European, in terms of standard of living. The brutal and shameful difference is among the more modest classes. There, yes, few can compete with us in terms of poverty and abandonment." By then, government and advertiser pressures had reduced the *Correio da Manhã* to a shadow of what it had once been. The newspaper had nothing to lose by publishing Pinheiro Neto's jeremiad. Yet even thriving newspapers and magazines had to publish evidence that abundance was in short supply; fantasies of incipient arrival at Rostowian "high mass consumption" had to be balanced by accounts of more prosaic issues affecting the lives of even relatively comfortable readers. "Why doesn't plenty arrive?" was the question that *Visão* asked in a 1967 cover story on problems in Brazilian provisioning, many of them identified in the Klein & Saks report fifteen years earlier. Six years later, at the miracle's dizzying peak, shortages of milk and meat affected even neighborhoods classed as "B," according to *Veja*, which also reported on miracle-era water rationing. With the 1973 oil shock, the lack of cheap gasoline led the government to turn on its pet industry, as technocrats argued that automakers had overemphasized passenger-car production while neglecting the building of buses, trucks, and tractors, calling on them to make smaller, more fuel-efficient cars, rather than the upmarket models over which Delfim Netto had exulted. As auto executives simmered, critics of the existing order saw the oil shock as an opportunity to abandon the "premature consumerism" of the miracle and its focus on a "limited stratum of the population" in favor of policies aimed at creating a truly mass market. It was not to be. Three years after the government's volte-face regarding the automobile industry's priorities, Minister of Planning Reis Velloso made a modified case for an audience of marketing professionals: "In the current stage of the automobile industry, nothing is more important than to lodge two ideas in the consumer's head: that of the small car and of less consumption of gasoline per car." There was nothing wrong with the automobile industry; it merely needed "to adapt itself to current circumstances," as retailers were, adopting such "modern mechanisms" as malls and supermarkets. By that point, according to Rio's Commercial Association, these developments belonged in the past tense, chain stores, shopping malls, and super- and hypermarkets having "completely transformed consumer habits" and defined the "current phase of the consumer society" in the cities of the southeast.[157]

————

Twenty years after Rabelo and Vasconcellos's evocation of the economy of abundance, abundance itself was in short supply. Dearth continued to be a part of everyday life for millions of Brazilian families. Given such conditions, the idea that Brazil was a consumer society may seem bizarre, but it was nevertheless widespread. "Brazil has a frankly consumer economy," wrote a longtime visitor in 1970. "The stores are well stocked and seemingly busy. In Rio de Janeiro and São Paulo the middle class seems well dressed, well fed, and actively spending money." As the geographic and social qualifications suggest, there were boundaries to Brazil's world of getting and spending, and it was no doubt with such boundaries in mind that another visitor called Brasília "the frontier of consumer civilization as Brazilians know it." For urban Brazilians of the comfortable classes, the experience of that civilization was formative, the artist Wanda Pimentel describing her background in 1970, at age twenty-six: "I was born here in Guanabara, I am of the middle class." For Pimentel, that meant that "the consumer society" had always been her habitat. Those born even fifteen years earlier, however, could remember a time before the "era of consumerism," when "to drink two soft drinks in one sitting was a scandal." Not for nothing did a 1971 seminar on marginality take as its subject the aged, an organizer explaining: "Although the aged person is not strictly speaking a marginal, in our consumer society he is beginning to be a problem of that type."[158]

Explaining the origins of such a society, and the estrangement accompanying it, led participants and critics back to the 1950s and the postwar era of which it was a part. In 1962, Genival Rabelo asserted his role as pioneer "insisting on the thesis of *consumerism*": "Here and now—I've repeated this for more than ten years—the problem is no longer to produce, but to consume." A decade later, a former APP president made a similar case for the cohort to which both men belonged, while making room for countrymen in other fields. "The Brazilian began to travel," Carlos Alberto dos Santos asserted of the 1950s, "and he began to see and learn how other peoples set out for industrial development. He began to perceive that if we really wanted to industrialize, we needed to create a consumer society. And a consumer society cannot live without advertising to accelerate the production-distribution-consumption function." For the critic José Lino Grünewald, writing in 1966, industrialization, U.S. influence, and the inflationary policies of pre-1964 governments lay behind the developments that Santos remembered fondly: "Within a few years, Brazilian society endured notable changes with the industrialization of the center-south region. . . . Here in the center of so-called progress, the machine and the philosophy of consumerism that it set in motion, in accord with the economic-social programming of the North American system, brought profound alterations. Especially in the anterior, inflationary period, the predominance of the conception of consumption over that of production brought about the euphoria of a party in full swing." Writing before Delfim Netto's turn as finance minister, Grünewald differed "that philosophy of consumerism with which the middle class was imbued" from the policies imposed by Roberto Campos: "the philosophy of the Government that installed itself . . . was not that of a return to euphoric consumerism." With the benefit of ten years' hindsight, he might have revised his perspective, perhaps coming around to his friend Paulo Francis's argument that there was little daylight between the regime's economic magi, the "Campos-Delfim model" being singular rather than plural. Whatever the case, he would have agreed with Francis's emphasizing the U.S. orientation of postwar Brazil's culture of consumption.[159]

By the 1970s, that culture reached beyond the social sectors targeted in the early postwar. For the economist Hélio Duque, writing in 1972, easy credit and aggressive advertising meant that Brazilians of little means were buying cars, "sacrificing even food and a more comfortable existence." Despite low wage rates, "through a series of artifices, the consumer society is making an illustrious spender of this people." While the editors of the alternative weekly *Politika* questioned whether "the multiplication of slums and of motorized wretches" was "the objective of those who want the much dreamed of Brasil Grande," the economist Paul Singer argued that the "tremendous alienation of public opinion, of youth, of the various social classes that ended up turning to consumerism during the years of the 'miracle'" was a goal of Médici-era policy.[160]

True to form, historians took up the question after economists and other social scientists. They also tended to take it up indirectly, with references to "consumerism," "consumer culture," and "consumer society" appearing in works concerned with mass entertainment, sociability, and material culture, among other subjects. Among monographs published in the 1980s and 1990s, Sérgio Augusto's loving chronicle of the Brazilian *chanchada*, a light, ludic variety of film that was, together with the radionovela, one of the great popular entertainments of the 1940s and 1950s, identifies the genre as having resulted, in part, from "our more effective tuning in to the consumer society." By 1953, according to Alcir Lenharo, consumerism was in sufficient evidence to feature in the teasing Carnaval ditty "O cinzeiro de Zazá." A dissertation published around the same time as Lenharo's book dates consumer society's emergence later, to the second half of the 1950s and the implantation of the "American model of mass production." Brian Owensby would appear to agree, declaring that "a full-blown consumer culture came of age" under Kubitschek. Among historians writing since the 1990s, Rafael Ioris followed Owensby in seeing "a Brazilian version of a culture of mass consumption" emerge amid Juscelino's Fifty Years in Five, while others have backdated that culture's inception, seeing it as occurring over a longer period of time, while expanding their area of analyses outward from Rio and São Paulo. For Ulpiano Bezerra de Menezes, commenting on a student's work on changes in domestic material culture between the 1870s and 1930s, it was over these years that, "more than anything, one may discern entry into the consumer society." In works by Amara Rocha, Alzira Alves de Abreu, and Jaílson Pereira da Silva, the emphasis is on tracing long processes rather than pinpointing moments of arrival; a parallel approach may be seen in Albertina Mirtes de Freitas Pontes's *A cidade dos clubes*, which situates "the emergence of consumer society" in Fortaleza amid two decades' worth of changes in urban architecture and sociability.[161]

One is left with a composite picture of long processes of cumulative cultural change rather than of near-instantaneous emergence, still less of maturity, metaphorical or actual. These processes and subprocesses were unfinished, but there can be little doubt that by the mid-1970s, Brazilian consumer capitalism had come into its own. Institutions, practices, products, behaviors, and patterns of thought unimaginable at earlier points in the history of Portuguese-speaking America had become everyday. Traditions and customs from Carnaval to Christmas had been reshaped. New professions, once ignoble, were now established and, in many corners, exalted. Identities had been remade. Such changes had been especially pronounced over the preceding twenty years and, indeed, many of the most salient features of Brazilian consumer capitalism and its culture had developed since the 1950s: the automobile industry and expanding car ownership, marketing as work and worldview, the shopping center and shopping-mall shopping. Careful investigation of even the seemingly most novel of these developments, however, reveals links and lineages without which the developments bridging the Kubitschek years and the economic miracle would have been impossible. The meanings attached to domestic manufacture of an increasing range of passenger cars built on dreams of individual ownership dating to the "Ford in Your Future" of the 1940s and earlier spectacles of mechanics and motion, glitter and glamour, brought up to date in the Automobile Salons ongoing in the 1970s. The impresario behind the latter fairs, Caio de Alcântara Machado, had cut his teeth in advertising, including for São Paulo's Assumpção group, which founded a chain of radio shops in the 1940s; as Lojas Assumpção's offerings diversified, it became an early television advertiser, alongside Mappin, Kibon, and Bombril. As practiced in Brazil, marketing had roots stretching back through the early professionalization of sales, market research, and advertising; as an element in the professional-managerial repertoire that enhanced an aspiring elite's bid for prestige and power, it had similar, and similarly early, antecedents. Precedents for the shopping mall, new in the 1960s, existed in the *conjuntos* and *galerias* of the 1950s and earlier. Shopping-center builders and managers—among them a founder of the Paulista Advertising Association—were able to count on the support of Sears-Brazil, which followed the parent-company view that "such centers represent an extension of the basic principles that governed establishment of Sears first retail stores," as well as of myriad other economic groups, from Lojas Americanas to Pão de Açúcar. Shopping-center shopping as a pursuit, meanwhile, incorporated elements introduced by Lauro de Carvalho at A Exposição, as well as by the managers and staff of Mappin, Mesbla, and O Rei da Voz's Midas Publicidade. Promoting shopping malls or marketing, AMCE's fairs or passenger automobiles, media elites were prepared to help at nearly every imaginable turn, as they had been before television and even radio, before the means of communication became *mídia*. In the mid-1930s, touting its services and *O Estado de S. Paulo*'s readership, the Ecléctica agency had presented the São Paulo daily as "everyone's newspaper" and thus "the right newspaper for advertising." Forty years later, the *Jornal do Brasil*'s advertising department described it as "Brazil's largest shopping center."[162]

What stands out most about the period beginning in the 1950s is the depth of support consumer-oriented business received from government. The passenger-automobile industry midwifed by Kubitschek and pampered by the military governments of the 1960s and 1970s is the most obvious example, but others abound. The Anhembi pavilion that housed the AMCE fairs and the millions they attracted was another, built with municipal-, state-, and national-government funding on public land.[163] Among the Brazilian citadels of marketing was EAESP, commissioned by Vargas's government in 1952 and housed by a federal-government ministry into the 1960s. Delfim Netto and the administrations he served played critical roles in the building of the marketing-driven Globo network. Beginning in the 1970s, the National Housing Bank invested in shopping centers, along the way hiring U.S. consultants to assess the field and share their expertise with interested parties in Brazil.[164] Nor were such instances of support isolated or one-off. Government support for shopping-center construction was part of a larger program for the modernization of Brazilian retail, including the turn to super- and hypermarketing. Export-quality hypermarkets, nationwide television broadcasting, and qualitative and quantitative benchmarks of the progress of the automobile industry were interpreted as evidence of Brasil Grande, not least by the country's advertising professionals, whose contributions to national greatness were highlighted in the Kubitschek government's award of the Ordem do Cruzeiro do Sul to JWT's Robert Merrick, and in subsequent collaboration between executives and officialdom.

All of which is not to say that governmental enthusiasm for and support of the Brazilian consumer capitalism of the 1950s, 1960s, and 1970s was unprecedented. If Kubitschek had exulted over the numbers of radio sets and refrigerators his countrypeople possessed in 1960 and, a dozen years on, military-government technocrats pointed to the expansion of television's reach and the growth and diversification of passenger-automobile manufacturing as evidence of national progress and the legitimacy of their regime, there were earlier precedents. Brazil's regimes of the 1930s and early 1940s—Vargas headed at least three—were attuned to commercial radio as a means of fostering a more cohesive sense of nationhood. The blank check given managers of state-owned Rádio Nacional testified to this interest, as did the preinstallation of "modern" radio sets—"of the renowned RCA-Victor trademark"—in working-class housing inaugurated by Vargas.[165] That Vargas himself, from the 1930s to his demise in 1954, had shown an interest in the domestic manufacture of U.S. passenger automobiles should be as clear. And, indeed, just as commercial radio had become a pastime for Brazilian urbanites by the time of Hermes Lima's late-1930s sojourn to the sertão, so too did passenger-car ownership—as aspiration and measure of middle-class arrival—become Brazilian over time, even as the consumerist "Paradise via Satellite" of TV-Globo would become as thoroughly a national institution as any to ever exist in the world's largest Portuguese-speaking country. Soon to reach similar status, if never to rival Roberto Marinho's fief, was the shopping center—the "new paradises" referred to in a mahrr-keh-*tching*-like lilt as "shoppings." The story of one such mall reintroduces familiar figures and forces in the making of Brazilian consumer capitalism between the interwar years and the economic miracle, while extending considerably past the latter.[166]

———————

The mall was the brainchild of José Luiz Moreira de Souza, of the Ducal group that had sprung from Lauro de Carvalho's A Exposição, becoming the UEB conglomerate, with interests in retail, manufacturing, tourism, real estate, and finance, in all these fields enjoying the support of the military regime as it sought to create Brazilian zaibatsu to counterbalance multinational capital. In the early 1970s, José Luiz decided that the time was right for his Rio-based group to bring the shopping mall fever gripping São Paulo to his adoptive hometown, much as his uncle had sought to re-create Macy's on the shores of Guanabara Bay. In 1972, to assist in his efforts to create a mall worthy of Brasil Grande, he enlisted the EAESP marketing professor Alberto de Oliveira Lima Filho, author of the first Portuguese-language book on shopping centers. All the while, José Luiz also drew on his connections in government.[167]

In 1973, plans for the shopping center made national news, in a *Veja* puff-piece that began, "The Americans invented the shopping-center system in 1923. . . . Today there are 14,500 of these commercial centers operating in the USA." Despite the precedent of São Paulo's Iguatemi mall, "the history of this commercial innovation in Brazil remains at its prologue," but a "decisive chapter is about to be written in Rio de Janeiro by the União de Empresas Brasileiras." In August, UEB was to begin construction on a site at the mouth of the easternmost tunnel linking Copacabana and Botafogo—the choicest piece of undeveloped real estate left within Rio's urban footprint—where the first enclosed mall in Rio's fashionable south would "exercise its attraction over a population of 388,000 people and 62,000 automobiles concentrated in eleven nearby neighborhoods." Over three levels, with a total area of 49,000 m², the mall would feature ninety stores, to pay rents based on total sales, which showed, according to Lima Filho, "that the UEB group has an interest in making the area a great commercial success and not merely a gigantic real-estate enterprise." But gigantic it was, to feature—atop the shopping mall—a forty-story office building that would make it Brazil's largest commercial-professional complex.[168]

Although construction did not begin that August, the month did see one promising development. Amid a "'Shopping Center' Seminar" hosted by Brazil's housing bank as part of a "Symposium on National Development," executives of UEB and the Japanese retail group Yaohan formalized a relationship hinted at in *Veja*. Under this contract, Yaohan, which was already active in São Paulo, would operate a two-in-one supermarket-department store to "anchor" the property for annual payment of US$1.68 million plus 2 percent of total sales.[169]

By that point, according to promotional materials, research and planning had been concluded, blueprints had been approved, and a construction firm had been contracted, but ground had not yet been broken. Getting the site's zoning changed from residential to commercial may have accounted for some delay, but approval from the state government came in November, and still construction did not begin. While additional red tape may have been at issue, when 1975 passed without any progress, it should have been clear that financing was the major problem. By then, Yaohan had dropped its commitment, its executives presumably knowing a zaibatsu gone bad when they saw one. Lima Filho had also decamped, to later complain that José Luiz's insistence on the grandiose office tower—slated to be Rio's tallest man-made structure— had undermined their plan for the malling of the city's south zone.[170]

It was not until 1976 that help arrived from the national government, which had been so solicitous of José Luiz's interests while Roberto Campos and Delfim Netto handled economic policy. Massive financing by the state-owned Caixa Econômica Federal made it possible for construction to get underway, now entrusted to the Norberto Odebrecht construction company, another military-government favorite. As work began on the physical plant, UEB's shopping-center subsidiary contracted a U.S. firm specializing in shopping-center marketing. Soon thereafter, UEB was the subject of a documercial similar to the one aired on behalf of Shopping Center Ibirapuera two years earlier. Spots and print advertisements promised, "The Globo Television Network will show Brazil going at full sail" in a program highlighting "what the UEB group is doing throughout Brazil. The Seridó Textile Industry, the greatest textile-industry facility in the Northeast. The UEB-Center with the Professional Center and Brazil's most modern and daring Shopping-Center."[171]

Behind this promotional bluster were signs that not all was well. The mainstream press kept up appearances, though *Veja*'s editor would later claim that the insolvency of UEB's Independência-Decred investment bank had been an open secret for years. Minister of Finance Mário Henrique Simonsen, together with Paulo Lira, the president of Brazil's Central Bank, continued to frequent the Association of Directors of Credit, Investment, and Financial Firms, a finance-sector interest group founded and presided over by José Luiz. Nevertheless, rumors regarding UEB's finances were circulating, leading the Central Bank to issue a February 1977 statement that it had no plans to take over the firm. In April, it was established—and confirmed by Simonsen and Lira—that the firm that owned Shopping Center Ibirapuera was in negotiations to purchase the UEB Center. By May, UEB's difficulties were threatening to become an embarrassment to the government, though Rio's newspaper of record still claimed that details of the conglomerate's financial difficulties were unavailable.[172]

The next morning, the government ordered the Central Bank to take over Independência-Decred, having provided it millions of dollars in 1977 alone attempting to keep it afloat. As officialdom and a relatively unmuzzled press (the regime had lifted most forms of censorship by then) looked deeper into the matter, it became clear not only that José Luiz's investment firm was insolvent but that the rot extended through UEB's commercial and industrial concerns, which had been built up by government favor only to become enmeshed in the tangle of speculation, fraud, and debt that brought down Independência-Decred. Much good money had been sent after bad, which phony financial instruments could only cover for so long, though some said that the government might have continued to assist UEB but for some political missteps on José Luiz's part. Whatever the case, when the dust settled, there was little left of the once-mighty conglomerate except the pharaonic shopping mall and office tower to which the government and José Luiz remained tied, the government seeking to recoup its lost millions, José Luiz hoping to retain ownership after repaying the Caixa Econômica Federal.[173]

And so construction of what was now called Rio Sul Shopping Center continued, paid for by the Caixa, in what was its largest-ever disbursement to a single lender, which promoters cynically attributed to its "social importance." Government support gave leading firms the assurance they needed to support the venture, and so Mesbla—representing "Brazil's largest chain of department stores"—agreed to occupy 20 percent of the mall's area. Soon thereafter, Lojas Brasileiras signed on to provide a second "anchor," followed by the Dutch-based C&A retail-clothing group, which had opened its first Brazilian store in Shopping Center Ibirapuera, and by Pão de Açúcar, representing "Latin America's largest chain of supermarkets." Smaller retailers followed, but they did so cautiously. Lacking the resources of Mesbla, C&A, Lojas Brasileiras, and Pão de Açúcar, the owners and managers of such operations were wary of the uncertainties brought by the second oil shock and José Luiz's obviously precarious position.[174]

Thus, when Rio Sul was opened to the public in April 1980, there were dozens of storefronts for which tenants had yet to be found. Such was the hurry to get money flowing in that the opening took place prior to completion of work on the facility—including on air-conditioning, restrooms, and lighting—while the office tower to be perched atop it remained mostly on the drawing board. While José Luiz's son Gustavo called the opening day "a true *happening*," some among the thousands of attendees expressed disappointment in the un-completed furnishings and empty shop-spaces. But three months later, there were two hundred businesses selling to, serving, and otherwise occupying the fifty-thousand-odd people who visited Rio Sul every day. By Christmastime, the mood—and Rio Sul's facilities—had improved, despite Brazil's economic doldrums. According to one account, there were few signs of recession amid the "Christmas *rush*" filling the "wide, air-conditioned galleries of the Rio Sul *shopping center*." On Saturday, December 22, more than two hundred thou-sand people visited the mall, setting the record for a single day, drawn by the promise of "*one stop buy*, or to purchase everything at once," from eighty-five lines of goods and services on offer from 220 stores and kiosks. At Mesbla, in particular, the movement of "so-called *big tickets*" was a welcome sight. By that point, despite its unimpressive opening, the shopping center was becom-ing part of everyday life for thousands of Rio residents, for sociability, leisure, and dining, as well as shopping. Christmas and the southern hemisphere's summer vacations added tourists to the mix, while a late Carnaval in 1981 meant that "February will be all consumption," to be followed by the "great summer liquidation sales," in the turn of the commercial calendar implanted in earlier retail revolutions, to culminate in another Christmas. As the shopping-center slogan put it, "Something's Always Happening at Rio Sul."[175]

The returns that would allow José Luiz to repay the Caixa Econômica Fed-eral seemed within reach, but construction lagged on the office tower. When it was finally completed, in 1982, Brazil stood on the brink of the worst economic crisis in its history, one that brought a definitive end to the economic growth that characterized most of its twentieth century. In such conditions, renting the new offices was an impossible task. As the economy worsened, José Luiz was again short, but he remained well connected enough to devise his own way out. In a three-way deal, he gave the shopping center and the office tower to the Caixa Econômica Federal as full payment for its financing; the Caixa then turned around and sold the mall to a holding company called Combrascan on a twenty-year mortgage, while retaining possession of the office tower; over the life of the mortgage, José Luiz's Empreendimentos Imobiliários Capri would manage the property and absorb a percentage of total rents. José Luiz's family also held a share in Combrascan, Gustavo having a stake in a firm that served as minority partner to the major shareowner, Brascan, a foreign-owned conglom-erate born of the Light & Power utility. With the Caixa Econômica Federal left with mostly unoccupied office space, while paying Combrascan for its "admin-istration," the Brazilian people were handed the bill for a commercial structure built in the likeness of Brasil Grande—the tenth-largest building in the world, as of 1985—for the idle time of classes A and B. It was thus a good deal more than "a turning point in the history of Rio commerce."[176]

Chapter 6

The Beginning of Things

In April 1978, the Third Brazilian Advertising Congress met at the convention center built for the AMCE fairs. The mood was downbeat, a contrast with the First Congress and its coincidence with the euphoria of the Kubitschek presidency, to say nothing of the Second, at which Delfim Netto praised the profession for enriching the world. Amid the after effects of the first oil shock, Brasil Grande began to seem small and vulnerable, the scenery and stage props of the miracle teetering, even as organizers—executives of Salles/Inter-Americana and TV-Globo, GM and JWT—planned the four-day meeting around a theme tardily acknowledging Brazilian conditions: "Advertising and the Economic, Social, and Cultural Reality of the Country," echoing calls for attention to "Brazilian reality" that had been reformist in the 1950s, radical in the 1960s.[1]

There was little radicalism, reformism, or reality at the opening ceremony, though there was the national government's minister of communications (one of four cabinet-level officials to attend). The first plenary session was similarly tame, or at least treated as such: no one appears to have registered the gruesome cynicism of Norton's Geraldo Alonso and TV-Globo's Roberto Marinho presenting a proposal, coauthored by Mauro Salles, for a cooperative code to regulate advertising in the public interest.

The fireworks, such as they were, came the following day, during a panel on "Advertising and the Economy." The panel began true enough to form, the chairman, a would-be marketing guru named Francisco Alberto Madia de Souza, telling his audience, "After this Congress, Brazilian advertising will never be the same." Equally rote were Souza's celebration of advertising's share of GDP and call for a greater place at the table for his cohort. But even amid familiar tropes was mention of the poverty in which most Brazilians lived. Souza's copanelists—including a business journalist and an ESPM professor—amplified that mention of poverty, while also drawing attention to the exclusion and inequality that were poverty's partners. It was the advertising executive Julio Ribeiro, however, who contributed the congress's most explosive intervention.[2]

Eight years earlier, as the economy surged, Ribeiro had all but shuttered his thriving agency, leaving behind a skeleton crew as he took key personnel to the United States "to acquire our own ability to sense the changes that will occur in our environment."[3] Now, the miracle having ended, he was concerned with Brazil: "What I wanted to express in this plenary is a deep concern, to the extent that we see, alongside euphoric pronouncements—that Brazil has finally reached 1 billion dollars' worth of investment in advertising, we are making a million automobiles a year, we are the ninth or tenth largest economy in the world, we are the builders and professionals of this prosperity—as I see it advertising is becoming an instrument of social dissolution."

Ribeiro was less concerned with any top ten Brazil might belong to—whether in GDP or advertising billings—than with its staggering levels of illiteracy, infant mortality, and poverty. Most Brazilians were only able "to consume the manufactured goods that our prosperous industry produces, to the detriment of other values essential to civilized man, such as health care and education," but yet they were exposed to their marketing all the same. While his audience was alienated from the masses, the latter were victimized: "How does this bulk of the population receive appeals on behalf of cigarettes, automobiles, and deodorant? I think that they must receive them as we do, that is, with the desire to buy them. And what is the social implication of this? It won't do to defend the idea that we are professionals who guarantee the northeasterner the right to not eat in order to buy a transistor radio. It won't do to defend the idea that this brutal mass of consumerist communication that we make is irrelevant, in terms of the distortion of social values." Rather than prosperity professionals, Ribeiro argued, he and his colleagues were "hired guns" of the economically powerful, though the very nature of their work made awareness of "the reality that surrounds us" extraordinarily difficult: "We are immersed in the water that we ourselves generate, that is, more than prosperity professionals, we are *ufanismo* professionals." As businessmen and professionals, he charged, "we were wrapped up in the 'oba, oba' of the economic miracle. We were educated in terms of having to think that high rates of gross domestic product and high rates of per capita income are the universal solution to all mankind's problems. Few took notice ... that there exist countries with per capita incomes that are only a small fraction of the per capita income of the USA in which the individual's quality of life is much better." Instead, Ribeiro described his cohort as entranced by "the spirit of 'The Brazil of the Future,' 'Consume Life,' and 'Be Happy by Buying Deodorant.'" Taking stock was a first step. "To be aware," he declared, "is the beginning of things."[4]

It is difficult to imagine an advertising, marketing, or media executive of Ribeiro's stature giving strident public voice to such ideas even four years earlier, except as a good-bye and good-riddance to the profession, ignored or interrupted by the jeering of colleagues, leading to the speaker's ostracism, if not a worse fate. The ending of the miracle was its precondition, without which Ribeiro's turn against the ufanismo that the miracle shared with the Kubitschek years would seem strange, subversive, even un-Brazilian. It was also enabled by the controlled opening of the country's politics and public life, as the dominant faction of the military elite pursued a slow, orderly, and tightly controlled relinquishing of formal power over government, to be followed by a return to barracks, bases, and business interests. But neither the critical bent of Ribeiro's speech nor the anxiety it betrayed was unprecedented. As early as 1937, in *Propaganda*'s debut issue, a leading Brazilian advertising man had warned against the shallow embrace of foreign methods. "We apply the results without accompanying the basic processes that out there serve as the bases for the monumental labor that American advertising is today," wrote João Alfredo de Souza Ramos. "Hence the mixture of styles, of conceptions, of quality, of 'uncontrollable results.'" More recently, the marketing preceptor Francisco Gracioso had written of the "intolerable tensions" of the profession and the anomie of city dwellers in an era of mass communication and incipient mass consumption. The well-to-do could seek succor from the psychiatric profession—"a typical subproduct of our civilization"—while for the rest, there was socially useful dissatisfaction: "We agree completely with those who say that advertising makes many folks unhappy, because they desire things they cannot buy. But, in all candor, what is wrong with that? The happy citizen is not necessarily the most useful one to society."[5] Thus, alongside the early emulation of all things U.S.A. and amid the miracle at its peak, spokesmen for the new professionals expressed concern about the unintended consequences of their Americanist enthusiasms and confessed that not all was sweetness and light, for themselves or for the objects of their efforts. The ability to hold two opposed ideas in one's mind while retaining the ability to function may or may not be the mark of a superior intelligence, as F. Scott Fitzgerald famously averred, but it undoubtedly characterized the professional cohort to which Gracioso, Ramos, and Ribeiro belonged.

Indeed, it was a characteristic rooted in the lives of two generations of professionals. These men and women, who came of age between the 1920s and the 1950s, were at once the creatures and creators of a culture of consumer capitalism identified with the United States and the carriers of older and opposing traditions, including as participant-observers of Brazilian intellectual life. By the 1940s, a few achieved national literary standing while continuing to work in advertising and sales promotion. Their multilayered experiences and expectations were reflected in reactions to critiques of changing modes of consumption and their promotion. The shallowest intellectual criticism might cut deep, even as it exaggerated the effectiveness of the new professionals' work and assisted in the creation of "consumer" as a meaningful category.

As Brazilian consumer capitalism became a subject for the creative arts in the 1960s and 1970s, deeper rumblings issued, ominous, inescapable, and unsettling, now as then.

Their Own Best Customers

The social origins and generational profile of the new professionals made them objects and agents of media and marketing interests, of business practices and products, of ideas of comfort and convenience, nearly all of them originating in North America, many of them identified with the United States for a long time after their introduction to Brazil even as they contributed to making the country what it was. As boys and girls, the new professionals thrilled to Hollywood movies and collected the ephemera of import culture, from movie programs to the American comics that edged aside *O Tico-Tico*, the children's weekly published in Rio beginning in 1905. Such was the beginning of a long turn away from Europe and toward the United States in which changes in material culture, consumption, entertainment, and comportment can be charted through the lives of men—and later women—who started their careers with GM and GE in the 1920s, worked for Ayer and McCann in the 1930s, built IBOPE and Norton in the 1940s, lectured and learned at the São Paulo Advertising School in the 1950s, and helped steer the commercialization of the press, the rise of radio broadcasting, and the growth of television. Before such work came experiences that were just as constructive, often on deeply personal levels.

The IBOPE founder Auricélio Penteado testified to aspects of these processes in 1951. "Raised on 'far-west' films and forming part of a generation that began to abandon the old and solid French culture of its parents," he wrote, "I always felt a nearly fanatical attraction for the things of the United States:—how they ate, the simplicity and nonchalance of their wardrobe, material comfort, idealism, the love of flowers, children, and animals, the enchanting innocence of American youth, the ability and capability of the American woman." His contemporary Renato Castelo Branco, though raised across the Brazilian subcontinent in Piauí, shared Penteado's childhood experiences: "We were Tom Mix, Mary Walcamp, Buck Jones, good guys, good girls and bad guys, as our heroes already came from American cinema." As a student in Rio in the 1930s, Castelo Branco observed the superimposition of new and old as a flâneur: "We went on foot, through Cinelândia, following the rua do Passeio, where the illuminated cinemas sparkled, exhibiting posters of Hollywood stars, its appearance of a mini Times Square." Castelo Branco remembered São Paulo similarly, with generational implications like

Penteado's, as young people frequented luxurious new cinemas, their dreams turning to Hollywood, their forebears' Francophilia yielding to Americanism. By that point, the *"glamour* that came from Hollywood" was casting its spells even in Rio Grande do Sul, among young men who had also grown up with the "famous *cowboy*" Tom Mix, their childhood romps re-creating the "tumult of *cowboys* and Apache Indians." That was the experience of Rodolfo Lima Martensen, years before creating the school that became ESPM.[6]

These experiences were formative. "To tell the truth I began at the Cinema Delícia, watching the movies," remarked Ricardo Ramos of growing up in Maceió, "and reliving that experience, at dances and in conversation, of the products and subproducts of Hollywood. Was it good, was it bad? I don't know, just as I don't know another me, I am this thing." Hollywood was thus, in the words of Julieta de Godoy Ladeira, who worked alongside Ramos at JWT before absorbing Martensen's curriculum and heading Thompson's creative department, "something ours," while also constitutive of "our things." Among "our things" remembered by Ladeira were Hollywood posters, old-time movie programs, and the cinema magazines: "They increased the week's expenses, but one bought magazines to speed things up, to already know something about upcoming films." As a child in São Paulo, Walter Clark Bueno "was crazy for cinema and a dedicated radio listener." "I saw lots of films before I experienced life," he recalled. "I saw *The Wizard of Oz*, I worried over Pinocchio's fate, I laughed with Mickey Mouse and Donald Duck. . . . I enjoyed *The Shadow* serial and all those series that opened cinema sessions: *Flash Gordon, Buck Rogers, Tom Mix*." When his family moved to Rio, Bueno encountered Copacabana's MGM movie palace, and its marvelous air-conditioning, as well as Ipanema's theaters, attending three times a week for "cinematographic marathons" exceeded only by the radiophonic ones that were a domestic staple.[7]

Ladeira and Bueno's testimonies begin with cinema but soon touch on other entertainments, from radio to the advertising-based ephemera of movie magazines. Ladeira's colleague Carlos Queiroz Telles remembered radio also, especially the *Tarzan* show of the 1940s, as well as his father receiving *Em Guarda*, the Portuguese-language magazine of the OCIAA, a bit of war-era Americanist propaganda also remembered by Ricardo Ramos.[8] But that was not all:

> The hammering away also came in the comics. Superman, Batman, and Captain Marvel were engaged in liquidating the furious Germans and treacherous Japanese. The allies were gods. Their enemies, stereotyped demons. Everything came down to Good and Evil. I was trained to perceive reality through the purest Manicheanism.

But the supreme gift of Yankee culture was called *Seleções de Reader's Digest*! It was required reading for the whole family. From it I learned to venerate the elevated ethical and moral standards of the *American way of life* and to consume imported models and dreams.

To reward my credulity, the advertisements guaranteed: "There's a Ford in your future!"[9]

Years before the war, Rodolfo Lima Martensen, dreaming of becoming an architect, delighted in the superior material culture on display in *American Home* and *House and Garden*. Renato Ignácio da Silva described growing up in São Paulo in the 1930s: "I had left behind *Tico-Tico* to follow the *Suplemento Juvenil*, of the modern ones, Flash Gordon and Buck Rogers, cycling through Jungle Jim, the Phantom, Tarzan, Mandrake, Dick Tracy, Slats, Bronco Piller, Prince Valiant. I already drank Ovaltine and I also followed the *Gazetinha Infantil*, a new magazine illustrated by Brazil's greatest comic-strip artists." In Rio, Paulo Ferreira read *Captain Marvel* comics while a neighbor's RCA-Victor radio set shared the Repórter Esso broadcast. After 1945, his mother having saved to make installment payments on a Brazilian-made set of her own, the Ferreira home echoed with soap operas. The radio also brought news of a Carnaval contest put on by the bottler of Crush, in which a neighborhood troupe won third prize for its improvised jingle, as Ferreira and his mother danced in costume. Back in São Paulo, Alex Periscinoto was impressed by advertising in the old newspapers he used in his household chores. "It was thus, on my hands and knees, that I discovered advertisements. I would read, observing the illustrations, the shape of the tire drawn in black and white, the shadows," he remembered, mentioning specific advertisements by JWT and the Panam agency. Later, he discovered a streetseller who traded in secondhand magazines: "Used magazines, half-torn, without their covers, but their condition didn't matter to me. What I really wanted was to enjoy Norman Rockwell's illustrations." "The discovery of American magazines," he claimed, "created an abyss between what was produced in Brazil and what those geniuses did out there." Outdoor advertising provoked similar wonderment in Sangirardi Jr.: "When I was a boy in São Paulo, oftentimes I would go [downtown], at night, just to admire the illuminated advertising signs. Those lights atop the buildings, forming figures that moved, letters that blinked, words that appeared and disappeared, were things that entertained me and had an indescribable enchantment." This wonderment prefigured the enjoyment Sangirardi derived as an adult from Rio's outdoor advertising and the radio programming introduced by Richard Penn, with whom he worked at Standard.[10]

Mass entertainment, changes in material culture, and accompanying experiences of marvelment thus went beyond child's play. As *O Estado de S. Paulo's* advertising columnist wrote, "The reading of foreign magazines, principally North American ones, always constituted a pleasure that I have never since relinquished. And not only because of the notable journalistic quality that they as a rule present, but also, oftentimes, for the high quality and good taste of their advertisements." The nascent culture of consumption could be part of becoming an adult and leaving childhood behind, as it was for Paulo Ferreira, who in 1949, at age thirteen, took the first bit of money he ever earned and bought, "in the Lojas Americanas in Méier, a handsome shirt for myself and, for my mother, two Pyrex dishes, at the time the maximum of American technology, which entered the Brazilian market with everything." Further on, his entry-level pay as an office boy at Shell's Brazilian subsidiary "allowed me such extravagances as buying, on installments, patent-leather shoes at the Clark shop on Rua do Ouvidor or Renner-brand shirts and slacks, with top-quality cloth, super-modern cuts, and impeccable finishing, at irresistible liquidation sales at Casa José Silva." When he got out of work, Cinelândia—"the Carioca Broadway"—was only five blocks away. By the mid-1950s, Ferreira was a Sydney Ross salesman, attending *soirées dansantes* in his off hours: "With Glostora-brand brilliantine in my hair and scented with Royal Briar, I behaved like a good boy and glided gracefully on the dance floor, entwined with young ladies from good families, devotees of the marvelous trio of Regina (soap, talcum powder, and perfume)." In São Paulo, about to be married, Rodolfo Lima Martensen oversaw the design of his first house, featuring "a most advanced kitchen for that time, as I ordered its design in the United States," and an exterior influenced by architectural ephemera he studied years earlier: "It was conceived in the style of the southern United States, with exposed brick, wide eaves, white windows and doors . . . a clear influence of the marvelous old catalog of the American Face Brick Association that I had ordered in the mail."[11]

Elements of these experiences were shared widely among city- and town-dwelling Brazilians who came of age between the 1920s and the 1950s. The literary critic Antonio Candido described Francisco Serrador's Cinelândia much as Paulo Ferreira and Renato Castelo Branco did, evoking its theaters: "Environments of dreams and luxury, with carpeting, comfortable seats, velvet curtains, uniformed ushers. And we also went to the famous old ones of yesteryear, the Pathé, the Parisiense. In Cinelândia, after the session, one went to the new, splendid ice-cream and confectionary shop [called] Americana, with the sensational novelty of *sundaes*, the opulent complication of which outdid the traditional simplicity of mere ice creams." Years before

Julieta Ladeira would save to buy movie magazines, Candido "not only read *Cinearte, Seleta, Cena Muda*, but the recent and portentious *Cinelândia*, published in Spanish by some grand international company, with glossy paper and incredible illustrations." In Porto Alegre in the 1950s, remembered Luiz Carlos Maciel, "I got out of class and went to have ice cream with *marshmallow* at the Lojas Americanas, because not only my classmates but the girls from the Colégio Madame Sevigné did the same." Maciel also thrilled to Hollywood's creations, James Dean becoming "the principal idol of my adolescence." A dozen years younger than Maciel, Alberto Villas missed the theatrical releases of *Giant* and *Rebel Without a Cause*, but his childhood in Belo Horizonte shared something with Maciel's adolescence: "The outings I went on with my mother always ended at the Lojas Americanas, more precisely, at its luncheonette. It was a luxury. I felt like I was in North America when I went in there. They served sandwiches, ice cream, and soft drinks at an enormous counter. I felt like a real man because I could already get up on those enormous stools with their soft cushions, one of each color, all by myself. Before approaching the counter, my mother would buy a chit at the cash register. We would sit down, and I always chose the *banana split*." It was therefore no exaggeration for a Brazilian journalist to claim, as Villas reached adulthood: "Most of us experience the profound influence of American culture, from its features of mechanical comfort to customs & manners and entertainments."[12]

Distinctions, however, must be made. By the 1960s, most city-dwelling Brazilians had been influenced by North American ways, but not to the same extent as the new professionals, who not only had been raised on Hollywood but were at work in producing consumption. In the 1940s, a proud few had worked for U.S. government agencies engaged in the war effort, most notably Orígenes Lessa, whose North American sojourn with the OCIAA produced the travelogue *O.K. América*, "a documentary of . . . the desire for greater comprehension and understanding among the peoples of the Hemisphere." Antonio Candido evoked the movie magazines of his youth, but he was not led to ask, as Julieta Ladeira would be, if their allure had led him to his career: "Did that attraction set me on a path to become an advertising executive?" For Jorge Martins Rodrigues, the answer would have been "yes": "In 1928, because I could read English, due to my yen for the movies and because I used to devour specialty magazines edited in the United States, I was hired as a translator by General Motors." Work in GM's advertising department, alongside Lessa and Aldo Xavier da Silva, led to a job at JWT as the automaker's account executive, followed by a return to GM, working in sales promotion and public relations, which took him all over Brazil and to the United States. Alex Periscinoto's fascination with the advertisements he pored over made learning English "an obsession." As a young man, he got a job illustrating advertising copy for Sears, then Clipper, before becoming Mappin's advertising head, which took him to the United States, and closer to acquiring English fluency, in what was the realization of "my great dream: to get to know Ohrbach's up close, in New York. I saw many of that store's advertisements in the American newspapers that I bought in São Paulo and I didn't believe that there could be anyone that competent in retail." The Ohrbach's department store led Periscinoto to the DDB agency, an experience he compared to the movie-houses of his childhood: "When I was a child and an adolescent, I loved cinema but I didn't have the money for tickets. So I went and asked for a job as an usher, so that I could watch the movies for free. There, at DDB, I felt the same thing. I wanted to be the usher." Periscinoto's longing would only grow, leading him, thirty-five years later, at the pinnacle of his success, to ponder impossibilities: "If I could do it all again, I would choose to have been born in the United States. Later, once I'd grown up, I would be an advertising man and go work alongside Bob Gage. . . . My greatest teachers, as I just said, were the Americans, especially the people I met at DDB." According to an old friend, Periscinoto's birthplace hardly mattered. He was "the most New Yorker of Brazilian advertising men," and "with the passion that he felt for William Bernbach he was able to bring a piece of the spirit of Madison Avenue" to Brazil.[13]

Formative experiences and a new language converged in making a calling, as well as a career, and the remaking of selfhood, as well as of society. As Amador Galvão de França, who joined Standard in 1943, remembered, "We were immersed in a new linguistic universe and had to memorize an entire glossary of foreign terms." "To words having to do with graphic production," as he put it, "we had to add others, all of them foreign, 'lay-out,' 'reprint,' 'release,' 'folds,' 'gimmick,' 'jingle,' 'spot,' 'prospect.' . . . We began our activities with much vigor, with the determined intention of getting to know, profoundly, our new occupation—in the final analysis, the art and technique of promoting useful things and riches, inducing men to produce more, sell more, and buy more." Fifteen years earlier, Aldo Xavier da Silva had much the same experience at GM's advertising department: "We only wanted a job, and we were really entering a profession. From then on, to observe, experience, and comprehend the peculiarities of that branch of communication became an everyday concern for us. We read whatever was at hand on the subject." In a third-person account, Silva described the cohort then beginning "to study advertising. Young men who knew English. Who read magazines from the United States. Who worked in American companies." "They became interested in advertising. They became impassioned with the art. They plunged into technical books and emerged as professionals, full of the distilled faith of neophytes, through the new, recently founded North American firms." "At that time," Renato Castelo Branco wrote of the 1930s and 1940s, "all of us, professionals and advertisers, were seized by the fascination of American technique. Back then, it represented the best *know-how* worldwide. It laid down the rules. It pontificated. And all of us went to work according to its primer." Referring to the 1940s, Genival Rabelo wrote, "What an enthusiast I was of the generous people of the North! What admiration I sustained for the things I read about the life, customs, history, everything that had to do with the United States! I learned, from the age of 20 to 22, notions of economy and advertising technique in American compendia. I memorized statistics that showed the economic development of that Country. I was, in the best sense of the term, a passionate Americanophile." From that point, it was a short step to throwing himself into the running of *Publicidade*: "The business began to define itself and I identified in such a way with the nature of the work that it imposed upon me, with the very reason for the business's existence, that paradoxically and mistakenly, it ceased to be a means to become an end, and, over the course of years, I gave it the best of my efforts." "I dove headfirst into advertising work," Emil Farhat wrote of his initiation into "the profession with the greatest future in Brazil." Thirty-four years at McCann followed, the last fifteen as president of its Brazilian subsidiary: "I dedicated my body and soul to a commercial activity as if it had been a spiritual task in which I had to put all the intellectual energies I had accumulated until then, or that I continued to accumulate. I was in a commercial corporation and I acted as if it was an institution with collective ends. Taking part in it engrossed me."[14]

Over these decades, the "know-how" referred to by Castelo Branco spread further. Arnaldo Vitulli acquired it starting as a Diários Associados "office-boy" in São Paulo in 1940, then as a sales manager in the advertising departments of other newspapers, before joining Geraldo Alonso's Norton Publicidade in 1947: "The mix of all that enriched my 'know-how' so much that when Geraldo went to work for the Galeria Carioca . . . he entrusted me with the management of the firm." When Alonso returned to São Paulo, he was replaced at Galeria Carioca by Pedro Nunes, whose experience included stints at Milton de Carvalho's A Capital, Lauro de Carvalho's A Exposição, and McCann-Erickson. "It was at McCann, as the head of its Radio Department, exactly during that auspicious phase, taking part in such a high-quality team of 'advertising-men' that I learned all of the broadest sense of the word 'planejamento' [planning], collaborating on programs like 'Um Milhão de Melodias' (Coca-Cola)." Other technical terms he adopted included "the trinomial: *sales promotion, advertising* and *merchandising*," "slogan," "Department Store," "show," "marketing," "display," "copy," "media," "jingle," "house-agency," "press-release," "out-door," "approach," and "layout." "Who, in recent times, talking with advertising folks," he asked, "hasn't heard talk of 'Layout,' 'Rough,' 'Approach,' 'Folder,' 'Media' (*midia*) and other American definitions making up the vocabulary that is becoming classic, that of the art of advertising?" For Walter Clark Bueno, over a career that took him from Rádio Tupi to Inter-Americana to TV-Globo, there were "spot," "dolly," "trainee," "off-set," "silk-screen," "layoutman," "scratchboard," "free-lancer," "paste-up," "fading," "link," "package," "script," "expert," "close[-up]," "strips," "pool," and "broadcasting."[15]

That employment of these terms exceeded their usefulness was clear, Nunes referring to the "vanity with which some advertising men demonstrate a certain pride when mentioning, habitually, in English, in the normal course of a lecture on advertising, something related to a promotion, a campaign, a piece of advertising." "Know-how" referred not only to technique but to a "system of work, a way of operating, a philosophy of selling," while the use of entirely nontechnical terms suggests stirrings deeper even than vanity. Armando d'Almeida and Nunes, independently of the other, used "chance" in ways that made clear that their referent was American opportunity rather than French fate. For d'Almeida, it was the "*chance* to develop their business"; for Nunes, "that 'chance'" was A Exposição–sponsored training "in the art of retail selling and executive management." For Orígenes Lessa in 1946, not only "copywriter" but "team" were keywords. Years later, he would refer to his own "appeal," revealing the easy fluency of someone able to crack a joke at his own expense in a second language. Referring to the early disciples of "the great school" of U.S. retail, Nunes commended the Carvalhos—Lauro, Milton, and Nilo—for their ability "to choose 'the right man in the right place.'" Simple flattery, perhaps, but not when Renato Castelo Branco's described his father's hardships: "He had to struggle from early on, to make a life for himself *the hard way*." Nor did Castelo Branco seem to be showing off when he referred to his own career as encompassing the work "of what the Americans call *jack of all trades*." The two framings suggest that for Castelo Branco, as for Ricardo Ramos, the JWT experience was personally formative: "I would not be the same if I hadn't lived through that Thompsonian phase." That it was professionally formative, Castelo Branco left no doubt: "All of us, from then on, gave ourselves over to fascination with American techniques. We chose American standards as the advertising ideal, as an objective to be reached, as a goal and a professional aspiration."[16]

Along the way, Brazilian Portuguese changed. In 1938, a writer for *Propaganda* made the erroneous assumption that "efficiente" (efficient) was a neologism introduced from English, such was its prominence in his new line of work. It was not, but there is no doubt that its usage increased over the twentieth century, during the hinge decade of which the Norton agency adopted the motto "Eficiência e Sinceridade" (Efficiency and sincerity), its take on McCann's "Truth Well Told." For an actual neologism, one need look no further than the name of another Brazilian agency, Cícero Leuenroth's Standard. In 1937, as the APP's first president, Orígenes Lessa used the term to refer to the development of national manufacturing, adding that advertising was making progress as well: "We have already reached a very high 'standard' of production, in Rio and São Paulo . . . in many modern fields we can say that one already does many things, in advertising, that honor national production." Six years later, Standard's Wilson Velloso quoted Lessa's words in a discussion of how far their profession had come and how far it still needed to go. By 1946, Armando d'Almeida had made "standard" a verb, *estandardizar*, while Lessa identified the "lack of standardization of newspapers" as an impediment to advertising.[17]

The model, once again, was the United States, which was clearer still when it came to the "standard" of living. Writing in 1942, when significant, long-term economic assistance from the United States in the postwar seemed possible, Genival Rabelo argued that "Practical Pan-Americanism" would promote an "increase in the 'standard' of living of the countries of Latin America," without which the region would be a poor trading partner. "Thereby, one does not need a great imagination," he argued, "to understand that an extraordinary consumer market may be developed, if one may raise the 'standard' of living of the Latin American countries a little. And this can only be achieved by the immediate industrialization of South America, which does not necessarily mean an industrialization that will end up competing with that of the United States." In another context, Rabelo made the case that Brazilians needed to reproduce the "'spirit of advertising' of the American people," which Celso Kelly linked to living standards: "Advertising has enriched the standard of living of civilized peoples. In the United States, the idea of comfort has earned a splendid market because advertising has shown the advantages of comfort." As Kelly switched to the first-person plural, Brazil and its standard of living took their place at the table: "Advertising shows us the way, annihilating distances and bringing the market and the factory closer together. Everyone considers themselves to have the right to enjoy the advantages of that which is most perfect. This is an aspiration that is becoming widespread. *Comfort and ease of communications* are considered by many to be the two great *tendencies of Western civilization*, in America above all. Advertising has a role to play in this sector. By raising the standard of living, it *civilizes*."[18]

That the new professionals idealized U.S. models of the good life, adopted the idea of the standard of living, and altered Brazilian Portuguese is indicative of the depth of their yearnings. The easy resort to Americanisms went beyond conceit or an instrumental bid for professional esteem and social standing. Brazilian advertising men were in some sense their own best customers, consumers of their own copy, or of copy cabled from Manhattan. The larger cohort of which they were a part, from employees to owners, submitted themselves to the discipline of sales promotion and the maxims of marketing in their professional lives, even as they sought to press both upon broader publics. When courses in sales promotion and executive management were introduced at A Exposição in the 1940s, remembered Pedro Nunes, "the example came from above, starting with the directors, who were the first to take classes, which was the case of Lauro de Souza Carvalho, José Carvalho, Júlio Maria and José Júlio de Azevedo e Sá." In 1957, two of Ducal's directors returned from the United States, "where they took the most modern courses on retail methods," and set to work organizing a convention, to share "revolutionary ideas" and to enjoin their fellow executives to "THINK BIG." Conventions like this one, according to Aldo Silva, were a key part of fostering "the modern business vision" among "enthusiastic teams." By the late 1950s, the executives and employees of CIN and Multi, as well as João Doria's eponymously named firm, worked to the same background music that greeted shoppers at Sears, Sirva-Se, and the Conjunto Nacional proto-shopping mall, the elevator music apparently prompting consumption and creativity at the same easy, predictable pace. At Multi, this "system of functional music" was counted among "modern methods that provide an agreeable environment for those who work there."[19]

It should thus come as little surprise that Dale Carnegie's *How to Win Friends and Influence People*—a "magnificent work," in a Brazilian admirer's words—and Napoleon Hill's *Think and Grow Rich* found a place on the new professionals' bookshelves alongside Claude Hopkins's *Scientific Advertising* and Charles Edwards and William Howard's *Retail Advertising and Sales Promotion*. The influence of self-help books and the North American milieu that produced them is evident across the new professions. Cícero Leuenroth, for one, claimed that what set Brazilians apart from the "great people" of the United States was that "there overabounds in the American that which we lack: optimism." For Walter Poyares, recently returned from the United States after years of admiring the country from afar, "Faith, my Brazilian friends, is what characterizes the American. Faith, which fills one's breast." This faith and the "citizen's confidence in himself and in his fellow citizens" formed "the most solid foundation of the progress of the North American people," manifest in "a different feeling of comfort, of material satisfaction, of technique at the service of man." Poyares need hardly have added: "If confidence is the moral foundation of the progress of the North American people, advertising is its stimulant." If advertising, confidence, faith, and optimism accounted for the differences between the two countries, then perhaps A Exposição's Júlio Maria de Carvalho had not been delusional on his return from the United States in 1947, when he declared, "I learned, my good man, that nothing is impossible."[20]

For more than a decade by that point, the new professionals and their allies had told all who would listen of the educational role of advertising and sales promotion. In the resulting jumble of pedagogy and publicity, the things themselves sometimes came to be eclipsed or upended. As João Alfredo de Souza Ramos wrote of advertising: "That same product, the properties of which it proclaims, serves as a pretext for the education of the people, for the raising of their degree of comfort and level of culture." "It is," he went on to say, "nothing more, nothing less than one of the great vehicles of our thought, and one would not even understand our lives as modern men without its existence." If, in the first of these two statements, the normal relationship between product and promotion was inverted, the second reversed that between profession and professional. The product became a means to advertise, rather than advertising a means to sell the product, while the creator—the modern man par excellence—was now mastered by his creation, without which existence is incomprehensible.[21]

Inadvertent tanglings of rhetoric aside, and with them the hyperbole that was the coin of the professional realm, there was something of the sorcerer's apprentice to Ramos's cohort. In 1952, PN's editors made a similar admission: "Our grandparents lived quite well, thank you, without all this entire complicated series of electric devices for use in the home. Many did not even know electricity. Today, we would feel unhappy without the Repórter Esso show, without the interminable radio soap operas, without whiskey over ice, in the end, without all those inventions that make life easier, making it more complicated." From radio news to bonded spirits on the rocks, the "men who decide"—as PN referred to its readers—were not as sovereign as they seemed. Indeed, when faced with the emblematic products of a superior material culture, they behaved as the consumers they claimed to control. As much is suggested by an account of a 1957 junket, sponsored by the APP and the Diários Associados, which took dozens of Brazilian advertising men and industrialists to the United States. Arriving in Miami, the first thing they did was rent new-model cars, "giving themselves over to the luxury of choosing the make, model, and color. . . . They look like millionaires, happily cruising the wide avenues."[22]

Public acknowledgment of such revelries, however, was rare. It was far more common for Brazilian professionals, like their North American counterparts, to exaggerate the distance that separated them from the "mass" by emphasizing their status as craftsmen, engineers, or scientists, men of work rather than play. This stance was clear in responses to a 1948 *O Globo* poll asking Rio residents what they would do with a sum of money that would make possible the fulfillment of a lifetime's worth of human needs or place almost any single desire within reach. "With one million cruzeiros," Pedro Nunes responded, "I would take a trip to the United States to polish my skills in advertising and sales." A copy artist "thought immediately of establishing a well-equipped agency and also making a research trip to the United States." Another advertising man expressed his interest in "a visit to Macy's, to get to know the organization of the big advertising agencies, to visit the great newspapers, to see how the chains of broadcasting stations work and what the exact sense of television is as an advertising vehicle." Contrived or not, these responses fit a larger pattern of professional self-presentation. "His only 'hobby' is work," declared a profile of McCann's Armando de Moraes Sarmento, using a turn of phrase familiar to his colleagues in New York. "Assis Paim Cunha's 'hobby' is work," the *Diario de Noticias*'s advertising columnist wrote of the founder of the Labor agency. "Men's fashion is his 'hobby' and his greatest joy is scoring a point in the struggle for the consumer's preference" was *PN*'s description of a retail chain's commercial director.[23]

Composite Characters

However hard they might strain, even the hobby-less—not to say humorless—among the new professionals remained Brazilian. Together with less single-minded colleagues, they may have bought into much of what they purveyed for firms foreign and domestic, on behalf of interests national and North American, but believing was not being, at least not yet, and identification was not identity, at least not completely. Even star pupils of the great school found some North American manners strange, off-putting, or incomprehensible. The most outstanding of the new professionals displayed attachments to place, political traditions, and cultural values that set them apart from North American executives, despite childhoods spent dreaming Hollywood dreams and grownup dedication to the principles of Claude Hopkins and Dale Carnegie.

The willing surrender of nationality encapsulated in Alex Periscinoto's fantasy of a North American rebirth was a minority position, even among the most ardent admirers of the United States. None dared state publicly that it would be all to the good if Brazil were to be absorbed into the North American union, though the topic was tabled, half-jokingly manner, at a Sales Directors' Club luncheon in Rio.[24] Across decades in which nationalist language exerted a seemingly unbreakable hold on public discourse, the new professionals claimed to be acting in the national interest, based on sincere attachment to birthplace and tradition. This attachment to place was manifest in the deep regional and local loyalties that have been the building blocks of a national imaginary in Brazil. Even after moving to Rio and São Paulo, and laboring to lose their provincial accents, the new professionals remained *gaúchos* and *potiguares*, *cearenses* and *baianos*, southerners and northerners, and especially northeasterners, not in opposition to Brazilianness, but enveloped in it, if not in easy ways. They were northeasterners, especially, because northeasterners were overrepresented in Rio's press, and so the cohort that entered the advertising profession after being drawn to journalism in the national capital included among its leading figures several proud sons of the northeast: Renato Castelo Branco, the first Brazilian to head JWT-Brazil, born in Piauí; João Doria, born in Bahia, who rose to the number-two position at Standard before starting his own agency; the sought-after copywriter Ricardo Ramos, born in Alagoas; and the longtime editor of *Publicidade* and its successor magazines Genival Rabelo, born in Rio Grande do Norte. Identification with their home states and through those patches of native ground to a region the very mention of which conjured up images of poverty and want, while positioning themselves as the professionals of such prosperity as existed in the country's southeast, was a reliable source of discomfort, most apparent in Rabelo's case but informing the outlook and aspirations of the others as well. For all four, it was part of who they were.[25]

Something of the extent to which North American ways remained strange even to adherents of American-style technicism comes through in Auricélio Penteado's description of his attraction to "things of the United States." U.S. foodways, apparel, and notions of comfort were all novel, different, distinct from the point of view of someone born in Rio in 1908. Even the most everyday of habits could signal difference, as when Julieta de Godoy Ladeira evoked working through lunch "alongside Americans who drink coffee with milk at noontime," bizarre dietary habits encapsulating opposite conceptions of time and work-discipline. The distinctiveness of such outlooks was not lost on all North Americans. As one of the Michigan State faculty on loan to EAESP noticed, Brazilian businessmen distinguished between themselves and their U.S. counterparts in mentality, bearing, and interests: "The American manager is regarded as an excessively single-minded fellow, a bit harried and not sufficiently interested in the arts." Even as Brazilian employers adopted psychotechnical examinations brought from abroad, such examinations were regarded as strange by some, and North American belief in their efficacy stranger still. "American stuff," in one account, the *psico-teste* symbolized North American impersonalism and scientism.[26]

In that account, the U.S. agency's insistence on the *psico-teste* also exemplified the high-handedness of "experts" from abroad and of foreign interests generally. It was hardly the only example. Touring his native northeast in 1949, Genival Rabelo was incensed by the situation he found in Fortaleza, where a U.S.-owned company was endangering public health by dumping combustible residues on oceanside dunes, with the complaisance of local officials. "The hostile and careless attitude that some foreigners adopt in contact with our people" was what Rabelo found galling, not, he carefully indicated, foreign investment: "I have nothing against the investment of foreign capital in Brazil. . . . Without a doubt, we are a country that is not very developed, for the progress of which it must count on the decided collaboration of foreign capital." Rabelo was also suspicious of Esso's activities, but he voiced his suspicions in terms that would have been recognizable to earlier generations of North Americans: the problem was a "trust" attempting to manipulate public opinion. For his part, despite years studying U.S. methods and IBOPE having earned Gallup's seal of approval, Auricélio Penteado was often frustrated by the unwillingness of North American executives to credit his firm's research. That the same "experts" received princely sums in comparison with their Brazilian coworkers was not lost on Penteado any more than it had been on Ivan Pedro Martins, who worked for Texaco a decade before IBOPE's founding. Despite Assis Chateaubriand's cheerleading, Brazil's Canadian- and U.S.-owned utility companies had their critics among the new professionals, as they did among urbanites generally. In 1954, Rabelo proposed the expropriation of the Light, but his support for foreign investment in the country's oil industry meant that he continued to be regarded by left-nationalists as the "finest flower of national sellout-ism," along with McCann's Emil Farhat and the supermarket impresario and Kubitschek speechwriter Augusto Frederico Schmidt.[27]

Brazilians of all political persuasions bristled at the "colonial" model adopted by foreign firms, including JWT, its offices "administered like a colonial empire, staffed by natives but . . . managed by Thompson men sent out from the U.S." By nearly all accounts, Robert Merrick, who headed JWT-Brazil from 1941 to 1961, was universally esteemed, despite his never having bothered to learn more than a few words of Portuguese, and Brazilian executives were gratified when the Kubitschek government awarded him the Ordem do Cruzeiro do Sul. Recalling Merrick's years in Brazil, Renato Castelo Branco described his staff: "Some of them were already renowned figures, but they gravitated for a long time in old Merrick's orbit. Others were practically his 'creatures,' or as he would say affectionately, *my boys*." This lasting affection is explained in part by Merrick's insistence upon JWT's turn from the colonial model, managing his retirement so that Castelo Branco succeeded him. The colonial model overturned, Castelo Branco claimed perquisites for Brazilian executives that had been contractual rights for their North American colleagues, including the expenses-paid overseas travel called "home leave." Pride in these achievements may have been one reason Castelo Branco was made the CNP's first president.[28]

Visiting the United States, whether on JWT's Brazilianized leave program or under other circumstances, members of the CNP-represented cohort marveled at material progress and comfort, but there were things that few Brazilians could admire. Firsthand experience of U.S. systems of racial discrimination could not but seem strange to Brazilian visitors, even those, like Genival Rabelo, who held to pseudo-scientific schemas of racial hierarchy into the postwar era. Then there was North American political intolerance, which Brazilians found even more mystifying than segregation. In 1947, Rabelo not only bristled at Jim Crow; he was repulsed by the rightward drift of the political climate, with talk of renewed war and the response, "He's a Communist!" answering his every query about former vice president Henry Wallace. Subsequent restrictions on the right to travel of North American Communists and of foreigners with the slightest connections to politically suspect individuals were regarded as even more absurd. Even as Joseph McCarthy's influence in the Senate crumbled, Auricélio Penteado suggested that his success had something to say of the character of the North American people ("hommo maccarthyensis") and their country ("McCarthyland"). While redbaiting went on in Brazilian professional circles—*PN* and the APP president Paulo Arthur Nascimento engaged in it at different points in time— it was of a comparatively restrained, less hysterical variety. Faced with the spectacle of the world's most powerful country tying itself in knots over ideological threats that were inflated or invented, Brazilian professionals, like many Western Europeans, could not but shake their heads.[29]

Brazilian incomprehension of McCarthyism was to some extent a rational response to an irrational phenomenon, but it also reflected a different political culture. Episodically, in the 1930s and 1940s, official anti-leftism in Brazil was as obsessive as its counterpart in the postwar United States, but it failed to work its way into the fabric of society and culture in the same way. One need look no further than the Rio office of the Inter-Americana agency. In 1953, a trainee-level job there introduced Walter Clark Bueno to the Left. "In that period," he wrote, "I first had contact with leftist ideas. At Inter-Americana, almost everyone was a Communist." He was soon collecting dues for the office cell, learning, "Not everyone at the agency was a card-carrying militant, but almost all were collection-time sympathizers. They contributed to the [party's] finances, paying their tithe religiously." The greatest of Inter-Americana's Communists was Ivan Pedro Martins, who had headed the country's Communist Youth in the era of the National Liberating Alliance (ANL), Brazil's version of the popular front, and who remained a party loyalist for years after returning from exile in the 1940s. Among the packed crowds Martins had addressed at ANL rallies in Rio were Emil Farhat and Renato Castelo Branco. Ten years later, while working for McCann, Farhat would help found the Democratic Left, an antiauthoritarian embryo of the postwar Brazilian Socialist Party, as would Guilherme Figueiredo, soon to begin a fifteen-year stint at the same U.S. agency. Ricardo Ramos was born too late to remember the ANL's brief existence, but was a fervent Communist from adolescence into adulthood, including a five-year stint at the party's *Tribuna Popular*, which he helped found as a seventeen-year-old cub reporter. Roberto Duailibi was active in a Communist Party cell while a secondary-school student, before joining Colgate-Palmolive's advertising department. By the time he passed through McCann in the 1960s, those politics were sufficiently deep in his past for him to befriend a copywriter of Trotskyist views. A grand old man among the new professionals, Jorge Martins Rodrigues was a leader of the Christian Democratic Party, which he steered toward support for Cuban self-determination as the threat of massive U.S. intervention hovered over the island following the defeat of the proxy invasion at the Bay of Pigs. Earlier in 1961, another veteran of the GM advertising department, Orígenes Lessa, had been among the signatories—most of them Communist Party members—of a petition protesting the botched invasion and laying responsibility for it at the feet of "North American imperialism."[30]

These commitments reflected a political culture that was less reactionary than that found in the United States, which in turn helped create a professional milieu that was relatively more open. The principal Brazilian trade magazines carried contributions from writers who were Communists and socialists during the years of the U.S. blacklists. These magazines' editors were hardly radicals, but they felt the need to debate Ivan Pedro Martins and discuss the relative merits of the Marxian idea of surplus value, which almost certainly failed to receive similar consideration in *Printer's Ink* or *Advertising Age*. In 1964, on the eve of the coup d'état that would begin two decades of military rule, the APP's president found himself unable to get its board to approve a motion in support of the March of the Family with God for Liberty, a right-wing mobilization aimed at the country's left-leaning president. That failure did not reflect leftist sympathies among the owners and upper management of major advertising agencies, still less support for continued constitutional government on the part of advertisers, but it did indicate distaste for the hard right among creatives. Carlos Queiroz Telles remembered watching the march with his partners in a small, recently founded agency, their clients and former bosses chanting anti-leftist slogans in "a pre-carnaval parade through the streets of the city." When the tanks rolled later that month, there was nothing to do but drink: while Telles and like-minded copywriters had poetized slogans for a revolution they imagined would be theirs, the other side had organized.[31]

There was no purge after the coup, however. As the literary critic Roberto Schwarz observed, in a much-cited essay written in 1969–1970, "the cultural presence of the left was not liquidated on that date, and what is more, from then to now it has not stopped growing." Schwarz exaggerated somewhat by adding, "In the sanctuary of bourgeois culture the left sets the tone," but it is unarguable that the professional-managerial cohort to which he, Telles, and their neighbors belonged stood well to the left of its North American counterpart. Indeed, one need only point to the two countries' editions of the monthly magazine of the middling to get a sense of the difference between the outlook of the U.S. middle class and Brazil's classes A and B, of which Schwarz and Telles were atypical members, but members all the same. According to the U.S.-trained director of *Seleções de Reader's Digest*, translations of the Vietnam-related stories featured in the flagship were unpublishable in Brazil, as such gung-ho support for a dirty postcolonial war was beyond the country's middle-class pale.[32]

In post-1964 circumstances, outrage over the U.S. war in Vietnam might compensate for the narrowing space afforded public criticism of oppressive conditions at home. As much is suggested by Telles's volume of poetry, produced and sold in poster format, *Viet-em-Mim* (a play on "Vietminh" and "mim," or me). It sold unforeseeably well, but its success did nothing to assuage the conflicts besetting Telles. He later recalled feeling like Jekyll and Hyde, half businessman and advertising executive, half writer and artist, in increasingly trying times. As a businessman, in his words, "I had to live together and cooperate amicably with a structure of power that worshipped according to the prayer book of torture and of the torturers, when it did not dribble its monthly tithe to the policemen of the organs of repression." His copywriting was at the service of the same, as was the work of his profession, which "was earning well with the economic progress of the country and played its cards, its creativity, and its talents in the maintenance of the regime and its systems." To creative struggles were added the puzzles and pressures of writing under official censorship (how to write scripts that would be meaningful to theatergoers without setting off the censors? what if yet another text was banned?). Then there were commitments to friends in jail, on the run, and underground, which were not easily shrugged off but carried with them the risk of suffering an array of nearly unimaginable fates.[33]

That Telles ran that risk sets him apart from most members of his professional cohort, few of whom were asked to hide a fugitive or courier messages abroad, much less accepted the dangerous charge. His literary interests, however, and even his literary success, as poet and playwright, were less remarkable. Whereas in the United States, advertising work was a notorious refuge for failed writers and artists, in mid-twentieth-century Brazil advertising and adjacent occupations were fields of employment for men and women of great accomplishment and promise in the creative arts. Few quit their calling altogether; of those who continued to write in their off hours, a handful were successful poets, playwrights, critics, essayists, and authors of creative fiction. The contrast with the United States can be drawn in a few strokes by reference to the *Cambridge History of Latin American Literature*'s chapter on the modern Brazilian short story. Of the fifty-odd writers born after 1899 deemed sufficiently important to be cited in an exceptionally compact essay, three made careers as advertising executives (Orígenes Lessa, Ricardo Ramos, and Julieta de Godoy Ladeira), while a fourth worked for Nestlé's in-house advertising department for over a decade (Marques Rebelo), a fifth spent a few years as a copywriter in the 1960s (João Antônio), and a sixth cofounded the Bahian agency Unigraf (João Ubaldo Ribeiro). A summary list of significant North American writers of the same period would not feature nearly as high a proportion of professional copywriters. In the United States, of course, there were many lucrative options for successful writers who needed more money than they could make from their craft, starting with Hollywood. Marcos Rey (pseud., Edmundo Donato), who did not make the *Cambridge History* but perhaps should have, pointed to Faulkner, Fitzgerald, and Dreiser when faced with criticism for side-jobbing in advertising and churning out scripts for radio, television, and the country's low-budget, mildly pornographic cinema. North American writers had Hollywood. Their Brazilian counterparts did what they had to.[34]

Thus Emil Farhat, Pedro Nunes, and Milton Pedrosa turned to careers in advertising, sales promotion, and media after publishing novels, Farhat's receiving a national prize from a committee of the great and the good of Brazilian letters. All three debut novels represented variations on the socially conscious literary regionalism of the 1930s, their authors elaborating upon a form identified with Pernambuco, Paraíba, and Bahia using local color culled from their own native ground. Renato Castelo Branco's first novel, *Teodoro Bicanca*, belonged to the same tradition, but it was written after he had worked in advertising off and on for over a decade. Like Farhat's, it won a national prize. In neither case was it coincidental that the genre to which these novels belonged allowed Castelo Branco and Farhat to give literary form to regional bonds, as well as to social and political leanings suspect in the Cold War–era United States.[35]

Castelo Branco also published poetry and book-length essays on national and regional history and ethnography, as well as a volume calling for South American politico-economic confederation (published by Brasiliense, a notoriously left-wing press). Jorge Medauar published poetry before turning to regionalist short stories of the cacao region of southern Bahia, where he was born. Ivan Pedro Martins, though born and raised in Minas Gerais, wrote two well-regarded regionalist novels of Rio Grande do Sul, where he spent years in hiding from the authorities after the ANL was banned, as well as short stories and a number of studies of the Brazilian economy. Guilherme Figueiredo wrote novels, short stories, poetry, and criticism, but his greatest literary success was as a playwright, beginning during the fifteen-year period he spent working for McCann and producing television shows.[36]

Two of the greatest literary talents to pursue advertising as a career were Ricardo Ramos and Julieta de Godoy Ladeira, best known for their precisely crafted short stories but who also published novels, criticism, and juvenile fiction. Each published short-story collections that won the coveted Jabuti Prize (Ramos in 1962 and 1971 for *Os desertos* and *Matar um homem*, Ladeira in 1963 for *Passe as férias em Nassau*). Ramos and Ladeira were also family to some of Brazil's foremost literary figures. Ramos's father, Graciliano, was one of the greatest Brazilian authors of midcentury; the Ramos family was joined by marriage to Jorge Amado, the most commercially successful of Brazilian novelists. Ladeira, after becoming one of the first women to graduate from the São Paulo Advertising School, the first female copywriter in JWT's São Paulo office, and the author of *Passe as férias em Nassau*, met and married Osman Lins, whose novels and short stories remain well regarded by critics, decades after his untimely death.[37]

Ladeira and Ramos, it bears repeating, were career copywriters, in the mold of Orígenes Lessa, whose double life as advertising man and literary figure culminated in election to the Brazilian Academy of Letters. Lessa, Ramos, and Ladeira worked in advertising steadily, decade after decade, while carving out time for their own writing. Emil Farhat and Renato Castelo Branco gave themselves over more completely to advertising, publishing only in the trade press between the late 1940s and the 1960s. For much of the same period, literary pursuits were relegated to a distant second place for Eliezer Burlá, Hernâni Donato, Oswaldo Alves, and J. G. de Araujo Jorge, among other successful authors-turned-advertising-men.[38]

Some simply passed through the field, turning to advertising at the start of their careers or other trying times. The journalist, cartoonist, and children's book author Ziraldo Alves Pinto worked for McCann—"where I discovered the world," he later said—as well as Grant and Standard, before getting a job at *O Cruzeiro*, following which he moonlighted in advertising. The writer and Communist militant Dias Gomes, desperate for work at a politically difficult moment, was hired at Standard by Sangirardi Jr.—"a man of the left, though he did not belong to the Party"—but did not take to the work and returned to writing for radio as soon as he could. Writing commercial radio scripts rather than reason-why advertising may seem a distinction without a difference, but it mattered to Dias Gomes. The writer Alina Paim, like Dias Gomes a lifelong Communist, worked for a time in the advertising department of a major nightclub interest. The bohemian journalists Rubem Braga and Paulo Mendes Campos each worked as copywriters at one point or another before finding more agreeable ways to piece together a living.[39]

The latter seems to have been a common aspiration. Renato Castelo Branco—"the dean of Brazilian advertising professionals"—tried to make a living as a translator for a while in the 1940s before returning to agency work. After more than a decade of working in advertising and sales, the poet Araujo Jorge was more successful in exiting the field, winning election to the national legislature in 1970, testament to his poetry's popularity, if not any other merits.[40]

While Castelo Branco tried translation as a means to escape advertising, others combined it with their day jobs. Wilson Velloso translated Kant, Orwell, and Bertrand Russell. The market researcher Octávio da Costa Eduardo translated Philip Hitti's *The Arabs*. Guilherme Figueiredo translated Shakespeare, Shaw, and Molière for the stage, and Jean-Jacques Servan-Schreiber and Pierre Mendès France for his Francophile compatriots. Having spent his salad days as a Communist street-speaker adapting Leninism to local idioms, Ivan Pedro Martins turned to Marshall McLuhan late in life, rendering *The Medium Is the Massage* and *War and Peace in the Global Village* into Portuguese.[41]

In these contexts, translation was more than piecework. It was a general duty of Brazil's lettered strata, who worked in at least three languages, another distinction between the new professionals and their U.S. counterparts. As Annibal Bomfim noted, "in their great majority, even in the cultured classes, North Americans are proudly ignorant of foreign languages; while most moderately cultured Brazilians know, at a minimum, French and English perfectly." Auricélio Penteado put it more pointedly: "In general, we read Portuguese, English, French, Spanish; they sometimes read English." The intellectualism epitomized by multilingualism was a matter of cultural values for some; for others it represented cultural capital, or a cultural means to capital. It was likely the latter gambit that led Geraldo Alonso, described even by admirers as culturally limited and politically reactionary, to bring prominent intellectuals the likes of Hernani Donato into the Norton agency.[42]

Socially speaking, the distance that took Donato from literature and journalism to advertising was slight. Before working in advertising in Rio, Guilherme Figueiredo traveled in São Paulo intellectual circles in which copywriters were fixtures; the friendships begun there were sustained through his years working for McCann, opening doors with Rio's literary elite. From the 1940s into the 1960s, São Paulo's "new" downtown was a space of sociability where the new professionals and established intellectuals rubbed shoulders with one another, drinking and carousing in the bars, cafés, and nightclubs evoked in Marcos Rey's fiction and remembrances. There, as in a constellation of drinking places stretching from Rio's city center southward to Copacabana, then west to Ipanema, executives from Brazilian- and U.S.-owned agencies mixed with prominent performing artists, songwriters, and authors. When Ricardo Ramos despaired of making enough money as a journalist to afford to get married, his father, at the height of his fame and having recently formalized his commitment to the Communist Party, shocked him by suggesting he try advertising. "Look up Emil Farhat, at McCann," he said, "or Orígenes Lessa, at Thompson. They're my comrades, tell them you're my son. They'll take care of you." Thereafter, Ricardo spent his days working under Lessa's supervision, while his father showed "a total knowledge of the milieu that was now open to me. He knew of Oswaldo Alves, Jorge Medauar, Alina Paim, Guilherme Figueiredo, Eliezer Burlá and others. He thought my having moved was a good thing." The kinds of favors and friendships Ramos recalled were not unique. A decade earlier, Lessa had helped the Trotskyist journalist Cláudio Abramo in the same way. As far as friendships were concerned, Caio Domingues—not yet the author of *Elementos de propaganda*—was close with some of his generation's favorite writers: Fernando Sabino, Paulo Mendes Campos, and the humorist Millôr Fernandes. Intellectual and ethylic interests brought together Carlos Drummond de Andrade and Manuel Bandeira, two of Brazil's most beloved poets, with Guilherme Figueiredo and the market-researcher Homero Icaza Sanchez, who created Globo's in-house institute.[43]

The milieux in which the new professionals aspired, played, and worked were thus very different from the United States. They were different. Many writers and artists among them were not failed writers or failed artists, like their North American counterparts, but rather novelists, short-story writers, poets, playwrights, illustrators, and painters who were born into a society where they could succeed in their calling but not survive on its fruits. The reactionary political culture of the United States was foreign even to those on the right of the political spectrum. While aspects of North American consumer capitalism reached deep into their professional identities and private lives, they remained Brazilians of a certain class, attuned to developments abroad and at home amid which they were formed and through which they fashioned themselves and their country.

Critics and Creators

Meanwhile, intellectuals fretted over changes to Brazil's commerce and culture effected by the new professionals. Some of their comments and critiques identified all-encompassing processes—massification and materialism, Americanization and the imposition of "the American way of life"—while others zeroed in on specific practices, including advertising, installment buying, and the profusion of North American English. The creation of new needs and fostering of new ways of being in the world came in for particular criticism, as embodying unwelcome shifts in values, as well as representing waste, misplaced priorities, and other obstacles to the realization of national potentialities. Comment along these lines ran from statements of vain regret to incisive criticism intended to inspire radical change. It also made for strange ideological bedfellows and may have assisted in the creation of "consumer" as a meaningful social category. From the 1960s onward, the new culture of consumption became a subject for creative artists, a handful of whom made it a major theme. Fiction and film, painting and poetry, thus lend the historian refractions of individual experiences of the new culture and estimations of its impact and reach.

Almost from the start, the twentieth century's means of communication came in for censure. According to conservative intellectuals of the upper crust, cinema worked as a fearsome solvent upon time-honored social relations. That was the view of the law professor Jorge Americano, writing in the silent-film era, who claimed that the "discovery of certain inventions and the ever-so-rapid evolution of certain others put the inferior strata in contact with the greater civilization, for which neither their sentiments were prepared nor their intelligence developed enough." Thereafter, as movies publicized "the unsuspected existence of the intimate life of comfort, luxury, riches, sumptuosity, and dissipation of the great homes," the lesser sort "knew of new pleasures, in the exclusive reach of the rich, and anxiously aspired to them. They experienced the desire for satisfaction with an unhealthy violence." Nearly forty years later, the economist Eugênio Gudin made the same case on a planetary level. Answering the question of "What are the most important characteristics of our time and what are their aspects in Brazil from a social point of view?" Gudin pointed to a turn from delayed gratification and thrift, the erosion of paternal authority, and the "the advent of cinema, radio, television, the airplane, making way for what has been called the demonstration effect, which is to say the ease with which the inhabitants of less-developed countries become aware (cinema, radio, television, or air travel) of the superior ways of life prevailing in richer countries." With this knowledge came "the feeling of nonconformity, which leads to discontent and to revolt."[44]

Identifying twentieth-century means of communication and transport with undesirable social and cultural changes was not the preserve of reactionary voices alone. Somewhere between corporatism and liberal socialism in the mid-1930s, the critic Sergio Milliet declared that love in its spiritual essence had been vanquished by the automobile, jazz, and radio—which also killed off reading and contemplation—while massification had led to the decadence of quality cinema. At decade's end, Milliet lambasted "imbecile advertising" in a riff on technological change and culture that divided it into two varieties, "that which seeks to inform us of that which we lack and that which has as its end creating a new need."[45]

At around the same time, the timidly progressive *O Observador Econômico e Financeiro* traced the decline of Brazilian radio under the influence of commercial imperatives: "Transformed into a vehicle for advertising, among us the radio completely lost its affinity with the book, as a superior instrument of culture. . . . It abandoned the lecture halls, fled from the chaired professor, hid itself from scientists, scorned the educator, left the sanctuary of symphony concerts and went to the slums to seek out *maxixe* [Afro-Brazilian dance music] and the decrepit stories of our melancholy forebears." The magazine's editorialists, apparently given relatively free rein on cultural matters, expressed a similar view of developments in cinema and publishing and their influence on youth, foreign films and comics producing "all of the pernicious effects of denationalization, of dissolution, of corruption of the national character."[46]

Fifteen years later, the psychiatrist Antônio Carlos Pacheco e Silva took on the movies and television, "powerful agents of collective action, which contribute in a decisive way to modify habits, customs, feelings, and conduct, not only of the individual but even of entire collectivities." "The effect of cinema combined with that of television," he continued, "makes itself felt in an imperceptible way, shaping the human personality." A homeopath of the human psyche, Pacheco e Silva held that despite all their potential for ill, "cinema and television may contribute such that humanity of our time, frustrated, skeptical, doubting, and disillusioned, given over to a dissolving materialism, not be dragged irredeemably to the abyss and to chaos." The novelist Amadeu de Queiroz, taking stock in a memoir written at around the same time, found no such upside: "The pretty futilities, created by artificial industry, that are fashions . . . the foolishness divulged by the radio . . . the influence of the films and actors of American cinema . . . the automobile obtained in an amoral fashion . . . [all of this together] is what drives young people to ruin, instilling in them ideas of an aggressive civilization." Meanwhile, an adoptive Paulistano suggested that "the moral crisis that is denounced generally perhaps has its roots, less in a transformation of mentality than in a change in living habits," specifically the turn away from traditional forms of housing to apartment living, in which—barring intervention by Brazilian architects—residents of lower floors "will dissolve into the collectivity, in automobile noise, in shop lights, in the agitated life of the city, which also penetrates the interior through the newspaper, through radio, through television."[47]

The disappearance of man into the mass, materialism, denationalization, and cultural leveling effected by commercial media—if asked, many Brazilian intellectuals would have identified these developments with the influence of the United States. Sergio Milliet, for one, made "Yankeeism" and "American civilization" shorthand for materialism and mass society in his 1930s interventions, while for others, "Americanization" stood for this bundle of developments. In additional cases, the term was used to refer to aspects of what Jorge Americano—perhaps wary of the potential for puns—called "modern life." The idea of "the American way of life" acquired something of the same plasticity, to be criticized in part or excoriated as a whole.[48]

As adherents of Old World fashion, Brazilian intellectuals of the interwar followed André Siegfried and other European observers of the United States. For Jeronymo Monteiro Filho, Siegfried's key insight was that the standardization of mass production had standardized the American public, to which Monteiro added a description of cookie-cutter towns, their main streets identifiable "by the constant 'Drug-Stores,' by the 'automatics,' by the always identical 'movies,' by the same façades, by the invariable signs, throughout the transcontinental territory." It was the bland face of the future: "Native expressions are being buried. Americanization proceeds, 'standardizing' the world. It is the surrender of individual self-assertion, in a holocaust for the profit of the overpowering 'leaders' of Wall Street, or . . . for the purpose of the material comfort of our descendants. . . . It will be the empire of monotony, labeled as the general progress of humanity." Francisco Emygdio da Fonseca Telles expressed similar horror at what he called "the Americanization of the world." Unlike Monteiro, Telles had never visited the United States, confessing, "I only discern the reflex of Americanism that comes to us from there." "But I may attest," he continued, "the extent to which the all-powerful concept, which in itself summarizes the breviary of the progressive man of our age, has been seen with distrust, with repugnance even, by some of the greatest contemporary minds." What followed was a brief on "modern materialism" made of quotes from Siegfried, Keyserling, and Gugliemo Ferrero, as well as the U.S. historian James Harvey Robinson.[49]

Telles had been inspired to address "Americanization" by the journalist Vivaldo Coaracy, who discussed "the conquest of the World" by "the American Spirit" in back-to-back installments of his column in *O Estado de S. Paulo*. Coaracy, however, was not a critic. Rather, he presented his perspective in a march-of-history framework that owed much to nineteenth-century sociology. While he nodded in the direction of the economic determinism he attributed to European thinkers and acknowledged economic calculations by U.S. actors, Coaracy saw material forces as only part of what was driving the overseas expansion of U.S. business, though the larger motor forces were lost even unto those men, "in remote offices in New York, Chicago, San Francisco . . . with a broader view of the facts, who know that these apparently dispersed and independent movements and operations are coordinated with vaster plans." The campaign would not end with the economic domination of the world by the United States, which Coaracy, for what it was worth, saw as less encompassing than earlier forms of dominion. Rather, Coaracy's horizon was the conquest of the world by "the American spirit," represented by the pairing of individualism and egalitarianism, grounded in a materialism tempered—paradoxically, he admitted—by mysticism. In the shorter term, "economic penetration [was] the vehicle for spiritual conquest," as was clear in Coaracy's discussion of film, with its echoes of Alberto Rosenvald, Julius Klein, and other believers in Hollywood's influence: "Well, if cinema is an excellent agent of commercial advertising, American industry's best salesman, preparing markets for the introduction of its products; it is with even greater efficiency a process for the divulging and penetration of the American Spirit with which it is impregnated. . . . It was thus that American habits, American sports, American fashions, American customs, the American conception of life, spilled forth and became well known around the globe. And these are nothing more than the clothing of the spirit." This clothing would then remake mankind through a process of transference, for just as North Americans' "love of material comfort" stemmed from their "materialist conception of life," so non-Americans' adoption of U.S. standards of material comfort would produce a materialist worldview on their part. The means by which individualism would be so transmuted was left unclear, but Coaracy made plain that he privileged it over materialism and egalitarianism, and thereby gave away his game, arguing that mass production and consumption had shown that capitalism, born of individualism, was capable of solving problems Communists believed it could never solve. There was a price to be paid (the raising of the material and mental state of the masses would provoke a lowering of the same conditions for the upper classes, and so American intellectual elites were not the equals of European elites), but as far as Coaracy was concerned, that price was more than paid by the fact that "the

American Spirit undertakes the conquest of the world as the powerful and aggressive paladin, vigorous and confident champion, of individualism," which was to say, of capitalism, lined up against Communism. Out of this contest, Coaracy concluded, would emerge the civilization of the future.[50]

Whatever one makes of Coaracy as a social theorist, he was ahead of his time politically. In the 1930s, reactionary screeds denouncing Americanization were more common than conservative appreciations of its anti-Communist potential. The educator and Catholic activist Laura Jacobina Lacombe, for example, amid a consideration of the impact of cinema, argued: "Even those people who consider themselves to be brave spirits have endured the influence of the 'Americanization' of our society. The ever-greater acceptance of habits, attitudes, or wardrobes, that were not characteristic of our people, is the work of cinema." It was, Lacombe discovered visiting the United States, nearly as predicted by the Protocols of the Elders of Zion, for was not the U.S. movie industry owned and run by Jews? The poet Murilo Mendes, like Lacombe a militant of the clericalist Dom Vital Center, was also affronted by the inversion of values he saw on all sides: "In this hurried age of Americanization of the spirit and of everything, 'to win' means to seize advantageous positions as if by assault, install oneself in a good automobile, and spread one's name in all directions over the radio."[51]

A dozen years later, Americanization remained something to be denounced as far as Mendes was concerned, now in a nationalist rather than a religious idiom, in an introduction to the work of Heitor Villa-Lobos, the maestro whose indigenous- and Afro-Brazilian-accented compositions had provided a soundtrack to the centralizing dictatorship of 1937–1945. According to Mendes, "Villa-Lobos restored to us the image of a Brazil that, with the sudden emergence of new customs, of Americanization, of the radio, etc., perhaps would have been lost forever if his artist's intuition hadn't recorded it."[52]

By that point, the defense of Brazilian traditions against "excessive Europeanization or Yankee-ization" had occupied Gilberto Freyre for years. Impassioned by northeastern ways, Freyre rallied to their defense against the stultifying influences of foreign culture. "American cinema—that is what today is molding boys' imaginations in Brazil—including in the Northeast." Popular poetry and folklore, he charged, were threatened by "cinema, novels, the cheap editions of detective stories," while Recife's cityscape was remade, "replacing the almost medieval vagaries of the old stone buildings with the Yankee furors of modern undertakings of steel-reinforced concrete."[53]

Writing in 1954, Freyre's friend and fellow traditionalist Afonso Arinos de Melo Franco identified "a different atmosphere" in Rio's high society, "imposed by the internationalization or, better put, the Americanization of

Carioca life," in which "nights pass in the smoke of American cigarettes and the passion for card games." Six years later he detected similar influences in his ancestral homeland, deep in Minas Gerais. There, with the roadbuilding linking Brasília to the coast, centuries-old mansions were demolished, giving way to empty lots and buildings of reinforced concrete and glass: "Meanwhile, new men, trucks, motor graders rip up the cobblestones and raise the dust of centuries. In American-style bars, with colored counters, orangeade and *ice cream* are sold. Traditional leather hats and boots encounter *blue jeans* and dark sunglasses. A young woman, of opulent backsides, squeezed tightly in blue nankeen-cotton pants, smiled to 'the senator' from the door of the bar and flicked her cigarette butt away with the tip of her fingers, in a careless gesture. Is she the daughter of some American engineer from the Três Marias dam works, or could she be a well-rounded cousin of mine from right here?"[54]

Similar criticisms issued from Communist intellectuals, albeit in a distinct argot. "North American imperialism," according to Octávio Brandão, "has as its aim the total Americanization of Brazil—to standardize everything." Among the tools of the United States and its agents were "newspapers corrupted by advertisements and subventions such as *O Globo* and the 'Diários Associados,'" as well as the Repórter Esso, *Seleções de Reader's Digest*, and *O Cruzeiro*, "full of stories of criminals and the scandals of North American actresses"; radio and its "stupid soap operas, of a decadent and whining romanticism"; and "films, paid for with the people's gold, [which] deform, denature, and devirilize Brazilian youth." The novelist Dalcídio Jurandir agreed: "The imposition of the North American way of life is done through the various methods of all-absorbing commercial advertising." It was clear in movies, the press, and especially radio: "From the commercial to the preponderance of all the garbage of the musical arrangements and the soap operas, imperialist domination makes itself felt day after day." The educational columnist of the party's *Imprensa Popular* blamed Brazil's "so-called 'elites,' the dominant classes": "they do everything to favor the diffusion among us of the means of degradation of our national culture, of propaganda of the North American way of life, through cinema, the press, radio, the 'comics.'" For the newspaper's movie columnist, however, it was a matter of U.S. skill: "It is needless to say that the Americans have a truly extraordinary commercial instinct. With well-planned advertising campaigns, they popularize their habits, their expressions, their idols. Thus occurred with Coca-Cola, with the young Frank Sinatra (who later revealed himself to be a very good actor), with 'rock and roll' and its representative, Elvis Presley."[55]

On the non-Communist left, the idiosyncratic São Paulo review *Anhembi* represented an attempt at marrying the French traditions dear to Sergio Milliet and Fonseca Telles with a modern, progressive politics. It was no less critical of North American influence than the traditionalists or the Communists. As its editor explained, softening a denunciation of French policy in Algeria with an appreciation for metropolitan culture and a slap at U.S. influence: "Our formation, intellectual or spiritual, if one likes, we owe exclusively to France. We, of ANHEMBI, belong to the civilization of Wine or of Olive Oil that is counterpoised, in Brazil, to the civilization of Coca-Cola and of 'Chiclets' that is more or less predominant among the younger generations, shaped by comic strips and an elementary and de-educating cinema." A year later, *Anhembi*'s defense of the national language, panicked and pedantic by turns, provided an inadvertent laundry list of some of the most representative institutions of Brazilian consumer capitalism: "At any moment, this emerges on the façades of large stores: 'Big liquidação.' Other large stores are even called: 'Magazine so-and-so.' The correct or, better put, the real foreign expression that even as such cannot be tolerated is 'Magasin,' much used in French . . . but thought to be too prosaic for these pedantic fools of commerce. But the barbarisms are to be found everywhere, dictated by national primitivism, such that we have even newspapers like the ridiculous *Shopping News* or magazines, like *Manchete*."[56]

Also on the left, the radical democrat José Honório Rodrigues confronted the issue of Americanization—"the rapid importation of new production techniques, new cultures and ways of life, especially the North American one"—in an essay on Brazilian history and aspirations: "The Americanization of Western culture brought about the rationalization of work, the valorization of economic life, especially mercantile and industrial activity, a stimulus to capitalism and to the overcoming of the past, but also all the evils of advertising, of the mentality of conspicuous consumption that favors inflation, the barbarization of commercial radio and television, the anxieties and the spread of alienation to the middle class."[57]

As José Honório's words were published, Vivaldo Coaracy returned to the subject of the "intensive process of *Americanization* of the world," his perspective having changed since his twin columns of 1930. The influence of nineteenth-century social thought had been tempered by an essentially humanistic outlook, with the resulting text more observation than analysis or intervention. For Coaracy, as for José Honório and many of their predecessors, Americanization was a world-encompassing trend, borne by cinema, popular magazines, music and dance, and cheap paperback books, as well as by advertising, commerce, and industrial products from appliances to automobiles. Such influences "provide the general mean of today's Brazilian public a clear vision of the United States, an idea of the environment, the habits, the existence of that land. Many of our people, even without having been there, know more things about the country of the dollars than in regard to vast regions of Brazil."[58]

By that point, Brazil's most conservative spokesmen had come around to the political calculus behind Coaracy's earlier intervention, and when it came to the United States they chose their words carefully, for to censure the United States had become tantamount to criticizing capitalism as well as Christendom and might provide cover for radical criticism of both while weakening the resolve of right-thinking Brazilians. As a spokesman for big business, the president of Rio's Commercial Association could criticize the United States and the extent of its influence, but only for a North American audience, while begging for more: "You have inundated our market with consumer goods and you have not invested enough to create national industries here. You aroused our discontent by putting pretty things in our windows. . . . Now we look to you to satisfy the needs that all people have a right to. When we see Americans with two cars, we Brazilians want two." On the ultramontane right, when the Catholic lay leader Gustavo Corção confessed his "little regard for innumerable aspects of the North American way of life," his confession was buried deep in a plea for closer relations with the United States, in contrast with the anti-Americanizationist screeds of his fellow militants of the Dom Vital Center thirty years earlier.[59]

Just a few years before, it had been possible for Brazil's nationalist left and its incense-scented right to deplore U.S. cultural influence together, as the two sides did in response to an unlikely bestseller published in 1957. A series of chapters stitched together into a full-fledged jeremiad, Pascoal Melantônio's *Geração "Coca-Cola"* was the work of a journalist, born to immigrant parents in the interior of São Paulo, who found that the cultural coordinates by which he mapped his life no longer met with the same esteem. Seeking an explanation, Melantônio found it in Americanization, which set in after 1918 and became especially harmful through its influence on youth, the Coca-Cola generation of his title. After World War I, "French influence disappeared completely and the Latin world ceased to exist for us. And in the year of grace 1957, what is it that we see? Simply this?—the people least disposed to become Americanized, became completely Americanized." At the time of Melantônio's writing, this Americanization was epitomized by adoption of the products and practices of U.S. commercial civilization: Melantônio's peers smoking U.S.-brand cigarettes, young women wearing "Yankee"-brand perfume; young men chewing Chiclets, following the latest Hollywood films, dancing to rock and roll, and wearing "extravagantly sporty clothes"; card-playing, Cadillac cars, contraband television sets, and blue jeans; comic books, *Seleções de Reader's Digest*, and "'big' . . . American novels." As "big" suggests, it transcended material culture, profoundly affecting language: "It is 'big' this way, it is 'big' that way. It is 'hello boy' here and 'hello boy' there. 'Okay' is a word that one hears at every instant."[60]

Melantônio's pamphlet-sized volume was a sensation, discussed by broadcasters and in São Paulo's most important newspapers, its initial run vanishing from bookstores. On the left, Fernando Góes welcomed Melantônio's "indignation with a series of transformations that we are witnessing," not least of which was "Yankee manners undermining our traditions." On the right, *Geração "Coca-Cola"* was welcomed as warmly in the *Correio Paulistano*, at that point tied ideologically and financially to São Paulo's archdiocese. It was still being discussed in the São Paulo press in 1958, by which time Rio's Tenentes do Diabo club had adopted the theme in its Carnaval procession for that year.[61]

This success owed much to the book's timing, *Geração "Coca-Cola"* reaching bookstores as a moral panic was gripping the newspaper-reading classes of the southeast, its title instantly synonymous with the words "Juventude Transviada," signifying errant youth (and the Brazilian theatrical-release title of *Rebel Without a Cause*). As Melantônio put it, "Deviant youth is headed to complete dissolution and ruin," and was a danger to others. This panic—in which Brazilian authorities, from parents to police chiefs, partook of broader transatlantic and inter-American anxieties regarding youth culture—increased in intensity in mid-1958 with the much-publicized death of a young woman who either threw herself or was thrown from the roof of a Copacabana apartment building after being set upon by two or more young men, described in the press as "part of the notorious deviant youth of Copacabana, that dances 'rock and roll,' wears bright-red shirts, chews gum, and wears 'blue-jeans.'" This gruesome story became grist for thousands of column inches in newspapers and magazines, as well as for new editions of *Geração "Coca-Cola,"* the second edition following the first very closely, the third making plain Melantônio's shift from a centrist, culturally conservative position to one on the left, clear in small editorial changes and the inclusion of long excerpts from a more recent denunciation of U.S. influence in Brazil, Cláudio de Araújo Lima's *Imperialismo e angústia*; throughout the book's publishing history, Melantônio and his admirers remained oblivious to the irony that *Geração "Coca-Cola"* was itself part of a cultural moment in which both the objects of anxiety (rock and roll, blue jeans) and the expressions of anxiety (panicked references to "deviant youth" and the idea of juvenile delinquency) were imported from abroad on their way to being appropriated for local consumption.[62]

Imperialismo e angústia was the era's most sustained discussion of Americanization and consumption. At once cultural commentary and psychosocial analysis of the Carioca middle class by a nationalist writer and psychiatrist, the book aimed to analyze the effects of U.S. influence over the previous thirty years. In a new era of imperialism, Lima believed, "the essential note of its activity was not that of the simple exportation of material, concrete, objective merchandise, like that of England at the height of the Victorian era." Rather, U.S. influence insinuated itself through "a new kind of merchandise: abstract, invisible, subjective merchandise, in forms until then unknown to history." This merchandise came in three varieties: new ways of life, including apartment living, different dietary habits, factory-made clothing, and such comforts of "the American way of life" as the motorized, rationalized kitchen; a new philosophy of life in which "to buy" was the most important aspect of existence, even at the cost of inflation; and a prefabricated ideology based on "the idea of individual freedom—raised to the extreme category of an inalienable myth." Where it all led was psychological anguish and the compulsive resort to dangerous escapism on the part of the urban middle class. Where it all began was Madison Avenue and Hollywood.[63]

In Lima's schema, commercial advertising was one part of a larger propagandistic effort. Indeed, because the Portuguese word "propaganda" can refer to official publicity or commercial advertising, it is not always clear to which he was referring, and in any case the distinction was moot as far as he was concerned. Other Brazilian intellectuals of the postwar era, however, zeroed in on commercial advertising as a contemporary scourge, apart from larger discussions of Americanization or massification. Writing in 1957, Gustavo Corção confessed his discomfort with modern advertising techniques and the profession's prestige: "But the advertisement, the announcement, the information is one thing, and the subliminal inculcation of the brand, of the magical value of a name, which constitutes a low blow, is another, completely different thing. And something even more aberrant is the valorization of those processes that have established a new kind of aristocracy." Corção soon came to his senses, serving as a guest of honor at Brazil's Second National Retail Commerce Convention, where he spoke from the same stage as McCann's Emil Farhat, lauding "the activities of distribution, advertising, communication, etc.," in a widely reprinted address.[64]

Writers on the left kept up their criticism: "An advertising firm constitutes an activity without the slightest benefit to the national economy, which gains only the sparse yield of taxes," charged *Anhembi*. "It is a mode of brokering, an economic activity that is, so to say, parasitic, that lives from commissions." Worse yet: "the greatest advertising budgets that exist in Brazil originate with the large American companies, which set aside enormous funds every year that they frequently use, less with the advertisement and advertising as an aim, than with the objective of buying newspapers, journalists, and even simple 'hacks.'"[65]

The month before *Anhembi* printed this defense of national journalism against North American advertising, it published an analysis of the *crediário*. While *Anhembi* recognized that inflationary conditions stimulated use of consumer credit, it condemned installment buying. On the one hand, argued *Anhembi*, the *crediário* encouraged families to live beyond their means, and the background investigations carried out by credit bureaus violated the sanctity of the home; on the other, the *crediário*'s costs were passed on to consumers, while firms received excess profits. The journal was not alone in criticizing the *crediário*, the progressive Catholic sociologist José Arthur Rios, among others, condemning it for contributing to inflation.[66]

Along the way, the manufacture of desire for new experiences and superfluous goods was held to have corroded Brazilian society. As the son and namesake of Antônio Carlos Pacheco e Silva described it: "Today's society is ever more immersed in the insatiable pursuit of material pleasures, yearnings strongly stimulated by the unchecked advertising that creates false needs, eagerly seeking to sell." Here, again, anxieties over consumption fed off international exchange, in this case "the works of the North American writer Vance Packard," author of the pop-sociology bibles *The Hidden Persuaders*, *The Status Seekers*, and *The Waste Makers*. "The lust for profit," Pacheco e Silva Filho argued, "has led to a veritable 'anything goes' in the advertising field. . . . Man is continually hammered away at, with repetitive slogans that seek to enslave him." Inspired by the Frankfurt School, he concluded that the ways of being in the world thereby produced were not just a dead end; they were deadening "to the extent that in human life concrete symbols of spurious material values come to predominate. To consume has become essentially the satisfaction of artificially stimulated fantasies, fantasies alien to the real, deeper state of being."[67]

Between 1955 and 1964, the Higher Institute of Brazilian Studies (ISEB) was a forum for discussion of many of the consumption-related issues raised by Pacheco e Silva and the North Atlantic authors who inspired him, including the waste, misplaced priorities, and obstacles to national progress and personal fulfilment represented by the acquisition—if not outright manufacture—of new needs. Founded in Rio as a branch of the Ministry of Education and Culture, ISEB was a center for research, teaching, and publication on development in its broadest sense, from economics to identity, sociology to philosophy. Initially conceived as a broad church (ISEB's advisory board, which never met, was a who's who of the Brazilian intelligentsia, left, right, and center), it became a focal point for the formulation and diffusion of left-nationalist doctrine. Accompanying this shift was growing hostility to foreign investment and increasing identification with the Communist Party, either of which would have been enough to seal its fate in the 1964 coup, during which its headquarters was sacked, never to reopen. As of its founding, however, those changes and the splits, purges, and autos-da-fe they entailed lay in the future. Contributors to ISEB's first major publication dealt with consumption primarily as an economic problem. In its introduction, for example, the sociologist Alberto Guerreiro Ramos described Brazil's characteristic "heteronomy" as reflected in consumption patterns adversely affecting its ability to import vital goods: "In the economic field, the waste of our resources that the existence of certain imported habits of consumption represent is significant. A considerable portion of our foreign exchange is spent on the importation of superfluous or sumptuary goods due to the heteronomy of the habits and taste of the Brazilian population." His colleague Ewaldo Corrêa Lima provided a more matter-of-fact brief, referring to the work of the UN Economic Commission on Latin America (ECLA) and noting that in Brazil, as in other "less developed" countries, "new forms of consumption expand with much greater speed than forms of production and thus there emerge social and economic tensions." Roberto Campos, not yet the neoliberal he would become, made the same point, though he cited Rostow rather than ECLA, adding the piquant whiff of cultural racism in his assertion that "the Mediterranean races in general seem to have a hedonistic vice that we did not escape," leading to high consumption relative to savings.[68]

Over the following years, it was the center's executive director, Roland Corbisier, who devoted the greatest attention to consumption as a cultural problem. As a young man, a dozen years before ISEB's founding, Corbisier had pondered his own existential anguish amid the material advance represented by industrializing São Paulo:

> With what right do we proclaim our dissatisfaction, if we are carried along by the great wave of "progress," if we find ourselves surrounded by all the conquests of technology, at the apogee of industrial civilization? Why do we insist upon calling attention to man and to human things, if we have the radio within reach, the airplane rumbling through the sky, the telephone screaming on the wall, the daily cinema, the luminescent advertising signs and the adding machine? . . . Why this tedium, this poor humor, this constant irritation, this destructive fury, if the immigrants are enriching themselves, the streets becoming broader, the buildings popping up and spreading like mushrooms, the confectionary shops filled with people, the Jews buying used clothes, the streetcars full of people, Brazil playing association football and helping the democracies in the struggle for the freedom of humankind?[69]

Corbisier's ISEB lectures suggest that the underdevelopment and inauthenticity inherent in "colonial" status had underlain that angst. Consumption—

material and cultural—was integral to colonialism, as Brazil exported primary goods while importing manufactured products: "To import a finished product is to import the way of being, the form, that incarnates and reflects the worldview of those who produced it. When we import, for example, the Cadillac, Chiclets, Coca-Cola, and cinema, we not only import objects or merchandise, but also an entire complex of behaviors and values that are implicated in these products."[70]

While Corbisier and ISEB were chiefly concerned with the cultural meanings and economic implications of changes in consumption, intellectuals to their right and left addressed the issue of how such changes were effected, making for one of the period's oddest intellectual pairings. This pairing arose in mid-1957, across two meetings of the National Confederation of Commerce's Technical Council, in which the indefatigable Gustavo Corção and Caio Prado Júnior, Brazil's premiere Communist historian, were probably shocked to find themselves in agreement. In these two meetings of the decoratively intellectual advisory board, the ideological opposites addressed the topic of advertising, Corção in contesting another counselor's idea of "the pedagogic mission that falls to elites," Prado amid a presentation on foreign investment.

For Corção, the idea of a "pedagogic mission" was noxious, inasmuch as he failed to distinguish a Brazilian elite that was up to the task and that such pedagogy summoned up the specter of hypnotism or, worse yet, of advertising. "Advertising is the process that a series of industrial and commercial organizations use these days to force upon us that which we do not need," he declared, adding that "modern advertising's technique of promoting . . . is one of modern society's great poisons." Prado, contesting Brazilian officialdom's openness to foreign capital, made much of what was not yet universally termed the "marketing" side of foreign direct investment: "There's the creation of a fictitious need, which compels us to make payments abroad. The Country's economy suffers the effects of a psychological deformation caused by the modern systems of advertising and product distribution." By that point, Prado had already woven considerations regarding Brazilian consumers into a longer series of economic arguments: "In the modern economy, the influence of the producer over the market is considerable. We know that the middle-class individual feels the influence of advertising—part of this manipulation of the making of the market—[and] is very important. Beyond this, these enterprises installed here [in Brazil] can much better engage in organization, in distribution, in sales, ultimately, of the commercial side of their business." Thus the Catholic rightist and the Communist shared a perspective in which advertising and allied sales techniques were seen as foisting unnecessary wants on hapless consumers, something occurring to "us"

(Corção) and the "middle class" (Prado) at a moment in which the culture of Brazilian consumer capitalism was a flicker of what it would become, parallels that resulted in part from what the two ideologues were reading or reading about (North Atlantic denunciations of massification) and then re-reading back onto Brazil.[71]

In terms of effects, it could be argued that critics as opposite as Corção and Prado, through their very critiques, partook in the cultural work of making *consumidor* ("consumer")—as opposed to older formulations like *freguês* ("customer")—a meaningful category of analysis. In this context, Corção's definition of advertising ("the process that a series of industrial and commercial organizations use these days to force upon us that which we do not need") bears comparison with a description made by Rodolfo Lima Martensen: "To sell, the advertising man seeks to place the likely buyer in a dilemma: 'he buys the advertised product or he will be in one way or another dissatisfied.'" So too does Prado's identification of middle-classness with susceptibility to consumerist appeals with an early IBOPE report, itself an advertisement for the market-research firm's services: "We call the attention of our clients for the levels attributed to the middle class. It is the one that consumes the most, that experiments the most, the most demanding one and the one with the greatest imagination. It is the one that most allows itself to be seduced by advertising."[72] In each pair of statements may be found parallel assumptions, voiced in diametrically different tones. For Corção and Martensen, modern advertising involved the inculcation of fictitious needs, a process that raised Corção's cultural-declensionist ire while leading Martensen to exalt the profession. For Prado and IBOPE, the middle class was particularly susceptible to advertising and thus the consuming class par excellence, to be regretted by the Communist historian and celebrated by the market-research firm. In both sets of pairs, but especially the latter, there is the emergence of the "consumer" and especially of the middle-class consumer as significant category and potential social subject. ISEB's emphasis on consumption may have further contributed to the making of consumer as a meaningful category, as the diagnoses of Araújo Lima and the Pacheco e Silvas undoubtedly did. Indeed, one reason the new professionals did not protest more often or with greater vehemence against accusations that they were manufacturing wants may have been the credence such criticism lent their claims of actually making the country's market and, indeed, creating its consumers, as the market-researcher Alfredo Carmo acknowledged.[73]

In 1964, the creation of consumers was celebrated by Rio's governor, Carlos Lacerda, weeks after his followers sacked ISEB's offices and classrooms. Anathema to the Brazilian left, Lacerda's celebration of working-class consumerism undermining revolutionary prospects found strange filmic succor in the documentary *Viramundo*, produced with the assistance of three young social scientists from the University of São Paulo. While the documentary's primary subject was the situation of rural migrants to industrializing São Paulo, it also, at least in part—here, perhaps, the influence of the junior professors was decisive—attempted to explain the political defeat of 1964 through the "false consciousness" of workers. This deficiency, the film would have one believe, stemmed from supposedly pre-political rural values, reinforced in the big city by charity, by the anesthetics of Catholicism, Afro-Brazilian spiritism and evangelical Protestantism, and by the individualistic push and pull of getting ahead and getting and spending, the last of which was captured in the testimony of an exceptionally fortunate migrant who worked his way up to a supervisory position in industry and comfortable domesticity: "I chose to build a good house facing the street in which to live. And in my house, I have a television, I have a refrigerator, and I have three children that I adore. But I like São Paulo a lot, this people I adore very much, a people that looks ahead, that helps those in need. I do not consider myself a Northerner but rather a Paulista and it is here that I intend to die." In identifying with his new home, the migrant was also identifying with what he believed were the values of its people, "who work ten, twelve, fifteen hours a day to have their houses nicely tidied . . . to go out with the wife and children on Sundays . . . to enjoy that which one calls life here. That is what is worthwhile."[74]

Creative Portraits

The denunciation of consumerism presented in *Viramundo* was not the last of its kind. Nor did denunciations of Americanization, denationalization, and massification, or of the specific scourges of advertising and installment buying, cease to issue from intellectuals. Far from it. But beginning in the late 1960s they were joined by portrayals of Brazil's culture of consumer capitalism and place in a planet-spanning consumer society that issued from creative artists. In fiction, there was Ignácio de Loyola Brandão's *Bebel que a cidade comeu* (1968), which provided the template for the feature film *Bebel, garota propaganda*, directed by Maurice Capovilla and released the same year as the book, six years before Capovilla would produce *Revolução do Consumo* to promote Shopping Center Ibirapuera. In the plastic arts, the work of Wanda Pimentel began to attract favorable attention at around the same time, while Carlos Drummond de Andrade engaged the new culture in a collection of poems published in 1973.

Loyola Brandão's *Bebel* purports to be the story of a beautiful daughter of brutish Spanish immigrants who becomes a professional model and a fixture on São Paulo's commercial television.[75] By the novel's narrative present

(1966), Maria Isabel ("Bebel" is her nickname) is past her prime, in a cycle of drink, pills, and promiscuity (mostly heterosexual, but including one lesbian relationship), literally and figuratively consumed—"eaten up" by the city and its culture industry, as indicated in the subtitle, in which "eaten up" would also slangily indicate sexual possession (that is, to be "eaten" would be to be "screwed"). Flashbacks to happier times show Bebel exulting in her public presence, on billboards from São Paulo to Rio's iconic granite mountainsides—counting 322 of them along the highway connecting the two cities—and on a television show meant to be recognized as *Noite de Gala*. As Bebel's portrayal as happy accomplice in her own commercialization suggests, the reader is not meant to see her as an innocent victim or to sympathize with her, a point driven home by her provoking a girlfriend's suicide. Instead of emerging as a morally complex character, Bebel is half child, half cipher, the improbable flatness of her character contrasting with the book's marginally more developed male characters: Bernardo, Marcelo, and Renato, rivals, casual but not close friends, and Bebel's sometime lovers.

Of the three, Bernardo is the one most closely drawn from the author's experience. At the novel's publication, Loyola Brandão had lived in São Paulo for over a decade, having left his native Araraquara at age twenty-one to seek his fortune, becoming a reporter for the local edition of *Ultima Hora*. Bernardo, like his creator, is from the provincial interior, an aspiring author scraping by in journalism. *Ultima Hora* is not named, but readers are meant to recognize it when Marcelo—in some ways Bernardo's double, also from the interior but uncompromisingly reckless in his political commitment—refers to the newspaper for which Bernardo writes as "half left, half whore." Among the settings meant to signal São Paulo's modern atmosphere is Rua Augusta, by then an established trope in Brazilian fiction: "Shopwindows explode in light with dresses, sweaters, stockings, cloths, jewelry, records, books, perfumes, furs. Imported, hand-made, mass-produced. Insignificant electric signs, the dimmer and more discrete the more elegant and expensive the *boutique*."[76] Typical of São Paulo, Rua Augusta also provides an opportunity to highlight the world of goods, of getting and spending, to which Bernardo returns later in the novel, telling Bebel:

I want money. You know what for? The longing I have for money is to buy love. Because it is through buying that one gets it. If I have money, I have a house, clothes, a car, and food. And security. Isn't that what women want? Security and a stand-up guy, who doesn't do anything crazy and buys them everything they want. It used to be I didn't want any of that. I thought that liking the woman was enough, the rest we would go about building with ease or difficulty. Both. Understand? Both together. But it never was like that. I was behind the times. A romantic. A romantic fool. We live our entire lives within the most formidable lie and it's no longer possible to flee from it.[77]

This want drives Bernardo to apply for a job at the advertising agency that employs his friend Armando, who started out in journalism with him and is now mulling over competing offers from leading agencies. The office where Bernardo visits Armando is a clean, well-lighted contrast with the squalid newsroom where he works. When Armando tells Bernardo he was rejected because he failed the psychotechnical exam, Bernardo protests ("But it's nonsense"), and Armando agrees: "I know. But this is an advertising Agency. The owners are Americans. And you know Americans believe in statistics, psychotecnics and other slobber." Still standing in Armando's office, Bernardo flashes back to their time together as journalistic tyros and then to Armando's leaving the field: "He went to an advertising agency. He said he was freeing himself from the newspaper, but he never freed himself from the greater feeling." It was the feeling of selling out: "I run into him. And each time we regard one another. Me: six years at the same newspaper, no longer a reporter, nor a columnist, but the managing editor. Just rotting away, knowing this and not reacting. There's one excuse: only my book matters, nothing else." That old dream, however, no longer offered the same consolation, and so Bernardo concludes, "I'm a streetwalking whore. Armando is a high-end call girl."[78]

Bebel may have been the first Brazilian novel launched simultaneously with a movie adaptation, albeit under a slightly different title, *Bebel, garota propaganda*. The change in title was no doubt done to preempt censorship and public outcry ("comeu" probably would have been rejected by censors and, in any case, would have been too much for movie posters), but it also suited the screenplay. The business of consumer capitalism figures more prominently in the film, which opens with a Max Factor advertisement. Its early scenes also include a photo shoot and a client meeting with the North American president of the company that manufactures "Love"-brand bath soap. After a cut to Bebel and the agency's creative head, Marcos, strolling through Shopping Center Iguatemi or a very well-lit *galeria*, he takes her back to his apartment, to rehearse the jingle "Love, Love, Love," among other things. The viewer then sees the shoot for a "Love" commercial and the billboard for the same campaign, each featuring Bebel.[79]

In parting the curtain on the worlds of advertising and television production, the movie version of *Bebel* took advantage of inherent qualities of the medium, as it did with stunning black-and-white shots of São Paulo in all its angular, imposing modernity and jarringly stark inequalities. To deal with the form's disadvantages relative to prose (the difficulty of re-creating first-person interior monologues and flashbacks, for example), the movie version availed itself of the conceit of a film within the film, a documentary about Bebel, which introduces a crew that interviews the principal characters.

The characters and their trajectories are also different. Most notably, Bernardo is a clownish figure in the movie, and his character's anguishing over goods and money, being and believing, buying in and selling out, are not reproduced filmically. Instead, Bernardo's sole intervention along these lines—a surprisingly direct criticism of the values the country's military rulers supposedly held most sacred—comes as Renato drives him through São Paulo in a stolen new-model convertible, the magic of its automatic roof prompting the cry "Long live Western, Christian . . . and decadent civilization!" The processes derided by Bernardo in the book are identified on film by Marcelo as "massification," which he sees as worthy of a herd of sheep ("uma carneirada").

In *Bebel* as film and fiction, modern life is devoid of anything to believe in or commit to in any meaningful, impactful manner. There is no going back, neither to the provincial interior of Bernardo's childhood, nor to the tenement of Bebel's. That the ostensible protagonist of novel and film is ultimately an object invites further reflection about the very possibility of conscious, deliberate human agency, but it also undoubtedly resulted from the male novelist's and director's inability to write and direct a credible female character. In the end, novel and film alike commodify Bebel for their own purposes in ways lost to their creators, a strange irony in works intended, at least in part, as critiques of consumerism and the commodification at work in and around the culture industry.

In this context, if the plastic artist Wanda Pimentel did not exist, one would have to invent her. Born into Rio's middle class in 1943, Pimentel began painting in her early twenties, and in doing so took what she saw as the most salient features of her milieu as her subject: "As a person, I have always lived within a society based on the compulsive act of consuming, therefore my subject was always what touches me directly, progress affecting mankind." It was a matter of class ("I'm from the middle class, which, as everyone knows, lives amid automatization and routine, surrounded by objects of comfort that place it at a distance from real life") and of gender ("as an artist and woman I also feel the influence of the consumer society"). Pimentel's early paintings, and especially those produced in the middle years of her series "Envolvimento" (1965–1975), are impossibly smooth and very bright, the coloring, she later said, "related to criticism of consumption." They typically take goods as their principal subject matter (an array of women's dress shoes, an automobile dashboard, an ironing board with rows of hanging feminine clothing), portrayed in sharp, flat geometric lines, offset by a glimpse in pale silhouette of some piece of the female form—toes, feet, or legs, which she modeled herself—the importance and personality of the inanimate objects outmatching the slight human presence. Humanity has thus been overwhelmed by goods, and individual women reduced still more. For the former, as Pimentel told an interviewer in 1970, "no culture can resist the instruments of mass communication. . . . Actively or passively, in this alienating whirlwind, all of us lose the chance to be." As for the latter: "The woman, above all, occupies a very prominent place in the consumer society, because she is used as an instrument and remains at the margin of a freedom she thinks she possesses." In subject matter and composition, comparisons have been made to Pop, as well as to Brazil's "Nova Figuração" movement, but Pimentel's contributions were sufficiently original to win several prizes. Their timeliness no doubt helped. As Fernando Cocchiarale wrote of "Envolvimento": "It discusses not only the relationship between the consumer society, then coming into being in the country, and the feminine condition, it also already detects the crisis of the subject, one of the contemporary world's central questions." Between criticism of the culture of Brazilian consumer capitalism and the broaching of the crisis of modern subjecthood, and in parallel with its treatment of the condition of women, Pimentel's work also subtly skewered the regime and its ideologues. How else to interpret her framing of Brasil Grande's characteristic products: the identification of alienation with the automobile, tedium with the television set?[80]

Pimentel, by her own admission, was born into Brazil's culture of consumer capitalism. The greatest poet to take it as his subject was not. Carlos Drummond de Andrade was born in 1902 in Minas Gerais, where he made a name for himself as one of Brazil's great modernist poets and where he lived until the mid-1930s, when he moved to Rio. In Rio, he became nearly as beloved for his slice-of-life newspaper stories (*crônicas*) as for his poetry, in which he showed a remarkable capacity for adaptation and growth, learning, for example, from the country's Concretist movement while continuing to show the fine ear for Brazilian Portuguese that was his hallmark. Perhaps due to his work as a *cronista*, perhaps even more so due to the deep humanism that animated nearly all his writing, he continued to show a vivid interest in novelties, good and bad, that were remaking the lives of those around him, at an age at which many men withdraw, retreating from present into past. The poems that open *As impurezas do branco* reflect this interest and his humanism as they alternate between irony and anguish, while borrowing—at least arguably—from the Tropicalist counterculture of the 1960s that represented itself as a revivication of the modernist movement in which he first achieved prominence. In the first, "Ao Deus Kom Unik Assão" (To the God Qom Uniq

Aishan), Drummond alluded to the culture of consumption ("And it consumes itself in consumption") on his way to a sendup of McLuhanism and the cult of communication more generally: "O meio é a mensagem / O meio é a massagem / O meio é a mixagem / O meio é a micagem" (The medium is the message / The medium is the massage / The medium is the mixing / The medium is the monkeying). In the second, "Diamundo: 24 h de informação na vida do jornaledor" (Dayworld: 24 hrs. of information in the life of the newspapereader), Drummond provided a disorienting pastiche of headlines, news items, and advertisements, in which weather data and air-pollution indices abut economic reporting and movie listings. Such juxtapositions make the accomplishments of the miracle scan as no less fatuous than the promises of real-estate agents, used-car salesmen, and astrologers, while factoids on childhood malnutrition, the death by drowning of holiday beachgoers, and the existence of slave labor in the interior are presented in the same clipped couplets and irregular stanzas as religious announcements, headlines on the oil crisis, and excerpts from the classifieds: "Precisa-se com urgência / homens de venda / homens de venda / homens de venda / homens de venda / homens de venda" (Urgently needed / salesmen / salesmen / salesmen / salesmen / salesmen).[81]

Counterpoints to this disconcerting conjugation of wordplay and ironic jokes with tragedies universal and particular appear later in the volume, in the short masterpieces "A palavra Minas," which returns to Drummond's native ground, and, on the facing page, "Fim de feira":

> No hipersupermercado aberto de detritos,
> ao barulhar de caixotes em pressa de suor
> mulheres magras e crianças rápidas
> catam a maior laranja podre, a mais bela
> batata refugada, juntam no passeio
> seu estoque de riquezas, entre risos e gritos.[82]

In these six lines, inequity is summoned from the first by reference to modern food shopping, the hyper- and supermarkets known to his readers bearing little resemblance to the improvised hypersupermarket for the indigent provided by the debris from an open-air market closing down for the day. Drummond's poor are scrawny but not unsmiling, hungry but not inhuman, neither brutalized nor beaten by adversity unimaginable to nearly anyone in his audience. It is not a cheap populism—indeed, it recalls José Honório Rodrigues's cultivated belief in the decency of the great mass of the Brazilian people as opposed to their leaders—but the apparent counterpoint to Drummond's "thin women and quick children" in *As impurezas do branco* would be the bizarre world of "Ao Deus Kom Unik Assão" and "Diamundo," inhabited by the poet and his audience, for whom the open-air market was meant.

Staging Consumerism

More than poetry or fiction, more than film or painting, theater lent itself to portrayal of Brazilian consumerism, a critic noting sardonically in 1970, "If it were up to the criticisms that the theater has untiringly aimed at it, the consumer society would be dead and buried already." The number of theatrical works dealing with the subject only increased thereafter. Within this larger body of work, three very successful plays stand out—indeed, they may be seen as a trilogy of sorts—the first two by Oduvaldo Vianna Filho, *Corpo a corpo* (first performed in 1970) and *Allegro desbum* (1973), the third Consuelo de Castro's *Caminho de volta* (1974). What stands out about these plays, beyond their success and thematic unity, is that their creators were writing from within as well as without the culture upon which their work turns. Oduvaldo Vianna Filho, son and namesake of the playwright who introduced the radionovela to São Paulo, had written for television for years, intermittently in the early 1960s, regularly for TV-Tupi beginning in 1968, and under contract to Globo from 1971. He was also, like his parents, a loyal member of the Moscow-aligned Communist Party. Consuelo de Castro had spent a few years in the party while pursuing a degree in social sciences at the University of São Paulo, where she was active in the student movement; with heightened repression in 1969, she moved to Rio and worked in advertising for a few years before returning to São Paulo and a job at the company that published *Time*-like *Veja* magazine.[83]

Vianna Filho's *Corpo a corpo*, its title suggesting hand-to-hand combat between well-matched antagonists, is a monologue, leavened by offstage voices, telephone calls, and other artifices. It takes place overnight in the Copacabana apartment of Luiz Toledo Vivacqua, a successful advertising executive. Born in Sergipe, Vivacqua left his home and family to make a life in Brazil's southeastern land of opportunity, earning a degree in sociology and producing television commercials while dreaming of making movies. The prompt for Vivacqua's long night, and the drug- and drink-fueled duel with himself that lasts the entirety of it, is learning that a close coworker, a model professional, is being fired for having criticized the volume of foreign advertising that their firm churns out. This situation forces Vivacqua to ask if he has the integrity to stand by his friend and quit in solidarity or remain at the agency and continue the uninspiring work that provides a comfortable life. This quandary opens the door to further questioning: of his loveless engagement to a woman to whom he is routinely unfaithful but whose hand holds the promise of social ascent; of his abandonment of his family and especially of his mother, alone, impoverished, and infirm in Sergipe; of his career, fostering unrealizable desires on behalf of unscrupulous bosses.

"What advertising, for the love of God!" he exclaims early in the play. "Advertising for people to be what they can't be?" While there are gestures at opposite resolution of these conflicts—in Vivacqua breaking up with his fiancée, telling off his supervisor, and reserving a plane ticket to Sergipe that will leave the next day—in the morning, after receiving word from the agency head that he is to fly to the United States and liaison with an agency there, he cancels his flight to Sergipe, calls his supervisor to make travel arrangements, and reconciles with his fiancée, whom he needs to help him pick out clothing for the trip. Though the play is plotted as tragedy—Vivacqua suffers doing what he must do—the monologue is darkly comic at points, as when the well-paid advertising executive refers to his means apart from his salary: "I have credit at A Exposição."[84]

Vianna Filho's *Allegro desbum* had the subtitle *se Martins Penna fosse vivo*—if Martins Pena were still alive—a reference to a nineteenth-century playwright celebrated for his humorous sketches of everyday life. As the subtitle suggests, *Allegro desbum* was written as an easy, slice-of-life comedy. Its protagonist—"Buja," short for the surname Azambuja—is in some ways Vivacqua's double, a successful advertising man who leaves a job making twenty thousand cruzeiros a month to drop out and be true to himself in a lower-middle-class apartment building, where he falls for Teresa, a young woman groomed by her domineering mother to marry a man making twenty thousand cruzeiros a month. As the mother remarks of her efforts: "We hustle and bustle, we save money, we buy exclusive designer clothes, shoes, but the marriage isn't happening, it seems like it's going to happen. . . . The guys come by, talk, smile, flowers, but what they want in the end is just to screw and nothing else." In addition to his halfhearted pursuit of Teresa, Buja spends his days hanging out with representatives of two countercultures (*desbum* would echo the Brazilianism *desbunde*, or "dropping out" of the 1970s), a hippie young woman and a homosexual man who manufactures dental prosthetics (thus called "Protético"). Buja's dropping out, however, proves purposeless: if, as he claims in the first act, his leaving advertising was because he did not want to end up in a mental institution; the play ends with him hanging his buttocks out his apartment window raving at passersby. The arc of the storyline is thus opposite to *Corpo a corpo*'s, and the cheap humor of *Allegro desbum* likewise sets it apart from the monologue, but there are intertextual references that indicate the plays are meant to be considered together, apart from their protagonists' professions. The most important of these place Rio—Brazil's Marvelous City—squarely in "underdeveloped" Latin America. In *Corpo a corpo*, Vivacqua sends out a drunken call for conversation on amateur radio, eventually answered by a Bolivian retiree (who, like Vivacqua's mother, has been abandoned by his progeny);

in *Allegro desbum*, Protético must get his lover bailed out of a Bolivian jail. The poorest country in South America is thus placed parallel to—indeed, in dialogue with—the Brazil of the economic miracle and Brasil Grande boosterism inescapable outside the theaters where the plays were performed.[85]

Whereas *Corpo a corpo* and *Allegro desbum* were set in apartments of the upper-middle and lower-middle classes, respectively, the three acts of Consuelo de Castro's *Caminho de volta* are set in a workplace, the offices and studio of an agency called Gomes Publicidade, on the brink of ruin despite boom times. As the agency's owner, Dr. Gomes, announces:

> People keep on buying things. You go to the open-air market, it's full of women filling their bags with tomato extract, steel wool, coffee filters. You go to automobile dealerships, and there's always some son of a bitch burying himself in debt to the top of the last hair on his head, to buy at least a Volkswagen. And Volkswagen is [a client of the agency] Alcântara. You go to the boutiques, and the young ladies are buying bras, panties, dresses. Fuck, everyone buying everything. Things for basic necessities, secondary, tertiary, tenth-place needs. . . . Never has there been such a great fever to consume among this people as right now! . . . The purchasing power of the people keeps growing. The middle class is less and less middling. And the bourgeoisie never had it so good, so full of refinements and life's necessities. The country is undergoing an economic miracle. Do you understand? And why is it only me that gets nothing out of this miracle? Now then, the country is struck by a sudden miracle, everybody producing, everybody buying, the credit system inventing tricks that even the devil casts doubts on, and here's Gomes, at a total standstill, going bankrupt, like an idiot.[86]

In addition to Gomes, four characters take their turns on stage, each an employee. The agency contact, Nandinho, is an adherent of a neotraditional Catholic movement who breaks every scruple at work. The creative head, Nildo, is professionally and morally spent, barely holding on to his job despite years without producing any campaigns of worth, only managing to do so thanks to the cover provided by the work of the play's dual leads, Marisa and Cabecinha. Marisa is from working-class Penha, where her father worked until he was unable to work any longer, his vision wasted by conditions at the Tecelagem Progresso (the Progress Textile Works), while the family sacrificed to send her to secretarial school; at the time of the play's action, she is an aspiring copywriter and a student of communication at USP, though in one scene she drunkenly models fabrics from the factory that consumed her father's eyesight and life (*vista* and *vida*) and offstage she agrees to sleep with the factory-owner to keep him committed to the agency. All the while, Marisa dreams of a storybook wedding to Cabecinha, the agency's art director, once an architecture student, now a successful commercial artist who no longer paints outside of work, and who declares that he is "against the consumer society" while trapped in credit-card debt. Marisa's dream of being a bride out of the pages of *Claudia* magazine is not her only fancy, nor is Cabecinha the only one who is trapped—or condemned to repetition, as the play's title suggests. Moving out of her drab family home and into a modernly furnished apartment, Marisa feels free; in a Vivacqua-like drunken monologue she imagines liberating her mother from household drudgery: "We're going to buy Mobilínea-brand furniture. What do you think, mom? You won't have to ruin your hands there at the washtub. We're going to hire a super washerwoman and buy a Bendix washing machine. . . . You're going to be able to watch television all day long." Even Gomes is trapped, as Nildo indicates when the agency head tries to fire him: "Isn't it pretty that I depend on you and you too have an owner? I think the capitalist system is just as fair as it can be, just as fair. Only it brings progress. Only it brings cleanliness and organization! No one can accuse anyone." To entrapment and betrayal as recurring themes in onstage dialogue are added intimations of offstage events meant to impress the immorality of the agency milieu upon the audience: a model's abortion, Marisa's much-regretted participation in a drunken orgy, Gomes's bloodlustful protagonism in the butchering of a racehorse that came up lame. This milieu, in turn, is of a piece with Brazilian capitalism in the age of Brasil Grande—"At the pace of Brasil Grande!" Nildo exclaims at one point—and the economic miracle's chasing after goods, described by Gomes and present in Marisa's every aspiration.[87]

The three scripts were products of different circumstances and inspiration, their authors writing with differing objectives in mind. On separate occasions, Consuelo de Castro stated that *Caminho de volta* was a denunciation of the commodification of human beings in the advertising business and a sendup of the miracle. Indeed, decades later she claimed that the miracle, rather than advertising per se, was her starting point for writing the script over three afternoons borrowed from her employers at Abril. Vianna Filho's *Allegro desbum* was intended to revive traditions and techniques in Brazilian comic theater at a time in which the genre was in low critical esteem, while *Corpo a corpo* was conceived in part as his retort to a misdirected staging of another script.[88]

As the latter suggests, entire universes of creation encompass playwriting and the public staging of theatrical works, in which the weight of authorial intent may vary tremendously, through readings, rehearsals, and reviews. Writers, directors, set designers, reviewers, and audiences engage in that vast interim, and so it was with these three plays, in interims culminating in critical accolades and box-office success. On the one hand, the three plays can be seen as part of a transition in the history of the Brazilian stage, from the univocally contestatory theater of the 1960s—politically satisfying for theatergoers but unthreatening to the powers that were—to the lighter, multiform, less blatantly message-driven productions of the 1980s. On the other—despite differences of genre and divergent inspiration on the part of their authors—the three plays came to be the object of strikingly similar readings.

The critic Yan Michalski, one of very few people to have witnessed Oduvaldo Vianna Filho's private reading of *Corpo a corpo* at Rio's Museum of Modern Art in 1970, later recalled "the density of the monodrama, originally written, everything leads us to believe, with a view to a plainly realist staging." Fausto Fuser, who saw one of the last rehearsals for the play's first commercial performance, came away convinced that it was "one of the most serious works of the national theater that we know of," but more than that, "an inestimable gift . . . to a better understanding of the Brazilian man of our time and our reality." For Juca de Oliveira, who starred in that production, Vianna Filho had "performed a veritable psychological surgery on Vivacqua." "He reveals," Juca continued, "a man involved in concrete. . . . And the search for this truth, which all of us propose, is an exercise in courage. One cannot conjure away a thing, confronting reality with rigor." Antunes Filho, the play's first director, made similar arguments, declaring, "I await someone informing me of the existence, in Brazilian theater, of the construction of a richer and more lifelike character, more objectively profound in his contradictions than Vivacqua." According to Antunes, with *Corpo a corpo*, "Oduvaldo Vianna emerges with a new attitude in Brazilian theater: a statistically realist, scientifically analytical attitude." For the critic Sábato Magaldi, Vianna Filho—as against proponents of the aggressively confrontational antitheater in vogue in the late 1960s—"did not abandon reason and sees in it the only possible way out." The result was "a melancholy portrait of Brazilian reality."[89]

Similar tropes—imputing realism, seriousness, Brazilian-ness, and timeliness, while appealing to the once-radical idea of "Brazilian reality"—enveloped the performances of *Allegro desbum* and *Caminho de volta*, despite differences of genre and the passage of time. Vianna Filho himself raised the question of genre in an interview published in advance of *Allegro desbum*'s opening night: "What is important is that the author consider reality up-close in order to study it. We cannot disregard any instruments that allow us to penetrate this reality. While there are more vigorous forms, comedy has its place and a determined role to fulfill." That role—as Vianna Filho's interviewer saw it—included helping spectators "understand a little more of the era and the social reality in which they live." *Allegro desbum* was not, according to its author, fictional in a strict sense, for its characters were people he "saw, knew, observed"; he thus wrote about "a lived reality." According to *Diario de Noticias*'s house critic, the result was a success, "one of the funniest and most Brazilian comedies that we know of," that "revitalizes Brazilian dramaturgy, insisting that it turn to our problems, to our people." When Consuelo de Castro's *Caminho de volta* debuted, *O Estado de S. Paulo* reminded readers of the "realistic language" of her theater, while the *Folha de S. Paulo* reported, "The piece focuses on an economic problem strictly tied to the average Brazilian man, putting on stage characters that are frustrated and neurotic, but deeply human and true." The play was thus, in the words of Jefferson Del Rios, "coherent with the Brazilian present," not least for its "extremely sarcastic commentaries on Brazilian reality." For Luiz Izrael Febrot, who saw in *Caminho de volta* the renovation of Brazilian theater, the play was additional evidence of Consuelo de Castro's "concern with Brazilian reality and with mankind," as well as public interest in "the recreation of reality and the discussion of ideas." Sábato Magaldi described the play as presenting "our reality without allegory or symbolism," seemingly out of nowhere: "Suddenly *Caminho de volta* . . . brings Brazil onto the stage once more and it is almost strange to witness this new breath of life and authenticity." In São Paulo's *Ultima Hora*, Alberto Guzik commented, "The text is directly descended from the best lineage of the Brazilian theater, which in recent times dedicated itself to investigate and analyze our reality." *Allegro desbum*'s thirteen-month run in São Paulo in 1976–1977 prompted similar commentary. According to its director, José Renato, Vianna Filho's objectives in writing the play had including showing "some aspects of the Brazilian problematic," allowing Renato "to bring some aspects of Brazilian reality to the stage again." Critical response suggests that the attempt was welcome. "*Allegro desbum* demonstrates a secure clarity," wrote Magaldi, "an always precise reference to the larger framing of reality and a sharp critique of everyday standards." It was, in another critic's words, "an honest and sincere reflection on the hard reality of our lives."[90]

The impression of widely shared experience recurred across the three plays' trajectories, from Fuser's "our time and our reality" through Magaldi's "our reality without allegory or symbolism." Juca de Oliveira, the first actor to star in *Corpo a corpo*, identified himself, his offstage castmates, and their contemporaries with Vivacqua, "including what is worst about us." Maria Bonomi, the set designer who—inspired by supermarket design—decked out Vivacqua's apartment-stage in polyester and acetate, identified him with a larger public: "All of us, who are a public of South-American-already-informed-almost-cultured-clean-shaven-professionals-who had ideals in our university days, of how they took away our ideals, of how we are now, our conflicts within our inevitable everyday existence of proposing things to others that we ourselves don't believe in. . . . All of us surrounded by objects that are necessary but that one doesn't need, which in reality don't resolve our problems as Humans but on which we depend."[91]

In 1973, introducing the first run of *Allegro desbum*, the director José Renato referred to the "system's cannibalism that swallows many of us." For the critic Febrot, *Caminho de volta* was in at least one sense a "reflexive critical portrait of the world of advertising as a microcosm of our society." Gracindo Júnior, who played Vivacqua in the second production of *Corpo a corpo*, made a similar case in 1975 to the one spelled out by Maria Bonomi four years earlier, though his starting point was an unorthodox, if not entirely unique reading of Vianna Filho's body of work: "*Corpo a corpo* can be considered a synthesis of everything he did. Vivacqua is the central character, he appears in almost all of Vianna's pieces from 1960 to now. In his anxieties and searchings, he has much to do with Vianna and with me. We are of the same generation and I think that the problems that Vivacqua (Viva) confronts have a broader dimension, which go beyond the world in which he is situated. He experiences the problem of a human being of our generation, and I can say that Aderbal [Júnior (the director)] amplified Vivacqua the advertising man into Viva, a man who struggles with ethical problems and attempts to be an individual in spite of massification."[92]

In 1971, Yan Michalski—without identifying himself with his subject—had identified Vivacqua as an "authentic and expressive exemplar of the young almost-intellectual lost in the contradictions of his generation and social class." He did not specify which class, but he hardly needed to, for others were eager to do so. Antunes Filho, as director of the first production of *Corpo a corpo*, explained, "Vivacqua is a poor creature of the middle class, attacked from one side and the other." According to Antunes, the play's realism hinged on its analysis, "like an x-ray, of the present-day Brazilian man of the middle class." For Fernando Peixoto, who directed the first production of *Caminho de volta*, the play was "a contribution to an understanding of the complex Brazilian middle class of today." In an interview introducing *Allegro desbum* on the eve of its first performance, Vianna Filho called it a depiction of "the current struggle of the Brazilian middle class, with some sectors struggling to join the consumer society and others trying desperately to escape from it." Shortly before opening night of the first São Paulo production of *Allegro desbum*, in 1976, by which time Vianna Filho had succumbed to cancer, its director explained that it contained an analysis of the conflict between acquisitive middle-class values—"ever more present in national reality"—and individuals attempting to distance themselves from the world of getting and spending.[93]

All three plays and both playwrights thus found the middle class—the consuming class par excellence, according to earlier critics—as their subject. Indeed, the middle class was a major focus of Vianna Filho and Consuelo de Castro's oeuvres. The literary scholar Maria Silvia Betti, for one, identified the "middle-class vein" that included nearly all of Vianna Filho's theatrical and television writing between 1965–1966 and 1974 as the most characteristic phase of his career. Consuelo de Castro's early plays, including *Caminho de volta*, were described as "critically portraying the day to day of the middle class" and showing a "preoccupation with mankind and Brazilian reality." But as the latter suggests, there was much elision at work. In the alchemy that transformed middle-class people in São Paulo and Rio—drawn from firsthand experience—into "the Brazilian man," who was equivalent to "Brazilian reality," Carlos Drummond de Andrade's "thin women and quick children" and millions more Brazilians who lived like them vanished. Brazilian reality, and Brazil thereby, became middle class, and while the complexes and contradictions of that class were to be regretted—including its "underdevelopment," in the term favored by Vianna Filho—the resulting social portrait was symmetrical with the standardized market-research scheme of 1970 and the most fanciful of miracle-era claims. Five months before his death, Vianna Filho reconsidered, identifying "the isolation of the middle class from the people, the great popular masses," as part of a larger problem: "To reduce a society of more than one hundred million people to a market of twenty-five million people, a very sophisticated and elaborate, very rich, very intense cultural process is required, to maintain, to make people accept being part of a ghost country, of a nonexistent country, of a country without problems." Only cultural work could achieve this outcome—"the refining of the means of communication, of the means of advertising"—making society all the more brutish. Dying, perhaps past the point of consistency, Vianna Filho could only hope that his work through the same mass media could help make Brazilian society "sharper, more perceptive, more rigorous." Consuelo de Castro, younger and much less sympathetic to her middle-class characters, offered only a curse: "Whoever collaborates with consumption will end up, sooner or later (usually sooner), being consumed."[94]

Slouching toward Veblen

Theater critics may have endorsed Consuelo de Castro's malediction— *Caminho de volta* won her the prestigious Molière Prize—but audiences preferred the antiheroic laugh parade of *Allegro desbum*, which broke box-office records. Mostly upper-middle-class audiences howled along to portrayals of their world, in what Yan Michalsky called "anticonsumerist consumption."

They would continue to do so through the release of a fourth play, *Arte final*, which Michalsky saw as making a tetralogy of the Vianna Filho-Consuelo de Castro trilogy. Whether that unity was real or contrived, the authorship and reception of *Arte final* provides a glimpse behind the curtain at how the new professionals responded to themes raised in Vianna Filho and Consuelo de Castro's scripts, for the author of *Arte final* had been a true insider, including as a copywriter at the Alcântara Machado agency envied by *Caminho de volta*'s Gomes. For Carlos Queiroz Telles, the script—a depiction of the political and personal compromises of an advertising man named Daniel Lima—combined therapy and autobiography: "It was the exorcism I needed to settle accounts with my years in advertising. The main character was a young copywriter . . . nonsense, it was me." "I put myself entirely in it, body and soul," he declared on another occasion, "saying things openly, without the need for grand flights of analogy. And I think [that these included] much material objectively denouncing what advertising did during the period of the Brazilian economic miracle." Years later, Renato Castelo Branco would turn to the same play to explain his sense of frustration: "For some years, as an advertising copywriter, I felt like Carlos Queiroz Telles's Daniel . . . unable to conciliate the advertising professional and the intellectual, the professional man and the moral one."[95] As the comments of one of the most admired of Brazilian advertising executives suggest, the country's new professionals were aware of and attuned to critical portrayals of their work. Indeed, their own, often-mordant self-criticisms in some cases anticipated the censure of such semi-outsiders as Consuelo de Castro, Vianna Filho, and Ignácio de Loyola Brandão. In other cases, they reacted defensively to intellectual critiques from right, left, and center. At the same time, in their dual position as abettors of big business and men and women of letters, some developed their own critiques. A national or even nationalist position emerged relatively early among the new professionals, with greater force in Rio than in São Paulo, but present in both centers. From Rio and São Paulo, the new professionals came to voice aesthetic concerns regarding manifestations of the culture they had helped create, to which an unresolved ethical questioning was joined amid reflections upon the impact of their work.

In Orígenes Lessa's *O feijão e o sonho*, first published in 1938 and republished countless times since then, one finds a fictionalized portrayal of Lessa's road not taken. Written during three weeks of shirking at JWT, *O feijão e o sonho* centers on a fictional doppelganger to Lessa, who chooses literature for himself and poverty for his family over the pursuit of a career and the comforts it would bring (in the terms of the novel's title, he chose his dream over his family's daily bread, represented by the Luso-Brazilian staple of beans). Nicknamed Juca, the main character is not a hero in the conventional sense, for while his family and especially his wife suffer as a result of his choices, he is at once bohemian and strangely spendthrift, drawn to goods his family cannot afford, including a household clock that produces an uproar—even this most modest household appliance is beyond their means—before bringing on a rare moment of conjugal contentedness. Along the way, Juca experiences "the supreme shame of his life," when, in debt to the butcher, he has no choice but to write "some little verses of advertising for the shop," for which he receives two pounds of beef. In the 1930s, dependent upon a copywriter's salary for his own sustenance, Lessa masked his critique in fiction written in Portuguese, which his North American superiors could not read, even as he attempted to hide his day job from literary friends. Later in life, however, by which time U.S. executives were thin on the ground in Brazil, he told all who would listen that he was planning to write a memoir of advertising, to be titled *Não coma, não beba, não use* (Don't eat, don't drink, don't use).[96]

Fictionalized self-criticism likewise featured in the work of Emil Farhat and Ricardo Ramos. In Farhat's second novel, *Os homens sós*, the criticism was metaphorical, Rio's low-end red-light district figuring as an "immense illuminated advertising sign" and what was beginning to be called "sales promotion" depicted as a confidence scheme. Ramos, by contrast, recorded advertising executives' self-deprecation in realist, autobiographical fiction that owed much to his father's work. In *As fúrias invisíveis*, he portrays an office—recognizably JWT's—where a few advertising executives watch pornographic films in the projection room after hours, prompting one to remark, "In any case, watching dirty films is the most decent thing we do at the agency." Like Castelo Branco in his memoir—and Bernardo, in Loyola Brandão's *Bebel*—Ramos recorded the feeling of prostituting himself, a sympathetic first-person protagonist of one of his stories claiming to have coined the jocular self-description "publicituto" (advertising professional/prostitute) in the 1950s.[97]

On other occasions, members of the same cohort responded in defense of their profession. In 1936, when the nutritional scientist Josué de Castro declared, while extolling milk consumption, that "honest advertising is unnecessary: milk needs no advertising," Orígenes Lessa responded with an essay defending advertising as worthwhile in all contexts and for all products, from milk to coffee to cars. Two decades later, Lessa published another brief for the defense in *Propaganda*: "Without the development and use of advertising, in a widespread and secure manner, we would fall into a situation of national calamity. Commercial and industrial advertising in our regime is a condition of economic vitality. And believe it or not, were one of these saviors of the fatherland who periodically infest the chapters of our history to show up and, among his dictatorial caprices, in a moment of greater insanity, resolve to prohibit all advertising activity for a year, Brazil would close for lunch and wouldn't reopen, for lack of anything to eat for dinner." The following year, Edmur de Castro Cotti wrote a long article defending advertising—"an art and a technique"—against the imprecations of the Catholic reactionary Gustavo Corção, in which he employed hallowed arguments about distribution and service alongside the McCann slogan, "Truth Well Told." Faced with the left-nationalist polemic *Imperialismo e angústia*, Eliezer Burlá responded with a relentlessly negative review, faulting Lima's work for being impressionistic, unscientific, backward looking, and inattentive to detail. A few months later, Manoel de Vasconcellos used his editorship of *PN* to respond to overseas critiques, defending advertising against charges leveled by Vance Packard and John Kenneth Galbraith.[98]

Even as the new professionals eagerly kept up with North American developments—even social criticism—and took the United States as their model of modern, consumer-oriented civilization, many strained to assert difference as well, even in cultural work in which so much was owed to foreign standards. The apparent and actual contradictions of the two stances were never fully faced, but they could produce results as uncontrollable as anything envisioned by João Alfredo de Souza Ramos in 1937, when he lamented the mimicking of North American form in the absence of attention to the content of the apparent civilizational progress of the United States. The assertion of difference might be directed inward or outward, aimed at Brazilians seen as unduly imitative or North Americans who were obtuse and heavy handed. From the accusation of North American heavy-handedness to the assertion that the same foreigners were excessively powerful was a further step, taken by few. Those who did paid dearly.

Armando d'Almeida likely spoke for most of his cohort in 1941, in a radio broadcast from the United States in which he asserted: "What we need is to take advantage of the experience of the United States, an experience that is the most rich and powerful one in the world, to construct our own greatness. To utilize the magnificent lessons of its technique, not to copy servilely what is done here, but to apply North American teachings to our realities." For all his countrymen had to learn, d'Almeida continued, "not even for this would I esteem, if you will forgive me the facile expression, an Americanized Brazil. That doesn't interest us nor does it interest the North Americans. We want a Brazilian Brazil, cultivating the spirit and tradition of its own aesthetic and sentimental riches, acting and dreaming with its own way of being idealistic, safeguarding its dear and particular physiognomy."[99]

As Orígenes Lessa had written a few years earlier, "the two peoples are different, of diverse formation, of diverse tendencies. It is not a question of superiority or inferiority, but of difference. Whoever thinks that this or that is superior matters little. The Brazilian tends really to see himself as inferior. What is good comes from Hollywood and Detroit." It was thus a short step to colleagues and national-capital clients "taking advantage . . . of what worked in the land of Uncle Sam," without the necessary work of carefully sifting through the good and the bad. For Olympio Guilherme, writing in the 1950s, this was "the error of 'Americanism,'" that "our advertising," despite its progress, "still continues to be fettered docilely to the American 'standard.'" "Formidable! It even looks like an American advertisement!" was a complement that set Rodolfo Lima Martensen's teeth on edge, not so much for the monkey-see, monkey-do approach it implied, as for its accuracy: "Our advertising follows the American methods of publicizing things that when it approaches perfection it may be mistaken, in its style, with American advertising." As a character in one of Lessa's short stories of the 1950s laments, tying together a set piece that would have rung wearyingly true to the traditionalist Afonso Arinos de Melo Franco, "Today everything is an imitation in this land. We are losing our personality . . ."[100]

Lessa's short story was intended for an entirely Brazilian audience, but his earlier assertion of difference had been directed at an audience composed of Brazilians and North Americans, carefully so, given the thin skin typical of members of the latter tribe. Finessing a dustup stemming from a slight allegedly committed by a luncheon speaker—a North American professor, as it would happen, who had called for "de-yankeefying the advertisement in Brazil"—Lessa made the case that advertising work might be done by professionals of either nationality, provided that they were attuned to Brazilian specificities: "Advertising, to obtain the best results, in Brazil, should be done in Brazilian terms, for Brazilians. So long as this desideratum is met, it would be fine even if it were not done by Brazilians." Some among his colleagues and countrymen went further. José Alfredo de Souza Ramos reacted angrily to a newspaper story on the Grant agency that seemed to credit all his profession's progress to foreign specialists. At each U.S. subsidiary, Ramos noted, Brazilians "constitute the entirety of their auxiliaries, who have not been mere executants, but rather excellent collaborators, bringing with them to the firms that they belong to, intelligence and good sense, and, above all, knowledge of the environment, which constitutes the primordial factor for those who know advertising's problems." A year later, Ramos criticized North American companies, for the "psychological error" of staffing top posts in their subsidiaries with executives who spoke no Portuguese or, worse still, attempted to get along with pidgin Spanish acquired elsewhere on the continent.[101]

The latter was the very essence of the "colonial model" that prevailed at JWT until Robert Merrick made way for Renato Castelo Branco, and Ramos's bringing the problem to light was one part of a long campaign for professional standing and esteem, to say nothing of individual advancement. But other airings of national-professional grievances obeyed no such logic. Rather, they seem to have resulted in equal measure from abiding frustrations and sudden disappointments on the part of well-placed professionals. In 1951, for example, the IBOPE founder Auricélio Penteado admitted that he was increasingly less secure in his enthusiasm for things North American. Making an exception for Richard Penn—the Colgate-Palmolive executive who had brought the radionovela from Havana to Rio and "after six months understood Brazil better than us and learned to speak and write Portuguese better than many educated Brazilians"—Penteado placed most of the blame for his disillusionment on "'export quality' Americans, which is to say, those who agree to accept jobs 'South of Rio Grande,' in some 'banana country.'" Overpaid, obtuse, and possessing an imagined monopoly on useful knowledge, the "South American expert" was the subject of one of the many satirical pieces Penteado placed in the trade press. This one had serious aspects, for the frustration that inspired it was real, and was accompanied by the expectation of improvement: "Am I irritated as I say all this? No, sirs, only impatient as I see a good cause lost, through stupidity. Am I being xenophobic? Not that either, because I wish the best for these American nincompoops and I would like to see our two peoples treating each other with mutual respect." Given Brazil's importance, Penteado argued, "It now time for us to treat one another as equals. It is now time that the United States send us the sympathetic, modest, intelligent, and understanding type who constitutes the standard of true American men of learning, and with whom it will be possible for us to maintain cordial and worthwhile relations, for the better approximation of our two Countries."[102]

What seems to have irked Penteado more than anything else was North American heavy-handedness, but beginning ten years after his broadside, North American power rather than manners would be at issue for a tiny minority among his cohort. The key figure was Genival Rabelo, copublisher of *PN* and its sister magazines, like Penteado a lifelong enthusiast of things North American. For Rabelo and a few others, the same heavy-handedness that had set off Penteado combined with unfair competition and Cold War politics to produce radicalization. The unfair competition came from U.S.-owned trade publications that Rabelo had earlier welcomed to the field, only to watch them siphon off undue portions of advertising billings. The Cold War politics—part of the radicalization-cum-internationalization of Brazilian politics between 1961 and 1964—were campaigns pursued by foreign and Brazilian businesses, including ones funded by the U.S. Central Intelligence Agency, involving advertising boycotts and threats thereof, which may have hurt Rabelo's publishing concern and certainly harmed the *Ultima Hora* newspaper chain. These pressures led Rabelo to rethink his earlier enthusiasm for *Visão* and other U.S.-owned publishing ventures. Where he had opposed the postwar constitution's ban on foreign ownership of news media, he now came to call for the enforcement of the letter of the law. In political terms, Rabelo's volte-face was even more dramatic. Through the postwar, he had been an outspoken advocate of the liberal-conservative center-right personified by Carlos Lacerda, breaking with lacerdista orthodoxy only in his tardy embrace of Kubitschek, whom he had earlier denounced. As late as 1962, Rabelo still plumped for *lacerdismo* in metropolitan Rio de Janeiro, while also supporting such national causes as agrarian reform, anathema to Lacerda. By 1963, however, Rabelo was an anti-lacerdista and a staunch supporter of the center-left constitutional president João Goulart. With Goulart's overthrow—which occurred with the fulsome support of the U.S. embassy, the Johnson administration, and local groups that had feasted on CIA funding in the years leading up to the coup—Rabelo lost *PN*, his last remnant of the publishing concern that had included *Vendas e Varejo, Indústria & Mercados*, and other ventures. He continued to denounce North American power and influence over the press for decades, through an officially sponsored visit to the Soviet Union that made him a Brezhnevian abroad even as he continued to use the expression "prosperity professional" unironically at home. In his struggle against foreign influence in the press, Rabelo was no angel, lashing out indiscriminately at naturalized Brazilians along with foreigners and the local agents of U.S. groups. But together with his friend João Doria—who invented Brazil's Sweethearts' Day while working in advertising and, as a left-nationalist federal deputy for his native Bahia, pursued legislative hearings on foreign influence in the press and broadcast media, before losing his seat and much else to the 1964 coup—Rabelo took a radical trajectory.[103]

The political terminus of Auricélio Penteado's trajectory was moderate by comparison, a preference for social democracy, Scandinavian, in the best of all worlds, failing that antipodean (New Zealander) or Latin American (Uruguayan, Costa Rican). The prompt for his turn from consumer capitalism appears to have been largely aesthetic: "All this that is occurring to the benefit of humanity is conventionally called PROGRESS, an abstract idea in the name of which mankind, slowly and over the centuries, is ceasing to be human and creating for itself a private little hell here on Earth. And to keep on going forward and develop the drivel of progress, man created a fabulous hormone, all-powerful and anti-enzymatic acting: Advertising, to which many of us, including me, sell talent."[104]

Penteado was a pioneer, similarly aesthetic objections to the artifacts of Brazil's new commercial culture eventually issuing from even his generation's least political professionals. Rodolfo Lima Martensen, for one, objected to the proliferation of outdoor advertising along the São Paulo–Santos highway and expressed his trepidation for what the future held for Rio's natural beauty. By the 1970s, such objections were no longer rare, Norton's art director asking, "Given that there is a law against air and water pollution, why isn't there a law against visual pollution?" All three kinds of pollution were discussed by the agency head Ênio Mainardi in an address titled "Packaging and the Environment," which he published as a *Propaganda* article dedicated to John Kenneth Galbraith, the object of trade-press contestation a decade earlier. Hoping that Brazil could avoid the mistakes of the North Atlantic countries, Mainardi cast a critical eye on their model: "Consumerism is going to turn its gears and cranks until it squeezes out the last drop. Everything will have to be purchased and destroyed, to be built again a little differently and then destroyed again, until men discover the advantages of a more intelligent use of GNP and of leisure." Mainardi knew well that his arguments flew in the face of those he called "the apologists of indiscriminate progress," as had Penteado two decades earlier, when he declared, "If this is progress, to hell with it."[105]

For Penteado and Mainardi, aesthetic objections to the culture they helped create and continued to serve led to a questioning of its ideological underpinnings. So too did ethical considerations. For both men it was not only foreign origins or ugly outcomes that made aspects of the new culture objectionable; it was obvious conflicts with basic human ethics. Penteado compared himself and his cohort to huntsmen, studying the psychology, habits, and responses of the public that was their quarry in order to better utilize "this tool of progress, this technique of persuasion, which could be so useful in the diffusion of hygienic, agricultural, and other teachings truly adequate to human well-being [that] is sometimes cheapened . . . in the sale to the people of a useless product that they cannot really afford to buy." Mainardi, relatively early on, came to believe "that the power of advertising is too great to be used exclusively for the consumerist promotion of necessity. That advertising is culture . . . and this culture needs to be contained, steered, controlled by dykes built by man's intelligence and not by the barrages of chance, the immediate interests of selling more."[106]

The ethical questioning of the new culture was perhaps the deepest of the self-criticisms emerging among the new professionals. Amid the polarization of the early 1960s, the U.S.-trained marketing professor Pólia Lerner Hamburger—the first woman admitted to the São Paulo School of Business— broke with decades of professional-managerial consensus when she suggested that advertising's promotion of unrealizable desires might lead to frustration and even social breakdown. Years later, her former colleague

Affonso Arantes expressed his objections to the entire process encapsulated in their shared field: "Contrary to what marketing specialists say, that marketing activities seek to suit products and services to the needs of the consumer, what we observe is that the greatest effort of the people who dedicate themselves to this activity consists in creating needs among these consumers for products and services that are not always essential. In reality, many are superfluous and others harmful. I also think that much of the pollution, of the waste that exists these days, is the result of marketing activities that create manufactured obsolescence and the rest of it." Genival Rabelo had also noted that "negative aspect of the influence of North American 'marketing': the excess of forged, unnecessary, manufactured obsolescence. . . . Products are made to last the absolute minimum, in an effort to create market turnover. It is, without a doubt, a dishonest principle."[107]

Marcus Pereira, for years *O Estado de S. Paulo*'s advertising columnist and the only major São Paulo executive to admit publicly, with Rabelo, that advertisers were exerting undue influence on the press, would eventually quit the field, citing similar concerns: "I didn't enjoy what I was doing, in good conscience it is very difficult to enjoy being the accomplice of interests that exist to stimulate consumption . . . in a society in which only a minority is in any condition to consume." In 1973, he closed his successful agency to produce Brazilian music. Looking back from 1980, he wrote, "Today, seven years later, I see TV advertising the superfluous in a Country in which an absolute majority of the population is not in any condition to acquire even that which is essential to life. And—the greatest crime of all—even charging for the display of products that, inevitably, the plots of the soap opera come to include. This deserved an ugly name, but it is called 'merchandising.'" Orígenes Lessa had made a similar case at the height of the economic miracle: "At one point in Brazil, one advertised for slaves. Now, served by powerful means of communication and persuasion, advertising makes slaves. Not of everyone, but it makes them. Of habits, customs, equipment, products, to say nothing of the field of ideas. Or—what is sadder still—it makes [people] slaves to a desire to buy." From making slaves to serving as the hired guns of powerful economic groups: it was a short distance from Lessa's constatations to Julio Ribeiro's denunciations at the Third Advertising Congress, just shy of recognizing what one authority called "the economic psychopathology of our daily lives."[108]

Along the way, reflecting on a life split between literary moonlighting and "a profession so often forced into lying and other forms of dishonesty," Lessa paused to consider young aspirants: "What am I going to say to the student of today, tomorrow's professional?" Having traded his dream for a metaphorical plate of beans forty years earlier, Lessa asked, "What can I say to those of our time? That they shouldn't eat lentils or caviar?"[109]

In that intergenerational context, self-flagellation scarcely mattered. At the moment of Lessa and Ribeiro's fullest questioning of their professional cause, it was already won. Thousands stood ready to take their places, among whom were increasing numbers of young men and women who had grown up—like the artist Wanda Pimentel—within the culture of Brazilian consumer capitalism, who did not remember a "before" and could scarcely ponder an "after," most of them lacking the intellectual and political formation that had informed earlier generations' views of past and future. Even for those earlier generations, there is scant evidence that the misgivings voiced by leading figures were universally felt. Indeed, self-doubt and second thoughts seem to have been minority positions. Perhaps more importantly, all but the most diffident or reckless spokespersons for the new professionals found means of conciliating politics and profession, Americanist enthusiasms and Brazilian belonging, aesthetic objections and economistic aims, moral questioning and missionary faith. Sangirardi Jr., perhaps steeled by his political beliefs, rejected the very idea that advertising was "a social and educational activity," or even that it could be. Rather, in the kingdom of this world, the point was to move merchandise. "Thus, observer, let us come down from this pedestal of sociologists and educators, to accept the worthy and true function of simple technicians, whose aim is to sell efficiently." National or nationalist misgivings might be whisked away by the assertion that Brazilian advertising was becoming universal or by the quick embrace of such national stereotypes as the hypersexualized *mulata*. Individual retreat to a bucolic Brazilian version of what was not yet called exurbia was Rodolfo Lima Martensen's final answer to the market-induced ugliness that had grown up around his first dream home, an option that matched escapes to Greenwich, Westchester, and points north by his Madison Avenue counterparts.[110]

And to ethical objections, the assertion of professional mission provided an answer. "Advertising is a serious, truly constructive activity that is indispensable to the economic development of Brazil," Orígenes Lessa asserted in a 1960 interview. At decade's end, Cícero Silveira called it "the industry of development." Not long thereafter, B. Godoy Prado asserted, "What is undeniable is that advertising is working together toward development." Addressing the National Confederation of Brazilian Bishops in 1977, Alex Periscinoto acknowledged the country's deep inequalities, but pointed to mass communication as "the one thing that is the same and equitable," for he and the very poor watched the same personalities, sports teams, and shows on TV-Globo: "And you know for sure that we receive, through mass communication, values and concepts that we didn't have before, messages and information that satisfy our ego, that fill our emptiness. Only communication does this. With the help of communication, I am not only going to help my fellow man—more than this, I am helping myself to become someone."[111]

No Brazilian gave voice to ideas of mission more often or at greater length than Renato Castelo Branco: in 1965, as the ABP's Advertising Man of the Year; in 1973, commemorating the APP's anniversary; in 1975, in the pages of *O Estado de S. Paulo*; in his memoir, published in 1981. According to Castelo Branco: "Advertising in Brazil created, in urban centers, this indispensable incentive to industrial expansion. And only through advertising can we create the incentives that will awaken immense areas of Brazil, still apathetic today, and lead them to participate effectively in the economic life of the country. I believe that economic development occurs within the following movement: *more people should possess more things and life should be easier and increasingly richer.* And there is abundant proof of the role that advertising has played in the distribution of more things to more people." Perhaps mindful of arguments like Sangirardi Jr.'s, Castelo Branco made pains to point out that this was not "to place advertising on a pedestal of altruism." Rather, "aggressive and intelligent advertising of a product or service, while it serves the producer's own interest through the increase in profitable sales, at the same time contributes in an important way to the national economy, educating a larger number of people, leading them to a higher standard of living."[112]

According to Castelo Branco's memoir, this reasoning was key to reconciling himself with his work. Even so, his memoir ends on a melancholy note, in allusions to lost dreams, misplaced ideals, and a life spent in the living. Ten years later, in a semiautobiographical novella, Castelo Branco placed his old arguments linking development, consumption, and advertising in the mouth of a character named Carlos Romero, as the character addresses a banquet hall filled with advertising luminaries. When Romero—like Castelo Branco in his JWT days, the head of a major U.S. agency's operations—wraps up his speech, it is greeted by loud applause, as Castelo Branco's had been in 1965, while the narrator, the novella's second double for its author, reflects: "When Romero finished his speech everyone applauded. But many, I thought, despite the clapping, must have responded intimately like the citizen next to me, who synthesized his feelings in one word: *Bullshit.*"[113]

Which was it? Mission or *merde*, to use the idiom that would have been more readily comprehensible to lettered Brazilians seventy years earlier? For Castelo Branco, it was both, it would seem, in a never-resolved inner conflict less dramatically intense than that depicted in Vianna Filho's *Corpo a corpo*, but one experienced rather than imagined. For others, there was work as a source of satisfaction, apart from meaning and only indirectly related to money. In Ricardo Ramos's novel *As fúrias invisíveis*, the sociologist Teodoro, forced to leave a teaching job and his native Pernambuco because of his leftist sympathies, becomes increasingly immersed in market-research work in São Paulo as it becomes like the social-scientific work he lost, in form if not in content. Ramos himself seems to have experienced copywriting as engaging, if also alienating, like most kinds of dependent, hired work. Julieta de Godoy Ladeira—Ramos's understudy at JWT, and a dear friend—derived similar satisfaction and suffering from her work, as well as something approaching freedom.[114]

Ladeira, true to her cohort, was raised amid the growth of Brazil's culture of consumption, but unlike many of the men and women she would later work alongside, she grew up in great comfort. Her father was a Portuguese-born broker, a member of the immigrant bourgeoisie that had emerged at the interstices of São Paulo's agrarian capitalism, while her mother was of the old regime of landlords and state administrators. As a child, Ladeira frequented the right clubs and attended the best schools, but she was also bookish and independent minded, finding the shelter that accompanied comfort to be suffocating. In later life, she liked to tell people that she had enjoyed working in her father's office as a girl and soon refused her allowance, rendered unnecessary by the money she earned tutoring schoolmates. Ladeira first traveled to Europe in her late teens or twenties. She may have run off to marry a man she already knew, or she met him in her travels, but whichever the case, she crossed the Atlantic alone as a young woman—which would have been nearly unheard of at that time—and returned to Brazil out from under the dominion of parents, grandmother, aunts, and uncles, at the price of an unhappy marriage that lasted through a short stretch of years in Rio and Belo Horizonte. When the marriage dissolved, Ladeira returned to São Paulo, but not to her childhood home, at least not permanently, instead living independently and earning her own livelihood, first as a secretary, then as a copywriter, attending the São Paulo Advertising School in the evenings. All the while, she was writing and reading, jealously guarding her evenings and weekends for her own creative work. In 1962, she published her first book, the prizewinning collection *Passe as férias em Nassau*. Soon thereafter, she was named head of JWT's creative department, by which time she was reputedly the highest-paid woman in Brazilian advertising, the salary she commanded increasing thereafter, through positions at Colgate-Palmolive and Multi. For this stubbornly independent daughter of the conjugation of traditional land- and office-holding and early twentieth-century commercial capitalism, however, her sometimes fascinating, often frustrating career in the making of Brazilian consumer capitalism was not an end to itself, but rather a means to the limited economic independence that would provide leisure for writing and—from 1965—enjoying companionate marriage to the novelist Osman Lins. Early in the marriage, which ended only in 1978, with Lins's death, she completed the novel *Entre lobo e cão*, released in 1971 by the prestigious José Olympio publishing house.[115]

The novel was a significant accomplishment, probably Ladeira's greatest writerly one. Superficially, it may seem memoir masquerading as fiction, a stream-of-consciousness through which the reader encounters a young woman raised in São Paulo's upper class before eloping to Europe, only to endure an unhappy marriage in Rio and Belo Horizonte, her stay in the latter interior city providing the novel's warmest, most equitable and human relationships, with the narrator's adoption into a neighbor's family while her husband travels for business. But there is more to the novel. Like Juca in Lessa's *O feijão e o sonho*—to which *Entre lobo e cão* is in every way superior—the life of Ladeira's double is antithetic to its author's: rather than engagement and autonomy, the protagonist of *Entre lobo e cão* retreats and eventually regresses to her parents' care. Unlike *O feijão e o sonho*, easy sentimentalism is absent from *Entre lobo e cão*, the atmospherics of which are ably captured by the title, "Between Wolf and Hound," an expression referring to the moment just before nightfall. Instead, the reader is exposed to nearly unremitting, often-intimate social cruelty in relations derived from colonialism and slavery: within the aristocratic extended family modeled on Ladeira's own; between masters, mistresses, and maids; among haves and have-nots generally.[116] Ladeira clearly intended *Entre lobo e cão* to be about more than one woman's experience. At key points, she indicates that her protagonist is representative of her class and its decadence amid what would have been called underdevelopment, while the weaving of the grand dates of national and international history into her narrative suggests an intention to speak to Brazil's history more generally. Evoking the Americanist and pro-Allied enthusiasms of the war years, her narrator recalls *Casablanca*'s "As Time Goes By" and Churchill's V for Victory, adding that then, "Imperialism still seemed different than Nazism to us."[117]

Along the way, institutions, artifacts, and attitudes characteristic of the development of Brazilian consumer capitalism—of the country's capitalism as observed, if not enjoyed, by people of all classes—stud her narrator's stream of consciousness. The lives of maiden great-aunts living in a middle-class Rio neighborhood are contrasted with her late grandmother's aristocratic quiescence in 1930s São Paulo. "My grandmother, her blueish-white hair, long sleeves, neutral colors, bobbin-net lace up her neck. They are of the same era, but Leninha and Estefânia seem as though they are from another, more courageous world. They have a washing machine, a television. They earn well. They like all the novelties, saving money to buy them. . . . They comment upon the national situation. They listen to radio, soap operas, they don't miss the news shows. Estefânia attends political clubs, goes to the Legislature, follows the debates, belongs to a Theosophical society." When her grandmother went out, it had been by hired car: "The chauffeur took off his cap, opened the door, helped her in. She went to Mappin or to Casa Alemã. Knowing her, the salesclerks invited her to sit down, brought over the merchandise. . . . The manager, cautiously, gave his opinion on the best choice. Even in the fabrics section one could hear the waltzes playing in the tearoom on the top floor."[118]

Arriving in São Paulo for the funeral of her grandmother's brother—mildly developmentally disabled, all but discarded by the family after his sister's death—Ladeira's narrator is thrust into the end-of-day crush of people exiting the downtown: "The eve of abjuration and the instinctive attachment to the immediate and palpable. The illuminated signage shows propane tanks, transmits news items, pours lightbulbs into teacups, gyrates stars, displays soft drinks, wines, torrents of pasta, stockings, green, white and golden signs, the city's totems. And the cars, the cafés, the streetcars, the stores and their shopwindows, the trembling of the hours, windows that go dark, useless telephones, the deserted offices." Approaching the former site of the Mappin department store, she remembers, "I was afraid of that glass door and in that building on the corner where one did not see the perfumed salon and the blonde wig next to the display of dyes I cried when they cut my hair." Further on was A Exposição, then: "The armoire travel trunks and toys of Casoy, Perella, Casa dos Fios. The sheets and bath towels of Casa Fortes, the Clark trademark." A meditation on mortality and decay gives way to an account of changes in a once-familiar retail landscape: "Casa Alemã is now Bazar Lord, the Brasserie was transformed into Ducal."[119] And further on: "Madame Genny's workshop, on Rua do Arouche (aluminum walls, plaster roundels) now is a Grande Venda de Retalhos, and the Casa Dirceu (they gave me candies before going to the dentist, candies in the shape of little naked dolls) is different and it is called Kopenhagen. The Instituto Ludovig remains. A Capital is A Exposição, the Viaduto bar is Casa Beethoven, but Casa Beethoven doesn't just sell records, acoustic guitars, accordions, ocarinas, Schmoll's sheet music, RCA Victor record needles. It displays refrigerators, heaters, television sets turned on day and night, entirely porcelainized automatic washing machines."[120]

In Rio, the Eucharist Congress of 1955 is "a kind of holiday card sent by General Motors or Coca-Cola, the large banks and the supermarkets, with angels and madonnas, psalms, nude babes, hands clasped together, words of Jesus Christ, of Saint Peter, underlined quotes from all the Apostles, hand-shakes between employees and bosses, messages of peace, of love and of goodwill on shipping boxes, on detergents, margarines, artichokes, prophy-lactics. I'm not able to see yet." Back in São Paulo, now able to see, family is defined: "Each one with their gift on certain dates. There are wakes in cases of death, loans are offered at childbirth or right before travel. Long conver-sations on the telephone, shopping done together, the exchange of informa-tion on treatments. Special offers, liquidations. Secrets always told." Life's meaning was different: "For my aunts, to get ahead also means to have more; to be good is to give away a little of what is left over. Above all, they fear pov-erty in old age. And for that they steal from one another, pray, make martyrs of their husbands so that they achieve, so that they hold out, dividing them-selves up among promissory notes come due, uniformed maids, mortgaged houses, daughters almost brides." Nor is the narrator immune: "I want to be able to dress better someday, to have a heavier, more modern coat." Indeed, reckless spending with a neighbor yields a passing moment of peace: "Walk-ing past shopwindows, mirrors, automobiles, I see myself illuminated by the day, penetrated by its light. I remember, with a free and humble serenity, the afternoon spent with my cousin at the dressmaker on Rua Augusta. Two women shopping. So simple."[121]

Just below were middle-class strivers, personified in childhood neighbors, their household headed by the owner of a machine shop who celebrated his Sunday freedom by not wearing overalls or bothering to shave: "They are trapped in the certainty that the family should have grenadine-red coverlets, Spanish dolls, and that a good father is one who works to get ahead, to earn more than the neighbor, the best is to earn more than the entire street and move, to buy the block, have colored stoves, refrigerators with 12 square feet of storage, light-colored, long automobiles. They need to buy milk in the morn-ing, bring bread home, go to the open-air market, exchange the propane tank, set aside savings." For "Life insurance, taxes, rental payments, dentist, lawyer, seamstress bills. Holidays, pharmacy, school fees, nonstop. Dubious compen-sations. And the next moment could be worse, the house mortgaged, the car not yet paid off, the children still unschooled. The wave breaking against the same points, year after year. That you give, that you pay, that you buy."[122]

Nearer at heart was the servant class, the *criadagem*, in the person of the narrator's girlhood nurse, her life and health spent, surrounded by portraits of the children she raised, clad in castaway clothes: "These coats, these blouses and skirts, belonged to your mistress. You almost never had money to buy new things. Only a dark coat, acquired on installments, remember? It lasted many years. And a lapis-blue dress. You liked to wear it to the cinema." "It's not enough," her narrator asserts, the stream of consciousness now reproducing her interventions and her nurse's responses: "I earned less than the others because I had been there a long time, I had raised the girls. They said it was like I was family. And if now they couldn't or didn't want to help you? You'd be on the street. Like so many others. Would that be fair, after spending your life serving? No one ever taught me, they never told me. I'd rather have died already so as not to bother anyone."[123]

And so the reader is left with individual portraits of what Ladeira's narrator elsewhere calls "Classes A, B, C. In several circles of hell."[124]

————

Amid a capitalism as savage as the inspiration of any nineteenth-century prophet, Ladeira registered a searing, searching retort nested in an artfully constructed narrative that, like all her literary creations, was enabled by work serving what she—with the playwrights Consuelo de Castro and Oduvaldo Vianna Filho—called "the system." For Ladeira, one was the condition of the other; just as for her narrator's great aunts, downward mobility is the price of the loosening of aristocratic strictures and living in a more courageous world. At *Entre lobo e cão*'s creation, the conditions it described—public squalor, private privilege, widening inequality, integral informality, and callousness unto cruelty, all interwoven with Brazilian consumer capitalism—would have been attributed to imperialism and underdevelopment. A half-century later, one would have to be blind to ignore that such features, imagined as nationally or macro-regionally particular in Ladeira's day, are to be observed in some of the other great automobile countries of the world, even in the other great American country, while abundance in its most favored twentieth-century trappings has become a near-certain formula for planetary ruin.

Postscript

Between the setting of Julieta de Godoy Ladeira's stream-of-consciousness and the shoddy hubris of José Luiz Moreira de Souza's UEB Center was a great deal of history, stretching through the economic crises that ended the Brazilian miracle of 1968–1973, culminated in the 1980s, and continued into the 1990s, crises that did little to lessen the appeal of the consumer society believed to be imminent in the early 1970s. Through these twenty years and on, observers from afar attested to the cultural hold consumerism had on Brazilians. By 1986, according to a Brazilian correspondent long resident in New York, "the 'American illusion'"—his borrowed term for what others called "the American way of life"—"is the dominant national aspiration. No one contests ideologically any longer that Brazil should be a rich country and that there exist a general and hypothetical popular access to material goods." The North American anthropologist Maureen O'Dougherty, a thoughtful observer of Brazilian upper-middle-class lives through the galloping inflation and stagnant growth rates of the 1980s and early 1990s, found the drive to consume high-end goods and services to be the most salient aspect of her subjects' identities and everyday existence; "consumption intensified" was how she characterized it. Through the second half of the 1990s and especially after 2003, as inflation was brought under control beginning in 1994 and growth resumed under the mildly redistributionist administration of Luiz Inácio Lula da Silva (2003–2011), foreign correspondents delighted in growing demand for carbonated soft drinks, color television sets, and new-model passenger cars, filing human-interest stories on Rio's favelas as sites of big-ticket consumption and gushing over "unfettered American-style consumerism" in once-sleepy portions of the country. The Lula-era boom in consumer demand also attracted the attention of the Anglo-Irish Marxist Perry Anderson, a longtime Brazil-watcher. "Purchase of electronics, white goods and vehicles was fanned," he wrote in 2016, "so along with much needed, genuine improvements in domestic living conditions, consumerism in its deteriorated sense spread downwards through the social hierarchy from a middle class besotted, even by international standards, with magazines and malls."[1]

These developments, of course, had a deeper history, however novel they might have appeared to the rapporteurs of the 1980s and after. As João Cruz Costa, born in São Paulo in 1904, remembered of the 1930s, "The system of selling on installments, an imitation of the *American way of life*, was assembled, providing the middle class and even the urban worker the appearance of prosperity." Even the most recent reportorial judgments—including Perry Anderson's verdict on Lula-era consumerism—have deeper histories. For Anderson, the besotting of the Brazilian middle class had been apparent as far back as his first encounter with the country, half a century earlier, when he found, in the urban southeast, a "middle class [that] is as large as that to be found in Western Europe and is at least as rich." The latter assertion is demonstrably false, but that it appeared to be the case to such an acute observer was due to a relative abundance of big-ticket items, the invisibility of consumer debt, and the ubiquity of the creature comforts of cheap domestic help. As our New York–based writer asserted of the expansion of U.S. and later of multinational capital in the immediate postwar era, "It brought consumer culture to the elites (which, in Brazil, includes the middle class) and, there's no way around it, the amorality of the same, which without the slightest difficulty transvested the pre-industrial, pre-shock of 1918 values under which we lived in my childhood and part of my adolescence," values that were formed in and informed by the intimate exploitation and mutual dependence of master-servant relations central to Julieta de Godoy Ladeira's fiction. The fact that such values could be transvested and levels of wealth superior to Western Europe's could be apparent but not real speaks to the making of twentieth-century consumer capitalism generally. The Norton agency slogan "Efficiency and Sincerity" (like McCann's "Truth Well Told") was just that, a slogan, rather than a description of the actual workings of advertising-driven, credit-enabled consumption. Given a glance at those actual workings, both the Brazilian slogan and the North American one bring to mind Oscar Wilde's Gwendolen, for in these matters of grave importance, surface style more than trumped sincerity.[2]

As Cruz Costa's remembrance of the 1930s suggests, the reach of the culture of consumption into people's lives went beyond upper- and middle-class "elites" even at a relatively early stage in the development of Brazilian consumer capitalism. Other evidence for that fact emerged in the company town built around Brazil's government-run steel complex in the 1940s, which was subject to periodic blackouts by the early 1950s because working-class homes in that state-capitalist citadel featured a relative surfeit of electric appliances. In São Paulo, meanwhile, an observer found, "There has been a slow but steady increase in the standard of living of the worker, in spite of the inflation. There is now a considerable market among the workers for the simple kinds of home appliances which a few years ago they could not have possibly bought." By 1959, another remarked, "the workers are generally much better off than they were a few years ago. The average worker here in São Paulo can now get a radio, a television set, a refrigerator. They get them on time, but they can get them, and these things are becoming common in workers' homes." For as long as the postwar republic lasted, skilled workers in industry enjoyed a prosperity that their neighbors measured in consumer durables and Christmas gifts, the future president Luiz Inácio Lula da Silva remembering of his adolescence in the industrial outskirts of São Paulo, before the 1964 coup, "Back then, the people in the automobile industry received some ten raises a year. They were the elite people. They had houses, the guy who first bought a television, the guy who first bought a car. Because it was close to our house, I used to watch the people from the vemag [plant] go by at Christmastime loaded with boxes of toys for their kids."[3]

Over the postwar, the world of goods helped drive mass migration out of the countryside into cities and towns. As the historian Paulo Fontes recorded, among the expectations of northeastern immigrants to São Paulo was "access, albeit modest, to the consumer goods that the development of Brazilian capitalism began to generate." By the early 1960s, according to the anthropologist Charles Wagley, those goods included radio sets, alarm clocks, wrist watches, nylon hose, "and other commodities which are symbols of the good life at home." Eight years later, Wagley added the television set to his list of goods obtainable by migrants to southeastern cities, products that continued to beckon symbolically to those left behind in the backlands.[4]

Part of the sugar-growing zone of the coastal northeast, if not its arid backcountry, enjoyed its first, fleeting taste of the fruits of Brazilian consumer capitalism in the early 1960s, when the minimum wage was extended to cane cutters and mill workers in Pernambuco. "The effect on Palmeiras [sic] was tremendous," a visitor to the sugar-zone town of Palmares reported. "There was a sudden increase in money spent in the town, all of the commerce of the town flourished, they began selling large quantities of clothing, shoes, sewing machines and other things for which there had not previously been a market." "It was a party," remembered another observer; "the roads filled up with trucks loaded with buckets and wash-basins, with innerspring mattresses and with every other luxury that the country people had always wanted to buy." "They bought tables and chairs, even water filters," a lifelong organizer recounted. "Transistor radios multiplied among them."[5]

Changes in material culture like these were of a piece with transformations operating across the lifetimes of Brazilians who came of age in the first half of the twentieth century, as new consumer goods, new patterns of behavior, and new ways of being in the world became so incorporated into everyday life as to be routine, the shifts in values they involved either experienced as entirely welcome or utterly invisible, save to intellectuals and other cranky types who nevertheless felt compelled to go along.

Among them was the inveterate bohemian Armando Puglisi, a lifelong resident of São Paulo's down-at-the-heels neighborhood of Bixiga, for whom there was an entire package of changes that could be traced back to the era of World War II and to the influence of the United States in music, film, and apparel, the coming of Coca-Cola, hot dogs, and outdoor advertising having been accompanied by the arrival of automobilism, conspicuous consumption, and manufactured obsolescence. Before the war, his mother had bought suits—"dead men's suits"—for him and his three brothers at pawn shops near downtown. "After the war, it began to be unsightly for a person to buy a used suit," Puglisi recalled. "Back then the pawn shops shut down because modernity arrived." Further on, the forced assent to new values reached into his home: "I'm going to tell you what my house was like back then: in the dining room the table was one way, the six chairs each one its own way, there was a sofa in the corner with two cushions, all torn up, the curtains my mother made with a piece of cloth. And so the money was enough because it was only for food, to pay school fees, and that was it, it wasn't like today. I'm hard up, but my house isn't so ugly. Why? Because my daughter is in college, in a little while she'll arrive with two or three friends of hers who study with her and you can't have a torn-up sofa. And so begins consumerism (is that the word for it?), which is what, in my opinion, ruined the world." Puglisi's ire was matched by that of the left-nationalist thinker, writer, and militant Darcy Ribeiro, in his inveighing against the interelite collusion of Brazil's commercial media and the arguably alienating, mystifying fare they traffic in. Nevertheless, when Ribeiro returned to his native Montes Claros in 1976 for the first time since being forced into exile a dozen years earlier, he spent hour after hour with his mother, holding her hand, watching television by her side as the Embratel system beamed Globo telenovelas to her household set. The world of the novelas had become her world and he was happy to share in it.[6]

It had become the world of millions of Brazilians. Indeed, the television soap opera had become Brazilian, and in so doing had shaped modern Brazil, as had earlier entertainments, conveniences, and commodities. For the memoirist Luiz Edmundo, writing in 1929, "American comfort" stood out among the aspects differentiating Rio and its people from Lisbon and European urbanites generally, while distinguishing national conditions from "colonial discomforts": "We wear clothes made of light fabrics, almost without lining. We banned the waistcoat, as well as gloves, gaiters, and hard-starched collars. . . . Aside from that, the Carioca won't go without the luxury of his refrigerator, not only to preserve the food that he eats, but also to refresh the liquids that he drinks. The one who doesn't have an electric refrigerator, gets one made of wood or zinc that, despite it being poor and primitive, still guarantees him the same benefits. Chilled water is served in all the cafés and even the most modest taverns and *bars*, for free. The use of the exhaust fan and the ventilator is common among us, like the telephone and the radio set."[7]

Over the years that followed, consumer credit, the five-and-dime store, commercial radio, soft-drink consumption, Sears, supermarketing, shopping malls, even "shopping" itself, would all become Brazilian. Taking the first of these as an example, within ten years of its introduction, the term *crediário* had slipped its origins as a commercial trademark and entered the Brazilian vernacular. By the postwar, according to one authority, credit sales were nothing less than "an institution in Brazil." But the importance of credit sales went beyond vulgarization or even institutionalization, changes in language and business practice: "The crediário appears in Brazilian society, not only as an economic phenomenon, but also a social one, a national aspiration, that brought integration to the Brazilian family, endowing it with comfort." As a "national aspiration," it helped fulfill what Jorge Martins Rodrigues called "the Brazilian population's new aspirations of consumption—aspirations that cinema, magazines, etc. generalize among our middle class and even in the bosom of that which one has somewhat depreciatively called 'the people.'"[8]

Through the agency of Rodrigues's "etc."—advertising, commercial radio, eventually television—Brazilianization worked on Brazilians, for even as exotic items, idioms, and entertainments became national, the country's commercial media began to effect changes in everyday ways of being that would have been otherwise impossible to enact. "Rádio Nacional had great national coverage," remembered the McCann executive Altino João de Barros. "Today, we owe the actual state of our language to Rádio Nacional," as regional accents were softened and selected modes of speech became Brazilian. This powerful nationalizing effect was almost entirely unscripted, and owed next to nothing to state-led efforts at centralization. In the words of the radio writer Mário Brassini, "Without receiving any specific instruction, no recommendation . . . we perform a service of national integration, Nacional carried out that integration. The very language came to be modified through Rádio Nacional." "Musical idols, advice columnists, comedy programs and soap operas," recalled Anna Verônica Mautner of her São Paulo childhood, "were relevant in the homogenization of a mentality and of a style that we may call 'Brazilian.'" This homogenization reached deeper into Mautner's home and homes like hers in the postwar, through television and colorful weekly magazines. Thus, in the words of Lia Faria, writing on behalf of women who came of age in the 1960s as aspiring schoolteachers, did the nationalizing effects of Brazil's consumer capitalism tend toward crowding out local and regional cultures: "The massification and consequent homogenization brought by the consumer society and the cultural industry eliminated differences and often restrict the diverse."[9]

What was so often seen as Brazilianization, however, was in fact a substitution of mostly novel aspects of a single part for a fictive whole, as could not but be the case in a national space of archipelagic regions undergoing rapid, wrenching change. A reified sense of Rio was imposed on the rest of the country, especially its points north, as Genolino Amado wrote of his native Sergipe in 1943:

> it was the radio that carried out the most singular revolution. Under its permanent and insidious quotidian influence, the local physiognomy, formed across the ages, imprinting its traits at the cost of so many traditions, upon reflection of so many aspects of history, of the physical environment, of the life that was spent there, was little by little decomposing, until it completely lost its character. . . .
>
> All this might not have great social importance, if there wasn't also establishing itself in Sergipe, as in all the other Brazilian provinces, a radiophonic conception of life. The smiling superficiality of the capital, its careless irreverence, the light froth of Carioca existence, is seeping into the soul of these backland folks, of the small cities and the distant towns, to which Brazil always turned for greater, purer inspirations.[10]

"Certainly, it would be puerile to blame 'broadcasting' for what is happening," Amado continued. "If radiophonic futility is so influential, even in the provinces, it is because Brazilian life at this moment lacks something to defend it in its spirit, that truly engages it, that gives it greater satisfaction than sambas and the soap-opera serials." Indeed, the situation seemed as critical in Rio, at least in Copacabana, a "poor Miami" where one took "cocktails in Americanized bars, with their falsely bohemian expression that doesn't recall Paris cabarets, but California 'drugstores.'" And so, the critic Murilo Mendes feared, "they want to Copacabanize, standardize, formulate, cretinize" the cultural diversity of the authentic regional cultures of the Brazilian archipelago. This Rio-centered standardization was what Anna Verônica Mautner would call a Brazilian style and mentality, a characterization to which she went on to add: "The kings and queens of radio homogenized ceaselessly from the center of irradiation that was the federal capital, Rio de Janeiro. Not only were the great transmitting stations there, but also the great magazine publishers, which divulged images of those whom we only knew by their voices." To these media, the cultural historian Cláudia Mesquita added Samuel Wainer's promotion-happy *Ultima Hora* chain, described as "fundamental for the 'nationalization' of the Carioca way of being, because its habits, dramas, and human types came to be 'exported' throughout the country with the establishment of the newspaper's national network." Before the advent of national television broadcasting, Wainer's promotion-oriented publishing concern "shortened the distance between Rio and other Brazilian locales and permitted its columnists to acquire importance throughout the country and for the 'culture of Carioquismo' to be assimilated as an element in the construction of national identity." By the time the Embratel system went online in 1969, the *Ultima Hora* chain was no more, and the newly national medium of television extended its efforts in a manner comparable only to the broadcasts of radio's golden age. Describing its effects in Pernambuco in 1973, the television executive Paulo Ferreira quoted an old pun ("the Brazilian people speak the Nacional language"), adding, "The same phenomenon repeated itself years later before my eyes, at the time of the installation of TV-Globo in Recife. Regional habits, manners, and manias came together in a single language, the Carioca one." By the 1980s, few corners of Brazil were immune to it, as Cláudio Abramo observed in Goiás: "The effect of TV is naturally bringing an end to regional habits. It is inevitable, to seek to struggle against it is foolishness." "It is what one calls civilization," he continued. "This is the process of the making of national identity."[11]

Abramo was slightly less than half-right. The homogenizing effects of Brazilian consumer capitalism and of the media summoned into existence to serve it were *part* of ongoing processes of national-identity formation. But the media also trafficked in ideas of regional unity-in-diversity dear to the likes of Murilo Mendes, as well as to the would-be centralizers of Brazil's authoritarian regimes of 1937–1945 and 1964–1985, ideas that contributed to the same processes. From the beginning, the selling of consumer capitalism had resorted to reified ideas of regional and local distinctiveness, as in advertisers' appeals to São Paulo state pride and to cultural forms envisioned as embodying Rio. As the major institutions of Brazilian consumer capitalism expanded into territories north of the two southeastern centers, they too grasped onto emblems of regional belonging: TV-Globo appropriating the iconic northeastern fishing vessels called *jangadas* to promote its Recife station, the Pão de Açúcar supermarket group using the backlands genre of chapbook poetry known as *literatura de cordel* to advertise supermarketing in Ceará. Neither group's executives needed the precious contraction "glocalization" to actualize what they were after.[12]

Meanwhile, the new culture of consumption came to attach itself especially to the city of São Paulo. As early as 1962, visiting São Paulo was described as synonymous with that culture for an audience of Rio women belonging to classes A and B: "We think about São Paulo in terms of commerce. Yes, shopping in the bandeirante Capital [i.e., the "Paulista" Capital] is always an invitation. To stroll Rua Augusta, on a misty afternoon, looking at the pretty shopwindows—very European—and the promenade of automobiles, of antique stores, and the parade of elegant women at five o'clock is without a doubt something that all of us like to do." In 1971, the same audience was offered apparently surprising news of a São Paulo hypermarket becoming a round-the-clock space of sociability: "What was not in anyone's plans was that a supermarket could become, for Paulistas, a place for a stroll. But it became exactly that." Here, just south of São Paulo's once-"new" downtown, was a place where couples ambled while exposing themselves to impulse buying, where "the Paulista finds . . . everything to satisfy his needs as a man of the consumer society." Two years later, the opening of São Paulo's newest shopping center led a specialist to explain that such structures responded to "urban populations' need for leisure, which provokes their integration to consumption." In 1974, *Manchete* described Shopping Center Iguatemi as the place to see the "latest manifestation of the native Paulista consumer society." Even as much of the rest of the country was made up of "subconsumers," and as pockets of real deprivation festered in and around the city of São Paulo, its marketing gave the appearance of advance, as the "sophistication of the Paulistano consumer society" lent itself to being seen as "not . . . a vast and standardized market, as one says around the way, but . . . a complex of submarkets, each with its own characteristics."[13] Therefore, it could be seen as

> our best laboratory for the examination of the first manifestations of the phenomenon among us. In standardization (the first stage of the consumer society) as in the diversification or individualization of the market (the second stage), the sale of goods and services, trumpeted by advertising and stimulated by the crediário, by direct-to-the-consumer credit or by the credit card, adds fuel to the fire under the cauldron of consumption. This reinforces what sociologists call the "propensity to consume more and more."
>
> In this case, consumption surpasses the limits of meeting material needs that cannot be put off and spills into the meeting of the psychological needs of a given "state of mind." That is: consumption taken as an instrument of social affirmation, of expressing one's personality, or even of manifesting a libertarian and permissive way of life. That of the "extra psychological benefit" sponsored by certain categories of product or service.[14]

Manchete's reporter went on to describe consumer behavior, in 1974, that Maureen O'Dougherty would see as typical of the "consumption intensified" that characterized São Paulo's upper-middle-class family life in the crisis-ridden 1980s and 1990s. And while some of the reporter's description was pure bluster, São Paulo was, if not ahead of its time, ahead of the rest of the country when it came to the advance of the new culture of consumption. Beachless, booming, and bereft of public entertainments commensurate to its size, it perhaps could not have been otherwise. However, as the anthropologist Gilberto Velho and his assistants found in their research in Copacabana in 1968–1970, consumerism and the culture industry had reached deep into the experience of middle-class families on Rio's southern beachfront as well, their informants returning again and again to the interrelated categories of commerce, consumption, and convenience in describing life on that once-idyllic beachfront. Indeed, more respondents identified Copacabana's retail trade than its natural attractions in explaining why they lived there. "It's the best commerce of Rio" was the typical reply.[15]

———

And so aspects of the new culture of consumption, even as they became Brazilian and contributed to Brazil's remaking, came to be identified especially with specific parts of the country, with select cities and certain locales within them. So too was that larger culture identified with particular Brazilians, nationally, regionally, and within favored corners of the urban southeast. It was no coincidence that *Manchete*'s reporter began his story on "The Paulistano Consumer" by portraying an automobile-owning "Paulistana housewife" of class A or upper B in her neighborhood supermarket—"the temple of the consumer society"—and that he never came around to offering a comparable profile of a male shopper. By that point, the idea that housewives specifically and women generally were the consuming category par excellence was a decades-old commonplace: "Research carried out across Brazil revealed that women purchase much more than men do. In addition, they exercise a powerful influence on most of the purchases that men make!" "Women . . . who understands them?" asked a Standard Propaganda advertisement in 1955. "That was in olden times. . . . Today women have ceased to be the 'eternal enigma.' Besides man's companions and collaborators, they are—above all—*the great buyers*!" In 1961, JWT presented a housewife facing mass-marketed products on a supermarket shelf: "The moment of truth . . . in marketing!" In 1964, Rio's decadent *O Jornal* made the empty promise of allowing advertisers to "speak DIRECTLY to the greatest buyer in the world," as the leading publication among "the feminine public," which it most certainly was not, while Marcia Rita—*O Globo*'s shopping columnist— offered retail-sales directors her professional knowledge "of the woman as purchaser, of the consumer," and her "experience as housewife, mother, [and] purchasing woman with 16 years on the job."[16]

As Marcia Rita's offer suggests, the idea of women and especially of housewives as the country's preeminent consumers was not simply put on in publicity, nor was it solely a projection of frivolousness and waste onto a supposedly weaker sex, as it had been following the postwar "flight of the dollars." It was an abiding understanding among the new professionals, if one that shifted with the times. In 1958, addressing his fellow advertising and sales professionals under the heading "Women Command," Marcus Pereira drew on his experience and a North American authority to present a brief for women as their most important demographic. Pereira's case was patronizing at points, but it also identified women as modern-minded actors who were influential in their own right, without exempting himself or his mostly male audience from the influence of the culture they had helped create: "To buy is an act of fundamental importance in all of our lives. For what we buy or what we keep from buying. Or for what women buy or keep from buying for us." Writing in 1962, Rodolfo Lima Martensen started from the claim that around 80 percent of the world's advertising was aimed at women and more than 90 percent of it was written by men to make the case—a far more sexist one, as it would happen—that too many of his (male) copywriting colleagues underestimated their quarry. "Be careful with the housewife!" he counseled. The inorganic intellectuals of the supermarket trade offered figures to their numbers-oriented audience, as in an April 1972 issue of *Supermercado Moderno*: "The typical supermarket consumer in Brazil is a lady who is more than 25 years old, married, with a family of 3 to 4 people, very concerned with the budget, with a level of education that includes elementary and secondary schooling, who in general goes to the supermarket 2 or more times per week." At decade's end, the director of Standard's research department summed up the conventional wisdom: "The housewife is the great buying agent and the middle-class housewife is the one who is most integrated into the consumer society."[17]

On this evidence, little would appear to have changed between 1958 and 1980 apart from manners and modes of speech. The writer of 1958, however, would have found it difficult to imagine that in little more than two decades, the research department of such a prominent agency would be led by a woman. But so it was that by 1980, that key position had been taken by Clarice Herzog, who brought formal training in the social sciences at the University of São Paulo as well as something of that institution's progressive mentality to her work on consumers generally and female consumers specifically, which went well beyond the objective, facts-and-figures approach of earlier researchers to plumb subjective questions of motivation, values, and even consciousness. "Women are innovative," Herzog told a reporter, "and like all modern consumers, open to adopting new things, be it as a consumer or as a member of society. Advertising, in turn, fulfills its role by accompanying society's constant changes and responding to its aspirations.

Its arguments vary as a function of the category of consumer good: for a more rational purchase—food, an automobile, etc.—appeals are more rational; for a more emotional purchase—cosmetics, clothing, 'superfluous items'—appeals also will be emotional."[18]

Orientations and approaches similar to Herzog's were apparent in a major study carried out by the LPM agency, its interpretations of evidence from a "discussion group" of housewives informed by sociology, by Freudian psychoanalysis and symbolism more generally, and—of course—by marketing. For the study's authors, as for the TV-Globo researchers who identified the same figure as comprising their station's major audience, the Brazilian middle-class housewife of the 1970s was in some ways more "modern" than her spouse, but she was also torn: "In effect, the woman senses that the new complex of values is opposed to the traditional ones. As a person, she wants to be modern and leave aside the 'drudgeries' of domestic life. . . . To return to old standards is impossible in an environment in which people prize what is modern. To abandon them is also impossible, because the woman's function in life is still defined by the role of housewife and mother."[19]

In the broadest sense, such stresses affected men and women: "The standards of modernity are valorized by manufactured obsolescence, by ever-faster and more-instantaneous communication. The most important roles of the individual housewife or male head of household tend to fuse into a single new and uniform role: that of consumer." But the situation of the middle-class housewife was different, because she brought these tensions directly to her domestic work, including to her role as primary child-rearer, whereas her spouse was assumed to sublimate them in work outside the home, and because the changes in her day-to-day activity and affective relations were so much greater:

> Thus, one compromise after another, she becomes modern and, in the process, alters her own role and relations within the family. Instead of staying at home picking through dried beans and rice, making soap, crushing tomatoes to make sauce, washing clothes, shelling peas and hearts of palm, etc., she purchases these services in the products that she acquires and which are, therefore, "more expensive than the homemade ones," for her.
>
> In performing her role, *doing* is no longer important, but rather *buying*. And the setting in which the housewife performs her role tends to shift from the home to the supermarket. "Shopping" comes to be one of her fundamental tasks. She navigates the streets (which in olden times was a place for drunks and bums) and drives an automobile to do her shopping, to look at shopwindows, to take the children to school, to pick up her husband, and even to visit friends.

In the process, however, her role remains the same one. Purchasing canned foods, she is still the one who feeds the family. Purchasing a textbook for her children and taking them to school, she is still the one taking care of their education. Dressing up to greet her husband at home or to go out with him, she is still the wife. And the home, with every-thing it contains, is still her specific domain.[20]

This ideal type, like any other, and perhaps more than most, may be crit-icized for any number of particulars (the omission of household servants, to start with), but it nevertheless is indicative of how far-reaching these changes were, of how deeply they delved into the domestic sphere, and—less obvi-ously—of how long they were in the making. Alongside incremental changes in material culture and household labor, from making soap in boiling caul-drons over open fires to buying factory-made soap, from scraping store-bought soap into flakes to purchasing powdered soap, from hand-scouring clothes with each of these applications to bringing home a machine that would wash them with detergent, were shifts in outlook, which occurred over the same three-quarters of a century. Such shifts, for the feminist writer and publisher Rose Marie Muraro, could be captured by changes in the readership of *Claudia* magazine's "progressive" columnist: "Carmen da Silva was read by university women in the 1960s and by housewives in the 1970s. Just look what a transformation the Brazilian woman underwent between 1965 and 1975." For Anna Veronica Mautner, writing as a memoirist, but drawing on her train-ing as a psychologist, changes like these began a generation earlier, in radio's golden age: "The world reached women inside their homes over the radio waves before they even went out to the world in mass." There, at home, "often-times around the radio," women came to hear "the voice of the other. The discovery of alterity without mutual exchange.... The radio's voice did not incite us to revolt nor to complaisance; it only made us conscious of being part of the world." Further on, magazines and television channeled the "Age of the Image." Recipes and domestic habits changed, as traditions passed from one generation to another "came to belong more and more to the past" and

the means of mass communication—radio, cinema, and incipient television—came to replace homely tradition. The condition of woman was transformed. Her functions as teacher, as mother, are absorbed by the *mass media.* . . . From being a person charged with preserving and maintaining, she becomes the one who perceives, imitates, and trans-forms. Women come to be more modern, and this trait comes to be seen as positive and desirable. As family members, we thereby pass from the dominion of women who had the duty of conserving—maintaining sacred the sacred—to women who were better to the degree to which they showed themselves apt to changes. With that, a good mother is one who evolves with the times, who learns with the *mass media*.

For Mautner, embedded in the changes fed by the commercial media, beginning with radio and continuing through television, were the preconditions for the sexual revolution and the arrival of contemporary feminism, and in all but the latter implications, it was nearly as foreseen by the Colgate-Palmolive executive Richard Penn, when he had rallied his Brazilian staff and their counterparts at Standard Propaganda and Rádio Nacional in the early 1940s: "We are going to reach women one way or another."[21]

The point is not simply that middle-class and upper-middle-class housewives were key objects of the new culture, as consumer capitalism's major purchasing agents—which they were, within certain limits—or even that "housewife" as identity underwent tremendous changes in Brazil—though it did—but that it was primarily through women that that culture breached the household gates and entered the most intimate spheres of family life. In purely economic terms, passenger-car production was unquestionably more important to Brazilian consumer capitalism than department-store shopping, but the country's Automobile Day has so far failed to overshadow Mother's Day, though the two commemorations fall on the same date in some years. Only Christmas compares as a commemorative bridging of public promotion and private celebration, commercialism and quiet domesticity, acquisitiveness and affection, to which it adds an unparalleled hold on children, "the market of tomorrow," described by Genival Rabelo in a column first published in *Shopping News* in 1956.[22]

The efficacy of the new culture therefore hinged on its elements being familiar, in the sense of being of the family, as well as in the sense of being well-known and, indeed, being seen in some ways as usual, ordinary, everyday. Diffused into omnipresence for urban Brazilians, it became part of the daily routines of its objects, even as its commercial commemorations marked the turns of the calendar year. It is up to believers to confirm whether cleanliness is next to godliness, but ubiquity of such an extent is almost certainly akin to hegemony, in the sense that human actors can scarcely imagine their lives entirely emptied of institutions and practices fashioned for the servicing of consumer capitalism, of getting and spending, of *more*. As diffuse as Brazil's consumer capitalism may thus appear, and has appeared for generations, its diffusion unto ubiquity operated through material and organizational infrastructures that had to be built up and maintained, and it was enabled by vast networks of interested parties.

By the late 1920s, these infrastructures included the near-national sales organizations of several foreign corporations—including General Motors, Ford, and Nestlé—that connected local dealers to headquarters in the southeast, through which poured products, promotional material, and sales techniques, to which General Electric added the innovation of corporate-run stores. U.S. firms, including the Hollywood studios, drew on the official and quasi-official organizational and logistical infrastructures of the State and Commerce Departments, the Chambers of Commerce, and National City Bank, while the Canadian- and U.S.-owned power companies—the Light and Bond & Share—contributed the electricity without which radio sets and refrigerators would not work, to which the two conglomerates added promotional efforts of their own. Beginning in the 1930s and accelerating in the postwar, expatriate- and Brazilian-run retail groups established regional and near-national chains (Lojas Americanas, Lojas Brasileiras, Ducal), while consumer-manufacturing interests (A. J. Renner, Carlos de Britto, Roupas Regência) expanded their sales organizations. From Sears in 1949 to C&A in the 1970s, foreign interests set out to impose their own methods on Brazil's retail trade. By the latter point in time, when the Dutch-based group implanted "European 'know-how'" in São Paulo's luxurious Shopping Center Ibirapuera, the scale and scope of sales and distribution operations had reached the point that a Gessy-Lever executive estimated that the Anglo-Dutch firm had reached half of the country's twenty million households through live demonstrations and free samples of OMO detergent. While perhaps something of an exaggeration, the fact that household-goods promotions like the ones mounted by Lever could reach millions of homes by the mid-1970s was enabled by the proliferation of supermarkets over the preceding quarter century, and especially the expansion of supermarketing beyond the São Paulo–Rio axis and into the interior of the south and southeast, as well as the capitals of Brazil's other states. In 1973, there were an estimated 6,350 self-service foodstores in the country, including hypermarkets and superettes as well as supermarkets. By late 1978, that number had risen to almost nine thousand, according to data gathered with the assistance of twenty state-level associations of supermarket retailers.[23]

As the latter suggests, infrastructures of such scale could not be created, maintained, or expanded without the gathering of increasingly large amounts of information, which is one reason why mapping Brazilian markets—and even of aspects of everyday life—occupied the attentions of the newly founded branches of U.S. advertising agencies in the interwar years. A dozen years on, IBOPE would begin the building of its expansive research operations, to be followed by others, from McCann-Erickson creating Marplan to Nestlé importing Nielsen. Along the way, their shorthand of letter-denominated strata—A, B, C, D, and often E—became the dominant way in which social difference was addressed in the commercial media from which Brazilians of all walks of life increasingly took their cues.

Commercial media infrastructures were no doubt most crucial in making for the ubiquity of the new culture, establishing a central place even in the lives of millions of Brazilians undesired by advertisers and usually unstudied by market researchers. An increasingly advertising-minded daily press, culminating in the oligopoly of *O Estado de S. Paulo*, the *Folha de S. Paulo*, *O Globo*, and the *Jornal do Brasil*, and complemented by weekly and monthly vehicles for advertising and enlightenment, including *Shopping News* and *Claudia*, was one pillar of this commercial media. Radio was another, one that was impossible to ignore in the glory days of Rádio Nacional, when the state-owned station was Brazil's Hollywood, but influential before and after the medium's golden age. Finally, there was television, ascendant over the 1950s and 1960s, absolutely dominant by the early 1970s, at which time the national government's Embratel system and Roberto Marinho's TV-Globo gave the country its first communications of undisputed national reach, beaming together a nation with international sport, national news, and—not least—*novelas* and their product-placement "merchandising."

While Globo programming was offered to any Brazilians who found themselves in front of a television set, credit determined who would become an active participant in the world of goods, rather than mere spectator. From the Argentine- and European-inspired—and U.S.-approved—creation of the crediário in the 1920s through the introduction of the credit card in the 1960s and 1970s, consumer credit and its promotion played vital roles in consumer capitalism's expansion. When such instruments were insufficient to meet the addled demand of Brazilian would-be consumers, middle-class Cariocas invented their own collaborative technique for car-buying, the *consórcio*, soon to be profitably adopted by automobile manufacturers and dealers, as well as to spread to other lines of goods, in the latter category assisting internal migrants in the acquisition of color television sets even as their wages were held down by official fiat. "Just imagine when I write to my family in Recife," remarked a northeastern-born worker in São Paulo's garment industry, "telling them that I'm watching television in color. Everybody's going to come, principally my mother, who loves novelas."[24] Ancillary to the provision of credit was the monitoring of potential customers and especially of delinquent accounts, at first the work of in-house credit bureaus, by the 1970s managed collaboratively through "credit-protection services" for the benefit of business.

These organizations and hundreds of others operating alongside them were created and maintained by shifting networks of stakeholders, staffers, and supporters. By the 1970s, the networks thus encompassed included anti-establishment creative artists—from orthodox Communists the likes of Oduvaldo Vianna Filho through the thirty-one flavors of the Brazilian counterculture—as well as the self-styled intellectuals of the country's military regime. Among the latter was General Carlos Meira de Mattos. This Freyrean military man predicted, on the eighth anniversary of the 1964 military coup, "Within ten years we will be ranked among mass-consumption societies, the world's most characteristic models of which are the United States, West Germany, and Japan," a pluralization of Brazilian models of the good life very much in line with the thinking of the heirs to Lauro de Carvalho, José Júlio de Azevedo Sá citing the West German economics minister Ludwig Erhard ("The right to consume is one of the inalienable rights of the human person") and José Luiz Moreira de Souza pointing to the Federal Republic of Germany, "where truly one reached a level of collective wealth, a level of *standard* of living, in which all may enjoy the comforts of civilization." If not exactly a turn away from the United States (José Luiz also mentioned the country that his uncle had called "the great school"), this recognition of consumerism's global spread was another step in its Brazilianization.[25]

In the 1910s, when U.S. officialdom and quasi-officialdom had first turned their attention to Brazil as a market, it had been because of its location, its size, and the imbalance of trade between the two countries, soon to be abetted by the opportunities presented by Europe's self-immolation. The trade commissioners and consuls who coordinated with one another and with interests in the United States and Brazil in order to expand U.S. exports were not interested in the creation of a consumerist market per se. Indeed, the language for such a thing was only then beginning to be invented in the United States. Rather, they sought to make U.S. business competitive with British and German business in general, including in metal goods and other product lines typical of nineteenth-century industry. It was the varieties of goods that were brought to Brazil and the apparatus created to promote them that ended up involving diplomats, bureaucrats, bankers, and their auxiliaries in the introduction of novel standards of style and civilization, new kinds of comfort and convenience, unfamiliar advances in technique and technology: GM's cars for every purse and purpose, Gillette safety razors, GE lamps; radio sets, refrigerators, wristwatches; testimonial advertisements, Stanley Resor's T-Square, reason-why advertising. Alongside these innovations, Hollywood brought a relative democratization of glamour and leisure, which was perhaps the greatest novelty of all. The interests involved—the offices of the Hollywood studios, Brazilian subsidiaries of U.S. corporations, the foreign-owned utilities that provided electric power and promoted the use of electrical appliances—were staffed and managed by Brazilians, North Americans, and European expatriates committed as a matter of professional course to these new standards. So too were the branches of the major U.S. advertising agencies as they opened offices in Rio and São Paulo between 1929 and 1935 at the behest of General Motors, Ford, and Standard Oil. Here, if not yet "the first great cohort of Brazilian advertising professionals" discerned by one veteran, was one nucleus thereof, the beginnings of a professional-managerial elite closely allied to its counterparts in journalism and the incipient mass media represented by commercial radio.[26]

Another nucleus was formed by the owners, managers, and employees of Brazilian-owned agencies, increasingly opting for North American models and manners of self-representation, joined beginning in the 1930s by their counterparts in Rio and São Paulo's retail trades, the inventors of the crediário, the term itself conjured up by Lauro de Carvalho some years before his first visit to the United States, from which he would return with merchandise, promotional methods, organizational techniques, and the inspiration to create a Macy's-like department store. As the example provided by Lauro and his brothers suggests, it was not only U.S.-owned and -directed firms that committed themselves to the emergent culture of consumption that João Cruz Costa described as synonymous with "the American way of life." Brazilian captains of commerce and industry, from the Carvalhos to Carlos de Britto, were early adherents of new methods, joining the representatives of such European firms as Lever and Nestlé. The Brazilian government, always solicitous vis-à-vis the country's increasingly commercialized press and the interests of the Hollywood studios, became a stakeholder in its commercial media with the acquisition of Rádio Nacional in 1940, allowing the station to become the country's most important cultural institution while airing hundreds of thousands of commercial appeals, including spots, slogans, jingles, and the sponsor's welcome that opened every radionovela episode. Nearly overnight, a centralizing, authoritarian regime became a more important agent in the diffusion of the new culture of consumption than the local representatives of the U.S. government had ever been, though the latter would make some signal contributions amid wartime appeals to hemispheric unity.

Across the postwar decades, as consumer capitalism confirmed its hold on Brazil, it came to be served by an oversized cohort of men and, increasingly, of women, who worked in advertising, sales promotion, market research, media management, design, and allied fields among the new professions. Marketing provided a professional-managerial optic and object of study; it was also touted as a means to speed up development and enhance the standing of the new professionals, leading figures among whom came to have the ear of powerful members of the post-1964 military governments, for which they helped create the slogans, images, and anthems of Brasil Grande. These images, in turn, would achieve truly national coverage over the government-created Embratel network. By that point, education had become another field to be colonized by the new culture, marketing having begun its long march through the institutions in the 1950s under the auspices of Point IV, "social communications" following in the era of military rule. Supermarkets, hypermarkets, and especially shopping centers came to involve some of the country's most economically powerful and politically influential groups as stakeholders in the new culture through the remaking of Brazilian cities, as real-estate magnates, contractors, and construction firms profited handsomely from the malling of urban space together with the successor firm to the old Light & Power trust, renamed Brascan, then, in 2009, Brookfield, at which point it held a stake in twenty-seven Brazilian *shoppings*.[27]

In 1973, marketing specialists predicted that within ten years, "Brazil will definitively enter the age of the *shopping center*." Despite the ending of the miracle amid that year's oil shock and subsequent economic havoc, Brazil seems to have exceeded expectations, for by 1987 not only had it entered the era of the shopping center; the era was held to have reached its peak, which may have been the overstatement of the year. Projections of that kind lent themselves to the opposite sort of error as well, another group of experts predicting in 1974 that Greater São Paulo (the state capital plus adjoining bedroom communities, industrial suburbs, and other satellites) might one day have "as many as 15 *shoppings*." By 2012, there were fifty-seven in the state capital alone, the jewel in the crown remaining Shopping Center Iguatemi, which by 1985 ranked fourteenth among shopping centers worldwide in profitability per square meter. There seems little likelihood of either the mushrooming of shopping malls or the megaprofits of Iguatemi ending anytime soon. What has vanished is the sense of the shopping center—*o shopping*—being American, or being exotic at all. In the absence of that understanding, Iguatemi became the trademark and standard for malls across the country.[28]

———

Accompanying the long fastening of a national culture of consumer capitalism upon Brazil's once-archipelagic regions has been a progressive winnowing of the imagination. Intellectuals who once nodded along with critiques emphasizing the inequity, irrationality, and misplaced priorities of the emerging order now see it as providing "greater freedom of movement, and of choice" and "helping to modernize the culture of our cities." Politicians with roots in social movements that sought to steel their members against "consumerism" now embrace it. To be sure, there is plenty of room for hybridity, resignification, dissent, indifference, and even dropping out, as well as for the fostering of new varieties of identity and community, particularly on the part of young people, but the same is true of the consumer capitalism of the contemporary United States. Gone from either country is the sense of there being anything beyond consumption, apprehended even by the most conventional of North American social scientists of midcentury.[29]

There will be something, though its definitive shape lies beyond the historian's ken. That this is the case means we may once more turn to creative work enabled by Brazilian consumer capitalism and inspired by earlier, antagonistic traditions. Amid the darkest years of her country's modern history, Julieta de Godoy Ladeira took as consolation and augury four lines composed by the great Carlos Drummond de Andrade near the nadir of the twentieth-century world.

> A injustiça não se resolve.
> À sombra do mundo errado
> murmuraste um protesto tímido.
> Mas virão outros.[30]

Notes

NBL-CPD	Nestlé Brasil Ltda., Centro de Pesquisa e Documentação, São Paulo
RAC-IBECA	Rockefeller Archive Center, International Basic Economy Corporation Archives, Sleepy Hollow, New York
RG59	Record Group 59, General Records of the Department of State, U.S. National Archives and Records Administration, College Park, Maryland
RG151	Record Group 151, Records of the Bureau of Foreign and Domestic Commerce, U.S. National Archives and Records Administration, College Park, Maryland
RG229	Record Group 229, Records of the Office of Inter-American Affairs, U.S. National Archives and Records Administration, College Park, Maryland
RJAP	Robert J. Alexander Papers (microfilm collection)
RRCAR	Records Relating to Commercial Attache's Reports
SMMC	Staff Meeting Minutes Collection
TDGC	Transcrição de Depoimentos a Glauco Carneiro
UFF	Universidade Federal Fluminense
UNICAMP	Universidade Estadual de Campinas
USP	Universidade de São Paulo

Chapter One

1. Late in Gilberto Freyre's life, the "Da outra America" series was collected in *Tempo de aprendiz: Artigos publicados em jornais na adolescência e na primeira mocidade do autor, 1918–1926*, 2 vols., ed. José Antônio Gonsalves de Mello (São Paulo, 1979). For republication elsewhere in Brazil, e.g., "Da outra America," *A Manhã* (Salvador), 10 June 1920, p. 1; "Uma correspondencia dos Estados Unidos," *A Razão*, 3 May 1920, p. 8.

2. Gilberto Freyre, "Da outra America," *Diario de Pernambuco*, 20 February 1921, p. 3 ("to . . ."); Freyre, "Da outra America," *Diario de Pernambuco*, 24 July 1921, p. 3 ("New York . . ."); Freyre, "Da outra America," *Diario de Pernambuco*, 1 September 1918, p. 2 ("Folks . . ." and "delicious . . ." [dated July 1918]); Freyre, "Da outra America," *Diario de Pernambuco*, 4 May 1919, p. 1 ("Each . . .").

3. Gilberto Freyre, "Da outra America," *Diario de Pernambuco*, 9 February 1919, p. 1; Freyre, "Da outra America," *Diario de Pernambuco*, 29 January 1922, p. 3 (quoted).

4. Gilberto Freyre, "Da outra America," *Diario de Pernambuco*, 13 February 1921, p. 3; Freyre, "Da outra America," *Diario de Pernambuco*, 12 February 1922, p. 3; Freyre, "Da outra America," *Diario de Pernambuco*, 30 July 1922, p. 3 (inc. "What . . . ," in English). Some of these features were already visible in the presses of Rio and São Paulo, but Freyre, a self-described "provincial . . . in the greatest of cities," had no direct experience of Brazil's southeast, his contrast between the "intellectual prostitution" of North American newspapers and their Brazilian counterparts overdrawn even at the time. See chapter 2; "provincial . . ." from Freyre, "Da outra America" (20 February 1921); "intellectual . . ." from Freyre, "Da outra America" (30 July 1922).

5. The first editions of the three volumes of Freyre's trilogy are *Casa-grande & senzala: Formação da familia brasileira sob o regimen de economia patriarchal* (Rio de Janeiro, 1933); *Sobrados e mucambos: Decadencia do patriarchado rural no Brasil* (São

Paulo, 1936); *Ordem e progresso: Processo de desintegração das sociedades patriarcal e semipatriarcal no Brasil sob o regime de trabalho livre; Aspectos de um quase meio século de transição do trabalho escravo para o trabalho livre; E da monarquia para a república* (Rio de Janeiro, 1959). Translations abound; in English, we have *The Masters and the Slaves: A Study in the Development of Brazilian Civilization*, trans. Samuel Putnam (New York, 1946); *The Mansions and the Shanties: The Making of Modern Brazil*, trans. Harriet de Onís (New York, 1963); and *Order and Progress: Brazil from Monarchy to Republic*, trans. Rod Horton (New York, 1970), respectively, as well as *New World in the Tropics: The Culture of Modern Brazil* (New York, 1959), referenced above.

6. Peter Burke and Maria Lúcia Pallares-Burke, *Gilberto Freyre: Social Theory in the Tropics* (Oxford, 2008), 209; Angela de Castro Gomes, ed., *Em família: A correspondência de Oliveira Lima e Gilberto Freyre* (Campinas, 2005), 113 ("American . . ."). Legacies of slavery and the influence of new standards of hierarchy and exclusion in the making of Brazilian consumer capitalism emerge periodically in the pages that follow, but they do not receive the sustained attention they deserve. Such consideration would necessarily extend over several additional volumes.

7. "Appoints Trade Consuls," *New York Times*, 27 September 1914, p. 14.

8. Leo Pasvolsky, "The World Depends on America," *Nation's Business*, April 1931, p. 138.

9. The phrase "making way for modernity" is from Roland Marchand's *Advertising the American Dream: Making Way for Modernity, 1920–1940* (Berkeley, Calif., 1985).

10. The major historiographical markers for this section's brief overview of Brazilian history, c. 1900–1980s, are laid down in the bibliographical essay that follows the notes.

11. E.g., *O Estado de S. Paulo*, 15 February 1929, p. 4 (quoted).

12. Carl von Koseritz, *Imagens do Brasil*, trans. Afonso Arinos de Mello Franco (São Paulo, 1943), 27–28; Alberto Ribeiro Lamego, *O homem e a Guanabara* (Rio de Janeiro, 1948), 226–243 (quote on 230); Luiz Edmundo, *O Rio de Janeiro do meu tempo*, 2nd ed., 5 vols. (Rio de Janeiro, 1957 [1938]), 1:66–67.

13. Nevin Winter, *Brazil and Her People of To-Day* (Boston, 1910), 52; Clayton Sedgwick Cooper, *The Brazilians and Their Country* (New York, 1917), 276–277.

14. Paul Walle, *Au Brésil, de l'Uruguay au Rio São Francisco* (Paris, n.d.), 152; Alfredo Moreira Pinto, *A cidade de S. Paulo em 1900* (Rio de Janeiro, 1900), 224–225; Mappin advertisement, *O Estado de S. Paulo*, 31 December 1913, p. 3; Manoel de Sousa Pinto, *Terra moça: Impressões brasileiras* (Porto, 1910), 336; Maria Claudia Bonadio, *Moda e sociabilidade: Mulheres e consumo na São Paulo dos anos 1920* (São Paulo, 2007), 74, 103–107; Jorge Americano, *São Paulo naquele tempo, 1895–1915* (São Paulo, 1957), 408.

15. Americano, *São Paulo*, 331.

16. Americano, *São Paulo*, 110–122; D. Brites (b. 1903), in Ecléa Bosi, *Memória e sociedade: Lembranças de velhos* (São Paulo, 1979), 235 ("Oven-roasted potato!"; "Pushbrooms, dustbrooms!"; "But what a beautiful tomato from my farm!"); José Maria Bello, *Memórias* (Rio de Janeiro, 1958), 45–47, 74; Patricia Acerbi, *Street Occupations: Urban Vending in Rio de Janeiro, 1850–1925* (Austin, Tex., 2017), esp. chap. 6.

17. William Guitteau and Nevin Winter, *Seeing South America* (Evanston, Ill., 1929), 85.

18. Roseli Boschilia, *A Rua 15 e o comércio no início do século* (Curitiba, 1996), 45–46; *Belo Horizonte & o comércio: 100 anos de história* (Belo Horizonte, 1997), 69, 72–73.

19. Cyro dos Anjos, *Explorações no tempo* (Rio de Janeiro, 1963), 78; Milton de Souza Carvalho, *História de um comerciante* (Rio de Janeiro, 1955), 24.

20. Nelson Palma Travassos, *No meu tempo de mocinho* (São Paulo, 1961), 225–229 (quotes on 225–226); João Carlos Tedesco, *De olho na balança! Comerciantes coloniais do Rio Grande do Sul na primeira metade do século XX* (Passo Fundo, 2008), 31–40; Limeira Tejo, *Retrato sincero do Brasil* (Rio de Janeiro, 1950), 146.

21. Arthur Ramos, *Introdução à antropologia brasileira*, 2 vols. (Rio de Janeiro, 1943–1947), 2:153; Mappin advertisement, *O Estado de S. Paulo*, 23 November 1924, p. 11.

22. Francisco Lagreca, *Porque não me ufano do meu paiz* (São Paulo, 1919), 158–159, 161.

23. Minutes of Representatives' Meeting, 20 August 1929, JWTA, SMMC, box 2; Jacob Eisenger, "Brazil: Challenge and Opportunity," *Commerce and Finance*, February 1939, p. 15.

24. "A casa de Mme. Rosenwald [*sic*]," *Gazeta de Noticias*, 12 October 1905, p. 2; "25 anos de glorias no Brasil," *Diario de Noticias*, 14 May 1940, sec. 2, p. 8; "Chegou hontem dos E. Unidos, o sr. Alberto Rosenvald," *A Manhã*, 9 February 1929, p. 5; "A nova directoria da Associação Commercial," *Folha da Manhã*, 31 May 1932, p. 2; "Necrologia," *Folha da Manhã*, 22 May 1948, sec. 1, p. 5; Companhia Paulista de Automóveis announcement, *Folha da Manhã*, 7 March 1948, sec. 4, p. 9; "Cinema," *Folha da Manhã*, 3 May 1931, p. 12 ("very . . ."); Alberto Rosenvald, "American Film Power," *Brazilian Business*, June 1922, pp. 24–25.

Chapter Two

1. "Steamer Notes," *Brazilian American*, 15 July 1922, pp. 32–33. Slightly different versions of the travel tale are in James Mooney, "Making the World Move Faster," *Nation's Business*, December 1928, pp. 21–22, 98, 100–102; Mooney, "The Automobile Remodeling Life," *New York Times*, 3 March 1929, XX14. For a capsule version, Mooney and Clarence Foss, "Economic Requirements of Automotive Road Vehicles Abroad" (paper presented to Society of Automotive Engineers Annual Meeting, Detroit, January 1929), while Argentine and Mato Grossense variations appear alongside one another in Mooney, "Man Yielding to Motor Influence," *New York Times*, 19 February 1928, XX13.

2. "Mooney Elected Director of General Motors," *Wall Street Journal*, 10 November 1923, p. 4; William Monaghan, "The Export Genius behind General Motors," *Forbes*, 15 August 1928, pp. 19–21; R. L. Duffus, "The Rise of a Billion-Dollar Corporation," *New York Times*, 18 November 1928, XX4 (quoted); B. C. Forbes, "How America's Biggest Export Job Is Handled," *Forbes*, 15 May 1929, pp. 13–16, 46, 48.

3. Ed Cray, *Chrome Colossus: General Motors and Its Times* (New York, 1980), 236, 250; "Net Profits of General Motors Double Fords for 1926," *News Bulletin*, May 1927, p. 20, JWTA; Duffus, "Rise."

4. That Mooney's visit was "the first time in history that an executive of the General Motors [Corporation] has ever visited a foreign country" is noted in "Mr. McReyn-

olds and Good Roads," *Brazilian American*, 4 July 1922, unpag., and "Steamer Notes," *Brazilian American*, 15 July 1922, p. 32. Canada did not count as a "foreign country" as far as U.S. automakers were concerned.

5. A. Fabian, "Automobile Trade Digest," *Brazilian Business*, September 1923, p. 37.

6. William C. Downs, "Automobiles in Rio de Janeiro," Report No. 101, Rio de Janeiro, 19 September 1916, RG151, RRCAR, box 54.

7. E. M. Van Voorhees, "Highways: Their Fundamental Importance to Brazil," *Paulista*, no. 1, 3rd quarter, 1930, p. 13.

8. A. Ogden Pierrot, "First Semester 1930 Automotive Survey," Rio de Janeiro, 31 July 1930, RG151, RRCAR, box 55; Pierrot, [document missing title page], Rio de Janeiro, 10 January 1929, RG151, RRCAR, box 54.

9. "World Automobile Statistics," *Brazilian Business*, July 1923, p. 13; Mooney and Foss, "Economic Requirements," appendix; David S. Green, "Automotive Market Trends in São Paulo," *Paulista*, no. 2, 1st quarter, 1931, p. 10.

10. Mira Wilkins and Frank Ernest Hill, *American Business Abroad: Ford on Six Continents* (Detroit, 1964), 93–95; J. P. Urner, "Recent Construction in São Paulo to House American Industries," *Paulista*, no. 1, 1st quarter, 1930, p. 12 ("modern . . ."); "Kristian Orberg, Reminiscences," FHA-BFRC, Accession 880, box 2 ("had . . ."); untitled enclosure to FSD 389, "Brazilian Automotive Industry," Rio de Janeiro, 18 September 1953, RG59, 832.3331/9-1853.

11. Wilkins and Hill, *American Business*, 147; "Brazil's First Automobile Show," *Brazilian Business*, September 1925, p. 18; A. Gaulin, "Automotive Exposition in Rio de Janeiro," Rio de Janeiro, 5 August 1925," and enclosed copy of exposition program, RG59, 832.6071/-[*sic*].

12. Richard Downes, "Autos over Rails: How US Business Supplanted the British in Brazil, 1910–1928," *Journal of Latin American Studies* 24, no. 3 (October 1992): 572 (quoted); Herndon W. Goforth to Secretary of State, São Paulo, 30 September 1926, and attachment, RG59, 832.154/73.

13. Cray, *Chrome Colossus*, 236 (quoted).

14. Untitled enclosure to FSD 389; Richard P. Butrick to Secretary of State, FSD 238, "U.S. Investment in São Paulo," São Paulo, 3 April 1957, RG59, 811.05132/4-357; Ademir Medici, *Migração e urbanização: A presence de São Caetano na região do ABC* (São Paulo, 1993), 269; David S. Green to Griffith Evans, São Paulo, 15 September 1931, RG151, RRCAR, box 57 ("model . . ."); "Outstanding American Industries, Utilities or Investment Groups Operating in the Country," 2 June 1930, enclosure to George S. Messersmith to Secretary of State, Buenos Aires, 5 June 1930, RG59, 632.111/1 ("one . . ." and "carry . . .").

15. *Brazilian-American*, 29 June 1929, p. 7.

16. Orígenes Lessa, "Em 1935 minha primeira grande promoção," *Propaganda*, June 1979, pp. 21–22; Fernando Teixeira Orlandi, quoted in Fernando Reis, "São Paulo e Rio: A longa caminhada," in *HPB*, 307–308; Rodolfo Lima Martensen, "O ensino da propaganda no Brasil," *O Estado de S. Paulo*, 20 December 1975, sec. "Suplemento do Centenário," 4.

17. Quasi-anonymous GM advertisement, *O Estado de S. Paulo*, 10 December 1926, p. 1; GM advertisement, *O Estado de S. Paulo*, 11 December 1926, p. 1; "Exposição de automoveis," *O Estado de S. Paulo*, 11 December 1926, p. 7; *General Motors do Brasil: 70*

anos de história (São Paulo, 1995), 24–26; "Exposição de automoveis," *Folha da Manhã*, 11 December 1926, p. 5.

18. "Grande Circo Chevrolet," in *General Motors do Brasil*, 23.

19. Ford advertisement, *O Estado de S. Paulo*, 10 December 1926, p. 3; Afranio Estevão Corrêa, *Os automóveis de Cuiabá, décadas de 20 e 30* (Rio de Janeiro, 1999), 83 (quoted); Manoel Julião Netto, *Do "cabeça de cavalo" ao "rabo de peixe"* (São Paulo, 1970), 140, 147–148.

20. "Mr. Sloan Looks across the Seas," *Printers' Ink*, 20 February 1930, p. 158; A. W. Childs, "Proposed Establishment of New Assembly Plant in Rio de Janeiro," Rio de Janeiro, 27 July 1935, RG151, RRCAR, box 65; Ralph H. Ackerman, "Economic Survey for 1935," Rio de Janeiro, 23 December 1935, RG151, RRCAR, box 65; Childs, "Automotive Survey for 4th Quarter of 1935," Rio de Janeiro, 4 February 1936, RG151, RRCAR, box 66; J. Winsor Ives, "Machinery for Tire Factory Being Installed," Rio de Janeiro, 14 February 1935, RG151, RRCAR, box 65; Ives, "American Concern to Undertake Merchandising of Tires through Filling Stations in Brazil," Rio de Janeiro, 22 March 1935, RG151, RRCAR, box 65; Childs, "Inauguration of New Rubber Plant," Rio de Janeiro, 10 March 1936, RG151, RRCAR, box 66.

21. Julião Netto, *Do "cabeça de cavalo"*, 155; A. W. Childs, "Dirigible 'Hindenberg,'" Rio de Janeiro, 3 April 1936, RG151, RRCAR, box 66; Childs, "Automotive Market Survey for First Half of 1935," Rio de Janeiro, 29 July 1935, RG151, RRCAR, box 65.

22. "Need of Automobile Financing Corporation in Brazil," *Brazilian Business*, March 1926, pp. 2–4; O. Ogden Pierrot, "Financing Auto Sales in Brazil," *Brazilian Business*, October 1929, pp. 27–28; DuWayne C. Clark, "Conditions in the Automotive Trade during the Fourth Quarter of 1934," Rio de Janeiro, 22 January 1935, RG151, RRCAR, box 65; Childs, "Automotive Survey for 4th Quarter of 1935."

23. Childs, "Automotive Survey for 4th Quarter of 1935"; Ralph H. Ackerman, "Economic Survey for 1936," Rio de Janeiro, 7 January 1937, RG151, RRCAR, box 68; Childs, "Automotive Vehicle Operation in Brazil," Rio de Janeiro, 6 January 1937, RG151, RRCAR, box 68; Childs, "Automotive Market Survey for Fourth Quarter of 1936," Rio de Janeiro, 22 January 1937, RG151, RRCAR, box 68; Childs, "Automotive Survey for the First Half of 1937," Rio de Janeiro, 23 July 1937, RG151, RRCAR, box 69; "Vias de comunicação," *O Observador Econômico e Financeiro*, July 1940, p. 140.

24. Minutes of Representatives' Meeting, 20 August 1929, JWTA, SMMC, box 2.

25. Rudolf E. Cahn, "Brazilian Publications," Rio de Janeiro, 17 August 1931, RG59, 832.91/3; Mario Carelli, *Carcamanos e comendadores: Os italianos de São Paulo da realidade à ficção, 1919–1930*, trans. Ligia Maria Pondé Vassallo (São Paulo, 1985), 62; JWTCB, "Investigation Made for Blue Star Line," São Paulo, 1931, JWTA, mr-223; David S. Green to Specialties Division, São Paulo, 5 April 1932, and attachment, "Advertising Media in Brazil," RG151, RRCAR, box 59.

26. Fernando Morais, *Chatô: O rei do Brasil* (São Paulo, 1994), 140–203 (quotes on 143, 187); Nelson Werneck Sodré, *Memórias de um escritor* (Rio de Janeiro, 1970), 48; *HPB*, 5, 214, 219, 269.

27. For a firsthand account, see Cunha Motta, *Os rapazes da imprensa* (São Paulo, 1990).

28. Reginal Gorham, "Advertising in Brazil," *Export Trade and Finance*, 28 September 1929, p. 12.

29. Gaulin, "Automotive Exposition," and enclosure.

30. Gaulin, "Automotive Exposition," and enclosure; Carlos Eduardo Leal and Sérgio Montalvão, "*O Globo*," in *DHBB*, 3:2540 ("popular," "to . . ."); advertisement for Moses's law practice, *Brazilian-American*, 22 July 1922, p. 47.

31. Morais, *Chatô*, quote on 143; Foreign Service Report No. 35, Rio de Janeiro, 4 June 1925, RG59, 832.911/11; Eileen Mackenzie, "Front-Page Fireball," *Inter-American*, June 1946, p. 23.

32. Association of National Advertisers, *Advertising and Merchandising in Brazil: Material Gathered by Harold McD. Brown, Corona Typewriter Company, for the Export Committee* (New York, 1921); Nathaniel P. Davis, "The Pernambuco Automobile Show and Good Roads Congress," Recife, 11 February 1926, RG59, 832.154/67; Ralph H. Ackerman to Brooke, Smith & French, "Automotive Advertising—Brazil," Rio de Janeiro, 6 January 1937, RG151, GR1914, box 2249.

33. Paul T. Cherington, "Are American Manufacturers Foolish Exporters?," *News Bulletin*, December 1922, pp. 11–15, JWTA; Cherington, "Some Lessons from Early New England Foreign Trading," *News Bulletin*, June 1923, pp. 11–15, JWTA; James L. Hutchinson, "Brass Tacks in Foreign Trade," *News Bulletin*, February 1923, pp. 9–11 (quoted), JWTA.

34. Russell Pierce, *Gringo-Gaucho: An Advertising Odyssey* (Ashland, Oreg., 1991), 20–21; "Conversation with Ken Hinks, 1/8/64," JWTA, Sidney Ralph Bernstein Company History Files, box 9.

35. "Greetings from Brazil," *News Letter*, 1 August 1929, p. 3, JWTA; Minutes of Representatives' Meetings, 20 August and 10 September 1929, JWTA, SMMC, box 2; "Off for São Paulo," *News Letter*, 15 September 1929, p. 4, JWTA; transcripts of interviews with Henry Flower, by Colin Dawkins, 20 July 1979 and 16 October 1979, JWTA, CDP, box 16; Harry W. Gordon, "JWTeers View Revolution in Streets of Sao Paulo," *J.W.T. News*, December 1930, p. 4, JWTA; Jackson Lears, *Fables of Abundance: A Cultural History of Advertising in America* (New York, 1994), 154.

36. "Deus lhe pague," *Propaganda*, June 1979, pp. 18, 20; J. Maxwell Kennard, "See How We've Grown in South America!," *News Letter*, 15 September 1929, p. 3 (quoted), JWTA.

37. Martensen, "Ensino," 4; "Augusto de Angelo," *J. Walter Thompson News*, May 1983, p. 10, JWTA.

38. Kennard, "See How We've Grown," 4; "Rio de Janeiro—Brazil" and "São Paulo—Brazil" (charts), JWTA, EGWP, box 76.

39. Harry Gordon, "How Much Should I Spend for Advertising in Brazil?," *Brazilian Business*, May 1931, p. 14; JWTCB advertisement, *Paulista*, no. 2, 1st quarter, 1931, back cover.

40. Minutes of Representatives' Meeting, 27 December 1927, JWTA, SMMC, box 1; JWTCB, "Investigation of the Face Cream Market in Brazil," São Paulo, July 1934, JWTA, mr-223. The milreis (one thousand reis, usually written 1$000) was the standard monetary unit in Brazil until 1942, during which time the conto (one thousand milreis, usually written 1:000$000) was the largest such unit and the tostão (one hundred reis, $100) the smallest.

41. Origenes [*sic*] Lessa, "Propaganda brasileira," *Propaganda*, January–February 1938, p. 2; "Homens de propaganda," *Propaganda*, December 1937, p. 22; H. B. Barton, "No Dynamite in Sao Paulo," *J.W.T. News*, March 1930, p. 7, JWTA.

42. Minutes of Representatives' Meeting, 20 August 1929, JWTA, SMCC, box 2; J. Walter Thompson Company, "International Advertising," New York, 1935, JWTA, mr-257; Colin Dawkins, memorandum on conversations with Samuel W. Meek, 5 May 1980, JWTA, CDP, box 15; Henry Flower, interview by Colin Dawkins, Greenwich, Conn., 20 July 1979, JWTA, CDP, box 16.

43. Kennard, "See How We've Grown," 3–4; Gordon, "How Much," 14.

44. JWTCB, "Investigation for Lehn & Fink," May 1931, JWTA, mr-223.

45. Carroll L. Wilson, "The International Operations of the J. Walter Thompson Company," 15 December 1945, JWTA, Samuel Williams Meek Papers, box 4; "Policies Regarding Repetition of Advertisements," 6 April 1931, JWTA, James Webb Young Papers, box 1; Chevrolet advertisement, *O Estado de S. Paulo*, 22 July 1934, p. 3; Chevrolet advertisement, *O Estado de S. Paulo*, 28 April 1935, p. 7; Brahma advertisement, *O Estado de S. Paulo*, 2 December 1934, p. 15; Blue Star Line advertisement, *O Estado de S. Paulo*, 12 January 1930, p. 2; Opel advertisement, *O Estado de S. Paulo*, 30 August 1933, p. 8.

46. Ralph Hower, *The History of An Advertising Agency: N. W. Ayer & Son at Work, 1869–1949* (Cambridge, Mass., 1949), 142–143; K. Orberg to B. R. Donaldson, São Paulo, 23 October 1940, FHA-BFRC, Accession 1394, box 2; Reis, "São Paulo e Rio," 318; Lessa, "Propaganda brasileira," 2 ("The best . . ." and "living"); Lessa, "Em 1935," 22 ("teacher . . ."); Martensen, "Ensino," 4 ("legendary . . .").

47. Martensen, "Ensino," 4 ("the most . . . ," "finishing . . ." and "'diplomas' . . ."); Renato Castelo Branco, *Tomei um Ita no norte: Memórias* (São Paulo, 1981), 170–171 ("gripped . . .").

48. Reis, "São Paulo e Rio," 319; Orberg to Donaldson, 23 October 1940.

49. "Homens de propaganda," *Propaganda*, September 1938, p. 11 ("the largest . . ."); N. W. Ayer and Son, "Sinopse da investigação e análise do mercado nacional de café," *DNC: Revista do Departamento Nacional do Café*, May 1934, pp. 563–671 (quotes on 565); I. D. Carson, "Advertising and the Brazilian Market," *Brazil*, March 1935, p. 9.

50. H. Braunstein to B. R. Donaldson, Rio de Janeiro, 23 October 1940, FHA-BFRC, Accession 1394, box 2 ("N. W. . . ."); Orberg to Donaldson, 23 October 1940 (remaining quotes).

51. Reis, "São Paulo e Rio," 319; Castelo Branco, *Tomei*, 170; Stephen Fox, *The Mirror Makers: A History of American Advertising and Its Creators* (New York, 1984), 174 ("natives"); Genival Rabelo, *Os tempos heróicos da propaganda* (Rio de Janeiro, 1956), 54.

52. U.S. Department of Commerce, *Advertising in Brazil* (Washington, D.C., 1937), 1 ("the gradual . . . ," "Although . . . ," and "American . . ."); Carson, "Advertising," 15 (remaining quotes).

53. Herbert Hoover, *The Memoirs of Herbert Hoover*, vol. 1, *Years of Adventure, 1874–1920* (New York, 1951), chaps. 5–8; Craig Lloyd, *Aggressive Introvert: Herbert Hoover and Public Relations Management, 1912–1932* (Columbus, 1973), esp. 45 ("to . . ."), 51 (coordination with JWT and Hollywood); William Leuchtenberg, *Herbert Hoover* (New York, 2009), 56 ("man . . .").

54. Herbert Hoover, *The Memoirs of Herbert Hoover*, vol. 2, *The Cabinet and the Presidency, 1920–1933* (New York, 1952), 79; William Leach, *Land of Desire: Merchants, Power, and the Rise of a New American Culture* (New York, 1993), 359.

55. Hoover, *Memoirs*, 2:79; Julius Klein, "Aspects of International Advertising," *Printers' Ink*, 4 June 1931, p. 33; Klein, "Fundamental Bases of Our Prosperity," *New York Times*, 15 December 1929, XX20.

56. Leach, *Land of Desire*, 361–362; Robert Neal Seidel, "Progressive Pan Americanism: Development and United States Policy toward South America, 1906–1931" (PhD diss., Cornell University, 1973), 140, 151–187. Quotes: "The New Pan-Americanism" (transcript of "A radio talk by Dr. Julius Klein . . . November 24, 1928 . . .") and "American Motorizing Mankind" (transcript of "A radio talk . . . July 21, 1928 . . ."), Hoover Institution, Julius Klein Papers.

57. Quotes: Isaac Marcosson, *Caravans of Commerce* (New York, 1926), 56–57. Consular offices: U.S. Department of Commerce, *Selling in Brazil* (Washington, D.C., 1925), 36.

58. Harry Collings, "United States Government Aid to Foreign Trade," *Annals of the American Academy of Political and Social Science* 127 (September 1926): 134–142 (quotes on 136).

59. J. R. McKey to W. L. Schurz, Washington, D.C., 11 May 1923, RG151, RRCAR, box 54.

60. U.S. Department of Commerce, *Annual Report of the Director of the Bureau of Foreign and Domestic Commerce . . . for the Fiscal Year Ended June 30, 1922* (Washington, D.C., 1922), 82; U.S. Department of Commerce, *Annual Report of the Director . . . for the Fiscal Year Ended June 30, 1923* (Washington, D.C., 1923), 123–125.

61. Julius Klein to William L. Schurz, Washington, D.C., 2 April 1923, RG151, RRCAR, box 54; Department of Commerce, *Annual Report . . . 1923*, 124; W. E. Embry to Director, São Paulo, 22 July 1925, RG151, RRCAR, box 54.

62. Randolph P. Butler to Director, São Paulo, 26 June 1931; David S. Green to American Association of Advertising Agencies, São Paulo, 29 July 1931; Green to Player-Tone Talking Machine Co., São Paulo, 14 December 1931; Butler to Automotive Division, São Paulo, 27 October 1931; Green to Specialties Division, São Paulo, 2 November 1931. Copies of all these letters are filed in RG151, RRCAR, box 57. For "Outstanding . . .": Walter J. Donnelly, "Annual Administrative Report for Fiscal Year 1937–38," Rio de Janeiro, 16 July 1938, RG151, RRCAR, box 71.

63. Some Bureau records on U.S. participation in the Centennial Exposition are in RG151, GR1914, boxes 2902–2903; quote from "U.S. Participation at the Centennial Exposition," *Brazilian Business*, September 1923, p. 80 (mislabeled 78).

64. Embry to Director, 22 July 1925.

65. David S. Green to the Automotive Division, São Paulo, 6 July 1931, RG151, RRCAR, box 57; Green, Weekly Report No. 23, São Paulo, 24 February 1932, RG151, RRCAR, box 60.

66. Ralph H. Ackerman, "Annual Administrative Report for the Fiscal Year-37," Rio de Janeiro, 13 July 1937, RG151, RRCAR, box 69.

67. "The American Chamber of Commerce for Brazil," *Nation's Business*, July 1916, p. 18.

68. Telegram, Gottschalk to Secretary of State, Rio de Janeiro, 29 May 1915 (date of receipt), RG59, 632.11171/2; "The American Chamber of Commerce for Brazil," *Nation's Business*, July 1916, p. 18; Gottschalk to Secretary of State, Rio de Janeiro, 26 June 1915, RG59, 632.11171/4 (inc. "as its . . ."); A. Gaulin, "American Chambers of Commerce Abroad," Rio de Janeiro, 24 February 1922, RG59, 632.11171/33 (other quotes).

69. J. E. Philippi to Director, Rio de Janeiro, 18 July 1919, RG151, RRCAR, box 54; E. M. Lawton, "American Chamber of Commerce in São Paulo," São Paulo, 14 March 1922, RG59, 632.11171/35.

70. Lawton, "American Chamber"; Earl Richard Downes, "The Seeds of Influence: Brazil's 'Essentially Agricultural' Old Republic and the United States, 1910–1930" (PhD diss., University of Texas, 1986), 408–410; *Paulista*, nos. 1 and 2 (3rd quarter, 1930, and 1st quarter, 1931); J. E. Philippi, "Business Methods in Brazil," *Brazilian Business*, September 1923, p. 4.

71. Harry B. Robertson, "The Power of Publicity," *Brazilian Business*, April 1921, pp. 13–16; "Eliminate the Wastes in Business," *Brazilian Business*, June 1925, p. 8; Julius Klein, "The Coming Trade Conflict in Latin America," *Brazilian Business*, May 1926, pp. 11–13; Klein, "The Economy of Knowledge in Business," *Brazilian Business*, March 1927, p. 6.

72. Julius Klein, "Economic Rivalries in Latin America," *Foreign Affairs* 3, no. 2 (15 December 1924): 241; James Matthews, "Credit Conditions in South American Countries," *Journal of Accountancy* 22, no. 6 (December 1916): 445; James Collins, *Straight Business in South America* (New York, 1920), 58–60, 95, 123–124; Frank O'Malley, *Our South American Trade and Its Financing* (New York, 1920), esp. 7, 8–10; Elmer Murphey, "The Way to Sell in Brazil," *System* (Chicago), November 1924, pp. 588–591, 644 (esp. 589); George Wythe, "Brazil's Recent Foreign Economic Policy" (PhD diss., George Washington University, 1938), 39; "Noyes Gives Views on Brazil Trade," *New York Times*, 5 March 1933, RE2.

73. Ducan McDowall, *The Light: Brazilian Traction, Light and Power Company Limited, 1899–1945* (Toronto, 1988), 225 ("nourished . . . ," in which "North American" refers to "promotion and technical expertise" from the United States and Canada); Ulysses Keener, "Hydroelectric Development in the State of São Paulo," *Paulista*, no. 1, 3rd quarter, 1930, pp. 15–16.

74. McDowall, *Light*, 260 (quoting Asa Billings); C. R. Cameron, "Bond and Share Activities in Paraná and São Paulo," São Paulo, 8 October 1930, RG59, 832.6463[-]Electric Bond and Share Co./3; Elias Chaves Neto, *Minha vida e as lutas de meu tempo* (São Paulo, 1978), 50; J. Winsor Ives, "Statistics Show Steady Growth in Consumption of Electrical Energy in Brazil's Two Leading Cities," Rio de Janeiro, 8 October 1936, RG151, RRCAR, box 67. The increase reflected in these statistics includes industrial, commercial, government, and household consumption of electricity.

75. Keener, "Hydroelectric Development," 16; Harvey Sheahan, "Industrialization versus Imports," Rio de Janeiro, 2 December 1932, RG151, RRCAR, box 59; Chaves Neto, *Minha vida*, 50.

76. David S. Green to H. E. Demarais, São Paulo, 15 January 1931, RG151, RRCAR, box 57; Sheahan, "Industrialization"; "Outstanding American Industries, Utilities or

Investment Groups Operating in the Country," 2 June 1930, enclosure to George S. Messersmith to Secretary of State, Buenos Aires, 5 June 1930, RG59, 632.111/1.

77. Theodore Geiger, *The General Electric Company in Brazil* (New York, 1961), 40, 78, 89–90; Sheahan, "Industrialization"; Rabelo, *Tempos*, 39; Armando de Moraes Sarmento, "As agências estrangeiras trouxeram modernidade, as nacionais aprenderam depressa," in *HPB*, 20–21.

78. Sheahan, "Industrialization"; Sarmento, "Agências," 20; Chaves Neto, *Minha vida*, 50; "Electrical Household Appliances," *Brazilian Business*, November 1926, p. 18; Ralph H. Ackerman, "The Changing Character of American Exports to Brazil," Rio de Janeiro, 13 August 1936, RG151, RRCAR, box 67; "A General Electric no Brasil," *O Observador Econômico e Financeiro*, July 1944, p. 94.

79. Isaac Marcosson, "Brazil in Evolution," *Saturday Evening Post*, 19 September 1925, p. 209 ("carrying . . .").

80. M. A. Cremer, "Status of Broadcasting and Markets for Radio Receiving Apparatus—Brazil," Rio de Janeiro, 1 April 1924, enclosure to R. A. Lundquist, Special Circular no. 210, Washington, D.C., 1 May 1924, RG151, GR1914, box 2477.

81. David S. Green, "The Radio Market in São Paulo," *Paulista*, no. 1, 3rd quarter of 1930, pp. 7–8.

82. Sheahan, "Industrialization"; J. Winsor Ives, "Radio Market Series—Brazil, Part II," Rio de Janeiro, 19 March 1936, RG151, RRCAR, box 66.

83. Ackerman, "Changing."

84. J. Winsor Ives, "Radio Market Series," Rio de Janeiro, 19 October 1937, RG151, RRCAR, box 69; A. W. Childs, "Economic Review for December," Rio de Janeiro, 15 December 1939, RG151, RRCAR, box 73 ("notable . . ."); Childs, "Economic Review for November," Rio de Janeiro, 17 November 1939, RG151, RRCAR, box 73 ("an . . ."); Ives, "Radio Broadcasting Stations in Brazil," Rio de Janeiro, 26 December 1939, RG151, RRCAR, box 73.

85. Cremer, "Status"; Antonio Pedro Tota, *A locomotiva no ar: Rádio e modernidade em São Paulo, 1924–1934* (São Paulo, 1990); J. Winsor Ives, "Radio Market Series—Brazil, Part I," Rio de Janeiro, 12 March 1936, RG151, RRCAR, box 66; Ives, "Radio Market Series" (19 October 1937). Byington: David S. Green to Machinery Division, São Paulo, 9 July 1931, RG151, RRCAR, box 57; Green to J. H. Smiley, São Paulo, 20 May 1932, RG151, RRCAR, box 59; British Chamber of Commerce of São Paulo and Southern Brazil, *Personalidades no Brasil/Men of Affairs in Brazil* (São Paulo, n.d.), 142.

86. Sheahan, "Industrialization"; J. Winsor Ives, "Short Wave Radio Reception in Brazil," Rio de Janeiro, 31 July 1937, RG151, RRCAR, box 69; Ives, "Radio Market Series" (19 October 1937); Rodolfo Lima Martensen, *O desafio de quatro santos: Memórias* (São Paulo, 1983), pt. 3; Bryan McCann, *Hello, Hello Brazil: Popular Music in the Making of Modern Brazil* (Durham, N.C., 2004), esp. chaps. 1–2; Lia Calabre de Azevedo, "No tempo do rádio: Radiodifusão e cotidiano no Brasil, 1923–1960" (tese de doutorado, UFF, 2002), quoting *O Globo* headline on 203.

87. McCann, *Hello*, 23.

88. Cremer, "Status"; Tota, *Locomotiva*, 54, 58, 84; David S. Green to Neville O'Neill, São Paulo, 17 July 1931, RG151, RRCAR, box 57.

89. U.S. Department of Commerce, *Broadcast Advertising in Latin America* (Washington, D.C., 1931), 8–10. This report mentions an unnamed U.S. automobile manufacturer, which *HPB* (175, 308) suggests was GM.

90. Tota, *Locomotiva*, 129, 131; A. W. Childs, "Brazil," *World Radio Markets*, 20 September 1938, p. 8 ("inclined . . .").

91. Ives, "Radio Market Series" (12 March 1936).

92. Ayer and Son, "Sinopse," 622–625; *HPB*, 178, 319.

93. Azevedo, "No tempo," 144, 147–148; Morais, *Chatô*, esp. 364–369; Glauco Carneiro, *Brasil, primeiro: História dos Diários Associados* (Brasília, 1999), esp. 174–180.

94. Quotes: Martensen, *Desafio*, 200; "Rádio Farroupilha," *O Observador Econômico e Financeiro*, December 1940, p. 65. Gessy: Roberto Simões, "Do pregão ao *jingle*," in *HPB*, 178. Philips: Paulo Cesar Ferreira, *Pilares via satélite: Da Rádio Nacional à Rede Globo* (Rio de Janeiro, 1998), 34. Lever: Martensen, *Desafio*, pt. 3. Nestlé: R. P. Castello Branco, "Os vehiculos que o Bueno esqueceu," *Propaganda*, January–February 1938, p. 6.

95. J. H. Wilson, *Herbert Hoover, Forgotten Progressive* (Boston, 1975), 112–113; Julius Klein, "The Romance of World Radio" (transcript of radio talk, 13 July 1929), Hoover Institution, Julius Klein Papers.

96. Julius Klein, "What Are Motion Pictures Doing for Industry?," *Annals of the American Academy of Political and Social Science* 128 (November 1926): 79; Marcosson, *Caravans*, 126; Leo Pasvolsky, "The World Depends on America," *Nation's Business*, April 1931, p. 49; Edward Lowry, "Trade Follows the Film," *Saturday Evening Post*, 7 November 1925, pp. 12–13.

97. A. de Almeida Prado, *Escolas de ontem e de hoje: Reminiscências e evocações* (São Paulo, 1961), 121–122; Julião Netto, *Do "cabeça de cavalo"*, 39; "A decadencia da importação de fitas francezas e italianas," *O Combate*, 15 September 1921, p. 1.

98. Alberto Rosenvald, "American Film Power," *Brazilian Business*, June 1922, p. 24 ("unloosed . . ."); copy of W. L. Schurz, "Summary of Import Market Condition in Brazil," Rio de Janeiro, 14 November 1922, attachment to Henry H. Morse to "Mr. Ackerman," [Washington, D.C.], 15 December 1922 ("American [films] . . ."), RG151, GR1914, box 1754; E. M. Lawton, "Moving Picture Industry in São Paulo," São Paulo, 5 March 1923 ("American productions . . ."), RG59, 832.4061/8 (misfiled with documents from 1930–1939); statistics based on U.S. Department of Commerce, *Motion Pictures in Argentina and Brazil* (Washington, D.C., 1929), 1.

99. J. Winsor Ives, "The Motion Picture Situation in Brazil," Rio de Janeiro, 22 November 1935, RG151, RRCAR, box 65.

100. William Mellniker, "Tinned Shadows," *Brazilian Business*, December 1931, p. 18; Walter J. Donnelly to Ambassador, Rio de Janeiro, 22 April 1938, RG151, GR1914, box 1305; Alberto Torres Filho to Walter J. Donnelly, Rio de Janeiro, 5 October 1938, RG151, GR1914, box 1305; William C. Burdett to Secretary of State, Rio de Janeiro, 11 September 1939, RG59, 832.4061-MOTION-PICTURES/93.

101. Anibal Machado, *O cinema e sua influencia na vida moderna* (Rio de Janeiro, n.d.), 27, 34; "Barra Funda," *O Combate*, 11 November 1919, p. 3.

102. Ives, "Motion Picture Situation."

103. Castelo Branco, *Tomei*, 39; Martensen, *Desafio*, 45, 50; Samuel Pfromm Neto, *Piracicaba de outros tempos* (Campinas, 2001), 79.

104. Quotes: Jonas da Silva Abreu, "O papel do cinema na construção da identidade da Cinelândia" (tese de mestrado, CPDOC, 2009), 58, 117, except "investigated . . . ," from Henry H. Morse to B. F. Sturevant Company, Washington, D.C., 17 November 1923, RG151, GR1914, box 1305.

105. Anne Merriman Peck, *Roundabout South America* (New York, 1940), 320; Sérgio Cabral, *No tempo de Ari Barroso* (Rio de Janeiro, 1993), 45–46.

106. Ernani Macedo de Carvalho, *Publicidade e propaganda*, 2nd ed. (São Paulo, 1947 [1935]), 66.

107. Department of Commerce, *Motion Pictures*, 6; Green to Specialties Division, 5 April 1932, and attachment, "Advertising Media in Brazil"; Sheila Schvarzman, "Ir ao cinema em São Paulo nos anos 20," *Revista Brasileira de História* 49 (2005): 173n1 ("primarily . . ."), 164 ("A country's . . .").

108. Department of Commerce, *Motion Pictures*, 6; Harvey Sheahan, "Motion Picture Situation, Brazil, 1931," Rio de Janeiro, 4 May 1932, RG151, RRCAR, box 61.

109. A. T. Haeberle to Secretary of State, São Paulo, 20 June 1923, RG59, 832.4061/9 (misfiled with documents from 1930–1939); Sheahan, "Motion Picture Situation."

110. C. J. North to F. L. Hernon, [Washington, D.C.], 5 August 1929, RG151, GR1914, box 1305 ("valuable . . ."); N. D. Golden to São Paulo Office, [Washington, D.C.,] 21 October 1929, RG151, GR1914, box 1649; John Nasht, "Hollywood's Carioca Fans," *Inter-American*, September 1943, p. 30 ("presenting . . .").

111. Henriqueta Chamberlain, *Where the Sabiá Sings* (New York, 1955), 145–146.

112. Manoel Bomfim, "Uncle Sam Film Actor," *Brazilian Business*, April 1922, pp. 22–23.

113. Monteiro Lobato, *A onda verde* (São Paulo, 1921), 42–43; Lobato, *Na antevespera*, 13th ed. (São Paulo, 1969 [1933]), 196–197.

114. Nelson Palma Travassos, *No meu tempo de menino* . . . (São Paulo, 1960), 263–265.

115. Clóvis de Athayde Jorge, *Consolação: Uma reportagem histórica* (São Paulo, n.d.), 170; Castelo Branco, *Tomei*, 164; Lessa, "Propaganda brasileira," 2.

116. "O Rio de Janeiro na república," *O Observador Econômico e Financeiro*, November 1939, p. 49.

117. Machado, *Cinema*, 34; Cícero Leuenroth, in *Brasil–Estados Unidos: Factores de amizade entre as duas grandes patrias americanas* (Rio de Janeiro, 1939), 143; Nasht, "Hollywood's Carioca Fans," 29.

118. Rosenvald, "American Film," 24–25.

119. Walter J. Donnelly, Weekly Report no. 46, Rio de Janeiro, 15 May 1939, RG151, RRCAR, box 72; "O Rio de Janeiro na república," *O Observador Econômico e Financeiro*, November 1939, pp. 47–48; "Notas editoriais," *O Observador Econômico e Financeiro*, March 1947, p. 8; "An Old Institution Dies," *Brazilian American*, 22 June 1929, p. 11.

120. Rosenvald, "American Film," 24; "Linking Two Nations with Celluloid Drama," *Brazilian Business*, March 1924, p. 2; Klein, "What Are Motion Pictures," 37; Brasil Gerson, *Vinte anos de circo* (São Paulo, n.d.), 121; J. A. de Souza Ramos, "A passo de tartaruga," *Propaganda*, November 1937, p. 14.

121. "U. S. Participation at the Centennial Exposition," *Brazilian Business*, September 1923, p. 78; Benjamin Fineberg, "Bringing Broadway to Brazil," *Paulista*, 1st quarter, 1931, p. 12; Sheahan, "Motion Picture Situation"; "Observações economicas," *O Observador Econômico e Financeiro*, November 1937, p. 113.

122. Corrêa, *Automóveis*, 43, 110–111; Rubem Braga, *A traição das elegantes* (Rio de Janeiro, 1967), 179–180; Pierrot, [document missing title page]; Pierrot, "Quarterly Automotive Survey, January—March, Inclusive," Rio de Janeiro, 5 April 1929, RG151, RRCAR, box 54; Carlton Jackson, "Material for Use in Connection with Monthly Economic Cable Report," Rio de Janeiro, 17 February 1933, RG151, RRCAR, box 62; "Linking Two Nations with Celluloid Drama," *Brazilian Business*, March 1924, p. 2; Leuenroth in *Brasil–Estados Unidos*, 143–144.

123. "United States and Brazil Have Joined Forces," *Brazilian Business*, December 1931, p. 15. On "Kodak," e.g., Sergio Milliet, *Terminus sêco e outros cocktails* (São Paulo, 1932), 336; Arthur Coelho, "O potencial do annuncio," *Propaganda*, April–May 1938, p. 2.

124. "What Shall We Do about Improving Business Conditions in Brazil?," *Brazilian Business*, March 1934, p. 67.

125. Peck, *Roundabout*, 268, 314, 320–321.

126. Hermes Lima, "Aspectos da vida sertaneja," *O Observador Econômico e Financeiro*, May 1938, pp. 54, 57; Lima, *Travessia: Memórias* (Rio de Janeiro, 1974), 131–132.

127. "Saudam o Cine Metro" (announcement by Cia. Constructora Nacional, its subcontractors, and their suppliers), *Diario da Noite*, 5 October 1936, p. 3; J. Winsor Ives, "Large American Film Company to Construct Model Theater in Rio de Janeiro," Rio de Janeiro, 13 August 1935, RG151, RRCAR, box 65; Ives, "Metro Goldwyn Mayer Inaugurate Motion Picture House in Rio de Janeiro," Rio de Janeiro, 1 October 1936, RG151, RRCAR, box 67; Aldene H. Barrington, "Large Buildings Projected or Under Construction in Brazil," Economic and Trade Note no. 39, Rio de Janeiro, 27 July 1937, RG151, RRCAR, box 69; Ives, "Motion Picture Notes," Rio de Janeiro, 22 September 1937, RG151, RRCAR, box 69; Frederico Branco, *Postais paulistas* (São Paulo, 1993), 52–55.

Chapter Three

1. "A organização do comércio varejista nos Estados Unidos," *Diario de Noticias*, 5 July 1938, p. 17, republished in *Brasil–Estados Unidos: Factores de amizade entre as duas grandes patrias americanas* (Rio de Janeiro, 1939), 499–506.

2. Lauro de Carvalho in *Brasil–Estados Unidos*, 499–506; Milton de Souza Carvalho, *História de um comerciante* (Rio de Janeiro, 1955), chaps. 8–10, 13; Humberto de Campos, *Perfis (Crônicas)*, ed. Henrique de Campos, 2 vols. (Rio de Janeiro, 1936), 1:116. "José Júlio de Azevedo e Sá" (transcription/summary of interview, n.d.), AHM-SDLM; "Um desfile de modas da Clipper," *Publicidade & Negócios*, September 1947, pp. 96–97; "Anúncios e campanhas," *Publicidade & Negócios*, October 1947, pp. 22–23.

3. U.S. Department of Commerce, *Advertising Methods in Argentina, Uruguay, and Brazil*, by J. W. Sanger (Washington, D.C., 1920), quotes from plates facing 65 ("The arrangement . . .") and 73 ("but no . . ."); James Collins, *Straight Business in South America* (New York, 1920), 108, 111 ("The idea . . ." and "Fascination . . .").

4. Collins, *Straight Business*, 107, 105, 112, 104, respectively.

5. J. Winsor Ives, "Rio de Janeiro Merchants Modernizing Store Fronts," Rio de Janeiro, 5 June 1934, RG151, RRCAR, box 64; U.S. Department of Commerce, *Advertising in Brazil* (Washington, D.C., 1937), 25.

6. "Em cinco anos as vendas aumentaram doze vezes," *Publicidade & Negócios*, November 1949, p. 43 ("shopwindows . . ."); Pedro Nunes, *35 anos de propaganda* (Rio de Janeiro, n.d.), 27 ("more . . ."); Department of Commerce, *Advertising in Brazil*, 25 ("manifesting . . ."); Ives, "Rio de Janeiro Merchants" ("a tendency . . .").

7. Lauro de Carvalho in *Brasil–Estados Unidos*, 506. Photographs: *Publicidade*, July 1942, pp. 12–13; *Publicidade*, July 1945, pp. 18–19; *Brazilian Business*, November 1947, pp. 24–25.

8. J. Winsor Ives, "The Brazilian Market for a Special Type Printing Device," Rio de Janeiro, 2 December 1936, RG151, RRCAR, box 67; "Em cinco anos . . . ," *Publicidade & Negócios*, November 1949, p. 43.

9. Milton de Carvalho interview in *Brasil–Estados Unidos*, 519 (quoted); Lauro de Carvalho in *Brasil–Estados Unidos*, 502–503.

10. "See Brazil as a Garment Market," *Brazil*, June 1946, p. 16; Mappin advertisements from *Folha da Manhã*, 6 November 1942, p. 5 ("North . . ."), 22 December 1943, p. 5 (Arrow shirts), 15 October 1944, p. 16 (blouses), 23 December 1941, p. 15 (toys).

11. Anne Merriman Peck, *Roundabout South America* (New York, 1940), 320 ("In . . ."); "Acaba de chegar a S. Paulo, procedente dos Estados Unidos . . . o sr. Paulo Franco, proprietário da 'Vogue,'" *Folha da Manhã*, 1 March 1942, p. 7; "Em pleno apogeu a moda norte-americana" (clipping labeled *Diário de S. Paulo*, 30 September 1942), AHM-SDP, texto 295, cx 1.

12. Female attendants: Frank Garcia, "Brazil's Women Score Gains," *New York Times*, 8 November 1936, D9; later this chapter, Beauty shops: "'Casa Anglo-Brasileira'–A inauguração, hontem, do Salão de Beleza 'Elizabeth Arden'" (clipping labeled *O Estado de S. Paulo*, 19 August 1939), AHM-SDP, texto 231, cx. 1 (quoted); Peck, *Roundabout*, 320; "O carnet Crediário" (Clipper advertisement), *Folha da Manhã*, 20 November 1948, sec. "Economia e Finanças," 5. Fashion shows: "Em pleno apogeu . . ."; "Maravilhoso desfile de modas norte-americana e nacional" (clipping labeled *Folha da Manhã*, 30 September 1942), AHM-SDP, texto 297, cx. 1; "Um desfile de modas da Clipper," *Publicidade*, September 1947, pp. 96–97 (quoted).

13. Mappin's "American Bar": *O Estado de S. Paulo*, 18 April 1939, p. 6. "English Tea Room": *O Estado de S. Paulo*, 18 August 1914, p. 3; Anna Veronica Mautner, *O cotidiano nas entrelinhas: Crônicas e memórias* (São Paulo, 2001), 17–23; Frederico Branco, *Postais paulistas* (São Paulo, 1993), 56–59. Clipper's nightclub: *Folha da Manhã*, 24 May 1946, p. 7. U.S. tour: "Pessoas inscriptas para a excursão aos Estados Unidos organizada por Exprinter Mappin Stores" (clipping, labeled *Fanfulla*, 2 April 1939), AHM-SDP, texto 173, cx. 1.

14. "Em cinco anos . . . ," *Publicidade & Negócios*, November 1949, pp. 38–39.

15. "Em cinco anos . . . ," *Publicidade & Negócios*, November 1949, p. 45; Nunes, *35 anos*, 78 (quoted); "Como nasceu o 'Artigo do Dia,'" *PN*, 20 November 1953, p. 71; "Revolução no comércio," *O Observador Econômico e Financeiro*, August 1949, p. 44.

16. "Em cinco anos . . . ," *Publicidade & Negócios*, November 1949, p. 43; Chandra Saksena (pseud., Louis James), *A organização e administração científica de indústria*

e comércio (Rio de Janeiro, 1940); Saksena, *A arte de vender a varejo* (Rio de Janeiro, 1942).

17. Nunes, *35 anos*, 68–69.

18. Carvalho, *História*, 50; "Em cinco anos . . . ," *Publicidade & Negócios*, November 1949, p. 43; Nunes, *35 anos*, 63 ("achieved . . ."); "A experiência norte-americana pode ser aproveitada no comércio de modas no Brasil," *Publicidade & Negócios*, September 1948, p. 32 ("applying . . ."); APP, *Depoimentos* (São Paulo, 1973), 83–86.

19. Carvalho, *História*, 79–80; Nunes, *35 anos*, 59–62, 67; "Sabe o que será o Artigo do Dia?" (Clipper advertisement), *Folha da Manhã*, 9 August 1946, p. 7; Willard Espy, *Bold New Program* (New York, 1950), 91 ("went . . ."). "Big" broadcasts and broadcast-ings: *Correio da Manhã*, 13 March 1947, p. 3; *Diario Carioca*, 8 September 1946, p. 5; *Diario de Noticias*, 4 March 1948, p. 8; *A Noite*, 27 May 1946, p. 8.

20. Mappin advertisement in British Chamber of Commerce of São Paulo and Southern Brazil, *Personalidades no Brasil/Men of Affairs in Brazil* (São Paulo, n.d.), 7; Carvalho, *História*, 107; Lauro de Carvalho in *Brasil–Estados Unidos*, 500, 504; Nunes, *35 anos*, 59.

21. Carvalho, *História*, 93–95; "O sr. Nilo Carvalho concede uma interessante ent-revista ao 'Diario Nacional,'" *Folha da Manhã*, 24 November 1927, p. 6; "José Júlio de Azevedo e Sá" (transcription/summary of interview, n.d.), AHM-SDLM; Nunes, *35 anos*, 25, 51; Lauro de Carvalho in *Brasil–Estados Unidos*, 505.

22. J. Winsor Ives, "1930 Proves Profitable Year for American Owned Chain Store Organization Operating in Brazil," Rio de Janeiro, 24 March 1931, RG151, RRCAR, box 56; Carl Crow, "Trunks Up," *Forbes*, 15 December 1940, pp. 14–15, 32 (quoted); "An American in Rio," *Time*, 2 December 1940, pp. 73–74.

23. "An American in Rio," *Time*, 2 December 1940, p. 73 ("laden . . ."); Crow, "Trunks Up," 14–15, 32 (inc. "Nada . . ."); "Lojas Americanas S.A.," *Folha da Manhã*, 12 June 1930, p. 5; "Lojas Americanas S.A.," *Folha da Manhã*, 2 September 1930, p. 2; Ives, "1930 Proves Profitable"; Lojas Americanas advertisement, *Folha da Noite*, 29 December 1934, p. 6; Milton Reynolds, *Hasta la vista* (New York, 1944), 104. On Brazil-ian currency during these years, see chapter 2, note 40.

24. J. Winsor Ives, "New Chain Store Organization in Brazil," Rio de Janeiro, 28 April 1931, RG151, RRCAR, box 58; Lojas Americanas S.A., "Relatório da diretoria relativo ao exercício de 1941," *Diário Oficial*, 20 March 1942, p. 4513.

25. "Lojas Brasileiras Sociedade Anonyma," *Diario Official*, 4 October 1930, p. 8697 ("articles . . ."); registration of trademark, "Lojas Brasileiras," *Diario Official*, 20 March 1930, p. 5854; "Tudo até 4$400," *PN*, 20 December 1952, pp. 26–28; "Como um modesto bancário fundou a mais importante cadeia de lojas do Brasil," *Vendas e Varejo*, May 1960, pp. 6–8; Lojas Brasileiras S.A., "Ao publico," *Folha da Manhã*, 13 March 1938, p. 8; "Lojas de Variedades Limitada," *PN*, 5 October 1953, pp. 47–48.

26. Benjamin Harris Hunnicutt, "If You Want to Do Business Successfully with Brazil," *Brazil*, May 1946, p. 7.

27. Dudley Maynard Phelps, *Migration of Industry to South America* (New York, 1936), 82–83; "Uma reunião de vendedores das Lojas General Electric," *Folha da Manhã*, 6 July 1933, p. 4; *Brazilian Business*, January 1938, p. 3; P. Rocha Gomide, "Publicidade pelo cinema," *Propaganda*, June 1938, p. 6.

28. *Belo Horizonte & o comércio: 100 anos de história* (Belo Horizonte, 1997), 102.

29. Cícero Leuenroth in *Brasil–Estados Unidos*, 141–146 (for Milton's interview, see 519–521).

30. Leuenroth in *Brasil–Estados Unidos*, 141–146; "Cícero Leuenroth," *Propaganda*, January 1971, pp. 8–9.

31. APP, *Depoimentos*, 45–48 (inc. "studying . . ."); Genival Rabelo, *Os tempos heróicos da propaganda* (Rio de Janeiro, 1956), 31, 38, 81–94; "'A Eclectica' nos Estados Unidos," *O Combate*, 1 July 1926, p. 4; "Homens de propaganda," *Propaganda*, June 1938, p. 22 ("visiting . . ."); "Empresas de propaganda," *Propaganda*, December 1937, p. 13; Victor Hawkins, "As difficuldades mechanicas da propaganda no Brasil," *Propaganda*, January–February 1938, p. 23; Ottilo Polato, "Uma approximação desejavel," *Propaganda*, July–August 1938, pp. 10–11 (inc. "We . . ."); "A inauguração das novas instalações da ECLECTICA," *Publicidade*, January 1941, p. 26.

32. Rabelo, *Tempos*, 38–39; "Nossa capa," *Publicidade*, January 1941, p. 4 ("educated . . . ," Chateaubriand); "Homens de govêrno—Atentai para o valor da publicidade," *O Observador Econômico e Financeiro*, July 1946, pp. 45 ("through . . ."), 38 ("felt . . ."); Inter-Americana advertisement, *O Observador Econômico e Financeiro*, January 1948, p. 95; "A S.A. Inter-Americana de Propaganda a seus clientes e amigos," *Publicidade*, September 1940, pp. 7–8, 18.

33. Fernando Reis, "São Paulo e Rio: A longa caminhada," in *HPB*, 327–328 (inc. "If . . ."); Standard advertisement, *Propaganda*, November 1937, inside cover; APP, *Depoimentos*, 86–89; Roberto Simões, "Do pregão ao *jingle*," in *HPB*, 180, 183; "Homens de governo . . . ," *O Observador Econômico e Financeiro*, July 1946, pp. 40 ("disciples"), 43 ("introduced . . .").

34. "A publicidade no Brasil," *O Observador Econômico e Financeiro*, January 1937, p. 52.

35. Reis, "São Paulo e Rio," 317 ("first . . ."), 334, 327, 334–335; Rodolfo Lima Martensen, *O desafio de quatro santos: Memórias* (São Paulo, 1983), 207–208 (on Siqueira); Heitor Mariz, "Ascese," *Propaganda*, March 1938, p. 17 ("efficiente" as neologism).

36. Martensen, *Desafio*, 228–230, 243; Lever advertisements in *O Estado de S. Paulo*, 7 June 1935, p. 4, and 28 June 1935, p. 5.

37. Martensen, *Desafio*, 243; Genival Rabelo, "Lintas parece que está O. K.," *Publicidade*, May 1945, pp. 27–29 (inc. "a bit . . .").

38. Jackson Lears, *Fables of Abundance: A Cultural History of Advertising in America* (New York, 1994); chapter 2 in this book.

39. Orígenes Lessa, "Em 1935 minha primeira grande promoção," *Propaganda*, June 1979, p. 22; Renato Castelo Branco, *Tomei um Ita no norte: Memórias* (São Paulo, 1981), 156.

40. Reis, "São Paulo e Rio," 310 (Lessa); R. P. Castello Branco, "A propaganda no successo industrial," *Propaganda*, December 1937, p. 9 ("It . . .").

41. "A S.A. Inter-Americana de Propaganda a seus clientes e amigos," *Publicidade*, September 1940, p. 7; Jorge Martins Rodrigues, "O Brasil através do para-brisa," *O Estado de S. Paulo*, 23 November 1958, p. 97.

42. Castelo Branco, *Tomei*, 177 ("We struggled . . ."); APP, *Depoimentos*, 87, 32, 49 ("We needed . . . ," "an entity . . . ," and "the valorization . . . *parasitic*," respectively).

43. "Associação Paulista de Propaganda," *Propaganda*, November 1937, pp. 18–19, 21; APP, *Depoimentos*, 87 (early member).

44. APP, *Depoimentos*: 56, 62 (English lessons); 32, 49, 56 (lectures, luncheons); 62 (formal courses).

45. APP, *Depoimentos*, 77; Benedito Barbosa Pupo, "A propaganda a serviço do consumidor," *Publicidade*, March 1946, pp. 18–19 (quoted); "Associação Brasileira de Propaganda," *Publicidade & Negócios*, March 1947, p. 33.

46. "Uma bella iniciativa," *Propaganda*, December 1937, p. 23.

47. "Notas editoriaes," *O Observador Econômico e Financeiro*, August 1938, p. 7 ("all . . ."); "A propaganda em marcha," *Propaganda*, July–August 1938, p. 3 (remaining quotes).

48. "O Dia da Propaganda," *Propaganda*, December 1937, pp. 14–15, 17; "Noticias diversas," *O Estado de S. Paulo*, 3 December 1938, p. 7; "Boletim da A.B.P." and "O que aprendi em 12 annos a serviço da propaganda," *Propaganda*, June 1939, pp. 23, and 13–16, respectively; "Noticias diversas," *O Estado de S. Paulo*, 3 December 1938, p. 7; "Notas editoriais," *O Observador Econômico e Financeiro*, December 1944, p. 3.

49. *Propaganda*, November 1937, p. 5; *Publicidade*, September 1940, p. 3; Fernando Reis, "Sobre o colunismo publicitário e as publicações especializadas," in *HPB*, 65 (quoting Genival Rabelo).

50. W. R. Poyares, "Quem é o especialista em propaganda?," *Publicidade*, September 1941, p. 5; "O papel educativo da propaganda," *Propaganda*, December 1937, p. 9 ("toward . . ."); Jorge Martins Rodrigues, "O papel da propaganda na melhoria das condições econômicas," *Propaganda*, December 1937, p. 10 ("the improvement . . ."); Mario Angelini, "A publicidade—Sistema técnico de venda," *Publicidade*, August 1943, p. 14 ("one of . . ."); Celso Kelly, "A publicidade e os tempos modernos," *Publicidade*, December 1943, p. 35 ("It . . ." and "*Comfort* . . .").

51. João Duarte Filho, "O 'slogan' e a propaganda," *Publicidade*, September 1940, p. 18 ("modern . . ."); Salvador Cosi Pintaudi, "Estudos de mercados (Market Analysis)," *Publicidade*, February 1943, p. 16; Dirceu Fontoura, "Sugestões para uma campanha," *Propaganda*, July–August 1938, pp. 4, 19; *Publicidade*, September 1940, p. 19.

52. "A propaganda é um serviço para a indústria," *Publicidade*, August 1944, p. 15.

53. "Os dez mandamentos do redactor de annuncios," *Propaganda*, November 1937, p. 23; John Benzon, "Lucros e prejuizos das agencias de publicidade," *Propaganda*, March 1938, pp. 2, 15; H. A. Batten, "Rumo a melhor compreensão da propaganda," *Publicidade*, February–March 1942, pp. 7–8, 22; "Linguagem da propaganda," *Propaganda*, June 1939, p. 36; "Linguagem da propaganda," *Propaganda*, July–August 1939, pp. 24–25; "97 productos em 26 jornaes," *Propaganda*, June 1939, pp. 22–25; "Relação das revistas, jornais, periódicos, rádios e alto-falantes do Brasil," *Publicidade*, May 1943, p. 11; A. P. Carvalho, "Cromotécnica," *Publicidade*, July 1946, pp. 16–18.

54. Origenes [*sic*] Lessa, "Como deve apresentar-se o vendedor," *Propaganda*, March 1938, pp. 4, 23; Lessa, *O livro do vendedor*, 3rd ed. (São Paulo, 1939 [1931]), 69, 96; "Linguagem da propaganda," *Propaganda*, June 1939, p. 36; *Publicidade*, September 1940, p. 3; "Vitrinas," *Publicidade*, December 1944, pp. 34–39; "A arte de expor no varejo," *Publicidade*, May 1945, pp. 23–25; "Vitrinas," *Publicidade*, July 1945, pp. 18–19; Sam Rosemberg, "Princípios essenciais na arte de vitrinas," *Publicidade*, January 1946, p. 12–15.

55. "Agostinho Pereira de Souza," *Publicidade*, January 1941, p. 17; "Vale a pena annunciar?," in *Propaganda* issues of November 1937, pp. 11–12, and September 1938, pp. 4, 21.

56. APP, *Depoimentos*, 56; "Que legislação assiste, no Brasil, a profissão de publicidade?," *Diretrizes*, 14 October 1943, p. 23; Humberto Bastos, "Ensaios econômicos" (1943), in *Os modernos: Apontamentos sobre a evolução cultural brasileira* (Rio de Janeiro, 1967), 103–107 (quoted); "Quantos radios existem no Brasil?," *Publicidade*, September 1940, pp. 5, 28; "O recenseamento geral de 1940 e a propaganda," *Publicidade*, January 1941, pp. 9–10, 18; *Publicidade*, December 1942, pp. 73–93.

57. *Propaganda*, July–August 1939, pp. 20–22, 34; "Mundo publicitário," *Publicidade*, September 1940, p. 17; "Homenagem da A.P.P. ao Prof. Candido Mota Filho," *Publicidade*, April 1943, pp. 22–24, 36; "O Presidente Getulio Vargas e a propaganda," *Publicidade*, December 1941, p. 7; W.R.P., "Pelo interior . . . ," *Publicidade*, March 1941, p. 8 ("March . . ."); W. R. Poyares, "Nós aos nossos," *Publicidade*, December 1941, p. 5 ("to . . .").

58. Genival Rabelo, "O 'espírito de publicidade' do povo americano," *Publicidade*, March 1941, p. 22; Rabelo, *O capital estrangeiro na imprensa brasileira* (Rio de Janeiro, 1966), 229 ("passionate . . ." and "What . . ."); "Regressou dos Estados Unidos o sr. Santos Costa," *Publicidade*, October–November 1943, p. 16.

59. *Propaganda*, November 1937, p. 5; Pintaudi, "Estudos," 16–17.

60. "Uma bella iniciativa," *Propaganda*, December 1937, p. 23 (quoted); "A psychologia da propaganda," *Propaganda*, July–August 1938, p. 16; "O que aprendi em 12 annos a serviço da propaganda," *Propaganda*, June 1939, p. 13.

61. "1.º Salão Brasileiro de Propaganda," *Propaganda*, July–August 1938, p. 4; "Associação Brasileira de Propaganda," *Publicidade & Negócios*, March 1947, p. 33; "Como foi festejado o 'Dia da Propaganda,'" *Publicidade*, January 1942, pp. 7–9, 13–14, 19.

62. Hunnicutt, "If You Want," 8 ("The . . ."); Paulo Zingg, "Revistas do Brasil," *O Observador Econômico e Financeiro*, October 1942, pp. 114–115 ("transformation . . ." through "services . . ."); "Notas editoriais," *O Observador Econômico e Financeiro*, December 1942, p. 6 ("decisive . . ." and "life . . .").

63. "Homens de governo . . . ," *O Observador Econômico e Financeiro*, July 1946, p. 56 ("Dr. Chateaubriand . . ." and "the . . ."); Altino João de Barros, "Uma visão da mídia em cinco décadas," in *HPB*, 126 ("obligatory . . ."); transcription of interview with Altino João de Barros by Ilana Strozenberg and Luciana Heymann, 14 July 2004, CPDOC-PHO (inc. "great . . .").

64. Samuel Wainer, *Minha razão de viver: Memórias de um repórter*, ed. Augusto Nunes (Rio de Janeiro, 1987), 49; Zingg, "Revistas," 117 ("first . . ."); Wilson Veloso, "Onde está o magazine nacional?," *Publicidade*, July 1943, pp. 6–7, 9 (remaining quotes); "Que legislação assiste, no Brasil, a profissão de publicidade?," in *Diretrizes*'s issues of 30 September 1943 (pp. 9, 18), 14 October 1943 (p. 23), and 4 November 1943 (p. 25).

65. "Linguagem da propaganda," *Propaganda*, June 1939, p. 36; "Na capa," *Publicidade*, August 1942, p. 4; Nunes, *35 anos*, 84.

66. Early 1940s estimates: "Quantos radios existem no Brasil?," *Publicidade*, September 1940, pp. 5, 28; Alvarus de Oliveira, "A surprêsas do recenseamento" (4 September

1940), in *Feira de idéias* (Rio de Janeiro, 1946), 45; "Mais da metade não foi registrada," *A Noite*, 12 October 1940, final ed., pp. 1–2; Murilo Reis, "O recenseamento geral de 1940 e a propaganda," *Publicidade*, January 1941, pp. 9–10; Rollo Smith, "Marketing Areas of Brazil," *International Reference Service*, January 1941, p. 3. Subsequent growth: "Basic Data on Political, Geographic, Social, and Economic Conditions [in] BRAZIL," June 1943, RG229, entry 3, box 513; J. R. Caldeira, "O 'cruzeiro anúncio,'" *Boletim Semanal*, 10 June 1944, p. 35; "Continuation of Good-Will Work in Latin America Seen after War," *New York Times*, 27 July 1944, p. 21; George Wythe, *Industry in Latin America*, 2nd ed. (New York, 1949 [1945]), 179. Nelson Rodrigues, "Rádio, poesia do subúrbio," *Diretrizes*, 11 December 1941, p. 19. São Paulo journalist quoted in Lia Calabre de Azevedo, "No tempo do rádio: Radiodifusão e cotidiano no Brasil, 1923–1960" (tese de doutorado, UFF, 2002), 75.

67. Azevedo, "No tempo," 76 (official data); Armin Ludwig, *Brazil: A Handbook of Historical Statistics* (Boston, 1985), 267 (active stations).

68. Lion de Araujo, *Processos de propaganda* (São Paulo, 1935), 121–122; Edmur de Castro Cotti, "As lições de um paralelo," *Publicidade*, December 1943, p. 113; *Revista do Rádio* in "Um quarto de século de rádio no Brasil," *Publicidade & Negócios*, May 1948, p. 26.

69. Walter Ramos Poyares, "Publicidade comercial," *O Observador Econômico e Financeiro*, September 1943, p. 24; radio director in "A indústria e o comércio precisam de rádio," *O Observador Econômico e Financeiro*, October 1945, p. 127.

70. Claudia Pinheiro, ed., *A Rádio Nacional: Alguns dos momentos que contribuíram para o sucesso da Rádio Nacional* (Rio de Janeiro, 2005), 20 (print advertising); Azevedo, "No tempo," 126 ("the largest . . .").

71. Barbosa and his coproducer in Luiz Carlos Saroldi and Sonia Virgínia Moreira, *Rádio Nacional, o Brasil em sintonia* (Rio de Janeiro, 1984), 32, 30, 31–32, respectively (see also 34–35 on record sales); Saroldi, "Por que a Nacional?," in Pinheiro, *Rádio*, 11.

72. Genival Rabelo, "Fatos & comentários," *Anuário de Publicidade*, December 1947, p. 18 ("our . . ."); Azevedo, "No tempo," 126–127 (Nacional's incoming correspondence); Walter Clark [Bueno], *O campeão de audiência* (São Paulo, 1991), 16 ("the station . . ."); Paulo Cesar Ferreira, *Pilares via satélite: Da Rádio Nacional à Rede Globo* (Rio de Janeiro, 1998), 25–26; "Um horário famoso," *A Noite Ilustrada*, 12 October 1948, p. 32 ("it was . . .").

73. Azevedo, "No tempo," 197–198; Bryan McCann, *Hello, Hello Brazil: Popular Music in the Making of Modern Brazil* (Durham, N.C., 2004), 24; Fernando Morais, *Chatô: O rei do Brasil* (São Paulo, 1994), 414–415; Glauco Carneiro, *Brasil, primeiro: História dos Diários Associados* (Brasília, 1999), 187–188.

74. "Homens de governo . . . ," *O Observador Econômico e Financeiro*, July 1946, p. 53 ("American . . ."); Azevedo, "No tempo," 164 ("great . . ."); Martensen, *Desafio*, pt. 3; Rabelo, *Tempos*, 17–19.

75. Rabelo, *Tempos*, 19; Edmur de Castro Cotti, "Imprensa contra rádio?," *Boletim Semanal*, 10 June 1944, pp. 18–19.

76. Leuenroth in *Brasil–Estados Unidos*, 143.

77. "Nossa indústria de publicidade," *O Observador Econômico e Financeiro*, May 1939, p. 43; Pintaudi, "Estudos," 16; Reis, "Recenseamento," 9–10.

78. "Nossa indústria de publicidade," *O Observador Econômico e Financeiro*, May 1939, p. 42; APP, *Depoimentos*, 50.

79. "Não é moamba, não, é um entrevistador do I.B.O.P.E.," *Anuário Brasileiro de Imprensa*, 1948, p. 42; "Biografias," *Publicidade*, July 1945, p. 33.

80. "Resumo geral da publicidade realizada por 342 produtos na imprensa diária de São Paulo, Santos e Campinas," May 1942 (quoted), AEL-IBOPE, CPU001; "A publicidade na imprensa diária de S. Paulo, Santos e Campinas durante o mês de abril de 1942," AEL-IBOPE, CPU001.

81. "Incorporação da CIPEX ao Instituto Brasileiro de Opinião Pública e Estatística" ("the public's . . ."), AEL-IBOPE, CPU001; "O que é o Instituto Brasileiro de Opinião Pública e Estatística," January 1945 ("permanent . . ." and "what . . ."), AEL-IBOPE, SX003; "What Program Are You Listening To?," *Brazilian Business*, July 1949, pp. 31–32 ("on-the-spot . . ." and "the public's . . .").

82. "What Program . . . ," *Brazilian Business*, July 1949, p. 32.

83. "What Program . . . ," *Brazilian Business*, July 1949, p. 31.

84. "What Program . . . ," *Brazilian Business*, July 1949, p. 31. For a contemporary non-IBOPE, nonagency study that relied on the A, B, C scheme: "Assim se espera 1946," *O Observador Econômico e Financeiro*, January 1946, pp. 18–29.

85. "How Does Your Product Sell in Brazil?," *Brazilian Business*, August 1948, pp. 19 ("the purchasing . . ."), 30; "Não é moamba, não, é um entrevistador do I.B.O.P.E.," *Anuário Brasileiro de Imprensa*, 1948, p. 40; "O que é o Instituto . . ."

86. "Serviço X" studies, 1943–1949, AEL-IBOPE, SX001–SX011; "How Does Your Product Sell in Brazil?," *Brazilian Business*, August 1948, p. 19; "Ever Take a Picture of Your Business?," *Brazilian Business*, August 1948, pp. 32–38.

87. "How Does Your Product Sell in Brazil?," *Brazilian Business*, August 1948, p. 19; "O que é o Instituto . . ." (quoted).

88. J. A. de Sousa Ramos, "O valor da investigação da opinião pública," *Digesto Econômico*, December 1946, pp. 115–116.

89. "Notícias do estrangeiro" in *Publicidade* issues of April 1946, p. 34, and January 1946, p. 34; "How Does Your Product Sell in Brazil?," *Brazilian Business*, August 1948, pp. 18–19.

90. "O que é o Instituto . . ."; "I.B.O.P.E. (Sociedade Civil Por Quotas)," December 1945, AEL-IBOPE, SX003; Azevedo, "No tempo," 173.

91. "O que é o Instituto . . ."; "Vale a pena annunciar?," *Propaganda*, November 1937, pp. 11–12 (inc. "modern . . ."); Rabelo, *Tempos*, 89; Simões, "Do pregão . . . ," 178; "Em cinco anos . . . ," *Publicidade & Negócios*, November 1949, p. 46.

92. "Não é moamba, não, é um entrevistador do I.B.O.P.E.," *Anuário Brasileiro de Imprensa*, 1948, p. 40 (quoted); "Sociedade Civil Por Quotas," AEL-IBOPE, SX005; "Sociedade Civil Por Quotas," AEL-IBOPE, SX008. According to the *DHBB* (3:3399–3400), as a law student in in the late 1910s and early 1920s, Machado Neto worked brokering between advertisers and publishers (his family then having little but their name to trade on). Machado's involvement in radio-set imports and retailing beginning in 1926 seems a likelier introduction to Penteado, though they may have known one another since childhood, each born into an old, if financially distressed, São Paulo family.

93. *Boletim das Classes Dirigentes*, nos. 1–2 (1950), AEL-IBOPE.

94. *Boletim das Classes Dirigentes*, no. 2 (6–13 November 1950): 7, AEL-IBOPE.

95. On one-off "teatro em casa": Rádio Nacional advertisement, *O Estado de S. Paulo*, 24 March 1938, p. 6; "Gente de rádio," *A Noite Ilustrada*, 22 September 1942, pp. 12, 14; Rabelo, *Tempos*, 19. On "Teatro Eucalol": "Rádio," *A Manhã*, 27 December 1941, p. 5; "Como os rádio-ouvintes apreciam os bons programas," *Cinearte*, September 1941, p. 34; "Gente de rádio," *A Noite Ilustrada*, 18 July 1944, p. 20; "Procopio Ferreira atuará no mais famoso programa do radio-teatro brasileiro," *Diario da Noite*, 20 January 1944, p. 5; Julio Pires, "Procopio Ferreira, logo mais, radio-ator," *Diario da Noite*, 24 January 1944, p. 5.

96. Richard Penn to "Sr. Redator," São Paulo, 15 June 1949, *Publicidade & Negócios*, June 1949, pp. 8, 10; Renato Ortiz, "Evolução histórica da telenovela," in Ortiz, Silvia Helena Simões Borelli, and José Mário Ortiz Ramos, *Telenovela: História e produção* (São Paulo, 1989), 26 ("We . . .").

97. "No ar, as novidades de 1940," *Propaganda*, February 1973, p. 52.

98. Simões, "Do pregão . . . ," 183; "Quando será o fim da novela 'Em busca da felicidade?,'" *Diario de Noticias*, 20 December 1942, p. 11 ("three . . ."); "Em busca de [sic] felicidade," *A Noite*, 10 April 1942, p. 2 (Penn, letters/day); Rabelo, *Tempos*, 17 (total mail).

99. "Gente de rádio," *A Noite Ilustrada*, 4 August 1942, p. 34; Lia Calabre, *O rádio na sintonia do tempo: Radionovelas e cotidiano, 1940–1946* (Rio de Janeiro, 2006), 139–151; Saroldi and Moreira, *Rádio Nacional*, 51; Mario Lago, *Bagaço de beira-estrada* (Rio de Janeiro, 1977), 97; Azevedo, "No tempo," 165; "No ar, as novidades de 1940," *Propaganda*, February 1973, p. 52 (executive).

100. "Radio," *O Estado de S. Paulo*, 14 September 1941, p. 3; Rádio São Paulo advertisements in *O Estado de S. Paulo*, 4 October 1941, p. 7, and 8 April 1942, p. 6; Deocélia Vianna, *Companheiros de viagem*, ed. Maria Célia Teixeira (São Paulo, 1984), 71–72.

101. Rádio Difusora advertisement, *Folha da Manhã*, 16 January 1942, p. 13; Renato Ortiz, *A moderna tradição brasileira*, 5th ed. (São Paulo, 1994 [1988]), 83–84 (Standard staff); "Visitas às novas instalações da Rádio Nacional," *A Noite*, 4 June 1942, p. 3 (quoted); *Teatro de Romance Peixe* advertisement, *A Noite*, 17 June 1942, p. 5.

102. Paulo Francis, *O afeto que se encerra: Memórias* (Rio de Janeiro, 1980), 35–36; Lago, *Bagaço*, 77; Azevedo, "No tempo," 249 (Lopes).

103. Jay Wainwright, "It's Catching!," *Brazil*, June 1947, p. 6.

104. Poyares, "Publicidade," 24.

105. Povina Cavalcanti, *Volta à infância: Memórias* (Rio de Janeiro, 1972), 24; José Aranha de Assis Pacheco, *Taquara rachada e outras memórias* (São Paulo, 1989), 136–137; Limeira Tejo, *Enéias: Memórias de uma geração ressentida* (Rio de Janeiro, 1956), 232.

106. Department of Commerce, *Advertising in Brazil*, 11.

107. Hermano Durval, "Marcas de fabricas," *O Observador Econômico e Financeiro*, November 1938, pp. 42–43.

108. Durval, "Marcas," 42–44.

109. Durval, 42, 45–46; Thorstein Veblen, *The Theory of Business Enterprise* (New York, 1904), 54–55.

110. Veblen, *Theory*, 64; Durval, "Marcas," 42–47.

111. Durval, "Marcas," 42–47.

112. Durval, 47.

113. R. M. Ferreira, "Produtos vendidos com marca registrada," *Propaganda*, March 1938, p. 19; *A Noite*, 12 June 1919, p. 5.

114. Angelini, "Publicidade," 14, 31.

115. Peixe advertisement, *Diario Carioca*, 17 July 1936, p. 2; "Goiabada, Peixe novo, lata 1.000" (retail product listing), *O Imparcial*, 31 May 1915, p. 9; Leite Moça product history, NBL-CPD, MDLM001.00.004; "Mantimentos," *Jornal do Brasil*, 2 November 1900, p. 4; Leite Moça advertisement, 28 July 1932, JWTA, mr-41; "Ever Take a Picture of Your Business?," *Brazilian Business*, August 1948, p. 34.

116. Advertisements from *Revista da Semana*: 12 September 1931; 10 June 1933; 25 November 1933.

117. "Preliminary Report on Royal Baking Powder," São Paulo, JWTA, mr-223; RBP advertisements from *Revista da Semana*, 18 June 1932 and 26 November 1932. Competitor's advertisements: *O Estado de S. Paulo*, 2 November 1928, p. 10; *Correio da Manhã*, 17 April 1929, p. 15; *O Estado de S. Paulo*, 6 October 1929, p. 15.

118. The information on Nestlé's expansion is from the company organ *Atualidades Nestlé*: August and October 1961, February, April, June, August, and December 1962 (NBL-CPD). Standard Brands: "A nova esplendida sede central da Standard Brands of Brasil [sic]," *A Noite*, 31 October 1939, p. 4. Nescau: Nescau product history, NBL-CPD, MDONE01.00.001. Santiago Development Corporation: "A Toddy Company vae installar sua fabrica no Brasil," *A Noite*, 17 August 1932, p. 2; "Ao publico," *A Noite*, 1 December 1933, 3rd ed., p. 2.

119. Eucalol toothpaste and bath soap advertisements in *Revista da Semana*, 4 November 1933 and 25 November 1933, respectively. Toddy: Nescau product history, NBL-CPD, MDONE01.00.001 (quoted); Toddy advertisement, *Revista da Semana*, 30 September 1933. Palmolive advertisements in *O Estado de S. Paulo*, 18 July 1937, p. 10, and *Revista da Semana*, 17 July 1937, p. 14. Palmolive and Colgate advertisements in *O Estado de S. Paulo*, 22 August 1937, p. 10. Colgate-Palmolive-Peet advertisements: *Revista da Semana*, 11 January 1941, p. 7; *A Noite Ilustrada*, 15 September 1942, p. 27. Coty: "A indústria dos perfumes," *O Observador Econômico e Financeiro*, June 1945, pp. 62–63; Coty advertisement, *O Estado de S. Paulo*, 18 July 1937, p. 10; JWT, "International Advertising," New York, 1935, JWTA, mr-257.

120. RBP advertisement, *Gazeta de Noticias*, 18 February 1919, p. 5; RBP advertisement, *Revista da Semana*, 18 June 1932; Toddy advertisement, *Revista da Semana*, 30 September 1933; Palmolive advertisement, *O Estado de S. Paulo*, 5 August 1937, p. 8; Palmolive advertisement, *O Estado de S. Paulo*, 15 January 1939, p. 11; RBP advertisement, *O Estado de S. Paulo*, 10 November 1939, p. 4.

121. Palmolive advertisement, *Revista da Semana*, 14 August 1937, p. 4; Eucalol advertisement, *O Estado de S. Paulo*, 25 August 1937, p. 14; Gessy advertisement, *A Noite*, 17 June 1940, p. 4; Colgate advertisement, *Revista da Semana*, 11 January 1941, p. 7; Peixe advertisement, *O Estado de S. Paulo*, 23 December 1937, p. 7; Nestlé advertisement, 18 August 1932, JWTA, mr-41; Toddy advertisement, *A Noite*, 26 January 1934, p. 6.

122. Eucalol advertisement (reprint), *Publicidade*, January 1941, p. 11; Lever advertisement, *A Noite*, 10 June 1940, p. 5; John Nasht, "Hollywood's Carioca Fans," *Inter-American*, September 1943, p. 30.

123. RBP advertisement, *Gazeta de Noticias*, 18 February 1919, p. 5; Backpulver advertisement, *O Estado de S. Paulo*, 2 November 1928, p. 10; Maizena Duryea advertisement, August 1932, JWTA, mr-41; Leite Moça advertisement, 28 July 1932, JWTA, mr-41; Gordura de Coco Carioca advertisement, *O Estado de S. Paulo*, 15 January 1939, p. 11; Johnson & Johnson advertisement, *O Estado de S. Paulo*, 14 September 1934, p. 2; RBP advertisement, *O Estado de S. Paulo*, 10 November 1939, p. 4; Palmolive advertisement in *O Estado de S. Paulo* issues of 27 August 1939, p. 11, and 24 December 1939, p. 14; Samuel Gorberg, *Estampas Eucalol* (Rio de Janeiro, 2000); Toddy announcement, *A Noite*, 3 July 1937, p. 6; Peixe advertisement, *O Estado de S. Paulo*, 21 September 1941, p. 6.

124. Duarte Filho, "O 'slogan'"; Ary Kerner, *Nos bastidores da publicidade* (Rio de Janeiro, 1943), 85–86; "Comércio e publicidade," *Digesto Econômico*, January 1945, pp. 25–29.

125. Royal Briar advertisement, *A Noite Ilustrada*, 1 November 1938, p. 14; Palmolive advertisement, *A Noite Ilustrada*, 15 September 1942, p. 27. Eucalol advertisements: *A Noite*, 9 September 1931, 2nd ed., p. 1; *Revista da Semana*, 4 November 1933; *O Estado de S. Paulo*, 26 January 1935, p. 9; *O Estado de S. Paulo*, 29 August 1936, p. 6; *O Estado de S. Paulo*, 25 August 1937, p. 14.

126. Omega-Tissot advertisement, *O Estado de S. Paulo*, 10 October 1935, p. 4; Mido Multifort advertisement, *Diario de Noticias*, 12 September 1943, p. 11; Peixe advertisement, *A Noite Ilustrada*, 30 April 1940, p. 45; Toddy advertisement, *A Noite*, 30 November 1938, p. 4; Malzbier advertisement, *A Noite Ilustrada*, 31 August 1943, p. 30; "Ice Cream in Brazil," *Business Week*, 21 November 1942, p. 24; Reynolds, *Hasta*, 104, 115; Colgate advertisement, *A Noite*, 10 May 1943, p. 4.

127. "Origem do jingle," *Publicidade & Negócios*, 1 October 1951, p. 51 ("that . . ."); Simões, "Do pregão . . . ," 178–187; Martensen, *Desafio*, pt. 3; Wainwright, "It's Catching!" ("radio . . ." through "As . . ."); interview in *Brasil–Estados Unidos*, 177 (Brazilian perspective on U.S. radio advertising, contrasted with "torment" of Brazil's).

128. "Lista de alto-falantes," *Publicidade*, December 1942, pp. 92–93; *Diretrizes*, 30 December 1943, pp. 8, 21, 23 (advertisements for Minas Gerais loudspeaker services); "O alto falante como veículo de propaganda," *Publicidade*, September 1943, pp. 12–14.

129. "City Bank's Branch as Business Factor," *New York Times*, 10 March 1915, p. 8; JWTCB, "Investigation for Lehn & Fink," May 1931, JWTA, mr-23; Department of Commerce, *Advertising in Brazil*, 22–23; F. M. Nogueira, "A guerra, o transito e a propaganda," *Publicidade*, December 1942, p. 66.

130. "A propaganda a ar livre no Brasil," *Propaganda*, July–August 1939, pp. 11–13 (quoted); "Á praça" (secção livre item), *O Estado de S. Paulo*, 8 August 1931, p. 8; Department of Commerce, *Advertising in Brazil*, 21–22; "Um marco de progresso na propaganda por cartazes e painéis," *Publicidade*, December 1943, p. 99.

131. Reginal Gorham, "Advertising in Brazil," *Export Trade and Finance*, 28 September 1929, p. 44; Araujo, *Processos*, 116; Department of Commerce, *Advertising in Brazil*, 22; Aldene A. Barrington, "Illuminated Signs to Be Free of Taxes during Coming Carnival Season," Economic and Trade Note no. 164, Rio de Janeiro, 27 December 1934, RG151, RRCAR, box 64; "Já se annuncia em São Paulo," *Propaganda*, January–February 1938, p. 19.

132. "Já se anuncia . . ." For "outdoor": "Linguagem da propaganda," *Propaganda*, July–August 1939, p. 24.

133. Carl Crow, "How Will Our Pan-American Trade Pan Out?," *Forbes*, 15 April 1941, p. 14.

134. Nunes, *35 anos*, 84, 168–170; "Coca-Cola já deu ao pais Cr$136,100.000,00," *Publicidade*, October 1948, p. 9; "Um marco de progresso na propaganda por cartazes e painéis," *Publicidade*, December 1943, p. 99; "As indústrias Coca-Cola no Brasil dirigem-se ao Exmo. Snr. Deputado Caffé [*sic*] Filho" (announcement), *O Estado de S. Paulo*, 19 October 1948, p. 10; Saroldi and Moreira, *Rádio Nacional*, 30–31 ("spearhead" and quote from Rádio Nacional producer); interview with Emil Farhat (McCann-Erickson) by Glauco Carneiro, 28 September 1982, NBL-CPD, TDGC, vol. 2; "Anúncios e campanhas," *Publicidade*, September 1943, p. 2 ("essentially . . ."); "Coca-Cola é uma indústria corajosa," *Publicidade*, April 1944, p. 5; Alvarus de Oliveira, "Coca-Cola e as ideologias politicas,"*Publicidade*, December 1948, pp. 18, 32 (inc. "among . . ."); Homero Homem, "Coca-Cola faz concorrência aberta e desleal, ao comércio varejista do país," *Revista de Economia Popular*, February 1951, p. 15. As war-era advertising could be written off in the United States (see later in this chapter), it is unlikely that Coca-Cola lost money in Brazil during these years.

135. Homero Homem, "Coca-Cola é um toxico, isto sim!," *Revista de Economia Popular*, December 1950, p. 19.

136. Marcus Pereira, *Lembranças de amanhã* (São Paulo, 1980), 190–191.

137. "Refrigerantes no Distrito Federal," *Publicidade & Negócios*, 15 July 1950, p. 22; W. R. Poyares, "Notas de um publicitário," *Publicidade & Negócios*, June 1949, p. 47.

138. "The New Pan-Americanism" (transcript of "A radio talk by Dr. Julius Klein . . . November 24, 1928 . . ."), Hoover Institution, Julius Klein Papers.

139. E.g., Sérgio Buarque de Holanda, *Raízes do Brasil* (Rio de Janeiro, 1936), an early version of which had the working title "Teoria da América"; Mário de Andrade, review of José Lins do Rego's *Riacho doce* (first published 12 November 1939), in *O empalhador de passarinho*, 3rd ed. (São Paulo, 1972 [1948]), 137; Sérgio Buarque de Holanda, "Considerações sobre o americanismo," *Diario de Noticias*, 28 September 1941, pp. 17–18 (reprinted as chap. 3 of *Cobra de vidro*, 2nd ed. [São Paulo, 1978 (1944)]); Florestan Fernandes, "Livros que valem" and esp. "Mais América," in *Folha da Manhã* issues of 1 July 1943, p. 7, 19 August 1943, p. 6. Sérgio Buarque and Florestan Fernandes were under forty when the works just cited were published, while Mário de Andrade was a youthful forty-six. For an older intellectual's pushback against "Americanism" and identification with Europe rather than the United States or Spanish America, see José Maria Bello, *Memórias* (Rio de Janeiro, 1958), 249, which draws on his diary of a 1947–1948 trip to the United States.

140. Nasht, "Hollywood's Carioca Fans," 29 ("It is . . ."); "South America IV: Brazil," *Fortune*, July 1939, p. 150 ("'okay' . . .); "American Moving and Talking Pictures in Brazil," 2 June 1930, enclosure to George S. Messersmith to Secretary of State, Buenos Aires, 5 June 1930 ("The talking . . ."—quoting unnamed Rio newspaper), RG59, 632.111/1.

141. "South America IV: Brazil," *Fortune*, July 1939, quotes on 150, 47 (respectively, "American . . ." and "a vast . . ."); "Leituras de ontem e de hoje," *O Observador Econômico*

e Financeiro, April 1942, pp. 45–48; Zingg, "Revistas," 115–117; "How U.S. Books and Magazines Sell in Brazil," *Brazilian Business*, April 1948, pp. 20–25 (inc. "an ever-increasing . . ."); Peck, *Roundabout*, 320, 341 ("like . . ." and "believe . . ."); Nelson Werneck Sodré, *Do tenentismo ao Estado Novo* (Petrópolis, 1986), 241.

142. Walter Rocha, "História do bairro Serrador," *Revista da Semana*, 8 November 1941, p. 33; Mário de Moraes, *Recordações de Ari Barroso* (Rio de Janeiro, 1979), 111–112; Carvalho, *História*, 58; "Lojas Duas Américas, o magazine chique da Rua Chile," accessed 27 June 2013, http://www.ibahia.com/a/blogs/memoriasdabahia/2012/09/04/lojas-duas-americas-o-magazine-chic-da-rua-chile/; Reynolds, *Hasta*, 86.

143. "Um desfile de modas da Clipper," *Publicidade & Negócios*, September 1947, pp. 96–97. Mattresses: Rabelo, *Tempos*, 30 (Clipper); *Diario da Noite*, 24 January 1943, p. 3 (Hollywood). Clipper and Hollywood cigarettes: "Vitrinas," *Publicidade*, March 1944, p. 23. Continental: *O Estado de S. Paulo*, 14 May 1949, p. 11. Lincoln: *O Estado de S. Paulo*, 22 August 1942, p. 3. Liberty: *O Paiz*, 6 August 1918, p. 6; "Uma gentileza da Cia. Souza Cruz," *Diario Carioca*, 17 July 1943, p. 3. José Jobim, *Brazil in the Making* (New York, 1943), 290–291.

144. E. Victor Saadeh, "Possible Infringement of American-Owned Trade Marks," Rio de Janeiro, 13 February 1942, RG59, 832.543/160; Saadeh, "Possible . . . ," 19 February 1942, 832.543/161; Saadeh, "Possible . . . ," 19 February 1942, 832.543/165; Saadeh, "Possible . . . ," 17 November 1949, 832.543/11-1749; Saadeh, "Possible . . . ," 9 January 1950, 832.172/1-950; Saadeh, "Possible . . . ," 17 January 1950, 832.172/1-1750; Saadeh, "Possible . . . ," 8 February 1950, 832.172/2-850; Saadeh, "Possible . . . ," 31 January 1950, 832.172/1-3150; Saadeh, "Possible . . . ," 15 February 1950, 832.172/2-1550.

145. Leite Moça product history, NBL-CPD, MDLM001.00.004; Manoel de Vasconcelos, "Agências americanas no Brasil," *Publicidade*, January 1944, p. 14.

146. Walter J. Donnelly to Ellis O. Briggs, Rio de Janeiro, 24 August 1940, RG59, 832.911/65; *Diretrizes*, September 1939, passim (quote on 59).

147. "No mundo da propaganda," *Propaganda*, April–May 1938, p. 18; Leuenroth in *Brasil–Estados Unidos*, 146; "A Empresa de Propaganda Standard expande-se," *Publicidade*, January 1941, p. 17; Reis, "São Paulo e Rio," 334; "As commemorações do Dia Pan Americano de Propaganda," *A Batalha*, 25 November 1939, p. 2.

148. Ottilo Polato, "Uma approximação desejavel," *Propaganda*, July–August 1938, p. 11.

149. "A Rádio Pan-Americana," *O Estado de S. Paulo*, 27 November 1942, p. 1; A Exposição advertisement, *O Estado de S. Paulo*, 28 February 1943, p. 14; "Demagogia—O mal do rádio brasileiro," *Diretrizes*, 4 November 1943, p. 26; "Rádio," *O Estado de S. Paulo*, 4 May 1944, p. 3; "A indústria e o comércio precisam de rádio," *O Observador Econômico e Financeiro*, October 1945, p. 127 (Rádio América); Clark, *Campeão*, 20–21 (Rádio Continental). See Vianna, *Companheiros*, 41–42, 53, on Oduvaldo's studying filmmaking in the United States.

150. *Folha da Manhã*, 16 January 1942, p. 13; "Como devemos anunciar na hora presente?," *Publicidade*, May 1942, pp. 15–16; Emil Farhat, *Histórias ouvidas e vividas* (São Paulo, 1999), 219–220; *PN*, 20 December 1952, p. 58.

151. "J. Walter Thompson Company do Brasil" (1961), JWTA, Information Center Vertical Files, box 10; Zingg, "Revistas do Brasil," 117 ("beating . . ."); "Homens de

governo . . . ," *O Observador Econômico e Financeiro*, July 1946, p. 55 (d'Almeida); Don Wharton, "The World Is Its Newsstand," *Nation's Business*, October 1946, p. 83.

152. Sodré, *Do tenentismo*, 246.

153. "Activities of the Coordinator of Inter-American Affairs in Brazil," 21 April 1943, RG229, entry 3, box 513; untitled memorandum, Robert F. Merrick to Colin Dawkins, 2 January 1980, JWTA, CDP, box 2; "Os lucros e as agencias americanas," *Publicidade*, June 1944, p. 24; Carroll L. Wilson, "The International Operations of the J. Walter Thompson Company: Analysis of an Expanding Venture," 15 December 1945, JWTA, Samuel Williams Meek Papers, box 4; Coordinator of Inter-American Affairs, "Annual Report [for Brazil, 1943]," RG229, entry 99, box 1259; John L. Sullivan to Nelson A. Rockefeller, Washington, D.C., 17 July 1942 (copy), RG229, entry 21, box 603 (quoted); Memorandum, Harold N. Elterich to J. C. Rovensky, "Reports on Increasing '43 Budgets," Washington, D.C., 27 January 1943, RG229, entry 21, box 603; B. R. Donaldson to K. Orberg, [Dearborn], 7 April 1943, FHA-BFRC, Accession 456, box 14; São Paulo Branch to Home Office, 7 June 1943, FHA-BFRC, Accession 456, box 14; J. C. Rovensky to "All Coordination Committees" [1943] (copy), RG229, entry 21, box 603.

154. Joseph C. Rovensky, "How the Rockefeller Advertising Plan for Latin America Is Being Implemented," *Export Trade and Shipper*, 17 August 1942, pp. 5–8; "Notas editoriais," *O Observador Econômico e Financeiro*, December 1943, p. 7 (quoted); "Anúncios e campanhas," *Publicidade*, September 1943, p. 3 (shoe-store); Roney Cytrynowicz, *Guerra sem guerra: A mobilização e o cotidiano em São Paulo durante a Segunda Guerra Mundial* (São Paulo, 2000), 2nd page of color plates (cooking-oil concerns).

155. GE advertisements in *O Estado de S. Paulo* issues of 19 August 1943, p. 7, 21 September 1943, p. 6.

156. "A General Electric anuncia para o após guerra," *Publicidade*, December 1943, p. 24; GE advertisement, *Revista da Semana*, 14 October 1944, p. 41; Philco advertisement (*Seleções*, June 1944), quoted in Azevedo, "No tempo," 66–67; Zenith advertisements in *O Estado de S. Paulo* issues of 15 July 1944, p. 8, 11 August 1945, p. 10; GM advertisement, *O Estado de S. Paulo*, 7 August 1945, p. 13.

157. Fred Gardner, "O Brasil, império econômico," *O Observador Econômico e Financeiro*, September 1945, pp. 145–147; "O presidente da Chrysler no Rio," *A Noite*, 30 March 1944, p. 2; "Sr. George P. Harrington," *O Estado de S. Paulo*, 27 March 1945, p. 6; "A propaganda é um serviço para a indústria," *Publicidade*, August 1944, p. 15 (quoted).

158. Poyares, "Publicidade," 24; "Que legislação assiste, no Brasil, a profissão de publicidade?," *Diretrizes*, 30 September 1943, p. 9; Carlos de Britto advertisement, *Diretrizes*, 30 December 1943, back cover.

159. "A General Electric no Brasil," *O Observador Econômico e Financeiro*, July 1944, p. 194; *Diretrizes*, 30 December 1943, quotes on 1.

160. GM advertisement, *O Estado de S. Paulo*, 23 October 1945, p. 13; Atlantic advertisement, *O Observador Econômico e Financeiro*, December 1945, inside cover.

161. "Depoimento de Augusto de Ângelo," Rio de Janeiro, 3 November 1988, IPHSP; GM advertisements in *O Estado de S. Paulo*, 18 December 1945, p. 5; GM advertisements in *O Estado de S. Paulo*, 8 February 1946, p. 5, and *Correio da Manhã*, 14 April 1946, p. 7; Genival Rabelo, "Robert F. Merick [*sic*] disse," *Publicidade*, September 1946, pp. 48–51;

"Regressou o gerente-geral da Colgate-Palmolive do Brasil," *Folha da Manhã*, 1 November 1946, p. 3.

162. *O Observador Econômico e Financeiro*, January 1946, pp. 22–23; August 1946, p. 68.

163. Shirley F. Woodell to Miss Beck, São Paulo, 7 February 1947 (2 of 2), JWTA, Shirley F. Woodell Papers, box 1; H. Monteiro to R. I. Roberge, São Paulo, 2 April 1945 ("duly . . ."), FHA-BFRC, Accession 46, box 300; Arnold Tschudy, "Brazilian-American Friendship: What of the Future?," *Brazil*, March 1947, pp. 16–17; "Chamber Notes," *Brazilian Business*, April 1945, p. 185.

164. "No Early Increase Seen in Import of U.S. Automobiles to Brazil," *Brazil*, June 1948, pp. 2–3; "How U.S. Products Sell in Brazil," *Brazilian Business*, February 1948, p. 18.

165. Manoel de Vasconcellos, "Subsistirá o sistema da economia privada?," *Publicidade & Negócios*, February 1947, p. 32.

166. Vasconcellos, "Subsistirá," 33.

167. "30 anos de publicidade no Rio de Janeiro," *Publicidade & Negócios*, August 1948, pp. 22–23, 26.

168. "Há um Ford em seu futuro! Mais . . . quando?," *Publicidade & Negócios*, 1 May 1950, pp. 6–11.

169. Humberto Bastos, *O pensamento industrial no Brasil* (São Paulo, 1952), 196–197; B. de Aragão, "A fuga do dólar," *O Observador Econômico e Financeiro*, July 1947, pp. 49–56; "Tendências dos negócios e da propaganda," *Anuário de Publicidade*, December 1947, p. 4.

170. Limeira Tejo, *Retrato sincero do Brasil* (Rio de Janeiro, 1950), 53–54; José Cândido Moreira de Souza, "Deflação por fora e inflação por dentro," *Vendas e Varejo*, August 1959, p. 6; Elias Chaves Neto, *Minha vida e as lutas de meu tempo* (São Paulo, 1978), 88; Gerson Moura, *Tio Sam chega ao Brasil: A penetração cultural americana* (São Paulo, 1984), 76.

171. Aragão, "Fuga do dólar," 55; Tejo, *Retrato*, 251; "Brazil's Foreign Trade during the Last Ten Years," *Brazil Trade Journal* 4, no. 4 (January–March 1948): 1–3; "Tendências dos negócios e da propaganda," *Anuário de Publicidade*, December 1947, p. 4.

172. "O nosso imperialismo," *O Observador Econômico e Financeiro*, December 1947, p. 5.

173. Tejo, *Retrato*, 55; Alvarus de Oliveira, "Não cremos na morte do Carnaval . . ." (25 February 1944), reprinted in his *Feira de idéias*, 34–35; Walter Clark [Bueno], *A vida de Walter Clark* (Rio de Janeiro, 1982), 20; "As águas fundam cidades," *O Observador Econômico e Financeiro*, February 1943, p. 41; Rodrigues, "Rádio," 19; "Teatro-Romance dos Produtos Marca Peixe" (advertisement), *A Noite*, 24 January 1945, p. 5.

174. "Quantos automóveis, rádios e telefones há na America?," *Digesto Econômico*, May 1945, p. 84 ("considered . . ."; "sense . . ."); H. Monteiro to R. I. Roberge, São Paulo, 2 April 1945 ("the public . . ." and "unchanged"), FHA-BFRC, Accession 46, box 300.

175. "No Early Increase Seen in Import of U.S. Automobiles to Brazil," *Brazil*, June 1948, p. 3 ("very . . ."); "Mais automóveis," *Publicidade & Negócios*, April 1949, p. 30 (remaining quotes).

176. Sol Bloom, *The Autobiography of Sol Bloom* (New York, 1948), 287 ("all bearing . . ."). "Artigo do Dia" advertisements ran in nearly every Rio newspaper; the products examples in the text are drawn from advertisements in the *Tribuna Popular*: 4 December 1945, p. 4; 16 December 1945, p. 7; 1 August 1946, p. 5; 1 September 1946, p. 4; 20 October 1946, p. 8; 24 December 1946, p. 8; 19 January 1947, p. 2; 2 March 1947, p. 5; 27 July 1947, p. 8. For A Exposição radio advertising: 2 February 1946, p. 5; 18 March 1947, p. 8.

177. Clark, *Campeão*, 15; Cecílio Elias Netto, *Memorial de Piracicaba* (Piracicaba, 2000), 240.

178. Arthur Ramos, *Introdução à antropologia brasileira*, 2 vols. (Rio de Janeiro, 1943–1947), 2:153–154, 156, 277.

179. Ramos, *Introdução*, 2:153–154, 156, 277.

Chapter Four

1. This paragraph and those following draw on textual and photographic evidence retained by Sears Holdings, as well as material from the press. For the former: Sears Archives, boxes 104, 3701, 3715–3718. For press coverage, beyond articles quoted in following paragraphs: "Inauguração das grandes lojas 'Sears, Roebuck,'" *O Estado de S. Paulo*, 16 March 1949, p. 8 (quoted here); "A Sears Roebuck provocou panico no comércio varejista de São Paulo," *Publicidade & Negócios*, March 1949, pp. 31–38, 40.

2. Photograph caption ("fluent . . ."), Sears Archives, box 3716; R. E. Wood to W. P. Flynn, Chicago, 22 January 1953, Sears Archives, box 3717.

3. "Paulistas in Wonderland," *Brazilian Business*, April 1949, p. 18; "Sears Opening at São Paulo," *Brazil*, June 1949, p. 18 ("to . . .").

4. "Good-Neighbor Sears," *Newsweek*, 28 March 1949, p. 70 ("any doubt . . ."); "Paulistas in Wonderland," 18 ("hundreds . . ."); also, airgram, Johnson to Secretary of State, Rio de Janeiro, 18 April 1949, RG59, 832.50/4-1849.

5. "A inauguração da 'Sears,'" *Diario de Noticias*, 7 June 1949, sec. 2, p. 1 (Morais); "Sears, Roebuck Rolls into Rio," *Life*, 27 June 1949, p. 32 ("near . . ." and "marched . . .").

6. "Annual Report, 1949," Chicago, 1950, Sears Archives; "Revolução no comércio," *O Observador Econômico e Financeiro*, August 1949, p. 41.

7. Emanuel Rapoport to T. V. Houser, Chicago, 16 September 1946, Sears Archives, box 3717; "Tendências dos negócios," *Publicidade*, November 1946, p. 34; "Letter from Brazil," *Fortune*, February 1947, p. 213; "Chamber Notes," *Brazilian Business*, May 1947, p. 18; K. Orberg to R. I. Roberge, [São Paulo], 7 May 1948, FHA-BFRC, Accession 12, box 32.

8. "Noticiário," *Publicidade & Negócios*, January 1949, p. 8; "Mais um grande anunciante," *Publicidade & Negócios*, February 1949, p. 21; *Quem é quem no Brasil* (1963), sec. "Quem é quem na publicidade e turismo," 5 (Chalmers).

9. "A Sears, Roebuck no Rio," *Publicidade & Negócios*, April 1949, p. 8; "A Sears não anuncia em rádio," *Publicidade & Negócios*, April 1949, pp. 24, 26.

10. "Sears, Roebuck Rolls into Rio," *Life*, 27 June 1949, p. 33; "Good-Neighbor Sears," *Newsweek*, 28 March 1949, p. 70; "Paulistas in Wonderland," *Brazilian Business*, April 1949, p. 18.

11. "Revolução no comércio," *O Observador Econômico e Financeiro*, August 1949, pp. 43–44.

12. "Brazil at a Glance," *Brazilian Business*, December 1948, p. 11; "Vendas no comércio a varejo," *O Observador Econômico e Financeiro*, August 1949, pp. 46–48 (inc. "the least-investigated . . .").

13. "Revolução no comércio," *O Observador Econômico e Financeiro*, August 1949, pp. 42, 44; "A Sears Roebuck . . . ," *Publicidade & Negócios*, March 1949, pp. 33, 38; "Um desfile de modas da Clipper," *Anuário do Rádio*, 1947, p. 96 (quoted); Loja Clipper advertisement, *Folha da Manhã*, 28 November 1943, p. 9.

14. Modas A Exposição Clipper advertisement, *O Estado de S. Paulo*, 21 December 1951, p. 10; "Serve Bem," *PN*, 10 November 1958, p. 59 (Casa José Silva); A Sensação advertisement, *Folha da Manhã*, 9 December 1951, p. 15; "As três Sensações de S. Paulo," *PN*, 5 September 1953, p. 32 ("to . . ."); "Sears, Roebuck and Co. International Operations, Store Information Sheet," August 1965, Sears Archives, box 3693; A Sensação advertisement, *O Estado de S. Paulo*, 15 July 1956, p. 48; A. P. Carvalho, "Novidades em promoção de vendas," *PN*, 5 October 1955, p. 70 (Mappin-Odeon); Modas A Exposição-Clipper advertisement, *PN*, 3 November 1958, pp. 17–18; "Prefiro vender fiado," *PN*, 17 November 1958, pp. 18–21.

15. Pedro Nunes, *35 anos de propaganda* (Rio de Janeiro, n.d.), 57 ("the . . ."); "Serve Bem," *PN*, 10 November 1958, pp. 58–59; "Como surgiu a Casa Barbosa Freitas," *PN*, 20 August 1955, pp. 74–75; "Vendas demais e dinheiro de menos," *PN*, 17 July 1961, p. 29; "Inaugurada a nova loja da 'Casa José Silva' em Copacabana," *PN*, 20 December 1956.

16. "American Goods Display by Mestre & Blatge," *Brazilian American*, 4 July 1922, unpag.; Walter J. Donnelly, Weekly Report No. 46, Rio de Janeiro, 15 May 1939, RG151, RRCAR, box 72; Manoel de Vasconcellos, "Tudo que um grande magazine precisa o Brasil já fabrica," *PN*, 20 September 1954, pp. 26–30, 32 (quoted); "A Christmas Gift for Rio," *Brazilian Business*, December 1954, pp. 14–17; "Mais uma grande loja no populoso e aristocrático bairro da Tijuca," *Ultima Hora*, 5 December 1958, p. 2; "Sears, Roebuck and Co. International Operations, Store Information Sheet," August 1965, Sears Archives, box 3693.

17. "José Júlio de Azevedo e Sá" (interview transcription/summary), AHM-SDLM; "A Sears no Brasil," Sears Archives, box 3717; "Thirteen Years Progressing with Brazil," Sears Archives, box 3717; Richard Earl Hattwick, "Marketing and Economic Growth: The Case of Sears, Roebuck and Company in Brazil" (PhD diss., Vanderbilt University, 1965), 98–100; "For the Well-Dressed Man," *Brazilian Business*, July 1951, pp. 19–20 (inc. "approximately . . ."); "Serve Bem," *PN*, 10 November 1958, pp. 58–59; "Não é possível despir o homem," *PN*, 20 February 1957, pp. 50–51; "Regressa dos EE.UU. o presidente d'A Exposição Modas S.A.," *Correio da Manhã*, 3 June 1949, p. 5 ("most . . ." and "one . . ."); "Prefiro vender fiado," *PN*, 17 November 1958, p. 21.

18. "Revolução no comércio," *O Observador Econômico e Financeiro*, August 1949, p. 44; "De operário a industrial," *Indústria & Mercados*, January 1961, p. 67; Charles Obertance, "Textile Pioneer Builds Gaúcho Industrial Complex," *Brazilian Business*, February 1962, p. 24; "Serve Bem," *PN*, 10 November 1958, pp. 58–59; Emanuel Rapoport to T. V. Houser, Chicago, 16 September 1946, Sears Archives, box 3717; "For the Well-Dressed Man," *Brazilian Business*, July 1951, pp. 19–20 (inc. "advertising . . .");

"Cinco anos de bons serviços em pról do aperfeiçoamento da roupa feita," *PN*, 5 December 1952, pp. 18–19; *Quem é quem no Brasil*, vol. IX (São Paulo, 1967), 23; Genival Rabelo, "Fatos e comentários," *Publicidade & Negócios*, November 1947, p. 8; "Em cinco anos as vendas aumentaram doze vezes," *Publicidade & Negócios*, November 1949, p. 46; José de Carvalho to "Sr. Diretor," *Vendas e Varejo*, January 1959, p. 7 ("I had . . ."); "A história do maior sucesso comercial dos últimos anos," *PN*, 27 February 1958, pp. 20–23 (inc. "I recommend . . .").

19. Hattwick, "Marketing," 143–145.

20. J. U. McManus to T. V. Houser and N. W. Jeran, Rio de Janeiro, 26 October 1949, Sears Archives, box 3717; "Anúncios & campanhas," *Publicidade & Negócios*, 15 March 1950, p. 27; João Carillo, "Verso e reverso," *Publicidade & Negócios*, 1 May 1950, p. 32.

21. A. P. Carvalho, "Novidades em promoção de vendas," *PN*, 20 January 1955, pp. 56–57; J. U. McManus to T. V. Houser, Rio, 29 August 1949, Sears Archives, box 3717; A. P. Carvalho, "Dá resultado o 'artigo do dia'?," *Vendas e Varejo*, February 1960, pp. 32–34; A. P. Carvalho, "Marketing," *PN*, 10 April 1961, p. 45.

22. "Não é possível despir o homem," *PN*, 20 February 1957, p. 50 (Casa Tavares); A. P. Carvalho, "Promoção de vendas," *PN*, 5 May 1957, p. 59 (Sears); Cícero Silveira, "Lojas & vitrinas," *Propaganda*, June 1956, pp. 14–15 (Clipper, Lojas Garbo, Isnard); Isnard advertisement, *O Estado de S. Paulo*, 8 April 1956, p. 68.

23. "6 mil mulheres consagram ontem as 'Goldwyn Girls,'" 15 May 1956 (clipping labeled *Ultima Hora* [São Paulo]), AHM-SDP, texto 513, cx. 2; Mappin announcement, *Folha da Manhã*, 15 May 1956, p. 3.

24. "Anunciou pela priveira [*sic*] vez," *PN*, 5 August 1955, p. 28; *Correio da Manhã*, 24 July 1955, sec. 1, pp. 1, 10, 14–15, sec. 2, p. 3, sec. 5, p. 14; "Anúncios e campanhas," *Publicidade & Negócios*, 15 July 1950, pp. 28, 30.

25. "Anúncios e campanhas," *Publicidade & Negócios*, 15 July 1950, p. 30 ("scoop"); "Como o Mappin vendeu 60% mais num mês normalmente fraco," *Vendas e Varejo*, February 1959, pp. 12–15; Alex Periscinoto, interview by Ilana Strozenberg and Luciana Heymann, 13 July 2004, CPDOC-PHO; Alex Periscinoto, *Mais vale o que se aprende que o que te ensinam* (São Paulo, 1995), 66, 264, 64–66 (respectively).

26. Vasconcellos, "Tudo," 28–29; "A Christmas Gift for Rio," *Brazilian Business*, December 1954, p. 16 ("to make . . ."); Mesbla advertisement, *Correio da Manhã*, 24 July 1955, sec. 1, p. 10; Sydney Clark, *All the Best in South America: East Coast* (New York, 1956), 109; "A Sears Roebuck . . . ," *Publicidade & Negócios*, March 1949, pp. 35–36; "Sears in Latin America: A Visual Presentation of Six Years Growth," Sears Archives, box 3701; Blue Room advertisement, *O Estado de S. Paulo*, 12 March 1950, p. 10; "Prefiro vender fiado," *PN*, 17 November 1958, p. 21; Naum Basbaum, *Noções da técnica no comércio de varejo* (São Paulo, 1954), 81–82 (quoted).

27. A Exposição-Modas Clipper advertisement, *Folha da Manhã*, 3 April 1949, sec. 1, p. 7; A. P. Carvalho, "Novidades em promoção de vendas," *PN*, 5 August 1955, p. 80 ("Bring . . ."); Meyer Stilman, *O comércio varejista e os supermercados na cidade de São Paulo* (São Paulo, 1962), 85 ("with . . ."); "A Christmas Gift for Rio," *Brazilian Business*, December 1954, p. 16 ("park . . ."); Mesbla advertisement, *Ultima Hora*, 7 December 1959, p. 12 ("Children's . . ."); "Registrando . . . ," *Ultima Hora*, 11 April 1960, p. 10 (Mesblinha).

28. Luiz Fernando Furquim, "O consumidor e os meios de comunicação," in *HPB*, 286–287.

29. "A Christmas Gift for Rio," *Brazilian Business*, December 1954, pp. 14–16 (inc. "frankly . . . ," "modeled," "The aisles . . ." and "Mesbla's . . ."); Vasconcellos, "Tudo," 26–28 ("A great . . . ," "to feminize . . ." and Wahl).

30. "Aqui, no coração da cidade, a mais elegante grande loja do Rio de Janeiro," *Publicidade & Negócios*, July 1949, pp. 30–36.

31. "A Sears Roebuck . . . ," *Publicidade & Negócios*, March 1949, pp. 35–36; Furquim, "Consumidor," 286.

32. "O crescimento vertiginoso das Lojas Ducal," *PN*, 5 December 1954, pp. 54–57 (quoted); Ducal-Tiradentes advertisement, *Diario de Noticias*, 7 November 1954, sec. 7, p. 7 ("largest . . ."); "Contratado em New York pela A Exposiçaõ Modas S.A.," *Diario Carioca*, 18 June 1954, p. 5 (quoted); "Grupo 'A Exposição'" advertisement, *Ultima Hora*, 5 January 1956, pp. 6–7; "A Ducal inverterá 20 milhões em publicidade no próximo ano," *PN*, 5 December 1956, p. 44; "Solenemente inauguradas ontem as Lojas Ducal de São Paulo," *Folha da Manhã*, 23 November 1956, p. 2.

33. "Aqui, no coração da cidade . . . ," *Publicidade & Negócios*, July 1949, p. 33.

34. CEBEC advertisement, *O Estado de S. Paulo*, 15 June 1954, p. 7; Sears advertisement, *O Estado de S. Paulo*, 1 August 1954, p. 44; "Na inauguração d'A Exposição Senador," *Correio da Manhã*, 24 October 1954, sec. 1, p. 10; Isnard Engenharia advertisement, *Correio da Manhã*, 22 January 1956, sec. 1, p. 11; "Tudo até 4$400," *PN*, 20 December 1952, p. 28 ("Everyone . . ."); Genival Rabelo, "Fatos & comentários," *PN*, 19 December 1960, p. 14 (Tônia Carrero).

35. Promúsica advertisement, *O Estado de S. Paulo*, 25 December 1958, p. 9; "Presidente da República ouve o 'Peixe-Vivo' e enquanto trabalha trata de descansar," *Jornal do Brasil*, 1 September 1957, sec. 1, p. 13 (Mesbla); "JK nada em Laranjeiras ao som do 'Peixe Vivo,'" *Revista da Semana*, 21 December 1957, p. 14 ("organized . . ."); "A música aumenta as vendas nas lojas," *Vendas e Varejo*, June 1959, p. 57 (Ducal).

36. Airpouch, Rio de Janeiro, 29 March 1950, "Primary Grades of Paper Used for Wrapping & Packaging," by Isabel L. Herwig, RG59, 832.392/3-2950; "'Bôlsas Pratix' abrem caminho no Brasil," *Vendas e Varejo*, October 1959, p. 70; "Grande sucesso das 'Bôlsas Pratix,'" *Vendas e Varejo*, January 1960, p. 36.

37. "A Sears Roebuck . . . ," *Publicidade & Negócios*, March 1949, p. 36; Victório Franceschini in *40 anos de supermercados no Brasil* (São Paulo, 1993), 174.

38. Otis Elevator advertisement, *Correio da Manhã*, 5 June 1959, p. 5; Joaquim Ferreira dos Santos, *Feliz 1958: O ano que não devia terminar* (Rio de Janeiro, 1997), 15; Clipper advertisement, *Folha da Manhã*, 19 December 1954, sec. "Assuntos Gerais," 9; Vasconcellos, "Tudo," 27 ("indispensable . . ."); "Tudo até 4$400," *PN*, 20 December 1952, p. 27; Basbaum, *Noções*, 81.

39. "Casa José Silva," *Ultima Hora*, 18 June 1951, p. 5; "Inauguração de mais uma moderníssima loja com 123 departamentos," *Folha da Manhã*, 1 December 1956, p. 5 ("a new . . ."); "Aspectos dos grandes magazines, no centro e bairros paulistanos," *Folha da Manhã*, 1 December 1956, p. 5 (remaining quotes); Eletro-Radiobraz advertisement, *Folha da Manhã*, 4 December 1956, p. 6.

40. Vasconcellos, "Tudo," 27–29; Yvonne Jean, "Vitrinistas e acompanhantes," *Ultima Hora*, 16 July 1957, sec. "*Ultima Hora* em Tabloide," 6 ("Rio . . ."); Gunther

Pamp, "Vitrina: Fator preponderante de vendas," *Propaganda*, June 1957, p. 12 ("Today . . .").

41. "Alfredo Brigantini ensina como executar uma vitrine," *PN*, 20 July 1955, p. 29; "Em cinco anos . . . ," *Publicidade & Negócios*, November 1949, p. 43; "O crescimento vertiginoso das Lojas Ducal," *PN*, 5 December 1954, p. 55; "A vitrina vende mais que certos empregados," *PN*, 20 November 1952, p. 44; "A opinião de comerciantes sobre a promoção de o 'Dia das Mães,'" *PN*, 20 June 1953, p. 29; Pamp, "Vitrina," 12.

42. "Sears in Latin America: A Visual Presentation of Six Years [*sic*] Growth," Sears Archives, box 3701; Modas Clipper advertisement, *O Estado de S. Paulo*, 12 September 1948, p. 13; A. P. Carvalho, "Novidades em promoção de vendas," *PN*, 5 October 1955, p. 70; "Já se pode fazer compras em São Paulo levando o carro até dentro da loja!" (clipping labeled *Ultima Hora* [São Paulo], 28 August 1955), AHM-SDP, texto 480, cx. 2.

43. "Anúncios e campanhas," *Publicidade & Negócios*, October 1947, pp. 22–23.

44. Consulate General to Department of State, São Paulo, 19 December 1952, FSD 204, "São Paulo Municipal Government Orders Night Closings of Retail Stores," by E. T. Kelsy, RG59, 832.00/12-1952.

45. W. P. Flynn to R. E. Wood, Rio de Janeiro, 27 October 1952 (quoted), and 13 January 1953, Sears Archives, box 3717.

46. "Em cinco anos . . . ," *Publicidade & Negócios*, November 1949, p. 46 (José de Carvalho); Owen Roche, "SENAC Sends Its Trainee to the United States," *Brazil*, December 1948, pp. 12–13; Vasconcellos, "Tudo," 28; "O crescimento vertiginoso das Lojas Ducal," *PN*, 5 December 1954, p. 56; "No mundo fabuloso do comércio varejista de New York," *PN*, 20 December 1956 ("fabulous . . ." through "most . . ."); "Os lojistas acordam cêdo e vão à aula," *PN*, 31 July 1958, pp. 28, 30 ("The Retail . . .").

47. José Luiz Moreira de Souza, "Rotação de estoque," *Vendas e Varejo*, May 1959, p. 4; Genival Rabelo, "Quando a inflação não atinge o varejo," *Vendas e Varejo*, October 1959, p. 66; "Vendas demais e dinheiro de menos," *PN*, 17 July 1961, p. 30.

48. "Em cinco anos . . . ," *Publicidade & Negócios*, November 1949, p. 46 (IBOPE); "A Ducal inverterá 20 milhões em publicidade no próximo ano," *PN*, 5 December 1956, p. 44 (quoted); "Otimismo hoje é atitude realista," *PN*, 7 March 1960, p. 18. On advertising agencies dedicating greater resources to research and founding research departments: e.g., Genival Rabelo, *Os tempos heróicos da propaganda* (Rio de Janeiro, 1956), 23, 41, 45, 52–53. On independent and quasi-independent institutes: "Depoimento de Arthur de Moraes Cesar," São Paulo, 6 December 1988, IPHSP; "A pesquisa de mercado e a venda," *Vendas e Varejo*, July 1959, pp. 16–21; "V. conhece seu mercado?," *O Dirigente Industrial*, February 1963, p. 63.

49. "Pesquisa interna entre consumidores," *Propaganda*, September 1956, pp. 60–61.

50. J. U. McManus to T. V. Houser and N. W. Jeran, Rio de Janeiro, 26 October 1949, Sears Archives, box 3717; "A Christmas Gift for Rio," *Brazilian Business*, December 1954, p. 16; Vasconcellos, "Tudo," 29.

51. Vasconcellos, "Tudo," 30, 32; "A Sears Roebuck . . . ," *Publicidade & Negócios*, March 1949, p. 32; Carl Kresl, "Brazil," São Paulo, 29 December 1950 ("Sears' . . ."), and "Thirteen Years Progressing with Brazil," 1962, Sears Archives, box 3717.

52. Genival Rabelo, "Fatos & comentários," *Publicidade & Negócios*, 15 March 1951, p. 20; "A Exposição inaugura uma escola de comércio para preparar vendedores e

chefes," *Correio da Manhã*, 29 October 1950, sec. 1, p. 7 (quoted); J. Benoliel, *Curso de aperfeiçoamento para vendedores de balcão*, 2nd ed. (Rio de Janeiro, 1954); "Escola para a formação de chefes," *Publicidade & Negócios*, 15 November 1950, p. 34; "No mundo fabuloso . . . ," *PN*, 20 December 1956.

53. "Novo curso de direção executiva para gerentes," *Noticiário Mappin*, 24 December 1955, p. 3, AHM; "Curso de direção executiva para gerentes de vendas," *Noticiário Mappin*, February 1956, p. 1, AHM; "Vendas demais e dinheiro de menos," *PN*, 17 July 1961, p. 24; Francisco Gomes de Mattos, "Método TWI para treinamento de vendedores," *PN*, 10 July 1958, pp. 32, 34; "A importância da arte de vender," *Noticiário Mappin*, May 1953, p. 2, AHM; "Pague a sua dívida com o progresso," *Noticiário Mappin*, November 1953, p. 3, AHM; "Adquira melhores hábitos de vender," *Noticiário Mappin*, December 1953, pp. 2, 4, AHM; "Grandiosa convenção da Ducal em Quitadinha," *PN*, 5 September 1957, p. 11; Manuel Árias, "A evolução do comércio varejista," *Vendas e Varejo*, May 1960, p. 2; Periscinoto, *Mais vale*, 58–63; Nunes, *35 anos*.

54. "Em cinco anos . . . ," *Publicidade & Negócios*, November 1949, pp. 40, 46; "O segrêdo do comércio a crédito," *PN*, 20 December 1952, p. 59; "O crescimento vertiginoso das Lojas Ducal," *PN*, 5 December 1954, p. 56; "A história do maior sucesso comercial dos últimos anos," *PN*, 27 February 1958, p. 23; "Prefiro vender fiado," *PN*, 17 November 1958, p. 21; Manoel Árias, "Uma loja com 18 gerentes," *PN*, 5 March 1953, p. 17; Silveira, "Lojas," 14; Hattwick, "Marketing," 147.

55. "Em cinco anos . . . ," *Publicidade & Negócios*, November 1949, p. 46; A Sensação advertisement, *O Estado de S. Paulo*, 6 January 1957, pp. 10–11; "Tendências dos negócios," *PN*, 5 July 1956, p. 40.

56. Milton de Souza Carvalho, *História de um comerciante* (Rio de Janeiro, 1955), 95; Adriano Vaz de Carvalho, "Vamos falar a verdade sobre o crediário," *Publicidade & Negócios*, 15 April 1950, p. 6; Enéas de Almeida, "Sim . . . 'Vamos falar a verdade sobre crediário,'" *Publicidade & Negócios*, 1 May 1950, p. 40; Silveira, "Lojas," 14.

57. Carvalho, "Vamos falar," 7; Hattwick, "Marketing," 137–139, 146–153; Carvalho, *História*, 145–147; "Lauro de Souza Carvalho assume a presidencia do Banco da Capital," *Revista de Economia Popular*, April 1950, p. 41; Geraldo Banas, "Capitais franceses no Brasil," *O Observador Econômico e Financeiro*, September 1958, p. 29; "Mappin Stores Becomes Brazilian," *Brazilian Business*, September 1950, p. 29.

58. "Criado em São Paulo o Serviço Central de Proteção ao Crédito," *PN*, 5 December 1955, p. 66; "Resultados cada vez mais amplos em defesa do comércio de vendas a prazo," *Vendas e Varejo*, November 1959, pp. 20–21; "Maior segurança de crédito em S. Paulo," *Correio da Manhã*, 20 June 1965, sec. "Econômico," 6; "Tendências dos negócios," *PN*, 5 July 1956, p. 39; "A história do maior sucesso comercial dos últimos anos," *PN*, 27 February 1958, p. 23; "Os lojistas acordam cêdo e vão à aula," *PN*, 31 July 1958, p. 30; "Serviço de Proteção ao Crédito," *Vendas e Varejo*, October 1960, pp. 22–24; Nunes, *35 anos*, 228; "Quando ter crédito é bom negócio," *PN*, 20 December 1962, p. 38.

59. "Maior segurança de crédito em S. Paulo," *Correio da Manhã*, 20 June 1965, sec. "Econômico," 6.

60. "Business Conditions in Brazil," *Brazilian Business*, March 1926, pp. 19–20; A. Ogden Pierrot, [document missing title page] Rio de Janeiro, 10 January 1929 (quoted), RG151, RRCAR, box 54; Carlton Jackson, "Material for Use in Connection

with Monthly Economic Cable Report," Rio de Janeiro, 17 February 1933, RG151, RRCAR, box 62; Alvaro Moreyra, *Tempo perdido* (Rio de Janeiro, 1936), 11; A Exposição advertisement, *O Estado de S. Paulo*, 24 February 1933, p. 2; "Indicador do Carnaval d' 'O Paiz,'" *O Paiz*, 10 December 1933, p. 10; "Notas editoriaes," *O Observador Econômico e Financeiro*, March 1936, p. 6.

61. A Exposição advertisements in *A Noite*, 14 February 1949, pp. 5 and 7, 21 February 1949, p. 2, and *Diario de Noticias*, 5 February 1950, sec. 2, p. 7, and 10 February 1950, sec. 1, p. 1; "Anúncios & campanhas," *Publicidade & Negócios*, 15 March 1950, pp. 26–27 (quoted); Nunes, *35 anos*, 85–88, 194–196.

62. "Anúncios & campanhas," *Publicidade & Negócios*, 15 March 1950, p. 26.

63. "Promoção de vendas no Carnaval," *Publicidade & Negócios*, 1 February 1951, p. 13; Sangirardi Jr., "Chumbo miudo," *Publicidade & Negócios*, 15 January 1952, p. 22.

64. "Comércio de Carnaval," *Conjuntura Econômica*, March 1954, pp. 33–42; "O rádio teatro não louva o rei da folia," *Diario Carioca*, 2 February 1958, sec. "Revista dos Espetáculos," 5.

65. "Christmas in Summer in Brazil," *Brazil*, December 1937, p. 16; "Em cinco anos . . . ," *Publicidade & Negócios*, November 1949, pp. 39, 43; Willard Espy, *Bold New Program* (New York, 1950), 90–91; "Papai Noel, idéia de propaganda," *Publicidade & Negócios*, 15 January 1952, p. 60. Brazil's Christmas traditions are largely unstudied. For pre-1930s traditions, I have drawn on memorial literature, e.g., Humberto de Campos, *Memórias inacabadas* (Rio de Janeiro,1941), 175–176; Jorge Americano, *São Paulo naquele tempo, 1895–1915* (São Paulo, 1957), 275–277, 280; Povina Cavalcanti, *Volta à infância: Memórias* (Rio de Janeiro, 1972), 39, 112–113, 147; Eugenio Gomes, *O mundo da minha infância* (Rio de Janeiro, 1969), 128; Maria Helena Cardoso, *Por onde andou meu coração: Memórias* (Rio de Janeiro, 1967), 98–100; Cyro dos Anjos, *Explorações no tempo* (Rio de Janeiro, 1963), 44–45; Augusto Frederico Schmidt, *O galo branco: Páginas de memórias* (Rio de Janeiro, 1957), 64–65, 162; Ernani Silva Bruno, *Almanaque de memórias: Reminiscências, depoimentos, reflexões* (São Paulo, 1986), 49; Edmar Morel, *Histórias de um repórter* (Rio de Janeiro, 1999), 28–29; Darcy Ribeiro, *Confissões* (São Paulo, 1997), 56–58. See also Brasil Gerson, *Vinte anos de circo* (São Paulo, n.d.), 109, and the oral histories in Ecléa Bosi, *Memória e sociedade: Lembranças de velhos* (São Paulo, 1979), 53, 57, 65, 79, 108, 170, 244–245, 303–304. A search of the online database of *O Estado de S. Paulo* for mentions of Papai/Papae Noel provides a rough index to the midcentury explosion of his cultural presence in Brazil: mentioned 4 times in the newspaper between 1910 and 1919, 18 times in the 1920s, 89 in the 1930s, 69 in the 1940s, 295 in the 1950s, and 420 in the 1960s (acervo.estadao.com.br, accessed 17 December 2013).

66. "O Natal no Rio de Janeiro," *PN*, 20 January 1953, p. 8; "História de uma promoção de vendas," *PN*, 5 February 1953, pp. 34–35 (inc. "We . . ."); "As mais lindas vitrinas do Natal," *PN*, 20 January 1954, pp. 8–9; "Comércio de Natal," *Conjuntura Econômica*, January 1953, pp. 32–33; "Perspectivas do comércio de Natal," *Conjuntura Econômica*, December 1953, pp. 31–32 (inc. "growing . . .").

67. A. P. Carvalho, "Novidades em promoção de vendas," *PN*, 20 March 1955, pp. 21–22; "Uma revista promove um magazine," *PN*, 5 August 1956; "A Christmas Gift for Rio," *Brazilian Business*, December 1954, pp. 14, 17; Carvalho, "Idéias e novidades," *PN*, 20 December 1955, p. 82; "Amanhã, Papai Noel irá ao Largo da Carioca,"

Correio da Manhã, 18 December 1955, sec. 1, p. 11 ("biggest . . ."); Carvalho, "Idéias & novidades," *PN*, 5 December 1956, p. 60 ("a spectacular . . .").

68. Maurício Rabello, "Promoção do Natal carioca," *Vendas e Varejo*, January 1959, pp. 9–11; "Papai Noel no Rio," *Vendas e Varejo*, January 1960, pp. 4–7.

69. A. P. Carvalho, "Idéias & Novidades," *PN*, 5 December 1956, p. 60; João de La Fontaine, "Copy-Clínica," *PN*, 26 December 1957, p. 34; Décio Pignatari, "Natal— magia promocional," *PN*, 24 November 1958, p. 46; Elsie Lessa, "Fim de ano," *SINGRA*, 1–7 January 1960, p. 3; "Papai Noel descerá hoje no Maracana," *Correio da Manhã*, 25 November 1962, sec. 1, p. 3; David St. Clair, "Christmas in the Tropics," *Brazilian Business*, December 1967, p. 10 ("In . . .").

70. APP, *Depoimentos* (São Paulo, 1973), 88–89 ("creating . . ."); "Dia das Mães," *Propaganda*, May 1956, p. 50; "O 'Dia das Mães' no Brasil," *Propaganda*, May 1958, pp. 12–13; Genival Rabelo, *A batalha da opinião pública* (Rio de Janeiro, 1970), 46–47; Genival Rabelo, "Fatos & comentários," *Publicidade & Negócios*, 1 September 1951, pp. 6–12 (Standard's president).

71. "A opinião de comerciantes sobre a promoção de o 'Dia das Mães,'" *PN*, 20 June 1953, p. 29; "Escolhido a cartaz para o 'Dia das Mães' de 1954," *PN*, 20 April 1954, p. 23; "A mãe brasileira do ano," *PN*, 20 April 1954, p. 45; "O 'Dia das Mães' como promoção," *PN*, 5 June 1954, pp. 38–42; "As pessoas—Os dias—As coisas," *PN*, 20 May 1955, p. 11; "O sentido promocional do 'Dia das Mães,'" *PN*, 20 April 1957, pp. 63–65; A. P. Carvalho, "Novidades em promoção de vendas," *PN*, 20 March 1955, p. 21; Carvalho, "Idéias & novidades," *PN*, 20 April 1956, p. 74. For *O Globo*'s then-new department: Roberto Martinho's introduction to Walter Poyares, *Imagem pública* (São Paulo, 1998), 9; "Um jornal moderno," *PN*, 5 September 1954, pp. 36–37.

72. "Anúncios e campanhas," *Publicidade & Negócios*, June 1948, pp. 34–35 (quoted); "Anúncios e campanhas," *Publicidade & Negócios*, June 1949, p. 38; "Pelas agências," *Publicidade & Negócios*, June 1949, p. 44; Genival Rabelo, "Fatos & comentários," *PN*, 20 March 1955, p. 20. Father's Day: "As melhores vitrinas cariocas para o 'Dia do Papai,'" *PN*, 20 September 1953, p. 76; Manoel de Vasconcellos, "Uma palavra do editor," *PN*, 5 September 1954, pp. 2, 4; A. P. Carvalho, "Novidades em promoção de vendas," *PN*, 20 September 1955, p. 73; "Diplomas e prêmios aos colaboradores do 'Dia do Papai,'" *PN*, 20 September 1956, p. 18.

73. "Campanhas & promoções," *Propaganda*, January 1957, p. 17; Kibon advertisement, *O Estado de S. Paulo*, 12 October 1956, p. 9; "Promoção do Dia da Criança," *PN*, 12 October 1959, p. 43. JWT's representing Kibon: "J. Walter Thompson Company do Brasil List of Clients," June 1961, *J. Walter Thompson Company do Brasil*, 1961, JWTA, Information Center Vertical Files, box 10.

74. A. P. Carvalho, "Novidades em promoção de vendas," *PN*, 20 December 1954, p. 62.

75. Basbaum, *Noções*, 92–93.

76. Cícero Silveira, "Quais as melhores épocas para promover vendas?," *Propaganda*, November 1957, p. 24; A. P. Carvalho, "Novidades em promoção de vendas," *PN*, 20 March 1955, p. 21.

77. "Em cinco anos . . . ," *Publicidade & Negócios*, November 1949, p. 39; Vasconcellos, "Tudo," 29–30; Francisco Gracioso, "A promoção de vendas no Brasil," *Propaganda*, February 1961, p. 16. For the "Calendário Promocional": in magazines, *Publicidade & Negócios-PN* (from 1954), *Propaganda* (from 1957), and *Vendas e Varejo*

(from 1959); in newsletters, "Um exito o calendârio promocional," *PN*, 20 January 1956, p. 72; in books, Ruy Chalmers, *Gerência de loja, técnica varejista e promoção de vendas em lojas de varejo* (Rio de Janeiro, 1966).

78. A. P. Carvalho, "Novidades em promoção de vendas," *PN*, 20 September 1955, p. 73.

79. Fiction: Silveira Peixoto, *Papai Noel é muito adulador!* (Curitiba, n.d.); Carlos Drummond de Andrade, "A mãe e o fogão" (1961) and "A outra senhora" (n.d.), in *Cadeira de balanço* (Rio de Janeiro, 1966), 90–91 and 155–157. "Class D": Carolina Maria de Jesus, *Child of the Dark*, trans. David St. Clair (New York, 1963 [1960]), 33, 96. Women: David José Lessa Mattos, *O espetáculo da cultura paulista: Teatro e televisão em São Paulo, décadas de 1940 e 1950* (São Paulo, 2002), 226; Bosi, *Memória*, 289. Interviewees: St. Clair, "Christmas," 10 (Raimundo Araujo); Bosi, *Memória*, 303–304 (D. Risoleta), 244 (D. Brites), 57 (D. Alice, for whom Bosi does not provide birth year). For Araujo's birth year: "Raimundo de Araujo," JWTA, EGWP, box 78.

80. Bosi, *Memória*, 238, 247; Cláudio Abramo, *A regra do jogo: O jornalismo e a ética do marceneiro*, ed. Cláudio Weber Abramo (São Paulo, 1988), 31; Manoel de Vasconcellos, "Uma palavra do editor," *Publicidade & Negócios*, 1 March 1951, p. 2 ("which . . ."); Paul Vanorden Shaw, "Fatores reais nas relações Brasil-EUA," *O Estado de S. Paulo*, 16 August 1956, p. 5.

81. Rabelo, *Batalha*, 16; "'O Estado de São Paulo' bateu todos os recordes de farturamento em nosso país," *PN*, 5 July 1955, p. 31.

82. "'O Globo'—Campeão das promoções," *PN*, 20 January 1957, p. 20; *O Globo*, 15 August 1953.

83. Carlos Lacerda, *A missão da imprensa*, 2nd ed. (São Paulo, 1990 [1950]), 73.

84. Samuel Wainer, *Minha razão de viver: Memórias de um repórter*, ed. Augusto Nunes (Rio de Janeiro, 1987), quote on 151; "'Ultima Hora'—Um novo tipo de jornal," *PN*, 20 March 1953, pp. 31–34 (inc. "35% . . ."); *Ultima Hora* advertisement, *PN*, 5 June 1953, p. 25 ("'round-table' . . ."); "'Ultima Hora' enterrou o espírito artesão na imprensa brasileira," *PN*, 20 July 1956, p. 49 (Wainer); "O 'Dia das Mães' e o novo salário-mínimo transformam a fisionomia do comércio," *Ultima Hora*, 7 May 1954, p. 7.

85. "'Shopping News' de São Paulo," *PN*, 1 November 1952, pp. 58–59 (inc. JWT quote); "São Paulo's First Cafeteria," *Brazilian Business*, July 1955, p. 16; "'Shopping News' do Rio com 120 mil exemplares," *PN*, 20 October 1956, p. 16; "Jornal, mesmo dado de graça, é a indústria mais lucrativa do Brasil," *PN*, 26 December 1957, pp. 40–42 (inc. "made . . ."); APP, *Depoimentos*, 70 ("higher . . .").

86. For the supplement's founding statement: *O Estado de S. Paulo*, 25 September 1953, "Suplemento Feminino," 2. For "Compare e . . . compre": Mary, "?," *O Estado de S. Paulo*, 23 October 1953, "Suplemento Feminino," 5 (quoted); Mary, "?," *O Estado de S. Paulo*, 6 November 1953, "Suplemento Feminino," 3; Mary, "Compare e . . . compre," *O Estado de S. Paulo*, 13 November 1953, "Suplemento Feminino," 3. On the *Jornal do Brasil*, Alzira Alves de Abreu, "Revisitando os anos 1950 através da imprensa," in *O moderno em questão*, ed. André Botelho, Élide Rugai Bastos, and Gláucia Villas Boas (Rio de Janeiro, 2008), 216; *Ultima Hora*'s tabloid debuted with the 16 October 1956 issue.

87. Hattwick, "Marketing," 138–139; Manoel de Vasconcellos, "Uma palavra do editor," *PN*, 20 March 1956, p. 2; Melo Lima, "O negócio de publicidade no Brasil,"

O Observador Econômico e Financeiro, July 1954, p. 58; "Quanto se gastou em publicidade no Brasil em 1957 [*sic*]," *Anuário de Publicidade*, 1957, p. 227; "Pelas agências," *PN*, 5 July 1955, pp. 25–26 (Wainer, *O Globo, Shopping News*); "Fatos e opiniões," *PN*, 21 November 1957, p. 5 (Moses).

88. Rabelo, *Tempos*, 75–76.

89. *Anuário Brasileiro de Imprensa*, 1948, p. 36; *O Cruzeiro*, 22 November 1958, p. 6; "Não encontrei em nenhum país tantas oportunidades comerciais como no Brasil," *Publicidade & Negócios*, 1 January 1952, p. 16 ("A single . . ."); "Espelho da imprensa," *Publicidade & Negócios*, 15 July 1952, p. 54; "Algumas novidades que merecem ser vistas," *PN*, 20 August 1955, pp. 30–32; J. Erkman, "Uma engrenagem complicada," *O Cruzeiro*, 22 November 1958, p. 74 ("Advertising . . ."); "'O Cruzeiro': Seu amigo de 30 anos," *O Cruzeiro*, 22 November 1958, p. 35.

90. "*Seleções* com uma tiragem de 350 mil exemplares," *Publicidade & Negócios*, 1 October 1951, pp. 39, 42; "'Seleções' com 410 mil exemplares," *PN*, 5 December 1953, pp. 26, 28; "Plano de 'merchandising,'" *PN*, 5 December 1953, pp. 27–28; "O departamento de circulação de 'Seleções,'" *PN*, 5 December 1953, p. 26; "600 mil exemplares," *Anuário de Publicidade*, 1957, p. 167.

91. "Espelho da imprensa," *Publicidade & Negócios*, 15 July 1952, p. 54 (Inter-Americana); Manoel de Vasconcellos, "Uma palavra do editor," *Publicidade & Negócios*, 15 May 1952, p. 4 (quoted).

92. "A'Mágica Revista do Amor' com uma tiragem de 100 mil exemplares," *PN*, 5 February 1953, p. 36; Rabelo, *Tempos*, 75.

93. "Little Duck—Big Deal," *Brazilian Business*, April 1952, pp. 19–20; Victor Civita, "O melhor cliente do mundo," *PN*, 20 March 1957, p. 23 ("the best . . ."); "90 mil exemplares a tiragem inicial de 'Capricho,'" *Publicidade & Negócios*, 15 July 1952, pp. 58–59 (inc. "a complete . . ."); "'Capricho': Um milhão de exemplares dentro de dois anos," *PN*, 12 June 1958, pp. 50–53; "Um cinema com meio milhão de poltronas," *PN*, 22 September 1958, four-page advertising insert at 32ff ("Monthly . . ."); "Capricho, mais um record de tiragem," *Propaganda*, November 1958, p. 22; "Uma revista que sextuplicou sua tiragem em quatro anos," *PN*, 5 December 1956, p. 17 (remaining quotes, save for "to belong . . . ," from "'Capricho': Um milhão . . . ," above, 51).

94. "'Cinelândia' sairá quinzenalmente a partir de abril," *PN*, 5 February 1953, p. 33; "Uma revista promove um magazine," *PN*, 5 August 1956, pp. 69–72; "'Show' de promoções em torno do 'Dia das Mães,'" *PN*, 20 June 1957, p. 21; *PN*, 10 October 1960, advertising insert at 28f; *Capricho-Você* advertisement, *PN*, 20 January 1957, pp. 37–39.

95. *Casa e Jardim* advertisement, *Propaganda*, October 1959, p. 4.

96. *Boletim das Classes Dirigentes*, no. 2 (6–13 November 1950): 7 ("poor . . ."), AEL-IBOPE; "O segrêdo do comércio a crêdito," *PN*, 20 December 1952, p. 58; "Brazil's Big Electronics Industry," *Brazilian Business*, August 1957, p. 20 ("a must . . ."). My estimate for 1948 represents a dialing back of that made by Manuel L. Leite on the basis of widely cited *Anuário do Rádio* data (Leite, "Rádio—O fabuloso veículo dos anos 30, 40, 50, 60, 70, etc., etc.," *Propaganda*, December 1974, pp. 48, 52) and accords with the 1951 estimate presented in Amara Rocha's *Nas ondas da modernização: O rádio e a TV no Brasil de 1950 a 1970* (Rio de Janeiro, 2007), 159. The estimate for the late 1950s and regional comparisons are from Frank Dunbaugh, *Marketing in Latin*

America (New York, 1960), 94. For conflicting estimates of ownership and production, e.g., Roberto Lobel to Department of State, Rio de Janeiro, 11 January 1950, "Annual Report on Radio Receiving Sets, Radio Receiving Tubes, and Radio Components," RG59, 832.335/1-1150; Charles E. Dickerson, Jr., to Department of State, Rio de Janeiro, 31 January 1951, "Annual Economic Report—1950," RG59, 832.00/1-3151; Samuel D. Eaton to Department of State, Rio de Janeiro, 26 February 1951, "Annual Report on Radio Receiving Sets, Radio Receiving Tubes, and Radio Components," RG59, 832.335/2-2651; Gertrude B. Heare to Department of State, Rio de Janeiro, 6 November 1951, and attachment, "Summary of Basic Economic Information—Brazil," RG59, 832.00/11-651; "Rádio, imprensa e cinema," *Conjuntura Econômica*, December 1952, pp. 69–71; "A indústria mecânica," *O Observador Econômico e Financeiro*, October 1950, p. 93; Heitor Ferreira Lima, "Fabricação de aparelhos domésticos," *O Observador Econômico e Financeiro*, August 1958, p. 37; Marcus Pereira, "O rádio do vizinho," *O Estado de S. Paulo*, 21 December 1958, p. 94; Herculano Borges da Fonseca, "Panorama of Economic Development of Brazil," *Brazilian-American Survey*, no. 10 (1959): 50; "Fatos & ideias," *PN*, 27 April 1959, p. 47; Antônio Andrade Nogueira, "Rádio brasileiro: Uma fôrça viva sob muitos prismas," *Propaganda*, June 1960, p. 8; Leite, "Rádio—O fabuloso," 52.

97. "Rádio, imprensa e cinema," *Conjuntura Econômica*, December 1952, p. 71; Nogueira, "Rádio," 8.

98. Paulo Cesar Ferreira, *Pilares via satélite: Da Rádio Nacional à Rede Globo* (Rio de Janeiro, 1998), 54–55; Walter Clark [Bueno], *O campeão de audiência* (São Paulo, 1991), 34; "A estação das multidões," *Veja*, 15 September 1976, 88–90, 92; Alcir Lenharo, *Cantores do rádio: A trajetória de Nora Ney e Jorge Goulart e o meio artístico de seu tempo* (Campinas,1995), 135; Rádio Nacional, "20 anos de liderança a serviço do Brasil (1936-1956)," quoted in Maria Arminda do Nascimento Arruda, *Metrópole e cultura: São Paulo no meio século XX* (Bauru, 2001), 128; "Depoimento de Gualter Leão," Rio de Janeiro, 9 November 1988, IPHSP.

99. "Rádio, imprensa e cinema," *Conjuntura Econômica*, December 1952, pp. 72–73; U.S. Department of Commerce, *Brazil: Information for United States Businessmen* (Washington, D.C., 1961), 143.

100. Clark, *Campeão*, 34–35 (inc. "was . . ."); J. R. Tinhorão, "Nos anos de ouro dos auditórios," *Jornal do Brasil*, 1 May 1977, sec. *Revista do Domingo*, 28–33 (inc. "a type . . . ," "and if . . ."); Ferreira, *Pilares*, 66 ("From . . ." and "to participate . . .").

101. Tinhorão, "Nos anos," 30 ("increasing . . ."); "O direito de nascer," *Publicidade & Negócios*, 1 September 1951, p. 32; Nestor de Holanda, "Mamãe Dolores—a que salvou Albertino," *A Noite Ilustrada*, 15 April 1952, pp. 8–11, 16 (inc. "Businessmen . . ."); "O rádio teatro não louva o rei da folia," *Diario Carioca*, 2 February 1958, sec. "Revista dos Espetáculos," 5.

102. Pereira, "Rádio"; "São estes os culpados," *A Noite Ilustrada*, 6 July 1948, pp. 23–24; "Tendências dos negócios e da propaganda," *Publicidade & Negócios*, July 1948, p. 2; Renato Ignácio da Silva, *Xerifes e coronéis* (Itaquaquecetuba, 1989), 148–149; "Os 'jingles' ameaçam os programas," *Publicidade & Negócios*, May 1949, p. 6; José Scatena, "O 'jingle' e as campanhas políticas," *PN*, 1 August 1952, p. 23; Scatena, "Nascimento, vida e glória do jingle," *Propaganda*, June 1956, pp. 28–30; Leo Erickson, "Marketing Management of the U.S. Firm's Brazil Subsidiary," in Claude McMillan and Richard

Gonzalez, *International Enterprise in a Developing Economy: A Study of U.S. Business in Brazil* (East Lansing, Mich., 1964), 151.

103. Clark, *Campeão*, 43; "Idéia grandiosa que se fez realidade," *Revista do Rádio*, 27 May 1952, pp. 40–41; Vasconcellos, "Tudo," 29; "Um negócio que progride em todo o mundo," *PN*, 5 August 1954, p. 112; "Notas e fatos," *Noticiário Mappin*, December 1953, p. 2, AHM.

104. Rocha, *Nas ondas*, 54 (Associados executive); Genival Rabelo, "Fatos & comentários," *Publicidade & Negócios*, 1 February 1951, pp. 14, 16; Rabelo, "Fatos & comentários," *Publicidade & Negócios*, 1 April 1951, p. 12; Jorge Edo interview, quoted in Mattos, *Espetáculo*, 72n; Ney Lima Figueiredo, *O poder da propaganda* (Rio de Janeiro, 1965), 58; Alcir Henrique da Costa, "TV Rio: 22 anos no ar," in Inimá Ferreira Simões, Alcir Henrique da Costa, and Maria Rita Kehl, *Um país no ar: História da TV brasileira em três canais* (São Paulo, 1986), 131 (Eucharist Congress); Glauco Carneiro, *Brasil, primeiro: História dos Diários Associados* (Brasília, 1999), 314 (Chateaubriand).

105. "Where Television Grows," insert in *J. Walter Thompson Company News*, 31 December 1951, JWTA; "Advertising & Marketing," *New York Times*, 26 January 1953, p. 31; "TV Advertising: How and Why?," *Brazilian Business*, February 1954, p. 22; J. Walter Thompson Company, *The Latin American Markets* (New York, 1956), 37; Department of Commerce, *Brazil*, 143 (USIA); "TV Comes of Age in Brazil," *Brazilian Business*, September 1957, p. 19; Tad Szulc, "Television's Progress in Brazil," *New York Times*, 26 January 1958, X13. The official Brazilian Institute of Geography and Statistics, by contrast, estimated that there were only 70,000 television sets in the country in 1956 (see Maria Elvira Bonavita Federico, *História da comunicação: Rádio e TV no Brasil* [Petrópolis, 1982], 139), which is suggestive of how morosely such information was gathered and of the volume of contraband.

106. "Where Television Grows"; "TV Comes of Age in Brazil," *Brazilian Business*, September 1957, p. 19; "TV Advertising: How and Why?," *Brazilian Business*, February 1954, p. 22; Lélia Abramo, *Vida e arte: Memórias* (São Paulo, 1997), 133; Hamilton de Souza, "Imagem—de Brucutu a Gagárin," *Propaganda*, May 1962, p. 14. "Televisitor" is my attempt at preserving the ring of the Brazilianism "televizinho" (literally, "teleneighbor").

107. "TV Comes of Age in Brazil," *Brazilian Business*, September 1957, pp. 18–22 (inc. for *O ceu é o limite*, *Um milhão Probel*, *Boliche Royal*); "Where Television Grows" (for association football); "TV Advertising: How and Why?," *Brazilian Business*, February 1954, pp. 22–24 (inc. for *Circo Bombril*); "Entre anunciantes," *PN*, 20 October 1953, p. 12 (*Sítio . . .*); Clark, *Campeão*, 78–79 (*Noite . . .*). For Clipper's Children's Festival and *Sítio*'s author, see this chapter and chapter 2, respectively.

108. "TV Advertising: How and Why?," *Brazilian Business*, February 1954, pp. 22–24; Guilherme Figueiredo, *A bala perdida: Memórias* (Rio de Janeiro, 1998), 132, 152–153; "Depoimento de Augusto de Ângelo," Rio de Janeiro, 3 November 1988, IPHSP; "Depoimento de Gualter Leão," Rio de Janeiro, 9 November 1988, IPHSP; "Depoimento de Caio Aurélio Domingues," Rio de Janeiro, 11 November 1988, IPHSP; "Surge a TV a com ela novos pioneirismos" and "Bob nos ensinou a delegar, a confiar e não encher," *Propaganda*, June 1979, pp. 32–33, 38, 40; "TV Comes of Age in Brazil," *Brazilian Business*, September 1957, pp. 18–22 (inc. quotes "all . . ." through "talent . . ."); "Entre an-

unciantes," *PN*, 20 October 1953, p. 12 (for *Sítio*); "Boliche Royal: 6.000 cartas por semana!," *Notícias JWT*, May 1956, JWTA; Oziel Peçanha, "Um pioneiro da TV," *Correio da Manhã*, 6 December 1964, sec. "Cultura-Diversão," 9.

109. "Depoimento de Caio Aurélio Domingues," Rio de Janeiro, 11 November 1988, IPHSP; "Bob nos ensinou . . . ," *Propaganda*, June 1979, p. 38; José Bonifácio de Oliveira Sobrinho, *O livro do Boni* (Rio de Janeiro, 2001), 75–77. List of advertisers from Souza, "Imagem," 11. On *garotas-propaganda*: Souza, "Imagem," 14 (quoted); Liba Frydman, "As 'garotas-propaganda' da televisão," *PN*, 5 October 1953, pp. 41–42; Marcos Margulies, "Garota-propaganda—Profissão ou estado de espírito," *O Estado de S. Paulo*, 1 June 1958, p. 113; Alexandre Bressan, "O produto garota-propaganda," *O Estado de S. Paulo*, 3 February 1985, p. 34; Oliveira Sobrinho, *Livro*, 75–76.

110. Szulc, "Television's Progress"; Heron Domingues, "A TV conquista o Brasil," *A Noite*, 29 May 1956, sec. 2, p. 1.

111. "Quanto se gastou em publicidade no Brasil em 1957 [*sic*]," *Anuário de Publicidade*, 1957, p. 227 (Tupi stations); Clark, *Campeão*, 71 (TV-Record); *Notícias JWT*, April and May 1956, JWTA; "The Latin American Way," *J. Walter Thompson Company News*, 2 July 1956, p. 2, JWTA; "A Ducal inverterá 20 milhões em publicidade no próximo ano," *PN*, 5 December 1956, p. 44.

112. "TV Comes of Age in Brazil," *Brazilian Business*, September 1957, pp. 18, 20; Szulc, "Television's Progress"; "Brazil Grows, Heads toward Economic Self-Sufficiency," *Advertising Age*, 12 May 1958, p. 84; Haroldo Holanda, "Televisão no Brasil já é negócio," *O Observador Econômico e Financeiro*, December 1959, p. 22.

113. "Nada vou copiar, mas tudo vou melhorar," *PN*, 24 April 1958, p. 47.

114. "Revolução nas cozinhas," *Anhembi*, April 1958, p. 340; "A Probel trabalha duro para você dormir macio," *PN*, 29 May 1958, p. 14.

115. Lima, "Fabricação," 33 ("symbolize . . ."); "modern comfort," e.g., advertisements in *Ultima Hora*, 22 September 1952, p. 3; 30 December 1952, p. 4; 3 September 1958, p. 4.

116. Lima, "Fabricação," 32–38; Julio Mesquita Neto, "A imprensa norte-americana," *O Estado de S. Paulo*, 16 December 1956, p. 21; "São Paulo's Walita," *Brazilian Business*, February 1953, pp. 18–19; "Confôrto e saúde ao apertar de um botão," *PN*, 11 May 1959, pp. 18–20 (Walita, quoted); "Arno on the March," *Brazilian Business*, June 1952, pp. 14–15; Probel advertisement, *Correio da Manhã*, 24 March 1957, sec. 1, pp. 10–11; J. U. McManus to T. V. Houser and N. W. Jeran, Rio de Janeiro, 26 October 1949, Sears Archives, box 3717; Hattwick, "Marketing," 90; Pyr Marcondes, *Uma história da propaganda brasileira* (Rio de Janeiro, 2001), 175–177 (Bombril); "Good News for Housewives," *Brazilian Business*, March 1953, pp. 12–13 (Pyrex); Rodolfo Lima Martensen, *O desafio de quatro santos: Memórias* (São Paulo, 1983), 275–278 (Lever).

117. "Confôrto e saúde ao apertar de um botão," *PN*, 11 May 1959, p. 19; "Frutas + legumes = VITAMINAS," *O Estado de S. Paulo*, 6 March 1949, p. 5; "Fórmula Arno para vender um bilião," 29 September 1958, p. 16; *Sugestões Mesbla* (Biblioteca Nacional's copy, dated 1951 in card catalog); "Mais de 2 milhões de eletro-domésticos vendidos," *PN*, 18 July 1960, pp. 24–25; Nescau product history, NBL-CPD, MDONE01.00.001.

118. Walita-A Exposição advertisement, *Ultima Hora*, 22 September 1952, p. 3; Bom Bril advertisement, *O Estado de S. Paulo*, 8 January 1952, p. 5; Waldir Dupont,

Geraldo Alonso: O homem e o mito (São Paulo, 1991), 55; Bendix advertisement, *Folha da Manhã*, 27 November 1955, p. 61.

119. Dupont, *Geraldo Alonso*, 55–56; "Industry's Rapid Rise to Success Reflects Brazil's Industrial Boom," *Brazilian Business*, June 1961, p. 33.

120. "O novo companheiro," *O Estado de S. Paulo*, 20 April 1958, p. 112.

121. "Um acontecimento inédito numa loja de varejo," *PN*, 8 December 1953, p. 23; Walita advertisement, *O Estado de S. Paulo*, 10 November 1953, p. 11 (quoted); Escolinha Walita advertisement, *Ultima Hora*, 18 June 1953, p. 3; "Confôrto e saúde ao apertar de um botão," *PN*, 11 May 1959, pp. 18–19; "Mais uma grande tournée dos revendedores Walita," *Notícias JWT*, April 1956, p. 3, JWTA; "Notas e notícias dos clientes," *Notícias JWT*, May 1956, p. 2, JWTA; Mônica Pimenta Velloso, *Mário Lago: Boemia e política* (Rio de Janeiro, 1997), 168–169 ("Walita Shopwindow"); Bressan, "Produto."

122. Walita advertisement, *Ultima Hora*, 26 August 1953, p. 2; Helena Sangirardi, *A alegría de cozinhar* (São Paulo, n.d.); Marialice Prestes, *Problemas do lar* (Rio de Janeiro, 1945); Isabel de Almeida Serrano, *Noções de economia doméstica* (São Paulo, 1946); Sensação do Lar advertisement, *Folha da Manhã*, 16 June 1957, sec. "Assuntos Gerais," 8–9; Empire television-set advertisement, *Jornal do Brasil*, 13 July 1962, sec. 1, p. 5. The São Paulo housewife's desire to keep a prized cook happy and in her employ figures in a popular novel set in 1957, though similar situations set members of the employing class to grumbling about the "servant problem." See Maria de Lourdes Teixeira, *Rua Augusta*, 3rd ed. (São Paulo, 1963 [1962]), 60; Benedito Orlando Costa, "O comércio de aparelhos eletro-domésticos no Rio de Janeiro," *PN*, 27 April 1959, p. 14.

123. Eletro-Radiobraz advertisement, *O Estado de S. Paulo*, 9 December 1958, p. 11 ("modern . . ."); Fernando Morais, *Chatô: O rei do Brasil* (São Paulo, 1994), 502; Rinso-retailer advertisement, *O Estado de S. Paulo*, 4 December 1959, sec. "Suplemento Feminino," 14; Costa, "Comércio," 14–15; José Louzeiro, "A verdadeira história do 'Ponto Frio,'" *PN*, 19 December 1957, pp. 10–12; "400 mil rádios e 60 mil TV vendidos anualmente no Rio," *Ultima Hora*, 28 November 1956, p. 6; ACADE advertisement, *Ultima Hora*, 6 December 1956, p. 9 (quoted).

124. Clark, *Campeão*, 78–80; Ferreira, *Pilares*, 82 (quoted).

125. A. P. Carvalho, "Novidades em promoção de vendas," *PN*, 20 November 1954, p. 33 (Mappin-Walita); Mesbla-Walita advertisement, *Correio da Manhã*, 22 February 1953, sec. 5, p. 3; "Maiores lucros com menores margens," *PN*, 12 October 1959, p. 15; Brastemp advertisement, *O Estado de S. Paulo*, 19 April 1955, p. 7; Gasbras advertisement, *Ultima Hora*, 29 June 1956, sec. 2, p. 4; "Brazil Grows, Heads toward Economic Self-Sufficiency," *Advertising Age*, 12 May 1958, p. 84 (Sarmento).

126. Rinso advertisement, *O Estado de S. Paulo*, 19 January 1958, p. 11; A. P. Carvalho, "Novidades em promoção de vendas," *PN*, 5 May 1955, p. 55; Sears advertisement, *Correio da Manhã*, 24 July 1955, sec. 5, p. 13; Sears advertisement, *O Estado de S. Paulo*, 30 October 1955, p. 35.

127. "O sucesso da inexperiência," *Vendas e Varejo*, March 1959, p. 17; "Tendências dos negócios," *PN*, 5 July 1956, p. 40 ("class . . ."); "Indústria de móveis precisa reequipar-se," *PN*, 27 March 1961, p. 25; "O segrêdo do comércio a crêdito," *PN*, 20 December 1952, p. 59; Vasconcellos, "Tudo," 30; Silveira, "Lojas," 14; Fernando Lemos,

"Uma inciativa fracassada," *PN*, 5 June 1958, p. 27; "A política de compra e venda diante da elevação dos preços," *PN*, 24 August 1959, p. 46; Auro Moura Andrade to "Sr. Diretor," *PN*, 5 October 1956, p. 8.

128. "O segrêdo do comércio a crêdito," *PN*, 20 December 1952, p. 59; A Exposição advertisement, *Correio da Manhã*, 21 September 1952, sec. 4, p. 3; "Tendências dos negócios," *PN*, 5 July 1956, pp. 39–40; Manoel de Vasconcellos, "Uma palavra do editor," *PN*, 20 March 1956, p. 2; Barbosa Freitas advertisement, *Ultima Hora*, 10 April 1956, p. 9; Ponto Frio advertisement, *Ultima Hora*, 16 July 1957, p. 11; "Brasil: Auto-suficiente em eletro-domésticos," *PN*, 26 June 1961, p. 27.

129. São Paulo: "Criado em São Paulo o Serviço Central de Proteção ao Crédito," *PN*, 5 December 1955, p. 66; "Resultados cada vez mais amplos em defesa do comércio de vendas a prazo," *Vendas e Varejo*, November 1959, pp. 20–21. Rio: "Facilitar o crédito aos bons pagadores e eliminar os maus," *Ultima Hora*, 10 April 1956, p. 9; "Os lojistas acordam cêdo e vão à aula," *PN*, 31 July 1958, p. 30; "Nova diretoria do Clube dos Diretores Lojistas do Rio de Janeiro," *Vendas e Varejo*, January 1959, pp. 18–19; "Serviço de Proteção ao Crédito," *Vendas e Varejo*, October 1960, pp. 22–24.

130. "Tendências dos negócios," *PN*, 5 July 1956, p. 38 (Monteverde); Floriano Nogueira da Gama to Valentim Bouças (via *PN*), *PN*, 5 December 1956, p. 4 (URA-PEL); Genival Rabelo, "A indústria pode parar, sem as vendas a prestação," *PN*, 20 June 1956, pp. 42–43 ("Industry . . ."); "Tendências dos negócios," *PN*, 5 July 1956, pp. 38, 40 ("What . . ." and "'Buy . . .'").

131. "Tendências dos negócios," *PN*, 5 July 1956, p. 39 ("a *philosphy* . . ." and *O Globo*); Wilson Velloso, "Crédito rotativo e outros créditos," *Vendas e Varejo*, February 1959, p. 21; "A 'Sears' e a convenção dos lojistas," *PN*, 16 November 1959, p. 17 (speaker referring to article Gudin published in *O Globo*, 28 August 1959).

132. "No mundo fabuloso . . . ," *PN*, 20 December 1956; Gama to Bouças, *PN*, 5 December 1956.

133. Comissão de Desenvolvimento Industrial, *O problema da alimentação no Brasil: Relatório de Klein & Saks*, 2nd ed. (Rio de Janeiro, 1956 [1954]); M. Lubomirski to E. G. Van Wagner, [São Paulo], 10 June 1953, RAC-IBECA, microfiche 9999-00-03; Olavo Ferraz to IBEC, São Paulo, 2 February 1954, RAC-IBECA, microfiche 9999-00-05; Richard W. Greenebaum to W. D. Bradford, São Paulo, 11 August 1954, RAC-IBECA, microfiche 9999-00-05; Irving Salert to Department of State, Rio de Janeiro, 18 August 1954, FSD 176, "Supermarket Sponsored by SAPS," RG59, 832.055/8-1854; Richard W. Greenebaum to W. D. Bradford, São Paulo, 29 September 1955, RAC-IBECA, microfiche 9999-00-06; Marek Lubomirski to Richard W. Greenebaum, São Paulo, 10 September 1956, RAC-IBECA, microfiche 9999-00-13; Marek Lubomirski to Richard W. Greenebaum, São Paulo, 27 September 1956, RAC-IBECA, microfiche 9999-00-13; "Report Prepared by J. E. Fernandes," March 1958, p. 22, RAC-IBECA, mr-J-114.

134. "Supermercados," *PN*, 5 March 1957, p. 17; "Um novo tipo de mercado na zona sul," *Correio da Manhã*, 28 April 1955, sec. 1, p. 2; "Copacabana e os super-mercados," *Correio da Manhã*, 28 July 1957, sec. 7, p. 6.

135. "Supermercados," *PN*, 5 March 1957, p. 17; "Copacabana e os super-mercados," *Correio da Manhã*, 28 July 1957, sec. 7, p. 6; "Pelos quatro cantos do Rio," *Correio da Manhã*, 6 January 1956, sec. 1, p. 9.

136. Manuel Arias, "Os supermercados em S. Paulo," *PN*, 5 September 1953, pp. 66–67 (Borges, Castro); interview with Maria Sylvia Pacheco de Castro, São Paulo, 22 March 1993, in *40 anos*, 158–59; interview with José Lemos, São Paulo, 18 March 1993, in *40 anos*, 139 ("Raul . . .").

137. Salert to Department of State, RG59, 832.055/8-1854; "Uma barraca em cada bairro," *Revista da Semana*, 24 July 1954, p. 46 ("the Federal . . ."); "Passo decisivo para o abastecimento do povo," *Ultima Hora*, 19 August 1954, p. 5 ("similar . . ."); "Supermercados," *PN*, 5 March 1957, p. 17 ("The Disco . . ."); "Registro social," *Correio da Manhã*, 21 September 1957, sec. 1, p. 15; "Regressa dos EE.UU. o dr. Vicente de Paulo Galliez," *Ultima Hora*, 20 March 1958, p. 2; "Report Prepared by J. E. Fernandes," RAC-IBECA, mr-J-114.

138. Arias, "Supermercados"; Stilman, *Comércio*, 262, 358; M.S.P. de Castro in *40 anos*, p. 160; "Mais cinco super-mercados do SAPS dentro de pouco tempo," *A Noite Ilustrada*, 7 September 1954, p. 26; "Estuda-se a possibilidade de instalação em Santos de um supermercado do 'SAPS,'" *O Estado de S. Paulo*, 14 November 1954, p. 12; "Mais um supermercado 'Disco,'" *Ultima Hora*, 29 December 1956, p. 5; "Supermercados," *PN*, 5 March 1957, p. 17 ("followed . . ." and "One . . .").

139. Interview with Mario Gomes d'Almeida, São Paulo, 30 November 1992, in *40 anos*, 161.

140. How supermarketing worked: "Moderniza-se o comércio varejista nesta capital," *Folha da Manhã*, 22 November 1953, sec. "Assuntos Especializados," pt. 1, pp. 1, 11; "Uma barraca em cada bairro," *Revista da Semana*, 24 July 1954, p. 46; "Aplaudem todos o super-mercado," *Ultima Hora*, 21 August 1954, p. 4; "Um novo tipo de mercado em Botafogo," *Ultima Hora*, 27 May 1955, p. 5. Advertising agencies: Arias, "Supermercados," 67; "Boa notícia para donas de casas e . . . maridos também!," *O Estado de S. Paulo*, 15 April 1956, p. 19; Almeida in *40 anos*, 161; Manoel de Vasconcellos, "Uma palavra do editor," *PN*, 5 March 1957, p. 2. Comparative advertising: Sirva-se advertisement, *O Estado de S. Paulo*, 6 April 1956, p. 8; Disco advertisement, *Ultima Hora*, 8 January 1957, p. 11; SAPS advertisement, *Correio da Manhã*, 3 July 1957, sec. 1, p. 12. Cooperative advertising: "Fornecedores do supermercado SírvaSe," *O Estado de S. Paulo*, 4 September 1953, pp. 8–9; "Parabéns a São Paulo," *Folha da Noite*, 2 August 1955, sec. 1, pp. 4–5; Arroz Brejeiro advertisement, *Correio da Manhã*, 28 April 1957, sec. 1, p. 5. Television advertising: Almeida in *40 anos*, 161; Manoel de Vasconcellos, "Uma palavra do editor," *PN*, 5 March 1957, p. 2; "Sessão das 5," *Ultima Hora*, 3 December 1956, p. 4 (quoted); "Boa notícia para donas de casas . . . ," *O Estado de S. Paulo*, 15 April 1956, p. 19. Promotions: A. P. Carvalho, "Novidades em promoção de vendas," *PN*, 20 January 1955, pp. 57–58 (quoted); Peg-Pag advertisements in *O Estado de S. Paulo*, 28 December 1954, p. 12, and 25 October 1955, p. 13; Disco advertisements in *Correio da Manhã*, 16 April 1957, sec. 1, p. 7, and 8 December 1957, sec. 5, p. 2; Mary, "Compare e . . . compre," *O Estado de S. Paulo*, 19 February 1954, sec. "Suplemento Feminino," 3; Peg-Pag advertisement, *Folha da Manhã*, 14 August 1955, sec. "Vida Social e Doméstica," 46; "Supermarkets for Brazil's Super City," *Brazilian Business*, January 1954, p. 29; Promúsica advertisement, *O Estado de S. Paulo*, 25 December 1958, p. 9; Peg-Pag advertisement, *Folha da Manhã*, 13 December 1955, sec. "Assuntos Gerais," 8.

141. A. P. Carvalho, "Novidades em promoção de vendas," *PN*, 20 January 1955, p. 57; "Passo decisivo para o abastecimento do povo," *Ultima Hora*, 19 August 1954, p. 5; Divisão de Propaganda do SAPS, *Ultima Hora*, 21 August 1954, p. 6; "Super Mercado do S.A.P.S." (paid announcement), *Correio da Manhã*, 22 August 1954, sec. 1, p. 6 (25,000); "Promete criar novos supermercados," *Ultima Hora*, 11 September 1954, p. 7; "O consumidor e as filas," *Correio da Manhã*, 10 September 1954, sec. 1, p. 5; "Mais cinco super-mercados do SAPS . . . ," *A Noite Ilustrada*, 7 September 1954, p. 26; Disco announcement, *Correio da Manhã*, 11 September 1956, sec. 1, p. 3; "Os supermercados chegaram e venceram," *PN*, 26 June 1958, pp. 14–16; Marek Lubomirski to Richard W. Greenebaum, São Paulo, 12 October 1956, RAC-IBECA, microfiche 9999-00-14; Marek Lubomirski to Arthur E. Anderson, São Paulo, 5 September 1957, and attachment, "Supermarkets in Operation in Brazil," RAC-IBECA, microfiche 9999-00-15; "Um símbolo de progresso da capital mineira," *Vendas e Varejo*, May 1960, p. 20 ("index . . ."); George W. Skora to Department of State, Salvador, 6 February 1957, FSD 24, "Economic Summary for January, 1957," RG59, 832.00/2-657; H. Gerald Smith to Department of State, Rio de Janeiro, 7 January 1957, FSD 746, "Monthly Economic Summary—December," RG59, 832.00/3-757; "As cifras do rádio," *Revista do Rádio*, 21 December 1957, p. 48 (inc. "Pague Pouco").

142. "Os supermercados chegaram e venceram," *PN*, 26 June 1958, p. 14; Stilman, *Comércio*, 258, 266–273; Ivan Duarte, "Com vistas aos pioneiros do auto-serviço no Brasil," *PN*, 24 November 1958, p. 30; Donald Taylor, "Retailing in Brazil," *Journal of Marketing* 24, no. 1 (July 1959): 56; Robert S. Hoard to Department of State, Porto Alegre, May 20, 1953, FSD 82, "Voluntary Preliminary Report on CAMPAL S.A.," RG59, 832.31/5-2053; "The Old and the New," *Brazilian Business*, January 1954, p. 30 ("revolutionizing . . .").

143. "Self-Service Stores Are Here to Stay," *Brazilian Business*, September 1965, p. 25; Loja Araujo advertisement, *Folha da Manhã*, 25 March 1953, sec. "Assuntos Especializados," 8; Sirva-se handbills (1953), RAC-IBECA, microfiche 9999-00-03 and 9999-00-04; Super-Mercado Tostão advertisement, *Ultima Hora*, 17 October 1956, sec. "Tabloide," 10; "Prossegue a revolução dos supermercados," *Ultima Hora*, 29 August 1961, p. 10 (cf. "Moderniza-se o comércio varejista nesta capital," *Folha da Manhã*, 22 November 1953, sec. "Assuntos Especializados," pt. 1, p. 1).

144. "Supermarkets for Brazil's Super City," *Brazilian Business*, January 1954, pp. 24–29 (inc. "that . . ."); Rubem Braga, "O super-mercado," *Diario de Noticias*, 18 May 1956, sec. 1, p. 2; "Supermercados," *PN*, 5 March 1957, pp. 16–18 (Disco); "Prossegue a revolução dos supermercados," *Ultima Hora*, 29 August 1961, p. 10; "Os supermercados chegaram e venceram," *PN*, 26 June 1958, pp. 14–16.

145. "As duas revoluções no mercado de discos," *PN*, 29 August 1956, pp. 64–65; A. P. Carvalho, "Promoção de vendas," *PN*, 17 October 1957, pp. 10, 12 (inc. "display . . ."); O Camizeiro advertisement, *Correio da Manhã*, 28 July 1957, sec. 1, p. 11 ("Super-Market . . ."); "Self-Service, a última novidade em matéria de comércio," *PN*, 20 August 1957, p. 84 ("I was . . ." and Helal).

146. Constâncio Pessutto (at NCR from 1951), in *40 anos*, 106–111; "Retrato atual do varejo nos EUA," *Vendas e Varejo*, December 1960, pp. 4–6 (inc. "Modern . . ."); "Inaugurada a fábrica da companhia 'Caixas Registradoras National S.A.,'" *O Estado de*

S. Paulo, 17 July 1958, p. 11; Victório Franceschini (NCR from 1946 onward, Casa Rio Prata-Sweda beginning in mid-1950s) in *40 anos*, 171–172; Casa Rio Prata-Sweda advertisement, *O Estado de S. Paulo*, 30 March 1958, p. 21; Casa Victor-Rena advertisement, *Ultima Hora*, 18 December 1956, p. 5.

147. M.S.P. de Castro in *40 anos*, 159; "Eleven Important São Paulo Groups," enclosure to Melville Osborne to Department of State, FSD 758, "Brazil's System of Economic Groups; Large São Paulo Groups, Brazilian Holding Companies," São Paulo, 13 December 1955, RG59, 832.053/12-1355; Flamengo advertisement *Folha da Manhã*, 15 May 1955, sec. "Assuntos Especializados," pt. 2, p. 11; Companhia Imobiliária Santa Cruz advertisement, *Correio da Manhã*, 7 October 1956, sec. 1, p. 5; "O prefeito Negrão de Lima inaugura as obras do centro comercial da Ilha do Governador," *Correio da Manhã*, 10 October 1956, sec. 1, p. 4; Santa Cruz advertisement, *Correio da Manhã*, 10 October 1956, sec. 1, p. 7; Orlando Macedo Incorporação e Vendas de Imóveis advertisement, *Correio da Manhã*, 11 November 1956, sec. 2, pp. 4–5; Construtora Veramar-Predial Steinberg advertisement, *Correio da Manhã*, 7 April 1957, sec. 3, pt. 1, p. 8; Sociedade Imobiliária ICCA advertisement, *Correio da Manhã*, 18 November 1956, sec. 3, pt. 1, p. 8; "Mais um lançamento da campanha," *Correio da Manhã*, 13 July 1957, sec. 1, p. 5; Construção e Incorporação Premier advertisement, *Correio da Manhã*, 20 October 1957, sec. 3, pt. 1, p. 12.

148. "Notícias do estrangeiro: Os supermercados da California," *PN*, 20 July 1953, pp. 66–67; Arias, "Supermercados"; "O Rio ainda não tem um super-mercado," *PN*, 20 November 1953, p. 8; Wilson Velloso, "O consumidor exigente faz o progresso da indústria," *PN*, 20 November 1953, p. 70; "As pessoas—Os dias—As coisas," *PN*, 20 January 1955, p. 12 ("accompanying . . ."); "Supermercados," *PN*, 5 March 1957, p. 16 ("The truth . . ."); "Produtos não alimentícios, tambem podem ser vendidos nos super-mercados," *PN*, 3 October 1957, pp. 18–19; Duarte, "Com vistas," 30–31 (inc. "The North . . .").

149. "Advertising on Rise in Canada and Brazil," *New York Times*, 13 December 1951, p. 52; "Brazil's Advertising Agencies," *Brazilian Business*, December 1952, p. 20; Lima, "Negócio," 54; Rabelo, *Tempos*, 49 (McCann); "J. Walter Thompson Company do Brasil," *J. Walter Thompson Company News*, 12 March 1951, JWTA; "News of Advertising and Marketing," *New York Times*, 8 December 1955, p. 64 (Almap); Manoel de Vasconcellos, "Uma palavra do editor," *PN*, 20 March 1956, p. 2; Vasconcellos, "Uma palavra do editor," *PN*, 20 December 1956, p. 2; Vasconcellos, "Uma palavra da redação," *PN*, 22 May 1958, p. 1.

150. Fernando Reis, "São Paulo e Rio: A longa caminhada," in *HPB*, 341, 353; "Brazil's Advertising Agencies," *Brazilian Business*, December 1952, p. 20; Lima, "Negócio," 59; Carlos Roberto Chueiri, "E, no princípio, era a verba . . . ," in *HPB*, 272.

151. Lima, "Negócio," 62 ("considerable . . ."); Bernardo Ludermir, "Propaganda como profissão no Brasil," *O Observador Econômico e Financeiro*, July 1959, p. 17; "Profissão pouco conhecida," *O Estado de S. Paulo*, 29 July 1966, sec. "Suplemento Feminino," 5 (Schützer quotes); "Depoimento de Hilda Ulbrich [Shützer]," São Paulo, 22 November 1988, IPHSP; interview with Hilda Ulbrich Schützer, by Ilana Strozenberg and Luciana Heymann, São Paulo, 14 July 2004, CPDOC-PHO; "Uma dona de casa contacto de agência," *PN*, 5 September 1953, pp. 54–55; Standard Propaganda advertisement, *PN*, 5 April 1955, cover. For increased salaries: Manoel de Vasconcellos,

"Uma palavra do editor," *Publicidade & Negócios*, 15 November 1951, p. 2; Vasconcellos, "Uma palavra do editor," *Publicidade & Negócios*, 1 January 1952, p. 2; Vasconcellos, "Uma palavra do editor," *Publicidade & Negócios*, 1 April 1952, p. 2; Lima, "Negócio," 62; [Marcus Pereira], "A profissão publicitária," *O Estado de S. Paulo*, 29 March 1959, p. 38; Ludermir, "Propaganda," 19.

152. Lima, "Negócio"; "Publicidade," *O Estado de S. Paulo*, 21 December 1958, p. 94; "Gloriosos 25 anos passados menores que os 10 anos futuros," *O Observador Econômico e Financeiro*, April 1960, p. 14; "Propaganda 58," *Propaganda*, December 1958, p. 10; "Agência em fóco: CIN," *Propaganda*, April 1959, p. 39.

153. "J. Walter Thompson Company do Brasil," *J. Walter Thompson Company News*, 12 March 1951, JWTA; Inter-Americana advertisement, *Brazilian-American Survey*, May 1956, p. 109; "Agência em fóco: CIN," *Propaganda*, April 1959, pp. 39–40; Reis, "São Paulo e Rio," 339–340; Publitec advertisement, *Propaganda*, November 1959, p. 15.

154. "Vendas mais eficientes e a mais baixo custo no Brasil," *Propaganda*, October 1956, pp. 46, 48 (quotes); ADVB announcement, *O Estado de S. Paulo*, 7 August 1956, p. 12; ADVB announcement, *Folha da Manhã*, 20 February 1957, sec. "Assuntos Especializados," 23.

155. "MPM—Agência de publicidade gaúcha terá âmbito nacional," *Diario da Noite*, 27 June 1957, sec. 1, p. 7; "Coquetel oferecido pela 'Ipiranga,'" *Correio da Manhã*, 5 May 1959, sec. 2, p. 11; Reis, "São Paulo e Rio," 346.

156. "Associação Comercial de São Paulo," *O Estado de S. Paulo*, 27 January 1946, p. 5; "Homenagem ao Sr. João A. da Costa Dória," *Publicidade & Negócios*, August 1949, p. 39; "Reconhecida de utilidade pública a Associação Paulista de Propaganda," *PN*, 5 July 1953, p. 17; "Orgão de utilidade pública a Associação Brasileira de Propaganda," *PN*, 3 October 1957, p. 4; Lima, "Negócio," 54 (quoted); "No mundo dos negócios," *O Observador Econômico e Financeiro*, January 1956, p. 82.

157. *Publicidade & Negócios*, 15 January 1950, cover ("Brazil's . . ."); Manoel de Vasconcellos, "Uma palavra do editor" *Publicidade & Negócios*, 1 July 1950, p. 2; Vasconcellos, "Uma palavra do editor," *PN*, 20 March 1955, p. 4; Vasconcellos, "Uma palavra do editor," *PN*, 20 July 1957, p. 1; Vasconcellos, "Uma palavra da redação," *PN*, 3 October 1957, p. 1; Genival Rabelo, "Fatos & comentários," *PN*, 8 August 1958, p. 29; Ludermir, "Propaganda," 18 (quoted).

158. On ABAP: "What Advertising Does for Brazilian Economy," *J. Walter Thompson Company News*, 6 July 1953, p. 5; Robert B. McIntyre, "Brazil's Ad Industry Faces Uphill Battle," *Editor & Publisher*, 15 December 1956, p. 30. For the 1951 events: "O Dia Pan-Americano da Propaganda," *Publicidade & Negócios*, 1 January 1952, pp. 65–68, 70–71; "Dia Pan-Americano da Propaganda, em São Paulo," *Publicidade & Negócios*, 1 January 1952, pp. 71–72. For associational activities generally: APP, *Depoimentos*, esp. 56–57, 95–96, 103–106, 115–116; Genival Rabelo, "Propaganda da propaganda," in *A volta por cima* (Rio de Janeiro, 1995), 147–148; Manoel de Vasconcellos, "Cresce o interêsse pelo estudo da técnica de publicidade," *Publicidade & Negócios*, February–March 1948, pp. 7–8; "Promover vendas finalidade geral do anúncio," *PN*, 20 March 1953, p. 12; "Entrega de certificados dos cursos IPET," *PN*, 5 September 1956, p. 80.

159. "A semana da propaganda de 1954," *PN*, 20 December 1954, pp. 23–26; "Como os homens de emprêsa encaram hoje a propanda," *PN*, 5 January 1955, p. 58.

160. ABP-ABAP advertisements in *O Estado de S. Paulo*, 7 December 1956, p. 12; *Ultima Hora*, 3 December 1956, sec. 3, p. 10; *Correio da Manhã*, 28 November 1956, sec. 1, p. 11. For McCann's role, see Rabelo, "Propaganda," 148.

161. *Ultima Hora*, 3 December 1956, sec. 3, pp. 10, 12.

162. P. M. Bardi, *História do MASP* (São Paulo, 1992); "Salão da Propaganda do Museu de Arte de S. Paulo," *Publicidade & Negócios*, 1 March 1951, pp. 18–19; Genival Rabelo, "Fatos & comentários," *Publicidade & Negócios*, 15 April 1951, p. 14; Rodolfo Lima Martensen, "Propaganda e insatisfação humana," *Publicidade & Negócios*, 1 February 1951, p. 32.

163. Martensen, "Propaganda."

164. Martensen, *Desafio*, 280.

165. Martensen, 280–282; Martensen, "Museu de Arte de São Paulo, Escola de Propaganda, Ante-Projeto," October 1951, ESPM-IC. The idea of a "Professional Advertising School" or a "University of Commerce" offering advertising training dated back to the early 1940s: "Que legislação assiste, no Brasil, a profissão de publicidade?," *Diretrizes*, 14 October 1943, p. 23; W. R. Poyares, "A necessidade de uma formação publicitária," *Publicidade*, March 1943, pp. 7, 16.

166. Martensen, "Museu de Arte . . . Ante-Projeto."

167. Martensen, *Desafio*, 279–289; Martensen, "O ensino da propaganda no Brasil," *O Estado de S. Paulo*, 20 December 1975, sec. "Suplemento do Centenário," 4; "Adiado o encerramento da exposição técnica de estudos sobre veículos de propaganda," *Folha da Manhã*, 20 January 1952, sec. "Noticiário Geral," 7 (USP pedagogists); "Seminário da escola de propaganda," *Folha da Manhã*, 30 August 1952, sec. "Economia e Finanças," 2 (Penteado); MASP Escola de Propaganda announcement, *O Estado de S. Paulo*, 19 June 1952, p. 4 (Loureiro); Peter W. Rodgers, "For Better and More Efficient Propaganda," *Brazilian Business*, December 1964, p. 15 (USP); Pereira, "Profissão." For the Diários Associados's advertising manager and *Propaganda*, masthead of November 1937.

168. "Publicidade—1958," *O Observador Econômico e Financeiro*, November 1958, p. 23 (on personnel shortages and resort to "elementos em fase de aprendizado" [i.e., the "trainee" system]). On the improvised partial solution to the artwork problem, see Benedito Ruy Barbosa et al., *Depois das seis* (Rio de Janeiro, 1964), 12, 52, 64, 132.

169. The foregoing is drawn from *Anais do Primeiro Congresso Brasileiro de Propaganda, 29–30–31 de outubro de 1957* (São Paulo, 1958), except "Consagra o congresso: A propaganda está a serviço da produtividade," *Ultima Hora*, 1 November 1957, p. 7 ("stands"); Antarctica advertisement, *Correio da Manhã*, 31 October 1957, sec. 1, p. 13; Chueiri, "E, no princípio," 272 ("not . . ."). Advertising Congress as long-standing aspiration: "Que legislação assiste, no Brasil, a profissão de publicidade?," in *Diretrizes*: 30 September 1943, p. 9, 14 October 1943, p. 23; 4 November 1943, p. 25.

170. Photograph, with annotation, Sears Archives, box 3715; Fred C. Hecht to Robert E. Wood, [Chicago?], 30 June 1949, Sears Archives, box 3717; Florence D'Eça, *The Diary of a Foreign Service Wife (Assignment to Brazil)* (Taunton, Mass., 1977), 224; "Rio Concedes Nothing," *Washington Post and Times Herald*, 28 August 1955, E3; Mauro Almeida, *E.U.A., civilização empacotada* (São Paulo, 1961), 60.

171. William Schurz, *Brazil, the Infinite Country* (New York, 1961), 286; A. P. Carvalho, "Dá resultado o 'artigo do dia'?," *Vendas e Varejo*, February 1960, pp. 32–34; Carvalho, "Marketing," *PN*, 20 February 1961, p. 53.

172. A Sensação advertisement, *Folha da Manhã*, 17 December 1950, p. 13; Anna Veronica Mautner, *O cotidiano nas entrelinhas: Crônicas e memórias* (São Paulo, 2001), 17–23 (inc. "democratic"); Genival Rabelo, "Parqueamento: Problema do varejo," *Vendas e Varejo*, October 1959, p. 72; Eneida (pseud., Eneida de Villas Boas Costa de Moraes), intro. to Paulo Berger, *Copacabana* (Rio de Janeiro, 1959), 17; Rabelo, *A volta por cima* (Rio de Janeiro, 1995), 152; *Publicidade & Negócios*, March 1949, p. 38; "Como remediar o esvaziamento do centro comercial," *Vendas e Varejo*, March 1962, pp. 7–13.

173. "Devolvida ao povo a casa do rapaz direito," *Ultima Hora*, 23 November 1954, p. 7; Ferreira, *Pilares*, 92; "Household Appliances," *Brazilian Business*, December 1956, p. 28; Mautner, *Cotidiano*, 19.

174. Genival Rabelo, "Fatos & comentários," *PN*, 21 November 1957, p. 16; "Publicitários com JK," *Ultima Hora*, 5 November 1957, p. 6; "Publicitários estiveram no Catete," *O Estado de S. Paulo*, 5 November 1957, p. 14.

Chapter Five

1. Genival Rabelo, "Fatos & comentários," *PN*, 26 June 1961, p. 20.

2. Manoel de Vasconcellos, "Uma palavra da redação," *PN*, 26 December 1960, p. 1.

3. Genival Rabelo, "Fatos & comentários," *PN*, 1 February 1960, p. 25; Rabelo, "Crediário é fator de progresso," *Vendas e Varejo*, April 1961, p. 40; Rabelo, "São Paulo e o Nordeste," *Vendas e Varejo*, August 1961, p. 14.

4. Manoel de Vasconcellos, "Uma palavra da redação," *PN*, 13 February 1958, p. 1; "O balanço de uma filosofia," *PN*, 14 November 1960, p. 2; "Duas solenidades presididas por Kubitschek," *O Estado de S. Paulo*, 23 October 160, p. 25; Genival Rabelo, *Onde o vento junta o cisco* (Rio de Janeiro, 1969), 133–137; *PN*, 5 December 1060, p. 13; Manuel Árias, "A cruzada de redenção," *Vendas e Varejo*, April 1962, p. 2.

5. João Pinheiro Neto, *Juscelino, uma história de amor* (Rio de Janeiro, 1994), 160.

6. Bernardo Ludermir, "Relações públicas," *O Observador Econômico e Financeiro*, August 1959, p. 24; Ney Peixoto do Vale, "Dois autênticos homens de relações públicas," *PN*, 16 May 1960, p. 37; "O ano que passou e o ano que passará," *Propaganda*, January 1961, 24, 26; Rodolfo Lima Martensen, "Porta dos fundos," *Propaganda*, May 1960, p. 48.

7. Walter Clark [Bueno], *O campeão de audiência* (São Paulo, 1991), 102; Renato Ignácio da Silva, *Xerifes e coronéis* (Itaquaquecetuba, 1989), 261–262.

8. "Posto de escuta," *Manchete*, 1 February 1958, p. 21; Murilo Melo Filho, "JK: A estrela sobe," *Manchete*, 27 February 1960, p. 87; J. M. [Justino Martins], "Conversa com o leitor," *Manchete*, 19 September 1959, p. 7; A. P. Carvalho, "Brasília: Uma cidade que surge sob o signo da propaganda," *PN*, 31 August 1959, p. 27; Martensen, "Porta," 48.

9. Carvalho, "Brasília: Uma cidade . . . ," 26–28 (inc. "the only . . . ," "once . . . ," "Radio's . . ."); "Vende de tudo para todos," *PN*, 20 July 1959, pp. 44–45 (Ecal); Carvalho, "Brasília: Uma realidade que surge," *PN*, 24 August 1959, p. 19 ("life's . . .").

10. Mary Thayer, "Brasilia Theatrical as Oklahoma," *Washington Post and Times Herald*, 28 April 1960, C24; "Portfólio de Brasília," *Propaganda*, May 1960, pp. 19–25.

11. "Portfólio . . . ," 19; Cláudio Lamas de Farias at al., *Eletrodomésticos: Origens, história e design no Brasil*, ed. Silvia Fraiha (Rio de Janeiro, 2006), 105; Walita advertisement, *O Estado de S. Paulo*, 10 April 1960, p. 15; "A indústria comercializa sua produção," *Indústria & Mercados*, October 1961, p. 22 (JWT executive); Melo Filho, "JK," 87.

12. Sérgio Augusto, *Este mundo é um pandeiro: A chanchada de Getúlio a JK* (São Paulo, 1989), 172; Fernando Henrique Cardoso, *The Accidental President of Brazil* (New York, 2006), 66; Edmundo de Macedo Soares, "A indústria de automóveis no Brasil," *Carta Mensal*, November–December 1957, p. 8; "Indústria automobilística," *Ultima Hora*, 30 November 1959, p. 18.

13. Glauco Arbix and Mauro Zilbovicius, eds., *De JK a FHC: A reinvenção dos carros* (São Paulo, 1997), 7; "Indústria automobilística," *Ultima Hora*, 30 November 1959, p. 18; Lúcio Meira, "Indústria automobilística brasileira," *PN*, 25 February 1963, p. 3; Lúcia Helena Gama, *Nos bares da vida: Produção cultural e sociabilidade em São Paulo, 1940–1950* (São Paulo, 1998), 307 ("All . . ."); Aluízio Flôres, "Em que pé se encontram as 30 metas de JK," *Manchete*, 26 September 1959, p. 85; Manoel de Vasconcellos, "Uma palavra da redação," *PN*, 27 February 1961, p. 1; Hugo Schlesinger, *Publicidade e promoção de vendas* (Rio de Janeiro, 1964), 66; "Mercado brasileiro de publicidade, 1967–1968," *Propaganda*, February 1968, p. 16; Ernani Silva Bruno, *História do Brasil: Geral e regional*, 7 vols. (São Paulo, 1966–1967), 5:182, 198, 7:211, 236.

14. Helen Shapiro, *Engines of Growth: The State and Transnational Auto Companies in Brazil* (Cambridge, 1994), tables A.5, A.6, A.10.

15. "Fabricação de automóveis no Brasil," *O Observador Econômico e Financeiro*, September 1950, p. 16; "A indústria mecânica," *O Observador Econômico e Financeiro*, October 1950, p. 92; "No mundo dos negócios," *O Observador Econômico e Financeiro*, November 1950, p. 14; "No mundo dos negócios," *O Observador Econômico e Financeiro*, December 1950, p. 9; "Tendências dos negócios," *Publicidade & Negócios*, 15 February 1951, p. 3; APP, *Depoimentos* (São Paulo, 1973), 70 (GM staffer).

16. "Visando à criação da indústria automobilística nacional," *Correio da Manhã*, 19 March 1952, sec. 1, p. 8; "Viajam para os Estados Unidos membros da Subcomissão de Jipes, Tratores, Caminhões e Automóveis," *Correio da Manhã*, 5 February 1953, sec. 1, p. 2; "Notas editoriais," *O Observador Econômico e Financeiro*, July 1952, pp. 4–6.

17. "O sr. Henry Kaiser no Catete," *Correio da Manhã*, 18 August 1954, sec. 1, p. 2; Elizabeth Cobbs, *The Rich Neighbor Policy: Rockefeller and Kaiser in Brazil* (New Haven, Conn., 1992), 203–217.

18. Shapiro, *Engines*, chap. 3 and table A.1.

19. Shapiro, chap. 3 and table A.1; Vemag advertisement, *O Cruzeiro*, 22 November 1958, pp. 12–13; Willys advertisement, *O Estado de S. Paulo*, 31 August 1957, p. 7; "Observações industriais," *O Observador Econômico e Financeiro*, March 1958, p. 27 ("in . . ."); U.S. Embassy to Department of State, Rio de Janeiro, 14 December 1959, FSD 595, "Monthly Economic Summary—November—1959," RG59, 832.00/12-1459 ("with . . ."); Romi-Isetta announcement, *O Estado de S. Paulo*, 9 September 1956, p. 19; "Estão sendo lançados os primeiros 'Vedette-Chambord,'" *PN*, 23 February 1959,

pp. 52–53; "O Brasil vai ter agora seu primeiro carro de luxo," *PN*, 18 July 1960, pp. 42–43; "Condecorado com a Ordem do Cruzeiro do Sul," *O Estado de S. Paulo*, 25 October 1960, p. 7; Clóvis Paiva, "Indústria automobilística," *O Observador Econômico e Financeiro*, November 1960, p. 43 ("affirming . . ."); "Gostos e tendências dos automobilistas no Rio e S. Paulo," *Indústria & Mercados*, February 1961, p. 41.

20. Willys advertisement, *O Estado de S. Paulo*, 27 March 1960, p. 7; "Um carro para marcar a posição social do dono," *Indústria & Mercados*, August–September 1962, pp. 36–37.

21. "Sem preconceito de cor," *PN*, 12 April 1962, pp. 28–30; "A campanha que fez uma verdadeira radiografia dos carros Volkswagen," *Indústria & Mercados*, August–September 1962, pp. 38–39 (inc. Cosi); Alex Periscinoto, *Mais vale o que se aprende que o que te ensinam* (São Paulo, 1995), 67–69, 80–82. Earlier European automobile advertising: A. W. Childs, "Dirigible 'Hindenberg,'" Rio de Janeiro, 3 April 1936, RG151, RRCAR, box 66; Peugeot advertisement, *Correio da Manhã*, 17 May 1949, p. 14.

22. "O Brasil expõe sua indústria automobilística," *PN*, 13 March 1961, pp. 41–42; "Salão do Automóvel foi grande sucesso," *PN*, 19 December 1960, p. 46; Tito Silveira, "Automotive Makers Go on Display at Salão do Automóvel," *Brazilian Business*, December 1960, pp. 25–29, 58; "Primeiro Salão," *O Observador Econômico e Financeiro*, December 1960, p. 34; Clóvis Paiva, "Salão de 61," *O Observador Econômico e Financeiro*, August 1961, pp. 33–34; "Exposição automobilística," *A Noite*, 23 January 1961, p. 2; Seweryn Szulc, "Arte e indústria," *Brazilian-American Survey*, no. 14 (1961): 35; "Museu da Arte Moderna homenageia promotores da exposição automobilística," *Correio da Manhã*, 16 June 1961, sec. 1, p. 7 (quoted).

23. "Allied in Progress," *Brazilian Business*, July 1963, pp. 26–31 (inc. "Mr. John . . . ," "purchasing . . ."); "EUA inauguram na Quinta da Boa Vista exposição que custou 500 mil dólares," *Ultima Hora*, 20 July 1963, p. 2; Paulo Francis, *Trinta anos esta noite* (São Paulo, 1994), 59.

24. "Dez anos de feiras," *Propaganda*, September 1967, pp. 20–22; "Uma idéia que surgiu na grande feira de Nova York," *Indústria e Desenvolvimento*, August 1969, pp. 19–20; "Caio Alcântara Machado," *Propaganda*, June 1973, pp. 16–20; Maria Claudia Bonadio, "O fio sintético é um show! Moda, política e publicidade (Rhodia S.A., 1960–1970)" (tese de doutorado, UNICAMP, 2005), chap. 2 (quote on 102).

25. Carlos Queiroz Telles, *Tirando de letra: Um manual de sobrevivência na selva da comunicação* (São Paulo, 1993), 70 ("great . . ."); "Rainha do algodão de 1959," *Manchete*, 19 September 1959, p. 87; "A feira nacional da indústria e o comércio," *Vendas e Varejo*, October 1962, pp. 4–9; "Notícias da indústria," *Vendas e Varejo*, October 1962, pp. 16–17; "Eis a FENIT," *Indústria e Desenvolvimento*, August 1969, pp. 12–15; interview with Edeson Ernesto Coelho, by Ilana Strozenberg and Luciana Heymann, Rio de Janeiro, 17 June 2004, CPDOC-PHO; Bonadio, "Fio sintético," esp. chap. 2 (inc. magazine quote) and appendix 1.

26. Bonadio, "Fio sintético," appendix 2; "Feira Nacional de Utilidades Domésticas," *Propaganda*, July 1959, p. 32 ("exposition . . ."); Farias et al., *Eletrodomésticos*, 96–97 (posters, *Casa e Jardim*); UD advertisement, *O Estado de S. Paulo*, 10 March 1960, p. 17.

27. "Sucesso (grande) da II Feira UD," *Propaganda*, June 1961, p. 37; "Domestic Utilities Fair Reflects a Growing South," *Brazilian Business*, June 1961, p. 38; Telles,

Tirando, 70; "III UD," *Folha de S. Paulo*, 28 April 1962, sec. 2. p. 5; "Lavadora atraiu na UD," *Propaganda*, June 1963, p. 27.

28. "Salão do Automóvel foi grande sucesso," *PN*, 19 December 1960, p. 46; "O Primeiro Salão do Automóvel," *O Estado de S. Paulo*, 9 December 1960, p. 21 ("it . . . ," *feérica*, and "photographic . . ."); Jayme Maurício, "Itinerário das artes plásticas," *Correio da Manhã*, 10 December 1960, sec. 2, p. 2; "Viram a segunda mostra de veículos 550 mil pessoas," *O Estado de S. Paulo*, 13 December 1961, p. 17; "Consolidação só ocorreu há 4 anos," *O Estado de S. Paulo*, 19 November 1970, p. 102.

29. Tavares de Miranda, "Reportagem," *Folha de S. Paulo*, 21 September 1961, sec. 2, p. 2; Florence Bernard, "São Paulo em 7 dias," *Correio da Manhã*, 8 October 1961, sec. 5, p. 7; "Grande afluência popular no Salão da Criança em SP," *Correio da Manhã*, 15 October 1961, sec. 2, p. 1 (quoted); "Os 'jornalistas mirins' revelam suas qualidades no I Salão da Criança," *Folha de S. Paulo*, 6 October 1961, sec. 1, p. 13; "Foi ver o Salão e virou 'repórter fotografico,'" *Folha de S. Paulo*, 12 October 1961, sec. 1, p. 8; Myriam Fragoso Xavier, "O Primeiro Salão da Criança," *O Estado de S. Paulo*, 13 October 1961, sec. "Suplemento Feminino," 5; Tavares de Miranda, "Reportagem," *Folha de S. Paulo*, 13 October 1961, sec. 2, p. 2 (inc. Guilherme de Almeida quote); "II Salão da Criança em SP," *Correio da Manhã*, 7 October 1962, sec. 1, p. 16; "O destaque do mês," *Propaganda*, November 1962, p. 15 ("undeniably . . ."); "Quem faz esses anúncios," *O Estado de S. Paulo*, 11 October 1968, p. 14 (remaining quotes).

30. "Uma idéia que surgiu na grande feira de Nova York," *Indústria e Desenvolvimento*, August 1969, p. 20; "Anhemby será sede das feiras," *Indústria e Desenvolvimento*, August 1969, p. 23; "Salão, desta vez com o Anhembi, grande notícia," *Anuário Brasileiro de Propaganda*, 1970–1971, p. 98 (inauguration); Anhembi advertisement, *O Estado de S. Paulo*, 19 November 1970, p. 11.

31. For design and the fairs, e.g., Jayme Maurício, "Itinerário das artes plásticas," *Correio da Manhã*, 16 July 1961, sec. 2, p. 2; Maurício, "Itinerário . . . ," *Correio da Manhã*, 25 October 1961, sec. 2, p. 2; "Viram a segunda mostra de veículos 550 mil pessoas," *O Estado de S. Paulo*, 13 December 1961, p. 17; Maurício, "Itinerário . . . ," *Correio da Manhã*, 17 October 1962, sec. 2, p. 2; Maurício, "Itinerário . . . ," *Correio da Manhã*, 4 April 1963, sec. 2, p. 2; "Eis a FENIT," *Indústria e Desenvolvimento*, August 1969, p. 15; Alexandre Wollner, *Alexandre Wollner: Design visual, 50 anos* (São Paulo, 2003), 127, 131. For this period in the history of design in Brazil generally: Décio Pignatari, *Informação, linguagem, comunicação* (São Paulo, 1969), 15–16, 89, 107–111; Wollner, *Alexandre Wollner*; Farias et al., *Eletrodomésticos*, 100–123; João Braga and Luis André do Prado, *História da moda no Brasil: Das influências às autoreferências* (São Paulo, 2011), chap. 5. On the industrial-design school: "Ensino," *Anuário Brasileiro de Propaganda*, 1968–1969, pp. 239–240; "Está nascendo a profissão de 'designer' brasileiro," *O Dirigente Industrial*, January 1969, pp. 43–44, 46; Pignatari, *Informação*, 5, 108; Wollner, *Alexandre Wollner*, 147–155, 179. For earlier "'export-quality' culture," see Daryle Williams, *Culture Wars in Brazil: The First Vargas Regime, 1930–1945* (Durham, N.C., 2001), chap. 6.

32. Kubitschek: Bonadio, "Fio sintético," 103; "JK falará no encerramento do II Salão do Automóvel," *Folha de S. Paulo*, 10 December 1961, sec. "Assuntos Diversos," pt. 1, p. 5; "O Senador Juscelino Kubitschek no II Salão de Automóvel," *O Estado de S. Paulo*, 12 December 1961, p. 24; "Entendimentos entre a câmara e a prefeitura," *O Es-*

tado de S. Paulo, 13 December 1961, p. 4. Goulart: "Goulart: 'Que o Brasil caminhe para a sua emancipação econômica," *Folha de S. Paulo*, 3 October 1961, sec. 1, p. 3; "Goulart continua indefinido: Desenvolvimento industrial," *Correio da Manhã*, 9 December 1962, p. 1. Subsequent presidents and ministers: "V Salão do Automóvel satisfaz presidente," *Correio da Manhã*, 27 November 1966, sec. 1, p. 5; José Lago, "Luxo e beleza no quinto salão," *Manchete*, 10 December 1966, p. 21; "Queiroz veio a São Paulo," *O Estado de S. Paulo*, 8 December 1966, p. 56; "O Salão e seu visitante mais ilustre," *O Estado de S. Paulo*, 23 November 1968, p. 10; "Um carro para cada gosto," *Manchete*, 7 December 1974, p. 102c.

33. Bonadio, "Fio sintético," 103–104 (journalist); "III UD," *Folha de S. Paulo*, 28 April 1962, sec. 2, p. 5.

34. "Feira de utilidades domésticas entusiasma público e expositor," *Diretor Lojista*, August 1974, p. 13; "500 mil pessoas visitaram o IV UD," *Vendas e Varejo*, August 1963, pp. 20, 22; "1º Salão do Automóvel," *O Estado de S. Paulo*, 13 December 1960, p. 5; "No II Salão do Automóvel," *Folha de S. Paulo*, 10 December 1961, sec. "Assuntos Diversos," pt. 1, p. 4; *Manchete* commemorative issue, *Brasil 70*, October 1970, p. 253 ("future . . ."); "O destaque do mês," *Propaganda*, November 1962, p. 15 ("a marvelous . . ."); Marcus Pereira, "Uma festa em que o melhor é ela própria," *O Estado de S. Paulo*, 8 April 1962, p. 84 ("The . . .").

35. Amara Rocha, *Nas ondas da modernização: O rádio e a TV no Brasil de 1950 a 1970* (Rio de Janeiro, 2007), 205; "Quem te viu e quem te vê," *Visão*, 2 December 1960, p. 20; "Os dez anos da TV no Brasil," *PN*, 6 February 1961, p. 16; Lia Calabre de Azevedo, "TV Excelsior," in *DHBB*, 5:5819; "O que 1960 nos reserva?," *Propaganda*, January 1960, p. 14; "O ano que passou e o ano que passará," *Propaganda*, January 1961, pp. 24–28.

36. "Os dez anos da TV no Brasil," *PN*, 6 February 1961, p. 16; "São Paulo Gets New TV Station," *Brazilian Business*, November 1967, p. 11; "Vinte anos de televisão," *Veja*, 23 September 1970, p. 63; Armin Ludwig, *Brazil: A Handbook of Historical Statistics* (Boston, 1985), 267 (official sources, 1968, 1974).

37. There are no accurate statistical series on television ownership for the period covered by this book. The convention has been to rely on figures on televisions in use produced by the association of Brazilian electronics manufacturers, but these data are entirely fanciful for the 1950s and deeply flawed for the years that follow, in part as a result of its relying upon the fanciful pre-1960 data as a starting point, in part—it would seem—because no attempt was made to account for large numbers of illegally imported sets. For chapter 4, I was able to put together a series for the years 1951–1958 based almost entirely on advertising agency sources (the specific figures are thus consistent and suggestive of actual trends), but such an approach was not possible for the period covered by this chapter, and so the preceding rough estimates were based on varied, often-inconsistent sources (including, for the later 1960s and the 1970s, the manufacturers' data), crossed with census data on household television ownership (from the 1960 and 1970 censuses, as cited in Ludwig, *Brazil*, 171) and additional household-ownership data from the sources cited in this chapter's notes 38 through 40: Ney Lima Figueiredo, *O poder da propaganda* (Rio de Janeiro, 1965), 58; Haroldo Holanda, "Televisão no Brasil já é negócio," *O Observador Econômico e Financeiro*, December 1959, p. 22; Department of Commerce, *Brazil*, 143; "Quem te viu e quem te vê,"

Visão, 2 December 1960, p. 20; "Os dez anos da TV no Brasil," *PN*, 6 February 1961, pp. 17–18; Weston C. Pullen Jr., "Memorando ao conselho de Time-Life sobre investimento na TV Globo," October 1965, in Joe Wallach, *Meu capítulo na TV Globo* (Rio de Janeiro, 2011), 223–224; Maria Elvira Bonavita Federico, *História da comunicação: Rádio e TV no Brasil* (Petrópolis, 1982), 140; "Vinte anos de televisão," *Veja*, 23 September 1970, p. 63; Francisco Gracioso, "A emprêsa na consumocracia (capítulo X)," *Propaganda*, May 1971, p. 27; Ramona Bechtos, "No Lack of Ad Media in Brazil," *Advertising Age*, 12 March 1973, p. 44; Mauro Salles, "Setor terciário da economia brasileira," *Propaganda*, August 1973, p. 44; Rede Globo advertisement, *Propaganda*, October 1974, p. 31. Easily accessible presentations of the manufacturers' data include Jacques Marcovitch, *Pioneiros e empreendedores: A saga do desenvolvimento no Brasil*, 3 vols. (São Paulo, 2003–2007), 3:318; Manuel L. Leite, "Rádio, 'uma voz que vai de um fim a outro fim do mundo,'" in *HPB*, 251. For some of the problems with the manufacturing-association's data and a bit on contraband, see José Silveira Raoul, "O desenvolvimento da televisão no Brasil," *O Estado de S. Paulo*, 4 October 1975, sec. "Suplemento do Centenário," 2; Federico, *História*, 139–140. The boast that Brazil's television market was growing faster than any other between 1965 and 1970 may be found in "A Denison Eletrônica está ficando rica às custas da Zenith," *Correio da Manhã*, 20 August 1971, sec. "Diretor Econômico," 18; "Entre as cores e o melhor nível," *Veja*, 12 January 1972, p. 48.

38. John Wells, "The Diffusion of Durables in Brazil and Its Implications for Recent Controversies Concerning Brazilian Development," *Cambridge Journal of Economics* 1, no. 3 (September 1977): 273 (slightly higher 1960 estimate, but cf. Ludwig, *Brazil*, 171), 260 (for 1972); Gracioso, "A emprêsa na consumocracia (capítulo X)," 27 (for 1970).

39. "Utilidades domésticas," *Indústria & Mercados*, August 1961, pp. 42, 40; Francisco Gracioso, "A emprêsa na consumocracia (capítulo V)," *Propaganda*, October 1970, p. 50.

40. Wells, "Diffusion," 263.

41. Marcos Margulies, "Garota-propaganda—Profissão ou estado de espírito," *O Estado de S. Paulo*, 1 June 1958, p. 113; "Antena de TV em teto de zinco," *PN* 13 February 1961, pp. 28–29; "O rádio continua crescendo," *PN*, 31 August 1959, p. 42; "Utilidades domésticas," *Indústria & Mercados*, August 1961, pp. 40, 42; Luiz Augusto Milanesi, *O paraíso via Embratel: O processo de integração de uma cidade do interior paulista na sociedade de consumo* (Rio de Janeiro, 1978), 116; "Continua a crescer o número dos 'televizinhos,'" *Visão*, 2 December 1960, pp. 22–23.

42. José Maria Campos Manzo, *Marketing: Uma ferramenta para o desenvolvimento* (Rio de Janeiro, 1969), 97; Salles, "Setor terciário," 44; Rede Globo advertisement, *Propaganda*, October 1974, p. 31; "Entre as cores e o melhor nível," *Veja*, 12 January 1972, p. 48 ("lower . . ."); Louise Brown, "New Products Go to Market," *Brazilian Business*, April 1963, p. 14.

43. Clark, *Campeão*, 182–183; José Bonifácio de Oliveira Sobrinho, *O livro do Boni* (Rio de Janeiro, 2001), 191; "Muitos e ruins," *Veja*, 7 November 1973, p. 103; David St. Clair, "TV: Infant Industry in Swaddling Clothes," *Brazilian Business*, November 1963, pp. 21–22; "O futuro de um império," *Veja*, 6 October 1976, p. 96; Maria Rita Kehl, "Eu vi um Brasil na TV," in Inimá Ferreira Simões, Alcir Henrique da Costa,

and Maria Rita Kehl, *Um país no ar: História da TV brasileira em três canais* (São Paulo, 1986), 174–176, 179, 185–190, 218–219.

44. Statistical series on billings by medium: "A TV cada vez engole mais," *Propaganda*, June 1969, p. 49; Federico, *História*, 153–155; Leite, "Rádio, 'uma voz,'" 231; Rocha, *Nas ondas*, 206. Decreasing per-household expense: Federico, *História*, 150.

45. *Enlatados*: "O ano que passou e o ano que passará," *Propaganda*, January 1961, p. 25; "Os dez anos da TV no Brasil," *PN*, 6 February 1961, p. 19; Paulo Cesar Ferreira, *Pilares via satélite: Da Rádio Nacional à Rede Globo* (Rio de Janeiro, 1998), 116; Oliveira Sobrinho, *Livro*, 142, 253; Wallach, *Meu capítulo*, 76–77, 93, 103, 117–118; "TV no Brasil é medíocre," *PN*, 27 May 1963, p. 23; Guy Playfair, "What's New? TV Globo Is, That's What!," *Brazilian Business*, January 1965, p. 22; "Clientes fazem notícias," *Boletim JWT*, July 1965, p. 2, JWTA. Videotape: "O ano que passou e o ano que passará," *Propaganda*, January 1961, p. 26; Clark, *Campeão*, 109–110, 112–113; Ferreira, *Pilares*, 97; Oliveira Sobrinho, *Livro*, 139–140, 190; St. Clair, "TV," 22; "Liderança com mais de 600 programas por mês," *Boletim JWT*, June 1967, p. 2, JWTA; "Veículação manteve liderança em rádio, televisão e 'outdoor,'" *Boletim JWT*, December 1967, p. 1, JWTA; Manuel Leite, "TV Brasil—ano 40," in *HPB*, 244–245.

46. "Primeiro filme seriado da TV vai sair logo," *Propaganda*, May 1961, pp. 6–7; "O Brasil já está produzindo 'enlatados' para TV," *PN*, 10 July 1961, pp. 32–33; "Chegou! 'O Vigilante Rodoviário,'" *Atualidades Nestlé*, February 1962, NBL-CPD; "O Vigilante Rodoviário," *Atualidades Nestlé*, June 1962, NBL-CPD; "Nestlé no I Salão da Criança," *Ultima Hora*, 24 October 1961, p. 8.

47. Variety shows: Leite, "TV Brasil," 245, 247; "Ficou," *Veja*, 8 August 1973, p. 74; Clark, *Campeão*, 108, 174, 214–215, 231–233; Oliveira Sobrinho, *Livro*, 201–210, 306–308; Wallach, *Meu capítulo*, 78–80, 90–91, 93–95. News and current-events broadcasts: João Moacir Medeiros, "Propaganda de varejo," in Alfredo Carmo et al., *Comunicação: As funções da propaganda* (São Paulo, 1970), 169; "Ficou," *Veja*, 8 August 1973, p. 74; "O novo marketing brasileiro," *Anuário Brasileiro de Propaganda*, 1973–1974, p. 10; Clark, *Campeão*, 213–214; Oliveira Sobrinho, *Livro*, 88; Wallach, *Meu capítulo*, 88, 132, 137. Musical programming: Leite, "TV Brasil," 245; Clark, *Campeão*, 174, 194–198, 228; Oliveira Sobrinho, *Livro*, 253, 263ff; Wallach, *Meu capítulo*, 103. Sports: Holanda, "Televisão," 22; Clark, *Campeão*, 219; Ferreira, *Pilares*, 152–153, 175.

48. Rodolfo Lima Martensen, *O desafio de quatro santos: Memórias* (São Paulo, 1983), 218; "Telenovelas: Instrutivas ou imbecilizantes?," *Propaganda*, August 1965, pp. 19–22, 27–28, 36; Clark, *Campeão*, 146–147, 178–184; Oliveira Sobrinho, *Livro*, 131–136, 173, 179–182, 211–223, 253, 255–261, 423; Ferreira, *Pilares*, 109, 230; Wallach, *Meu capítulo*, 89–90, 102–103, 121–129; "Glória na hora de verdade," *Veja*, 12 November 1969, p. 77; "Os filhos do Direito de Nascer," *Veja*, 7 May 1969, pp. 27–30.

49. Wallach, *Meu capítulo*, esp. chap. 1; Ferreira, *Pilares*, 159–192; Clark, *Campeão*, 158–299; also, Kehl, "Eu vi um Brasil."

50. José Ulises Alvarez Arce, "Televisão: Ano 25/10 de conquistas de comercialização," *Anuário Brasileiro de Propaganda*, 1975–1976, pp. 66–67; Walter Clark Bueno in *Anuário Brasileiro de Propaganda*, 1973–1974, p. 10; Wallach, *Meu capítulo*, 124–125; Ferreira, *Pilares*, esp. 172–173, 176–177; Federico, *História*, esp. 97–99.

51. Ferreira, *Pilares*, 174; St. Clair, "TV," 22; "Walter Clark: 'Homem de Vendas do Ano,'" *Propaganda*, December 1973, p. 49.

52. Wallach, *Meu capítulo*, 140–146; Ferreira, *Pilares*, 173; Clark, *Campeão*, 285; Kehl, "Eu vi um Brasil," 182 (diretor).

53. On the recording industry: Clark, *Campeão*, 265–266; Wallach, *Meu capítulo*, 129; Oliveira Sobrinho, *Livro*, 391ff; "O futuro de um império," *Veja*, 6 October 1976, pp. 91–92. For "merchandising": "O futuro . . . ," 91–92; Oliveira Sobrinho, *Livro*, 193. On research: Clark, *Campeão*, 240–242; Ferreira, *Pilares*, 191–192; Oliveira Sobrinho, *Livro*, 421–423; "O futuro . . . ," 87 ("It . . .").

54. Ferreira, *Pilares*, 67; "Thompson Clients Sponsor Radio Broadcast of Brazil's Victory in World Soccer Contest," *J. Walter Thompson Company News*, 11 August 1958, p. 1, JWTA; Michel de Montaigne, "A dança do futebol," *PN*, 15 February 1960, p. 24; "Rádio Nacional e Melhoral" (advertisement), *Propaganda*, August 1962, p. 1.

55. Manuel L. Leite, "Rádio—O fabuloso veículo dos anos 30, 40, 50, 60, 70, etc., etc.," *Propaganda*, December 1974, pp. 48, 52; Medeiros, "Propaganda," 161; Janice Perlman, *Favela: Four Decades of Living on the Edge in Rio de Janeiro* (Oxford, 2010), xvi ("everything . . ."); Francisco Gracioso, "Para onde vai a propaganda," *Propaganda*, December 1965, p. 22; Gracioso, "A emprêsa na consumocracia (capítulo V)," 52; Samir Razuk, "O rádio desperta emoções profundas," *Anuário Brasileiro de Propaganda*, 1975–1976, p. 72.

56. Federico, *História*, 154–155; Michel de Montaigne, "Televisão: Veículo feminino?," *PN*, 6 July 1959, p. 41; Sinésio Ascêncio, "Publicidade radiofônica," *Propaganda*, August 1961, pp. 17–21; Umberto Gargiulo, "Nunca se ouviu tanto rádio como agora," *Propaganda*, September 1961, pp. 13–15; "O direito de nascer," *Propaganda*, June 1963, p. 25; "Favela: Poesia de tristeza da terra carioca," *PN*, 3 September 1962, p. 29; [Marcus Pereira], "Os veículos do século," *O Estado de S. Paulo*, 13 July 1958, p. 96; Gracioso, "A emprêsa na consumocracia (capítulo V)," 50; Wells, "Diffusion," 260, 262; Ferreira, *Pilares*, 139–143.

57. Arnaldo Bloch, *Os irmãos Karamabloch: Ascensão e queda de um império familiar* (São Paulo, 2008), 200, 202; Murilo Melo Filho "A *Manchete* na onda Brasília," in *Aconteçeu na Manchete: As histórias que ninguém contou*, eds. José Esmeraldo Gonçalves and J. A. Barros (Rio de Janeiro, 2008), 371–375; J. M. [Justino Martins], "Conversa com o leitor," *Manchete*, 7 May 1960, p. 7 (Kubitschek).

58. Cláudia Mesquita, *De Copacabana à Boca do Mato: O Rio de Janeiro de Sérgio Porto e Stanislaw Ponte Preta* (Rio de Janeiro, 2008), 204; F. Teixeira Orlandi, "Veículos impressos," *Propaganda*, October 1960, p. 7; Rabelo, *Onde*, 210–212 (inc. "The fact . . . ," "market . . . ," "what happened . . ."); Bloch, *Irmãos*, 208; "Etiquêta lançou moda de inverno," *PN*, 5 June 1961, pp. 32–34.

59. Abril advertisement, *Propaganda*, January 1974, p. 1; Abril advertisement, *PN*, 20 January 1957, pp. 37–39 (inc. "women . . ."); Ana Rita Fonteles Duarte, *Carmen da Silva: O feminismo na imprensa brasileira* (Fortaleza, 2005), esp. 19–20 (inc. "The explosive . . ."), 169–170; Abril advertisement, *Propaganda*, October 1967, pp. 12–13; Maria Celeste Mira, *O leitor e a banca de revista: A segmentação da cultura no século XX* (São Paulo, 2001), 51–58 (inc. "the Brazilianizing . . ."); Carmen da Silva, "A protagonista," *Claudia*, September 1963, in *O melhor de Carmen da Silva*, ed. Laura Taves Civita (Rio de Janeiro, 1994), 17–23; Teresa Barros, "Casamento não é razão de viver" (interview with Carmen da Silva), *Correio da Manhã*, 5 May 1968, sec. "Feminino," 1; Carla Beozzo Bassanezi, *Virando as páginas, revendo as mulheres: Revistas femininas*

e relações homem-mulher, 1945–1964 (Rio de Janeiro, 1996); Darcy Ribeiro, *Aos trancos e barrancos: Como o Brasil deu no que deu* (Rio de Janeiro, 1985), item 1954; Carmen da Silva, "Parabéns a todas nós" (1971), in *O melhor . . .* , 41.

60. "O ano dos veículos especializados," *Propaganda*, February 1961, p. 30; "Número 7 da revista Quatro Rodas," *O Estado de S. Paulo*, 17 February 1961, p. 24; *Mecânica Popular* advertisement, *O Estado de S. Paulo*, 26 November 1961, p. 14; "Em português a revista *Visão*," *Publicidade & Negócios*, 1 March 1952, pp. 47–48; Genival Rabelo, *O capital estrangeiro na imprensa brasileira* (Rio de Janeiro, 1966); "'Visão'— Agora semanal," *Propaganda*, June 1957, p. 11; "Presente de Natal não é problema," *Visão*, 14 December 1967, pp. 36–39.

61. "Tudo," *PN*, 5 August 1956, p. 56; "Publicidade," *O Estado de S. Paulo*, 8 March 1959, p. 56; Mira, *Leitor*, 75–84; "Retrospecto," *Anuário Brasileiro de Propaganda*, 1968–1969, p. 15; "Abril," *Propaganda*, October 1973, pp. 36–37; Abril advertisement, *Propaganda*, November 1969, pp. 24–25 (quoted).

62. On the IVC: transcription of interview with Altino João de Barros by Ilana Strozenbert and Luciana Heymann, 14 July 2004, CPDOC-PHO; IVC announcement, *Ultima Hora*, 21 March 1963, p. 11; Pedro Nunes, *35 anos de propaganda* (Rio de Janeiro, n.d.), 230–231. According to an expert, the "big four" newspapers received 70 to 80 percent of their income from advertising: Mauro Salles, "Opinião pública, mercado e comunicações," *Revista da Associação Comercial*, October 1976, p. 21. On *A Notícia* and *O Dia*: Emil Farhat, "Jornais: Odisséia e epopéia," in *HPB*, 207.

63. "'Folhas' têm novos donos," *PN*, 3 September 1962, p. 11; Bechtos, "No Lack of Ad Media," 35; Engel Paschoal, *A trajetória de Octavio Frias de Oliveira*, 2nd ed. (São Paulo, 2007 [2006]), quotes on 12–13.

64. Leite, "TV Brasil," 246; Rabelo, *Onde*, 212 ("student . . ."); Carlos Roberto Chueiri, "E, no princípio, era a verba . . . ," in *HPB*, 276 ("very . . ."); "Prêmio Propaganda—1970," *Propaganda*, January 1971, p. 12 ("contributed . . ."); Sérgio Ricardo Rodrigues Castilho, *"Marketing político": A construção social do "mercado eleitoral" no Brasil, 1954–2000* (Rio de Janeiro, 2014); Manoel de Vasconcellos, "Uma palavra da redação," *PN*, 26 December 1960, p. 1; Vasconcellos, "Uma palavra da redação," *PN*, 15 December 1958, p. 1.

65. "Linguagem da propaganda," *Propaganda*, June 1939, p. 36; Clark, *Campeão*, 43; "Roberto Duailibi," *Anuário Brasileiro de Propaganda*, 1970–1971, p. 74; Bonadio, "Fio sintético," 133; Francisco Gracioso, "Marketing no Brasil: Evolução, situação atual, tendências," in *HPB*, 85–97; Chueiri, "E, no princípio," 272–275.

66. Manoel de Vasconcellos, "Uma palavra do editor," *Publicidade & Negócios*, 20 December 1952, p. 2; Armando de Moraes Sarmento to "Sr. Diretor," *Publicidade & Negócios*, 20 January 1953, p. 2; Genival Rabelo, *A volta por cima* (Rio de Janeiro, 1995), 147 ("global . . ."); Raimar Richers, *O que é marketing* (São Paulo, 1981), 15; Ole Johnson, "Homens de negócio," *Propaganda*, May 1956, p. 44; Vasconcellos, "Uma palavra da redação," *PN*, 10 November 1958, p. 1; Associação Brasileira de Marketing, *I Congresso Brasileiro de Marketing e Comercialização: Hotel Nacional, Rio de Janeiro, maio, 16, 17 e 18, 1977* (published proceedings); Vasconcellos, "Uma palavra da redação," *PN*, 26 December 1960, p. 1 (*"comercialização global"*); Roberto Simões, *Iniciação ao marketing* (São Paulo, 1970), 15–16; Francisco Gracioso, *Marketing: Uma experiência brasileira* (São Paulo, 1971), 14; "Encontro técnico," *Veja*, 20 June 1973, p. 106.

67. Sarmento to Sr. Diretor; José Roberto Whitaker Penteado, "Administração de Empresas," *PN*, 2 January 1958, p. 28; Raimar Richers, "A emancipação do administrador mercadológico," *Revista de Administração de Empresas* 1 (May–August 1961): 36–38 (cf. "Report of the Definitions Committee," *Journal of Marketing* 13, no. 2 [October 1948]: 209). Richers's preferred definition paraphrased Paul Mazur's "Distribution is the delivery of a standard of living" ("Does Distribution Cost Enough?," *Fortune*, November 1947, p. 138).

68. Carlos Roberto Chueiri, "Propaganda é uma ponte entre a fábrica e o mundo," *O Dirigente Industrial*, April 1969, p. 47; José Maria Campos Manzo, *Marketing: Uma ferramenta para o desenvolvimento* (Rio de Janeiro, 1969), quotes on 12; Mário Pacheco Fernandes, "Marketing," *Indústria e Desenvolvimento*, June 1970, pp. 22–23; Harry Simonsen Jr., "Marketing," in Carmo et al., *Comunicação*, 31–33; Roberto Duailibi and Harry Simonsen Jr., *Criatividade: A formulação de alternativas em marketing* (São Paulo, 1971), 32 (cf. 18, 28); Francisco Gracioso, "A emprêsa na consumocracia (capítulo I)," *Propaganda*, August 1970, pp. 48, 50; Gracioso, "A emprêsa na consumocracia (capítulo II)," *Propaganda*, September 1970, pp. 44, 46; Otto Scherb, "A queda de circulação de revistas," *Propaganda*, November 1970, p. 15.

69. Caio Domingues, *Elementos de propaganda* (Rio de Janeiro, 1959), 7, 10–11, 90–98; Genival Rabelo, "Fatos & comentários," *PN*, 1 February 1960, p. 25; "Das mais desenvolvidas a indústria gráfica e de embalagens de S. Paulo," *Indústria e Desenvolvimento*, May 1969, p. 27; Ruy Chalmers, *Marketing: A experiência universal de marketing na conquista sistemática dos mercados* (São Paulo, 1969); Simões, *Iniciação*, 18–19; Simonsen, "Marketing," 37–38.

70. Genival Rabelo, "Fatos & comentários," *PN*, 1 February 1960, p. 24 ("first . . ."); Martensen, *Desafio*, 243; Nunes, *35 anos*, 148; Gracioso, "Marketing no Brasil," 86–87; APP, *Depoimentos*, 24 ("In Brazil . . ."); "Museu de Arte de São Paulo, Escola de Propaganda, Ante-Projeto," October 1951, ESPM-IC; "Escola de Propaganda faz dez anos," *PN*, 18 October 1962, p. 29; "ESPM," *Propaganda*, March 1973, pp. 16–18, 20–21.

71. Chalmers, *Marketing*, 11–12; "Novo curso de direção executiva para gerentes," *Noticiário Mappin*, 24 December 1955, p. 3, AHM; "Curso de direção executiva para gerentes de vendas," *Noticiário Mappin*, February 1956, p. 1, AHM; "Curso de direção para chefes de departamentos do Mappin" (clipping labeled *Ultima Hora* [São Paulo], 4 June 1956), AHM-SDP, texto 522, cx. 2; Instituto Técnico de Aperfeiçoamento de Vendas advertisement, *Folha de S. Paulo*, 23 September 1962, sec. "Assuntos Diversos," pt. 1, p. 11; "Os lojistas acordam cêdo e vão à aula," *PN*, 31 July 1958, p. 28; "IPET festeja hoje quinto aniversário de fundação," *Diario de Noticias*, 20 February 1960, sec. 2, p. 1; "Varejo em foco," *Vendas e Varejo*, February 1964, p. 47; ADV-Rio announcement, *Diario de Noticias*, 1 November 1964, p. 4; "Mauro Salles fala no Curso Superior de 'Marketing,'" *Revista Brasileira de Vendas*, October 1966, p. 20; J. Favaro, "ABC do marketing integrado," *Revista Brasileira de Vendas*, January 1965, pp. 35–36; "Novos livros de marketing," *Revista Brasileira de Vendas*, March 1965, p. 6; Einar Udnaes, "Marketing—Um fator esquecido no planejamento dos países subdesenvolvidos," *Revista Brasileira de Vendas*, April 1966, pp. 17, 20–21; "ADVB Federação," *Marketing*, August–September 1967, p. 6.

72. "Executives Go Back to School," *Brazilian Business*, December 1954, pp. 23–24, 57; Johnson, "Homens," 44–45; "São Paulo's School of Business Administration

Expands," *Brazilian Business*, December 1956, pp. 16–17; "A Escola de Administração de Empresas, de São Paulo," *PN*, 5 January 1957, pp. 53–54; "Brazil's City of Go-Getters," *Business Week*, 13 July 1957, p. 63; Vergil D. Reed to Samuel W. Meek, East Lansing, Mich., 27 August 1958, JWTA, EGWP, box 1; Reed, "São Paulo School to Become Latin America's First Business College," *Brazilian Business*, September 1960, pp. 30–33, 55–56; Reed, "A universidade como um centro de serviço para o comércio e o governo," *Brazilian-American Survey*, no. 11 (1960): 109–112; Peter Rodger, "The Making of a Businessman," *Brazilian Business*, November 1962, pp. 21, 23–24; "FGV preparada para enfrentar o século XXI," *Indústria e Desenvolvimento*, January 1971, p. 8; Richers, *O que é marketing*, 8 ("as . . ."). See also Alyza Munhoz, "Pensamento em marketing no Brasil: Um estudo exploratório" (tese de mestrado, EAESP, 1982), esp. 223–313, for excerpts from interviews with seven of the first EAESP assistant professors to specialize in marketing.

73. Eduardo Buarque de Almeida, "Apresentação," in Joaquim Caldeira da Silva, *Gerência de vendas: Visão prática de um profissional* (São Paulo, 1986), 13.

74. Paulo Afonso Lajes de Aguiar, interviewed by Glauco Carneiro, 28 June 1982, NBL-CPD, TDGC, vol. 3; José Garcia de Silva Lemos (quoted), interviewed by Glauco Carneiro, 3 November 1982, NBL-CPD, TDGC, vol. 2.

75. "Convenção de gerentes de Nestlé em S. Paulo," *Vendas e Varejo*, May 1960, p. 19; "EmM [Emile Meyer] arregaça as mangas e mostra o que é 'marketing integral,'" *Atualidades Nestlé*, May–August 1963 (quoted), NBL-CPD; Jean-Pierre Brulhart, untitled transcription of speech, *Atualidades Nestlé*, April 1972, p. 58, NBL-CPD; "Vademecum do Vendedor," MDWNB00.00.000012, NBL-CPD; "Nossa cozinha do futuro foi show à parte na UD," *Atualidades Nestlé*, July–August 1968, pp. 20–21, NBL-CPD; "Nescau teve gosto de feste no II Salão da Criança," *Atualidades Nestlé*, January–April 1963, NBL-CPD; "Nestlé comandou o espetáculo no VI Salão da Criança," *Atualidades Nestlé*, 1966, p. 22, NBL-CPD; "Criança reina no Salão," *Atualidades Nestlé*, 1967, pt. 2, p. 10, NBL-CPD; "Nossa presença no Salão da Criança," *Atualidades Nestlé*, December 1968, pp. 14–15, NBP-CPD; Gracioso, *Marketing*, 46; "Histórico" (of Centro Nestlé de Economia Doméstica), in HNSC, NBL-CPD; "Economia doméstica—Relações com consumidores (experiência brasileira)," in HNSC, NBL-CPD; Débora Fontenelle, interviewed by Glauco Carneiro, 27 October 1982, NBL-CPD, TDGC, vol. 1; *Seleções do Reader's Digest* advertisement, *Propaganda*, July 1961, pp. 30–31; Roger Anderfuhren (quoted), interviewed by Glauco Carneiro, 3 December 1982, NBL-CPD, TDGC, vol. 2; "A. C. Nielsen: De como se levantar informações," *Supermercado Moderno*, April 1973, p. 32.

76. Martensen, *Desafio*, 229, 243; Almeida, "Apresentação," 13–14; Gracioso, "Marketing no Brasil," 86; José Garcia de Silva Lemos interview, NBL-CPD; "V. conhece seu mercado?," *O Dirigente Industrial*, February 1963, p. 62; "O novo marketing brasileiro," *Anuário Brasileiro de Propaganda*, 1973–1974, pp. 15–16; Simonsen, "Marketing"; Simonsen, "Algumas ideias sobre a função de planejamento de produtos no âmbito da filosofia de marketing," *Marketing*, August–September 1967, pp. 20–21; Simonsen, "Propaganda e marketing," *Propaganda*, June 1969, pp. 42, 44–45; Duailibi and Simonsen, *Criatividade*; Munhoz, "Pensamento," 269–270, 292–297; "Associação dos Dirigentes de Venda," *O Estado de S. Paulo*, 28 January 1970, p. 11; *Anais do Primeiro Congresso Brasileiro de Propaganda*, 32, 46; "Reed (Thompson): Brasil deve

formar dirigentes," *Propaganda*, September 1961, p. 15; Reed, "São Paulo School," 32; Gracioso, "Marketing no Brasil," 86 ("among . . ."); Ricardo Ramos, "Do reclame à comunicação," *Anuário Brasileiro de Propaganda*, 1970–1971, p. 66 ("carried . . ."); Doria Propaganda advertisement, *Diario de Noticias*, 29 May 1959, sec. 1, p. 5; Standard advertisement, *PN*, 6 July 1959, cover; McCann advertisement, *Propaganda*, May 1960, p. 2; "A Denison altrapassará 1/2 bilião este ano," *PN*, 19 June 1961, p. 29; JWT advertisement, *Propaganda*, July 1961, p. 4; Francisco Gracioso, "A promoção de vendas no Brasil," *Propaganda*, February 1961, p. 18.

77. Manoel de Vasconcellos, "Uma palavra da redação," *PN*, 22 August 1960, p. 1; Cezar Augusto Freire, "Marketing," *O Estado de S. Paulo*, 24 September 1972, p. 46. For "philosophy," "Fórmulas não são infalíveis," *O Estado de S. Paulo*, 24 September 1972, p. 46; social science, Richers, "Emancipação," 51.

78. Gracioso, *Marketing*, 42–48.

79. *Seleções* advertisements in *PN*, 19 June 1961, pp. 24–25, and *Propaganda*, July 1961, pp. 30–31; Arce, "Televisão."

80. "Depoimento de Valentim Lorenzetti," São Paulo, 27 October 1988 (quoted), IPHSP; "Depoimento de Sidrak Berberian," São Paulo, 18 October 1988, IPHSP; "10.000," *Boletim JWT*, February 1965, p. 2, JWTA.

81. Alfred Chandler, *The Visible Hand: The Managerial Revolution in American Business* (Cambridge, Mass., 1977); Rabelo, *Volta*, 51; Ney de Lima Figueiredo, "Introdução," in Carmo et al., *Comunicação*, 21; Escola Superior de Vendas advertisement, *O Estado de S. Paulo*, 7 January 1962, p. 5; Gracioso, *Marketing*, 36–37, 51; Richers, "Emancipação," 35.

82. Manzo, *Marketing*; Francisco Gracioso, preface to Chalmers, *Marketing*, 15; Luiz Carlos Bresser Pereira, "Desenvolvimento econômico e o empresário," *Revista de Administração de Empresas* 4 (May–August 1962): 79–91; W. W. Rostow, "O conceito de um mercado nacional e as suas implicações no crescimento da economia," *Revista de Adminstração de Empresas* 25 (October–December 1967): 155–169; Raimar Richers, "Transformação social pela abertura de novos mercados," *Revista de Administração de Empresas* 27 (April–June 1968): 97–127; Manoel de Vasconcellos, "O problema ideológico," *PN*, 30 July 1962, p. 10; Enaldo Cravo Peixoto, "A SUNAB e as classes produtoras," *Revista das Classes Produtoras*, September 1969, p. 24; Emil Farhat, *O país dos coitadinhos: Algumas idéias sôbre o Brasil* (São Paulo, 1966), 151; Gracioso, *Marketing*, esp. 18–25.

83. Curso Superior de Marketing announcement, *O Estado de S. Paulo*, 14 July 1968, p. 10; Humberto Dantas, "Documentos da nova revolução industrial," *Indústria e Desenvolvimento*, September 1968, p. 3; Gastão Nunes dos Santos Brun, "Diferenças regionais e regionalismo obtuso," *Indústria e Desenvolvimento*, August 1971, p. 23; Ivan Pedro de Martins, *O amanhã é hoje: Brasil 1970* (Rio de Janeiro, 1970); Genival Rabelo, *A batalha da opinião pública* (Rio de Janeiro, 1970), 254; Aldo Xavier da Silva, *Comunicação nos negócios* (Rio de Janeiro, 1974), 38; Manzo, *Marketing*, 13.

84. Silva, *Comunicação*, 104 (also, 40); "Faturando notícias," *Diretor Lojista*, October 1974, p. 31; Kehl, "Eu vi um Brasil," 217.

85. Manoel de Vasconcellos, "Uma palavra da redação," *PN*, 10 November 1958, p. 1; Chueiri, "Propaganda," 47; Simonsen and Duailibi, *Criatividade*, chaps. 13–14.

86. Simões, *Iniciação*, 16; Richers, *O que é marketing*, 7, 15; Cultrix advertisement, *Propaganda*, March 1972, p. 42; "Livros," *Propaganda*, September 1972, p. 4.

87. Bernardo Ludermir, "Propaganda como profissão no Brasil," *O Observador Econômico e Financeiro*, July 1959, pp. 18–19; [Marcus Pereira], "A profissão publicitária," *O Estado de S. Paulo*, 29 March 1959, p. 38; Telles, *Tirando*, 72; Ramona Bechtos, "Brazil's Marketing Scene Reflects Nation's Growth," *Advertising Age*, 12 February 1973, p. 60.

88. *Carta Mensal*, May 1957, pp. 33–34 (Corção); Rabelo, *Batalha*, 32; Marinette Bouças in *O Observador Econômico e Financeiro*, November 1958, p. 5 ("big men," in English); *PN*, 29 August 1960, pp. 13–15; *PN*, 5 September 1960, pp. 12–13; *PN*, 12 September 1960, pp. 12–14; *PN*, 19 September 1960, pp. 12–13; *PN*, 26 September 1960, pp. 13–14; Genival Rabelo, "Fatos & comentários," *PN*, 26 February 1962, p. 122; "1961 será ano bom," *PN*, 9 January 1961, p. 26 (Burlá); Leôncio Basbaum, *Uma vida em seis tempos: Memórias*, 2nd ed. (São Paulo, 1978 [1976]), 252.

89. "Relações públicas em 'O Estado de S. Paulo,'" *Propaganda*, March 1958, p. 16; Francisco Gracioso, "O fator humano no desenvolvimento da propaganda," *Propaganda*, November 1962, p. 39; Otto Scherb, "A explosão do ensino de comunicação no Brasil," *Propaganda*, September 1962, p. 10; Rodolfo Lima Martensen, "O ensino da propaganda no Brasil," *O Estado de S. Paulo*, 20 December 1975, sec. "Suplemento do Centenário," 5; "Uma visão profissional do negócio brasileiro," *Anuário Brasileiro de Propaganda*, 1975–1976, p. 6; Nemércio Nogueira, "Os empresários começam a descobrir as vantagens das técnicas de relações públicas," *Anuário Brasileiro de Propaganda*, 1975–1976, p. 62.

90. [Marcus Pereira], "Publicidade: Os pequenos carregadores de chumbo," *O Estado de S. Paulo*, 6 April 1958, p. 58; Manoel de Vasconcellos, "Uma palavra da redação," *PN*, 11 April 1960, p. 1; "O volume de propaganda no mundo," *Propaganda*, February 1961, p. 20; "Brazilian Ad Industry Zooms to New High in Volume," *Advertising Age*, 4 June 1962, p. 4; Peter Bart, "U.S. Ad Men See Giants to South," *New York Times*, 8 April 1963, p. 63; "Brazil's Anti-Inflation Measures Test Admen," *Advertising Age*, 30 May 1966, pp. 58, 60; "450 milhões de dólares; 1,2% sobre o PNB," *Propaganda*, February 1972, p. 19; Fernando Reis, "São Paulo e Rio: A longa caminhada," in *HPB*, 366; Gracioso, *Marketing*, 54–55, 137 (inc. "Brazilians . . .").

91. "Louras ou morenas?," *Propaganda*, July 1958, pp. 6–12.

92. Lindberg Faria, "Enriqueça aprendendo ilustração," *O Estado de S. Paulo*, 19 March 1961, p. 111 (Castelo Branco); "Brasil fará 1.º Congresso Latino-Americano de Propaganda," *Propaganda*, June 1961, p. 13 (Alonso); "Em foco," *Propaganda*, August 1965, p. 3.

93. Gracioso, "Promoção," 16.

94. "Histórico," HNSC, NBL-CPD.

95. Altino João de Barros, "Uma visão da mídia em cinco décadas," in *HPB*, 133, 138, 140; "A Clipper reformula seus métodos," *Vendas e Varejo*, October 1962, pp. 22–23; "Ponto Frio," *Vendas e Varejo*, July 1964, p. 6; "Mesbla lidera os magazines," *O Dirigente Industrial*, October 1967, p. 137; "Peg-Pag," *Supermercado Moderno*, April 1969, p. 24; "Retrospecto," *Anuário Brasileiro de Propaganda*, 1968–1969, p. 19; José Roberto Penteado Filho, *Previsão de vendas* (São Paulo, 1971), 19.

96. "Bacharelandos," *Boletim JWT*, November 1965, p. 3, JWTA; partially transcribed interview with Geraldo Toledo in Munhoz, "Pensamento," 298–302; Walter Poyares, *Imagem pública* (São Paulo, 1998); Nogueira, "Empresários," 62; Martensen, "Ensino," 4–5. For "brain trust" (in English): Marinette Bouças in *O Observador Econômico e Financeiro*, October 1958, p. 5. For the growing presence of social-science graduates in consumer-oriented firms: "O que é pesquisa de mercado," *Atualidades Nestlé*, 1967, pt. 2, p. 5, NBL-CPD; "Histórico," HNSC, NBL-CPD; Renato Ortiz, *Trajetos e memórias* (São Paulo, 2010), 129–30.

97. "Mercado brasileiro de publicidade, 1967–1968," *Propaganda*, February 1968, p. 17; Ramona Bechtos, "Brazil Agencies Big on Creativity," *Advertising Age*, 26 February 1973, p. 160; Bechtos, "Brazilian Agencies Growing Faster than U.S. Shops," *Advertising Age*, 19 February 1973, p. 46. On CIN: "CIN," *Propaganda*, October 1959, pp. 37–40. Denison: "Uma agência que já nasceu grande," *PN*, 27 April 1959, pp. 68–69; "A Denison ultrapassará 1/2 bilião êste ano," *PN*, 19 June 1961, p. 29. DPZ: Reis, "São Paulo e Rio," 357–359. Mauro Salles: "Depoimento do empresário Mauro Salles," São Paulo, 11 September 1985, in Cleber Aquino, *História empresarial vivida*, 5 vols. (São Paulo, 1986–1991), 3:209–247; "De 'foca' a secretário de 'O Globo,'" *PN*, 17 April 1961, p. 29; *Mecânica Popular* advertisement, *O Estado de S. Paulo*, 26 November 1961, p. 14; "Discurso de posse de Mauro Salles," *Propaganda*, August 1967, p. 56; Rabelo, *Onde*, 128–130; Robert E. Dennison to Dan Seymour, São Paulo, 28 January 1970, JWTA, EGWP, box 2 (also, same box: E. G. Wilson to John Devine, New York, 29 January 1970). For agency rankings: T. Teixeira e Silva, "A New Rhythm for Brazil," *Brazilian Business*, November 1969, p. 20; "450 milhões de dólares; 1,2% sobre o PNB," *Propaganda*, February 1972, p. 20; Jomar Pereira da Silva, "O anúncio da publicidade brasileira," *Revista da Associação Comercial*, January 1975, p. 8.

98. Reis, "São Paulo e Rio," 331, 350, 355–356; Bechtos, "Brazil's Marketing," 60; Ricardo Ramos, "Um século de propaganda no Brasil," *O Estado de S. Paulo*, 20 December 1975, sec. "Suplemento do Centenário," 3.

99. "Terá supervisão sobre América Latina e Europa," *Ultima Hora*, 18 June 1959, p. 2 ("Brazil's . . . ," "reflection . . ."); "Banquete em homenagem a Sarmento," *PN*, 13 July 1959, p. 6; "Consagração a um publicitário brasileiro," *Ultima Hora*, 25 June 1959, p. 8; "Sarmento eleito para comandar," *Correio da Manhã*, 14 December 1963, sec. 1, p. 10; "É pura propaganda, logo é verdade," *Veja*, 5 March 1969, p. 26 (Farhat); "As fitas mais criativas do mundo," *O Estado de S. Paulo*, 21 October 1971, p. 12; "Caderno especial," *Propaganda*, July 1973, pp. 30–65.

100. Renato Castelo Branco to Peter Dunham, Rio de Janeiro, 8 November 1960 (quoted), JWTA, EGWP, box 1; Renato Castelo Branco, *Tomei um Ita no norte: Memórias* (São Paulo, 1981), 177; Martensen, *Desafio*, 292; "Cr$300 milhões em propaganda grátis," *Boletim JWT*, June 1965, p. 1, JWTA; "Conselho estimula consumo," *Boletim JWT*, July 1965, p. 1 (Castelo Branco), JWTA; "Propaganda da propaganda," *Propaganda*, August 1968, pp. 11–12; "CNP," *Anuário Brasileiro de Propaganda*, 1968–1969, pp. 229–231 (inc. "advertising . . ."); CNP advertisement, *Propaganda*, October 1968, p. 56; "NYO Campaign for MPA Sparks Brazil Ad Council Effort," *J. Walter Thompson Company News*, 11 October 1968, p. 4, JWTA.

101. Castelo Branco, *Tomei*, 177; Martensen, *Desafio*, 292; José Lino Grünewald, "Gerações & concepções," *Correio da Manhã*, 19 July 1966, sec. 1, p. 6 ("euphoric . . .");

Waldir Dupont, *Geraldo Alonso: O homem e o mito* (São Paulo, 1991), 28; Murilo Melo Filho, "Os senhores embaixadores," *Manchete*, 9 November 1974, p. 17; "Propaganda, na hora de mudar," *O Estado de S. Paulo*, 25 February 1969, p. 15; "Propaganda e desenvolvimento," *Propaganda*, May 1971, pp. 10–12, 14–16.

102. Salles, "Setor," 39–46; "Publicitário revela previsões do plano," *O Estado de S. Paulo*, 6 September 1974, p. 11; "Imune a pressões," *Veja*, 11 September 1974, p. 30; "Uma indústria moderna," *Veja*, 18 September 1974, pp. 28–30; "Opinião pública, mercado e comunicação," *Revista da Associação Comercial*, October 1976, pp. 18–25; "Em doze meses, sinais de revitalização," *Veja*, 26 October 1977, pp. 46–47.

103. Carlos Fico, *Reinventando o otimismo: Ditadura, propaganda e imaginário social no Brasil* (Rio de Janeiro, 1997); Nina Schneider, *Brazilian Propaganda: Legitimizing an Authoritarian Regime* (Gainesville, Fla., 2014); Thomas Skidmore, *The Politics of Military Rule in Brazil, 1964–1985* (Oxford, 1988), 110–112 (see also 345–346 [notes 15–22], for citations of additional authorities); Gilnei Rampazzo, "A imagem oficial, retocada para o consumo," *O Estado de S. Paulo*, 16 October 1977, p. 8 ("fallen . . ."); Ferreira, *Pilares*, 178–179; Telles, *Tirando*, 167–168; "O comunicar exige amor," *O Estado de S. Paulo*, 16 October 1970, p. 7 ("the most . . .").

104. "Negócios," *Propaganda*, July 1944, p. 37; "Convenção dos lojistas," *PN*, 12 October 1959, pp. 10–12; "1961 será ano bom," *PN*, 9 January 1961, p. 23; "Exposição Clipper," *PN*, 13 December 1962, p. 20; "A regulamentação espontânea das vendas a crédito e suas implicações sociais e econômicas," *Vendas e Varejo*, April 1963, p. 44; "Conselho Diretor," *Revista das Classes Produtoras*, June 1970, pp. 60, 62–63.

105. Affonso Celso, *Porque me ufano do meu paiz* (Rio de Janeiro, 1900); Rabelo, *Batalha*, 202–203 ("In the . . ."); Maria Victoria Benevides, "O governo Kubitschek: A esperança como fator de desenvolvimento," in *O Brasil de JK*, ed. Angela de Castro Gomes (Rio de Janeiro, 1991), 17; Autran Dourado, *Gaiola aberta: Tempos de JK e Schmidt* (Rio de Janeiro, 2000), 38, 111 ("Schmidt . . ."); "Morre de colapso cardíaco Augusto Frederico Schmidt," *Correio da Manhã*, 9 February 1965, sec. 1, p. 2 ("speaking . . ."); "Empresários comemoram 1.º aniversário da revolução," *Revista das Classes Produtoras*, April 1965, p. 40 ("task . . .").

106. "Gloriosos 25 anos passados menores que os 10 anos futuros," *O Observador Econômico e Financeiro*, April 1960, pp. 13–14; "Em foco," *Propaganda*, August 1965, p. 3; *Direção* special issue ("Brasil/66"), December 1965; "A capa de Sergio," *Boletim JWT*, January 1966, p. 3, JWTA; "São Paulo Art Director in NYO," *J. Walter Thompson Company News*, 21 October 1966, p. 3, JWTA.

107. "O Brasil está à beira do abismo," in *O Estado de S. Paulo*, 12 January 1969, p. 13, and *Veja*, 22 January 1969, pp. 4–5.

108. "Retrospecto," *Anuário Brasileiro de Propaganda*, 1969–1970, pp. 56–57; Embratel advertisement, *O Estado de S. Paulo*, 26 March 1969, p. 11; Lloyd advertisement, *Revista das Classes Produtoras*, November 1969, p. 27; Sângia advertisement, *O Estado de S. Paulo*, 10 August 1969, p. 88; Centro da Barra advertisement, *O Estado de S. Paulo*, 9 December 1969, p. 15.

109. Souza Cruz advertisement, *Revista das Classes Produtoras*, September 1970, back cover; Civilização Brasileira advertisement, *Revista das Classes Produtoras*, September 1970, p. 44; "Homenagem da ADECIF," *Revista das Classes Produtoras*, June 1969, p. 43 (Moreira Souza); "Caio de Alcântara Machado: Vamos dar mais café

aos brasileiros," *Revista das Classes Produtoras*, July 1969, p. 46; "Moreira Salles pede fim do processo de estatização," *Revista das Classes Produtoras*, August 1969, p. 41; Ernesto Rosario Manzi [to the editors], *O Estado de S. Paulo*, 18 December 1971, p. 23.

110. Meira, "Indústria" ("dream . . ."); "Brazil's Auto Industry at the Crossroads," *Brazilian Business*, September 1966, p. 17 ("number . . ."); "Nosso automóvel investe no presente e aposta no futuro," *Indústria e Desenvolvimento*, November 1970, p. 4 ("most . . .").

111. "Este é o carro que faltava," *Publicidade Industrial*, March 1967, pp. 36–38; Preben Vils, "Ford Motor do Brasil," *Brazilian Business*, November 1967, p. 13; "GM trabalhou muito para lançar o Opala," *O Dirigente Industrial*, October 1968, p. 92; "Where Ford Is Hot on VW's Heels," *Business Week*, 16 May 1970, p. 44; "Novo Volks sedan sairá dia 8," *O Estado de S. Paulo*, 26 July 1970, p. 30; Joaquim Carlos da Silva, *Marketing nas empresas brasileiras* (Rio de Janeiro, 1971), 86 ("everyone . . ."); "Mercado adulto," *Jornal do Brasil*, 7 July 1970, sec. 1, p. 6; "Exportação, o novo otimismo," *O Estado de S. Paulo*, 9 July 1970, p. 22 ("The . . ."); "Nosso automóvel investe no presente e aposta no futuro," *Indústria e Desenvolvimento*, November 1970, p. 7 (inc. Delfim); Lago, "Luxo," 22.

112. "Going Shopping with Lady Luck," *Business Week*, 16 December 1967, pp. 152, 156, 158; Klaus Kleber, "A primeira geração do consumo," *Administração e Serviços*, June 1980, pp. 8, 10; Cassio Muniz announcement, *Jornal do Brasil*, 12 September 1965, sec. 5, p. 6; Mauro Ribeiro, "Automóveis," *Correio da Manhã*, 4 July 1972, sec. 1, p. 8 (inc. Delfim Netto); Ramona Bechtos, "Key Consumer Goods Growing Fast in Brazil," *Advertising Age*, 5 March 1973, p. 48.

113. Julio Casoy, "Supermercados: História, ficções e realidade," *Folha de S. Paulo*, 11 November 1976, p. 32; "Pão de Açúcar!," *Supermercado Moderno*, May 1969, p. 36; Mauro Salles, "O Brasil na era do consumismo," *Anuário Brasileiro de Propaganda*, 1971–1972, p. 72; "Diálogo para o desenvolvimento dos supermercados," *Supermercado Moderno*, November 1972, pp. 54, 58; "Peg-Pag," *Supermercado Moderno*, April 1969, p. 23; "Governo tem programa para fortalecer a pequena indústria," *Supermercado Moderno*, January 1973, pp. 31, 33; "Financiamento para supermercado," *Supermercado Moderno*, July 1973, p. 5; Joelmir Beting, "O consumidor paulistano," *Manchete*, special issue "Retrato de São Paulo" (1974), 139; "Super Supermercado Peg-Pag," *Supermercado Moderno*, June 1971, pp. 30–43 (quote on 34); "Jumbo," *Supermercado Moderno*, August 1971, pp. 32, 34, 37–38, 41–42, 44–45 (quote on 38).

114. "Perspectivas ilimitadas de desenvolvimento comercial para v.," *Supermercado Moderno*, January 1973, p. 10; Jeff Radford, "The Hypermarket Comes to Brazil," *Brazilian Business*, August 1972, pp. 18–21; "O Jumbo de São Paulo," *Supermercado Moderno*, July 1973, pp. 53, 55; "Jumbo," *Supermercado Moderno*, August 1971, p. 32; "Os homens que tratam dos elefantes," *Supermercado Moderno*, July 1973, p. 56; "O Brasil exporta supermercados," *Boletim Cambial*, 2 April 1959, repr. in *Ultima Hora*, 7 April 1959, p. 3; Disco advertisement, *Correio da Manhã*, 20 August 1959, p. 7; Disco advertisement, *Revista das Classes Produtoras*, December 1970, p. 29.

115. "O grupo Ducal e o lojista do ano," *Vendas e Varejo*, February 1964, pp. 2–5, 8, 10–14, 16, 18; "Brazil Hails Its Kings of Credit," *Business Week*, 14 November 1964, pp. 134, 136, 141; "Trabalho de 15 anos mostra que o grupo Ducal nada tem de estranho," *Revista das Classes Produtoras*, November 1965, pp. 22–23; "Redução de custos

leva lojas de eletrodomésticos à fusão," *Revista das Classes Produtoras*, November 1966, pp. 28–29 (inc. "The consuming . . ."); "União diabólica," *Veja*, 10 June 1970, p. 45; "O forte do tecido," *Veja*, 30 June 1971, p. 66; "De como a Ducal aumentou suas vendas em mais de 200% depois de conglomerar-se," *Supermercado Moderno*, January 1973, p. 66; "A Ducal não é mais aquela," *Propaganda*, June 1973, pp. 27–30 (inc. "popular . . ."); "Duas contradições que derrubaram um império," *Folha de S. Paulo*, 15 May 1977, p. 37; "O maior estouro do mercado," *Veja*, 18 May 1977, pp. 100–106; "Bolsa financeira[,] setor de lojista," *Correio da Manhã*, 10 October 1964, sec. 1, p. 11. On government support for mergers and zaibatsu-style conglomerates: Mario Henrique Simonsen and Roberto de Oliveira Campos, *A nova economia brasileira* (Rio de Janeiro, 1974), 69–70, 206–207; Brasil, *Projeto do II Plano Nacional de Desenvolvimento, 1975–1979* (Rio de Janeiro, 1974), 27, 39, 43–44, 46; *Supermercado Moderno*, January 1973, pp. 58, 60, 62, 66–68.

116. Bloch, *Irmãos*, 208, 211; Ferreira, *Pilares*, 174 (quoted).

117. Ferreira, *Pilares*, 174, 178–179; *Manchete* commemorative issue, *Brasil 70*, October 1970; *Veja*, 14 October 1970; "Prêmio Propaganda—1970," *Propaganda*, January 1971, p. 26. Also on Almap's Volkswagen comercial (widely available online), see Jaílson Pereira da Silva, *Um Brasil em pílulas de 1 minuto: História e cotidiano em publicidades das décadas de 1960–80* (Recife, 2010), 157–160.

118. "Walter Clark: 'Homem de Vendas do Ano,'" *Propaganda*, December 1973, pp. 48–49 (inc. "director . . ."); Clark, *Campeão*, 231–232, 235, 239, 252–253 (remaining quotes); Oliveira Sobrinho, *Livro*, 309–311; Ferreira, *Pilares*, 174–175, 187, 189.

119. "Retrospecto," *Anuário Brasileiro de Propaganda*, 1968–1969, p. 27; Ferreira, *Pilares*, 152–153 (inc. "commercial . . ."); "Vá também ao México, é só ligar a televisão," *Placar*, 5 June 1970, pp. 18–19; "Retrospecto," *Anuário Brasileiro de Propaganda*, 1970–1971, pp. 80, 98; "Rádio, uma guerra ingrata," *Placar*, 5 June 1970, p. 19; "Depoimento de Gualter Leão," Rio de Janeiro, 9 November 1988, IPHSP; "Depoimento de José Yosan dos Santos Fonseca," Rio de Janeiro, 8 November 1988, IPHSP; *Placar*, 20 March 1970.

120. Ferreira, *Pilares*, 175; Sérgio Francisco Costa, "Comunicação x bandeira x Copa do Mundo," *Atualidades Nestlé*, July 1970, p. 18, NBL-CPD; Manoel Julião Netto, *Do "cabeça de cavalo" ao "rabo de peixe"* (São Paulo, 1970), 243.

121. Fico, *Reinventando o otimismo*, 137; Goyana advertisement, *O Estado de S. Paulo*, 23 June 1970, p. 10; Lipton advertisement, *O Estado de S. Paulo*, 23 June 1970, p. 18; Ourodur advertisement, *O Estado de S. Paulo*, 23 June 1970, p. 19; Empresas BMG advertisement, *O Estado de S. Paulo*, 23 June 1970, p. 21; Rádio Televisão Bandeirantes advertisement, *O Estado de S. Paulo*, 23 June 1970, p. 26; "Prêmio Propaganda—1970," *Propaganda*, January 1971, p. 28; "Brazil Players Can't Kick About Gifts," *New York Times*, 28 June 1970, sec. 5, p. 6.

122. Telles, *Tirando*, 167–168 (inc. Costa); "Retrospecto," *Anuário Brasileiro de Propaganda*, 1970–1971, p. 96; Carlos Monforte, "Como no sabão, a qualidade é tudo," *O Estado de S. Paulo*, 16 October 1977, p. 8.

123. ABM, *I Congresso*, 44; Charles Albert de Andrade, "Shopping center também tem memória: Uma história esquecida dos shoppings nos espaços intra-urbanos do Rio de Janeiro e São Paulo nos anos 60 e 70" (tese de mestrado, UFF, 2009), 21 ("shopping-center culture").

124. "Cá entre nós . . . ," *Vendas e Varejo*, April–May–June 1964, p. 29; Milton Costacurta, "Febre de galerias em São Paulo," *Propaganda*, August 1963, p. 35; Haïdine da Silva Barros Duarte, "A cidade do Rio de Janeiro: Descentralização das atividades terciárias," *Revista Brasileira de Geografia* 36, no. 1 (January–March 1974): 68–69; Cynthia Augusta Poleto Aleixo, "Edifícios e galerias comerciais: Arquitetura e comércio na cidade de São Paulo" (tese de mestrado, USP, 2005), esp. 94–99, 128–139, 160–228; Demósthenes Magno Santos, "A história da Construtora Alfredo Mathias, 1950–1985" (tese de mestrado, USP, 2013), 84–95, 158–169; Grandes Galerias advertisement, *O Estado de S. Paulo*, 10 June 1960, pp. 26–27; Galeria Menescal advertisement, *Ultima Hora*, 9 November 1951, p. 5. Marketeer's disapprobation: Meyer Stilman, *O comércio varejista e os supermercados na cidade de São Paulo* (São Paulo, 1962), 90; Luiz Carlos Bresser Pereira, "Tendências e paradoxos do varejo no Brasil," *Revista de Administração de Empresas* 13, no. 3 (July–September 1973): 137.

125. "A Glimpse at the São Paulo of Tomorrow," *Brazilian-American Survey*, May 1956, pp. 64–65; Promúsica advertisement, *O Estado de S. Paulo*, 25 December 1958, p. 9; "Centro de Promoção de Vendas," *PN*, 17 October 1957, 14; "1.700 revendedores em convenção," *Propaganda*, June 1959, p. 40; "In Brazil . . . ," *Engineering News-Record* (New York), 29 November 1956, p. 44; Andrade, "Shopping," 72–74 (inc. "symbol . . ."); "Highlights of Progress," *Brazilian Business*, September 1956, p. 26; "Escritórios profissionais e comerciais em Copacabana," *Ultima Hora*, 16 June 1955, p. 2; Cidade de Copacabana advertisements in *Correio da Manhã*, 28 July 1957, sec. 7, pp. 5 ("the 1st . . ."), 14 ("social-commercial . . ."), 9 ("commercial . . .").

126. Andrade, "Shopping," 79–80; "O shopping center no Brasil," *Visão*, 10 November 1975, p. 91; "Shopping Center do Méier reúne escrete de lojistas," *Vendas e Varejo*, October 1965, pp. 14–15; "O 'shopping center' como instrumento do varejo moderno," *Vendas e Varejo*, June 1963, insert at 24f ("adapting . . . ," "first . . ."); "Lacerda inaugura hoje no Méier shopping center," *Jornal do Brasil*, 27 August 1965, sec. 1, p. 5 (inc. "from . . ."); untitled column by Léa Maria, *Jornal do Brasil*, 31 August 1965, sec. "Caderno B," 3 ("play . . ."); "Lacerda inaugura shopping center do Méier," *Jornal do Brasil*, 28 August 1965, sec. 1, p. 5 (inc. "multitude"); "Hoje a feira da bondade," *Ultima Hora*, 28 August 1965, p. 2 ("great multitude"); Mário Rodrigues Rocha, "'Shopping centers' & propaganda cooperativa," *Propaganda*, December 1965, p. 39 (inc. "the . . .").

127. Alberto de Oliveira Lima Filho, "An Analysis of the Development of Controlled Retailing Systems in the Greater São Paulo Metropolitan Area" (PhD diss., Michigan State University, 1972), 216–226; Andrade, "Shopping," 80–83, 140; Santos, "História," 99–101; Alfredo Mathias advertisements in *O Estado de S. Paulo*, 24 January 1965, p. 11 (door-to-door), 14 February 1965, p. 9 (INESE); SCI advertisement, *O Estado de S. Paulo*, 27 November 1966, pp. 12–13; "Shopping Center vai faturar oito bilhões," *O Estado de S. Paulo*, 27 November 1966, p. 35; "O 'shopping' abriu com festa," *Folha de S. Paulo*, 28 November 1966, sec. 1, p. 3; "Shopping Center já funciona," *O Estado de S. Paulo*, 29 November 1966, p. 13 (inc. "the . . .").

128. "O 'shopping center' como instrumento do varejo moderno," *Vendas e Varejo*, June 1963, insert (on the importance of foot traffic to SCM); Lima Filho, "Analysis," 226 (cars and SCI); "Cidades de vendas," *Veja*, 30 January 1974, pp. 40–41 (inc. Mathias quote); APP, *Depoimentos*, 24, 31–33, 40–41; Homero Psillakis, *Shopping center e o*

varejo brasileiro (Rio de Janeiro, 1984), 38; Albertina Mirtes de Freitas Pontes, *A cidade dos clubes: Modernidade e "glamour" na Fortaleza de 1950–1970* (Fortaleza, 2005), 78; Santos, "História," 102; "O planejamento técnico em busca da eficiência de vendas," *Visão*, 10 November 1975, pp. 10–11 (inc. "who . . ."); Isabel Dias de Aguiar, "Para cada classe, um 'shopping,'" *Folha de S. Paulo*, 10 November 1974, p. 45 (inc. "It . . . ," "*Shopping . . .*"); "Estuda-se plano sobre 'shoppings,'" *O Estado de S. Paulo*, 4 March 1973, p. 34; ABM, *I Congresso*, 118.

129. "Concepção social e humana do problema do apartamento," *Ultima Hora*, 22 October 1956, sec. 2, p. 4 (Mindlin); "Shopping centers," *O Estado de S. Paulo*, 6 April 1958, p. 58; Hélio de Oliveira Passos, "O que é e como funciona o shopping center," *Vendas e Varejo*, May 1961, pp. 52–55 (inc. "this . . ."); Léa Maria column, *Jornal do Brasil*, 31 August 1965, sec. "Caderno B," 3; "O comércio segue no caminho do sol," *O Estado de S. Paulo*, 4 July 1965, p. 22; "O 'shopping' abriu com festa," *Folha de S. Paulo*, 28 November 1966, sec. 1, p. 3; "Shopping center vai faturar oito bilhões," *O Estado de S. Paulo*, 27 November 1966, p. 35.

130. SCM advertisement, *Correio da Manhã*, 18 November 1962, sec. 1, pp. 10–11; Shopping Center de Niterói advertisement, *Correio da Manhã*, 2 August 1964, sec. 1, p. 19; SCRB advertisement, *O Estado de S. Paulo*, 10 January 1965, p. 23; SCI advertisement, *O Estado de S. Paulo*, 27 November 1966, pp. 12–13; Pão de Açúcar advertisement, *O Estado de S. Paulo*, 27 November 1966, p. 21 ("modernization"); Casa Tavares advertisement, *Jornal do Brasil*, 12 September 1965, sec. 1, p. 7; SCI advertisement, *O Estado de S. Paulo*, 27 November 1966, p. 11; SCRB advertisement, *O Estado de S. Paulo*, 24 January 1965, p. 11; Léa Maria column.

131. "Rede de otimismo na televisão" (announcement), *O Estado de S. Paulo*, 13 June 1965, p. 5; Marcos Eduardo Neves, *Vendedor de sonhos: A vida e a obra de Roberto Medina* (São Paulo, 2006), 76–77; "Revolução do Consumo" (advertisement), *Jornal do Brasil*, 21 August 1974, sec. 1, p. 3.

132. "Missa de galo no 'Super Shopping Center,'" *Ultima Hora*, 23 December 1959, p. 8; "Missa do galo inaugurou modern igreja de Arena," *Ultima Hora*, 26 December 1960, p. 4; José Mauro, "Na hora H," *Ultima Hora*, 29 April 1961, p. 3; "Também Pelé vai participar do Festival do Escritor Brasileiro," *Correio da Manhã*, 23 July 1960, sec. 1, p. 3; "Festival do Escritor Brasileiro foi um espetáculo inédito na vida da cidade," *Correio da Manhã*, 27 July 1960, sec. 1, p. 3; "Quinhentos escritores reunidos," *Ultima Hora*, 24 July 1961, p. 9; Super Shopping Centers Populares advertisement, *Ultima Hora*, 21 June 1965, p. 3; Andrade, "Shopping," 102–103; "Papai Noel já chegou," *O Estado de S. Paulo*, 30 November 1966, p. 13; "Shopping ganha o prêmio," *O Estado de S. Paulo*, 6 January 1971, p. 12.

133. "O Jumbo de São Paulo," *Supermercado Moderno*, July 1973, pp. 53, 56; "Cidades de vendas," *Veja*, 30 January 1974, p. 40.

134. "O planejamento técnico em busca da eficiência de vendas," *Visão*, 10 November 1975, p. 84 ("The . . ." through "It . . ."); paid announcement by SCI, *O Estado de S. Paulo*, 22 April 1965, p. 8; "Desenvolvimento metropolitano cria condições para o surgimento de novas formas de varejo," *Supermercado Moderno*, April 1973, p. 21; "A evolução do varejo," *Revista da Associação Comercial*, January 1977, p. 17; Jorge Franke Geyer, "Shopping center e desenvolvimento social," *Revista da Associação Comercial*, March 1981, p. 28.

135. "Shopping center vai faturar oito bilhões," *O Estado de S. Paulo*, 27 November 1966, p. 35 ("a family . . ."); "Rua Iguatemi, 1191," *O Estado de S. Paulo*, 25 November 1966, sec. "Turismo," 2 ("a person . . ."); Radford, "Hypermarket," 20; "O planejamento técnico em busca da eficiência de vendas," *Visão*, 10 November 1975, pp. 86, 91 (Continental); "Compras e lazer sem poluição, frio ou calor," *Indústria e Desenvolvimento*, April 1974, p. 14.

136. "E a cidade já está comprando à noite," *O Estado de S. Paulo*, 30 April 1969, p. 14 (inc. "Nighttime . . . ," "Finally . . ."); "São Paulo tem 24 horas de supermercado," *Supermercado Moderno*, July 1969, pp. 34–40 (inc. "Our . . . ," "São . . .").

137. *O Estado de S. Paulo*, 3 October 1971, p. 50; Albert, "Shopping," 127; "Público varia em preferência," *O Estado de S. Paulo*, 24 November 1967, p. 10; "O Jumbo de São Paulo," *Supermercado Moderno*, July 1973, p. 60.

138. "O Jumbo de São Paulo," *Supermercado Moderno*, July 1973, p. 55; Lima Filho, "Analysis," esp. 226–227; "Porque o Banco Real escolheu o Shopping Center Ibirapuera" (advertisement), *O Estado de S. Paulo*, 13 October 1974, p. 5; Pereira, "Tendências," 136–139.

139. Simonsen and Campos, *Nova economia*, 20; Joseph Novitski, "Brasilia, Far from Anywhere, Is Becoming Somewhere," *New York Times*, 31 July 1970, p. 2; "Booming Brazil Finds a Key to Growth," *Business Week*, 13 March 1971, p. 92; Elizabeth Hardwick, "Sad Brazil," *New York Review of Books*, 27 June 1974, p. 9.

140. Serviço de Pesquisa Entre Consumidores, Grupo III, Produtos Domésticos e Alimentícios, Nº 50, Rio de Janeiro, July 1956, AEL-IBOPE, SPC009; "São Paulo: Quem compra e até quanto pode comprar," *PN*, 20 August 1962, pp. 20–23 (Prodimec); "Antena de TV em teto de zinco," *PN*, 13 February 1961, pp. 28–29 (Norton); "Novidades em pesquisa no Brasil," *PN*, 11 April 1960, pp. 12–15 (Marplan).

141. Serviço de Pesquisa Entre Consumidores, Grupo I, Produtos de Toucador, Nº 60, São Paulo, May 1956, AEL-IBOPE, SPC010; Serviço de Pesquisa Entre Consumidores, Grupo I, Produtos de Toucador, Nº 111, São Paulo, July–August 1960, AEL-IBOPE, SPC018; "O 'Ipeme' vai pôr a nu o problema das favelas," *PN*, 20 September 1957, pp. 58–59; Otto Scherb, "Classes sócio-econômicas e orçamentos familiares," *O Observador Econômico e Financeiro*, March 1959, pp. 33–36; "O conceito de classes sócio-econômicas," *PN*, 18 May 1959, p. 37; "Pesquisas sobre o padrão de consumo no Brasil," *Propaganda*, May 1959, p. 20; "A renda familiar no Brasil," *Propaganda*, June 1959, pp. 42–43; "Antena de TV em teto de zinco," *PN* 13 February 1961, pp. 28–29; "São Paulo: Quem compra e até quanto pode comprar," *PN*, 20 August 1962, pp. 20–23; R. B. Prado, "A evolução sócio econômica do Brasil," *Revista Brasileira de Vendas*, May 1966, pp. 15–17; *O público e a propaganda: Pesquisa realizada pela J. Walter Thompson em novembro de 1967* (São Paulo, 1967), JWTA; Ernest John Cowan, "Market Research and the Brazilian Consumer Market," *Brazilian Business*, February 1961, pp. 23, 56; Cowan, "Consumer Research Firms in Brazil Seeking New and More Effective Advertising Techniques," *Brazilian Business*, May 1961, p. 41; "A indústria comercializa sua produção," *Indústria & Mercados*, October 1961, pp. 32–33; Pergentino Mendes de Almeida and Hilda Wickerhauser, "Finding a Better Socio-Economic Status Classification System for Brazil," *Marketing and Research Today* 19, no. 4 (November 1991): 240; Carlos Eduardo Meirelles Matheus in "Paraíso perdido," *Folha de S. Paulo*, 31 August 1980, sec. "Folhetim," 9.

142. "A pesquisa está mudando seus critérios," *Propaganda*, June 1970, p. 27.

143. "A pesquisa está mudando seus critérios," *Propaganda*, June 1970, pp. 28–29; "O consumidor brasileiro e o não consumidor brasileiro," *Anuário Brasileiro de Propaganda*, 1971–1972, p. 40.

144. "Paraíso perdido," *Folha de S. Paulo*, 31 August 1980, sec. "Folhetim," 9 ("standard . . ."); Carlos Guilherme Mota, *Educação, contraideologia e cultura: Desafios e perspectivas* (São Paulo, 2011), 191; "O consumidor brasileiro e o não consumidor brasileiro," *Anuário Brasileiro de Propaganda*, 1971–1972, p. 40; Carlos Eduardo Meirelles Matheus, "O novo marketing e o consumidor (novo?)," *Anuário Brasileiro de Propaganda*, 1973–1974, p. 49.

145. "E a culpa é do termômetro?," *Veja*, 22 September 1971, p. 48; ABM, *I Congresso*, 97–98, 100; Emil Farhat, "Os milheiros ocultos de um jornal," *Anuário Brasileiro de Propaganda*, 1975–1976, p. 71; "Empresas & negócios," *Folha de S. Paulo*, 10 August 1979, p. 29; Mauro Rubens de Barros, "Qual a sua classe social?," *Folha de S. Paulo*, 16 September 1979, p. 42; Nelson Blecher, "Pesquisa redefine tamanho da classe média," *Folha de S. Paulo*, 29 August 1991, sec. "Dinheiro," 12; Almeida and Wickerhauser, "Finding," 240–242, 248–250; Nelson Blecher, "Anunciantes rejeitam redefinição de classes," *Folha de S. Paulo*, 30 September 1991, sec. "Dinheiro," 8 (also, same page, "Ibope resistiu a novas regras" and "Mudança gera polêmica"); "Dissidentes da Abipeme fundam nova entidade," *Folha de S. Paulo*, 15 January 1992, sec. "Dinheiro," 3; "Ibope defende os interesses das redes de TV," *Folha de S. Paulo*, 16 January 1992, sec. "Dinheiro," 5; Milanesi, *Paraíso*, 31, 76, 180; Federico, *História*, 92; Silva, *Brasil*, 196; Marcos Flamínio Peres, "1930 foi mais importante que 1889," *Folha de S. Paulo*, 23 October 2010, E6.

146. Maureen O'Dougherty, *Consumption Intensified: The Politics of Middle-Class Daily Life in Brazil* (Durham, N.C., 2002); Brian Owensby, *Intimate Ironies: Modernity and the Making of Middle-Class Lives in Brazil* (Stanford, Calif., 1999); Barbara Fields, *Slavery and Freedom on the Middle Ground: Maryland in the Nineteenth Century* (New Haven, Conn., 1985), xii.

147. "O volume da publicidade nos vários países do mundo," *Anuário de Propaganda*, 1957, p. 142; "O volume de propaganda no mundo," *Propaganda*, February 1961, p. 20; Francisco Gracioso, "A emprêsa na consumocracia," *Propaganda*, February 1971, p. 34; "450 milhões de dólares, 1,2% sobre o PNB," *Propaganda*, February 1972, pp. 19–10; "Igual ao dos EE.UU. o padrão dos anúncios feitos pela Thompson, no Brasil," *PN*, 20 August 1955, pp. 20–21; "Paralelos entre propaganda americana e brasileira," *Propaganda*, November 1958, p. 21; "Diferenças entre Brasil e Estados Unidos," *Propaganda*, February 1959, p. 32; "A 'tecnomidiacracia' é uma aberração," *Propaganda*, October 1970, p. 33; Manoel de Vasconcellos, "Uma palavra do editor," *PN*, 5 January 1956, p. 4 (Walita); "Em histórias em quadrinhos o Brasil é uma segunda América," *PN*, 20 July 1957, pp. 10–11; "Indústria de discos já é maior de idade," *O Observador Econômico e Financeiro*, June 1960, p. 24; "Carro nacional expande mercados," *Propaganda*, March–April 1961, p. 23; "Brasil fará 1.º Congresso Latino-Americano de Propaganda," *Propaganda*, June 1961, p. 13; Hernane Tavares de Sá, "66: o ano brasileiro," *Direção* special issue, December 1965, p. 36; Lago, "Luxo," 21–22.

148. Manoel de Vasconcellos, "Uma palavra da redação," *PN*, 11 April 1960, p. 1; "Vende de tudo para todos," *PN*, 20 July 1959, pp. 44–45; "Publicitário chega dos EUA

afirmando que TV no Brasil não perde para a americana," *Propaganda*, December 1965, p. 13 (quoted); "O 'shopping center' como instrumento do varejo moderno," *Vendas e Varejo*, June 1963, insert (quoted); "Madureira ganha novo e espetacular 'shopping-center,'" *Vendas e Varejo*, November 1963, p. 15 ("the . . ."); "Cidades de vendas," *Veja*, 30 January 1974, p. 40 (quoted); "Know-how traz produtividade e lucros maiores," *Supermercado Moderno*, January 1974, p. 16; "Brasileiros foram aos EUA ver que problemas terão amanhã," *Supermercado Moderno*, August 1972, p. 34; "Carta do diretor," *Supermercado Moderno*, March 1973, p. 4.

149. Vergniaud Gonçalves, "Uma civilização sobre rodas," *PN*, 5 September 1955, p. 76; "Várias solenidades marcaram o 5.º aniversário de Brasília," *O Estado de S. Paulo*, 22 April 1965, p. 8; Carlos Lacerda, "Civilização do trabalho livre" (1963), in *Palavras e ação* (Rio de Janeiro, 1965), 164–169; Marcelo Coimbra Tavares, "JK presta contas," *Manchete*, 6 February 1960, esp. 57; Lacerda, "A entrevista de Orly" (1964), in *Palavras e ação*, 137–138.

150. Lacerda, "O que penso e o que farei," in *Palavras e ação*, esp. 17–18; APP, *Depoimentos*, 129; "Walter Clark: 'Homem de Vendas do Ano,'" *Propaganda*, December 1973, p. 49; Rocha, *Nas ondas*, 95, citing *Anais da sessão da Comissão de Comunicações da Câmara Federal* (1975).

151. Manoel de Vasconcellos, "Uma palavra do editor," *PN*, 5 February 1956, p. 4; APP, *Depoimentos*, 26; Beting, "Consumidor," 140.

152. Manoel de Vasconcellos, "Uma palavra do editor," *PN*, 5 February 1956, p. 4; "O esporte favorito de fazer compras," *PN*, 5 July 1954, p. 52; "Declaração de Genival Rabelo sobre o pleito da ABP," *Ultima Hora*, 1 July 1961, p. 12; "1ª Convenção do Comércio Lojista do Nordeste," *Vendas e Varejo*, July 1961, p. 14; Rabelo, "Fatos & comentários," *PN*, 7 August 1961, pp. 22–23; "Maioridade da economia brasileira," *PN*, 28 August 1961, pp. 26–28, 30.

153. Gracioso, "A emprêsa na consumocracia (capítulo II)," 41; Salles, "Brasil," 6.

154. "Perspectivas ilimitadas de desenvolvimento comercial para V.," *Supermercado Moderno*, January 1973, pp. 9–11; "O novo marketing brasileiro," *Anuário Brasileiro de Propaganda*, 1973–1974, p. 30; Celso Sorrenti, Ouhydes Fonseca, and Afonso de Souza, "Modelo, esse objeto de consumo," *Propaganda*, May 1973, pp. 26–28.

155. "Brasil, país desenvolvido?," *O Estado de S. Paulo*, 27 December 1969, sec. "Anos 70, promessas e dúvidas," 14; *Seleções* announcement, *O Estado de S. Paulo*, 28 February 1969, p. 9.

156. "Até filosofia é importante no supermercado," *O Estado de S. Paulo*, 3 October 1971, p. 50; "Mercado adulto," *Jornal do Brasil*, 7 July 1970, sec. 1, p. 6; "Comércio moderno," *Jornal do Brasil*, 29 December 1971, sec. 1, p. 6; "Falta defesa para comprador," *O Estado de S. Paulo*, 3 October 1971, p. 50.

157. "Lojistas reunidos no Rio aprimoram técnica de venda" and "Esquistossomose faz vítimas em 99% do povo sergipano," *Correio da Manhã*, 7 September 1965, sec. 1, p. 10; João Pinheiro Neto, "Comentário," *Correio da Manhã*, 21 December 1972, p. 6; "Por que a fartura não vem," *Visão*, 19 May 1967, 24–28; "Carta ao leitor," *Veja*, 8 August 1973, p. 19; "A carne, um prato bem polêmico," *Veja*, 8 August 1973, pp. 91–96; "A seca nas torneiras," *Veja*, 10 September 1969, p. 46; "Agua, finalmente," *Veja*, 7 April 1971, pp. 38–39; "Digerindo a nova harmonia," *Opinião*, 16 September 1974,

p. 6; "Caminhos do reajustamento," *Opinião*, 16 September 1974, pp. 6–7; "Os automóveis e o milagre," *Opinião*, 16 September 1974, p. 7 ("premature...," "limited..."); ABM, *I Congresso*, 44; "Uma das instituições mais importantes no seu papel de terminal de consumo," *Revista da Associação Comercial*, January 1977, p. 17. On the romantic Americanist aura of the Pampulha complex in the 1940s, see Marco Antônio Tavares Coelho, *Herança de um sonho: As memórias de um comunista* (São Paulo, 2000), 44.

158. Charles Wagley, "If I Were a Brazilian Today," in *An Introduction to Brazil*, rev. ed. (New York, 1971 [1963]), 309; Novitski, "Brasilia"; Isabel Montero, "Vanda [*sic*] Pimentel," *Jornal do Brasil*, 25 July 1970, sec. "Caderno B," 8; Boris Fausto, interviewed by Angela de Castro Gomes and Keila Grinberg, São Paulo, June 2006, in *Leituras críticas sobre Boris Fausto*, ed. A. C. Gomes (São Paulo, 2008), 153; "Seminário sobre a velhice começa em São Paulo reunindo 5 especialidades," *Jornal do Brasil*, 9 March 1971, sec. 1, p. 14.

159. Genival Rabelo, "Fatos & comentários," *PN*, 5–12 March 1962, p. 50; APP, *Depoimentos*, 104; Grünewald, "Gerações"; Paulo Francis, *O afeto que se encerra: Memórias* (Rio de Janeiro, 1980), 33, 83–84.

160. Hélio Duque, "'Facilidades' levam o povo a dever cada vez mais," *Politika*, 17–23 April 1972, p. 21; Paul Singer, in *Retrato do Brasil: Da monarquia ao estado militar*, vol. 4, *Depoimentos* (São Paulo, 1984), 29.

161. Augusto, *Este mundo*, 18; Alcir Lenharo, *Cantores do rádio: A trajetória de Nora Ney e Jorge Goulart e o meio artístico de seu tempo* (Campinas,1995), 73; Norton Ribeiro de Freitas Jr., *O capital norte-americano e investimento no Brasil: Características e perspectivas de um relacionamento econômico, 1950 a 1990* (Rio de Janeiro, 1994), 18; Owensby, *Intimate Ironies*, 245; Rafael Ioris, *Transforming Brazil: A History of National Development in the Postwar Era* (New York, 2014), 9; Ulpiano Bezerra de Meneses, preface to João Luís Máximo da Silva, *Cozinha modelo: O impacto do gás e da eletricidade na casa paulistana, 1870–1930* (São Paulo, 2008), 13; Rocha, *Nas ondas*, esp. 28, 191–192; Alzira Alves de Abreu, "Revisitando os anos 1950 através da imprensa," in *O moderno em questão*, ed. André Botelho, Élide Rugai Bastos, and Gláucia Villas Bôas (Rio Janeiro, 2008), 211; Silva, *Brasil*, 194–196, 202; Pontes, *Cidade*, esp. 119–120.

162. "Annual Report, 1955," Chicago, 1956, Sears Archives; A Ecléctica advertisement, *O Estado de S. Paulo*, 12 April 1935, p. 10; *Jornal do Brasil* advertisement, *Manchete*, 2 November 1974, pp. 36–37.

163. "Anhemby será sede das feiras," *Indústria e Desenvolvimento*, August 1969, p. 23; "A controvertida compra de prejuízos," *Visão*, 4 August 1975, p. 48.

164. "Estuda-se plano sobre 'shoppings,'" *O Estado de S. Paulo*, 4 March 1973, p. 34; "Mercado atrai as populações," *Jornal do Brasil*, 21 August 1973, sec. 1, p. 27; "Rosen crê que Brasil supera o atraso em comercialização," *Jornal do Brasil*, 23 August 1973, sec. 1, p. 27; "Economistas são convocados a tratar do planejamento urbano," *Jornal do Brasil*, 24 August 1973, sec. 1, p. 20.

165. "Villa Operaria Waldemar Falcão," *O Imparcial*, 31 December 1938, sec. 6, p. 10 (quoted); "Casas operarias," *O Observador Econômico e Financeiro*, January 1939, pp. 154–157.

166. For "Paradise via Satellite," cf. Milanesi, *Paraíso*; "new paradises" and "shoppings," Anna Veronica Mautner, *O cotidiano nas entrelinhas: Crônicas e memórias*

(São Paulo, 2001), 13; also, "Estuda-se plano sobre 'shoppings,'" *O Estado de S. Paulo*, 4 March 1973, p. 34.

167. "As origens e a queda da UEB" and "Qual pode ser o destino da UEB," *Jornal do Brasil*, 12 May 1977, sec. 1, p. 33; "O maior estouro do mercado," *Veja*, 18 May 1977, pp. 100–106; "Duas contradições que derrubaram um império," *Folha de S. Paulo*, 15 May 1977, p. 37; Alberto de Oliveira Lima Filho, *Shopping centers: E.U.A. vs. Brasil* (Rio de Janeiro, 1971).

168. "Shopping carioca," *Veja*, 20 June 1973, pp. 104–105.

169. "Túnel novo ganha logo 'shopping-center'" and "Costa Cavalcanti destaca pioneirismo do BNH," *Diario de Noticias*, 26 August 1973, p. 5; "UEB e Yaohan assinam contrato de areendamento" (announcement), *Jornal do Brasil*, 30 August 1973, sec. 1, p. 21.

170. "UEB e Yaohan assinam . . ."; Ducal-Companhia Brasileira de Roupas annual statement, 18 April 1974, *Jornal do Brasil*, 23 May 1974, sec. 1, p. 9; UEB annual statement, 6 January 1975, *Jornal do Brasil*, 2 February 1975, sec. 1, p. 33; Ducal-Companhia Brasileira de Roupas annual statement, 28 April 1975, *Jornal do Brasil*, 25 May 1975, sec. 1, p. 33; "Duas contradições que derrubaram um império," *Folha de S. Paulo*, 15 May 1977, p. 37.

171. Banco Independência-Decred announcement, *Jornal do Brasil*, 11 May 1976, sec. 1, p. 15; "Caixa Econômica financia construção do maior centro comercial da América Latina," *Jornal do Brasil*, 29 May 1976, sec. 1, p. 20; "CRB, Ducal e Bemoreira estimam em Cr\$1,5 bilhão faturamento de 76," *Jornal do Brasil*, 21 September 1976, sec. 1, p. 22; "UEB-Center contrata Nordal Associates Inc." (announcement), *Jornal do Brasil*, 14 July 1976, sec. 1, p. 5; Especial UEB advertisement, *O Estado de S. Paulo*, 22 August 1976, p. 38.

172. Andréa Lepeti, "Grupo UEB: Contando os trocados," *Opinião*, 10 December 1976, p. 11; José Roberto Guzzo, "Carta ao leitor," *Veja*, 18 May 1977, p. 19; "O maior estouro do mercado," *Veja*, 18 May 1977, pp. 101, 105; "BC desmente intervenção no grupo Ducal," *Jornal do Brasil*, 19 February 1977, sec. 1. p. 18; Gilberto Menezes Cortes, "UEB faz acordo com Veplan e solução sai na semana que vem," *Jornal do Brasil*, 9 April 1977, sec. 1, p. 16; "Informe econômico," *Jornal do Brasil*, 13 April 1977, sec. 1, p. 22; "Informe econômico," *Jornal do Brasil*, 10 May 1977, sec. 1, p. 14; "Távora acha defesa da Sudepe mais difícil," *Jornal do Brasil*, 10 May 1977, sec. 1, p. 19.

173. "Duas contradições que derrubaram um império," *Folha de S. Paulo*, 15 May 1977, p. 37; "O maior estouro do mercado," *Veja*, 18 May 1977, pp. 100–106; "Qual pode ser o destino da UEB," *Jornal do Brasil*, 12 May 1977, sec. 1, p. 33; "Informe econômico," *Jornal do Brasil*, 4 February 1978, sec. 1, p. 16; "Grupo UEB levanta concordata de suas empresas industriais," *Jornal do Brasil*, 15 May 1979, sec. 1, p. 17; "BC define conselho da Capri esta semana," *Jornal do Brasil*, 16 May 1978, sec. 1, p. 23; "CEF diz que UEB paga dívida em 1 ano," *Jornal do Brasil*, 29 April 1980, sec. 1, p. 23; "'Shopping' deverá pagar gastos com liquidação," *O Estado de S. Paulo*, 24 July 1980, p. 42.

174. "Mesbla assina contrato para instalar seu novo magazin no Rio Sul Shopping Center" (announcement), *Jornal do Brasil*, 2 May 1978, sec. 1, p. 7; "Lojas Brasileiras S.A.—Lobrás—assina contrato para instalar sua maior loja no Rio Sul Shopping Center," (announcement), *Jornal do Brasil*, 11 July 1978, sec. 1, p. 5 (inc. "social . . .");

Rio Sul advertisement, *Jornal do Brasil*, 23 August 1978, p. 7; Rio Sul advertisement, *Jornal do Brasil*, 11 January 1979, sec. 1, p. 9.

175. "Rio-Sul inaugura sem luz e com muitas lojas fechadas," *Jornal do Brasil*, 30 April 1980, sec. 1, p. 8; "Sabor de vitória," *Veja*, 30 April 1980, p. 72; "Sem praia, solução é shopping-center," *O Estado de S. Paulo*, 18 July 1980, sec. "Turismo," 7; "Rio-Sul supera expectativas e vendas vão a Cr$2 bilhões" and "'Shopping' já é opção de lazer para carioca," *Jornal do Brasil*, 28 December 1980, sec. 1, p. 18; Teresa Bastos, "Brasil na era dos shoppings," *Revista da Associação Comercial*, November 1982, p. 49 (slogan).

176. "Combrascan vai pagar à CEB dívida do Rio Sul," *Jornal do Brasil*, 28 December 1983, sec. 1, p. 13; "Novos donos do Rio Sul vão investir mais em 'shopping,'" *Jornal do Brasil*, 30 December 1983, sec. 1, p. 16; "Trânsito livre," *Veja*, 4 January 1984, p. 60; "CEF dá 20 anos para Combrascan amortizar a dívida do Rio Sul," *Jornal do Brasil*, 14 January 1984, sec. 1, p. 16; "Rio Sul custa à CEF Cr$69 milhões por mês em administração," *Jornal do Brasil*, 19 June 1985, sec. 1, p. 14; "CEF abre licitação para tentar a venda da 'Torre Rio-Sul,'" *O Estado de S. Paulo*, 3 December 1985, p. 43; Carlos Kessel, "História do comércio no Rio de Janeiro," in *Um balcão na capital: Memórias do comércio na cidade do Rio de Janeiro*, ed. José Carlos Cabral and Karen Worcman (Rio de Janeiro, 2003), 17 (quoted).

Chapter Six

1. *Anais do III Congresso Brasileiro de Propaganda* (São Paulo, 1978).

2. *Anais do III Congresso*, 28–31.

3. "Uma agência brasileira nos USA," *Propaganda*, August 1970, pp. 17–18, 20, 22.

4. *Anais do III Congresso*, 32–33, 35–36 (in translating Ribeiro's speech, I have altered editor- or stenographer-imposed punctuation and capitalization to restore probable cadence as spoken).

5. J. A. de Souza Ramos, "A passo de tartaruga," *Propaganda*, November 1937, p. 14; Francisco Gracioso, *Marketing: Uma experiência brasileira* (São Paulo, 1971), chaps. 1, 5, 10 (quotes on 24, 56, 123).

6. Auricélio Penteado, "Os norte-americanos são mesmo burros ou é só aparência?," *Publicidade & Negócios*, 15 December 1951, p. 22; Renato Castelo Branco, *Tomei um Ita no norte: Memórias* (São Paulo, 1981), 39, 141–142, 164; Rodolfo Lima Martensen, *O desafio de quatro santos: Memórias* (São Paulo, 1983), 107, 45, 50.

7. Ricardo Ramos, "Cinema Delícia," in *Memórias de Hollywood*, ed. Julieta de Godoy Ladeira (São Paulo, 1988), 22; Ladeira, "Hollywood: Coisa nossa, nossas coisas," in *Memórias*, 11–15; Ladeira, "Sessão corrida," in *Memórias*, 62–63; Walter Clark [Bueno], *O campeão de audiência* (São Paulo, 1991), 17–22, 27.

8. Carlos Queiroz Telles, *Tirando de letra: Um manual de sobrevivência na selva da comunicação* (São Paulo, 1993), 14–15; Ramos, "Cinema," 21.

9. Telles, *Tirando*, 15.

10. Martensen, *Desafio*, 99; Renato Ignácio da Silva, *Xerifes e coronéis* (Itaquaquecetuba, 1989), 153; Paulo Cesar Ferreira, *Pilares via satélite: Da Rádio Nacional à Rede Globo* (Rio de Janeiro, 1998), 25–31, 34–36; Alex Periscinoto, *Mais vale o que se aprende que o que te ensinam* (São Paulo, 1995), 47, 55–56; Sangirardi Jr., "Chumbo miúdo," *Publicidade & Negócios*, 1 June 1952, pp. 18–19.

11. Marcus Pereira, *Lembranças de amanhã* (São Paulo, 1980), 166; Ferreira, *Pilares*, 43–74; Martensen, *Desafio*, 253–254.

12. Antonio Candido, "Cinematógrafo," in Ladeira, *Memórias*, 90–91; Luiz Carlos Maciel, *Geração em transe: Memórias do tempo do tropicalismo* (Rio de Janeiro, 1996), 37, 271; Alberto Villas, *O mundo acabou!* (São Paulo, 2006), 186; Paulo Francis, "A causa é a mesma," *Correio da Manhã*, 17 March 1968, sec. 4, p. 1.

13. Orígenes Lessa, *O.K. América: Cartas de Nova York* (Rio de Janeiro, 1945); Ladeira, "Sessão corrida," 63; APP, *Depoimentos* (São Paulo, 1973), 67–68; Periscinoto, *Mais vale*, 55–57, 67–69, 35, 115; Petit, preface to Periscinoto, *Mais vale*, 11–12. On wartime service by Lessa and others: "Na capa," *Publicidade*, April 1942, p. 2; "Pelas agências," *PN*, 5 July 1953, p. 23; "Caio Domingues," JWTA, EGWP, box 78; APP, *Depoimentos*, 61; Robert J. Alexander, notes on a conversation with Ruy Dâmaso, Rio de Janeiro, 28 March 1966, RJAP, mr-3.

14. APP, *Depoimentos*, 139; Aldo Xavier da Silva, *Comunicação nos negócios* (Rio de Janeiro, 1974), 15; Silva, "A propaganda como negócio," *Publicidade*, September 1940, p. 5; Castelo Branco, *Tomei*, 171; Genival Rabelo, *O capital estrangeiro na imprensa brasileira* (Rio de Janeiro, 1966), 229; Rabelo, *Onde o vento junta o cisco* (Rio de Janeiro, 1969), 98; Emil Farhat, *Histórias ouvidas e vividas* (São Paulo, 1999), 278, 283; "A figura do dia," *Ultima Hora*, 8 April 1953, p. 2 ("The . . .").

15. APP, *Depoimentos*, 153; Pedro Nunes, *35 anos de propaganda* (Rio de Janeiro, n.d.), 84–87 (inc. "It . . .") and passim; Clark, *Campeão*.

16. Nunes, *35 anos*, 124 ("vanity . . ."), 126 ("system . . ."), 68 ("that . . ."), 50 ("to choose . . ."); "Homens de governo—Atentai para o valor da publicidade," *O Observador Econômico e Financeiro*, July 1946, pp. 56 (d'Almeida), 42 and 50 (Lessa); APP, *Depoimentos*, 37 ("appeal"); Castelo Branco, *Tomei*, 31, 175; Ricardo Ramos, "Faz bem nos sentirmos da Thompson," *Publicidade*, June 1979, p. 40; Castelo Branco in *Jeca Tatu e a propaganda brasileira* (São Paulo, 1982), unpag.

17. Heitor Mariz, "Ascese," *Propaganda*, March 1938, p. 17; Waldir Dupont, *Geraldo Alonso: O homem e o mito* (São Paulo, 1991), 58; Fernando Reis, "São Paulo e Rio: A longa caminhada," in *HPB*, 327–328; "Associação Paulista de Propaganda," *Propaganda*, November 1937, p. 19; Wilson Velloso, "Seis anos depois," *Publicidade*, December 1943, p. 36; "Homens de governo . . . ," *O Observador Econômico e Financeiro*, July 1946, pp. 38 (d'Almeida), 58 (Lessa).

18. Genival Rabelo, "Pan-americanismo prático," *Publicidade*, May 1942, pp. 11, 16; Rabelo, "O 'espirito de publicidade' do povo americano," *Publicidade*, March 1941, p. 22; Celso Kelly, "A publicidade e os tempos modernos," *Publicidade*, December 1943, p. 35.

19. Nunes, *35 anos*, 68; "Grandiosa convenção da Ducal em Quitadinha," *PN*, 5 September 1957, p. 11; Silva, *Comunicação*, chap. 7; Promúsica advertisement, *O Estado de S. Paulo*, 25 December 1958, p. 9; "Nova agência de publicidade," *O Estado de S. Paulo*, 19 December 1957, p. 8.

20. Silveira Costa, "A necessidade do estudo da propaganda no Brasil," *Publicidade*, January 1941, p. 17; Leuenroth in *Brasil–Estados Unidos*, 142–146; Walter Poyares, "Notas de um publicitário," *Publicidade & Negócios*, October 1949, pp. 31–32; Genival Rabelo, "Fatos e comentários," *Publicidade*, November 1947, p. 8.

21. J. A. de Sousa [*sic*] Ramos, "Propaganda na indústria e no comércio," *Digesto Econômico*, March 1945, pp. 73–76.

22. "O segrêdo do comércio a crêdito," *PN*, 20 December 1952, p. 58; Humberto Gargiúlo, "Publicitários brasileiros nos EE.UU.," *PN*, 20 June 1957, pp. 54, 56–57. For "men who decide," *PN* advertisement, *O Observador Econômico e Financeiro*, December 1957, p. 45.

23. M. Vasconcellos, "Os homens de propaganda querem aprender," *Publicidade & Negócios*, February–March 1948, p. 1; "No mundo dos negócios," *O Observador Econômico e Financeiro*, January 1956, p. 82; "Gente de propaganda," *Diario de Noticias*, 25 June 1961, p. 2; "Nova força no comércio de roupas em São Paulo," *PN*, 25 June 1962, p. 28.

24. Rabelo, *Onde*, 102–103.

25. Castelo Branco, *Tomei*; Castelo Branco, *A chimica das raças* (São Paulo, 1937); Castelo Branco, "O Piauí," *O Observador Econômico e Financeiro*, November 1940, pp. 66–74; Castelo Branco, *O Piauí: A terra, o homem, o meio* (São Paulo, 1970); Genival Rabelo, "Fatos & comentários," *PN*, 26 February 1962, p. 122 (Doria); Ricardo Ramos, *As fúrias invisíveis: Romance* (São Paulo, 1974), esp. chap. 19; Ramos interview in *Viver e escrever*, 2 vols., ed. Edla van Steen (Porto Alegre, 1981), 1:166–167; Rabelo, "O Nordeste é um grande mercado," *Publicidade*, May 1944, pp. 26, 32, 44, 46; Rabelo, "Fatos & comentários," *PN*, 24 November 1958, pp. 26–27; Rabelo, "Fatos & comentários," *PN*, 19 July 1962, p. 50; Rabelo, "Fatos & comentários," *PN*, 30 July 1962, p. 50. The terms *gaúchos, potiguares, cearenses,* and *baianos* refer to native sons (and daughters) of the states of Rio Grande do Sul, Rio Grande do Norte, Ceará, and Bahia, respectively. For the unlearning of provincial accents, also Martensen, *Desafio*, 198–199; on northeasterners' overrepresentation in Rio's press corps, Limeira Tejo, *Enéias: Memórias de uma geração ressentida* (Rio de Janeiro, 1956), 164.

26. Penteado, "Norte-americanos," 22; Julieta de Godoy Ladeira, *O desafio de criar* (São Paulo, 1995), 116–117; Claude McMillan, Jr., "The American Businessman in Brazil," *Business Topics* 11, no. 2 (1963): 77; Genival Rabelo, *A volta por cima* (Rio de Janeiro, 1995), 22.

27. Genival Rabelo, "Fatos & comentários," *Publicidade & Negócios*, September 1949, p. 14; Rabelo, "Fatos & comentários," *Publicidade & Negócios*, 1 April 1950, pp. 22–23; Penteado, "Norte-americanos," 24 (inc. "experts"); Ivan Pedro Martins, *A flecha e o alvo: A intentona de 1935* (Porto Alegre, 1994), 77–78; "A Light é agente de uma conspiração internacional contra a industrialização do Brasil," *PN*, 5 July 1953, pp. 6–13, 16; Manoel de Vasconcellos, "Uma palavra do editor," *PN*, 20 July 1953, p. 2; "A Light é responsavel pela falta de energia," *PN*, 20 July 1953, pp. 40–42, 44 (based on *Jornal do Brasil* series); "Jânio Quadros acusa a Light," *PN*, 20 August 1953, pp. 12–14; Rabelo, "Fatos & comentários," *PN*, 20 October 1954, pp. 7–8; Anderson Mascarenhas, "Caem as máscaras dos sabotadores," *O Semanário*, 16–23 February 1961, p. 4.

28. Stephen Fox, *The Mirror Makers: A History of American Advertising and Its Creators* (New York, 1984), 174 ("administered . . ."); Renato Castelo Branco to Peter Dunham, Rio de Janeiro, 22 November 1960, Robert F. Merrick to Samuel W. Meek, São Paulo, 30 January 1961, R. F. Merrick to S. W. Meek, São Paulo, 17 July 1958, Robert F. Merrick to Samuel W. Meek, Miami, 31 May 1960 (all four letters from JWTA, EGWP,

box 1); Genival Rabelo, *Os tempos heróicos da propaganda* (Rio de Janeiro, 1956), 67; Orígenes Lessa, "Bob Merrick," *PN*, 21 November 1961, p. 19; Castelo Branco, *Tomei*, 181–182, 207–208.

29. Rabelo, *Onde*, 186; Rabelo, "Fatos & comentários," *Anuário de Publicidade*, 1947, pp. 12, 14; Rabelo, "Fatos & comentários," *PN*, 30 January 1958, p. 18; Penteado, "Norte-americanos," 22; R. Magalhães Júnior, "A outra 'cortina de ferro,'" *Diario de Noticias*, 4 October 1949, sec. 2, p. 1; "A outra cortina de ferro," *Diario de Noticias*, 11 October 1949, sec. 2, pp. 1–2; Rabelo, "Fatos & comentários," *PN*, 12 June 1958, p. 20; Penteado, "O 'hommo maccarthyensis,'" *PN*, 5 July 1954, pp. 12–14; "Projeto contra as agências de publicidade no Brasil," *PN*, 20 June 1955, p. 20; "Eddie, APP e os comunistas," *Vendas e Varejo*, March 1964, p. 37.

30. Clark, *Campeão*, 53–54; Martins, *Flecha*; Castelo Branco, *Tomei*, 65–68, 141–142, 156–157; Farhat, *Histórias*; "Manifesto da Esquerda Democrática" (Rio, 1945); Ricardo Ramos, *Graciliano: Retrato fragmentado* (São Paulo, 1992), 78, 207; interviews with Roberto Duailibi, by Luciana Heymann and Verena Alberti, Rio de Janeiro, 14 and 18 October 2004, CPDOC-PHO; *O Estado de S. Paulo*, 19 September 1961, p. 4; Nelson Werneck Sodré, *A ofensiva reacionária* (Rio de Janeiro, 1992), 184–185.

31. Ivan Pedro de Martins, "O pensamento industrial no Brasil," *Publicidade & Negócios*, 15 July 1952, pp. 42, 46, 48; Alceu Marinho Rego, "O não consumidor no país das maravilhas," *PN*, 5 August 1953, pp. 89, 96; Tito Batini, "Propaganda e cinema," *Propaganda*, May 1956, pp. 34–35; Martins, "Um programa de desenvolvimentismo," *PN*, 30 January 1958, p. 16; Genival Rabelo, "Fatos & comentários," *PN*, 30 January 1958, p. 18; Martins, "Um programa de desenvolvimento," *PN*, 6 March 1958, p. 16; Rabelo, "Fatos & comentários," *PN*, 6 March 1958, p. 18; Manoel de Vasconcellos, "Uma palavra do editor," *PN*, 3 October 1960, p. 1; APP, *Depoimentos*, 132–133; Telles, *Tirando*, 105.

32. Roberto Schwarz, "Cultura e política, 1964–1969," in *O pai de família e outros estudos* (Rio de Janeiro, 1978), 62; Antônio Torres, "Vamos para Portugal, lá é mais barato," *Politika*, 25 September–1 October 1972, p. 15.

33. Telles, *Tirando*, 164–66.

34. K. David Jackson, "The Brazilian Short Story," in *Cambridge History of Latin American Literature*, 3 vols., ed. Roberto Gonzalez Echevarría and Enrique Pupo-Walker (1996) 3:207–232; "O retorno de Marcos Rey," *O Estado de S. Paulo*, 16 February 2003, D3.

35. Emil Farhat, *Cangerão* (Rio de Janeiro, 1939) and 3rd ed. (1967), unpag. front matter; Aurélio Buarque de Holanda, "Apresentação," in Nunes, *35 anos*, 8; Benedito Ruy Barbosa et al., *Depois das seis* (Rio de Janeiro, 1964), 178, 228; Castelo Branco, *Piauí*, 6.

36. Castelo Branco, *Tomei*; Castelo Branco, *Um programa de política exterior para o Brasil* (São Paulo, 1945); Maria Odete Medauar, Maria Matilde Medauar, and Jorge Medauar Jr., *Jorge Medauar em prosa e verso* (Ilhéus, 2006); Antonio Hohlfeldt, *Trilogia da campanha: Ivan Pedro de Martins e o Rio Grande invisível* (Porto Alegre, 1998); "A publicidade é anti-literária?," *Propaganda*, November 1964, p. 24; Guilherme Figueiredo, *A bala perdida: Memórias* (Rio de Janeiro, 1998), esp. 570, 573–576.

37. Barbosa et al., *Depois*, 120, 240; Aroldo José Abreu Pinto, *Literatura descalça: A narrativa "para jovens" de Ricardo Ramos* (São Paulo, 1999), 24–28; Ramos, *Gra-*

ciliano; "São Paulo Copy Chief's Stories Capture Literary Prize," *J. Walter Thompson Company News*, 17 January 1964, p. 3, JWTA; "Resultados dos exames de habilitação à Escola de Propaganda," *O Estado de S. Paulo*, 8 March 1959, p. 56; "Curriculum antigo," IEB-FJGL, cx. 8; Julieta de Godoy Ladeira, "Retrato," IEB-FJGL, cx. 13; "Nota bi-ográfica," in Ladeira, *10 contos escolhidos* (Brasília, 1984), 13–16. For listings of Jabuti prize winners: http://premiojabuti.com.br/edicoes-anteriores/.

38. "A tradição é nossa ligação com o futuro e não com o passado" (interview with Lessa, by Bella Jozef), *O Estado de S. Paulo*, 31 July 1983, sec. "Cultura," 8–9; Barbosa et al., *Depois*, 32, 52, 96, 214, 228; *DHBB*, 3:2861.

39. Herberto Sales, *Subsi Diário: Confissões, memórias & histórias* (Rio de Janeiro, 1988), 70; Ziraldo (pseud., Ziraldo Alves Pinto), *Ziraldo*, ed. Samira Youssef Campe-delli and Benjamin Abdala Jr. (São Paulo, 1982), 8, quoted; Dias Gomes, *Apenas um subversivo* (Rio de Janeiro, 1998), 148–149, 156–157; Jorge Medauar, "Os intelectuais e a propaganda," in *HPB*, 15–17; Figueiredo, *Bala*, 131–132.

40. Castelo Branco, *Tomei*, 188–190; *DHBB*, 3:2861.

41. *O pensamento vivo de Kant*, ed. Julien Benda, trans. Wilson Velloso (São Paulo, 1940); George Orwell, *1984*, trans. Wilson Velloso (São Paulo, n.d.); Bertrand Russell, *Ensaios céticos*, trans. Wilson Velloso (São Paulo, 1957); Philip Hitti, *Os árabes*, trans. Otavio da Costa Eduardo (São Paulo, 1948); Guilherme Figueiredo, *A pluma e o vento* (Rio de Janeiro, 1977), 8–9, 15; Martins, *Flecha*; Marshall McLuhan and Quentin Fiori, *O meio são as massa-gens*, trans. Ivan Pedro de Martins (Rio de Janeiro, 1969); McLuhan and Fiori, *Guerra e paz na aldeia global*, trans. Martins (Rio de Janeiro, 1971).

42. Annibal Bomfim, "Política de boa vizinhança," *Publicidade*, November 1943, p. 118; Penteado, "Norte-americanos," 23–24; Dupont, *Geraldo Alonso*.

43. Figueiredo, *Bala*; Mario da Silva Brito, *Diário intemporal* (Rio de Janeiro, 1970), 83; Brito, *Conversa vai, conversa vem* (Rio de Janeiro, 1974), 20–21, 131; Mário de Andrade, *A lição do guru: Cartas a Guilherme Figueiredo, 1937–1945* (Rio de Janeiro, 1989); Telles, *Tirando*, 92; Marcos Rey, *Café na cama* (São Paulo, 1960); Rey, *O enterro da cafetina* (Rio de Janeiro, 1967); Lúcia Helena Gama, *Nos bares da vida: Produção cultural e sociabilidade em São Paulo, 1940–1950* (São Paulo, 1998), 303–304 (Rey's remem-brances); Clark, *Campeão*, 58–59, 84–85; Jorge Medauar, *Ensaios* (Ilhéus, 2000), 38–40; Ramos, *Graciliano*, 128–129; Cláudio Abramo, *A regra do jogo: O jornalismo e a ética do marceneiro*, ed. Cláudio Weber Abramo (São Paulo, 1988), 24; "Nas agências," *Pub-licidade & Negócios*, 5 July 1953, p. 23; Carlos Drummond de Andrade, *O observador no escritório* (Rio de Janeiro, 1985), 22, 76, 144.

44. Jorge Americano, *A lição dos factos* (São Paulo, 1924), 135–136; Eugênio Gu-din, "Reflexões incertas," *Carta Mensal*, April 1962, pp. 9–10.

45. Sergio Milliet, *Marcha á ré* (São Paulo, 1936), 198; Milliet, *Ensaios* (São Paulo, 1938), 151–155; Milliet, "O radio de botão," *O Estado de S. Paulo*, 16 July 1939, pp. 4–5.

46. "Notas editoriaes" of *O Observador Econômico e Financeiro*, January 1938 and June 1939.

47. A. C. Pacheco e Silva, "O cinema e a televisão na vida social," *Anhembi*, Decem-ber 1954, pp. 218, 228; Amadeu de Queiroz, *Dos 7 aos 77: Recordações e comentários, 1880–1950* (São Paulo, 1956), 119–120; Roger Bastide, "Estética de S. Paulo," *O Estado de S. Paulo*, 27 June 1951, p. 5.

48. Milliet, *Marcha à ré*; Americano, *A lição dos factos*, 135.

49. Jeronymo Monteiro Filho, "E a americanização prosegue . . . 'standardizando' o mundo," *O Jornal*, 9 February 1930, sec. 2, p. 1; F. Telles, "A americanização do mundo," *Diario Nacional*, 12 June 1930, p. 3.

50. V. Cy., "A conquista do mundo," *O Estado de S. Paulo*, 25 May 1930, p. 28; V. Cy., "O espírito americano," *O Estado de S. Paulo*, 1 June 1930, p. 6.

51. Laura Jacobina Lacombe, "O cinema," *O Jornal*, 19 July 1935, p. 3; Murillo [*sic*] Mendes, "O grande catholico Ismael Nery," *O Jornal*, 6 April 1935, p. 3.

52. Murilo Mendes, "Formação de discoteca," *A Manhã*, 21 September 1947, sec. "Letras e Artes," 5.

53. Gilberto Freyre, *Região e tradição* (Rio de Janeiro, 1941), 33, 163, 194.

54. Afonso Arinos de Melo Franco, *Um estadista da república: Afrânio de Melo Franco e seu tempo*, 3 vols. (Rio de Janeiro, 1955), 3:1544–1545; Franco, *A alma do tempo: Memórias* (Rio de Janeiro, 1961), 284.

55. Octávio Brandão, "O imperialismo norte-americano é o inimigo mortal do povo brasileiro," *Voz Operária*, 6 February 1954, p. 5; Dalcídio Jurandir, "O programa," *Voz Operária*, 26 June 1954, supplement, 3; "Educação e ensino," *Imprensa Popular*, 20 October 1954, p. 4; "Cinema," *Imprensa Popular*, 16 October 1957, p. 4.

56. "Jornal de 30 dias," in *Anhembi*, May 1958 and September 1959 (571 and 126, respectively).

57. José Honório Rodrigues, "Características nacionais," in *Aspirações nacionais: Interpretação histórico-política* (São Paulo, 1962), 60.

58. Vivaldo Coaracy, *Encontros com a vida: Memórias* (Rio de Janeiro, 1962), 117–118.

59. Walter Guzzardi Jr., "The Crucial Middle Class," *Fortune*, February 1962, p. 212; Gustavo Corção, "O discurso do presidente," *O Estado de S. Paulo*, 22 March 1961, p. 5.

60. Pascoal Melantônio, *Geração "Coca-Cola"* (São Paulo, 1957), quotes on 12–13.

61. Antonio D'Elia, "Franciscanismo e Cocacolismo," *Correio Paulistano*, 26 January 1958, sec. 2, pp. 2, 6; Ferreira, *Pilares*, 90. Fernando Góes's comments on *Geração "Coca-Cola"* (from São Paulo's *Ultima Hora*, 11 September 1957) are reprinted on the back cover of the book's second edition. On *Correio Paulistano* and the archdiocese: Richard P. Butrick to Department of State, FSD 190, "Daily CORREIO PAULISTANO under New Ownership," São Paulo, 24 February 1956, RG59, 932.61/2-2456.

62. Melantônio, *Geração*, 34; Arlindo Silva, "Juventude transviada ataca de noite," *O Cruzeiro*, 26 July 1958, pp. 30–33; Melantônio, *Geração . . .* , 2nd ed. (1959), 85; Melantônio, *Geração . . .* , 3rd ed. (1963).

63. Cláudio de Araújo Lima, *Imperialismo e angústia* (Rio de Janeiro, 1960), quotes on 15, 16, 38, 47, 59.

64. Gustavo Corção, "Pecados sem pecadores," *Diario de Noticias*, 21 July 1957, sec. "Suplemento Literário," 1; "O mercado interno do Brasil preocupa os lojistas," *PN*, 7 November 1960, pp. 48–51; Corção, "O comerciante no mundo moderna," *Vendas e Varejo*, November 1960, pp. 48–50; Corção, "Cabe ao comerciante um papel de relevo na vida econômica e social do Brasil," *Diario de Noticias*, 20 November 1960, sec. 3, pp. 1, 7; Corção, "Cabe ao comerciante . . . ," *Revista da Associação Comercial*, January 1961, pp. 13–14.

65. "Jornal de 30 dias," *Anhembi*, April 1958, p. 328.

66. "Jornal de 30 dias," *Anhembi*, March 1958, pp. 98–102; José Arthur Rios, "A inflação brasileira vista por um sociólogo," *Carta Mensal*, July 1972, p. 10.

67. A. C. Pacheco e Silva Filho, "Tensões e neuroses," *O Estado de S. Paulo*, 5 May 1967, p. 18.

68. Guerreiro Ramos, "A problemática da realidade brasileira," in Instituto Superior de Estudos Brasileiros, *Introdução aos problemas do Brasil* (Rio de Janeiro, 1956), 25; Ewaldo Corrêa Lima, "Política do desenvolvimento," in Instituto Superior de Estudos Brasileiros, *Introdução aos problemas*, 65; Roberto Campos, "Cultura e desenvolvimento," in Instituto Superior de Estudos Brasileiros, *Introdução aos problemas*, 230.

69. Roland Corbisier, "Panfleto contra o mundo moderno," São Paulo, 1943, in *Autobiografia filosófica: Das ideologias à teoria da praxis* (Rio de Janeiro, 1978), 129.

70. Corbisier, *Formação e problema da cultura brasileira*, 3rd ed. (Rio de Janeiro, 1960 [1958]), 69.

71. "Comentários," *Carta Mensal*, May 1957, pp. 123–126; Caio Prado Júnior, "Investimentos estrangeiros no Brasil," *Carta Mensal*, June 1957, pp. 12–37.

72. Rodolfo Lima Martensen, "Propaganda e insatisfação humana," *Publicidade & Negócios*, 1 February 1951, p. 32; "Serviço X" study, AEL-IBOPE, SX001.

73. Alfredo Carmo, "A pesquisa dos efeitos da propaganda," *Propaganda*, July 1967, p. 18.

74. Carlos Lacerda, "A entrevista de Orly" (1964), in *Palavras e ação* (Rio de Janeiro, 1965), 137–138; *Viramundo* (1965, dir. Geraldo Sarno, assisted by Octavio Ianni, Juarez Brandão Lopes, Cândido Procópio).

75. Ignácio de Loyola Brandão, *Bebel que a cidade comeu* (São Paulo, 1968).

76. Brandão, *Bebel*, quotes on 179, respectively. For Brandão's background, see van Steen, *Viver*, 1:39–58. For earlier novelistic descriptions of Rua Augusta: Théo-Filho, *Experiência em São Paulo* (Rio de Janeiro, 1961), 154, 208; Maria de Lourdes Teixeira, *Rua Augusta*, 3rd ed. (São Paulo, 1963 [1962]).

77. Brandão, *Bebel*, 170–171.

78. Brandão, quotes on 252–254.

79. *Bebel, garota propoganda* (1968, dir. Maurice Capovilla).

80. Quotes from Isabel Montero, "Vanda [*sic*] Pimentel," *Jornal do Brasil*, 25 July 1970, sec. "Caderno B," 8; Antonio Gonçalves Filho, "Wanda Pimentel mostra o outro lado da tela," *O Estado de S. Paulo*, 19 November 1992, D2 ("related . . ."); Fernando Cocchiarale in Daniel Labra, Frederico Morais, and Fernando Cocchiarale, *Wanda Pimentel* (Niterói, 2010), unpag. For overviews of Pimentel's work, see, in addition to Labra, Morais, and Cocchiarale's introduction, Frederico Morais and Vera Beatriz Siqueira, *Wanda Pimentel* (Rio de Janeiro, 2012).

81. Carlos Drummond de Andrade, *As impurezas do branco*, 2nd ed. (Rio de Janeiro, 1974 [1973]), 3–19.

82. Andrade, *Impurezas*, 113. "In the open-air hypersupermarket of detritus, / to the clatter of crates in sweaty rush / thin women and quick children / pick after the biggest rotten orange, the most beautiful / rejected potato, they gather on the sidewalk / their stock of riches, amid laughter and shouting."

83. Yan Michalski, "Comunidade, antes e depois do corpo," *Jornal do Brasil*, 15 December 1970, sec. "Caderno B," 2; Deocélia Vianna, *Companheiros de viagem*, ed.

Maria Célia Teixeira (São Paulo, 1984); Dênis de Moraes, *Vianinha: Cúmplice da paixão* (Rio de Janeiro, 1991); Yan Michalski, "Consuelo de Castro: Sempre urgente, sem rupturas," in Consuelo de Castro, *Urgência e ruptura* (São Paulo, 1989), 14–16; Consuelo de Castro, interview by Luis Francisco Carvalho Filho and Daisy Perelmutter, São Paulo, 17 August 2006, Biblioteca Mário de Andrade, Projeto Memória Oral.

84. Oduvaldo Vianna Filho, "Corpo a corpo," typescript, 21 June 1969, USP, Escola de Comunicações e Artes.

85. Oduvaldo Vianna Filho, "Alegro [*sic*] desbum, ou se Martins Pena fosse vivo," typescript, Biblioteca Padre Alberto Antoniazzi, Pontifícia Universidade Católica de Minas Gerais.

86. Consuelo de Castro, *Caminho de volta* (Porto Alegre, 1974), 116–117.

87. Castro, *Caminho*, quotes on 35 ("against . . ."), 97 ("We're . . ."), 114 ("Isn't . . ."), 59 ("At . . .").

88. "A publicidade é o tema da peça," *O Estado de S. Paulo*, 17 October 1974, p. 16; Consuelo de Castro, interview; "Vianninha, em ritmo allegro de desbum," *Diario de Noticias*, 22 August 1973, p. 15; Sandra Rodart Araújo, "*Corpo a corpo* (1970) de Oduvaldo Vianna Filho: Do texto dramático à encenação do Grupo Tapa de São Paulo (1995)" (tese de mestrado, Universidade Federal de Uberlândia, 2006), 42.

89. Yan Michalski, "Entre Santos e São Paulo," *Jornal do Brasil*, 17 December 1971, sec. "Caderno B," 2; Fausto Fuser, "A descoberta de um ensaio: 'Corpo a corpo,'" *Folha de S. Paulo*, 22 November 1971, p. 17; "Antunes dirigirá 'Corpo a Corpo," *O Estado de S. Paulo*, 13 October 1971, p. 7 (Juca); "Uma personagem e muitos fantasmas," *O Estado de S. Paulo*, 18 November 1971, p. 17 (Antunes); Sábato Magaldi, "O que há de tão especial nesta peça?" [*Jornal da Tarde?*], 8 December 1971, quoted in Araújo, "*Corpo a corpo* (1970)," 110.

90. Tamar de Castro, "A angústia cotidiana em ritmo de comédia" (Vianna Filho interview), *Jornal do Brasil*, 9 August 1973, sec. "Caderno B," 2; Aldmomar Conrado, "Vianninha, em ritmo allegro de desbum," *Diario de Noticias*, 18 August 1973, p. 15; "A publicidade é o tema da peça," *O Estado de S. Paulo*, 17 October 1974, p. 16; "No Aliança, as muitas voltas de um caminho," *Folha de S. Paulo*, 18 August 1974, p. 31; Jefferson Del Rios, "O caminho de volta," *Folha de S. Paulo*, 25 August 1974, p. 37; Luiz Izrael Febrot, "Renovação no teatro brasileiro," *O Estado de S. Paulo*, 1 December 1974, sec. "Suplemento Literário," 5; Sábato Magaldi, *Jornal da Tarde*, 1974, in Consuelo de Castro, *Urgência*, 569; Alberto Guzik, *Ultima Hora*, 1974, in Consuelo de Castro, *Urgência*, 570; Yan Michalski, "'Alegro': [*sic*] consumo anticonsumista," *Jornal do Brasil*, 3 May 1977, sec. "Caderno B," 2 (13-month run); "Comédia satiriza o consumo," *O Estado de S. Paulo*, 13 March 1976, p. 10 (Renato); Sábato Magaldi, "O alegre repouso de Vianinha," *Jornal da Tarde*, 24 March 1976, in *A crítica de um teatro crítico*, ed. Rosangela Patriota (São Paulo, 2007), 138; Alberto Guzik, "*Alegro desbum*, alegre Vianinha," *Ultima Hora*, 12 April 1976, in Patriota, *Crítica*, 134.

91. Fuser, "Descoberta"; Sábato Magaldi, *Jornal da Tarde*, 1974, in Consuelo de Castro, *Urgência*, 569; "Antunes dirigirá 'Corpo a Corpo,'" *O Estado de S. Paulo*, 13 October 1971, p. 7 ("including . . ."); "Uma personagem e muitos fantasmas," *O Estado de S. Paulo*, 18 November 1971, p. 17; Maria Bonomi, "A questão da cenografia," *Folha de S. Paulo*, 22 November 1971, p. 17.

92. José Renato, introduction to Rio première, in *Alegro desbum . . . ou "se Martins Pena fosse vivo . . ."* (program, São Paulo, 1976), Museu Lasar Segall, Biblioteca Jenny Klabin; Febrot, "Renovação"; *Jornal do Brasil*, 13 March 1975, sec. "Caderno B," 10.

93. Michalski, "Entre Santos"; "Uma personagem e muitos fantasmas," *O Estado de S. Paulo*, 18 November 1971, p. 17; Fernando Peixoto, "Um cavalo estraçalhado na Hípica," Rio de Janeiro, March 1974, in Consuelo de Castro, *Caminho*, 14; Castro, "Angústia"; "Comédia satiriza o consumo," *O Estado de S. Paulo*, 13 March 1976, p. 10.

94. Maria Silva Betti, *Oduvaldo Vianna Filho* (São Paulo, 1997), 315; "A publicidade é o tema da peça," *O Estado de S. Paulo*, 17 October 1974, p. 16; Febrot, "Renovação"; "Entrevista a Ivo Cardoso," in Vianna Filho, *Vianinha: Teatro, televisão, política*, ed. Fernando Peixoto (São Paulo, 1983), 180–181, 184; "Na Aliança, as muitas voltas de um caminho," *Folha de S. Paulo*, 18 October 1974, p. 31.

95. "Cinco receberão o 'Prêmio Molière,'" *O Estado de S. Paulo*, 16 April 1975, p. 9; Moraes, *Vianinha*, 242; Michalski, "Alegro"; Michalski, "Ser ou não ser publicitário," *Jornal do Brasil*, 5 November 1978, sec. "Caderno B," 2; Telles, *Tirando*, 199; Marco Antônio Guerra, *Carlos Queiroz Telles: História e dramaturgia em cena, década de 70* (São Paulo, 1993), 144 ("I . . ."); Castelo Branco, *Tomei*, 166.

96. Orígenes Lessa, *O feijão e o sonho*, 7th ed. (Rio de Janeiro, 1968 [1938]), quotes on 33, 36; "A tradição é nossa ligação com o futuro e não com o passado," *O Estado de S. Paulo*, 31 July 1983, sec. "Cultura," 9; "Empresas de propaganda," *Propaganda*, December 1937, p. 13; "Origenes [*sic*] Lessa," *Anuário Brasileiro de Propaganda*, 1970–1971, p. 67; Lessa interview, van Steen, *Viver*, 1:125.

97. Emil Farhat, *Os homens sós* (Rio de Janeiro, 1945), 65, 247; Ramos, *Fúrias*, 60–67; Castelo Branco, *Tomei*, 156; Ramos, "Os amantes iluminados," in *Amor à brasileira*, ed. Guido Fidelis and Caio Porfírio Carneiro (São Paulo, 1987), 15.

98. Origenes [*sic*] Lessa, "Ensaio sobre a publicidade," *Diario Carioca*, 14 June 1936, p. 24; Lessa, "A propaganda e o futuro do Brasil," *Propaganda*, March 1956, p. 18; Edmur de Castro Cotti, "Bilhete cordial para um inimigo gratuito," *Propaganda*, September 1957, pp. 14–15; Eliezer Burlá, "Um psiquiatra ataca a propaganda," *PN*, 12 December 1960, pp. 26–27; Manoel de Vasconcellos, "Uma palavra do editor," *PN*, 22 May 1961, p. 3.

99. "Assim eu vejo o Pan-Americanismo," *Publicidade*, September 1941, p. 26.

100. Lessa, "Propaganda brasileira," 12; Olympio Guilherme, "O êrro do 'americanismo' na publicidade brasileira," *Publicidade & Negócios*, 1 April 1952, p. 10; Rodolfo Lima Martensen, "Porta dos fundos," *Propaganda*, January 1960, p. 48; Lessa, "O milagre," in *Zona sul* (Rio de Janeiro, 1963), 68.

101. Lessa, "Propaganda brasileira," 12; João Alfredo de Souza Ramos, "Propaganda," *Publicidade*, June 1943, pp. 4–5; Ramos, "A propaganda no Brasil e o êrro psicológico dos americanos," *Publicidade*, September 1944, pp. 30–32.

102. Penteado, "Norte-americanos," 22–24. In the terms of Penteado's title ("Are the North Americans Actually Dumb or Does It Just Look That Way?"), the problem was—despite exceptions such as Penn—that "'export quality' Americans" were thick headed and heavy handed.

103. Rabelo, *Capital*; Edward G. Wilson, "Memorandum for the Files," 25 April 1962, JWTA, EGWP, box 2; Rabelo, *Onde*; Rabelo, "Fatos & comentários," *Publicidade &*

Negócios, 1 November 1950, pp. 14–15; Rabelo, "Fatos & comentários," *PN*, 5 August 1954, pp. 10, 12, 14; Rabelo, "Fatos & comentários," *PN*, 26 September 1960, p. 16; Rabelo, "Fatos & comentários," *PN*, 11 June 1962, p. 50; editorial cartoon (by "Ferraz"), "O 'Publicitário do Ano,'" *PN*, 11 January 1963, p. 5; "Planejamento," *PN*, 4 February 1963, pp. 18–19; Rabelo, *Batalha*, esp. 46–50, for "prosperity . . ."; Rabelo, *Volta*. Chased into exile by the 1964 coup, João Doria turned from advertising and radical-reformist politics to para-psychology and the "mind power" movement. His son and namesake is currently (June 2019) governor of São Paulo, having deserted Brazil's center-right for tropical Trumpism.

104. Auricélio Penteado, "Se isto é o progresso, para o diabo com êle!," *PN*, 20 June 1955, p. 38.

105. R. L. Martensen, "Porta dos fundos," *Propaganda*, October 1962, p. 64; Helga Miethke (Norton's art director) in *Propaganda*, April 1971, p. 45; Ênio Mainardi, "A embalagem e o meio ambiente," *Propaganda*, March 1973, pp. 44–46.

106. Penteado, "Se isto é o progresso," 38; Ênio Mainardi, "Público desenvolverá contra-remédio da propaganda," *Anuário Brasileiro de Propaganda*, 1969–1970, p. 28. Having shed his youthful left-liberalism, Mainardi would go on to put his talents at the service of some of Brazil's most hidebound, morbidly corrupt politicians, as well as produce pro-gun advertising that was pulled under court order for exploiting anti-black racism. Fernando Rodrigues, "'Sou candidato para ganhar,' diz Maluf," *Folha de S. Paulo*, 19 May 2000, A15; Bruno Paes Manso, "Collor tenta presença no rádio e na TV," *O Estado de S. Paulo*, 15 August 2000, A6; "Justiça manda retirar outdoor sobre armas," *O Estado de S. Paulo*, 30 July 1999, A11.

107. Pólia Lerner Hamburger, "A propaganda como elemento de frustração," *Revista de Administração de Empresas* 10 (January–March 1964): 55–68; Affonso Arantes in Alyza Munhoz, "Pensamento em marketing no Brasil: Um estudo exploratório" (tese de mestrado, EAESP, 1982), 287–288; Rabelo, *Batalha*, 33.

108. Marcus Pereira, "Há pressão: Provas," *Propaganda*, August 1963, pp. 18–19; Pereira, *Música: Está chegando a vez do povo* (São Paulo, 1976), 35–36; Pereira, *Lembranças*, 6; APP, *Depoimentos*, 42; Robert Heilbroner, *The Worldly Philosophers: The Lives, Times, and Ideas of the Great Economic Thinkers*, 6th ed. (New York, 1986 [1953]), 230.

109. APP, *Depoimentos*, 42.

110. Sangirardi Junior [*sic*], "Chumbo miúdo," *Publicidade & Negócios*, 15 April 1952, p. 10; R. L. Martensen, "Porta dos fundos," *Propaganda*, November 1961, p. 56; "Como achar mulata modelo," *Propaganda*, January 1970, pp. 12–13; Martensen, *Desafio*, 337–338.

111. "Um nome da propaganda," *Jornal das Moças*, 30 June 1960, p. 4; "É pura propaganda," *Veja*, 5 March 1969, p. 25; APP, *Depoimentos*, 97; Periscinoto, "A Palestra dos Bispos," in *Mais vale*, 148.

112. "Advertising Man Lists Five Challenges," attachment to José F. Kfuri to Peter Dunham, São Paulo, 22 December 1965, JWTA, EGWP, box 77; APP, *Depoimentos*, 26–27 (inc. "Advertising . . ."); Renato Castelo Branco, "Propaganda e desenvolvimento," *O Estado de São Paulo*, 20 December 1975, sec. "Suplemento do Centenário," 5 ("to place . . ." and "aggressive . . .").

113. Castelo Branco, *Tomei*, 166–167, 256–257; Renato Castelo Branco, *O comunicador: A vida numa agência de propaganda, vista pelo decano dos publicitários brasileiros* (São Paulo, 1991), 100–103.

114. Ramos, *Fúrias*, chap. 18; this chapter (notes 16 and 97); Ramos, *Circuito fechado* (São Paulo, 1972).

115. Julieta de Godoy Ladeira, *Entre lobo e cão* (Rio de Janeiro, 1971). No study exists of Ladeira's life and work. My overview is based primarily on her unindexed papers, esp. "Curriculum antigo," IEB-FJGL, cx. 8; "Retrato," IEB-FJGL, cx. 13; "Lembranças de uma publicitária," IEB-FJGL, cx. 18. See also her "Voltas ao redor do centro," in *Vamos ao centro*, ed. Cremilda Medina (São Paulo, 1994), 279–284.

116. The emotional economy of the servant-employing household was an established theme in Ladeira's short fiction. See especially, "O que tem de ser," in *Passe as férias em Nassau* (Rio de Janeiro, 1962), 19–32.

117. Ladeira, *Entre*, quotes on 38, 101.

118. Ladeira, 38–39.

119. Ladeira, quotes on 56–57, 136.

120. Ladeira, 142.

121. Ladeira, quotes on 42, 153–154, 71.

122. Ladeira, quotes on 113, 115.

123. Ladeira, 152.

124. Ladeira, 107.

Postscript

1. Paulo Francis, *O Brasil no mundo* (Rio de Janeiro, 1985), 81–82; Maureen O'Dougherty, *Consumption Intensified: The Politics of Middle-Class Daily Life in Brazil* (Durham, N.C., 2002); James Brooke, "U.S. Investors Stampede into Brazil," *New York Times*, 17 April 1995, D5; Diana Jean Schemo, "Brazil's Economic Samba," *New York Times*, 7 September 1996, pp. 35, 37; Todd Benson, "Courting the Poor, a Retailer Rises to No. 3 in Brazil," *New York Times*, 14 July 2004, W1, W7; Andrew Downie, "Boom Times for Brazil's Consumers," *New York Times*, 24 May 2008, C3; Rachel Glickhouse, "Favela Consumer Class on the Rise in Brazil," accessed 5 March 2013, http://www.csmonitor.com/World/Americas/Latin-America-Monitor/2013/0227 /Favela-consumer-class-on-the-rise-in-Brazil; Simon Romero, "Reshaping Brazil's Retail Scene," *New York Times*, 15 September 2013, A6; Perry Anderson, "Crisis in Brazil," *London Review of Books*, 21 April 2016, p. 16.

2. João Cruz Costa, *Pequena história da república* (Rio de Janeiro, 1968), 138; [Perry Anderson], "Historical Introduction, 1930–1964: The Legacy of Vargas," in João Quartim, *Dictatorship and Armed Struggle in Brazil*, trans. David Fernbach (New York, 1972), 18; Paulo Francis, *O afeto que se encerra: Memórias* (Rio de Janeiro, 1980), 83–84. Authorship of the introduction to Quartim's book is attributed to Perry Anderson in Gregory Elliott, *Perry Anderson: The Merciless Laboratory of History* (Minneapolis, 1998), 303, in reference to an edition published in London in 1971.

3. Oliver Dinius, *Brazil's Steel City: Developmentalism, Strategic Position, and Industrial Relations in Volta Redonda, 1941–1964* (Stanford, Calif., 2011), 181; Robert J.

Alexander, notes on conversation with William G. Winslow, São Paulo, 28 April 1956, RJAP, mr-2; Robert J. Alexander, notes on conversation with [illegible], described as a "businessman," São Paulo, 28 August 1959, RJAP, mr-2; Mário Morel, ed., *Lula, o metalúrgico* (Rio de Janeiro, 1981), 33.

4. Paulo Fontes, *Um nordeste em São Paulo: Trabalhadores migrantes em São Miguel Paulista, 1945–1966* (Rio de Janeiro, 2008), 77; Charles Wagley, *An Introduction to Brazil* (New York, 1963), 115; Wagley, *An Introduction to Brazil*, rev. ed. (New York, 1971 [1963]), 106.

5. Robert J. Alexander, notes on conversation with Caio Prado Júnior, São Paulo, 17 November 1965, RJAP, mr-3; Darcy Ribeiro, *Aos trancos e barrancos: Como o Brasil deu no que deu* (Rio de Janeiro, 1985), item 1654; Gregório Bezerra, *Memórias*, 2nd ed. (São Paulo, 2011 [1979]), 518.

6. Armando Puglisi, *Memórias de Armandinho do Bixiga*, ed. Júlio Moreno (São Paulo, 1996), 38–39, 52; Darcy Ribeiro, *Confissões* (São Paulo, 1997), 463.

7. Luiz Edmundo, *De um livro de memórias*, 5 vols. (Rio de Janeiro, 1958), 4:1227–1228.

8. Manoel de Vasconcellos, "Uma palavra do editor," *PN*, 20 March 1956, p. 2; "Maior expansão para os eletrodomésticos," *Correio da Manhã*, 20 December 1964, sec. "Econômico," 3; Jorge Martins Rodrigues, "Perspectivas . . . ," *Propaganda*, November 1957, p. 9.

9. Transcription of interview with Altino João de Barros by Ilana Strozenbert and Luciana Heymann, 14 July 2004, CPDOC-PHO; Amara Rocha, *Nas ondas da modernização: O rádio e a TV no Brasil de 1950 a 1970* (Rio de Janeiro, 2007), 48–49 (Brassini); Anna Veronica Mautner, *O cotidiano nas entrelinhas: Crônicas e memórias* (São Paulo, 2001), 30, 19, respectively; Lia Faria, *Ideologia e utopia nos anos 60: Um olhar feminino* (Rio de Janeiro, 1997), 160.

10. Genolino Amado, "A morte da província," in *Os inocentes do Leblon: Crônicas do Rio* (Rio de Janeiro, 1946), 137–138.

11. Amado, "A morte da província," 137–138, and "O amor em Botafogo" (April 1944), in *Inocentes*, 235; Murilo Mendes, "Formação de discoteca," *A Manhã*, 21 September 1947, sec. "Letras e Artes," 5; Mautner, *Cotidiano*, 30; Cláudia Mesquita, *De Copacabana à Boca do Mato: O Rio de Janeiro de Sérgio Porto e Stanislaw Ponte Preta* (Rio de Janeiro, 2008), 238; Paulo Cesar Ferreira, *Pilares via satélite: Da Rádio Nacional à Rede Globo* (Rio de Janeiro, 1998), 57; Cláudio Abramo, *A regra do jogo: O jornalismo e a ética do marceneiro*, ed. Cláudio Weber Abramo (São Paulo, 1988), 233.

12. Ferreira, *Pilares*, 201–208; Gilmar de Carvalho, *Publicidade em cordel* (São Paulo, 1994), 138–150. For commercial appeals playing on Paulista state pride and Carioca cultural forms, e.g., *PN*, 20 February 1954; Aélio de Brunno, "Rio 400 anos em promoções e informações," *Propaganda*, December 1965, pp. 32–33.

13. "Semana para você," *Correio da Manhã*, 21 October 1962, sec. 5, p. 7; "Agora o hipermercado," *Jornal do Brasil*, 3 March 1971, sec. "Caderno B," 5; "O templo do integrado consumo ao lazer," *Jornal do Brasil*, 20 June 1973, sec. "Caderno B," 10; Joelmir Beting, "O consumidor paulistano," *Manchete*, special issue "Retrato de São Paulo" (1974), 139–140. For "subconsumers" and "sub-consumption," e.g., "Tendências dos negócios," *PN*, 5 July 1956, p. 40; "Caixa alta," *PN*, 14 March 1963, p. 1; Limeira Tejo, *Retrato sincero do Brasil*, 5th ed. (Rio de Janeiro, 1978 [1950]), 186, 206, 222; Renato Castelo Branco, *Tomei um Ita no norte: Memórias* (São Paulo, 1981), 167.

14. Beting, "Consumidor," 140.

15. Beting, 140–141; O'Dougherty, *Consumption*; Gilberto Velho, *A utopia urbana: Um estudo de antropologia social* (Rio de Janeiro, 1973), quote on 66.

16. Beting, "Consumidor," 138; *O Jornal-Feminino* advertisement, *Publicidade & Negócios*, 1 October 1950, p. 7; Standard Propaganda advertisement, *PN*, 5 April 1955, cover; JWT advertisement, *Propaganda*, July 1961, p. 4; *O Jornal* advertisement, *Vendas e Varejo*, January 1964, p. 3; Marcia Rita, "Uma palavrinha de apresentação," *Vendas e Varejo*, April–June 1964, p. 28.

17. Marcus Pereira, "As mulheres mandam," *O Estado de S. Paulo*, 23 November 1958, p. 97; R. L. Martensen, "Porta dos fundos," *Propaganda*, May 1962, p. 40; "Perfil do consumidor," *Supermercado Moderno*, April 1972, p. 61; Wanda Jorge, "De olho no preço," *Folha de São Paulo*, 31 August 1980, sec. "Folhetim," 5.

18. Jorge, "Olho," 6. Clarice Herzog is well known to Brazilians as the widow of Vladimir Herzog, whose murder in official custody in 1975, after the defeat of the armed opposition to the military regime, generated an uproar that marked the beginning of the end for polite-society apologetics for continued state repression. That it did should be credited in part to her brave refusal to acquiesce to the regime's fiction, which held that Vladimir had hung himself in his cell. In fact, his death was the result of brutal methods of torture, administered as a matter of routine in the interrogation of the politically suspect.

19. Pergentino Mendes de Almeida, "A dona de casa diante das inovações," *Propaganda*, April 1971, pp. 31–35.

20. Almeida, "Dona de casa," 32–33.

21. Almeida, 32; Rose Marie Muraro, *Memórias de uma mulher impossível* (Rio de Janeiro, 2000), 119; Mautner, *Cotidiano*, 29–30, 19, 22–23 (respectively).

22. Genival Rabelo, "Fatos & comentários," *PN*, 20 December 1956, p. 16.

23. C&A advertisement, *O Estado de S. Paulo*, 15 August 1976, p. 15; Ramona Bechtos, "Key Consumer Goods Growing Fast in Brazil," *Advertising Age*, 5 March 1973, p. 48; "Lojas por auto-serviço vendem Cr$35,8 bilhões em 1973," *Supermercado Moderno*, April 1974, p. 16; "O balanço do supermercado brasileiro," *Superhiper*, November 1978, p. 18.

24. "Going Shopping with Lady Luck," *Business Week*, 16 December 1967, p. 1; "Entre as cores e o melhor nível," *Veja*, 12 January 1972, pp. 44–45 (quoted).

25. Carlos de Meira Mattos, "Revolução, democracia e poder," *O Estado de S. Paulo*, 9 April 1972, p. 27; "A regulamentação espontânea das vendas a crédito e suas implicações sociais e econômicas," *Vendas e Varejo*, April 1963, p. 45; "O Brasil na hora da decisão," *Vendas e Varejo*, February 1964, p. 25. Mattos would go on to choose Gilberto Freyre as his principal adviser when he defended a doctoral thesis in political science (*DHBB*, 3:3640–3641).

26. Orígenes Lessa, "Em 1935 minha primeira grande promoção," *Propaganda*, June 1979, p. 22.

27. Brookfield advertisement, *O Estado de S. Paulo*, 23 June 2009, B6–B7.

28. "Shopping center," *Jornal do Brasil*, 30 September 1973, sec. "Revista de Domingo," 4; Vicente del Rio, Carlos Eduardo Ferreira, José Kós, and James Miyamoto, "Nascimento e apogeu do shopping-center," *Módulo* 94 (1987): 34–47; "Empresários destacam as vantagens dos shoppings," *Diretor Lojista*, November 1974, p. 47; Beatriz

Piccolotto Siqueira Bueno, *São Paulo, um novo olhar sobre a história: A evolução do comércio de varejo e as transformações da vida urbana* (São Paulo, 2012), 100; Silvana Maria Pintaudi, "Os shopping-centers brasileiros e o processo de valorização do espaço urbano," *Boletim Paulista de Geografia* 64 (1986): 36.

29. Fernando Henrique Cardoso, *Autoritarismo e democratização* (Rio de Janeiro, 1975), esp. chap. 2; Francisco Weffort, preface to *Cinquenta anos de supermercados no Brasil* (São Paulo, 2002), 9; Morel, *Lula*, 90; Walt Whitman Rostow, *The Stages of Economic Growth* (Cambridge, 1960), 11–12, 90–92.

30. Julieta de Godoy Ladeira, *Entre lobo e cão* (Rio de Janeiro, 1971), 1; from "Consolo na praia" (1943?), first published in Drummond's *A rosa do povo* (Rio de Janeiro, 1945). "Injustice is not resolved. / In the shadow of the erring world / you murmured a timid protest. / But others will come."

A Further Note on Archival and Periodical Sources

The research for this book was eased by the fact that the archives of several of the most important institutional actors in the making of Brazilian consumer capitalism are open to the public. These include the Ford Motor Company, the J. Walter Thompson Company, and the Instituto Brasileiro de Opinião Pública e Estatística. Official U.S. sources—from the Bureau of Foreign and Domestic Commerce, the State Department, and the Office of the Coordinator of Inter-American Affairs—complemented these materials, as did archival material from other private collections, but the resulting picture was incomplete. While the Sears Archives, in Hoffman Estates, Illinois, provided invaluable detail, it was insufficient for the history of Brazilian retail. One promising lead—the archive of Garbo S.A., successor firm to Nilo de Carvalho's Modas A Exposição Clipper—became a dispiriting dead end, the collection apparently having been destroyed, discarded, or misplaced at some point after its listing in *Guia dos documentos históricos na cidade de São Paulo, 1554–1954*, ed. Paula Porta Fernandes (1998), 696.

And so, on retailing and other matters, I came to rely heavily on the press, including, especially, the trade press, most notably a series of magazines published in Rio de Janeiro beginning in the 1940s, consulted at the New York Public Library, Escola Superior de Propaganda e Marketing, Biblioteca Nacional, Library of Congress, and Nettie Lee Benson Collection of the University of Texas. One of these magazines—at points, reputedly the largest circulating trade magazine published anywhere in the world outside the United States—changed titles over the years, during which it was published first as a monthly, then fortnightly, finally on a weekly basis: founded as *Publicidade* in 1940, it became *Publicidade & Negócios* in 1947, and *PN* in 1952 (its sister publications, *Vendas e Varejo* and *Indústria & Mercados*, kept the same titles over their shorter runs). In this book's notes, where references to items from *PN* for 1956 lack page numbers, it is because they were missing from the collection I consulted for the later 1950s, at the Escola Superior de Propaganda e Marketing, because they were either cut off when the issues were bound or offset from the printable area of the page.

Next most important to these magazines was the *Fortune*-style monthly *O Observador Econômico e Financeiro*, published in Rio from 1936 to 1962, and the two series of the São Paulo advertising magazine *Propaganda* (1937–1939, 1956–). Other Brazilian trade, industry, and business-interest publications that figured in my research include *Administração e Serviços, Anuário Brasileiro de Imprensa, Anuário Brasileiro de Propaganda, Anuário de Publicidade, Anuário do Rádio, Boletim Semanal* (of the São Paulo Commercial Association), *Brazilian American, Brazilian-American Survey, Brazilian Business, Carta Mensal* (of the Technical Council of the National Confederation of Commerce), *Conjuntura Econômica, Digesto Econômico, Direção, Diretor Lojista, O Dirigente Industrial, Indústria e Desenvolvimento, Marketing, Paulista, Publicidade Industrial,*

Revista Brasileira de Vendas, Revista da Associação Comercial (of Rio de Janeiro), *Revista das Classes Produtoras, Revista de Administração de Empresas, Revista do Comércio* (of the National Confederation of Commerce), and *Visão*.

The trade press, like the Brazilian press more generally, was overwhelmingly concentrated in Rio and São Paulo. Given that fact, adhering to the convention of identifying place of publication at each citation would have added thousands of words to this book's notes, to no appreciable payoff. Instead, I have adhered to that convention only when dealing with periodicals published outside the Rio–São Paulo axis, except where place of publication is provided in or implied by the title (the *Diario de Pernambuco* is published, of course, in Recife, capital of the state of Pernambuco). Of the remaining titles, these were published in Rio: *Anuário Brasileiro de Imprensa, Anuário de Publicidade, Anuário do Rádio, A Batalha, Boletim Cambial, Brazilian American, Brazilian-American Survey, Brazilian Business, Carta Mensal, Cinearte, Conjuntura Econômica, Correio da Manhã, O Cruzeiro, Diario Carioca, Diario da Noite, Diario de Noticias, Diario Official/Diário Oficial, Diretor Lojista, Diretrizes, DNC: Revista do Departamento Nacional do Café, Gazeta de Noticias, O Globo, O Imparcial, Imprensa Popular, O Jornal, Jornal das Moças, Jornal do Brasil, Manchete, A Manhã, Módulo, A Noite, A Noite Ilustrada, Opinião, O Paiz, Politica, A Razão, Revista da Associação Comercial, Revista da Semana, Revista das Classes Produtoras, Revista de Economia Popular, Revista do Comércio, Revista do Rádio, O Semanário, SINGRA* ("Suplemento Intergráfico"), *Tribuna da Imprensa, Tribuna Popular, Ultima Hora,* and *Voz Operária*. That leaves the following São Paulo titles: *Administração e Serviços, Anhembi, Anuário Brasileiro de Propaganda, Boletim Semanal, O Combate, Correio Paulistano, Diario Nacional, Digesto Econômico, Direção, O Dirigente Industrial, O Estado de S. Paulo, Folha da Manhã, Folha da Noite, Folha de S. Paulo, Indústria e Desenvolvimento, Jornal da Tarde, Marketing, Paulista, Placar, Publicidade Industrial, Revista Brasileira de Vendas, Revista de Administração de Empresas, Veja,* and *Visão*. (Here and elsewhere, titles are spelled as they appeared on periodical mastheads, rather than in accord with the orthographic standards of their day or subsequent reforms.)

Researchers will search library catalogs in vain for the magazine *Supermercado Moderno* (São Paulo, 1969–2018). I consulted the collection belonging to the Associação Brasileira de Supermercados, in São Paulo, which continues to publish *Superhiper* (1974–).

Bibliographical Essay

Readers may have noticed that this book's endnotes are leaner than those found in much recent historical scholarship. This was deliberate. Wherever possible, citations have been limited to archival materials, items from the press, and other primary-source documentation. The running commentary on other historians' work featured in most monographs these days ("For a fascinating account of X, see Professor Y's book, Z . . .") has been omitted on the assumption that readers will not have picked up this book to discover my thoughts on the historiography of Brazilian identity, inter-American relations, or the sixties, much less what I make of this or that social-scientific method, theoretical approach, or critical technique. Rather, my assumption has been that readers who glance at the notes—and not all will—will do so in search of citations; in a limited number of cases, they will also find additional explanation.

As far as method, theory, and technique are concerned, with Barbara Fields I believe that "whatever our motives or purposes for undertaking a particular investigation, whatever our wrestling with the tools needed for the work, yea and whatever our categories of analysis, we should be drawing our audience's attention to the past, not to ourselves. What belongs on display is not the categories of analysis, but the new understanding of the past that our categories of analysis have guided us to." She adds,

> If I contract with someone to do the plumbing in my new house, I surely hope that the plumber is fully conversant with tools, materials, and sound technique. But when I show the new house to my friends, I do not expect the first exclamations to be: "What glorious solder! What uncommon flux! What stylish elbow fittings!" Categories of analysis are the tools of our trade. But when they live and breathe and jostle human beings in our finished work, we are inviting our guests to gape through holes in the walls of the new house and marvel at the pipes and fittings. In that case, we have not only forgotten what the tools were for, but why we wanted a new house in the first place. ("Categories of Analysis? Not in My Book," in ACLS Occasional Paper no. 10.)

I quote Fields at such length not only for the sensible point she delivers gracefully and in good humor but also because the same idea may be shown to have a Brazilian pedigree, in a "Timid Preface" that the great Darcy Ribeiro began by declaring, "Finally we have in our hands a doctoral thesis that is good to read. To achieve this, it was remade, domesticated, the methodological scaffolds were hidden away so that one could see the building" ("Tímido prefácio," in Lia Faria, *Ideologia e utopia nos anos 60: Um olhar feminino* [Rio de Janeiro, 1997], 13). And so the scaffolding and soldering of this book have been hidden away.

Nevertheless, some further explanation seems in order, and may be laid out, I hope, without gutting the construction raised over the preceding chapters. In particular, it seems appropriate to acknowledge some of the scholarship on which my work rests, to offer suggestions for further reading and—perhaps—for future research, and especially to gesture at the Portuguese-language historiography that has come into being since the 1990s, when I began the work that led, by twists and turns, to this book. The growth of Brazilian higher education and the flourishing of the country's historical scholarship over recent decades have been exciting to watch, but the latter's ever-increasing size and scope make mastery elusive. What follows represents a starting point, rather than the final word.

Starting Points, Counterpoints

As the acknowledgments indicate, I began researching U.S. advertising in Brazil as an undergraduate. It was then that I was introduced to Jackson Lears's *Fables of Abundance: A Cultural History of Advertising in America* (New York, 1994), the first book I encountered that made advertising the subject of serious scholarship rather than of meretricious or muckraking journalism. I wrestled with it at the time and for some time to come, inspired by it, allowing it to influence my work, and investigating the larger project of which it was part, including the volume Lears coedited with Richard Wightman Fox, *The Culture of Consumption: Critical Essays in American History, 1880–1980* (New York, 1983), in which advertising is characterized as "the central institution of consumer culture" (xiii). Over time—and this was probably due more to faults of my own than of Lears's work—I found myself frustrated by the lack of explication of the making of that larger culture. A project that was unfurled with gestures toward "conceiving consumption as an ideology and a way of seeing, [while] direct[ing] attention to the powerful groups that over the last century have promoted the cultural and institutional framework of contemporary Americans' lives" (also on xiii), culminated in an artfully constructed and often beautifully written set of ruminations on advertising's roles in and as North American culture, but one in which that larger framework is only dimly seen. Hence this book's worrying away at frameworks, institutions, interconnections, and their power. In thinking about these issues, I also learned from Lears's rereading of Antonio Gramsci ("The Concept of Cultural Hegemony: Problems and Possibilities," *American Historical Review* 90, no. 3 [June 1985]: 567–593), even as Brazilian scholarship has provided constant reminders that Lears's Gramsci is not the only one we have.

I encountered *Fables* at the suggestion of Louis A. Pérez Jr., then immersed in what many believe to be his masterwork, the meticulously documented account of the cultural tangling of Cuba and the United States titled *On Becoming Cuban: Identity, Nationality, and Culture* (Chapel Hill, N.C., 1999). In that book's introduction, Pérez addressed the monographic charm: "There has always been a temptation to address these issues separately, in monographic form: a study of, for example, Protestant missionaries, or tourism, or baseball and boxing, or music or popular culture, or the influence of motion pictures. But such an approach seemed incapable of yielding the desired outcome: namely, to understand the context and complexity of these linkages as a totality, as a system, and to see how connections worked together" (5). Readers will note this book's emphasis on connections—and cumulativeness—in the making of Brazilian consumer capitalism and an attempt to see the latter systematically, as well as my emulation of Pérez's prodigious research, if not any match of it. This study, however, is a less ambitious one than *On Becoming Cuban*, in which the practices and products of a consumer culture identified with the United States are considered alongside Cubans' experiences of and reflections on schooling, travel, and self-government, to name only a few further subjects. The totality of U.S. influence upon Brazil—beyond commerce, consumption, and their promotion—exceeds the scope of this book.

In Pérez's book, and to some degree in modern Cuban history, the yen for U.S.-style market culture was embodied in El Encanto, the Havana department store destroyed by fire three days before Fidel Castro proclaimed the Cuban Revolution to be socialist, four days before the proxy invasion at the Bay of Pigs. My own work on the centrality of the retail trade to the making of Brazilian consumer capitalism was profoundly influenced by William Leach, *Land of Desire: Merchants, Power, and the Rise of a New American Culture* (New York, 1993), and its congenial emphasis on power and the institutional coalitions that underlay the culture of consumer capitalism in the United States. Years before that book's publication, Leach announced his vision of a "fully dialectical, historical assessment of consumption" encompassing the critical, declensionist position that would inform *Land of Desire* and attention to "those patterns of consumer life that implied a new freedom from self-denial and from repression, a liberation that promised to expand the province of rewarding work and of individual expression for women," the latter of which he explored separately, and somewhat half-heartedly, in an article that would remain sectioned off from his larger work ("Transformations in a Culture of Consumption: Women and Department Stores, 1890–1925," *Journal of American History* 71, no. 2 [September 1984]: 319–342 [quotes on 320]). In my charting of the creation of a Brazilian culture of consumer capitalism, I have attempted to juggle both, especially when dealing with women who were in some ways counterparts to the subjects of Leach's article. It is no accident that this book ends, twice, with the copywriter and creative author Julieta de Godoy Ladeira.

At the time of publication of Victoria de Grazia, *Irresistible Empire: America's Advance through Twentieth-Century Europe* (Cambridge, Mass., 2005), I thought completion of a short book on the North American origins of Brazilian consumer culture was in sight. As it turned out, I still had to wrestle with my first book, to recast this project, to do more research, to stew. I also had to do some thinking about my work in relation to de Grazia's. Readers of both books—I hope I won't be the only one—will notice parallels and points of departure as the two volumes explore similar developments. De Grazia's, of course, follows the U.S. "Market Empire" from one end of Europe to the other, jumping from country to country, through a collection of finely wrought episodes held out as particularly telling; this book tracks a parallel turn to consumerism in a single nation-state, diachronically, cumulatively, while tracing connections between the actors and interests that people its pages. One of the cumulative arguments that this book makes—that the cultural work that went into the making of a national variant of U.S.-style consumer capitalism eventually helped define "Brazil"—could, I believe, be extended to de Grazia's: that is, that twentieth-century consumerism made Europe "Europe." How else to understand Spanish technocrats and social scientists of the late Franco years describing processes seen as culminating in consumerism as "Europeanization"? Or Jean-Christophe Agnew's quip that "the language of commodities" furnished "the Esperanto of European unity"? (Jean-Christophe Agnew,

"Coming Up for Air: Consumer Culture in Historical Perspective," in *Consumption and the World of Goods*, ed. John Brewer and Roy Porter [New York, 1993], 34; for Spain, e.g., Alfonso Ortí Benlloch, "Política y sociedade en el umbral de los años setenta: Las bases sociales de la modernización política," in *Cambio social y modernización política: Anuario político español, 1969*, ed. Miguel Martínez Cuadrado [Madrid, 1970], 24–87).

Twentieth-Century Brazil

The task of writing a worthwhile synthesis of twentieth-century Brazilian history, in any language, is an open challenge to future scholars, who will find much of their statistical material in Francisco Vidal Luna and Herbert Klein, *The Economic and Social History of Brazil Since 1889* (Cambridge, 2014), which draws in part on Thomas Merrick and Douglas Graham's classic *Population and Economic Development in Brazil: 1800 to the Present* (Baltimore, 1979). See also *Estatísticas do século XX* (Rio de Janeiro, 2003), available in .pdf on the website of the Instituto Brasileiro de Geografia e Estatística (www.ibge.gov.br), a valuable source of additional historical data. Thomas Skidmore's two volumes (*Politics in Brazil: An Experiment in Democracy, 1930–1964* [Oxford, 1967] and *The Politics of Military Rule in Brazil, 1964–1985* [Oxford, 1988]) still provide the best narrative history of postwar politics, thickened with consideration of the problems of economic development and policy-making, though readers of Portuguese interested in the period of military rule must now also consult the journalist Elio Gaspari's pentalogy: *A ditadura envergonhada* (São Paulo, 2002), *A ditadura escancarada* (São Paulo, 2002), *A ditadura derrotada* (São Paulo, 2003), *A ditadura encurralada* (São Paulo, 2004), and *A ditadura acabada* (Rio de Janeiro, 2016). Searchers after a general overview of Brazil's twentieth century may be best served by Darcy Ribeiro's unorthodox, often-funny compilation, *Aos trancos e barrancos: Como o Brasil deu no que deu* (Rio de Janeiro, 1985). Ribeiro's subtitle, "How Brazil Ended Up as It Did," identifies the major problem animating my work as well as his.

There exist several collections and collaborative works in which historians consider aspects of twentieth-century Brazilian history. The first serious collaborative history of Brazil was the eleven-volume *História geral da civilização brasileira* (São Paulo, 1960–1984), conceived and organized by Sérgio Buarque de Holanda. Its coverage of post-1889 history, in vols. 8–11, editorship of which Sérgio Buarque delegated to Boris Fausto, is limited, but repays consideration. Not for nothing does the series remain in print. For a livelier attempt at overviewing the same period, see the third and fourth volumes of the *História da vida privada no Brasil*, gen. ed. Fernando Novais (São Paulo, 1997–1998): *República, da belle époque à era do rádio*, ed. Nicolau Sevcenko, and *Contrastes da intimidade contemporânea*, ed. Lilia Schwarcz, both published in 1998.

The same year saw publication of an instigating edited collection on the 1920s, *A década de 1920 e as origens do Brasil moderno*, ed. Helena Carvalho De Lorenzo and Wilma Peres da Costa (São Paulo). For a collection on the dictatorship of 1937–1945, see *Repensando o Estado Novo*, ed. Dulce Pandolfi (Rio de Janeiro, 1999). On the 1950s: André Botelho, Élide Rugai Bastos, and Gláucia Villas Boas, eds., *O moderno em questão: A década de 1950 no Brasil* (Rio de Janeiro, 2008); Wander Melo Miranda, ed., *Anos JK: Margens da modernidade* (São Paulo, 2002). The dictatorship begun in 1964 receives similar treatment in Daniel Aarão Reis, Marcelo Ridenti, and Rodrigo Patto

Sá Motta, eds., *A ditadura que mudou o Brasil: 50 anos do golpe de 1964* (Rio de Janeiro, 2014). On the entire period 1945–1985, see Edmar Bacha and Herbert Klein, eds., *Social Change in Brazil, 1945–1985: The Incomplete Transition* (Albuquerque, N.Mex., 1989).

Since publication of the *História da vida privada*, we have had two additional collaborative histories. First, there is *O Brasil republicano*, 4 vols., ed. Jorge Ferreira and Lucilia de Almeida Neves Delgado (Rio de Janeiro, 2003). More recently, there is the *História do Brasil nação, 1808–2010*, 5 vols. (São Paulo, 2011–2014), a series edited by Lilia Schwarcz that includes volumes covering the years 1889–1930, 1930–1964, and 1964–2010, edited by Schwarcz, Angela de Castro Gomes, and Daniel Aarão Reis Filho, respectively.

Were that reference works on modern Brazilian history were as abundant as edited volumes and collaborative histories. There is, however, one work on Brazil's history since 1930 that is indispensable, the *Dicionário histórico-biográfico brasileiro: Pós-1930*, 2nd ed., 5 vols. (Rio de Janeiro, 2001 [1984]). I have not burdened the endnotes of this book with citations documenting every single time I paused to check a fact in its pages. The most current English-language guide to the historiography is Barbara Weinstein, "Postcolonial Brazil," in *The Oxford Handbook of Latin American History*, ed. Jose Moya (Oxford, 2011), 212–256, which updates Thomas Skidmore's "The Historiography of Brazil, 1889–1964," published over successive issues of the *Hispanic American Historical Review* 55, no. 4 (November 1975): 716–748; and 56, no. 1 (February 1976): 81–109. Readers may also want to consult the bibliographical essays published in *The Cambridge History of Latin America*, ed. Leslie Bethell, vol. 9, *Brazil since 1930* (2009), 545–590. The English-language compendium edited by Armin Ludwig (*Brazil: A Handbook of Historical Statistics* [Boston, 1985]) served Skidmore well in his work; I too have drawn on it here, complemented by the previously mentioned Instituto Brasileiro de Geografia e Estatística data.

The early history of Brazilian consumer capitalism is very much a tale of the two cities of São Paulo and Rio de Janeiro. The interpretations of their histories provided in two major overviews, Richard Morse's *From Community to Metropolis: A Biography of São Paulo, Brazil*, rev. ed. (New York, 1974 [1958]) and Eulália Lobo's *História do Rio de Janeiro: Do capital comercial ao capital industrial e financeiro*, 2 vols. (Rio de Janeiro, 1978), await revision by scholars able to take advantage of the historiographical riches of the last four decades.

For the latter, on Rio, see especially Sidney Chaloub, *Trabalho, lar e botequim: O cotidiano dos trabalhadores no Rio de Janeiro da belle époque*, 2nd ed. (Campinas, 2001 [1986]); Patricia Acerbi, *Street Occupations: Urban Vending in Rio de Janeiro, 1850–1925* (Austin, 2017); Jeffrey Needell, *A Tropical Belle Epoque: Elite Culture and Society in Turn-of-the-Century Rio de Janeiro* (Cambridge, 1987); José Murilo de Carvalho, *Os bestializados: O Rio de Janeiro e a República que não foi* (São Paulo, 1987); Teresa Meade, *"Civilizing" Rio: Reform and Resistance in a Brazilian City, 1889–1930* (University Park, Penn., 1997); Amy Chazkel, *Laws of Chance: Brazil's Clandestine Lottery and the Making of Urban Public Life* (Durham, N.C., 2011); Angela de Castro Gomes, *A invenção do trabalhismo*, 3rd ed. (Rio de Janeiro, 2005 [1988]); Julia O'Donnell, *A invenção de Copacabana: Culturas urbanas e estilos de vida no Rio de Janeiro, 1890–1940* (Rio de Janeiro, 2013); Sueann Caulfield, *In Defense of Honor: Sexual Morality, Modernity, and*

Nation in Early-Twentieth-Century Brazil (Durham, N.C., 2000); Marieta de Moraes Ferreira, ed., *Rio de Janeiro: Uma cidade na história*, 2nd ed. (Rio de Janeiro, 2015 [2000]); Carlos Eduardo Sarmento, *O Rio de Janeiro na era Pedro Ernesto* (Rio de Janeiro, 2001); Jerry Dávila, *Diploma of Whiteness: Race and Social Policy in Brazil, 1917–1945* (Durham, N.C., 2003); Brodwyn Fischer, *A Poverty of Rights: Citizenship and Inequality in Twentieth-Century Rio de Janeiro* (Stanford, Calif., 2008); Ana Maria da Costa Evangelista, *Arroz e feijão, discos e livros: História do Serviço de Alimentação da Previdência Social, SAPS, 1940–1967* (Rio de Janeiro, 2014); Jorge Ferreira, ed., *O Rio de Janeiro nos jornais: Ideologias, Culturas políticas e conflitos sociais, 1946–1964* (Rio de Janeiro, 2011); Cláudia Mesquita, *De Copacabana à Boca do Mato: O Rio de Janeiro de Sérgio Porto e Stanislaw Ponte Preta* (Rio de Janeiro, 2008); Leandro Benmergui, "The Alliance for Progress and Housing Policy in Rio de Janeiro and Buenos Aires in the 1960s," *Urban History* 36, no. 2 (2009): 304–326. Kenneth Serbin, "Church-State Reciprocity in Contemporary Brazil: The Convening of the International Eucharistic Congress of 1955 in Rio de Janeiro," *Hispanic American Historical Review* 76, no. 4 (November 1996): 721–751, provides background on a Rio event that surfaces in chapters 4 and 6 of this book.

On São Paulo, see the pioneering statewide study by Joseph Love, *São Paulo in the Brazilian Federation, 1889–1937* (Stanford, Calif., 1980), as well as Warren Dean, *The Industrialization of São Paulo, 1880–1945* (Austin, Tex., 1969); George Reid Andrews, *Blacks and Whites in São Paulo, 1888–1988* (Madison, Wisc., 1991); Anne Hanley, *Native Capital: Financial Institutions and Economic Development in São Paulo, Brazil, 1850–1920* (Stanford, Calif., 2005); Jaime Rodrigues, *Alimentação, vida material e privacidade: Uma história social de trabalhadores em São Paulo nas décadas de 1920 a 1960* (São Paulo, 2011); Barbara Weinstein, *For Social Peace in Brazil: Industrialists and the Remaking of the Working Class in São Paulo, 1920–1964* (Chapel Hill, N.C., 1996); Paulo Fontes, *Um nordeste em São Paulo: Trabalhadores migrantes em São Miguel Paulista, 1945–1966* (Rio de Janeiro, 2008), available in English translation as *Migration and the Making of Industrial São Paulo*, trans. Ned Sublette (Durham, N.C., 2016); Paula Porta, ed., *História da cidade de São Paulo*, vol. 3, *A cidade na primeira metade do século XX* (São Paulo, 2004); Marisa Midori Deaecto, Lincoln Secco, Marcos Silva, and Raquel Glezer, eds., *São Paulo: Espaço e história* (São Paulo, 2008). For an overheated, but not uninteresting, portrayal of cultural change in interwar São Paulo, see Nicolau Sevcenko, *Orfeu extático na metrópole: São Paulo, sociedade e cultura nos frementes anos 20* (São Paulo, 1992). Lúcia Helena Gama's *Nos bares da vida: Produção cultural e sociabilidade em São Paulo, 1940–1950* (São Paulo, 1998) is not history in any conventional sense, but there is no better guide to the life of São Paulo's "new" downtown of the 1940s and 1950s. São Paulo's quadricentennial of 1954, including its promotional aspects, is studied in Silvio Luiz Lofego, *IV Centenário da Cidade de São Paulo: Uma cidade entre o passado e o futuro* (São Paulo, 2004) and Barbara Weinstein, *The Color of Modernity: São Paulo and the Making of Race and Nation in Brazil* (Durham, N.C., 2015), chaps. 6–8.

Brazil's pre-Lenten Carnaval receives historical treatment in Rachel Soihet, *A subversão pelo riso: Estudos sobre o Carnaval carioca da belle époque ao tempo de Vargas*, 2nd ed. (Uberlândia, 2008 [1998]); Olga Rodrigues de Moraes von Simson, *Carnaval em branco e negro: Carnaval popular paulistano, 1914–1988* (Campinas, 2007); and Zélia Lopes da Silva, *Os carnavais de rua e dos clubes na cidade de São Paulo: Metamor-foses de uma festa, 1923–1938* (São Paulo, 2008). For major developments in music: José Ramos Tinhorão, *História social da música popular brasileira* (Lisbon, 1990); Carlos Sandroni, *Feitiço decente: Transformações do samba no Rio de Janeiro, 1917–1933* (Rio de Janeiro, 2001); Marc Hertzman, *Making Samba: A New History of Race and Music in Brazil* (Durham, N.C., 2013); Bryan McCann, *Hello, Hello Brazil: Popular Music in the Making of Modern Brazil* (Durham, N.C., 2004), chaps. 2–5; Christopher Dunn, *Brutality Garden: Tropicália and the Emergence of a Brazilian Counterculture* (Chapel Hill, N.C., 2001); Gustavo Alonso, *Cowboys do asfalto: Música sertaneja e moderniza-ção brasileira* (Rio de Janeiro, 2015). Hermano Vianna, *The Mystery of Samba: Popu-lar Music and National Identity in Brazil*, ed. and trans. John Charles Chasteen (Chapel Hill, N.C., 1999), goes well beyond music and social dance.

Two English-language works on another national pastime have appeared recently. Gregg Bocketti's *The Invention of the Beautiful Game: Football and the Making of Mod-ern Brazil* (Gainesville, Fla., 2016) is a careful study of the early development of asso-ciation football and its imbrication with discourses of Europhile exclusion and national mythmaking. In *The Country of Football: Soccer and the Making of Modern Brazil* (Berkeley, Calif., 2014), Roger Kittleson traces similar conflicts and contradictions through a history of Brazilian association football down to our time.

Middle-classness in Rio and São Paulo is the subject of Brian Owensby, *Intimate Iro-nies: Modernity and the Making of Middle-Class Lives in Brazil* (Stanford, Calif., 1999), a cultural approach that wraps up more or less at the starting point of Waldir José de Quadros's master's-level thesis in economics, "A nova classe média brasileira, 1950–1980" (UNICAMP, 1985). For representative samples of the exciting production on working-class history coming out of the University of Campinas in the 1990s and early 2000s, see Claudio Batalha, Fernando Teixeira da Silva, and Alexandre Fortes, eds., *Culturas de classe: Identidade e diversidade na formação do operariado* (Campi-nas, 2004); Elciene Azevedo, Jefferson Cano, Maria Clementina Pereira Cunha, and Sidney Chalhoub, eds., *Trabalhadores na cidade: Cotidiano e cultura no Rio de Janeiro e em São Paulo, séculos XIX e XX* (Campinas, 2009).

Women's history has been the subject of two major edited volumes: Mary Del Priore, ed., *História das mulheres no Brasil* (São Paulo, 1997); and Carla Bassanezi Pinsky and Joana Maria Pedro, eds., *Nova história das mulheres no Brasil* (São Paulo, 2012). The transition from women's history to the history of gender among U.S.-based historians of Brazil was announced in Susan Besse, *Restructuring Patriarchy: The Modernization of Gender Inequality in Brazil, 1914–1940* (Chapel Hill, N.C., 1996), which also glances at upper-class women's consumption, while Caulfield's *In Defense of Honor* represents that transition's completion. James Green, *Beyond Carnival: Male Homosexuality in Twentieth-Century Brazil* (Chicago, 1999), initiated the field of gay history among U.S. scholars of Brazil while capturing a parallel transition from the social-historical con-cern with the experience of previously understudied groups to the cultural-historical turn to gender and sexuality as categories of analysis.

The earliest monographs on the politics and political economy of the Brazilian post-war were the work of scholars in other fields, especially political science, but also eco-nomics, sociology, and even philosophy. See especially the essays in Francisco Weffort, *O populismo na política brasileira*, 3rd ed. (Rio de Janeiro, 1980 [1978]), the earliest of which were first published in the mid-1960s; Caio Navarro de Toledo, *ISEB: Fábrica de ideologias*, 2nd ed. (São Paulo, 1978 [1977]); Maria Victoria de Mesquita Benevides, *O governo Kubitschek: Desenvolvimento econômico e estabilidade política, 1956–1961* (Rio de Janeiro, 1979); Benevides, *A UDN e o udenismo: Ambigüidades do liberalismo brasileiro, 1945–1965* (Rio de Janeiro, 1981); Benevides, *O PTB e o trabalhismo: Partido e sindicato em São Paulo, 1945–1964* (São Paulo, 1989); René Armand Dreiffus, *1964, a conquista do estado: Ação política, poder e golpe de classe*, trans. Else Ribeiro Pires Vieira et al., 6th ed. (Petrópolis, 2006 [1981]); Regina Sampaio, *Adhemar de Barros e o PSP* (São Paulo, 1982); Vera Lúcia Michalany Chaia, *A liderança política de Jânio Quadros, 1947–1990* (Ibitinga, 1991); and, in English, Kathryn Sikkink, *Ideas and Institutions: Developmentalism in Brazil and Argentina* (Ithaca, N.Y., 1991), which contrasts the developmentalist success of the Kubitschek presidency in Brazil with the failure of Arturo Frondizi's in Argentina.

Maria José Trevisan, *50 anos em 5: A Fiesp e o desenvolvimentismo* (Petrópolis, 1986) was one of the first treatments of postwar political economy to emerge from a Brazilian history department. More recently, Courtney Campbell has returned to the subject of Toledo's *ISEB*, in "From Mimicry to Authenticity: The Instituto Superior de Estudos Brasileiros on the Possibility of Brazilian Culture, 1954–1960," *Luso-Brazilian Review* 51, no. 1 (2014): 157–181. Oliver Dinius provides a very fine study of the workings of Brazil's state-led developmentalism and welfare statism (its *desenvolvimentismo* and its *trabalhismo*, respectively), in *Brazil's Steel City: Developmentalism, Strategic Power, and Industrial Relations in Volta Redonda, 1941–1964* (Stanford, Calif., 2011), while Joseph Love casts comparative light on certain of the ideas that made way for and then underlay postwar developmentalism in *Crafting the Third World: Theorizing Underdevelopment in Rumania and Brazil* (Stanford, Calif., 1996). On the industrial development of Brazil's third-most-important city, we have Marshall Eakin, *Tropical Capitalism: The Industrialization of Belo Horizonte, Brazil* (New York, 2001). Postwar politics and the assumptions of earlier social scientists are reexamined by leading historians in *O populismo e sua história: Debate e crítica*, ed. Jorge Ferreira (Rio de Janeiro, 2001), the editor of which went on to publish *O imaginário trabalhista: Getulismo, PTB e cultura política popular, 1945–1964* (Rio de Janeiro, 2005). On the Kubitschek presidency, see also Rafael Ioris, *Transforming Brazil: A History of National Development in the Postwar Era* (New York, 2014).

Something of the cultural history of the postwar through the slide into military dictatorship, together with the cultural effects of the latter, is captured in Heloisa Buarque de Hollanda, *Impressões de viagem: CPC, vanguarda e desbunde, 1960–1970*, 3rd ed. (Rio de Janeiro, 1992 [1980]); and Marcelo Ridenti, *Em busca do povo brasileiro: Artistas da revolução, do CPC à era da TV* (Rio de Janeiro, 2000). In "Cultura e política, 1964–1969: Algumas esquemas" (1970), the literary critic Roberto Schwarz provided an on-the-spot interpretation of the cultural history of the early years of the military dictatorship, published years later in *O pai de família e outros estudos* (Rio de Janeiro, 1978), 61–92, and much cited since. The cultural politics of the years of military rule were the subject of a conference hosted by the University of Maryland to mark the fortieth anniversary of the military coup, two contributions to which were later published alongside two more recent articles on the era of the dictatorship in a special section of the *Hispanic American Historical Review* 92, no. 3 (August 2012): 403–535.

Of the four articles, Bryan McCann's "The View from the Corner Bar: Sérgio Porto's Satirical *Crônicas* and the *Democradura*" (507–535) should be read alongside Cláudia Mesquita's book on Porto's Rio (*Da Copacabana à Boca do Mato*, mentioned earlier), while Benjamin Cowan's "'Why Hasn't This Teacher Been Shot?': Moral-Sexual Panic, the Repressive Right, and Brazil's National Security State" (403–436) previewed his book, *Securing Sex: Morality and Repression in the Making of Cold War Brazil* (Chapel Hill, N.C., 2016). Even more recent—released after this book's chapters were drafted— is Christopher Dunn, *Contracultura: Alternative Arts and Social Transformation in Authoritarian Brazil* (Chapel Hill, N.C., 2016).

The preeminent Brazilian historian of the military regime is Carlos Fico, who offers an overview of the coup d'etat and its aftermath in *O golpe de 64: Momentos decisivos* (Rio de Janeiro, 2014). His "La classe média brésilienne face au régime militaire" (trans. Armelle Enders), *Vingtième Siècle: Revue d'histoire* 105 (2010): 155–168, offers an up-to-date, culturally informed portrait of a group first treated by Waldir José de Quadros in his unpublished doctoral thesis, defended before the economics faculty of the University of Campinas in 1991, "O 'milagre brasileiro' e a expansão da nova class média." Fico's own doctoral thesis, which focuses on the regime's propaganda apparatus, was published as *Reinventando o otimismo: Ditadura, propaganda e imaginário social no Brasil* (Rio de Janeiro, 1997); pro-regime propaganda has since been the subject of Nina Schneider, *Brazilian Propaganda: Legitimizing an Authoritarian Regime* (Gainesville, Fla., 2014). Arena, the pro-regime party organized in 1965, is the subject of Lucia Grinberg, *Partido político ou bode expiatório: Um estudo sobre a Aliança Renovadora Nacional (Arena), 1965–1979* (Rio de Janeiro, 2009). The regime's celebration of the sesquicentennial of Brazilian independence is covered in Janaina Martins Cordeiro, "Lembrar o passado, festejar o presente: As comemorações do sesquicentenário da independência entre consenso e consentimento" (tese de doutorado, UFF, 2012). Another recent Brazilian doctoral thesis, Pedro Henrique Pedreira Campos, "A ditadura dos empreiteiros: As empresas nacionais de construção pesada, suas formas associativas e o estado ditatorial brasileiro, 1964–1985" (UFF, 2012), examines relations between the state and construction firms, powerful groups that emerge in this book for their stake in the supermarketing and malling of Brazilian cities and suburbs.

Relations with the United States are the subject of a sizable if uneven historiography. Moniz Bandeira's *Presença dos Estados Unidos no Brasil: Dois séculos de história* (Rio de Janeiro, 1973) remains the most comprehensive overview. Readers may also want to consult Joseph Smith's *Brazil and the United States: Convergence and Divergence* (Athens, Ga., 2010). Monographs covering particular periods in government-to-government relations include Joseph Smith, *Unequal Giants: Diplomatic Relations between the United States and Brazil, 1889–1930* (Pittsburgh, 1991); Stanley Hilton, *O ditador e o embaixador* (Rio de Janeiro, 1987); Kenneth Callis Lanoue, "An Alliance Shaken: Brazil and the United States, 1945–1950" (PhD diss., Louisiana State University, 1978); Gerald Haines, *The Americanization of Brazil: A Study of U.S. Cold War Diplomacy in the Third World, 1945–1954* (Wilmington, Del., 1989); W. Michael Weis, *Cold Warriors and Coups d'Etat: Brazilian-American Relations, 1945–1964* (Albuquerque, N.Mex., 1993); Carla Simone Rodeghero, *Capítulos da guerra fria: O anticomunismo brasileiro sob o olhar norte-americano, 1945–1964* (Porto Alegre, 2007); Ruth

Leacock, *Requiem for Revolution: The United States and Brazil, 1961–1969* (Kent, Ohio, 1990); Phyllis Parker, *Brazil and the Quiet Intervention, 1964* (Austin, Tex., 1979); Jan Knippers Black, *United States Penetration of Brazil* (Philadelphia, 1977); Carlos Fico, *O grande irmão: Da Operação Brother Sam aos anos de chumbo* (Rio de Janeiro, 2008). Aspects of the World War II–era alliance and the historical moment of which it was a part are treated in Frank McCann, *The Brazilian-American Alliance, 1937–1945* (Princeton, N.J., 1973); Theresa Louis Kraus, "The Establishment of United States Army Air Corps Bases in Brazil, 1938–1945" (PhD diss., Univ. of Maryland, 1986); Antonio Pedro Tota, *O imperialismo sedutor: A americanização do Brasil na época da segunda guerra* (São Paulo, 2000), English ed., *The Seduction of Brazil: The Americanization of Brazil during World War II*, trans. Lorena Ellis (Austin, 2009); Seth Garfield, *In Search of the Amazon: Brazil, the United States, and the Nature of a Region* (Durham, N.C., 2013); Marina Helena Meira Carvalho, "*Right man* com bossa: As representações do Brasil e do *American way of life* nas propagandas comerciais em revistas de variedades brasileiras, 1937–1945" (tese de mestrado, Universidade Federal de Minas Gerais, 2015). On postwar U.S. cultural diplomacy, see Fernando Santomauro, *A atuação política da Agência de Informação dos Estados Unidos no Brasil, 1953–1964* (São Paulo, 2015). Unofficial relations between the two countries feature in Elizabeth Cobbs, *The Rich Neighbor Policy: Rockefeller and Kaiser in Brazil* (New Haven, Conn., 1992); Earl Richard Downes, "The Seeds of Influence: Brazil's 'Essentially Agricultural' Old Republic and the United States, 1910–1930" (PhD diss., University of Texas, 1986), a noteworthy advance upon Victor Valla's "Os Estados Unidos e a influência estrangeira na economia brasileira: Um período de transição, 1904–1928" (tese de mestrado, USP, 1969) and *A penetração norte-americana na economia brasileira, 1898–1928: Sempre de acordo ou nobre emulação?* (Rio de Janeiro, 1978); Isabel Lustosa, *A descoberta da América: O lugar dos EUA no modernismo brasileiro* (Rio de Janeiro, 1995); Micol Seigel, *Uneven Encounters: Making Race and Nation in Brazil and the United States* (Durham, N.C., 2009); Gerson Moura, *Tio Sam chega ao Brasil: A penetração cultural americana* (São Paulo, 1984); Flávia de Sá Pedreira, *Chiclete eu misturo com banana: Carnaval e cotidiano de guerra em Natal, 1920–1945* (Natal, 2005); Cristina Meneguello, *Poeira de estrelas: O cinema hollywoodiano na mídia brasileira nas décadas de 40 e 50* (Campinas, 1996); Júlia Falivene Alves, *A invasão cultural norte-americana* (São Paulo, 1988). See also Antonio Pedro Tota's *O amigo americano: Nelson Rockefeller e o Brasil* (São Paulo, 2014), a subject likewise approached in Gerard Colby and Charlotte Dennett's journalistic doorstopper, *Thy Will be Done: The Conquest of the Amazon; Nelson Rockefeller and Evangelism in the Age of Oil* (New York, 1995).

North American competition with British interests in the 1910s and after is discussed in Emily Rosenberg, "Anglo-American Economic Rivalry in Brazil during World War I," *Diplomatic History* 2, no. 2 (1978): 131–152; Alan Manchester, "Anglo-American Rivalry in Brazil," *World Affairs*, September 1934, 179–182; Manchester, *British Preëminence in Brazil, Its Rise and Decline: A Study in European Expansion* (Chapel Hill, N.C., 1933), chap. 12. Subsequent commercial—and geopolitical—rivalries are outlined in Stanley Hilton, *Brazil and the Great Powers, 1930–1939: The Politics of Trade Rivalry* (Austin, Tex., 1975), which includes an illuminating foreword by the greatest of Brazilian historians of the mid-twentieth century, José Honório Rodrigues. On Britain's earlier commercial hegemony, see, in addition to Manchester's *British Preëminence*,

Richard Graham's Rostowian compendium, *Britain and the Onset of Modernization in Brazil, 1850–1914* (Cambridge, 1968), which remains worthwhile despite its conceptual apparatus, and Gilberto Freyre, *Ingleses no Brasil: Aspectos da influência britânica sobre a vida, a paisagem e a cultura do Brasil* (Rio de Janeiro, 1948), the first volume of a characteristically unfinished series. Graham and Freyre's books go beyond the economic, offering key evidence of the cultural impact of the British presence. On French cultural influence, see Emilia Nogueira, "Alguns aspectos da influência francesa em São Paulo na segunda metade do século XIX," *Revista de História* 16 (1953): 317–342, rev. ed. in Emilia Viotti da Costa, *A dialética invertida e outros ensaios* (São Paulo, 2013), 177–207; Francisco de Assis Barbosa, *Alguns aspectos da influência francesa no Brasil: Notas em torno de Anatole Louis Garraux e da sua livraria em São Paulo* (Rio de Janeiro, 1963); José Murilo de Carvalho, "Da cocotte a Foucault," in *Pontos e bordados: Escritos de história e política* (Belo Horizonte, 1998), 390–395; Laurent Vidal and Tania Regina de Luca, eds., *Franceses no Brasil: Séculos XIX–XX* (São Paulo, 2009). The Canadian utility company that accompanied rather than contested U.S. primacy in Brazil is the subject of Duncan McDowall, *The Light: Brazilian Traction, Light and Power Company Limited, 1899–1945* (Toronto, 1988), drawn upon in the broad-brush business history *Global Electrification: Multinational Enterprise and International Finance in the History of Light and Power, 1878–2007*, by William Hausman, Peter Hertner, and Mira Wilkins (Cambridge, 2008).

Americanism and Consumption, at Home and Abroad

U.S. economic and cultural expansion in interwar Brazil was part of a larger series of outward thrusts, each conditioned by developments at home. If there is a better overview of the domestic scene that served as launch pad for the overseas expansion of the 1920s than William Leuchtenburg's *The Perils of Prosperity, 1914–1932*, 2nd ed. (Chicago, 1993 [1958]), it has eluded me. Aspects of that extrusion, including to Brazil, are treated monographically in Robert Mayer, "The Origins of the American Banking Empire in Latin America: Frank Vanderlip and the National City Bank," *Journal of Interamerican Studies and World Affairs* 15, no. 1 (February 1973): 60–76; Henry Leslie Robinson, "American and Foreign Power Company in Latin America: A Case Study" (PhD diss., Stanford University, 1967); James Schwoch, *The American Radio Industry and Its Latin American Activities, 1900–1939* (Chicago, 1990); Kristin Thompson, *Exporting Entertainment: America in the World Film Market, 1907–1934* (London, 1985). For the policy side of the story, see Joseph Brandes, *Herbert Hoover and Economic Diplomacy: Department of Commerce Policy, 1921–1928* (Pittsburgh, 1962); Burton Kaufman, *Efficiency and Expansion: Foreign Trade Organization in the Wilson Administration, 1913–1921* (Westport, Conn., 1974); Joan Hoff Wilson, *American Business and Foreign Policy, 1920–1933* (Lexington, Ky., 1971). Emily Rosenberg, *Spreading the American Dream: American Economic and Cultural Expansion, 1890–1945* (New York, 1982), represents an early synthesis. A long view of U.S. foreign direct investment may be found in Mira Wilkins's two-volume history, *The Emergence of the Multinational Enterprise: American Business Abroad from the Colonial Era to 1914* and *The Maturing of the Multinational Enterprise: American Business Abroad from 1914 to 1970* (Cambridge, Mass., 1970–1974). For the radical technocratic origins of the idea of "the economy of abundance" decades before its resignification by Brazilian prosperity profession-als, I relied upon Robert Westbrook, "Tribune of the Technostructure: The Popular Economics of Stuart Chase," *American Quarterly* 32, no. 4 (1980): 387–408.

As indicated, the work of William Leach and Jackson Lears introduced me to the historiography on advertising and consumer culture in the United States, for the for-mer of which I also recommend Roland Marchand, *Advertising the American Dream: Making Way for Modernity, 1920–1940* (Berkeley, Calif., 1985) and Pamela Walker Laird, *Advertising Progress: American Business and the Rise of Consumer Marketing* (Baltimore, 1998). On public relations, see Marchand, *Creating the Corporate Soul: The Rise of Public Relations and Corporate Imagery in American Big Business* (Berkeley, Ca-lif., 1998). Leach's *Land of Desire* is only one of an ever-increasing number of books on the rise of what he called "the culture of consumer capitalism"; among the many other excellent books dealing with aspects of the subject are Susan Strasser, *Satisfaction Guaranteed: The Making of the American Mass Market* (Washington, D.C., 1989), Gary Cross, *An All-Consuming Century: Why Commercialism Won in Modern America* (New York, 2000), and Lizabeth Cohen, *A Consumer's Republic: The Politics of Mass Con-sumption in Postwar America* (New York, 2003). No attempt was made to master the larger literature, which looks to become a field unto itself, complete with its own mono-graph series and professional journals. For a pointed overview, inspired in part by Co-hen's *A Consumer's Republic*, see David Steigerwald, "All Hail the Republic of Choice: Consumer History as Contemporary Thought," *Journal of American History* 93, no. 2 (September 2006): 385–403.

Beginning in the 1990s, scholars of twentieth-century consumption and consumer cultures in the United States and Europe established dialogues resulting in two edited volumes: Susan Strasser, Charles McGovern, and Matthias Judt, eds., *Getting and Spending: European and American Consumer Societies in the Twentieth Century* (Cam-bridge, 1998); Martin Daunton and Matthew Hilton, eds., *The Politics of Consump-tion: Material Culture and Citizenship in Europe and America* (Oxford, 2001).

Broader in geographic scope and deeper in temporal span, the Cultures of Consump-tion program directed by Frank Trentmann joined historians with anthropologists, geographers, and others in a five-year collaborative examination of consumption world-wide, producing dozens of books and articles. John Brewer and Frank Trentmann, eds., *Consuming Cultures, Global Perspectives: Historical Trajectories, Transnational Exchanges* (Oxford, 2006), offers a good introduction to the program's work. Part cul-mination, part continuation, Trentmann's *Empire of Things: How We Became a World of Consumers, from the Fifteenth Century to the Twenty-First* (New York, 2016) is a his-torical tour de force—erudite, inspiring, and engagingly written—and a substantial artifact of consumption in its own right. For a more compact introduction to some of the issues animating the book, salutary reminders of the normative charge of the idea of consumerism, and a longer view of the historiography than that found in Steiger-wald's overview (above), see Trentmann, "Crossing Divides: Consumption and Glo-balization in History," *Journal of Consumer Culture* 9, no. 2 (July 2009): 187–220.

At a mid-range between the expansiveness of the Cultures of Consumption program and the relatively narrow U.S.-European collaborations of the 1990s was a German His-torical Institute (GHI)–sponsored workshop that met in Washington in 2008 and produced *Decoding Modern Consumer Societies*, ed. Hartmut Berghoff and Uwe

Spiekermann (New York, 2012), which included contributions from scholars of Japan and Africa, as well as the United States and Germany. An expanded version of my presentation to the GHI workshop was published as "Consumer Culture, Market Empire, and the Global South," *Journal of World History* 23, no. 2 (June 2012): 375–398. As the midsection of its title suggests, the essay formed part of my larger engagement with de Grazia's *Irresistible Empire*.

Commercial and Material Cultures in Brazil

For commercial cultures of the turn of the twentieth century, see Acerbi, *Street Occupations*; Marisa Midori Deaecto, *Comércio e vida urbana na cidade de São Paulo, 1889–1930* (São Paulo, 2002); Heloisa Barbuy, *A cidade-exposição: Comércio e cosmopolitanismo em São Paulo, 1860–1914* (São Paulo, 2006); Milena Fernandes de Oliveira, *O mercado do prestígio: Consumo, capitalismo e modernidade na São Paulo da "Belle Époque"* (São Paulo, 2014); Carina Marcondes Ferreira Pedro, *Casas importadoras de Santos e seus agentes: Comércio e cultura material, 1870–1900* (Cotia, 2015); João Carlos Tedesco, *De olho na balança! Comerciantes coloniais do Rio Grande do Sul na primeira metade do século XX* (Passo Fundo, 2008). To these scholarly works should be added Ernesto Senna's early account of nineteenth-century Carioca commerce, *O velho commercio do Rio de Janeiro* (Rio de Janeiro, n.d.).

Vânia Carneiro de Carvalho, *Gênero e artefato: O sistema doméstico na perspectiva da cultura material (São Paulo, 1870–1920)* (São Paulo, 2008), and João Luís Máximo da Silva, *Cozinha modelo: O impacto do gás e da eletricidade na casa paulistana (1870–1930)* (São Paulo, 2008), are fine studies of aspects of domestic material culture; in some ways, Silva's work provides the back story to my discussion of Brazil's foreign-owned electric-utility monopolies in chapter 2 of this book. On those companies, see also McDowall, *Light*; Ricardo Maranhão, "Estado e capital privado na eletrificação de São Paulo," in *História de empresas e desenvolvimento econômico*, ed. Tamás Szmrecsányi and Ricardo Maranhão, 2nd ed. (São Paulo, 2002 [1996]), 381–408; Judith Tendler, *Electric Power in Brazil: Entrepreneurship in the Public Sector* (Cambridge, Mass., 1968).

The literature on Brazilian automobilism, and especially the automobile industry, is vast. The economist Helen Shapiro's *Engines of Growth: The State and Transnational Auto Companies in Brazil* (Cambridge, 1994) is one of the most thorough studies. Among works by historians, Joel Wolfe's *Autos and Progress: The Brazilian Search for Modernity* (Oxford, 2010) may be read alongside Cobbs, *The Rich Neighbor*, chap. 5; Richard Downes, "Autos over Rails: How US Business Supplanted the British in Brazil, 1910–1928," *Journal of Latin American Studies* 24, no. 3 (October 1992): 551–583 (a revised version of chap. 7 of his previously cited dissertation); Flávio Limoncic, "A civilização do automóvel: A instalação da indústria automobilística no brasil e a via brasileira para uma improvável modernidade fordista, 1956–1961" (tese de mestrado, Universidade Federal do Rio de Janeiro, 1997); Benedicto Heloiz Nascimento, *Formação da indústria automobilística brasileira* (São Paulo, 1976); Marco Sávio, *A cidade e as máquinas: Bondes e automóveis nos primórdios da metrópole paulista, 1900–1930* (São Paulo, 2010). Glauco Arbix and Mauro Zilbovicius's edited volume, *De JK a FHC: A reinvenção dos carros* (São Paulo, 1997), published on the fortieth anniversary of domestic automobile manufacturing, brings together the work of economists (among them Shapiro), sociologists, political scientists, engineers, and the historian Antonio Luigi Negro. Caren Addis's interesting revisionist study *Taking the Wheel: Auto Parts Firms and the Political Economy of Industrialization in Brazil* (University Park, Penn., 1999) touches on a good deal more than the automotive-parts sector strictly defined.

The first publication by a historian of Brazil to consider "consumer culture" at any length was Anna Cristina Camargo Moraes Figueiredo, *"Liberdade é uma calça velha, azul e desbotada": Publicidade, cultura de consumo e comportamento político no Brasil, 1954–1964* (São Paulo, 1998), which examined commercial advertising in weekly magazines in attempting to "understand . . . the elements that made up the imaginary of the urban middle classes in the ten years that preceded the military coup of 1964" (15). More recently, João Manuel Cardoso de Mello and Fernando Novais have provided a panorama of Brazil in the throes of consumerism during the years covered by the later chapters of this book, in "Capitalismo tárdio e sociabilidade moderna," in Schwarcz, *Contrastes da intimidade contemporânea*, 559–658 (see esp. 562–574).

Advertising is discussed in the thesis Maria Arminda do Nascimento Arruda presented to the faculty of the University of São Paulo for a degree in the social sciences in 1979, first published as *A embalagem do sistema: A publicidade no capitalismo brasileiro* (São Paulo, 1983) in the series "História e Sociedade," revised for a second edition (1985), and since reissued (2015). In *A cidade como espetáculo: Publicidade e vida urbana na São Paulo nos anos 20* (São Paulo, 2001), Marcia Padilha takes a less schematic, and somewhat more historical, view of the advertising of the 1920s in São Paulo. The activities of the leading U.S. agency in Brazil during the following decade are the subject of my "Marketing Modernity: The J. Walter Thompson Company and North American Advertising in Brazil, 1929–1939," *Hispanic American Historical Review* 82, no. 2 (May 2002): 257–290, while Patrícia Sunha de Negreiros Lopes, "A agência McCann-Erickson do Brasil: Um estudo sobre a profissionalização do campo publicitário brasileiro (1935–1964)" (tese de mestrado, CPDOC, 2016), takes a longer view of the history of JWT's longtime rival. André Iribure Rodrigues's "MPM Propaganda: A história da agência dos anos de ouro da publicidade brasileira" (tese de mestrado, Universidade Federal do Rio Grande do Sul, 2002), though defended in a department of communications, takes a substantially historical approach to the trajectory of the one major Brazilian agency to emerge outside of the Rio–São Paulo axis. Jaílson Pereira da Silva, *Um Brasil em pílulas de 1 minuto: História e cotidiano em publicidades das décadas de 1960–80* (Recife, 2010), looks at television advertising.

Historical study of advertising's adjacent fields in Brazil is in its infancy. The country's premiere market and public-opinion research firm is the subject of Silvia Rosana Modena Martini's doctoral thesis in sociology, "O IBOPE, a opinião pública e o senso comum dos anos 1950: Hábitos, preferências, comportamentos e valores dos moradores dos grandes centros urbanos (Rio de Janeiro e São Paulo)" (UNICAMP, 2011), which concludes on the basis of IBOPE data that the possession of durable goods became the measure of "development" and well-being during the 1950s as Brazil joined the worldwide making of "the consumer society." Although presented for a business degree, Aylza Munhoz's "Pensamento em marketing no Brasil: Um estudo exploratório" (tese de mestrado, EAESP, 1982) is an essentially historical study of the early development of marketing at the São Paulo School of Business. Sales promotion, public relations, and the rest of the twentieth-century "marketing mix" await monographic treatment.

Over the last decade, Maria Claudia Bonadio has established herself as the leading social and cultural historian of Brazilian fashion. Her *Moda e sociabilidade: Mulheres e consumo na São Paulo dos anos 1920* (São Paulo, 2007) provides an illuminating look not only at women's consumption in São Paulo in the 1920s but on the city's commercial scene more generally. That book was originally her master's thesis, which she followed with "O fio sintético é um show! Moda, política e publicidade. Rhodia S.A. 1960–1970" (tese de doutorado, UNICAMP, 2005), an imaginative, rigorously researched examination of the advertising and publicity efforts sponsored by the Brazilian subsidiary of Rhône-Poulenc to convince Paulistanas and others to wear synthetic fibers. These efforts included Rhodia's participation in AMCE's textile-industry fairs, which I examine in chapter 5, drawing in part on Bonadio's thesis, since expanded into *Moda e publicidade no Brasil nos anos 1960* (São Paulo, 2014). A master's student of Bonadio's, Maíra Zimmermann, has produced *Jovem Guarda: Moda, música e juventude* (São Paulo, 2013), which looks at youth culture, consumption, fashion, and music in the 1960s, since elaborated upon in "Rebeldia pronta para o consumo: A construção da cultura juvenil no Brasil dos anos 1950–1960" (tese de doutorado, UNICAMP, 2016). Bonadio is also the author of an early consideration of that apparently more attractive of the new professions of the Brazilian postwar, modeling: "Dignidade, celibato e bom comportamento: Relatos sobre a profissão de modelo e manequim no Brasil dos anos 1960," *Cadernos Pagu* 22 (2004): 47–81.

The brick-and-mortar of twentieth-century changes in urban space connected with changing commercial regimes is discussed in four theses, one in public history and cultural patrimony, two in architecture and urbanism, and one in geography. See, respectively, Jonas da Silva Abreu, "O papel do cinema na construção da identidade da Cinelândia" (tese de mestrado, CPDOC, 2009), which provides a very fine overview of the making of Cinelândia; Cynthia Augusto Poleto Aleixo, "Edifícios e galerias comerciais: Arquitetura e comércio na cidade de São Paulo, anos 50 e 60" (tese de mestrado, USP, 2005), chap. 4, on the development of commercial *galerias* in São Paulo's "new" downtown; Demósthenes Magno Santos, "A história da Construtora Alfredo Mathias, 1950–1985" (tese de mestrado, USP, 2013), on the life's work of the developer whose most lastingly famous work is Shopping Center Iguatemi; and Charles Albert de Andrade, "Shopping center também tem memória: Uma história esquecida dos shoppings nos espaços intra-urbanos do Rio de Janeiro e São Paulo nos anos 60 e 70" (tese de mestrado, UFF, 2009), which, despite its title, focuses on Rio's early experiments in shopping-center planning and construction, undoubtedly a "forgotten history." Architecture also figures prominently in Albertina Mirtes de Freitas Pontes, *A cidade dos clubes: Modernidade e "glamour" na Fortaleza de 1950–1970* (Fortaleza, 2005), originally a thesis presented at the department of history at the Universidade Federal de Ceará.

Artistic portrayals of the new culture of consumption have not yet occupied the attention of historians, with the notable exceptions of Rosangela Patriota and her students at the Universidade Federal de Uberlândia (UFU), who have contributed several key monographs on the work of Oduvaldo Vianna Filho, considered briefly in this book's chapter 6. See especially Patriota, *Vianinha: Um dramaturgo no coração do seu tempo* (São Paulo, 1999); Patriota, ed., *A crítica de um teatro crítico* (São Paulo, 2007); Sandra Rodart Araújo, "*Corpo a corpo* (1970) de Oduvaldo Vianna Filho: Do texto dramático à encenação do Grupo Tapa de São Paulo (1995)" (tese de mestrado, UFU, 2006); Amanda Maíra Steinbach, "'Olhar nos olhas da tragédia': A ressignificação de *Medeia* por Oduvaldo Vianna Filho" (tese de mestrado, UFU, 2012). On Vianna Filho, see also Maria Silvia Betti, *Oduvaldo Vianna Filho* (São Paulo, 1997); Carmelinda Guimarães, *Um ato de resistência: O teatro de Oduvaldo Vianna Filho* (São Paulo, 1984); Dênis de Moraes, *Vianinha: Cúmplice da paixão* (Rio de Janeiro, 1991); Leslie Hawkins Damasceno, *Cultural Space and Theatrical Conventions in the Works of Oduvaldo Vianna Filho* (Detroit, 1996). The career of Vianna Filho's father and namesake receive historical treatment in Flavia Veras, "As conexões teatrais entre Rio de Janeiro, São Paulo e Buenos Aires através do trabalho de Oduvaldo Vianna (1923–1946)," a paper drawn from the research for her "'Fábricas da alegria': o mercado de diversões e a organização do trabalho artístico no Rio de Janeiro e em Buenos Aires (1918–1945)" (tese de doutorado, CPDOC, 2017). Another playwright featuring in this book's sixth chapter, Carlos Queiroz Telles, is the subject of Marco Antônio Guerra, *Carlos Queiroz Telles: História e dramaturgia em cena, década de 70* (São Paulo, 1993). In contextualizing Vianna Filho and Telles's work within twentieth-century Brazilian theater, I was assisted by Jacó Guinsberg and Rosangela Patriota's book of essays, *Teatro brasileiro: Ideias de uma história* (São Paulo, 2012).

The Press, Cinema, Radio, and Television in Brazil

On the press, Nelson Werneck Sodré, *História da imprensa no Brasil*, 4th ed. (Rio de Janeiro, 1999 [1966]), remains the essential starting point. On São Paulo, see also Freitas Nobre, *História da imprensa de São Paulo* (São Paulo, 1950); Paulo Duarte, *História da imprensa em São Paulo* (São Paulo, 1972); Heloisa de Faria Cruz, ed., *São Paulo em revista* (São Paulo, 1997); and my "Pages from a Yellow Press: Print Culture, Public Life, and Political Genealogies in Modern Brazil," *Journal of Latin American Studies* 46, no. 2 (May 2014): 353–379.

On the 1950s, see Alzira Alves de Abreu, "Revisitando os anos 1950 através da imprensa," in *O moderno em questão*, ed. Botelho, Bastos, and Villas Bôas, 211–235; Alzira Alves de Abreu, Fernando Lattman-Weltman, Marieta de Moraes Ferreira, and Plínio de Abreu Ramos, *A imprensa em transição: O jornalismo brasileiro nos anos 50* (Rio de Janeiro, 1996); Anna Paulo Goulart Ribeiro, "Jornalismo, literatura e política: A modernização da imprensa carioca nos anos 1950," *Estudos Históricos* 31 (2003): 147–160; Ribeiro, "Modernização e concentração: A imprensa carioca nos anos 1950–1970," in *História e imprensa: Representações culturais e práticas de poder*, ed. Lúcia Maria Bastos Neves, Marco Morel, and Tania Maria Bessone Ferreira (Rio de Janeiro, 2006), 426–435. Alzira Alves de Abreu, *A modernização da imprensa, 1970–2000* (Rio de Janeiro, 2002), its title notwithstanding, takes the 1950s as the starting point for a quick overview of changes in the press over the last fifty years. An essay, rather than a work of history, Carlos Eduardo Lins da Silva, *O adiantado da hora: A influência americana sobre o jornalismo brasileiro* (São Paulo, 1991), provides a journalist's perspective on changes in the twentieth-century press, including but not limited to the "American influence" of its title.

On *O Globo*, there is the semiofficial portrait of its owner by the in-house journalist Pedro Bial, *Roberto Marinho* (Rio de Janeiro, 2004); for *O Estado de S. Paulo*, Maria

Helena Rolim Capelato and Maria Lígia Prado, *O bravo matutino: Imprensa e ideologia no jornal O Estado de S. Paulo* (São Paulo, 1980). For the *Folhas*, we have Carlos Guilherme Mota and Maria Helena Capelato, *História da Folha de S. Paulo, 1921–1981* (São Paulo, 1981), as well as Engel Paschoal's biography of its leading figure from the 1960s onward, *A trajetória de Octavio Frias de Oliveira*, 2nd ed. (São Paulo, 2007 [2006]).

On the Diários Associados, see the biography of its founder, Fernando Morais, *Chatô: O rei do Brasil* (São Paulo, 1994), a "bestseller" in Brazil on which I have relied, as well as the conglomerate's official history, by the journalist Glauco Carneiro, *Brasil, primeiro: História dos Diários Associados* (Brasília, 1999). In 1931, the Diários Associados absorbed Brazil's oldest continuously published newspaper; its hundred-and-fifty-year history is covered in Arnoldo Jambo, *"Diario de Pernambuco": História e jornal de quinze décadas* (Recife, 1975). On *Diretrizes* and *Ultima Hora*, see the posthumously published memoir of Samuel Wainer, *Minha razão de viver: Memórias de um repórter*, ed. Augusto Nunes (Rio de Janeiro, 1987). Wainer's *Ultima Hora*–era experiment in magazine publishing is discussed in Jefferson José Queler, "Do consumidor de mercadorias ao leitor de jornal: Peculiaridades da indústria cultura nas páginas do semanário *Flan* (1953–1954)," *Topoi* 26 (January–July 2013): 105–118.

For *Seleções*, we have Mary Anne Junqueira, *Ao sul do Rio Grande: Imaginando a América Latina em "Seleções"; Oeste, wilderness e fronteira, 1942–1970* (Bragança Paulista, 2000), and Silvio Luiz Gonçalves Pereira, "*Seleções do Reader's Digest, 1954–1965: Um mapa da intolerância política*" (tese de doutorado, USP, 2006). For *Manchete* and the Bloch organization's other publications, see the family history, by one of Adolpho Bloch's nephews, Arnaldo Bloch, *Os irmãos Karamabloch: Ascensão e queda de um império familiar* (São Paulo, 2008), as well as José Esmeraldo Gonçalves and J. A. Barros, eds., *Aconteçeu na "Manchete": As histórias que ninguém contou* (Rio de Janeiro, 2008). On *Manchete* and the Kubitschek presidency, there is Pedro Augusto Gomes Santos, *A classe média vai ao paraíso: JK em "Manchete"* (Porto Alegre, 2002). On magazines generally, see Maria Celeste Mira, *O leitor e a banca de revista: A segmentação da cultura no século XX* (São Paulo, 2001).

On women's magazines, Tania Regina de Luca provides an excellent overview and, in her notes and bibliography, a guide to the specialist literature, in "Mulher em revista," in Pinsky and Pedro, *Nova história das mulheres no Brasil*, 447–68. Chronologically more limited, but no less worthwhile, is the monograph by Carla Beozzo Bassanezi, *Virando as páginas, revendo as mulheres: Revistas femininas e relações homem-mulher, 1945–1964* (Rio de Janeiro, 1996). Originally a master's thesis in history, Ana Rita Fonteles Duarte, *Carmem da Silva: O feminismo na imprensa brasileira* (Fortaleza, 2005), considers the career of *Claudia*'s most important columnist.

Radio has become an important topic among historians of Brazil. Together with McCann's *Hello, Hello Brazil*, see Lia Calabre de Azevedo, "No tempo do rádio: Radiodifusão e cotidiano no Brasil, 1923–1960" (tese de doutorado, UFF, 2002); Lia Calabre, *O rádio na sintonia do tempo: Radionovelas e cotidiano, 1940–1946* (Rio de Janeiro, 2006); Geni Rosa Duarte, "Sons de São Paulo: A atividade radiofônica paulista nos anos 1930/40," *Revista de História Regional* 8, no. 2 (2003): 9–47; Alcir Lenharo, *Cantores do rádio: A trajetória de Nora Ney e Jorge Goulart e o meio artístico de seu tempo* (Campinas, 1995); Antonio Pedro Tota, *A locomotiva no ar: Rádio e modernidade em São Paulo, 1924–1934* (São Paulo, 1990).

Rádio Nacional has been the subject of several books, including Miriam Gold-feder, *Por trás das ondas da Rádio Nacional* (Rio de Janeiro, 1981), originally a master's thesis in communication; Claudia Pinheiro, ed., *A Rádio Nacional: Alguns dos momentos que contribuíram para o sucesso da Rádio Nacional* (Rio de Janeiro, 2005); Luiz Carlos Saroldi and Sonia Virgínia Moreira, *Rádio Nacional, o Brasil em sintonia* (Rio de Janeiro, 1984). On radionovelas, in addition to Lia Calabre's book cited earlier, see Zenilda Poci Banks Leite Belli's master's thesis in communications, "Radionovela: Análise comparativa da radiodifusão na década de 40" (USP, dated 1980, defended 1981).

On radio and television, see Maria Elvira Bonavita Federico, *História da comunicação: Rádio e TV no Brasil* (Petrópolis, 1982), and especially Amara Rocha, *Nas ondas da modernização: O rádio e a TV no Brasil de 1950 a 1970* (Rio de Janeiro, 2007), a historian's advance on earlier communications-studies approaches. On television alone, Inimá Ferreira Simões, Alcir Henrique da Costa, and Maria Rita Kehl, *Um país no ar: História da TV brasileira em três canais* (São Paulo, 1986), provides histories of the Tupi and Globo networks, as well as of TV-Rio and TV-Excelsior. For Globo, see also Kehl, "Um só povo, uma só cabeça, uma só nação," in *Anos 70*, 7 vols., ed. Adauto Novaes and Jorge Ferreira (Rio de Janeiro, 1979–1980), 5:5–29. On telenovelas: Renato Ortiz, Silvia Helena Simões Borelli, and José Mário Ortiz Ramos, *Telenovela: História e produção* (São Paulo, 1989); together with Kehl's "Três ensaios sobre a telenovela," in Simões, Costa, and Kehl, *Um país no ar*, 277–323, and "As novelas, novelinhas e novelões: Mil e uma noites para as multidões," in *Anos 70*, ed. Novaes and Ferreira, 5:49–73. On theater, television, and their interconnections in postwar São Paulo, see David José Lessa Mattos, *O espetáculo da cultura paulista: Teatro e televisão em São Paulo, décadas de 1940 e 1950* (São Paulo, 2002), which combines scholarship and participant history: an earlier version of the book was a doctoral thesis in history, but it is also colored by Mattos's experience as a child television actor in São Paulo beginning in 1954. Sergio Miceli, *A noite da madrinha* (São Paulo, 1972), an early sociological study of Brazilian television, should be read alongside Luiz Augusto Milanesi's quasi-ethnographic study, *O paraíso via Embratel: O processo de integração de uma cidade do interior paulista na sociedade de consumo* (Rio de Janeiro, 1978), as well as Maria Celeste Mira, *Circo eletrônico: Sílvio Santos e o SBT* (São Paulo, 1994). In *A televisão no Brasil: 50 anos de história, 1950–2000* (Salvador, 2000), the communications scholar Sérgio Mattos provides a wide-ranging overview of the larger literature on television (177–251), including his own voluminous production, much of which is available in English. Also in English, and pioneering in their day, are the works of Mattos's communication-studies colleague, Joseph Dean Straubhaar, which are glossed in Straubhaar, "Mass Communication and the Elites," in *Modern Brazil: Elites and Masses in Historical Perspective*, ed. Michael Conniff and Frank McCann (Lincoln, Neb., 1989), 225–245.

Brazilian historians have considered the cinema, including in Sheila Schvarzman, "Ir ao cinema em São Paulo nos anos 20," *Revista Brasileira de História* 49 (2005): 153–174, and Sérgio Augusto, *Este mundo é um pandeiro: A chanchada de Getúlio a JK* (São Paulo, 1989). This interest is yet to be matched by U.S.-based historians of Brazil, at least not in print, though we look forward to the contributions of Paula Halperín, an Argentine historian who presented her PhD dissertation, "Modernization and Visual Economy: Film, Photojournalism, and the Public Sphere in Brazil and Argentina, 1955–

1980," to the history faculty of the University of Maryland in 2010. Books on Brazil by scholars working in English in the field of cinema studies include Randal Johnson, *The Film Industry in Brazil: Culture and the State* (Pittsburgh, 1987), and Robert Stam, *Tropical Multiculturalism: A Comparative History of Race in Brazilian Cinema and Culture* (Durham, N.C., 1997).

Finally, any discussion of cinema, the press, radio, and especially television in Brazil must acknowledge the sociologist Renato Ortiz's work on mass culture and the culture industry. Our periodization and points of emphasis differ, but I recommend Ortiz's *A moderna tradição brasileira*, 5th ed. (São Paulo, 1994 [1988]), as an essential reference on these issues, and on modern Brazil more generally. Among Ortiz's many other books are a nicely written memoir, *Trajetos e memórias* (São Paulo, 2010), which unfortunately does not cover his turn to mass culture and the culture industry as areas of professional interest, as opposed to an obvious feature of life in the urban southeast when he returned to Brazil from Europe in the mid-1970s.

Official Histories

In the early 1990s, the Brazilian government formalized regulations allowing private interests to offset their tax bills by spending equivalent sums on "culture." One result of this initiative—referred to universally in Brazil as the Rouanet Law—was a surge in publication of commemorative, coffee-table histories, distributed free of charge to clients, friends, and perhaps a library or two. The intellectual quality of these volumes has been, for obvious reasons, uneven: some texts are carefully researched, some not, the same going for similar books published under earlier fiscal artifices or motivated by more purely promotional interests. Indeed, Julieta de Godoy Ladeira, who was involved in the production of similar tomes before passage of the Rouanet Law, was led to ask, "But if, on the one hand, this initiative can be called cultural—up to what point can it be?"

On this matter, as in much else, Julieta Ladeira was probably right. However, given the anemic state of Brazilian business history, and the fact that exceedingly few firms permit independent researchers access to their archives, Rouanet Law volumes and books like them often constitute the most complete public record of important businesses and lines of business. Lavishly illustrated, often with reproductions of otherwise unavailable documentation, they offer iconographic and archival glimpses unavailable anywhere else. For these reasons, I have drawn on this body of work in the writing of this book and in the broader reading that informed it, painfully aware that I was using contemporary promotional materials to write a critical history of the cultural—and promotional—work involved in raising of the edifice of Brazilian consumer capitalism.

Particular firms are considered in *General Motors do Brasil: 70 anos de história* (São Paulo, 1995); Zuleika Alvim and Solange Peirão, *Mappin: Setenta anos* (São Paulo, 1985); Humberto Werneck, *Gessy Lever: História e histórias de intimidade com o consumidor brasileiro* (São Paulo, 2001); Fernando Morais, *Souza Cruz 100 anos: Um século de qualidade* (São Paulo, 2003); Fernando Garcia, ed., *Anos depois: A vida econômica de Souza Cruz em 102 anos* (São Paulo, 2005); *O futuro sem fronteiras: A história dos primeiros 50 anos da Brasmotor* (São Paulo, 1996); Glauco Carneiro,

J. Macedo: Uma saga empresarial brasileira (São Paulo, 1989); Elias Awad, *Samuel Klein e Casas Bahia: Uma trajetória de sucesso* (Osasco, 2003); Helena Tassara, *Perdigão: Uma trajetória para o futuro* (São Paulo, 1996); Célia de Assis, ed., *A história da Tigre: A força e o valor de uma marca* (São Paulo, 1997); Assis, ed., *Uma história de realizações: Empresas Petróleo Ipiranga 60 anos* (São Paulo, 1997).

Commerce, as a subject, is most often considered in Rouanet Law–type books on local and regional associational bodies, for example: Herculano Gomes Mathias, *Comércio: 173 anos de desenvolvimento; História da Associação Comercial do Rio de Janeiro, 1820–1993* (Rio de Janeiro, 1993); *História da Federação do Comércio do estado de São Paulo: Fecomercio, 70 anos, 1938–2008* (São Paulo, 2008); Lígia Maria Leite Pereira, *Associação Comercial de Minas, 1901–2001: Uma história de pioneirismo e desenvolvimento* (Belo Horizonte, 2001); Angelina Nobre Rolim Garcez, *Associação Comercial da Bahia, 175 anos: Trajetória e perspectivas* (Rio de Janeiro, 1987); Fernanda Cristina Scalvi, ed., *Uma história de crédito: 50 anos do SCPC* (São Paulo, 2006).

Some such productions, however, take on the subject of commerce generally. For perspectives that purport to be national, see Mario de Almeida, *O comércio no Brasil: Iluminando a memória* (Rio de Janeiro, 1995); Arthur Bosisio Júnior, *O Comércio e suas profissões: Imagens, Brasil, 1500–1946* (Rio de Janeiro, 1983); and, on retail specifically, Ignácio de Loyola Brandão, *Memórias do varejo no Brasil: Uma abordagem cultural através do tempo* (São Paulo, 2015), which the author of *Bebel* wrote on behalf of the French super- and hypermarket giant Carrefour under the Rouanet Law's auspices. On Rio, see José Carlos Cabral and Karen Worcman, eds., *Um balcão na capital: Memórias do comércio na cidade do Rio de Janeiro* (Rio de Janeiro, 2003); and João Máximo, *Cinelândia: Breve história de um sonho* (Rio de Janeiro, 1997), a Rouanet volume on Francisco Serrador's most lasting legacy. For São Paulo: Beatriz Piccolotto Siqueira Bueno, *São Paulo, um novo olhar sobre a história: A evolução do comércio de varejo e as transformações da vida urbana* (São Paulo, 2012), which includes invaluable storefront-by-storefront mappings of Paulistano commerce at key moments; Antonio Hélio Junqueira, *100 anos de feiras livres na cidade de São Paulo = 100 Years of Street Markets in the City of São Paulo* (São Paulo, 2015); Mauro Malin, *Memórias do comércio* (São Paulo, 1995), which includes consideration of the commerce of the cities of the Paulista interior, the subject of Julio Dias Gaspar and Silvana Issa Afram, *Memórias do comércio. Os caminhos do interior: Araraquara, São Carlos e região* (São Paulo, 2000), the first volume in a spin-off series. On the capital of Minas Gerais, there is the nicely done *Belo Horizonte & o comércio: 100 anos de história* (Belo Horizonte, 1997); on Salvador, Jafé Borges and Glácia Lemos, *Comércio baiano: Depoimentos para sua história* (Salvador, 2002). Finally, on the capital of Paraná, there is Maria de Lourdes M. Chaves, *Voltando ao passado: Histórico de determinadas indústrias e casas comerciais de Curitiba* (Curitiba, 1995).

For reasons that should be clear, advertising has been the subject and purpose of more than its share of promotional histories, including: *100 anos de propaganda* (São Paulo, 1980); Nelson Varón Cadena, *25 anos da melhor propaganda brasileira* (São Paulo, 1992); Cadena, *450 anos de propaganda na Bahia* (exhibition catalogue, Salvador [1998?]); Cadena, *Brasil: 100 anos de propaganda* (São Paulo, 2001). On the ubiquitous market-research firm, there is Silvana Gontijo, *A voz do povo: O Ibope do Brasil* ([Rio?], 1996). The major sales promotion and marketing association, Associação de Dirigen-

tes de Vendas e Marketing do Brasil (known as the Associação dos Diretores de Vendas do Brasil at its founding) published its own institutional history: *50 anos em
evolução com o Brasil* (São Paulo, 2006). Marketing and the most beloved of sports are
the subject of *70 anos de seleção: O marketing no futebol* (Rio de Janeiro, 1984).

In 2011, the Casas Pernambucanas retail concern sponsored the publication of a history of Brazilian fashion, João Braga and Luis André do Prado, *História da moda no
Brasil: Das influências às autoreferências* (São Paulo, 2011), which updates Silvana Gontijo, *80 anos de moda no Brasil* (Rio de Janeiro, 1987), including by considering menswear as well as women's fashion. For fashion on Rio's beaches, see Marcia Disitzer, *Um
mergulho no Rio: 100 anos de moda e comportamento na praia carioca* (Rio de Janeiro,
2012).

Brazilian supermarketing has received the Rouanet treatment not once but twice,
in *40 anos de supermercados no Brasil* (São Paulo, 1993) and *Cincoenta anos de supermercados* (São Paulo, 2002), while the Ponto Frio home-appliances chain sponsored the
publication of Cláudio Lamas de Farias, Eduardo Ayrosa, Gabriel Carvalho, and José
Abramovitz, *Eletrodomésticos: Origens, história e design no Brasil*, ed. Silvia Fraiha.
(Rio de Janeiro, 2006). Packaging is the subject of Pedro Cavalcanti and Carmo Cha-
gas, *História da embalagem no Brasil* (São Paulo, 2006). Aspects of telecommunications are treated in Henry British Lins de Barros, ed., *História da indústria de
telecomunicações no Brasil* (Rio de Janeiro, 1989), sponsored by Xerox.

Further Afield

U.S.-based historians of Brazil are expected also to be expert in the history of Spanish
America; in my case, an interest in the history of Brazilian consumerism was developed in dialogue with work on North American market culture in Cuba. These expectations and inspiration have led to fruitful reading in the Latin American
historiography through the formulation, research, and writing of this work. Students
who would like an introduction to twentieth-century changes in material culture in
the region, including evidence of individual countries' experiences of twentieth-
century consumerism, should start with Arnold Bauer, *Goods, Power, History: Latin
America's Material Culture* (Cambridge, 2001), chaps. 5–7. Bauer was also a contributor to Benjamin Orlove's valuable edited collection, *The Allure of the Foreign: Imported
Goods in Postcolonial Latin America* (Ann Arbor, Mich., 1997). The diffusion through
Latin America of the most characteristic of twentieth-century goods is treated in Guill-
ermo Giucci, *The Cultural Life of the Automobile: Roads to Modernity*, trans. Anne
Mayagoitia and Debra Nagao (Austin,Tex., 2012). In "The Products of Consumption:
Housework in Latin American Political Economies and Cultures," *History Compass* 6,
no. 1 (2008): 207–242, Marie Eileen Francois provides an interesting, centuries-long
overview of domestic labor in the region and its place in the production of tangible and
intangible goods. Thomas O'Brien, *The Revolutionary Mission: American Enterprise
in Latin America, 1900–1945* (Cambridge, 1996), examines attempts by U.S. corporations to impose distinct patterns of labor, habitation, leisure, and consumption in
mostly enclave areas of Spanish America. O'Brien's sequel, the synthesis *The Century
of U.S. Capitalism in Latin America* (Albuquerque, N.Mex., 1999), includes discussion
of Brazil as well as other areas of extra-enclave influence in Latin America. Catherine

LeGrand directs readers' attention to the dynamism and connectedness masked by the "enclave" label in an important essay published in a late twentieth-century state-of-the-field on inter-American cultural history in the United States ("Living in Macondo: Economy and Culture in a United Fruit Company Banana Enclave in Colombia," in *Close Encounters of Empire: Writing the Cultural History of U.S.-Latin American Relations*, ed. Gilbert Joseph, Catherine LeGrand, and Ricardo Salvatore [Durham, N.C., 1998], 333–368). Among LeGrand's co-contributors was William Roseberry, earlier the author of an outline essaying what a more comprehensive, sophisticated inter-American history might look like, which I have found inspiring at points: "Americanization in the Americas," in Roseberry, *Anthropologies and Histories: Essays in Culture, History, and Political Economy* (New Brunswick, N.J., 1989), 80–121. For more recent perspectives from Latin America, see María Barbero and Andrés Regalsky, eds., *Americanización: Estados Unidos y América Latina en el siglo XX; Tranferencias económicas, tecnológicas y culturales* (Sáenz Peña, 2014), which features Spanish- and Portuguese-language essays on problems related to "Americanization" in Latin America, as well as overviews of the larger literature on the subject in other geographical contexts.

Of the individual Spanish American countries, Argentina has inspired the largest historical literature related to consumption, its promotion, and the emergence of consumer capitalism. Fernando Rocchi, "La americanización del consumo: Las batallas por el mercado argentino, 1920–1945," in Barbero and Regalsky, eds., *Americanización*, 150–216, goes well beyond the issue of "Americanization" to present a panorama of changes in consumption and its promotion over a crucial quarter-century in Argentina's history. For the Argentine activities of the J. Walter Thompson advertising agency during the 1920s and 1930s, see Ricardo Salvatore, "Yankee Advertising in Buenos Aires," *Interventions: The International Journal of Postcolonial Studies* 7, no. 2 (2005): 216–235, and Jennifer Scanlon, "Mediators in the International Marketplace: U.S. Advertising in Latin America in the Early Twentieth Century," *Business History Review* 77, no. 3 (2003): 387–415 (title notwithstanding, Scanlon's article, like Salvatore's, focuses on JWT in Argentina). Matthew Karush, *Culture of Class: Radio and Cinema in the Making of a Divided Argentina, 1920–1946* (Durham, N.C., 2012), makes a convincing case for the role of Argentine mass culture during the same quarter-century glossed in Rocchi's essay—fully commercial and in dialogue with U.S. cultural exports—in enabling the antielitist, nationalist, and redistributionist political culture associated with the "populism" of Juan and Eva Perón in the 1940s and after. The history of consumption under their new regime is explored in Eduardo Elena, *Dignifying Argentina: Peronism, Citizenship, and Mass Consumption* (Pittsburgh, 2011), and Natalia Milanesio, *Workers Go Shopping in Argentina: The Rise of Popular Consumer Culture* (Albuquerque, N.Mex., 2013). Youth culture, including consumption, in the period after the Peronist golden age has been explored movingly by Valeria Manzano. See her "The Blue Jean Generation: Youth, Gender, and Sexuality in Buenos Aires, 1958–1975," *Journal of Social History* 42, no. 3 (2009): 657–676, and *The Age of Youth in Argentina: Culture, Politics, and Sexuality from Perón to Videla* (Chapel Hill, N.C., 2014). The parallel story of Brazilian "youth"—a story skirted in this book—awaits a historian of Manzano's range, though Maíra Zimmermann (above) has composed some important chapters. Laura Podalsky's *Specular City: Transforming Culture, Consumption, and Space in Buenos Aires, 1955–1973* (Philadelphia, 2004), a conceptually and thematically busy "cultural studies project" (xii), pushes through the earlier insight of Adolfo Prieto that the essential starting point for understanding the Argentine 1960s was the coming of consumerism, if in nationally attenuated form ("Los años sesenta," *Revista Iberoamericana* 125 [October–December 1983]: 889–901).

Cuba's tangled experience of U.S. material and market culture is treated in Pérez's *On Becoming Cuban*; in Joshua Nadel, "Importing Modernity: Commerce and Consumer Culture in Rural Cuba," *SECOLAS Annals* 37 (2005): 121–144, which makes the well-founded point that the "Cuban experience of [consumer-oriented] modernity, if filtered through the United States experience, was nevertheless contemporaneous with it"; and in Marial Iglesias Utset, *A Cultural History of Cuba during the U.S. Occupation, 1898–1902*, trans. Russ Davidson (Chapel Hill, N.C., 2011). More recently, on television in Cuba—where, as in Brazil, it was born commercial, along U.S. lines—we have Yeidy Rivero, *Broadcasting Modernity: Cuban Commercial Television, 1950–1960* (Durham, N.C., 2015).

For Mexico, elements of consumption and a "consumer culture" of sorts—or, more precisely, of sorts of consumer cultures—at the turn of the twentieth century are explored in Steven Bunker, *Creating Mexican Consumer Culture in the Age of Porfirio Díaz* (Albuquerque, N.Mex., 2012). In *Mexico at the World's Fairs: Crafting a Modern Nation* (Berkeley, Calif., 1996), Mauricio Tenorio-Trillo unpacks nationalism and modernity, and not only in Mexico, providing a short account of Brazil's Centennial Exposition of 1922 along the way (chap. 12), before Mexico's "becoming more urban, industrial, consumerist, and relatively literate than ever before" (252). The activities of the J. Walter Thompson and Sears, Roebuck companies in midcentury Mexico are discussed in Julio Moreno, *Yankee Don't Go Home! Mexican Nationalism, American Business Culture, and the Shaping of Modern Mexico, 1920–1950* (Chapel Hill, N.C., 2003). Mexico's shared border with the United States was the prompt for *Land of Necessity: Consumer Culture in the United States-Mexico Borderlands*, ed. Alexis McCrossen (Durham, N.C., 2009).

An earlier Mexican-themed collection, Gilbert Joseph and Daniel Nugent's *Everyday Forms of State Formation: Revolution and the Negotiation of Rule in Modern Mexico* (Durham, N.C., 1994), was an important part of my scholarly salad days, as it was for many if not most of this country's mid-1990s initiates into the study of Latin American history. Of the chapters in *Everyday Forms* that were based on original research, only one, by Armando Bartra—a true odd man out, who took Mexican *historietas* (comics) as his starting point—looked at issues related to market culture. The remainder examined rural politics, some of them brilliantly, in attempting to explain the making of Mexico's "great arch"—a term the editors drew from Philip Corrigan and Derek Sayer's *The Great Arch: English State Formation as Cultural Revolution* (Oxford, 1984), in which E. P. Thompson's metaphor for bourgeois revolution and bourgeois culture in Britain was drained of nearly all its color and life (cf. Thompson, "The Peculiarities of the English," *Socialist Register* 2 [1965]: 311–362). My own work, in part, aims to show that the development of Brazil's culture of consumer capitalism, over a period of fifty-odd years across the twentieth century, was something like its "great arch," its "cultural revolution," the cumulative, connected, constitutive result of the efforts of retail magnates and supermarket managers, artists and architects, advice columnists and advertising executives, assisted by representatives of the U.S. government at an early stage, later by Brazilian mayors and governors, presidents and ministers, whose efforts built a cultural edifice still with us today.

Indeed, I would argue not only that Thompson's metaphor fits this project better than its grafting onto episodes in Mexican rural history or a fancifully linear account of English state-making, but that it is in the developments described in this book, rather than the conceptual dead ends of "populism" or "nationalism" (of which the contributors to *Everyday Forms* and the co-authors of *The Great Arch* were mostly innocent), that we find the necessary framework within which hegemonic processes emerge, in Brazil and elsewhere in Latin America, by the varied heirs to Thompson's peculiar bourgeoisie, while recognizing that the influence of U.S. market culture also produced outcomes entirely opposite, as in Cuba. For Mexico, we may cite Alan Knight arguing, at around the same time that copies of *The Great Arch* reached readers: "Meanwhile, [in the 1930s, 1940s, and after,] the regime built roads and distributed radios, and in doing so undoubtedly strengthened national integration and national markets. But the roads and the radio brought a different culture: Americanized, consumerist, aural (and later visual) rather than oral and written—yet still strongly Catholic. Over time, this new 'Great Tradition' . . . established itself" ("Popular Culture and the Revolutionary State in Mexico, 1910–1940," *Hispanic American Historical Review* 74 no. 3 [August 1994]: 393–444 [quote, 443]). In Brazil, the same occurred, and in both cases there was a great deal more to it, encapsulated not quite adequately in Knight's allusive "resourcefulness of the market" (the final words of his "Popular Culture and the Revolutionary State").

Loose Ends

Readers will have noted my quoting from memoirs by leading figures in advertising, retailing, and the broadcast media, the publication information for which may be found in the notes. Some of the authors of these works also contributed to the *História da propaganda no Brasil*, ed. Renato Castelo Branco, Rodolfo Lima Martensen, and Fernando Reis (São Paulo, 1990), the chapters of which veer between chronicle, memoir, and participant history. Erazê Martinho's *Carlito Maia, a irreverência equilibrista* (São Paulo, 2003) is as much a memoir as a biography of an unrepresentative advertising professional, as well as an entertaining read.

On print journalism, although these works are quoted less often, I found a number of memoirs to be useful in getting a personal sense of the changes outlined in the historical scholarship. Future historians interested in the topic will want to examine the ones by Cláudio Abramo, Vivaldo Coaracy, Guilherme Figueiredo, Paulo Francis, Hermes Lima, Edmar Morel, Cunha Motta, Herberto Sales, and Samuel Wainer (cited in the notes) and the following volumes, while keeping their eyes open for memoirs that may have eluded me: Martins Alonso, *Ao longo do caminho: Memórias* (Rio de Janeiro, 1976); Tito Batini, *Memórias de um socialista congênito* (Campinas, 1991); Ernani Silva Bruno, *Almanaque de memórias: Reminiscências, depoimentos, reflexões* (São Paulo, 1986); Carvalho Netto, *Norte oito quatro* (Rio de Janeiro, 1977); Licurgo Costa, *Licurgo Costa: Um homem de três séculos (memórias)* (Florianópolis, 2002); Paulo Duarte, *Memórias*, 10 vols. (São Paulo, 1974–1980 [vol. 10 published in Rio]); Geraldo Ferraz, *Depois de tudo* (Rio de Janeiro, 1983); Mario Hora, *48 anos de jornalismo: Memórias de um "dromedário"* (Rio de Janeiro, 1959); Heitor Ferreira Lima, *Caminhos percorridos* (São Paulo, 1982); João Pinheiro Neto, *Bons e maus mineiros (& outros brasileiros)* (Rio de Janeiro, 1996); Joel Silveira, *Na fogueira: Memórias* (Rio de Janeiro, 1998); Silveira, *Memórias de alegria* (Rio de Janeiro, 2001); and the same author's collection, *Tempo de contar* (Rio de Janeiro, 1985). Also worthwhile are the oral-history collections *Eles mudaram a imprensa*, ed. Alzira Alves de Abreu, Fernando Lattman-Weltman, and Dora Rocha (Rio de Janeiro, 2003), and *Elas ocuparam as redações*, ed. Abreu and Rocha (Rio de Janeiro, 2006).

Acknowledgments

This book's dedication to Louis A. Pérez Jr. reflects years of inspiration, guidance, and friendship, as well as the original prompt to study the commercial transformation of twentieth-century Brazil. That prompt was issued one afternoon in the spring of 1996, when—casting about for a topic for an honors thesis—I visited Lou in his office on the fifth floor of Hamilton Hall. At the time, like most any aspiring historian of Latin America in this country, I was interested in rural peoples, resistance, and rebellion in the circum-Caribbean, especially Mexico and Central America. Earlier in the academic year, I had written a seminar paper addressing these concerns, while also exhausting the supply of locally accessible primary-source materials in those pre-digital days. That sunny afternoon, Lou suggested I visit Duke University's Special Collections Library, where the holdings of the J. Walter Thompson Company, an advertising agency active in South America beginning in the 1920s, had not yet attracted the attention of Latin Americanist historians. Through twists and turns, that prompt led to this larger examination of Brazil's remaking amid the global spread of U.S.-style consumer capitalism.

Over these years, I have counted on the generous friendship, counsel, and support of Barbara Weinstein. Indeed, it is unlikely that I would still be in the field were it not for Barbara's caring support and good humor. The gargantuan task of ploughing through two drafts of this book—the first a considerably longer one—seems slight by comparison with everything else, but it undoubtedly made this a better book, for which I am now additionally indebted. If I ever finish the book on belonging in São Paulo researched and planned as this one was written and revised, it will be for her.

Jerry Dávila is another colleague whom I have been well fortuned to count as a friend for over twenty years. He too braved heroic sallies through two drafts and made signal suggestions for improvement. I look forward to a day when we can once more spend a good stretch of time in Brazil together, this time with Liv, Ellen, Alex, and Robert Seamus, as well as Kim.

Other friends helped this work along in their own ways. Circumstances prevented Oliver Dinius from submitting a draft to one of his characteristically sharp reads, but our discussions of the subject and related matters were inspiring. Jeff Strickland and Richard Conway—fast friends and dear departmental colleagues—accompanied my writing on a sometimes-daily basis, in the process aiding more than they perhaps knew.

Before I landed in New Jersey, I was awarded a year in residence at the Center for Humanistic Inquiry at Emory University, where I imagined I would wrap up an abbreviated version of something like this book. The center's generous support and the intellectual energy provided by its other resident fellows turned out to be more foundational than finishing-stage, however, and so I must thank its then-director, Martine Brownley, for her patience, as well as for all that the center provided me during that year, for which Keith Anthony, Amy Erbil, and Colette Barlow are due thanks as well.

Among the things I learned while in residence at Emory was that I needed to broaden my research. Brief research trips to Brazil were complemented by a semester-long Fulbright fellowship sponsored by the history department of the University of São Paulo. I am deeply grateful to Maria Helena Machado for the invitation and to John Monteiro for his friendly support, as well as to Tom and Felicity Skidmore, Luiz Valente, and Barbara Weinstein for their efforts during the application process. In São Paulo, Patricia Grijo of the Comissão Fulbright was a great help, while Sueli de Freitas Alves at the Brazilian consulate in Washington assisted in getting a newborn baby a visa in a hurry; Margaret Dickson of the Council for International Exchange of Scholars was also of great logistical assistance. Prior to the Fulbright, some of the research on the U.S. side was funded by grants from Duke University's John W. Hartman Center for Sales, Advertising, and Marketing History and from Montclair State University.

Archivists and librarians at some two dozen institutions assisted my research. They included Ellen Gartrell and Jacqueline Reid at the Hartman Center, Arlene May at Sears Archives, Linda Skolarus at the Benson Ford Research Center, Ronald Bulatoff at the Hoover Institution, Beth Jaffe at the Rockefeller Archive Center, Gabriela Giacomini de Almeida at the Instituto de Estudos Brasileiros, Paulo Simões de Almeida Pina at the Biblioteca Jenny Klabin, and Linda Gill at the Nettie Lee Benson Collection of the University of Texas. I thank Pollyanne Cristina B. Teixeira, Suelen Rodrigues, and Barbara Moraes of the Biblioteca Padre Alberto Antoniazzi (Pontifícia Universidade Católica de Minas Gerais) for making available a scan of their rare copy of the script of Oduvaldo Vianna Filho's *Allegro desbum*. The Instituto Cultural of the Escola Superior de Propaganda e Marketing was a key research site, where I was ably attended by its staff and by then-director Nilma Marli de Jesus, and where I was befriended by Carlos Roberto Chueiri. At the Museu Paulista, I must thank Shirley Ribeiro Soares and especially Tatiana Vasconcelos dos Santos; at Nestlé's São Paulo headquarters, Sandra A. de Souza and especially Solange Peirão and her team at the Centro de Pesquisa e Documentação. Solange Peirão also provided access to transcripts of interviews with advertising professionals produced by her historical-research consultancy in the 1980s, an especially generous step for which I remain very grateful. Closer to home, Kevin Prendergast, Siobhan McCarthy, and Arthur Hudson of the interlibrary loan office at Harry A. Sprague Library continue their diligent labors in pursuit of what must often seem bizarre requests, building on the work of their counterparts at the Robert W. Woodruff Library. This book would have been additional years in the making without their dedication.

Portions of this research were presented at the usual academic conferences, as well as in looser fora hosted by the Arquivo Público do Estado de São Paulo, the Casa de Rui Barbosa, the Centro de Pesquisa da História Contemporânea do Brasil, the German Historical Institute, the New School for Social Research, the Pontifícia Universidade Católica de São Paulo, Seton Hall University, the University of Delaware, and the University of Bern. I can only give the broadest of thanks to the overly generous audiences I encountered through presentations of both kinds, though several commentators, chairs, co-panelists, and organizers are mentioned in the paragraph immediately following. In addition, I would like to recognize Carol González Velasco, Flavia Veras, and Sandra Gayol, who included me in their stimulating panel at the second meeting of the Asociación Latinoamericana e Ibérica de Historia Social, and James Green,

Monica Grin, Isabel Lustosa, and Mônica Schpun, for their organization of an engaging meeting in Rio de Janeiro where I was able to sketch out some of this book's principal arguments for an audience studded with leading specialists in twentieth-century Brazilian history. Jim Green's contributions did not end there—they also included facilitating access to Brown University's copy of the film *Bebel, garota propaganda* (1968) and the opportunity to present an overview of this project at Brown's Thomas J. Watson Institute for International Studies.

Many others contributed over the years. Among those whose names have not escaped me are Alexandre Moreli, Álvaro Pereira do Nascimento, Amilcar Araujo Pereira, Amy Chazkel, Antonio Pedro Tota, Beth Mofacto, Brian Owensby, Bryan McCann, Charles Capper, Colin Snider, Elizabeth Cancelli, Esperanza Brizuela García, Fernando Santomauro, Flavia Rios, Gabriel Passetti, Gillian McGillivray, Giovana Xavier, Gregg Bocketti, Hartmut Berghoff, Henrique Espada Lima, Hugh Bator, Ian Merkel, Jeff Lesser, Jerry Bentley, Joan Ficke, Joanne Caruso, Joel Wolfe, John Chasteen, Kirsten Schultz, Larissa Rosa Correa, Lars Schoultz, Lauro Ávila Pereira, Leonie Herbers, Ligia Prado, Márcio Siwi, Mary Colón, Matheus Gato de Jesus, Matthew Restall, Michael Hall, Michael Whelan, Micol Seigel, Mike Peters, Molly Ball, Patricia Acerbi, Paulo Fontes, Rafael Ioris, Robert Friedman, Rosangela Patriota, Seth Garfield, Shannan Clark, Stella Krepp, Sue Goscinski, Susan Brunda, Susan Strasser, Tania Regina de Lucca, Tatiana Seijas, Teresa Cribelli, Thomas Monteiro, Tom Rogers, Tori Langland, Uwe Spiekermann, Valeria Manzano, Vitor Izecksohn, Xenia Salvetti, and Zachary Morgan. Apologies to anyone whom I may have overlooked—it has been a long and sometimes trying journey.

That editing and production have been the journey's shortest stretches is thanks to Elaine Maisner, assisted by Andrew Winters. Elaine was a quick enthusiast of this project and has been dedicated in her pursuit of its success, more than living up to her reputation in the field. Also at the University of North Carolina Press, I would like to thank Iris Levesque, Cate Hodorowicz, Dino Battista, Jay Mazzocchi, and Anna Faison.

At this milestone, it is a joy to recognize further friendships made and sustained over these two decades, those of Elizabeth Johnson and Reese Ewing, Matt Kadane and Claire Lesemann, Brian and Michelle Doyle, Josh and Laura Neelon, Roni and Ana Paula Bastos, Bianca and Michael Bator. Elizabeth and Reese helped this work along year after year; as importantly, they and their children, Julian and Annika, along with everyone else just mentioned, helped me forget about it for moments here and there, as did my sister and her family, Barbara, Monty, Teddy, Max, and now Corinne.

My mother and father, by contrast, were keen to remind me of it, which I suppose remains part of the job. As of this writing, it also recalls a beloved adviser's evocation of his own parents' lively interest in his second book. Thank you both for the habitual reminders and that warm recollection, and for everything else.

And then there's Kim, who hung the moon and stars, and Seamus, who feels the same way. I am fortunate beyond my dreams.

James P. Woodard
Montclair, New Jersey
June 2019

Index

ABA. *See* Brazilian Association of Advertisers
ABAP. *See* Brazilian Association of Advertising Agencies
ABI. *See* Brazilian Press Association
ABP. *See* Brazilian Advertising Association
Abramo, Cláudio, 167, 328, 378
Abramo, Lélia, 180
Abril, 173–74, 203, 209, 239–43, 245, 273, 352
ACADE. *See* Association of Merchants of Household Electrical Appliances
A. C. Nielsen Company, 249, 385
A. D'Almeida (agency), 81–82, 85–92
Aderbal Júnior, 355
ADVB. *See* Association of Sales Directors of Brazil
advertising, 3–4, 21, 35–66, 70–71, 80–92, 166–67, 185–86, 201–13, 254–62; agencies, 5, 26, 52, 79, 96–97, 101, 155, 228, 385, 388; automobile, 29, 31, 224–25; cinema and, 61–62, 332; congresses, 209–10, 212–13, 250, 261, 294, 305–6, 364; cooperative, 189, 197–98; criticism of, 329–30, 334–36, 338–39, 341–43, 352, 356; for domestic appliances, 185–88, 190–91; instructions for consumers in, 111, 185; jingles, 113, 177–78; outdoor, 29, 106, 113–16, 220, 291, 310, 363, 375; for post–World War II era, 122–25; pricing in, 110–11; print, 42, 62, 76, 79, 92–93, 98, 106, 121, 167–74, 197–98, 220, 227–28, 239–40, 242–43, 273, 299, 386; radio, 56–58, 76, 93–96, 102–6, 177–78, 229, 238; retail, 71–74, 76, 79, 131–32, 136, 142–45, 152–54, 157–65, 209; slogans, 112–13, 127; shopping-center, 279–81;

soft drink, 117; supermarket, 197–99; television, 179, 181–83, 198, 229, 233–37; testimonial, 44, 83, 111–12, 294, 387; trademarks and, 107–10, 119; women's employment in, 84, 138, 202, 308, 367
air conditioning, 66, 123, 149, 151, 153, 275, 303–4, 309
A. J. Renner (industrial group), 141, 203, 311, 385
Alcântara Machado (agency), 197, 357. *See also* Almap
Alcântara Machado Comércio e Empreendimentos (AMCE), 226–27; fairs, 216, 225, 227–31, 234, 243, 249, 274, 290, 299–300, 305
Alfa Romeo, 224
Almap, 201, 203, 225, 229, 254, 259, 271, 274. *See also* Alcântara Machado
Alonso, Geraldo, 257, 261, 305, 314, 327
Alpargatas, 176, 197, 251
Alves, Francisco ("Chico"), 68, 188
Alves, Oswaldo, 326, 328
Amado, Genolino, 377–78
Amado, Jorge, 326
ambient music, 149, 198, 275, 317
AMCE. *See* Alcântara Machado Comércio e Empreendimentos
American Association of Advertising Agencies, 49, 244–45
American Chambers of Commerce in Brazil, 46, 50–52, 121, 385; magazine of (*Brazilian Business*), 51, 58, 65, 126, 147, 276; members of, 50–51, 91
American Institute of Public Opinion (Gallup organization), 101, 286, 321
Americanization, 5–6, 65, 133, 329, 331–38, 343, 359, 377

American Marketing Association, 245
Americano, Jorge, 329, 331
"American way of life": Brazilian interest
in and exposure to, 118, 121, 310;
Brazilian professionals on, 215, 246;
buying on installments as imitation,
388; criticism of, 334, 336, 338; in
OCIAA propaganda, 122
Anderson, Perry, 372–73
Andrade, Auro Moura, 190
Andrade, Carlos Drummond de, 227, 328,
343, 347–48, 356, 390
Angelini, Mario, 109
Anhembi, 334–35, 338–39
Anhembi convention center, 229–30,
300, 305
Anjos, Cyro dos, 17
ANL. *See* National Liberating Alliance
Antarctica (brewer and soft-drink
manufacturer), 113, 189, 210, 220
Antônio, João, 325
Antunes Filho, 353, 355
APP. *See* Paulista Advertising Association
Aragão, B. de, 129
Aranha, Oswaldo, 223
Arantes, Affonso, 364
Araujo, Raimundo, 167
Arno, 184–85, 203, 212
Artplan, 281
Associação Brasileira Cinematograph-
ica, 60
Associados group. *See* Diários Associa-
dos; Emissoras e Diários Associados
association football (*futebol*, soccer), 13,
149, 176, 180, 234, 264, 268, 271–74.
See also World Cup competitions
Association of Merchants of House-
hold Electrical Appliances (ACADE),
188, 191
Association of Sales Directors of Brazil
(ADVB), 203, 247, 250, 252, 272
Assumpção & Cia., 41, 51, 299
Atlantic Refining Company, 41, 44, 51, 125
automobile imports, 27–28, 31
Automobile Industry Executive Group
(GEIA), 223–25

automotive industry, in Brazil, 221–26,
230, 266–68, 296, 384
automotive industry, U.S., 5, 20, 25–26,
31, 127, 224, 267
Automotive Materials Industry Executive
Commission (CEIMA), 223

Babo, Lamartine, 61
Bandeira, Manuel, 328
Barbosa, Haroldo, 95
Bardi, Lina Bo, 206–7
Bardi, Pietro, 206–9
Barros, Adhemar de, 134–35
Barros, Altino João de, 376
Barroso, Ari, 61
Basbaum, Leôncio, 255–56
Batista, Linda, 159
Bebel, garota propaganda, 343, 345–46
Bebel que a cidade comeu. See Brandão,
Ignácio de Loyola
Bennaton, Jocelyn, 80
B. F. Goodrich, 44, 51
"big tickets," 138, 183
Blanco, Leandro, 103
Bloch, Adolpho, 172–73, 239–40, 271
Blue Star Line, 41, 44
Bob's, 277
Bombril, 181, 184–85, 197, 209,
220, 299
Bomfim, Annibal, 327
Bomfim, Manoel, 63
Bond & Share, 385. *See also* Emprezas
Electricas Brasileiras
Bond Stores, 142
Bonomi, Mari, 354–55
Borges, Raul, 195–96
Braga, Rubem, 199, 327
Brahma, 41, 44, 113, 328
Brandão, Ignácio de Loyola, 343–46,
357–58
Brandão, Octávio, 334
branded goods, 17, 21, 71, 74, 102–3,
106–13, 116, 117–20, 130–32, 146,
177–78, 189, 197, 219–20. *See also*
specific product names, e.g., Coca-Cola
Brascan, 304, 389

Harvard University, 47, 56
Hawkins, Victor, 81
HBS. *See* Harvard Business School
hegemony, ubiquity as akin to, 384
Herzog, Clarice, 381–82, 507n18
Herzog, Vladimir, 507n18
Higher Advertising and Marketing
 School (ESPM), 247, 205, 309. *See also*
 São Paulo Advertising School
Higher Institute of Brazilian Studies
 (ISEB), 339–42
Hollywood, 20, 51, 59–67, 72, 74, 118–19,
 121, 132, 243, 308–9, 312, 319, 325, 332,
 338, 360, 375; celebrities, 44, 83; films,
 26, 95, 102, 117, 133, 181, 195, 197, 236,
 336; glamour, 44, 72, 309, 387; gossip,
 168, 243; Rádio Nacional as Brazil's,
 386; studios, 5, 47, 51, 121–22, 385,
 387–88. *See also* cinema
Hoover, Herbert, 46–48, 51, 58

IBM, 87
IBOPE. *See* Brazilian Institute of Public
 Opinion and Statistics
Imparcial, O, 34
Imperialismo e angústia (Lima, C.),
 337–38, 359
Independência-Decred, 271, 302–3
Industrial Development Commission,
 194, 222
Indústria & Mercados, 214, 217, 243,
 293, 362
inequality, 218, 241, 285, 305, 345, 348,
 365–66, 371, 389
inequity. *See* inequality
INESE. *See* Instituto de Estudos Sociais e
 Econômicos
inflation, 12; advertising budgets and,
 201; consumer credit usage and, 137,
 184, 191–93, 339; as difficulty in market
 research, 286; stock control and, 154;
 pre-1964, 297, 335, 338, 373; under
 military rule, 235, 261, 265–66; in 1980s
 and 1990s, 372
Instituto de Estudos Sociais e Econômicos (INESE), 155, 277, 286

Instituto de Pesquisas de Opinião e
 Mercado (IPOM), 155, 174, 286
Inter-Americana, 120, 172, 203, 206, 209,
 219, 238, 315, 322. *See also* Salles/
 Inter-Americana
International Basic Economy Corpora-
 tion, 141, 223
International Monetary Fund, 216
Interpublic, 260
Ipiranga (petroleum company), 203, 238
IPOM. *See* Instituto de Pesquisas de
 Opinião e Mercado
ISEB. *See* Higher Institute of Brazilian
 Studies
Isetta, 224

James, Louis, 16
JMM, 282
Johnson & Johnson, 41, 112, 132, 164,
 197, 251
Jorge, J. G. de Araujo, 326–27
Jornal, O, 33, 35–36, 380
Jornal do Brasil, 33, 167, 170, 212, 242,
 386; as Brazil's largest shopping center,
 299; on production of millionth VW,
 267, 295. *See also* Rádio Jornal do
 Brasil
Jornal do Commercio, 33, 36
Jovem Guarda, 234, 238
Jovem Pan. *See* Rádio Pan-Americana
Julião Netto, Manoel, 273
Jurandir, Dalcídio, 334
J. Walter Thompson (JWT, Thompson),
 5, 38–39, 47, 62, 81, 96, 99, 114, 173,
 180, 202–4, 259–60, 286, 310, 321, 380;
 in Brazil compared to the United
 States, 288–289; "colonial" model of
 staffing and, 45, 321–22, 360–61; Day of
 the Child and, 164; early operations in
 Brazil, 39–44; employees and former
 employees of, 39, 80–82, 85–86, 156,
 171, 173, 176, 20, 204, 244, 246, 250,
 260, 265, 289, 300, 305, 309, 312, 315,
 320–22, 326, 357, 366–67; growth in
 billings in 1950s, 201; IBOPE and, 99,
 101, 218; offices of, 39, 53, 358; relations

284–90, 295–96, 324, 341–42, 346, 355–56, 368, 370–71, 385–86

social communications. *See* communications

Sodré, Nelson Werneck, 118, 121

soft drinks, 1, 57, 106, 116–17, 131, 146, 189, 209–10, 296, 312, 372, 376. *See also* Coca-Cola

Souza, Francisco Alberto Madia de, 305

Souza, Gustavo Moreira de, 303–4

Souza, José Cândido Moreira de, 263

Souza, José Luiz Moreira de, 148, 264–66, 271, 301–4, 372, 387

Souza Cruz (British-American Tobacco), 266, 273

Standard Brands, 38, 109–10, 121, 181

Standard Oil, 37, 45, 50–51, 65, 82, 88, 388. *See also* Esso; Repórter Esso

Standard Propaganda, 82, 202, 259, 316; absorbed by Ogilvy & Mather, 259–60; claims regarding women consumers, 202, 380–81; clients, advertising and other services for, 103–4, 109–13, 124, 163–64, 227, 240–41; employees and former employees of, 82, 85, 145, 157, 160, 187, 202–3, 218, 310, 313, 316, 320, 326–27, 384; and IBOPE, 5; radio broadcasting and, 103–4, 113, 131; U.S. office, 120. *See also*, Leuenroth, Cícero

streetselling, 16–20, 87, 113, 310

supermarkets, 193–201, 268–70, 275, 300, 379, 385

Supermercado Moderno, 282, 294, 381

Supermercados Copacabana, 194, 198

Sweethearts' Day, 163–66, 362

Sydney Ross, 210, 311

Szulch, Tad, 179–80

Tejo, Limeira, 18, 106, 128–29

telenovelas, 3, 5, 180, 234–37, 270, 282, 375, 386

television ownership, 179–80, 220, 232–33, 239, 372–74, 386, 462n105, 475–76n37

Telles, Carlos Queiroz, 254, 309–10, 323–25, 357

Telles, Francisco Emygdio da Fonseca, 331–32, 335

Texas Company, 51

Theory of Business Enterprise, The (Veblen), 107

Thompson. *See* J. Walter Thompson

Time-Life, 235–36

Toddy, 110–13, 209, 229

trademark applications, 106–7, 119

Trans-Amazonian Highway, 271–72

Travassos, Nelson Palma, 17–18

Tribuna da Imprensa, 168

Tribuna Popular, 132, 323

Tropicalismo, 227, 234, 347

Tschudy, Arnold, 126

TV-Excelsior, 231, 236

TV-Globo, 235–36, 271, 301, 305, 315, 349, 365, 378, 382, 386. *See also* Globo media group, Rede Globo

TV-Itacolomi, 179, 231, 233

TV-Paulista, 179, 198

TV-Record, 179, 182, 198, 205, 238

TV-Rio, 179, 183, 189, 206, 231

TV-Tupi, 178–79, 182, 188, 198, 200, 349

Twentieth Century Fox, 60

UEB. *See* União de Empresas Brasileiras

ufanismo, 264–65, 306–7

Ultima Hora, 168–70, 187, 196, 200, 206, 209, 226, 242, 260, 276, 344, 354, 362, 377–78

União de Empresas Brasileiras (UEB), 270–71, 301–3

Unilever, 83, 235, 245

Union of Electrical Appliance Retailers (URAPEL), 191, 193

United States and Brazil Steamship Line, 50

United States Banknote Company, 50

United States Information Agency, 179

Universal Films, 59

University of São Paulo (USP), 208–10, 258, 261, 286, 343, 349, 351, 381

URAPEL. *See* Union of Electrical Appliance Retailers

U.S. Exposition (1963), 226